DATE DUE

THE POLITICS OF
A GUARANTEED
INCOME

THE POLITICS OF
A GUARANTEED INCOME

INCOME

The Nixon Administration
and the Family Assistance Plan

DANIEL P. MOYNIHAN

Vintage Books
A Division of Random House
New York

FIRST VINTAGE BOOKS EDITION, August 1973
Copyright © 1973 by Daniel P. Moynihan
All rights reserved under International and Pan-American
Copyright Conventions. Published in the United States by
Random House, Inc., New York, and simultaneously in
Canada by Random House of Canada Limited, Toronto.
Originally published by Random House, Inc., in 1973.
Library of Congress Cataloging in Publication Data
Moynihan, Daniel Patrick.
    The politics of a guaranteed income.
    Includes bibliographical references.
    1. Guaranteed annual income—United States.
2. Public welfare—United States. 3. United States—
Social policy. I. Title.
[HC110.I5M65 1973b]   362.5   73–5704
ISBN 0–394–71931–X
Manufactured in the United States of America

Grateful acknowledgment is made to the following sources for permission
to reprint:

Basic Books, Inc.: Excerpts from *Rationalism in Politics* by Michael Oakeshott,
1962.

Andrew F. Brimmer: Address delivered at Tuskegee Institute, March 22, 1970,
"Economic Progress of Negroes in the United States: The Deepening Schism."

The Brookings Institution: From *The State of Welfare* by Gilbert Y. Steiner.
Copyright © 1971 by The Brookings Institution, Washington, D.C.

Commentary: From "The Limits of Social Policy" by Nathan Glazer, September 1971. Copyright © 1971 by the American Jewish Committee.

Fortune Magazine: From "The Looming Money Revolution Down South" by
Richard Armstrong, in *Fortune*, June 1970. Copyright © 1970 by Time, Inc.

Holt, Rinehart and Winston, Inc.: From *The Vantage Point* by Lyndon Baines
Johnson. Copyright © 1971 by HEC Public Affairs Foundation.

Minnesota Sentinel Publishing Co.: From "Workfare Welfare Makes Sense,"
editorial in *Twin Cities Courier*, August 23, 1969.

William Morris Agency, Inc.: From *The Inhabitants* by Julius Horwitz. Copyright © 1960 by Julius Horwitz.

The New Republic: "Comment: The Greening of Education," in *The New
Republic*, November 13, 1971. Copyright © 1971 by Harrison-Blaine of New
Jersey, Inc. "Nixon's Family Assistance Bill: An Attack by Lucy V. Katz, A
Defense by Daniel P. Moynihan," in *The New Republic*, July 18, 1970. Copyright © 1970 by Harrison-Blaine of New Jersey, Inc.

G. P. Putnam's Sons: From *Irrational Ravings* by Pete Hamill. Copyright ©
1971 by Pete Hamill.

Random House, Inc.: From "In Memory of W. B. Yeats," in *Collected Shorter
Poems 1927–1957* by W. H. Auden. Copyright 1940 by W. H. Auden. Copyright renewed 1968.

Science News: "Social Work—Choosing a New Way," in *Science News*, June 7,
1969. Copyright © 1969 by Science Service, Inc.

The Washington Post: From "What's Happened to the 'Good Guys'?" by Alice
M. Rivlin, in *The Washington Post*, December 21, 1969. Copyright © 1969 by
The Washington Post.

Acknowledgments

With the exception of the telegram on page 251, all quotations in the narrative are from written sources, generally from my notes and papers. I have trusted to memory for nothing, save for this one item which I learned by heart at the time. In portions of the narrative I quote extensively from press accounts. In each instance it was my understanding at the time that the statements and events recorded had in fact occurred. A number of skilled journalists followed these events, and their accounts have much value in and of themselves. For the reader, however, the main point to note is that an item that appeared in the press was widely known about at the time, whereas conversations, meetings, documents not so reported were known to only a limited circle.

As will be evident, I have relied heavily on three earlier works bearing on my general subject, Stephen K. Bailey's *Congress Makes a Law,* John F. Manley's *The Politics of Finance,* and Gilbert Y. Steiner's *The State of Welfare.* I have found their perceptions durable, indeed indispensable.

As participant history this has been perforce a one-man exercise, and its failings are those of one man only. I am, however, indebted to Jason Epstein, Nathan Glazer, Norman Podhoretz, Lee Rainwater, and James Q. Wilson, who read the manuscript. Leslie Lenkowsky checked it for the errors of transcription that plague any one-man enterprise of mine. This, at all events, is the task he undertook. In the end he did far more, holding me to the most rigorous standards of evidence with respect to issues whose complexity I came to perceive in the light of his relentless and not always gentle questioning. That I am much indebted to this formidable young scholar will be evident.

Margaret E. Carnduff typed the manuscript with cheerful efficiency, and Lynn Y. Sakai made Xerox copies with vast patience. If this work pleases anyone, they should know that Edward Jay Epstein first suggested it. I am, finally, much indebted to the wisdom and scholarship of Seymour Copstein.

DANIEL P. MOYNIHAN

Cambridge, Massachusetts
March 1972

For Liz, with love

In the deserts of the heart
Let the healing fountain start,
In the prison of his days
Teach the free man how to praise.

W. H. Auden

Contents

THE POLITICS OF
A GUARANTEED
INCOME

Introduction

In the course of the 91st Congress, the United States almost established a guaranteed income. The proposal, known as the Family Assistance Plan, was set forth by President Richard Nixon in a television address on August 8, 1969, not quite seven months after taking office. Eight months later, on April 16, 1970, the House of Representatives approved the legislation by almost a two-to-one vote. It then faltered, only finally to fail in the Senate, albeit the debate went on to the very last moments of the 91st Congress, which did not end until January 2, 1971, nineteen days before the 92nd Congress began.

An account of the history of the Family Assistance Plan, or FAP as it came to be known, must hence be one of failure. The law was not enacted.

Yet in an only slightly different perspective the notion of failure would appear inappropriate. The 91st Congress had seemed destined for prolonged and bitter partisanship as between the parties, and between the Congress and the president. To those whose primary concern was the restoration of a measure of social peace, it had seemed the most that could be hoped for was a passive acceptance by all concerned that nothing much by way of legislation, good or bad, was going to be dealt with seriously during these years. The new president had conducted a largely negative campaign, directing himself to the failings of the previous administration, under which the Nation had spiraled into a condition of portentous unrest. The world's most powerful democracy had entered a period of assassination, riot, and protest: war abroad and increasingly the conditions, certainly the rhetoric, of war at home. An opposition party seeking office needed to do little more than stress these facts. It was a time to keep things from coming apart; a time to head off disaster: hardly a time to contemplate a quantum leap in social policy.

The Democrats seemed to sense the bleak prospects of the season, bleak both for themselves and for any significant forward movement in social policy. If the Republican campaign had been negative, that of the Democrats was hardly a campaign at all. Their convention had been the scene of horror, tumult, dissimulation, and political failure. Scarcely anyone was not somehow to be blamed, and, blaming one another, the shattered components of the majority party went off in varied directions expecting defeat, and in many instances half hoping for it.

The outcome was closer than expected, but not different. The Republican candidate won with a bare plurality. On the face of it, the electorate had voted overwhelmingly against social change and, in the case of the largest third-party movement in half a century, one of the three or four largest in the history of the Republic, many had voted for something very like social regression. As if to formalize the prospect of a truly historic stalemate, for the first time since the administration of Zachary Taylor an incoming president faced a Congress in which the opposition party controlled both houses.

And yet this same president proposed, and one body of that Congress passed, and the other might well have passed, one of the half-dozen or dozen most important pieces of social legislation in American history. It adduced much favorable comment in the United States, although the more complex analyses tended to come from abroad. A Yugoslav Marxist, for one, was reported as commenting within his circles that were it to pass it might well be the most important social legislation in history in that it would finally free the individual and his family from the myriad and inescapable forms of coercion which society exerts through the employment nexus. Be that as it may—a quality of the proposal was that it was not accompanied by any especially large promises—it did mark a coming of age of American social policy. For the longest time we had been importers of ideas, as we had been importers of capital. That radical politics in

America with rare exceptions has been a European import is not greatly to be disputed. But this is true equally of reformist politics. The bold reform programs of the thirties and forties and fifties and beyond (we are just, for example, getting to health insurance) have consisted to a dispiriting degree of ideas Lloyd George borrowed from Bismarck.

The Family Assistance Plan was different. It was singularly an American idea, and of recent origin. Its passage would set a standard of social policy against which the rest of the world might measure itself. Indeed, such stirrings were quickly to be discerned in western Europe once the American initiative occurred. In 1971 the Liberal government of Canada introduced a bill establishing a Family Income Security Plan, to be known as "FISP," a cousin to FAP. In Britain a Conservative government established "FIS," the Family Income Supplement, a similarly related scheme for low income families with children where "the head of the family is in full-time work." In the Spring of 1972 the British Chancellor of the Exchequer announced his government's intention to move to a full negative income tax credit scheme, a proposal even closer to FAP, and even more refined in its specifics. (The Chancellor did not fail to take note of charges from the Left that under the previous Labour government there had been a "growing gap between the rich and poor in Britain," a paradox of social policy that had come to puzzle statesmen and scholars alike in many parts of the world.)[1]

It is in this sense that FAP did not fail in the 91st Congress. It began there. Technically a revenue measure, it had to originate in the House, and to be dealt with by the Committee on Ways and Means, from which it emerged as H.R. 16311, introduced by the chairman and the ranking minority member, Wilbur D. Mills of Arkansas and John W. Byrnes of Wisconsin. Eventually it failed of enactment, but scarcely was lost from sight. As the 92nd Congress convened it reappeared, this time as H.R. 1, the bill with pride of place in the legislative cycle. *Newsweek* Magazine declared that if enacted, "It will constitute a humanitarian achievement unrivaled since the New Deal." These words concluded the *Newsweek* cover story of February 8, 1971, entitled: "WELFARE: There Must Be a Better Way." The cover story of *Time* on February 8 was devoted to the same subject: "The Welfare Maze." It began, "The U.S. welfare system is a living nightmare that has reached the point of the involuntary scream and chill awakening." The cover story of *U.S. News and World Report* of the same date announced *its* main story: "Welfare Out of Control—Story of Financial Crisis Cities Face."

If it had happened before that all three national news magazines featured the same cover story, it surely was not on the subject of welfare. That they should do so at the outset of 1971 reflected a state of alarm and perceived crisis significantly different from the attitudes which greeted the president's proposal for welfare reform just eighteen months earlier. Now for the first time the national news media were seriously focused upon the subject. And yet the presidential speech, and the message to Congress that followed, had been similarly without precedent. No president, no administration, had ever before addressed the subject of welfare in a sustained, purposive manner. (Kennedy had sent a message to Congress in 1962 proposing rehabilitative and preventive services for welfare recipients, but it did not touch on the central problem of providing enough money to the poor.) Nor in any significant sense had there been an informed and concerned public to follow the subject. Welfare had been nobody's business. It remained so until an extraordinary and precipitous sequence of events in the 1960s brought it near to the top of the agenda of national social problems and political issues.

It might at first appear that a *too* familiar sequence was being followed, that once again only crisis could command the attention of an overdistracted public, or summon the innovative energies of a dispersed system of government, at once harried and inattentive. Such a view would be mistaken. It is true enough that it was not until the welfare rolls commenced the startling increases of the late 1960s that much heed was given to the subject, or that it became possible to begin a substantive, serious political discussion. But to a marked degree the crisis had been foreseen—and foretold—and had been the subject of fairly powerful analysis. A number of social scientists had seen what was coming, and had put forth a range of proposals as to what might be done. None was forthwith adopted, but when the time came, as it did, that a general clamor arose to do *something,* government was not at a total loss.

This is a perhaps underappreciated role of the academic

disciplines. People are not at their best when startled. It is at such moments that the ordinary decencies of life, which Orwell perceived to be not ordinary at all but rather a precious achievement which few societies attain, tend to break down. Ugly questions arise. Who is guilty? Who is to blame? Who is to be punished? When, however, such troubles have been anticipated, however dimly, they acquire a certain normal-seeming quality when they come to pass. When, further, there is on hand a set of propositions as to what might be done to meet the suddenly perceived emergency, things go better all around. It is for such purposes that men o'warsmen practiced at their guns. Society need not always be blind, need not constantly lurch from obliviousness to panic and back.

The development of FAP is an instance of such forehandedness. It may be, then, that there is a general purpose to be served in recounting the history so far: things to be learned that may be of use in comparable efforts in other fields; things also that may help to summon the extraordinary assertion of social purpose which the final enactment of FAP will require, and which it would entail. The event was singular and yet quintessential. There is as much or more to be learned from it as from any event in recent domestic politics.

One of the primary contentions of political science is that things don't change very much, or, rather, very fast. Many insist that it shall be otherwise. An impasse follows. Our knowledge, as has been said, is no match for their ignorance. The experience of Family Assistance, however, suggests that each side in this argument might usefully give a bit, might learn something from the other. For here an extraordinary, discontinuous, forward movement in social policy *did* occur, and in the very least promising of circumstances. Those who call for "fundamental social change" could, if they so desired, point to the events leading up to the proposal and near enactment of the Family Assistance Plan as evidence that "fundamental," rather than merely "incremental," social change *is* a realistic option for American society at this time. The history of FAP does somewhat challenge our normal skepticism, and offers at very least the prospect of instruction.

This prospect is enhanced by the unusual circumstance that two political scientists, Bill Cavala and Aaron Wildavsky, attempted beforehand to *predict* how the President, the Congress, and the public would deal with the issues involved.[2] They went about this task—the presumed test of a genuine science—with care and insight. Their prediction, however, proved wrong on a number of crucial points. This suggests that some of the premises on which it was based may have to be revised. Here it may be that social scientists can learn something about their science. On other points, however, the prediction proved quite correct. *Here* it is at least possible that those whose behavior was predicted will learn something about themselves.

Cavala and Wildavsky began their paper, entitled "The Political Feasibility of Income by Right," with the "basic assumption" that "the political process will continue to function in ways only incrementally different from its operation in the past." This followed the assertion of Charles E. Lindblom, in his classic essay "The Science of 'Muddling Through'."[3] Lindblom, writing in 1959, held that "Democracies change their policies almost entirely through incremental adjustments. Policy does not move in leaps and bounds." There are always those who are impressed by the "ideological rhetoric [which] pervades political debate," but, Lindblom insisted, and all, or almost all the evidence has demonstrated, "incremental politics" dominate.[4]

Few measures would constitute so sharp a break in social policy as the establishment of a guaranteed income. In the context of a general theory, and on the basis of specific evidence which they gathered, Cavala and Wildavsky concluded that there was virtually no chance of such a measure being proposed, much less enacted. They wrote in 1969: "Income by right is not politically feasible in the near future. The President will not support it and Congress would not pass it if he did. The populace is hugely opposed." Some fifty congressmen were interviewed. Most, when the idea of a guaranteed income was explained to them, were themselves "hugely opposed." Even those liberals who supported the idea did not expect anything to come of it. Asked the chance of such a measure passing the House of Representatives they would reply: "None, zero, absolutely no chance." Three considerations in particular militated against any such possibility. First, the authors reasoned, "Policies that provide unearned income run counter to widely held and deeply felt American values, such as achievement, work, and equality of opportunity."

Second, great sums would have to be raised by taxation to pay for such a scheme. Third, "Labor unions fear that a guaranteed income would render them superfluous. Militant black leaders take the same position for a similar reason."

Few social scientists would have challenged this analysis. Yet at the very moment (March 1969) Cavala and Wildavsky were interviewing congressmen, a plan for a guaranteed income was being presented to the president of the United States. Five months later he proposed it. Nine months after that the House passed it.

Cavala and Wildavsky were, of course, right in their prediction that the measure would not finally be enacted, at least by the 91st Congress. They correctly predicted that trade unions would be alarmed. They were correct in their prediction that militant black leaders would oppose a proposal to give money to the black poor. The authors were also certainly right in their perception that "Guaranteed income plans unfortunately provide no assurance of producing political credit for their supporters." Nixon did get some initial support from "liberals" for proposing FAP, but he lost at least as much among "conservatives." After a point the president was being denounced from both sides, many liberals having found their own reasons for opposition. In the end the bill was defeated in the Senate Finance Committee by liberal votes. Welfare militants were jubilant. Inevitably enthusiasm for the measure waned somewhat in the White House. (Enthusiasm waned even more in the Congress, and here Cavala and Wildavsky provide clues on which to base new predictions. Congressmen pay close attention to debates such as that over FAP. They see more than they say. They saw in the 91st Congress that anyone trying to replace the welfare system with a guaranteed income would be attacked by welfare militants with a violent and abusive rhetoric that would do damage to a liberal or moderate reputation. In particular, any suggestion that income maintenance be associated with work incentives would be excoriated as repression. Cavala and Wildavsky write:

The position of the radicals has been enviable. They get credit for improving welfare conditions and for opposing the system—that is, they have learned the ultimate political trick of combining the advantages of power with the benefits of opposition.

Accordingly, or so it might be hypothesized, the congressional center moved in the direction of providing massive day-care facilities for the poor, as in the proposed Comprehensive Child Development Act, which provide services *only* to those who work, thereby avoiding arguments over who should.) Even so, a guaranteed income *was* proposed by a president and *did* pass one body of the Congress.

John F. Manley, in a paper presented to the 1970 meeting of the American Political Science Association, addressed the question of reconciling the Cavala and Wildavsky predictions with the actions of Nixon and the Congress—and, for that matter, the public.[5] He implied that if Cavala and Wildavsky had had more *facts* at the time they wrote, their basic hypotheses would have led them to different predictions. They did state, for example, that standard assumptions about the incremental behavior of the political system "ignore the role which domestic crisis has come to play in our political system." The president's decision was in fact based on a conviction that the great growth in welfare dependency, and the anticipated continued growth (which, if anything, the White House underestimated), did indeed reflect a domestic crisis of much wider implications than those normally associated with the issue. On the subject of a guaranteed income, they quote one congressman as saying, "If the president was for it, then we could stand up with him." This suggests that taken in *sequence* outcomes would be different than predicted. Once the president had proposed a guaranteed income, the Congress would find it easier to support the proposal, which is what happened. Most importantly, Cavala and Wildavsky underestimated the role which presidential rhetoric would play. They saw that the term "guaranteed income" had become ideologically charged. It had come to stand for the proposition that people ought not to have to work for a living. American public opinion has shown a persistent tendency to associate political radicalism with the abolition of the wage system, an essentially utopian ideal, or with bohemian disdain for the work ethic. Any president proposing a "guaranteed income" in *those* terms would press *that* button, and that would be the end of his proposal. But nothing required that a guaranteed income be *called* a guaranteed income. The term was in no sense proprietary. It was merely one of a number of designations that could

be used to describe and label an assortment of income mainte-
nance schemes. "Guaranteed income" was the one label that said
"Poison." Accordingly the president declared that the Family
Assistance Plan was *not* a "guaranteed income."

This will confuse some readers and trouble others, inasmuch as it *was,* a fact the president knew well enough. That he
should have said it was not will seem to some disingenuous, or
worse. But from an only slightly different point of view it will be
seen that the president's proposal was *not a guaranteed income in
the meaning the public had come to attach to that term*. The
heart of the proposal was to supplement the income of persons
already working, and it sincerely looked to the prospect of finding
work for others who were not working. As will be explained,
there was *no* work requirement *per se* in the legislation, but the
central income supplement provision was surrounded by incentive structures designed to increase the feasibility and desirability
of work. In a pattern of response which political science has now
firmly identified, the American public, which had been overwhelmingly opposed to something called a "guaranteed income,"
just as overwhelmingly approved the Family Assistance Plan with
the provisions proposed by the president, and in the terms by
which he described those provisions.[6]

Manley is surely correct in suggesting that the events surrounding the proposal of the Family Assistance Plan indicated
that "a model of 'abnormal' decision-making is needed." He
correctly states that the Family Assistance experience shakes our
previous understanding of the relation of politics to policy.

[T]he political process, in the case of family assistance, yielded a
nonincremental change in welfare policy, thereby violating the incrementalist model and raising questions about its utility in providing
operating assumptions for predicting policy outcomes. However applicable incrementalism is to the day-to-day decisions of government it
is not, by definition, applicable to the unusually significant, though
statistically unusual, calculated risks taken by policy-makers. It may
be that the lesson of family assistance is that incrementalism is worse
than useless for explicating the most significant decisions government
makes; the blinders it entails exaggerate the barriers to basic policy
change and distort the degree to which the "big" decisions are
possible in the American political system.

What the family assistance plan reveals is that national policy-making institutions have a high but limited tolerance for the intolerable. If needs are pressing enough and if existing programs are inadequate enough, the politically unfeasible may become feasible. To some critics of American political institutions, this may be construed as damning with faint praise. Be that as it may, it is nevertheless true that political scientists have not given sufficient emphasis to substantive consideration of policy questions as a variable that helps explain the actions of policy-makers. Political necessities and advantages, group pressures, institutional rivalries, and electoral considerations all do their part in accounting for public policy. But so too does scrutiny of problems and solutions.

If I have any understanding of what happened, this *is* what happened. Scrutiny of the problem and possible solutions led to a major departure in policy. For years now Michael Polanyi has contended that this kind of event does occur, and has large consequences. "People," he will say, "change their minds." Here is such an instance. It is worth recording, while the "raw data" of what it felt like can still be retrieved.*

I write of course about events in which I participated and make no pretense of "disinterested objectivity," much less of a "value-free social science." At the same time I hope it will be found that my account is accurate. I was there; I describe what I saw. My task at the time was to see things as clearly as I could manage; to delude myself as little as possible. I did not, then, comment on everything I "saw," and I do not now. There are things I have not felt free to disclose, and things I have chosen not to disclose. Beyond this there are details about which I am simply not sure enough to state anything with confidence. In the

* The events leading to and from the proposal of FAP have a conceptual unity that admits of separate treatment as a long range development in social policy. The proposal was made, however, as part of an over-riding *short term* strategy to bring down the level of internal violence. This is a matter to be dealt with many years hence, if ever. Many readers will nonetheless divine that this *had* to be the case. To avoid misunderstanding, two points about this short-term strategy should be made. First, it was my judgment that urban rioting would tend *not* to reoccur barring exceptional events or singularly clumsy government. Second, although FAP was designed to help the poor, and especially the black poor, I assumed it would have no short-term impact of any particular consequence on the behavior or attitudes of this group. The short term impact would be on middle and upper class persons taking the measure of the new administration.

main these are small matters, turning largely on personality: interesting but not important. I am satisfied that nothing has been left out that is necessary to the understanding of the events I describe, to the extent, of course, that the events are understandable or that I understand them.

Arthur Schlesinger, Jr., has recently defended the role of the "participant-historian," which is experiencing something of a revival despite "a certain skepticism and resistance from professional historians."[7] He writes from his own experience that, "To take part in public controversy, to smell the dust and sweat of conflict, to experience the precariousness of decision under pressure may help toward a better understanding of the historical process." In my case a certain duress may be pleaded. In the decades 1950–1970, I spent thirteen years in government, for the most part at the political level, first as an aide to Averell Harriman, governor of New York, later in the administrations of presidents Kennedy, Johnson, and Nixon. I believe I am the only person to have served in sub-Cabinet or Cabinet of all three. As a teacher I find these experiences are the largest store of knowledge on which I have to draw, much as my colleagues may draw on their own experience in developing the methodology of the social sciences, which during this same period moved forward at least somewhat.

Hence I do not apologize for a study that offers nothing by way of methodological innovation. (I hardly dare to think of its other limitations, but that is a different matter.) If I understand it correctly, the history of science records that the pleasing symmetry of disinterested development of pure scientific knowledge followed by gradual transformation into applied practice, moving down a nicely graduated scale of social and intellectual status—physicist to engineer to operative—is more a recent phenomenon than otherwise. Earlier developments, and doubtless many today, were nothing so tidy. Solving practical problems, early technicians established many relationships which theorists thereupon systematized. There is an equivalent in social science.

A participant historian is likely to be of most use when simply recording "the dust and sweat of conflict." Subsequent analysts, not themselves involved, are more likely to make sense of what actually happened, but for this the participant's account and his interpretation can be helpful, even indispensable. The participant-historian presents his facts—and himself—for subsequent scrutiny. I do not at this point expect to take any great pleasure in such accounts when and if and as they appear. "Use every man after his desert," said the Prince to Polonius, "and who should 'scape whipping?" Not I. Not most of those with whom I shared office in Washington in the 1960s. Too much life was lived in that decade: we came out of it as from too much drink, able to live at all only on condition of living less. Already hideous charges are being made about men I know to be . . . what? Innocent? No. Not guilty. No one is innocent after the experience of governing. But not everyone is guilty. My private list is confined only to those who, looking back in self-exculpating horror, claim only to have been *giving* orders or whatever formulation serves to suggest that while they were in charge, others were to blame. Kennedy would say over and again: to govern is to choose. Men who will not abide by this condition are less than what is required.

For the moment we have what we have, and I offer herewith an account of the proposal and the fate of the Family Assistance Plan. I write in praise of democratic government. Much of what is written at this time is designed to discredit government or has the effect of doing so. I do not object to this. I object to the absence of countervailing effort. There are no villains in this book. To my understanding all those involved, myself included, pursued their personal interests, usually at a less than exalted level. I am not aware of any society in which different practices obtain. I do believe, however, that American government in this period managers to an exceptional degree to accommodate self-advancement with the advancement also of large and generous social ideals. I propound no notion of systemic genius which spares us the fate of less fortunate peoples. I only state that my experience of American government is that it is a decent process, and commands my regard.

I believe also that the history of Family Assistance provides evidence that American government is potentially capable of the "fundamental social change" which is so much demanded by some groups, and for which I believe a persuasive case can be made. However—I speak now both as a political liberal and a political scientist—I see little prospect that this will occur until those who espouse such change come to know more of what is involved, what is required. In the fall of 1971 Senator Edmund S. Muskie, addressing a dinner of the Liberal party of New York, stated that, "The blunt truth is that liberals have achieved virtually no fundamental change in our society since the end of the New Deal." Is this true? If so, why? Is it possible that loud, even strident, insistence on social change is becoming a mask for social privilege in America? The French have a phrase for it: "Think left, live right." Is that what is happening? Is liberalism increasingly the property of a privileged class that really does not want change, that wants only the appearance of doing so? Such things happen. It can also happen that advocates of great change will oppose with rending passion any change they conceive to be insufficiently great and interpret as a device for putting off the apocalyptic day of final change which is, of course, a persistent human vision. This for certain happened to the Family Assistance Plan. Its most passionate opponents were those who declared themselves in favor of more, not less, than it provided.

There may be a pattern of social behavior here, as the following passage will suggest.

The President's message and the recommendations of the committee were well received by the entire country. They were praised by congressional leaders of all parties and in editorials in leading newspapers, with only a few dissents. The program recommended was acclaimed as sound and conservative, and most of the criticisms were that it did not go far enough. Only considerably later was any conservative opposition manifested. Very early, however, stories appeared regarding the dissent of the "experts" and the advisory council, and as time passed more and more criticisms were levied at the program. By March, practically all newspaper and magazine comments were critical, although always with a note that the objectives sought were sound. Most frequently the criticisms centered upon the alleged lack of thorough consideration and the division among the advocates of social security, and concluded by urging delay.

This is from Edwin E. Witte's account *The Development of the Social Security Act* which describes the tumultuous seven months from the time the measure was proposed by President Franklin D. Roosevelt to its enactment by Congress.[8] Had the experts prevailed then in urging delay the Roosevelt generation would probably have lost its chance for the fundamental social change which the Social Security Act embodied. One is hard put to guess when such a chance would have come again. Not soon.

More than three decades later legislation of comparable importance came before the Congress. This time the "experts" prevailed, in a curious alliance of left and right. The legislation was put off. What will be the consequence is not yet known. All that can be said is that this may be one pattern of events.

References for Introduction

1. News Release, Department of National Health and Welfare, Ottawa, Canada, "Family Income Security Plan Unveiled: More Money for Needy Families," undated (1971). The development and details of FISP are discussed in John Munro, *Income Security for Canadians,* Ottawa, Department of National Health and Welfare, 1970. See also United Kingdom, Department of Health and Social Security, "Family Income Supplement: for families with children," Leaflet FIS 1, February 1972, and *Hansard,* 27 March 1972, Remarks of Mr. Barber on the Budget Resolutions and Economic Situation, pp. 40–42.
2. Bill Cavala and Aaron Wildavsky, "The Political Feasibility of Income by Right," *Public Policy,* Spring, 1970, pp. 321–354.
3. Charles E. Lindblom, "The Science of 'Muddling Through'," *Public Administration Review,* Spring, 1959, p. 84. The concept of incrementalism is treated thoroughly in Lindblom's later book, *The Intelligence of Democracy,* New York, The Free Press, 1965.
4. Charles E. Lindblom, "Policy Analysis," *American Economic Review,* June, 1958, p. 301.
5. John F. Manley, "The Family Assistance Plan: An Essay on Incremental and Nonincremental Policy-Making," Washington, D.C., The Brookings Institution, mimeographed, undated (1970), pp. 6, 10.
6. "American public opinion often operates on two levels simultaneously, and frequently in a rather schizophrenic fashion, a distinction which developed from a study conducted in 1964 by the Institute for International Social Research." Albert H. Cantril and Charles W. Roll, Jr., *Hopes and Fears of the American People,* New York, Universe Books, 1971, pp. 40–41.
7. Arthur Schlesinger, Jr., "The Historian As Participant," *Daedalus,* Spring, 1971, pp. 339, 348.
8. Edwin E. Witte, *The Development of the Social Security Act,* Madison, University of Wisconsin Press, 1962, p. 76.

I

The Problem of Dependency

The issue of welfare is the issue of dependency. It is different from poverty. To be poor is an objective condition; to be dependent, a subjective one as well. That the two circumstances interact is evident enough, and it is no secret that they are frequently combined. Yet a distinction must be made. Being poor is often associated with considerable personal qualities; being dependent rarely so. This is not to say that dependent people are not brave, resourceful, admirable, but simply that their situation is never enviable, and rarely admired. It is an incomplete state in life: normal in the child, abnormal in the adult. In a world where completed men and women stand on their own feet, persons who are dependent—as the buried imagery of the word denotes—hang.*

The emergence of poverty as a social and political issue in the early 1960s was an event of some complexity. Had not Kennedy been a Roman Catholic and been required to prove himself in Protestant West Virginia, there probably would not have been very much national attention paid to the decline of Appalachia; certainly there would not have been an Area Redevelopment Administration (one of Kennedy's few legislative

---

* If American society recognized home making and child rearing as productive work to be included in the national economic accounts (as is the case in at least one other nation) the receipt of welfare might not imply dependency. But we don't. It may be hoped the women's movement of the present time will change this. But as of the time I write, it had not.

17

achievements, long since swallowed up in the bureaucratic maze). Writers helped: Harrington, Caudill, others. Even so, there was debate in the White House as to whether the theme of the 1964 election should be poverty or the problems of the suburbs. Poverty was chosen—at least as one theme—and program work was under way at the time of the assassination. Kennedy's years had produced something very like a constitutional crisis. Congress just wasn't responding to presidential initiatives, and there seemed no way to get it to respond. Then the shock of his death loosened things up. The issue of poverty was there waiting; it proved attractive to the new president, and to the Congress as well. It was a unifying subject. The poor were deserving of help, and various kinds of help were contrived. More accurately, a great number of laws were enacted in the name of helping the poor.

There may also have been at work at this time a more general social phenomenon. As asserted by the *Encyclopedia of the Social Sciences* in the 1930s, "An increase in perceived poverty is a phenomenon particularly characteristic of American life during periods of so-called prosperity." "So-called" or genuine, prosperity does seem to have this effect. Concern for the poor, however, does not necessarily or even commonly extend to those who are dependent, that is to say those who own nothing and earn nothing and depend on society for their livelihood. When such persons are very young or very old, allowances are made. But when they are of the age when other persons work to earn their way and, further, if they are dependent during periods when work is to be had, dependency becomes a stigma.

This is the heart of it. The issue of welfare involves a stigmatized class of persons. The recipients know this. Or rather they share this judgment. Of late, perhaps, some do not. And yet the manner and the tactics of those who assert that welfare is a right that certain citizens are entitled to are somehow unconvincing. Over and again what occurs is an effort to humiliate or intimidate others who are not dependent, especially if they are in some symbolic or functional way those depended upon. It cannot too often be stated that the issue of welfare is not what it costs those who provide it, but what it costs those who receive it.

This is a widely shared impression. It is the basis of most

judgments on the subject. Almost the first *fact* about welfare dependency, however, is that apart from gross statistics on the number of recipients, and characteristics such as age, sex, and place of residence, there is astonishingly little dependable information. The actual processes of welfare dependency—how it comes about, what it is, how it is sustained, what diminishes it—remain virtually unexamined. Some few persons have ventured into the field, often at cost to themselves, and rarely with any great reward in terms of findings. In large terms there is nothing unusual about this absence of knowledge. What forms of human behavior *are* understood? Even so, in most areas of social policy there are quite extensive research efforts which recurrently produce results of proximate value; but not in the area of welfare dependency.

A variety of reasons may be adduced for this, of which the first is simply that for quite a long while it was generally assumed that, as a permanent social problem, dependency was disappearing. Thus, in the mid-1950s the governor of New York decided to seek an increase in the salary of the heads of his departments of Health and of Mental Hygiene. These two areas were of great public interest at the time. There had been impressive scientific advances in the treatment of afflictions such as poliomyelitis and mental illness. Both incumbent commissioners were men of large achievement. A raise was in order. The governor's office was accordingly surprised to receive an almost bitter communication from the Commissioner of Social Welfare (as the title then was) who asserted, correctly, that the salary of the three commissioners had traditionally been the same. To raise the pay of the first and second, but not the third, would be a blow to the prestige of the Department of Social Welfare. He conceded that welfare was no longer an issue of comparable importance, certainly not of comparable public concern, but insisted that there was a principle involved and asked that it be adhered to. (The Commissioner won his point, but he had had to make it.)

Indeed welfare had all but vanished as a political issue in New York by the mid-1950s. Some signals made their way to Albany that all was not well in the slums. Heroin addiction seemed unaccountably to be rising. A Department of Health official was dispatched to Britain to look into the system of legal-ized drug use. (He returned with a negative report.) But there was as yet no inkling of the massive social disorganization to come and little perception that it would be closely associated with race. (In 1957 a 164-page symposium in the *Annals of the American Academy of Political and Social Science,* entitled "Metropolis in Ferment," devoted seven paragraphs to the subject of the Negro in the City.) The theory of the Social Security Act of 1935 seemed to be working out. Social Security was a straightforward insurance plan for providing workers with income in their old age, and to care for their widows and dependent children should they die. The authors of the legislation foresaw the day when almost all workers and their dependents would be eligible for such benefits. In the interval there would be a number of persons who were old, disabled, widowed, some of whom would be caring for dependent children, but who would not be eligible. Interim programs would be necessary to care for them, and these were included in the Social Security Act: Old-Age Assistance; Aid to the Blind; Aid to Dependent Children. (Aid to the Permanently and Totally Disabled was added in 1950.) The presumption, and for a long while the experience, of these "categorical programs" was that they would gradually decline and perhaps eventually disappear. By the mid-1950s this certainly seemed to be happening. From 1955 to 1970 the number of persons receiving Old-Age Assistance declined in round figures from 2,540,000 to 2,100,000. The number receiving Aid to the Blind dropped from 100,000 to 81,000.

The "withering away" assumption persisted into the mid-1960s. In November 1965, John V. Lindsay, mayor-elect of the City of New York, set up a task force to advise him on problems of poverty. At a final session, which Lindsay attended, one member raised the problem of welfare. There were then (December 1965) 531,000 persons receiving welfare in the city, and the number had been rising. There was no apparent reason for this, the adviser declared: something was going askew; the family structure of the poor was apparently weakening, this was going to be a problem for the new mayor. Were there other views? Lindsay asked. There were. In strong terms it was asserted that the rising welfare rolls merely reflected the incompetence, possibly the corruption, of the previous administration, which the new mayor would replace. Tammany: that had been the problem, and that problem would soon be over. This was an agreeable view. The task force went on to other matters.

If there were men in the room who knew better, it would have been near to bad form for them to have said so. The subject under discussion was family structure, and this was a subject which American public men had avoided with a diligence rare in the affairs of any nation, and singular in ours.

A distinction is to be made between a generalized cultural piety about family life, and specific social policies directed to family concerns. The two need not be complementary; most often, in American experience, they have been in conflict. An unlikely assemblage of political, cultural, religious, and philosophical influences have converged on this topic. The laws against primogeniture and entail enacted by the Colonial assemblies, the prohibition in the Constitution against the granting of titles of nobility, reflected a generalized distrust of "great" families, the political unit of an aristocratical system, but this was only the negative side. The positive attitudes of the laissez-faire democracy that developed in the nineteenth century were equally resistant to public concern with matters that were increasingly defined as inviolate and private. The age of immigration reinforced the pattern. Successive ethnic and religious groups coming to the country tended to bring distinct family patterns with them; a political order that sought to prescribe in such matters would have found it increasingly difficult to do so. A pattern of avoidance arose. The inordinate difficulties of adoption in America derive mostly from this historically accidental set of circumstances. The Catholic orphan, the Protestant couple, the Jewish judge, the black social worker. There was, to be sure, some regulation. Protestant legislatures forbade birth control and abortion, and restricted divorce. Later, Catholic influence helped sustain such rules, but this only made the issues more sensitive.

Overlying these patterns peculiar to American experience was a general development in social thought, liberal on the one hand, Marxist on the other, which increasingly concentrated attention either on the lone individual or on abstract collectivities—the market, the electorate, the state, the universe—all to the exclusion of the family in between. Thirty years ago Alva Myrdal noted this tendency:

The state and the individual were always the two poles of interest. Social and political controversy was occupied with the question of the interrelationship of these two social entities. Whether the issue be stated as democracy versus authoritarianism, individualism versus collectivism, or competition versus cooperation, the dualism was un-varied—state and individual. What distribution of power and respon-sibility should there be between those two? That there might be still another competing center of attention—namely, the family—was mostly lost sight of. Similarly, the family was strangely neglected in education and in literature. There was, it is true, outward respect for the family with a whole system of verbal generalities, taboos, and moralities; but it remained outward only. The content of education was devoid of any attempt to disseminate knowledge which would prepare for better functioning of the intimate relationships within the family. The family was exalted in literature in the form of idyls; but in the idyls there was the essential falsity of Puritanism. Neither the problems nor the values of the family were treated with such re-spectful honesty as might enhance its competitive value.[1]

That the tradition persisted may be seen in the comparative fate of the two Myrdal books commissioned by the Carnegie Corporation in the late 1930s. *An American Dilemma* by Gun-nar Myrdal was an instant success, and continues to be widely read and influential. By contrast, the hardly less distinguished volume by Alva Myrdal was barely noted at the time it appeared, and has lived almost an underground existence since. Gunnar Myrdal wrote about the position of the Negro in American life, a subject of continued and at times preoccupying concern to American liberalism. Alva Myrdal's book, *Nation and Family,* addressed the issue of family policy.

By mid-twentieth century American liberalism had come to associate the idea of family policy not just with political con-servatism, but with Catholic conservatism. This was a fair enough reading of political history in nineteenth-century Europe, but it responded even more to the rise of Catholic political power in the United States. This brought to American public life a tentative assertion of Catholic social thought, in which the family is seen as the basic social unit, whose interests take priority, surely, over those of the marketplace; but also, in curious ways, over those of the state and the individual. This aroused suspicion, even alarm, among liberals, especially those of Protestant and

Jewish background, facing, in the Democratic party, a substantially Catholic infrastructure. Unfortunately, perhaps, Catholics did not produce an intellectual class that could expound its views on a competitive basis with Protestant and Jewish publicists. The most elemental of misunderstandings persisted. (Even now Catholic clergy, following the papacy, are given to denouncing the doctrines of "liberalism," especially as they apply to family matters. What the bishops have had in mind is laissez-faire capitalism of the vintage of Jeremy Bentham. At least until the time of John XXIII American liberals have somehow got the impression that what was being denounced was the minimum wage. That the enactment of the minimum wage, and practically the entire corpus of equivalent social legislation, was in large part due to Catholic legislators, is something neither liberals, nor Catholics, nor Catholic liberals seem ever quite to comprehend.) When in 1966 Americans for Democratic Action at length turned its attention to the subject of family policy, there emerged a resolution calling for enlightened legislation facilitating "abortion, birth control, and divorce." The failure of understanding was at times near total.*

The difficulty was compounded by the rise of a humanitarian concern, never so strong as in the present time, to protect "the good name of the poor." Curiously, this began as a reaction to the same laissez-faire moralism that so troubled the bishops. Early social welfare efforts in the United States tended to locate the sources of dependency in the habits of the poor. There was a case to be made for this view. Drink, to cite an example, was and is a formidable source of poverty and dependency. It was and is especially destructive to families. The temperance movement was onto something real. The family of the sober working man was far better off than that of the drunken one. And yet there is a sense in which social conditions create drunkenness, and that too is real. Little has been added to the controversy since *Major*

---

* During the period covered by this narrative women's liberationist views began also to influence this subject, again in such a way as to heighten its sensitivity. Many objected to the notion, implicit or explicit in much of the literature on family policy, that a female headed family is somehow incomplete. A perfectly understandable objection, but one which hardly makes the condition of the *dependent* female headed family any the more enviable. A case could be made that the welfare system institutionalizes the exploitation of women. This would be my view.

Barbara. Regardless of the evidence, however, opposition to the moralistic tone of welfare assistance appeared early, and by the beginning of the twentieth century had become the mark of "advanced" thinking in the field. An individual might be seen as having traits which caused him difficulty, but these tended to be ascribed to social or, later, psychopathic, conditions over which he had little control.

The Great Depression made the proposition that the unemployed are somehow not looking for work seem absurd, as indeed it was at the time, while, in general, advances in economics have increasingly portrayed joblessness as the consequence of national decisions that have nothing whatever to do with the character traits of the jobless. Again, this may not be wholly the case, but it is not to be doubted that the sensibilities of American social reformers have grown increasingly offended by definitions of social problems which seem to locate the source of difficulty in the behavior of the individual in trouble rather than in some abstraction made up of persons not in trouble. This concern is hardly unique to American social attitudes, but it is felt with special intensity here. Dependency amounts to failure, a fate seemingly more dreaded among us than others. Americans feel the need to deny failure, or to ascribe it to the most generalized sources. If there is a pattern among us it is that of denying the existence of a problem as long as possible, and thereafter quickly ascribing it to some generalized failing of society at large.

This instinctive avoidance is never more powerful than when the matter at issue touches on sexual behavior—which family matters necessarily do. As far back as social records go, poverty, especially urban poverty, has been associated with illegitimacy, desertion, and failure to provide, subjects so painful to humanitarians that many seemed able to confront the reality only by denying that it was in any way a failure of those who experience it, as in the formulation that family patterns of the poor represent an admirable, even enviable, rejection of bourgeois repression. Others contrived to know only as much about such matters as was absolutely necessary. This pattern became chronic within government. Where the tendency of most bureaucracies is to exaggerate the gravity of problems with which they deal, the tendency of welfare bureaucracies has been rather the opposite. One Secretary of Health, Education, and Welfare concluded toward the end of his tenure that his officials were so extremely reluctant to face the realities of dependency that they persistently underestimated prospective rises in the welfare rolls. A tradition of being "color blind" enabled those in the Federal bureaucracy who so wished to conceal from themselves the degree to which dependency had become associated with race, while a tradition of liberal-minded tolerance caused them to deny that problems such as illegitimacy existed.

As with most patterns of self-deception, this ended as self-defeating. The time came when the question of a generalized failure of the social system had to be confronted, but when it did the task fell to others. Welfare dependency became a "crisis" in the mid-1960s *not* because it was consuming large amounts of money, or involved large numbers of people. The amounts of money were trivial, and the numbers not that large. Welfare had to be defined as a crisis because of the rate at which the rolls commenced to grow. "The heart of it," Robert L. Bartley writes, "is that such growth has powerful overtones of social disintegration." Here surely was an opportunity to argue that the individual caught up in the system was not to blame, but the habit of analysis had been lost (or never acquired) among those nominally closest to the subject.[2] The whole matter had become just too painful.

It was thus that American society was peculiarly unprepared to respond to the rise of welfare dependency that occurred with such suddenness in the mid-1960s. The difficulty was not primarily or even significantly an unwillingness to *do* anything about the problem. Rather, it was an inability to *think* about it to any purpose. Nathan E. Cohen and Maurice F. Connery have described this as "a schism in our thought in which some processes of our society are perceived as subject to understanding and control and others subject only to some vague, unknowable dynamics to which we can only hope to respond."[3] The cost of this schism was, and continues to be, considerable. It involved, for one thing, the intellectual denial of a primary social reality, namely that family structure and functioning have consequences for children, and that, by and large, families function best in traditional arrangements. (Persons who have benefited from such arrangements sometimes find it easy to disparage them. A Southern saying goes, "A dollar ain't much if you got one.") Just as significantly, among social activists the presumption was reinforced that family matters were not to become public questions. Thus, when the United States Supreme Court early in 1971 upheld the constitutionality of a New York State law providing for periodic home visits to welfare recipients, there was an audible response that another blow had been struck against civil liberties. *The Times,* in its news columns, described the decision as evidence of an emerging "conservative" majority on the court. A *Times* editorial resisted this view, pointing out that the welfare worker in the case was seeking to visit a child that had at various times suffered a skull fracture, a dent in the head, and a "possible" rat bite. Justice Harry A. Blackmun had ruled that "the dependent child's needs are paramount, and only with hesitancy would we relegate those needs, in the scale of comparative values, to a position secondary to what the mother claims as her rights." The *Times* editorial defended this judgment, but the more general opinion was revealed in the news story. The "liberal" decision would have been to bar the social worker, as "government has no business interfering with family life." In this there was to be seen an odd continuity between the laissez-faire liberalism of the nineteenth century and the far more interventionist liberalism of the twentieth.[4]

In sum, it was scarcely to be expected that the 1965 task force advising Mayor-elect Lindsay on poverty problems would be equipped to anticipate what was to become not merely his most serious poverty problem, but the central malaise of his administration. Before Lindsay took office the welfare rolls had been climbing at about 3,000 to 5,000 recipients per month. In mid-1966 the rate more than doubled. Then it almost doubled again. It dropped back in 1969, only to rise again in 1970. Five years after his task force had met, the 531,000 New Yorkers on welfare had become 1,165,000.* An end of sorts came on

---

* The increase was expected to continue with the caseload reaching 1,340,000 by mid-1973—one New Yorker in six. By October 1971, the number of welfare recipients had already passed 1,228,000. From a slightly different perspective, Nicholas Kisburg has calculated that in 1960 the ratio of private sector wage and salary employment to public assistance recipients in New York City was 9.7 to 1. By 1971 the ratio was 2.6 to 1.

December 29, 1970, when the mayor announced his rejection of the proposed budget of the Human Resources Administration which asked $2.1 billion for welfare costs. In the course of the decade the population of the city had grown hardly at all. (There was an increase of some 85,000 persons.) But the welfare rolls had grown from one person in thirty, to one in twenty, to one in ten, one in nine, one in eight, one in seven. The new budget foresaw a rise to one in six. Officials talked of one in five.

The mayor said stop. "The City of New York and taxpayers can no longer meet the rising costs of welfare," he declared, and went on, in effect, to repudiate the central position he had adopted with respect to welfare in the five stormy years of his administration. His had been the most humane, accepting, even approving, of attitudes. In one way or another he had repeatedly affirmed that welfare was a right. Those entitled to it should get it, and should be helped to do so. (Under Lindsay, the city adopted a simple declaration device whereby a person wishing to obtain welfare simply affirmed that he or she was eligible.) The mayor now reversed his position. He was going to find ways to turn people down. He instructed the Corporation Counsel "to determine the city's legal ability, in light of Federal and state laws, to refuse to pay for increased welfare costs or accept additional welfare cases because of its financial condition." "We are sick to death," he declared, "of having Federal and state law ram down our throats the cost of a program which doesn't work."

That it was not working, few would deny, and yet it was not less obvious the mayor was accepting a counsel of desperation. As early as 1961, Joseph Mitchell, the city manager of Newburgh, a small city in the Hudson Valley, had called attention to the uses of attacks on "welfare chiselers" as a "respectable" device for tapping anti-Negro sentiment among voters. This was hardly the posture, public or private, of John V. Lindsay. Yet he was instructing his attorney to find grounds for turning away the destitute and abandoned women and children of his city. On February 24, 1971, the mayor walked from City Hall to the Federal Court House at Foley Square, where he filed a lawsuit on behalf of the city contending that the Federal and state laws mandating welfare payments are unconstitutional. He cited the dictum of Chief Justice John Marshall in *McCulloch v. Mary-*

land that "the power to tax involves the power to destroy." Welfare costs, he said, were destroying New York City.*

Lindsay had little choice save to act as he did. It had become the practice by 1970 to ascribe the increasing welfare load to new pride, militancy, and organization among the poor in the city, yet the evidence hardly supported this. Five days after the mayor's declaration, a member of the editorial board of *The Times* said what there was to say.

The only figures which almost exactly parallel welfare figures are those for desertion and illegitimacy. The economic situation seems to have some impact on welfare rolls. City officials report that many of those now coming on to the rolls explained that they had lost jobs or run out of unemployment insurance benefits. But just as welfare rates rise steadily, regardless of the economic situation, so have illegitimacy and desertion rates. Most of those on welfare are women with children. There has been a startling 83 per cent increase in female-headed families among inner-city Negroes in recent years.

The day following the mayor's announcement, *The Times,* which had persistently backed his accepting attitude toward welfare, indicated that it, too, was out of patience. Its lead editorial, entitled "The Welfare City," was waspish.

The existing job situation in New York is not so bad—nor are all of those on welfare so helpless—that there is any excuse for having one person in seven on public assistance, much less contemplating a growth that will make the ratio one in six or even five.

Welfare dependency had become a dominant fact of the city; a central condition that affected all other conditions. Government itself was the first to be affected, as direct welfare expenditures grew to dominate the budget. From fiscal year 1960 to 1970, income-support and welfare-related activities increased sixfold. In short order the welfare proportion of the

* The Mayor had no case, as the court eventually found. "Welfare" is part of the Social Security program in which States are theoretically free to participate or not as they wish.

budget surpassed that for education, and by the end of the decade was half again as large.*

New York had known earlier periods of great distress. In the aftermath of the British occupation, in the doldrums of Jefferson's Embargo, quite astounding proportions of the population received some form of public relief, while the proportion of welfare recipients in the 1930s depression has yet to be surpassed. Still the experience of the 1960s was different. This was not a period of hard times, but rather of sustained economic growth, high employment, and general prosperity. Welfare dependency had become a phenomenon separated from the experience of the larger society, just as welfare recipients had come to live apart from the rest of the population. The symbol of welfare dependency was the female-headed family. The numbers of such grew and grew, until in 1969 the New York *Daily News* would report, not in anger or even disapproval, but simply as a statement of fact, "A quiet social revolution is taking place in the slums of the nation, especially those here in New York City: desertion and illegitimacy are soaring at the expense of the traditional family structure."

As the decade came to an end, avoidance of these aspects of dependency became less possible. What had been unmentionable was openly discussed. In 1970, Henry Cohen, Director of the Center for New York City Affairs at the New School for Social Research and former Deputy Human Resources Administrator for the city, published an analysis of welfare which reported that 60 percent of New York's illegitimate births occurred to women on welfare rolls. "The rate of out-of-wedlock births," he wrote, "has been increasing among all segments of the population, and in 1968 exceeded 40 percent among nonwhites, 25 percent among Puerto Ricans, and 6 percent among whites." It appeared new ratios would be even higher. The following year Jule M. Sugarman, Human Resources Administrator and Commissioner of Social Services, made public a staff study showing that "welfare births," which in 1959 accounted for 5.76 percent of all births in the city, had by 1969 risen to 17.07 percent. Of these, 69.15 percent were out-of-wedlock, a proportion also growing.

* City welfare payments from only its own funds amounted to 28 percent of New York's total costs in 1970, state and Federal sources assuming the bulk of the expense.

To a dangerous, divisive degree the older ethnic working-class groups of the city found by the end of the decade that they appeared to be paying for the support of a vast dependent population of female-headed families, and a shadow population made up of the presumably absent fathers, who had been relieved of the trouble and expense of raising their children. To the affluent there might seem little cause for dismay in all this, but the great proportion of New Yorkers were hardly affluent. (In the late 1960s, the earnings of many blue-collar workers were declining in real terms. Between 1960 and 1970 the weekly take-home pay of the envied workers in contract construction, nationwide, increased only from $96.17 to $122.76 in constant 1957–1959 dollars.) Blacks no less than whites were burdened and puzzled. In his book *The Inhabitants,* published in 1960, Julius Horwitz depicted a black social worker, struggling to raise his children, holding down two jobs to pay the mortgage on a house in Flatbush, baffled by what was even then a baffling, inherently conflicting, unprecedented phenomenon.

"I came home about 2:45 this morning. We had a snack before we got to bed. My wife gets up when I come in, which I think is nice of her. Then I don't feel like a hired bastard crawling off to sleep on the cornhusks. I told her about a girl I had seen yesterday. Eighteen years old, a nice girl, a girl born right here in New York City. Her natural father told her to go to hell. Her stepfather supported her until just three days ago and then he told her to go to hell, she was eighteen, and goodbye. Her mother helped shove her out the door. The girl got grabbed in a hallway when she was fourteen and she had a baby on her fifteenth birthday and that ended high school for her. Then some boy from the Bronx got into her when she was sixteen and that was baby number two. I went out to see her. She and the two kids were sleeping on the floor of a girl friend who had a furnished hotel room on West 110th Street. Three adults told this girl to go to hell, turned their backs, and beat it. Now this girl has two boys starting to grow up. How's she going to make it? I talked about it with my wife until 3:30 in the morning. And this morning I realized I can't do a god-damn thing for her except put her on the budget, and from my experience in the matter, I don't expect God to do a damn thing."

Bronson picked up the thick black manual on his desk.

"Look at this son-of-a-bitching thing. I think it was written in hell in some air-conditioned, stainless steel, windowless room. This is the damndest book. I've been studying this book for the past couple of weeks instead of just using it. This book . . . contains the absolute minimum fixed prices necessary to maintain subsistence living in present-day New York City—which is one of the richest biggest cities in the entire history of the world, period. This book is the papa for 350,000 people right here in New York City getting assistance. And I'll bet my pay that there are tens of thousands of people right here in New York who don't even live up to the minimum standards that we lay down but who would rather eat old newspapers than apply for welfare. Do you see what I'm driving at, . . . ? We're not giving what's necessary, we're just giving what's minimum. Because those tens of thousands who live below the minimum have got what I call what's necessary for living. Do you know why I've been studying this manual, because my actual take-home pay is below the minimum of what I would get if I went downstairs and signed an application. So it's not money. And now I become lost."[5]

And with him countless others. Soon the racial and ethnic imbalance of the dependent population became unmistakable, and such explanatory powers as those categories may have was readily enough invoked.

But in truth as the 1960s progressed troubling disparities arose in the distribution of social benefits. By the end of the decade, social services had expanded so greatly that a dependent family that optimized its situation—public housing, Medicaid, food stamps, and such-like—could have an equivalent income at least equal to and probably above that of the average New York family. This had to have political consequences. The 1969 mayoralty election was the first in the city's history to be decided primarily by the intensity of racial conflict. The standard-bearer of the Democratic party, the oldest organized political party in the world, the party that for on to two centuries had spoken for the poor and submerged of the city, took the other side. The consequences of welfare were beginning to spread far beyond the welfare class.

And yet how little the recipients seemed to benefit from even the most generous standards. Barely weeks after Lindsay's announcement that the city could no longer afford an increase in the rolls, *The Times* reported that the Human Resources Ad-

ministration had put up a welfare mother and her four children
at the Waldorf-Astoria Hotel at a cost of $152.64 for two days.
The mayor was not amused; indeed, he suspected malicious
intent. City Hall issued a statement reporting, "The Mayor expressed deep anger and outrage over the incident, which he
denounced as 'colossal bad judgment or worse' on the part of the
city employees involved. He demanded an accounting of the
incident within twenty-four hours." A routine of sorts ensued.
Suspensions; threatened strike; picketing; reinstatements. In the
end, nothing changed. (Nor had there been any plot against the
mayor.) Mrs. Cleola Hainsworth went to stay at her girlfriend's
where she had wanted to go in the first place. The rent would be
$100 a week for two rooms, less than the average of more than
$660 a month the city was paying for welfare families in some
forty hotels. But it added up to so little for the families themselves. In the end Horwitz's case worker would own his house.
The welfare family would own nothing.

The problems of the city inevitably became those of the
state. In early March 1971, Governor Nelson A. Rockefeller let
it be known that he was considering, in the words of the *Times*
report, "a drastic revision of the state's welfare philosophy that
could cut the influx of welfare recipients into the state and require able-bodied persons on welfare to accept employment in
private industry or state-created jobs." In a statement, the governor declared that the existing welfare system "will ultimately
overload and break down our society"; it was not even helping
the recipient; rather, it was promoting "permanent dependence
on the government."

Rockefeller spoke as the senior governor in the nation, and
one of the most liberal leaders of either party.* But he and his
aides spoke with a bluntness, even a harshness, that was new.
The favorite statistic of welfare administrators—how small a
proportion of persons on relief are capable of work—was rejected almost with contempt. "The social workers don't make
surprise visits," said one administration source, "they tell them
they'll be there next Wednesday." Presumably surprise visits—
the "midnight raids" that for years had been a liberal symbol of

* One who was proposing, as well, a 40 percent increase ($324 million) in
welfare expenditures in his 1971 budget.

government oppression of the poor—would once again be in order. Yet more drastic was the governor's proposal to restrict migration into the state, despite a Supreme Court decision that had struck down "residency requirements" for welfare.[6] Newcomers seeking welfare, a source said, would be given emergency aid—"like lunch"—and a ticket back where they came from. The proposal, in the judgment of *The New York Times,* was "patently unconstitutional." Nonetheless, two weeks later the governor proposed a one-year residency requirement. Citing the finding of the Supreme Court that a "compelling state interest" was a prerequisite of a valid residency requirement, he asserted there was just that: "This step is essential to protect the state's economic and social viability." The legislature agreed. (A statute was enacted, and was duly declared unconstitutional: the governor's object was primarily to make a point.)

Welfare was no longer a residual and declining concern of state government. (One of the governor's 1971 proposals was to bring the Commissioner of Social Services under his direct control, the position having been for years a presumed nonpolitical post responsible to the state Board of Social Services.) He proposed to create an Inspector General of Welfare Administration with an investigating staff "to insure proper expenditure of welfare funds." Work was to be given primary emphasis in the welfare system. The power of local social-services districts to declare an individual unable to work was to be restricted. Every employable public-assistance recipient was to report to the State Employment Service every two weeks to pick up his check, rather than having it mailed to him. Every employable recipient was to have an interview with the Employment Service every two weeks. Any such person who quit his job without good cause or refused a job he was able to perform would be denied welfare. Again, the legislature agreed.

The men in Albany were serious in their alarm. One put it: "We're actually creating secondary effects in overloading the system, which is now affecting other citizens because of a breakdown in services." It was not an unreasoned judgment, nor did it only concern police, fire, and school services. Secondary effects were to be observed in the political system as well. When politicians of the right had proposed measures such as Lindsay and Rockefeller were now advocating, they were easily enough dismissed as reactionaries and racists. But surely not these men. In an editorial, "Welfare's Bankruptcy," *The Times* of March 12, 1971, acknowledged what was happening.

It is not the figurative bankruptcy of the cities and states in terms of dollars that must be of such concern now. It is, instead, an emerging bankruptcy of spirit and thought on the part of political leaders trapped in impossible budgetary binds.

Weeks later, the New York state legislature in a "budget revolt" imposed a 10 percent reduction in welfare payments to dependent families, primarily those in New York City.*

Trouble was hardly confined to New York: it was merely more pronounced there, had first become evident there. By 1970 the percentage rise in welfare rolls in New York City was running behind that for typical large cities. While this can be a statistical artifact, it also reflected a changed reality. By the end of the 1960s, welfare dependency had become a national phenomenon. In the twelve months ending June 30, 1970, the number of Americans receiving public assistance rose to a record 12.2 million, an increase of 2 million, or 20 percent, in a single year. The cost rose to $12.8 billion. In over one-quarter of the states the rolls went up by one third or more, Texas as well as Michigan, Maine along with Washington and Oregon; no part of the nation was unaffected. Again, the New York pattern held. During this period the number of recipients of Old-Age Assistance increased hardly at all—less than one percent—while the recipients of Aid to the Blind actually declined. Eighty-five percent of the overall increase came in the category of Aid to Families with Dependent Children. The number of such families had risen in twelve months by 27.3 percent.

In some measure this increase reflected an economic recession, especially in states such as Washington where employment

* At this time Hawaii also established a one-year residency requirement for welfare, directed not, however, toward the Aid to Families with Dependent Children (AFDC) population so much as to "welfare hippies" (the term used by Lieutenant-Governor George Ariyoshi), who had been arriving in considerable number to take advantage of the beaches and of a general assistance law similar to that of New York. "There must be no parasites," declared State Senator Wadsworth Yee, "in paradise."

in the aerospace industries had fallen off sharply, but the trend over time was unchanged. The increase in AFDC rolls for the fiscal year 1966 had been 4.5 percent; for 1967, 11.7 percent; for 1968, 13.2 percent; for 1969, 17.7 percent. In good years and bad, the number rose. The Administrator of the Social and Rehabilitation Service of HEW saw a future "no brighter." Welfare costs, he asserted, "could double again in the next five years, and the rolls could rise by another 50 to 60 percent." In particular, the pattern of rising illegitimacy and desertion was almost everywhere to be encountered, as was the pattern of racial and social imbalance in the welfare population. In the course of the decade the proportion of AFDC families living in metropolitan areas, primarily the inner cities, rose from three fifths to almost three fourths; the number of families with father absent, by about the same. By 1970 about 48.1 percent of the family heads covered by AFDC were white; 45.2 percent, Negro; and 6.7 percent, other races.

Although New York has perhaps a greater aura of wealth about it, few other large cities in the nation have the per capita income of Washington, D.C. Yet three days after Mayor Lindsay's announcement, the Washington *Post* reported that in 1970 the AFDC rolls in the capital had grown by 66 percent. (According to the *Post,* 95 percent of these AFDC applicants were black.) If poverty had seemed a straightforward affair, clearly welfare dependency was not. *Across the nation it had become a general rule that as poverty declined, welfare dependency increased.*

The War on Poverty of the 1960s was officially announced in the Economic Report of the President of January 1964. The Council of Economic Advisers defined as poor any family of two or more persons with income for the year less than $3,000. This was computed on the basis of a study by the Social Security Administration which had estimated $3,165 as the minimum income needed (in 1961) for a nonfarm family of two adults and two children. The SSA had in turn based its calculations on the U.S. Department of Agriculture's Economy Food Plan which had emerged from its 1955 survey of food consumption. The poverty level was set at three times the cost of the Economy Food Plan. (In time, adjustments were made for family size and increases in the Consumer Price Index, but the basic concept continued in force.)* By this standard, poverty declined steadily and sharply in the 1960s. In 1959 almost a quarter of the American population, 39,490,000 persons, was below the poverty level. By 1969 the proportion had declined to 12.2 percent, and the numbers to 24,289,000. This decline was sharpest for non-whites: in 1959, 56.2 percent were in poverty; a decade later, 31.1 percent. (As a percent of total, however, the "share" of poverty among "Negro and other races" rose slightly from 27.9 percent to 31.4 percent.)

This was a period of great concern about poverty, especially black poverty. A profusion of programs came forth from Washington, some of which had measurable consequences. Some may even have contributed to the decline of poverty, but almost certainly the most important influence in this respect was a long, sustained period of economic expansion which phased into a wartime boom. Whatever else is to be said about war, it makes social statistics look good. Between 1960 and 1969 the number of nonwhite craftsmen and operatives, the basic blue-collar occupations which make up about one third of the work force, increased 40 percent, whereas the number of whites in such jobs rose only 7 percent. The real earnings of nonwhite men averaged a 55 percent gain during this period, double the increase for whites. In 1968 an event of significance occurred. The median income of young husband-wife black families outside of the South reached parity with those of white families. In 1969 even more impressive gains occurred. Outside the South, the median earnings of husband-wife Negro families headed by a male twenty-five to thirty-four years of age were 91 percent of the pay of their white counterparts, while for similar families with a head age fourteen to twenty-four years, the midpoint of black income reached 107 percent that of whites. This was surely the first time in the history of the United States that a broadly defined category of blacks had higher incomes than did their white equivalents.

* In 1970 the economy experienced the first recession in a decade, in the course of which the number of persons in poverty increased by 1.2 million to a total of 25.5. This increase was evenly distributed among the various poverty classes. The Federal Interagency Standard "poverty level" for a nonfarm family of four rose from $3,743 in 1969 to $3,968 in 1970. Thus at the outset of the new decade the $3,000 poverty definition of the original Economic Opportunity Act had risen to $4,000.

Another milestone was passed in 1968, one very much less promising. That year, for the first time, a majority of poor Negro children lived in female-headed households.

This is the key to what happened in the 1960s. Opportunities opened to those equal to them, for the white poor as well as for the black. (Statistics for the latter are in ways the best clue to what is happening among the former.) In rough terms, young families headed by a male were most nearly equal to the opportunities that opened. Families headed by older persons were in a less good position to move up, while families headed by a female were in no position at all. From 1959 to 1969 the number of male-headed white families in poverty dropped 49.7 percent; Negro and other races dropped 54.8 percent. But the number of female-headed white families living in poverty rose slightly, and the number of poor female-headed black families increased by one third. At the end of the 1950s, two thirds of poor Negro families were headed by a man. By the end of the 1960s more than half were headed by a female. These were not just poor families: they were dependent ones. The nature of poverty had changed. Especially among minorities, but as a general phenomenon also, poverty among children and young adults was associated with dependency, not unemployment. These were the welfare poor.

Two further facts about poverty emerged clearly by the end of the 1960s. The families of the poor with children were large, and for the most part they either lived in the South or had come from there. Both facts were also particularly characteristic of the black population.

By the end of the 1960s black Americans were living in a state almost of population siege. In 1970 nonwhites comprised 11 percent of the civilian noninstitutional population age sixteen and over—that is to say, the adult population. But they made up 15.8 percent of the population under sixteen. If black earnings were rising, family size still militated against person-for-person equality of income. Again, this situation was most pronounced among the poor. The 1960 Census demonstrated that black families at lower levels of social and economic status consistently had more children than their white counterparts, while just the opposite was the case at higher levels. (Black families ceased to reproduce themselves after passing income levels of about $7,000 per year. By contrast, the size of white families, after declining also, began to increase at about this point.) *

Number of children ever born, for married women living with their husbands, 35 to 44 years old, by socioeconomic status, 1960.

Socio-economic status	NUMBER OF CHILDREN	
	Per 1,000 white wives	*Per 1,000 nonwhite wives*
90–99 (high)	2,440	1,538
80–89	2,328	1,827
75–79	2,315	2,148
70–74	2,373	2,158
60–69	2,444	2,355
50–59	2,564	2,591
40–49	2,734	2,834
30–39	2,904	3,051
25–29	3,104	3,277
20–24	3,297	3,450
10–19	3,607	3,983
0–9 (low)	4,358	4,867

SOURCE: U.S. Bureau of the Census, *U.S. Census of Population: 1960, Subject Reports,* Socioeconomic Status, Final Report PC(2)-5C, table 13, pp. 194–95.

In 1960, married women would have had to produce 2.27 "children" each in order to maintain the United States population at its present level.

The 1960s was a period of marked demographic change, curiously parallel to and interconnected with changes in income and employment. Things got better and worse. The most significant event was a sharp decline in population growth, accom-

---

* The Bureau of Census has constructed a socioeconomic status scale for the 1960 population. Each interval of ten corresponds, approximately, to a thousand dollars of income, starting at the bottom and rising. When reproduction rates are measured against this scale, a pronounced pattern emerges.

panied by a sustained economic expansion. As a result, for the period 1959–1968 the base population of the Nation (defined as the civilian population residing outside institutions and members of the Armed Forces living off post or with their families on post in the United States) increased 12 percent, while the national aggregate money income rose 49.4 percent. Alexander Radomski has calculated that for this period the number of income recipients increased twice as fast as population, and the number of women recipients increased 2.7 times as fast as men. "Dependency ratios" declined sharply. In 1959 there had been, for whites, 98 persons of all ages without income for every 100 with; by 1968 this ratio had dropped to 76. For Negroes and other races the decline was from 106 to 94. Among white persons the number of children decreased from 58 per 100 income recipients to 47; among Negro and other races from 73 to 68. Although changes in nonwhite birth rates lagged behind those of whites when they did come they were, if anything, more pronounced. Between 1959 and 1964 the number of nonwhite children increased 18.9 percent. Between 1964 and 1968 the increase was only 2.4 percent. (In New York City, although the number of welfare births rose, the percent of welfare mothers giving birth to a child during the year dropped from 18.2 percent in 1964 to 11.2 percent in 1970.) During the period median income of white men increased 25 percent; white women, 33 percent; nonwhite men, 57 percent; nonwhite women, 71 percent.[7]

These are the great ratios of a society; these define the possible. What emerges as having been possible in the 1960s was a redress of social imbalance on a scale approaching grandeur. Little, or little enough, of what occurred was the result of avowed social policy, but actual outcomes were startlingly in line with such policy. If somehow an opposite impression appeared to dominate events toward the end of the period—that is to say the impression of social conditions steadily worsening, and a society approaching apocalypse—the explanation has to do, in some measure at least, with the contrary movement that persisted and grew more pronounced among the dependent poor.

The number of persons classified as poor in the span 1959 to 1968 decreased by 36 percent. The number of public-assistance recipients rose 41 percent. This is about the gist of it, allowing that the welfare-*associated* population—the invisible men, the families cycling in and out—is considerably larger than the number of recipients at a given time.

Despite declining fertility rates for both groups, the disparity between whites and nonwhites actually grew during much of this period as well as over the century. (In 1920–1924 the ratio of white to nonwhite births for women fifteen to forty-four years of age was 1:1.21; in 1967 it was 1:1.44.) Illegitimacy became a serious problem for all groups: a *new* rather than a received disposition. Here again the pattern of opposite tendencies appears. Illegitimacy rates rose for whites during the 1960s but declined for Negro and other races. (A decline in overall birth rates will normally produce a decline in illegitimate rates as well.) However, the illegitimacy *ratios* for both groups increased every year from 1960 to 1968. By the latter year 5.3 percent of all white and 31.2 percent of all nonwhite births were illegitimate. Among Negro and other races, 48 percent of *first* births were out of wedlock, which would suggest that fully half that female population began childbearing in circumstances predisposed to dependency. Once again the contrasting trends are to be noted: illegitimacy ratios increased in part because the proportion of women of childbearing age who remained unmarried increased, but also because of a general decline of fertility, "mainly marital" in the words of the Bureau of the Census, which reduced the base against which the illegitimacy ratio is calculated.[8] (The United States was not alone in this development. In Britain, the illegitimate as a percentage of all live births, after remaining stable through the first half of the century, nearly doubled between 1951 and 1968, rising from 4.9 percent to 8.4 percent.) A range of developments in the field of birth control, combined with public and private family planning programs, had created the opportunity to limit family size. The circumstances of those who took advantage of the opportunity improved, at least in relative terms, far more than that of those who did not, or could not.

Race, family size, family structure: all these were correlates of poverty. But none was nearly so powerful in aggregate terms as the mere fact of geographic region. All in all, by the end of the 1960s half of all the nation's poor families—two in five of the poor whites, and two in three of the poor blacks—lived in the sixteen states plus the District of Columbia which Federal statistics define as the South. Of those most poor, which is to say rural families earning less than half the poverty level income, 60 percent lived in the South, which altogether had only a third of the American population. The North–South gap was worse for blacks than for whites. In 1968, Southern white families on average had only $85 in income for every $100 going to white families elsewhere; for black Southern families this amount was only $66. Outside the South, in 1968, one black family in four had an income of $10,000 or more per year; in the South there was only one such family in eight. The proportion of Southern white families who were poor was half again the proportion for all white families, while among blacks, being Southern increased the likelihood of being poor by a third.

Poverty in the South is not so much associated with unemployment as with low wages and low earnings. Even so, Southern poverty, like poverty elsewhere, is also associated with dependency. Of the ten states with the highest percentage of welfare recipients at the end of 1969, eight were Southern. Of the four Federal categorical programs, there were fifty-four recipients per 1,000 persons in the South, compared with thirty-three elsewhere. Louisiana led all the states in Old-Age Assistance, with 410 persons out of every 1,000, sixty-five or older, receiving Federal benefits. Half the recipients of this category of aid lived in the South.

Not so with children. The distinctive pattern of welfare assistance in the South has been to aid the aged and neglect the young. Of every 1,000 children under eighteen in the South, only sixty-seven were receiving AFDC support, compared with seventy-eight elsewhere. If the relative North–South proportions of the "adult categories" had obtained, instead of sixty-seven children per thousand, there would have been 156. What support the children received was often pitiful. Of the ten states with the lowest average AFDC payment, all were in the South. In Mississippi the payment was $8.50 per child per month.

As the 1960s progressed, poverty came to be better understood. It was seen to be a dynamic rather than static condition. In a given year as many as a third of poor families were "new arrivals," which is to say families that had not been poor the previous years. Correspondingly, as the overall numbers declined, an even larger number of families would have "left" poverty in such a year. The population "at risk" was significantly larger than the number of poor at any given moment. Families cycled in and out: something like that. No one knew for certain. During intervals of personal hard times welfare became a prime or sole source of income. Studies of AFDC families showed that half received assistance for less than two years. Something led into dependency and then led out of it. For some, presumably, the pattern repeated itself. No one could say for how many, but one fact did emerge most powerfully from the studies of this period: the AFDC program was far and away the most significant antipoverty effort of the Federal government, and was the core element of a national family policy. One child in five reaching maturity at the end of the 1960s had at one time been supported by AFDC. Among black youth the proportion may have been as high as two thirds. Again, using nonwhite data as a surrogate for low-income and poor persons generally, there could be no doubt of the immense, if unintended, influence of this singular form of income maintenance.

That the influence was unintended is nothing unusual. In the course of the 1960s the Federal government was to find itself in thrall to "hidden" policies in the widest range of foreign and domestic affairs. (Thus, Selective Service, a simple device for getting soldiers at below market costs, emerged as a national youth policy of incomparable consequence to the lives of young persons, and eventually to the foreign and domestic policies of the Nation.) That "hidden policies" would profoundly affect children was in some ways the central theme of Alva Myrdal's *Nation and Family*. In the nature of modern society, she had argued, no government, whatever its wishes, can avoid doing things that profoundly influence family relationships. These patterns of activity add up to family policy, which in turn "can be nothing less than a social policy at large."

No one intended that the AFDC program should become the central family policy of the United States in the 1960s. To the pattern of avoidance of family issues generally the evolution of AFDC added a pattern of inadvertence. The program began almost as an afterthought. As the depression of the 1930s persisted, a political movement for Federal old-age pensions arose, modeled on veterans' pensions, the oldest, most widely based, and until then almost the only, welfare activity of the national government. An alternative idea of a social-insurance system patterned on European practice was widely accepted in liberal circles at this time, and President Roosevelt moved to head off a pension plan by creating Social Security. The Old-Age Assistance provisions of the Act provided in effect a pension for the aged destitute of the time, but the long-range principle was to be one of social insurance rather than of relief.

Even so, relief was much in the air. The drafters of the Social Security Act were primarily concerned with problems of the dependent aged, but, influenced by the Children's Bureau, then in the Department of Labor, agreed to provide for destitute children as well. "Mothers' Pensions" had originated in the Progressive Era and by the 1930s had been established in all but two states, Georgia and South Carolina. Their purpose was to allow dependent children to remain with their mothers. There was also an element of singling out the deserving poor for special treatment. One student writes, "The mere act of receiving a Mothers' Pension grant bestowed prestige, so high were the moral and child-rearing expectations."[9] Divorced and deserted women were eligible for such support, but at the outset of the Depression, in four fifths of the families aided, the mother was a—presumedly respectable—widow. There was a large element of local option in the system, such that by the time of the Depression fewer than half the counties with the authority to provide support were actually doing so. The case for Federal assumption of some part of the cost was clear enough, and this was done in the form of the Aid to Dependent Children provision of the Social Security Act.

The new program was permanent and its cost, in the form of claims submitted by individual states for the Federal share of payments, provided under increasingly complex formulae, was an automatic charge on the Treasury. What bills came in were paid; that was about the end of it. The administrative arrangement so diffused responsibility that no one was particularly accountable for the program. A vertical relationship between bureaucracies at different levels of government gradually formed, and took over management of the program. At the Washington level this immensely complex social program, and the social problem it reflected, became a matter for career officials in the Bureau of the Budget, the Treasury Department, and the Social Security Administration, the last dedicated then as now to keeping its program "out of politics."

It took no great effort to do this where ADC was concerned. From the outset Congress was much involved with the old-age provisions of Social Security. Coverage was steadily expanded, and the pattern commenced of increasing benefit levels every other year as elections approached. ADC was different.* A fair but not especially telling point could be made that ADC recipients did not vote. (Not, at least, until 1950 when the mother, as well as the children, became eligible for benefits and the program was renamed Aid to *Families* with Dependent Children or, AFDC.) More important, as time passed, a program that had simply been without interest began to fill up with peril. The recipients changed. The West Virginia widow in the God-fearing hills became a black, likely as not unmarried, mother in the depths of the corrupting city. Gilbert Y. Steiner of the Brookings Institution described the view from Washington in the mid-1960s: "Public assistance introduces problems of race, of sex, of religion, and of family relationships. It is hard to think of four areas most American politicians would rather avoid."[10]

(Early in 1971 a member of the editorial board of *The New York Times* wrote on its Op-Ed page:

Welfare can be called an outrage because: it offers the equivalent of a tax-free income estimate as high as $5,624 to a family of four which may or may not have actually been deserted by its father; it holds out a bonus for additional illegitimate children; any recipient can double a monthly payment by claiming to have lost a check; it has even included, in extreme cases, fringe benefits beyond those in any union contract, such as a weekend at the Waldorf-Astoria or a ski trip to Vermont.

Eighty percent of the welfare rolls in New York City, he declared, are made up of women and children. "They are on welfare principally because of desertion and illegitimacy." The answer to the crisis, he went on, lay in family planning, day care, and job training. Mayor Lindsay, he asserted, had "done next to

---

* Indeed, substantial efforts had to be made by supporters of ADC to prevent its being left out of the regular "cost-of-living" increases in benefits paid under the other categories of assistance.

nothing to expand his city's family-planning services. Schools, where early pregnancy is increasingly a problem, offer no family-planning counseling." The editor was treading on the most frangible, opaque issues of social policy. To cut down welfare "and the misery it represents," he was in fact proposing to reduce the number of black Protestant and Catholic Puerto Rican children born in New York City. Who has the right to use public funds to ensure that relatively more children will be born to one ethnic or social group in the city, and fewer to some other? Such decisions are now routinely made, but by men—budget officials and legislators in the main—who prefer not to think too closely about what they do. The political and social culture has provided almost no guides *for* thinking about such subjects. In the meantime, a white Protestant editor of a Jewish-owned newspaper in New York might talk about the subject, but a "WASP" or Jewish politician would hardly be advised to do so.) [11]

There was, finally, little pressure for politicians to become involved. As with many areas of public activity, a profession had developed in the field of social welfare, complete with a hierarchy of graduate schools, professional associations, and certification procedures. As professions go, it was not the least demanding. It drew on middle- and upper-class persons for many if not most of its recruits, typically persons of strong attachment to ideals of social justice. What it lacked was a working model of social behavior which would enable the practice of social welfare to produce definable social consequences. The result had been a sequence of often brief enthusiasms for this or that "school," ranging from the complexities of Freudian case-work to the simplicities of the social gospel, each period seemingly destined to be followed by a flurry of evaluations suggesting that nothing of much consequence happened one way or another.

Professions, in such circumstances, tend to keep nonprofessionals at something of a distance. The social-welfare profession was not an exception. In 1962, Congress, which in this case is to say the Committee on Ways and Means of the House of Representatives, for the first time became seriously concerned that the AFDC program seemed to be getting out of hand. Asked their professional advice, the social-welfare profession assured the committee (as did the Kennedy Administration) that what was needed was more and better social work. Congress accepted this advice. The result was the Social Security Amendments of 1962, providing greatly increased Federal support for training and for programs in the social services. But as the welfare crisis of the 1960s mounted, it became plain enough that the social-welfare profession could not even explain events, much less control them. Something was going wrong which the profession could neither account for nor cope with. As the decade moved on, Congress was to look back at the 1962 Amendments with a feeling of having been misled. It had sought the best professional counsel, had responded generously and things had only got worse. But nothing mysterious had occurred, and certainly nothing dishonorable. It was simply that the profession had overestimated how much it knew or could hope to know.

If social-welfare practice could not make the welfare system work, it was inevitable that persons, including those within the profession, would begin questioning the system itself. Such questioning grew in intensity, even fury, as the decade passed. The American Public Welfare Association sponsored a serious study of the AFDC program, *An American Dependency Challenge* by M. Elaine Burgess and Daniel O. Price, which appeared in 1963. The authors argued that the AFDC program was not working, and concluded it could not be made to. At the Columbia School of Social Work a group of radical theorists associated with Richard A. Cloward contended that the system should be made *not* to work, in effect, be sabotaged, by bringing as many persons as possible onto the rolls, thus forcing the city and state governments toward bankruptcy and the political system toward radical reform. Intermediate views abounded. Even the most balanced of these analyses, however—as for example the report of Burgess and Price—had a quality of abstractness about them which at bottom revealed itself as the familiar pattern of avoidance.[12] The political system was repeatedly told that something had to be done, but was not told why. That is to say, it was not told that welfare dependency might represent a social problem larger than the sum of individual difficulties. To uncertainty of knowledge was added an obvious fear, or at least anxiety, about the probable reaction. The political environment was seen as fundamentally hostile.

There was a measure of truth in this, but also an element of bias, even possibly of projection. Whatever else the social-welfare profession was, it was preeminently respectable. In cities such as New York, it had had from the outset fairly close ties with social elites, as in the familiar charity balls, the exquisitely groomed planners of which are still faithfully photographed by The *Times*. The profession, and the considerable number of persons associated with it in bureaucracies such as the Children's Bureau, seemed to fear that "the politicians," and "the public"— the electorate—would balk at funding welfare if they learned too much about illegitimacy and such, and so in a sense, kept the whole matter quiet. Yet it is not clear just who was disturbed by what. Professions, like other institutions, tend to retain some of the characteristics of the eras in which they formed. The social-welfare profession had never quite overcome the posture of the municipal reform movement of the early 1900s that politics was "unclean" and that professionals might for a wide set of purposes supplant politicians. Whatever the case, a kind of *faux* gentility was preserved. The signs in the halls of social welfare read *Silence*.

In such circumstances it was reasonable to expect politicians to take some initiative on their own, and this occurred. The United States at the time was the only industrial democracy in the world that did not have a system of family allowances. The *theory* of Family Allowance developed in Europe as an accommodation of the social theory (in this case Catholic) that holds it to be the responsibility of society to provide families with an adequate income to the modern industrial practice that gears wages to the productivity of the worker without regard to differing levels of need. A married man with five children presumably can be said to need, and also from the point of view of some social theory, to deserve, more income than does a bachelor. Family allowances, typically, are flat payments of so much per month per child. The *practice* began in Europe under fairly conservative regimes, usually a pronatalist policy. Soon enough, however, it became a standard feature of social-democratic welfare policies. (Not infrequently, as in the case of Mrs. Myrdal's Sweden, it served both causes. The Swedes of the 1930s thought they were dying out, as indeed they were, however slowly.)

Formulas varied considerably from country to country, but in Europe a consistent feature is that the more children a family has the more money it receives. Following the introduction of reduced family railroad fares and the French Family Medal, innovations of the 1920s, France, in 1932, established a general system of family allowances for workers in trade and in industry, and with the adoption of the Family Code in 1939 commenced a "coherent and continuous family policy" which was and remains fundamentally pronatalist.

There is nothing concealed about this policy. A 1966 French government manual declares:

It was . . . during the international crisis years of 1938 and 1939 that the French people as a whole came to a full realization of the seriousness of the population situation. The Family Code, as the defensive reaction of a Nation whose frontiers were threatened, is above all a scheme to promote the birthrate, and it is typical that it should have been published on the very eve of the outbreak of the Second World War, as was also the addition to the Government of a Minister for Families on 6th June 1940—during the most dramatic hours of the invasion.[13]

Such policies had discernible consequences, perhaps most notably in France, where family allowances remain quite high. Within a decade of the adoption of family allowances income differentials of workers with families had quite changed. In 1939, incomes, at the level of the basic wage, were only moderately greater for men with families than for the unmarried: a family with four children had an income 30 percent greater than a bachelor. By 1949 such a family had twice the income of an unmarried man.[14] Although rising wage levels and inflation in Western Europe have led to a general decline in the proportion of income represented by family allowances, they remain a prominent feature of social policy, with wide political support.

Family allowances were introduced in Canada during World War II, partly as a gesture to French Canadians, and became enormously popular. Senator Richard L. Neuberger of Oregon came upon the idea, and in the mid-1950s introduced a Senate resolution, cosponsored by such colleagues as John F. Kennedy and Hubert H. Humphrey, proposing a congressional inquiry into the matter. Neuberger is said to have thought it would take him fifteen years to get a children's allowance adopted, but he died soon after taking up the issue. Nothing directly came of his initiative, but the idea persisted.

With the advent of the Kennedy Administration a general searching about in such areas began. Within the Labor Department, preoccupied with the slow, painful climb down from the unemployment levels of the time, a view arose that policy-makers had become too much concerned with aggregate measures of employment, a surrogate measure for the general level of economic activity, and too little concerned with actual income flows to workers' households. In 1963 the position of Assistant Secretary of Labor for Policy Planning and Research was established, and with it a Policy Planning Staff. As the new Assistant Secretary, I turned first, with some encouragement from the labor movement, to the subject of family income.

In the winter of 1963–1964, the Policy Planning Staff of the Department developed a position paper on "Family Allowances in the United States." The first bureaus of labor statistics established in the United States had arisen largely from the desire of the early trade unions that the government regularly calculate the living costs of workers in order that they might bargain against an official standard of need. In this way the City Workers Family Budget was developed, and from it a variety of consumption-oriented indices. However, concern with family income levels subsequently receded under the combined impact of Keynesian economics, with its emphasis on employment rates, and the developing ability to measure such rates. Now, however, the Labor Department had some success in reviving the subject. Here and there the formulation took root that the United States was "the only industrial democracy in the world without a system of family allowances," a phrase intended both to reassure and to unsettle.[15]

The attractions of the family allowance lay in simplicity, in universality, and in the possibility of arguing that it was, after all, a practice long since established among such sensible folk as the Canadians and the Dutch. These were also its disadvantages. As it made no distinction between the poor and the nonpoor, it was of necessity relatively "inefficient" as an antipoverty device. Being universal, it suggested a "baby bonus" and with that the prospect of the teeming working-class quarters so disagreeable to social-welfare enthusiasts. Perhaps just as important, since it was a measure that had already been conceived and put into practice, there were simply limits to the enthusiasm which family allowances could arouse in clever minds.

Happily, there existed an alternative that had occurred two decades earlier to the singularly clever mind of the economist, Milton Friedman. In 1943, working in the Treasury Department on income-tax matters, he became concerned about the problem of fluctuating earnings. Given graduated tax rates, persons whose incomes rose and fell from one year to the next paid more tax over a long period than persons with equivalent gross earnings whose annual income was steady. This inequity was especially pronounced among low-income workers who moved back and forth from a zero tax bracket to a positive one. Friedman conceived of a negative income tax to even things up. In a good year such a worker would pay taxes *to* the Treasury; in a bad one, the *Treasury* would pay taxes to him. By the late 1940s it had further occurred to Friedman and his fellow economist George Stigler that a negative income tax could do more than smooth some of the bumps in the citizen's experience with Form 1040. It could become a permanent device for eliminating poverty: that is to say, it could be paid routinely to persons whose income *never* entered the positive brackets. The striking feature of the idea is that it introduced incentives for the poor to increase their incomes. Just as the positive graduated income tax steadily took more from the taxpayer as his income mounted, but never *all* the additional increment of income, so the negative income tax would give less as earning increased, but never to the point of canceling *all* advantage of increased earnings. (At this time most AFDC programs operated on the principle that earnings of a welfare recipient would be deducted, dollar-for-dollar, from welfare payments. As it cost money, in most circumstances, to work, there was a disincentive for the welfare recipient to do so unless earnings would be considerably higher than welfare payments themselves.)

The negative income tax was a spanking good idea, with much of the clarity and symmetry of the economic vision of the time. It proposed precisely the kind of abrupt disengagement from past practices that professions and bureaucracies managing a problem rarely conceive on their own. It addressed itself directly to the question of incentives: the obverse of the issue of dependency. Important as were the qualities of the idea, still more important was its origin. Friedman was a skilled and respected economist; he was also a convinced and combative political conservative. (He was to become, for example, a close adviser to Senator Barry Goldwater in the presidential campaign of 1964.)[16]

Should the political history of America in the period after World War II be written by the standards that period applied to earlier eras, which is to say should a serious effort be made to identify the locus of intellectual and ideological movements without prejudice to their source, it will surely be observed that in the course of the 1960s the left adopted almost wholesale the arguments of the right. This was not a rude act of usurpation, but rather a symmetrical, almost elegant, process of transfer. The extreme left adopted stances of the extreme right; the traditional left, those of the traditional right; the moderate liberals, those of moderate conservatives. By the end of the 1960s, an advanced student at an elite Eastern college could be depended on to avow many of the more striking views of the Liberty League and its equivalents in the hate-Roosevelt era; for example, that the growth of Federal power was the greatest threat to democracy, that foreign entanglements were the work of demented plutocrats, that government snooping (by the Social Security Administration or the United States Continental Army Command) was destroying freedom, that the largest number of functions should be entrusted to the smallest jurisdictions, and so across the spectrum of this viewpoint. Although the parallel may be taken to the point of caricature, an essential and ironical truth remains. The 1950s and 1960s was a period when conservative thinking had neither social nor intellectual status. A fairly traditional liberalism, of the kind to be associated with John F. Kennedy, was dominant in the national media and the academy, with the only discernible challenge a resurgence of a somewhat unformed left associated less with dogma than with tactic. The preservation of conservative doctrine was left to quirky Catholics and Texas millionaires. Goldwater's candidacy was derided precisely on the grounds that the consequences of his election would be so dreadful that none could take it seriously.

Yet within months of their victory the liberal victors were

openly embarked on a demented military adventure in Asia which would have seemed unthinkable even for right-wing fundamentalists. (One might say especially for persons of such persuasion: it is not conservative administrations who have taken America to war in the twentieth century.) Simultaneously, social unrest, notably among the urban black populace, began a spiraling ascent which Democrats had thought could only come with the advent of a regressive Republicanism. In sum all the worst things liberals had intimated might occur were conservatives elected, did occur almost the moment the conservatives were defeated. The question arose, naturally enough, as to which side was which.

Vagaries of politics aside, a larger movement of opinion was in evidence. The democracies had fared well enough in the postwar period, yet almost every national capital came to be suffused with a curious sense of failure. At the close of the 1960s, the French Prime Minister Jacques Chaban-Delmas, in an address to the National Assembly, was to describe his nation as a "blocked society." The state? "An octopus, and an inefficient one." In London, British socialism had about exhausted its credibility, if not its good intentions. But this was the point: increasingly the issue put to government was not what would it promise, but what could it deliver? Increasingly the judgment of observers was skeptical.

By 1968, when the election outcome in the United States was the reverse of that of 1964, a more chastened, if not more thoughtful, mood had settled on politics and politicians. In an article which appeared in *The Public Interest* just as Richard Nixon took office, and which he commended to his Cabinet, Peter Drucker asserted that modern government was everywhere a failure, that all it had proven able to do effectively was to wage war and inflate the currency.

There is mounting evidence that government is big rather than strong; that it is fat and flabby rather than powerful; that it costs a great deal but does not achieve much. There is mounting evidence also that the citizen less and less believes in government and is increasingly disenchanted with it. . . . This disenchantment may well be the most profound discontinuity in the world around us.[17]

In the summer of 1968 a Gallup Poll reported that "big government" more than "big business" or "big labor" was seen by the public as posing the greatest threat to the future. This was depicted as a "sharp" change from public opinion at the close of the Eisenhower era, when "big labor" was seen to be by far the greatest danger, with 41 percent of the public naming it, and only 14 percent identifying "big government." In the course of the 1960s this ranking had quite reversed. Forty-six percent of the public came to see "big government" as the main threat to the Nation, with 26 percent naming "big labor," and only 12 percent "big business." This view was shared almost equally by Democrats and Republicans, and was most pronounced among Independents. Clearly the New Frontier and the Great Society had aroused fears as well as hopes.[18]

In these circumstances a critique of government arose addressed to the question of method. What would *work?* An assertion came forth, labeled conservative but in historical terms almost classically liberal, that government administration did not work, while the market did. Or, by and large, that the one worked better than the other. The assertion turned on the issue of incentives, the argument being that the incentive structure of the market was vastly the more powerful. A further argument, which in retrospect may be adduced on behalf of the new conservatism, is that diffusing responsibility for social outcomes tends to retard the rise of social distrust when the promised or presumed outcome does not occur. The modern welfare state was getting into activities no one understood very well. It had not reached the point of picking every man a wife, but it was getting close enough to other such imponderables to find itself increasingly held to account for failure in areas where no government could reasonably promise success.

The conservative argument had heft. This became ever more evident in the course of the 1960s as the Federal government undertook an unprecedented range of social initiatives designed to put an end to racial and ethnic discrimination, to poverty, and eventually also to unequal levels of achievement as among groups variously defined by race, class, religion, national origin, and sex, primarily through a strategy of providing new, or "enriched," social services.[19]

The problem of the services strategy came down to one of efficiency: how well did it work? Hot lunches seemed to work. They could be defined as a good in themselves. Head Start? Not clear. Public housing? Yes, and yet, no. Legal services? Perhaps. (Did not the neighborhood and the country lawyers of old provide the political infrastructure that brought stability, influence, and power to surprising places? Would those young Yale lawyers on a two-year tour do that? Would local lawyers spring up?)

The answers were rarely clear. Unavoidably the burst of service activities in the 1960s was followed by some scrutiny of the results. The services strategy was challenged on a variety of grounds. First there was the transparent self-interest of the service dispensers. With astonishing consistency, middle-class professionals—whatever their racial or ethnic backgrounds—when asked to devise ways of improving the condition of lower-class groups would come up with schemes of which the first effect would be to improve the condition of the middle-class professionals, and the second effect might or might not be that of improving the condition of the poor. The programs of OEO were quintessentially of this kind. Few would survive the scrutiny of cash-flow analysis. Head Start soon came to cost $1,600 a year or more per presumed beneficiary. Who got the $1,600? To whom did the cash actually go? To the poor child? To the poor mother? (A certain number of "paraprofessionals" were brought into such programs, but why?) *To whom did the benefit flow?* Did the child do better in school? No, not really. (That was the ineluctable conclusion to be drawn from evaluation studies.) What then? Project Follow-Up. More jobs for persons with Master's degrees. *To whom would the benefit flow?* In the meantime, there was a discernible rise in dissatisfaction, with an eventual distrust of an educational system that promised what it did not deliver, that obtained ever-increasing portions of the GNP, but seemingly did not produce "more" education with each increment of public money. It is easy enough to take the critique of a services strategy to the point of caricature. Much of modern government consists of services once performed privately, if at all. There are efficiencies and equities in present arrangements that few would dispense with. Yet there are absurdities also, and inequities. No very extensive public discussion of this issue had arisen by the late 1960s. Those who questioned this or that program were too frequently charged with opposing the purposes of the program, which was a retaliation, not a response, but the questioning had begun.

The antipoverty program enacted in 1964 came to embody many of the ambiguities and uncertainties of an ambitious services strategy directed to the problems of poverty. A good deal of money was being expended. It could *not* be shown that it was going to the poor. It *was* going, in large degree, to purchase services, which could *not* be shown to benefit the poor. And yet what was the alternative?

In this context, the idea of an *income* strategy arose. A year-long seminar on poverty and race at the American Academy of Arts and Sciences helped to sort out the subject. Legal strategies had uses: obtaining rights in being. Services, similarly, could be of value up to a point. But for most persons living in poverty it appeared that a direct income strategy would show the largest return. It would in any event show some return, and an immediate one. This was an outcome government might desire on many grounds. In retrospect the negative income tax appears very much an idea whose time to come was the late 1960s.

There is an irony about these respective positions. The services strategy has been quintessentially that of political liberalism in the middle third of the twentieth century. And yet the actual *effect* of service programs such as education is probably to reallocate resources *up* the social scale, taxing, as it were, factory workers to pay school teachers. (Even the economic value directly attributable to the education received by the children of these workers was, in fact, much more doubtful than was generally assumed.) By contrast, the conservative sponsors of an income strategy (specifically, a negative income tax) were proposing that most radical of social measures: income redistribution *down* the social scale. This may have been perceived by writers on the political left such as Robert Theobald, who argued in the Kennedy years that the high unemployment rates of the period were but a precursor of a general disappearance of low-skilled jobs resulting from automation.[21] This argument, at least in the short term, proved wrong; but the unemployment of the time was real enough, as was the poverty, and the Federal government struggled for an answer. The negative tax idea gained currency, and lost some of the "conservative" pedigree that derived from Friedman.

A formative event occurred in March 1967 when, on the occasion of the 100th anniversary of the New York State Board of Social Welfare, Governor Nelson A. Rockefeller convened a meeting at Arden House "to help plan new approaches to public welfare in the United States." To a governor of New York State the need for such approaches, the realization that the AFDC program was, in James Tobin's formulation, "an insane piece of social engineering," was evident enough. It was beyond fixing; it needed to be replaced. For such a task there was little help to be expected from established cadres of social-welfare administrators and experts, whose primary reference point was the founding of the Social Security system in 1935, and whose general preoccupation had been that of expanding and perfecting that system. The trade unions, the civil-rights organizations, the philanthropic world: such possible sources of assistance were generally uninterested even when informed. The governor's inspiration was to turn to the heads of the large capitalist enterprises of the nation, a community with few ties, certainly, to the Social Security system, having bitterly opposed its establishment, but now including among its members men of generous disposition on social issues, a tendency much accentuated by the onset of urban rioting. (A somewhat loose but valid generalization could be made that among the Arden House conferees those who had been most successful in business tended to be the most progressive on social issues. The steering committee, for example, was headed by Joseph C. Wilson, Chairman of the Board of Directors and Chief Executive Officer of Xerox Corporation. Its members included Joseph L. Block, Chairman of the Executive Committee of Inland Steel Company; Philip M. Klutznick, Chairman of the Urban Investment and Development Company of Chicago; Gustave L. Levy, Chairman of the Board of Governors of the New York Stock Exchange; and Albert L. Nickerson, Chairman of the Board and Chief Executive Officer of Mobil Oil Corporation.)

The governor put to the group the question: "If the problem of public welfare was given to you, what would you recommend as sound public policy in the next decade?" He had turned to them, he declared, because, "It is largely the private sector of the nation that has historically demonstrated ingenuity and inventiveness, the resources and resourcefulness that made America what it is today." This remark, if a bit mindless—the America of that day had produced among other things the misery the conference was concerned with—did nonetheless reflect the fact that the businessmen involved were given to being businesslike about most problems presented to them, and were singularly uninvolved with, as well as uncommitted to, the received social-welfare system which they were to consider.

The Conference went to work. "What are the facts?" There were none. ("Solid research," the steeering committee concluded, "is virtually unknown in public welfare.") Thereupon a presumption arose against the competence of the traditional public-welfare advocates. If they had no facts, what could they know? In short order the Conference turned to the subject of income maintenance. A reasonably detailed debate took place on the merits of a negative income tax as against a system of family allowances.* The steering committee in its report concluded that either would do, inasmuch as both would establish uniform national minimum standards, and both would be universal or near-universal in coverage. (Existing welfare programs then covered only one fourth of those "living below an acceptable standard.") The committee, however, declared that "it leans in the direction of a negative income tax." It emphasized that "Such a system should contain strong incentives to work. . . ."[22]

Wilson's steering committee did not disband, but rather constituted itself an ongoing lobby for the replacement of the existing welfare system with a program of automatic income maintenance. Its report, with its central proposal for "the acceptance as a national goal of the objective that basic economic support on the poverty level, at least, be assured all our people," was made the agenda of a meeting of the Public Policy Forum of the Committee for Economic Development in May 1968. (On this occasion Marion B. Folsom spoke on behalf of the continued extension and improvement of the Social Security system, and defended the essential soundness of social insurance as the central principle for social-welfare policy, but nonetheless acknowl-

---

* Milton Friedman spoke for the former, I for the latter.

edged the probable need for an income maintenance system such as envisaged by the Arden House group. His tendency was rather in the direction of children's allowances, but proposed also that "experimentation and further study . . . be given to new approaches, such as the negative income tax.")[23] In this way, and others, the business elite of the nation acquired familiarity with the subject of welfare dependency, and commenced a fairly pronounced movement toward a response which by most previous standards would have to have been judged radical if not revolutionary.

The impact of an idea in part reflects the reputation of those who advance it. The poverty program, with its great emphasis on services, was not seen to succeed; nor did progressive urban government fare especially well. The worst riots seemed often to occur in the "best" cities. By contrast, economists and corporate executives appeared to know what they were doing, and the country proved able to use their advice. As the decade passed the case for direct income redistribution to help the poor grew stronger, and its adherents more influential. The family allowance won a measure of support, but in overwhelming numbers economists preferred the negative income tax.[24] It was an economist's idea. It began to acquire an aura of inevitability. It was too large a proposal for the Johnson Administration to put forth in its last period: such initiatives come at the beginning of administration. Even so, the presumption grew that at some early point some president would have to face up to the issue.

In his Economic Message of January 1967, President Johnson announced that he would establish a Commission on Income Maintenance Programs. Later that year, OEO quietly began a negative income tax experiment among a thousand families in New Jersey. No one was in a hurry. The Democratic Platform adopted later that year endorsed in principle the idea of family income support but avoided specifics.

To support family incomes of the working poor a number of new program proposals have recently been developed. A thorough evaluation of the relative advantages of such proposals deserves the highest priority attention by the next Administration. This we pledge to do.[25]

This was a respectable pace of progress, but events overran it. Before the next year was out, a president was to espouse a guaranteed family income. But it was a Republican president. This was the result of many forces, but first of all the crisis in welfare.

Citations—Chapter I

1. Alva Myrdal, *Nation and Family,* New York, Harper and Brothers, 1941. Paperback edition, Cambridge, The M.I.T. Press, 1968. Foreword by Daniel P. Moynihan, p. xii.
2. Commenting on efforts to improve the AFDC program in the fifties and sixties, Gilbert Steiner has called the period one of "tireless tinkering," emphasizing the lack of critical analysis that accompanied reforms such as the Social Security Amendments of 1962. Gilbert Y. Steiner, *The State of Welfare,* Washington, D.C., The Brookings Institution, 1971, Chapter 2.
3. Nathan E. Cohen and Maurice F. Connery, "Government Policy and the Family," *Journal of Marriage and the Family,* February 1967, p. 11.
4. *The New York Times,* January 13, 25, 1971. The case is *Wyman v. James,* 400 U.S. 309 (1971). For a discussion of this and related literature see Nanette Dembitz, "The Good of the Child Versus the Rights of the Parent: The Supreme Court Upholds the Welfare Home-Visit," *Political Science Quarterly,* September 1971, pp. 389–405.
5. Julius Horwitz, *The Inhabitants,* Cleveland and New York, World, 1960, pp. 118–20.
6. *The New York Times,* March 28, 1971. The case is *Shapiro v. Thompson,* 394 U.S. 618 (1969).
7. Alexander Radomski, "Income and Poverty 1958–68," *Welfare in Review,* January–February 1971, pp. 13–17.
8. Bureau of the Census, Current Population Reports, *Special Studies, Fertility Indicators, 1970,* Series P-23, No. 36, April 16, 1971.
9. Winifred Bell, *Aid to Dependent Children,* New York, Columbia University Press, 1965, p. 13.
10. Gilbert Y. Steiner, *Social Insecurity: The Politics of Welfare,* Chicago, Rand McNally, 1966, p. 4.
11. John A. Hamilton, "Welfare's Outrage," *The New York Times,* February 22, 1971. In 1969 the New York State legislature also voted to cut welfare assistance. In an intense closing debate, a Bronx Democrat, a Negro, told the Assembly, "This is an anti-Negro bill, an anti-Puerto Rican bill, an anti-poor bill." A Reform Democrat Assemblyman said, "If we pass this bill today, then God have mercy on the souls of every member of this chamber." (*The New York Times,* March 30, 1969.) The bill was passed.
12. There is nothing uncommon in this: it would be extraordinary for there not to be such lacunae. Morris Janowitz makes a similar observation on the lack of sociological analysis of military organizations in the late 1950s. "In the United States the development of the social sciences is linked to the liberal tradition which, in general, has sought to handle the problem

of military institutions by denial." Morris Janowitz, *Sociology and the Military Establishment,* New York, Russell Sage Foundation, 1959, p. 15.

13. *Social Welfare in France,* La Documentation Française, Paris, 1966, p. 439.
14. *Ibid.,* p. 485.
15. I have discussed these developments in a foreword to James C. Vadakin's study, *Children, Poverty and Family Allowances,* New York and London, Basic Books, 1968.
16. Friedman stated the arguments in behalf of a negative income tax in his widely read book, *Capitalism and Freedom,* Chicago, University of Chicago Press, 1962, chapter 12.
17. Peter F. Drucker, "The Sickness of Government," *The Public Interest,* Winter 1969, p. 3.
18. The Gallup Poll, " 'Big Government' Named Greatest Threat to Nation," Princeton, New Jersey, August 18, 1968.
19. A thorough discussion of this emerging area of Constitutional law, in the context of education, is contained in John E. Coons, William H. Clune, III, and Stephen D. Sugarman, *Private Wealth and Public Education,* Cambridge, Massachusetts, Harvard University Press, 1970, part II.
20. See Daniel P. Moynihan, *On Understanding Poverty, Perspectives from the Social Sciences,* New York, Basic Books, 1969, and James S. Coleman, *Resources for Social Change,* New York, Wiley-Interscience, 1971.
21. Robert Theobald, *Free Men and Free Markets,* Garden City, New York, Doubleday, 1963. Theobald later edited a symposium on the subject, *The Guaranteed Income,* Garden City, New York, Doubleday, 1966.
22. Report from the Steering Committee of the Arden House Conference on Public Welfare, undated, pp. 9, 12, 22–3.
23. Statement of Marion B. Folsom, Committee for Economic Development Public Policy Forum, May 8, 1968, mimeographed, p. 8.
24. Steiner discusses the development of agreement among economists in support of a negative income tax in *The State of Welfare,* pp. 95–100.
25. "Toward a More Perfect Union," The Platform of the Democratic Party, as Presented to the Democratic National Convention, Chicago, 1968, p. 48.

II

The President's Options

One of the persisting anomalies of American as of British democracy is that the party of ardor is frequently the one to make the cold decisions that come along in political life, while the party of reserve is not less commonly entrusted with the generous initiatives. A situation of this kind arose with respect to the problem of dependency. Democrats could at least talk about poverty; the subject brought out much that was attractive in them. By contrast, the issue of dependency recurrently evoked fearful or even vengeful responses. The best of the Democrats were frequently at their worst when dealing with this issue. Surely few men in recent history have so ardently and sincerely espoused the cause of the poor and the excluded, especially where this condition interacts with racial and ethnic prejudice, than Robert F. Kennedy. Yet in the course of the 1968 Presidential primary contests he was led to denounce the idea of a guaranteed annual income, contrasting his position with that of Eugene J. McCarthy, who advocated it. In a speech in Boston on April 11, McCarthy proposed that the Federal Government "determine a minimum income which it will assure for all Americans." That same day Kennedy was telling an audience of Michigan Democrats which, according to *The Times,* "greeted his speech with whoops of approval," that the welfare program of the thirties was a failure in the sixties, and that what was needed was a system of financial incentives to "make it possible for private industry to bring jobs and housing, and therefore hope, into our ghettos." His program would not be costly, he claimed, but would "increase the total wealth of the nation" by reducing welfare expenditures. On May 19, Kennedy issued a policy statement which *The Times* described as "scorning a guaranteed annual income." His was an employment strategy. "The answer to the welfare crisis," his statement declared, "is work, jobs, self-sufficiency and family integrity; not a massive new extension of welfare; not a great new outpouring of guidance counselors to give the poor more advice." He would find jobs for the working poor. He would not supplement their income.[1]

Kennedy's views on this subject were consistent through the years of his life, but it was also the fact, which Eugene McCarthy was not to forget, that he was now using these views in opposition to another candidate of the left, contrasting his hardheaded, even conservative position with the extravagances of his opponent. It was normal for Democratic politicians to assume that a guaranteed income would be perceived as a "massive new extension of welfare," and simply judicious to join the anticipated attack by describing it, as Kennedy did in his position paper, as a proposal to "pay men to sit at home."*

A similar concern was to be encountered in the report of the National Advisory Commission on Civil Disorders which appeared in March of the election year. The Commission, headed by Otto Kerner of Illinois, with Mayor Lindsay as vice-chairman, did not hesitate to declare its belief that "Our present system of public assistance contributes materially to the tensions and social disorganization that have led to civil disorders." It called for a "National System of Income Supplementation" to aid both the working poor and the dependent poor, but in doing so invoked none of the fashionable theories or theorists of the time, but rather the thin-lipped integrity of former Republican Senator Robert A. Taft of Ohio, who in 1949 had proposed that the Federal government maintain a "minimum standard floor under subsistence" so as to guarantee all Americans a "minimum standard of decent living," and "all children a fair opportunity to get a start in life."

* As one who campaigned for Kennedy during this period, I should note this was hardly the central thrust of his social proposals. Campaign rhetoric notwithstanding, Kennedy was open to consideration of ideas such as the negative income tax and revenue sharing. And yet, he did make the charge against McCarthy.

The Republican problem in 1968 was the opposite of that of the Democrats. In the 1964 campaign they had allowed the Democrats to make them appear to be opposed to social-welfare programs generally, and specifically to Social Security. Clearly this was not a winning strategy. Moreover, the urban riots had taken place in the interval and the business community had begun to look upon issues of social welfare as priority matters which could be a challenge to creativity as well as to common sense. The Nation seemed in terrible trouble, and no one could say why. By habit, businessmen sought out seemingly irrational, inefficient practices and asked whether these might be the source. In July 1968 a *Fortune* article, "A Way Out of the Welfare Mess," began: "Seldom has a nation governed by rational men created an institution so erratic in its operation, and so perverse in some of its social effects, as the U.S. welfare system." In an article in *Look* Magazine at about this time, George Harris reported "Richard Nixon's closest advisers have been urging him to campaign hard for a guaranteed income." The economist Pierre Rinfret was reported to view the negative tax as a powerful countercyclical device, much in the manner of unemployment insurance. Others adduced other grounds. Harris nicely pointed to the power of the proposal to attract persons of divergent political viewpoints and varied professional concerns.[2]

The Ripon Society, which describes itself as a Republican research and policy organization of "young members of the business, academic, and professional communities," was an early advocate of a negative tax. A research paper issued in April 1967 proposed such a scheme as an alternative to "the mismanaged, miscellaneous, and ineffectual War on Poverty that has been put forth by the Johnson Administration." In a novel but admissible interpretation, the paper argued that "The Negative Income Tax is not a new concept; already almost sixty countries have a similar program known as the family allowance." It emphasized the range of political appeal.

The Negative Income Tax has gained the support of many of the nation's most respected economists, both Republican and Democratic. Henry Wallich, a member of President Eisenhower's Council of Economic Advisers, supports the idea. One of its first proponents was University of Chicago economist Milton Friedman, Barry Goldwater's chief economic adviser during the 1964 presidential campaign. . . . Yale economist James Tobin, a recent member of the Council of Economic Advisers, has written extensively advocating the idea. Harvard's Daniel Moynihan and Dr. Martin Luther King have suggested variations of the plan.[3]

At the outset of 1968, John Price, a founder of the Ripon Society, proposed, at a dinner meeting with Nixon, that the negative income tax and the volunteer army were the two issues that might unite the liberal and conservative wings of the Republican party. (Price later became Counsel to the Urban Affairs Council of the Nixon Administration and exercised great influence in the development of the Family Assistance Plan. He was also a steady source of support within the White House for a volunteer army, which Nixon also proposed. Unity continues to elude his party.)

Among congressional Republicans, and within the party organization, a most influential proponent of the negative income tax was Melvin R. Laird of Wisconsin, Chairman of the House Republican Conference, but he was almost alone in his interest. The congressional Republicans had been consistently inept in the social-welfare politics of the 1960s. The Democrats had come along with one proposal after another, and had enacted most of them over Republican opposition.* Much was at stake in these encounters. In the aftermath of their legislative victories, the Democrats had been able to create a whole new

---

* If Democratic conflicts ran deep, Republican incompetence ran deeper. A low point of some note was reached on March 17, 1964, on the opening day of hearings by the House Committee on Education and Labor on the Economic Opportunity Act of 1964. It was a moment of high political drama, of a kind the Capitol can occasionally provide. The new president was sending the brother-in-law of the previous one to unveil to the Congress an ambitious and attractive program, his first domestic initiative. He had brought together as sponsors a Southern conservative in the House and a Northern liberal in the Senate who put aside, symbolically, the issues of race to unite in an effort to rid the Republic of poverty. The Nation was coming out of the shock of the assassination, and the deadlocked politics that had preceded it. Spring had come after a long winter. At length the committee chairman, Rep. Adam Clayton Powell, Democrat of New York, turned to the Republicans for comment. A senior Representative began by reading to us from John 12:8, "For the poor always ye have with you." We were presumably to understand that Jesus opposed the poverty program. Sitting alongside Sargent Shriver at the witness table, I found myself neither angered nor disturbed, but simply unbelieving.

generation of bureaucracies within the government, and client groups outside it. This was true not least of the cohorts of young college graduates who were summoned to fight poverty, fix up Latin America, educate Africa, revive Appalachia, integrate Alabama, and finally—the undoing of it all—to bring democracy to Southeast Asia. The congressional Republicans, debilitated and in ways corrupted by having been out of power for the better part of four decades, were no match for the dazzle of the New Frontier or the Great Barbecue that followed. By all indications, an entire generation of middle- and upper-class youth, offspring of Republican parents, moved during this period to the Democratic party or beyond. It may surely be argued that this occurred in part because the Democrats gave them something to do. The war turned this cohort against the Johnson Administration, but not against the Democratic party. The consequences of this shift are likely to be significant in American politics for the remainder of the century.

Laird could sense this; enough to see that if the Republican party was to remain competitive in American politics it would have to be *for* programs of its own, not merely opposed to those of Democrats. This might seem, in retrospect, no very great insight, but it was a thought that had not occurred to Republican leaders in a very long while. He could not hope to outdo the Democrats in their whirlwind style of the 1960s, and he had to assume that his own party would rebel at creating yet another generation of marginal bureaucracies. Even Democrats were beginning to question that approach, and the services strategy which it embodied. He had to come up with a distinctive alternative program, one which embodied also an alternative style of government.

An income strategy seemed made to order. As the 1968 campaign began, he published a collection of essays entitled *Republican Papers,* drawing on congressmen and academics to "define the problems and offer solutions for the domestic crises facing today's America." Included was "The Case for the Negative Income Tax" by Milton Friedman. Some years earlier Friedman's views had come to the attention of the labor leader Ralph Helstein. "That's it," Helstein was reported as saying, "this conservative has provided us with a way to get guaranteed income."[4]

In November the more conservative candidate was elected president. The campaign had not been notable for analytic or speculative discourse. The Democrats had in effect forfeited the presidency. In order to win it was only necessary for the Republican candidate to do nothing seriously wrong. As it turned out, saying *nothing* was close to doing something seriously wrong. Nixon was barely elected, and carried almost no one into office with him. Congress remained solidly in control of the opposition Democrats. The leaders of this party, and those of much influence within it, disliked or detested the incoming president in a degree that had few counterparts in American history. The prospects seemed hardly favorable for radical social change.

And yet these precisely were the circumstances necessary to bring forth a radical proposal and to ensure it a respectful hearing. As the decade came to a close, the public life of the United States was characterized by unease and apprehension. The Nation had become involved in a dreadful war which it could not win, and from which it seemingly could not disengage. A vast transformation in racial attitudes had moved far enough to permit and even to encourage violent denunciation of the society that had fostered the earlier attitudes. This was accompanied by dramatic and seemingly mounting violent actions, including vast urban riots. The social reforms of the mid-decade had been oversold, and, with the coming of the war, underfinanced to the degree that seeming failure could be ascribed almost to intent. There was indeed considerable social change going on, and much of it in the direction most desired by those who were most discontent, but it was progress clearly linked to the economic boom brought on by the war, which made it difficult for many to take much satisfaction in it. A recrudescence of crude and abusive Marxist rhetoric seemingly drove out thought in that part of the political spectrum ranging from left to far left, while in the South there was a massive movement toward a comparably vulgar and absolutist racialism. These ostensibly disparate movements held many positions in common. They were singularly contemptuous of the liberal centrists whose influence had been more or less preeminent in Washington for many years. Each, in its way, affected regional politics. In the North not a few such liberals were converted, silenced, or defeated. In the South a tradition of moderation and political competence which had marked the era when Sam Rayburn was Speaker of the House and Lyndon B. Johnson Majority Leader of the Senate was seemingly destroyed. (It was not, but who could know this at the time?)

These were primarily problems for Democrats. The Republicans, having won the election, could at least experiment with unity, and were in any event required to govern. Their prospects were less than splendid. They had no program, far less a mandate to put one into effect. They had almost no thinkers, almost no writers, almost no reputation for a sophisticated or even compassionate view of social policy. The aftereffects of the 1964 campaign still lingered. And yet they were also relatively free. Having proposed no program, they had made few commitments. Having no intellectual base, no informed and disputatious constituency alert to departures from orthodoxy, the Republican Administration that took office was not only in a position to be pragmatic, but almost required to be. Certainly they were not required to persist in or be protective about an insane social arrangement such as the welfare system had become. Some satisfaction—the Democrats having done nothing—and possibly some advantage might be had from a sudden sharp departure from previous policy, a style few suspected in the new president, but which for good or ill was to mark his first years in office.

Nixon had said little about welfare during the campaign until the very end. On October 25 he proposed the adoption of "national standards," contrasting the pitiful payment levels of Mississippi with the relatively generous ones of New York. On October 28, in one of the radio addresses which he used for thoughtful statements about complex issues, he offered two propositions. First, the government must provide help to those who cannot help themselves, "the poor, the disabled, the aged and the sick," in a way "that preserves the dignity of the individual and the integrity of the family." Second, "it should offer opportunity and incentive for those who can, to move off welfare rolls onto private payrolls." In his address he proposed "equivalent" rather than "equal" payments. No great note was taken of either statement, but the proposal for equalization, modest as it may seem, was extraordinarily in advance of any proposal ever made by an incumbent president. And yet almost any candidate running in 1968 might have endorsed the two basic propositions, and it is fair to assume that in the prolonged ordeal of primaries and conventions and the final runoff, most did. Inexorably, welfare dependency was making its way to the center of national politics, not in the form of a proposal to do something, but as a condition about which something had to be done. At length, one of the candidates would be elected, whereupon after decades in custody of the bureaucracy, the issue would come to the presidency. In this sense Richard Nixon was fated to deal with welfare.

It was not to be foreseen how he would respond, yet this, too, was in part settled by the time he took office. In the choice of his Cabinet and White House staff he more or less precluded any attempt to reverse the course or extent of government commitment to the resolution of the more salient social problems of the 1960s.

(Although this was in ways the central fact of his Administration, it remained a most obscure one, partly because of a combined interest both he and his opponents had in keeping it obscure. It was possible to perceive the adoption of an income strategy as a restoration of primitive Republican principle, and certainly possible to depict it as such. At least some Democrats were disposed to this, but so also were Republicans seeking to reassure those in their party who with reason thought they had elected a quite different president than Nixon would turn out to be. One of the arts of government is to avoid the humiliation of the interests that lose out in the clash of policy. There is no general pronouncement to be made about this process save that it is not of necessity a mark of dishonesty in politics—often it is just the opposite—and that it is difficult to do. A measure of cynicism is the price of achievement in politics. Politicians alone seem to know this. To pursue moral objectives with much hope of success it is necessary to be informed minutely as to the purposes of others, and thus is to be privy to much that is unattractive. So much, that many find their own self-assurance threatened and either choose not to know that without which they cannot succeed, or transform their own loss of innocence into a presumption of universal guilt. Some, that is, deny the existence of evil and others the existence of grace. The art of politics is to live with the reality of both. It is recurrently required of a leader that he abandon either his integrity or his followers; that he do what he pledged to do, or do what he has come to feel he ought to do. To choose the latter course often requires the courage to know that not everything need be made to appear what it is. In such circumstances symbolic rewards may go to one group while "actual" rewards go to quite a different one. With luck those who have lost are consoled, and those who have won are not deceived. In the events to be described in this volume Nixon had little such luck.)

The decision not to repudiate the social goals of his predecessors was signaled, but never quite articulated. Was there a choice? Was it possible at long last to be perfectly clear? Perhaps not. Whatever the case, comparatively clear decisions *were* made. There was *not* to be a restoration. There *was* to be continuity. By choosing this course the president made it yet more certain that he would have to face the issue of welfare, for the issue had become central to the questions of poverty and of racial equality.

The argument for continuity was basically prudential. The nation was shaken: possibly approaching instability; simultaneously immobilized and yet coming apart. Domestic violence had been rising on a straight trajectory and none could say it would not continue so. The domestic programs of the Kennedy and Johnson era had not prevented such deterioration, may even somehow have contributed to it, but they *had* achieved great visibility and great symbolic meaning as promises that somehow things would be better, or, at least, as testimonials that somebody cared. Some such programs were near to quixotic, as for example Model Cities, but these tended to be the ones most believed, and more importantly the ones that had come to involve the greatest number of people in devising dreams of a better tomorrow. To kill such programs would have been to kill the dream, and there had been enough killing. Nixon decided to carry on.

The decision was embodied in the appointment of a series of "task forces" to prepare reports for the president-elect on issues to which he would want to give priority attention. The choice of subjects—Urban Affairs, Education, Health, Resources and Environment, Manpower, *et al.*—was itself determinant. It was in almost every respect a "liberal" agenda. The election campaign was somewhat in evidence. Subjects such as "Black Capitalism," a Republican-sounding proposition, were given some prominence, but this and others like it were in no way divergent from the general trend of government-supported programs to improve the condition of the Negro. The choice of task-force members was, if anything, more decisive. Republicans were included, and typically headed the individual task forces, but a wide assortment of Democrats, ranging from political activists such as Richard Goodwin to institutional liberals such as Alan Pifer, head of the Carnegie Corporation, was also present. Much as Kennedy had taken Republicans into his cabinet, Nixon was now taking Democrats into his counsel.

He hardly had a choice if he wished for much by way of social-science advice. The rapid growth of this academic profession in the postwar period—no other nation experienced anything comparable—was accompanied by an equally pronounced movement toward liberal and, notably in the case of sociologists, left politics. On January 11 the president-elect dined with his task-force advisers at the Hotel Pierre. "I am an intellectual, too," he said, in brief remarks, but indicated his understanding that few of those present would have voted for him. Few would have. Seymour Martin Lipset and Everett Carll Ladd, Jr., in analyses of a faculty-opinion survey carried out for the Carnegie Commission on Higher Education, found that Nixon was supported by only 19 percent of social scientists in 1968. Seventy-one percent of this group described themselves as left or liberal. Among Jewish social scientists—a numerous and vigorous group—this political tendency was yet more pronounced, while among young social scientists even more than that. This was to have consequences for the president. He was to put forth a complex social-science proposal, which was to be judged by a profession that by and large loathed him. A kind of dissonance was to arise. The president—this one—would rarely forget that a full 68 percent of the public described itself as "middle-of-the-road," "fairly conservative," or "very conservative" in the Gallup Poll, while social scientists were of just the opposite tendency. In such circumstances the rhetorical demands on a president setting forth a radical proposal—demands, that is, to satisfy a conservative or moderate majority of the public and a liberal or left majority of a profession—involved risks so high as to appear in retrospect almost foolhardy.[5] Whatever else may be said, a majority of those in the hotel ballroom would have been present for a similar fête which almost surely would have been convened, and for precisely the same purpose, had the president-elect been Hubert H. Humphrey.

Certainly most members of the Task Force on Public Welfare (whose report leaked the following day) would have been on hand for a Humphrey celebration. The chairman was Richard P. Nathan of the Brookings Institution, a student of social policy who had been Associate Director for Program Research of the Kerner Commission. He had been recommended for the job by John Gardner, Secretary of HEW in the Johnson Cabinet. The task-force members included Mitchell I. Ginsberg, then Administrator of the Human Resources Administration, that is to say the welfare department, of New York City; James L. Sundquist, also of Brookings, who had been a member of the task force that drew up the poverty program in the months immediately after the assassination of John F. Kennedy; and Robert Patricelli, Minority Counsel to the Senate Subcommittee on Employment, Manpower, and Poverty. Ginsberg and Sundquist were active Democrats, Nathan and Patricelli no less active Republicans. (Nathan was to become Assistant Director of the Bureau of the Budget, and a crucial supporter of the Family Assistance Plan in the months to come. Patricelli joined Robert H. Finch's staff at the Department of Health, Education, and Welfare. Along with John G. Veneman, a California legislator who become Undersecretary of HEW, he managed the legislation in the Congress.)

The Nathan task force was fully capable of devising and setting forth large proposals, but did not do so. Whatever the case against the existing welfare system, the cost of radical transformation was too great for a group of persons, no one of whom was close to the president-elect, to propose with any expectation of success. The national economy and the Federal budget were both in difficulty. The Vietnam war had brought on a succession of sharp budget deficits followed by price inflation and now by the beginnings of unemployment. There is a normal Republican disposition to be anxious about matters such as inflation and deficits, if not especially about unemployment, but by any standards the economy in the winter of 1968–1969 was unbalanced, and threatening. Any advisory group, Democratic or Republican, would have hesitated before calling for large new expenditure. The task force said as much:

Heretofore, consideration of basic reforms of the nation's troubled Public Assistance system has concentrated on broad and very costly proposals. We believe that a highly significant start can be made on Public Assistance reform at a cost which should permit some action in this area in the relatively near-term future, assuming continued economic growth and somewhat reduced defense spending.

The most salient shortcoming of the welfare system as it then existed was the gap between the states with the lowest payments and those with the highest. The New Deal legislation, in the manner of the time, had left it to state government to determine levels of benefits, with the Federal government a passive contributor of a proportion of the total. Three decades later the variance in payments between high and low states was almost ten to one. Following the president-elect's October statements the task force proposed that the Federal government establish minimum benefit standards of AFDC and the categorical programs for the aged, blind, and disabled with full Federal assumption of the cost of the latter.

The gathering political support for basic change can be detected in the fact that the task-force proposals, set forth almost with forbearance, with consciousness of the shortage of funds, nonetheless contemplated an unprecedented increase in expenditure. Minimum AFDC standards alone would have cost the Federal budget $1.4 billion per year. Moreover, the task force made clear that it looked forward to complete Federal financing of all welfare programs, and went on to suggest that even this might prove insufficient.

It is the conviction of some members of the Task Force that incremental improvements in the Public Assistance programs will fail in the long run to provide a basic income maintenance system that encourages family stability, stresses work incentives, and enables the development of efficient service delivery and modern program management. . . . If the implementation of the Task Force's recommendations and similar measures does not provide satisfactory progress, we believe the new Administration should turn its attention to longer-run alternatives, such as . . . the negative income tax, children's allowances, etc.

The president was inaugurated January 20, 1969. With the oath of office he assumed responsibility for a nationwide problem of welfare dependency which, if not out of control, was evidently worsening. He himself had made few commitments on the subject, but in the intellectual baggage train of his party there was to be found an impeccably Republican proposal for a guaranteed income which in its potential was incomparably more sweeping, more radical, than any welfare measure yet proposed by the opposition Democrats, certainly more sweeping and radical than any so far enacted. Further, the president-elect had resolved to set up a machinery for policy and program formulation with respect to domestic matters that all but ensured that at some point he would confront the guaranteed income as a specific policy option.* Both circumstances were crucial.

The policy machinery was the Urban Affairs Council which he established January 23, as his first executive act. The UAC was more or less modeled on the National Security Council. In domestic as in foreign affairs, fewer and fewer issues of the kind likely to concern a president were such as to fall within the exclusive or even the predominant jurisdiction of any of the Cabinet departments or the various executive agencies. This had led to a steady growth in the size and influence of the White House staff, a development which a succession of presidents (now to include Nixon as well) had been in the habit of deploring and abetting. Nixon, as his predecessors, did at first hope for a strong Cabinet and assembled one of relative strength if not glamour. By regularly meeting in council with his domestic Cabinet officers, he hoped both to strengthen their positions and possibly to avoid the difficult situations that arise in dealing with individual Cabinet members with respect to matters that involve the interests of several. The Council was accordingly constituted as the President, the Vice-President, the Attorney General, and the Secretaries of Agriculture, Commerce, Labor, Housing and Urban Development, Transportation, and Health, Education, and Welfare.

The Council was charged to assist the president in the development of "a national urban policy." The idea of *policy* was central. The president's "talking points" prepared for the

---

* My appointment as an adviser to the president also seemed to increase the likelihood that he would consider various alternatives to the existing welfare system, although our conversations prior to my agreeing to serve in his Administration did not deal at any length with that topic.

January 23 meeting began by noting that the census of 1920 had revealed that a majority of Americans had come to live in cities, but that half a century later the Federal government was still responding to this changed reality in inadequate and self-defeating terms, piling one program on top of another, hoping for the best, but with no sustained view of what would be best or of what combination of forces would most likely achieve such an outcome. Without, that is, an urban policy.

The American national government has responded to urban concerns in a haphazard, fragmented, and often woefully shortsighted manner (as when the great agricultural migrations from the rural South were allowed to take place with no adjustment or relocation arrangements whatever). What we have never had is a policy: coherent, consistent positions as to what the national government would hope to see happen; what it will encourage, what it will discourage. Having a policy in urban affairs is no more a guarantor of success than having one in foreign affairs. But it is a precondition of success.

Nixon in office was beginning to change. The cautious, negative campaign was behind him. Ahead lay his reputation in American history. He had watched the near-sighted decisions of the Eisenhower years gradually close off his chances for the presidency in 1960; he was concerned that the same style should not now take over his own Administration. It seemed hardly appropriate to the 1970s, and it hadn't worked in the 1950s either. Hadn't, at all events, worked for him.

He said as much to his new Council, stressing the importance of getting into position quickly. The "magic time" to change policies, he said on January 23, and to take the political "heat" for doing so, would be the first few months of the Administration. The Nation, he felt, recognized the need for change. "We don't," he added, "want the record written that we were too cautious."

Nine subcommittees of the Council were appointed, each headed by the Cabinet officer principally concerned, if there was such, and made up of other Cabinet officers with responsibilities or personal interests in the area. The subcommittee assignments —again—reflected a basic decision to go forward with the political agenda, if not the administrative methods, of the 1960s: Future of the Poverty Program; Future of the Model Cities Program; Minority Business Enterprise; Welfare; Crime; Voluntary Action; Internal Migration; Surplus Food and Nutrition; Mass Transit. These were described as "Near-Term" issues. Another group was established to consider the "Long-Term Issue" of "Transition to Peacetime Economy at the End of Vietnam Hostilities." The prospect of a "peace-and-growth" dividend still seemed viable, and it was assumed that somewhere down the road major initiatives in social policy would be made possible by the availability of these funds. Thus the atmosphere of severe fiscal restraint relaxed somewhat. This was to influence greatly the work of the subcommittee on welfare headed by Robert Finch, the new Secretary of Health, Education, and Welfare, the closest of the president's political associates, and among the oldest of his friends.

With his policy and program machinery cranked up in the area of urban affairs, the president could and did turn his attention to concerns of defense and foreign policy, and the economy. The Administration was soon embroiled in divisive and depleting conflicts with Congress over the antiballistic missile (ABM) and the retention of an income-tax surcharge. Yet from the first meeting of the Urban Affairs Council the issue of welfare absorbed the new president in a direct and personal way. Like his Republican predecessors Eisenhower and Hoover, he had been born in modest circumstances. Unlike them he had grown up in the Great Depression. Unlike them, further, he took office in an atmosphere of social malaise that suggested something deeply the matter with the Nation. The nominating conventions of the two major parties had taken place in an atmosphere of siege, intrigue, even suspicion of subversion. Inside, the crowds were riddled with army agents awaiting the next assassination attempt or worse. Outside, the police battled or skirmished with mobs. There had been deaths in Miami, beatings in Chicago. Elsewhere a third party of utterly regressive views was finding a place on the ballot of every state in the Nation. Nixon's campaign theme had been law and order, as reasonably it might, for the Republic was seemingly approaching instability.

Yet traditional liberal opinion insisted on depicting the theme of "law and order" as a code word for official lawlessness or, as it came to be known, repression. As James Q. Wilson writes, "Empathy (though not outright approval) governed the

liberal response to urban riots and campus disorders. . . ."
When the police in turn misbehaved, not infrequently in response to elaborate taunting and provocation, the liberal response was "rage."[6] Not six, not five years earlier progressive
political forces in America had attained a historic unity and
strength of purpose in asserting the *rule of law* with respect to the
civil rights of blacks in the South. Now the very notion seemed
increasingly abandoned as liberals explained, and excused, and
avoided the reality that the law could be broken even by persons
for whom one felt great compassion. Such liberals had every
reason to think of themselves as the governing class of the
Nation, but seemed unwilling any longer to govern. There was
not merely a crisis of objective events, but an ideological crisis
also. More than that, and yet less, a collapse of morale, a failure
of nerve, that revealed, *au fond,* a failure of understanding.

The Nation's largest city, once again, provided the most
distressing evidence. Some weeks before the inauguration a
group of administrators, academicians, and intellectuals met to
discuss a special issue of *The Public Interest* devoted to New York
City. Paul Weaver, a young political scientist, summarized the
day's discussion in a minute that shortly thereafter was read by
the president-elect. For all its overtones of Leo Strauss, it reflected sober opinion.

1. The social fabric of New York City is coming to pieces. It isn't just
"strained" and it isn't just "frayed"; but like a sheet of rotten canvas,
it is beginning to rip, and it won't be too long until even a moderate
force will be capable of leaving it in shreds and tatters. . . . Among
a large and growing lower class, self-reliance, self-discipline, and industry are waning; a radical disproportion is arising between reality
and expectations concerning job, living standard, and so on; unemployment is high but a lively demand for unskilled labor remains
unmet; illegitimacy is increasing; families are more and more matri-
focal and atomized; crime and disorder are sharply on the rise. There
is, in short, a progressive disorganization of society, a growing pattern
of frustration and mistrust. . . . This general pathology, moreover,
appears to be infecting the Puerto Rican community as well as the
Negro. (It is a stirring, if generally unrecognized, demonstration of
the power of our welfare machine.) A large segment of the population is becoming incompetent and destructive. Growing parasitism,
both legal and illegal, is the result; so, also, is violence.

2. Something comparable is happening in the political arena. New York used to be the very model of moderate, materialistic, incremental Madisonian politics. Only the goo-goos challenged the whole system, but not out of self-interest, and rarely intemperately. Otherwise, participation was limited to the pursuit of limited self-interest; live-and-let-live logrolling was both fact and value; and conflict was avoided as much as possible. But today, there is the "spirit of confrontation," in which self-interest and a desire to change the system are merged in groups which depend for their existence on pursuing a "conflict" strategy. The result is that, to the extent this pattern exists, political executives are less free to determine the mix of (partly inconsistent) values and interests which best defines the public interest; public tranquility is unsettled; and political cohesion is threatened. The consequence is to increase the tension between responsibility and responsiveness in government. Thus, Lindsay orders a "no-arrest" policy at precisely the point when law and order are manifestly in decay; it "cools" the city "off" in the short run but may heat it up in the long run. The general problem is whether representative government can maintain a country or city which is divided against itself and which discounts its long-term interest so heavily.

3. Are we then witnessing the ultimate, destructive working out of the telos of liberal thought? The viability of liberal thought rested on the ability of the country which adopted it to be largely self-regulating, self-maintaining, and self-improving. As long as the typical individual was formed and directed in socially useful ways by more or less autonomous operations of private subsystems of authority, a government which permitted great freedom and engaged largely in the negative and peripheral activity of the umpire was possible. It was also possible for citizen and statesman to live with a rhetoric which denied the existence, functions, and basis of those private subsystems. Being traditional, those subsystems were (on the rhetoric's terms) "irrational"; being particularistic, they were not "universal"; constituting and maintaining differences among men, they fostered "inequality"; and forming character and directing energy as they did, they were "authoritarian." *The thoroughly liberal society, in short, cannot know what makes it work.* Now, in parts of New York City, those subsystems are absolutely breaking down. At the same time, the rhetoric is getting an ever stronger and more blinding grip on "informed" opinion as well as on partisan opinion. The rhetoric leads to policies which actually hasten the dissolution of the subsystems.

That the society is breaking down means that the liberal state will no longer do. It must, on pain of anarchy or civil war, be replaced by a regime which explicitly recognizes the necessity of the subsystems and which is prepared to create substitutes for those subsystems when they break down. Our problem is that informed opinion is moving in precisely the opposite direction.

It was in this way, lastly, that the subject of the family forced itself onto the agenda of the American national government. Of the "private subsystems of authority" that make for orderly public behavior, the family is the one commonly assumed to be the most significant. It is an argument not without support in social science, but, more important, it is an almost automatic popular assumption. Generations beyond counting appear to have ascribed the ills of the time to laxness in child-rearing or breakdown in family structure. But in the face of an unquestioned rise in social disorder, and a concomitant rise in welfare dependency primarily associated with family breakdown, the proposition assumed a cogency and urgency beyond the homily stage.

The president, for example, had campaigned for law and order, but he knew no way to bring it about. No one did. Presumably the police could do more. Clearly there were ways for government to *appear* to be trying harder. But there was little knowledge of any kind available to the Federal government as to how actually to reduce either the true or perceived incidence of violent urban crime. A particular variety of conservative could talk tough (e.g., pretrial detention); a comparable breed of liberal could talk soft (e.g., drawing attention to "shocking" rates of "white-collar crime") but mostly this was role playing. Anyone with the least perception was soon enough forced to realize that in the end the "private subsystems of authority" either would dispose the urban populace to traditionally acceptable behavior or would not. Not just crime, but a whole range of urban ills seemed to come down to this central reality. Either people would take care of their houses, or they would not. Either they would send their children to school in an educable state, or they would not. Either they would find jobs, or they would not. Better housing, better schools, better jobs, and more of each, no doubt contributed to the probability of success, and up to a point were preconditions of success, but after that point the incentives, whatever exactly they were, built into the private subsystems exercised ever greater influence over behavior, and the public systems correspondingly less.

Of these private subsystems, none, presumably, was as powerful as family. There lay the heart of the matter, and, as an issue of policy, it presented itself to the presidency as a crisis in welfare. This was, at one remove, an aspect of a racial-ethnic crisis that had produced ominous strains in the American polity. Thus precisely those considerations that had kept the subject out of the political sphere for so long now at length brought it to the very center.

In December the president had appointed me as his Assistant for Urban Affairs, and later, with the establishment of the Urban Affairs Council, Executive Secretary of that body. Shortly after taking office he appointed Dr. Arthur F. Burns as Counsellor, with special responsibility for program development. Thus commenced a protracted debate over policy. The subjects under debate ranged as widely as the domestic concerns of the Federal government, but somehow repeatedly focused, as did so much, on the problem of welfare. Much of the debate was concerned with tactical objectives. The economist was concerned about the economy, feared inflation, feared for business confidence, and took it as given that for the president to propose a large spending program in any area, notably one associated with the "tax and tax, spend and spend" style of the Democrats, would send out precisely the wrong signal from the White House. He had seen Nixon defeated eight years earlier, not by his campaign platform, but by the unemployment rate. The political scientist cared perhaps insufficiently for such matters, but was in any event absorbed with the evident erosion of political authority in America, the seeming inability of liberals to comprehend and defend liberalism, the real enough prospect of a polity regressing toward protracted violence and irresolvable conflict. Government needed a success: an achievement that would directly touch the lives of people in ways they could comprehend and appreciate and use. The Nation had begun a war on poverty. Why not win it? So many subjects were caught up in that one issue: race, cities, violence, not least the ability of government to govern. All this pointed to some form of direct income supplement. Any of a number of variations would do; the principle was the important thing. The thought of establishing that principle at a moment when the national government was widely assumed to have entered a period of stalemate and futility was not without a heroic quality. The center might hold.

The president had no view; at least none he disclosed. He was, however, preoccupied with effectiveness in government. He told his first Cabinet meeting, "We let the people down," meaning by "we" the men of government. The country, he felt, was ready for candid discussion. He wanted his Administration to be "a producing, honest, candid bunch of people." He proposed to "test what we do in terms of what we can accomplish." At the same meeting he heard Paul W. McCracken, the new Chairman of the Council of Economic Advisers, say that some form of income maintenance would be necessary if the Administration was to curb inflation without making the unemployed pay the cost. Such an economic argument would of course be complicated. On an opposite tack, there were presumably political gains to be had from "cracking down" on the "welfare mess." Reports on this from New York City seemed to confirm his own campaign rhetoric, and that of conservatives generally. There was cheating, fraud, waste, theft. This issue seemed to call for strong measures. To move in on it might make the most sense. Surely anything different would make more sense than the situation he had inherited.

From the outset welfare absorbed more of his interest than any other domestic issue. Five days before the inauguration he had sent a memorandum to me, Finch, Attorney General John Mitchell, and his legislative assistant Bryce Harlow asking for a "thorough investigation" of the "New York welfare mess," which he suspected was typical of that all over the country. We were not to be bemused by protestations from the bureaucracy or the mayor that the amounts of money involved were "chickenfeed." "The American people," he wrote, "are outraged and, in my view, they should be." Responses were to be on his desk January 31. Strangest of events: where previous administrations had contrived, sometimes by considerable effort, to ignore the subject of welfare, this one would begin by concentrating on it. I was in a position to encourage this interest, and did so. But at bottom the president was responding not to the interests of an aide, but to a social reality that no longer could be ignored. Further, had not a particularly mindless form of liberalism got itself into this "mess"? That was the word he used. Not, surely, without some satisfaction.

He asked what had gone wrong in New York City? Would a get-tough policy do any good? I responded on January 31, his twelfth day in office. There were no very good answers to his questions. In the eighteen years between 1948 and 1965 the welfare rolls of the city had increased by a quarter million; in the two years that followed they grew by another quarter million. It was not a matter of immigration, nor of Medicaid publicity, nor of welfare militancy. There was enough evidence to reject exogenous explanations of this kind, but not enough to establish that some internal dynamic of the social structure of the city was at work. There were some indications that case workers had become more lenient. The rate of rejection of AFDC applicants had dropped from 40 percent in 1965 to 23 percent in 1968. This might reflect the mayor's policy, which was hardly hostile to welfare; it might reflect an administrative breakdown; but it might also reflect an increased proportion of eligible applicants. Certainly there were many more female-headed households; a steadily larger proportion of illegitimate children. It could be argued that the poverty program encouraged the poor to assert their rights. Did it encourage them also to break up their families in order to establish rights? There were no hard answers.

The most likely source of the problem was the wage structure. "It is increasingly clear," my memorandum summed up, "that the amount of money a low skilled male family head can earn in a city such as New York is not enough to maintain a family at what are now expected standards of living." The most recent City Workers Family Budget for the New York–Northeastern area estimated the need of a family of four at $10,195. The median income of male-headed families in New York was $7,136: for nonwhites it was $5,333, for Puerto Ricans, $4,366. Take-home factory pay was estimated at $90.01 per week. With small earnings on the side, now legally sanctioned and encouraged, a welfare family of four did better than that. On balance it was hard to make much of a case for "getting tough." "The fact is," I summed up, "the more one knows about welfare the more horrible it becomes: but not because of cheating, rather because the system destroys those who receive it, and corrupts those who dispense it."

If there was anything new in this first report to the president it was the emphasis on income. For most of the period since the Great Depression unemployment seemed to have been the master problem, but in the course of the 1960s the power of unemployment to account for dependency weakened and then vanished altogether. The memorandum pointed out to the president that during the 1950s there had been an almost perfect correlation between the monthly rise and fall of male unemployment rates and the rise and fall in the number of new AFDC cases. (The original analysis had used nonwhite unemployment rates, but the relationship was about the same for the whole population.) As male unemployment rates had gone up, so had the number of new AFDC cases. Down, down. Up, up. The correlation was among the strongest known to social science. It could not be established that the men who lost their jobs were the ones who left their families, but the mathematical relationship of the two statistical series—unemployment rates and new AFDC cases—was astonishingly close. Then with the onset of the 1960s the relationship weakened abruptly, and by 1963 vanished altogether. Or, rather, reversed itself. For the next five years the nonwhite male unemployment rate declined steadily and the number of AFDC cases rose steadily. On February 1 a graph illustrating the change was sent to the president.[7]

This caught his eye. On February 3 he asked for a further memorandum explaining as much as could be explained about this sudden reversal which seemed to contradict the most basic assumptions as to the sources of social stability and instability.

This document, drafted for me by Paul Barton, of the Department of Labor Policy Planning staff, entitled "The Relationship of Employment to Welfare Dependency," was ready for the president March 1. It illustrates both the extent and the limits of government analysis of social issues at this time. The social-science analysis of the great presidential commissions that had succeeded one another through the crisis years of the late 1960s had often been surprisingly weak. There existed no mode of causal analysis with anything approaching sufficient explanatory or predictive power to cope with the subjects under inquiry.

Cases opened under AFDC compared with unemployment rate for nonwhite males

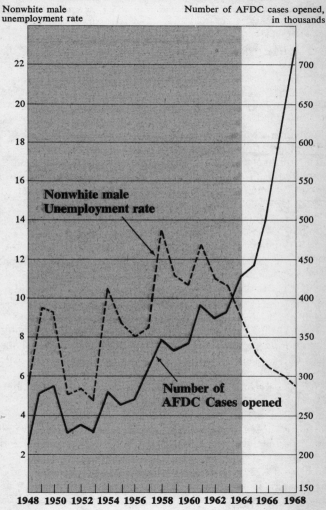

Nonwhite male unemployment rate

Number of AFDC cases opened, in thousands

Nonwhite male Unemployment rate

Number of AFDC Cases opened

1948 1950 1952 1954 1956 1958 1960 1962 1964 1966 1968

Some commissions did better than others, but often the popular reception, which is to say primarily that of the national press, varied inversely to the quality of the social science. The more simplistic the analysis the more enthusiastically it was received. In any event, the nature of the problems posed for the commissions—crime, rioting, violence—was of such sensitivity that whole sectors of the subject remained off limits. By contrast, analyses prepared for a president's personal scrutiny in theory at least did not need to pretend to knowledge that did not exist, nor to avoid subjects that could not be raised in public.

The final conclusion of the March 1 report was that "the information available is inadequate for understanding what is happening." If such information ever was to become available, it would not likely become so during the president's term of office, certainly not in the early months when he wished to assume a legislative initiative. He would have to rely on judgment informed by certain kinds of statistics that would tend to rule out some possibilities, and point to others. There would be no certainty.

The strongest *probability* was that the welfare rolls were growing as a result of a combined "increased demand and increased supply." Thus as welfare payment levels rose, the number of persons below such levels, and therefore eligible for welfare, rose accordingly. As the acceptance rate increased—slowly at first, then rapidly—from 55 percent in the 1950s to 73 percent in the later 1960s, more persons were declared eligible. In both instances the supply of welfare was enlarged. Simultaneously the demand for welfare grew as the number of female-headed families in metropolitan areas increased. From 1961 to 1967, 93 percent of the AFDC rise was in cases where the father was absent from the home. The number of illegitimate births during that period had risen 42 percent. (White illegitimate births had been advancing at a faster pace than nonwhite, although the latter accounted for 55 percent of the total of illegitimate births.) In 1961, 69 percent of the unmarried mothers on AFDC were black (possibly 75 percent by the end of the decade). It was generally known at this time that poor white female-headed families were less likely to be receiving AFDC support than those headed by poor nonwhites. If the Northern urban poor increasingly was black, even the same aggregate level of poverty would produce an increase in the demand for welfare.

The most emphatic finding of the report was in a sense no finding at all, but merely the acknowledgment of the implications of postwar birth rates. The female children born in the post–World War II "baby boom" were now themselves having children. Young, unmarried females are by definition exposed to the risk of illegitimacy; young married couples are most exposed to the risk of family breakup. There were now many many more persons exposed to such risks. For example, the Negro population in central cities in the ages of fifteen to twenty-four increased by 44 percent from 1960 to 1968. *Most significantly, the demographic data promised that this situation would grow more strained before it eased.* Based on 1967 statistics, it appeared that among nonwhites the age group five to fourteen, which stood ready to take the place of the fifteen-to-twenty-four group, was half again as large. The 1970s would be a period of continued and probably intensified demographic strain among the urban poor. Thus teen-agers had accounted for 18 percent of nonwhite unemployment at the outset of the decade, but will account for 31 percent by 1976. (At this time Paul McCracken confirmed for the White House staff the vulnerability of young nonwhites to economic shifts. The period January to October 1967 had witnessed the most recent sustained rise in the number of unemployed. For all persons the increase had been 14 percent. For nonwhite teen-agers it had been 57 percent.)

The estimated nonwhite female population under five was precisely that of the group five to nine, which suggested that in the early 1980s the demographic siege would begin to lift, and urban blacks would be entering a period of lessening pressures of this kind. The data argued convincingly, however, that the 1970s were likely to be even more difficult demographically than the 1960s had been.

It appeared that to the degree such difficulties led to welfare dependency, the phenomenon would soon be more widespread. Between 1960 and 1966 New York and California combined accounted for 46 percent of the total increase in AFDC recipients. But between 1966 and 1968 the case load began to shift. New York, to be sure, had the largest percentage increase. But among the highest ten states four were Southern: Texas, Georgia, Louisiana, Alabama. Kentucky and South Carolina were in the next tier. Welfare was likely, then, to become much more of a *national* problem.

A separate memorandum to the president compressed the findings of the report:

In sum, the bulk of AFDC recipients are now made up of persons not associated with husbands or fathers with an attachment to the labor market. They are drawn from a population that is rapidly growing in size. As a result, changes in the labor market no longer affect the number of AFDC recipients.

Within the limits of available information, that seemed to be the inescapable conclusion.

The president next asked, had there then been a change in the social acceptability of welfare? Were people less reluctant to get on and stay on? His own attitudes on the subject were very much those of his youth, which he would describe, somewhat loosely, as "the Puritan ethic." To be on welfare was at very least a mark of failure, and in certain circumstances a badge of shame. It is just such "antiquated" notions that had made him an object of sustained dislike among liberals. On the other hand his attitudes were much closer to those of welfare recipients themselves than of those who viewed them from afar. In this sense the president knew more about the subject. It was precisely because he viewed welfare as a terrible experience that he was prepared to risk more in an effort to transform it than any other president of his era had been. The liberal pattern of avoidance of the subject of welfare was in ways a form of indifference combined with self-certification. Nixon—whatever else—had no such airs. Welfare was awful: that he knew on taking office. In short order he was considering radical measures to do something about it.

On March 11 the president was provided with a memorandum, "Attitudes Toward Welfare." Here, for once, good research was available, although it was hardly a guide for action. Public opinion, it appeared, was conflicted: strongly sympathetic toward the truly needy, strongly critical of lay-abouts, ne'er-do-wells, welfare cheaters, and so through the range of characterizations by which those who are not dependent disapprove of those who, without apparent cause, are. As none save those directly involved in welfare administration could have any but the vaguest notion as to the mix of the welfare rolls between these two extremes, perceptions of existing reality were almost by definition unstable.

The National Opinion Research Center had been following the subject for thirty years, and had concluded that what was involved was not conflict between social groups, but a widely shared individual ambivalence. An NORC paper summarized

. . . [T]he following conflicting patterns emerge: overlapping support for welfare expenditures and for restrictive measures; simultaneous adherence to a work-incentive ideology and to support for welfare; absence of any clear correlations among support for restrictive measures, welfare support, and the ideological dimensions; and moderate class and age cleavages on support for expenditures, for restrictive measures, and the ideology. All these patterns suggest that the major tension in welfare attitudes is located not between groups of the population but within the individual himself.

On the one hand, the individual is moved to generosity by his perception of the endurance and extent of poverty. He is willing to charge his government with the task of alleviating genuine want wherever it exists, and he is willing to pay increased taxes to facilitate such a program. On the other hand, he is imbued with the tradition of economic incentive and its relationship to self-reliance; and he is suspicious and even resentful of persons who, unlike himself, are in need. He quickly discredits the integrity of welfare recipients and enthusiastically supports policies that not only control welfare-cheating but make the receipt of welfare difficult and embarrassing.

A paper presented in 1967 to the Pacific Sociological Society had similarly concluded: "age, education, income . . . religious preference . . . do not, on the whole, relate to difference in attitude toward welfare." It did however note that "Negroes and whites both see welfare as supporting mostly Negroes, and tend to denigrate welfare recipients. The Negroes may well feel that the stereotypes of welfare recipients held by whites reflect unfavorably on all Negroes." It was well established that the most disapproving attitudes were to be found among the poor themselves. The paper continued: "Lower-income Negroes who are not receiving welfare are attempting to maintain a certain social distance from those who do."

It seemed unlikely, my memorandum continued, that "a social phenomenon as impressive as the growth of the welfare population" would have occurred without some change in attitudes toward dependency, but they had not been found. Jacobus tenBroek, a student of the history of welfare, who argued for fundamental changes in the legal basis of welfare systems, had nonetheless been clear that welfare clients viewed even their statutory rights as a form of privilege. Most significantly, it was evident that *during the 1960s public opinion had grown more skeptical about problems of poverty*. The NORC put the question: "In your opinion, which is more often to blame, if a person is poor—lack of effort on his part, or circumstances beyond his control?" In 1964, 36.9 percent of whites had judged it to be a matter of effort. Three years later this proportion had grown to 43.5 percent. Among Negroes the proportions were lower, but the trend to greater severity was even more pronounced. Only 8.9 percent of blacks had thought effort, or lack of it, responsible for poverty in 1964. In three years this proportion doubled to 19.6 percent. Blacks who thought "circumstances" to blame declined from 45 percent to 35 percent. At every income level the great majority of persons thought that men on relief who are physically able to work "Must take any job offered which pays the going wage." Significantly, however, persons with high incomes were more likely to oppose such a proposition than those with low incomes. In 1964 only 6.6 percent of persons with incomes under $3,000 opposed a compulsory work provision. Among persons with incomes over $10,000, the proportion opposed was 15.7 percent.

Among welfare recipients these attitudes were even more pronounced. Lawrence Podell of the City University of New York had by early 1969 completed an extensive study *Families on Welfare in New York City*. He established, first, that contrary to the stereotype of one generation of welfare recipients breeding another, welfare was a new experience for most of those involved, especially for Negroes and Puerto Ricans who had migrated to New York City. These were not "hardened" recipients. Over half the publicly assisted mothers agreed with the statement "Getting money from welfare makes a person feel ashamed." Over eight in ten agreed "People should be grateful for money they get from welfare." Fifty-six percent of whites, but 70 percent of blacks, agreed "A lot of people getting money from welfare don't deserve it."

Podell found the "work ethic" very much intact among welfare mothers, at least in terms of responses to questionnaires. Seven in ten mothers "preferred to work for pay rather than stay at home." Given the availability of "appropriate" day-care facilities, "six in ten mothers with preschool children preferred to work."[8]

Information was accumulating now. The March 11 memorandum concluded:

The two facts tugging us in different directions on policy decisions are simply that first, there is terrible poverty, not restricted geographically to any part of the country, urban or rural, and secondly, that there is both outright cheating by some of those on welfare, and that there are some legal loopholes in the welfare laws which prove an incentive for going on welfare as opposed to working.

The March–April 1969 issue of *Welfare in Review,* an HEW journal, featured two articles, the first by Perry Levinson, the second by Thomas S. Langner and associates reporting the results of carefully designed inquiries into the effects of welfare dependency on children. Some such work had previously been done, but now for the first time relatively "hard" data were coming to hand. A prefatory statement about the articles took note that both had come to essentially the same conclusion: "Children in families receiving public assistance suffer from more social and emotional problems than children in families not receiving public assistance, however low their income."

Levinson in a longitudinal study of a southeastern metropolitan area, "Mountain View," of a quarter million population, divided his sample among students whose families had received AFDC payments, students from families who had applied but had been rejected, and those who had never applied. The children from AFDC families had by far the most behavioral problems, such as dropping out of school, delinquency, school disciplinary difficulties, premarital pregnancy, and such. Further, Levinson found, "The longer the family receives assistance, the more likely it is to have children with [these] . . . kinds of problems. . . ." Of 144 possible instances of difficulty he found "students from AFDC families scored highest 87 times; students from rejected families, 41 times; and students from the non-recipient families, 7 times."

In a study of psychiatric impairment among Manhattan children, Langner found a similar pattern of differences between children from welfare and low-income, nonwelfare families, especially pronounced in such areas as the development of speech, sight and hearing and abilities for functioning in school. The widely held belief, or hope, that the father absence in AFDC families was somehow made up for by other males did not survive the inquiry. Defining a father figure as a "natural father, or father substitute—a stepfather or boyfriend of the mother, including a common-law husband—who had been present in the home for at least a year," the results were emphatic. Fifty-six percent of AFDC families had no father figure, compared with 25 percent of low-income families (under $6,500 per year) and 8 percent for high-income families, that is those with incomes over $6,500. The study was careful to insist that "Broken homes, *in themselves,* may not be a noxious influence," but the combination of welfare with other such qualities narrowed the odds dramatically. Langner's findings, as Levinson's, suggested that welfare itself introduced a new dynamic into the experience of children which made things harder for them, rather than otherwise. Research was beginning to get at the phenomenon of dependency. Langner concluded:

The problems and handicaps of welfare (AFDC) children do not originate in their low-income status only. The children in low-income nonwelfare families are less impaired than the welfare children in *total impairment,* a difference even more marked when specific aspects of impairment are examined. For certain aspects of impairment, however, low-income status is of primary importance. The welfare children also differ from the nonwelfare children on the basis of diagnostic impressions. They seem to have a higher incidence of serious disorders such as psychosis and appear to be more isolated, mistrustful, and anxious than the nonwelfare children.

The greater impairment and less healthy personality of the welfare children is the result of a great number of forces affecting them. An analysis of symptomatology in the mothers suggests that welfare mothers may have more psychiatric impairment than nonwelfare mothers. Also, family structure differs. Welfare children appear to be more independent of their mothers; nonwelfare mothers appear to control their children more than welfare mothers. The employment status of the welfare mothers also seems to affect impairment: children of working mothers have less impairment.

Finally, the data corroborate the commonsense hypothesis that the presence of a father figure in the home is of great importance in the welfare family. Children from families including a father or father substitute are less impaired than children from families without a father figure. The presence or absence of the father, though, does not explain all conditions. The ability of the father to provide for his family and to fill adequately the role of a father may be of even more significance then his mere presence in the home. Thus, attempts to overcome dependency on welfare should not concentrate solely on providing income to families in need. They should also provide opportunities for family members to gain the self-respect and assurance they need to function effectively in society. Once eligibility and income cease to be the exclusive aims of social services, caseworkers can better perform the duties for which they were trained. This means that great changes must be made in our welfare laws and in the attitudes of legislators and the public toward the poor.[9]

(Later, an HEW study of achievement motivation among thirteen- to sixteen-year-old males living in AFDC families added further to the case against welfare. Long-term exposure to AFDC acted as a sharp depressant to the achievement motivation of young males; Negro youth remained relatively unaffected, but Anglo and Mexican-American youth on long-term welfare expected less and were doing less than their nonwelfare peers.)[10]

At this time, research also established the degree to which the rise in welfare rolls was associated with changing populations. Irene Lurie, in a Brookings Institution study, showed that the number of AFDC families could rise much faster than the rise in the number of poor female-headed families because black families in such a situation were more likely to be receiving welfare than whites (in 1959, 52 percent, as against 33 percent). In the period 1959 to 1966, moreover, the number of poor female-headed white families had declined, while the number of poor female-headed black families had increased, especially those with four or more children. But still this did not mean there was more poverty: simply more dependency.

The slight increase [1959–1966] in the total number of poor families headed by women is composed of a decrease of poor white families of 58,000 and an increase of poor nonwhite families of 82,000. The increase in the number of poor nonwhite families is not the result of an increase in the proportion of nonwhite families which are poor. In 1959, 80 percent of nonwhite female headed families were poor, and the poverty rate fell to 70 percent by 1966. Rather it is the result of a 31 percent increase in the number of nonwhite female headed families, that is, of an increase in the breakdown of the Negro family. The number of nonwhite female headed families increased at twice the rate of white families, leading to an increase of 16 percent in the number of poor nonwhite families.[11]

This phenomenon was in turn associated with a growth in the relative advantages of becoming dependent on AFDC support. Podell estimated that 70 percent of the new AFDC cases in New York City involved abandonment by husbands and fathers. Increasingly, seemingly, such a move presented itself as a rational economic choice. Elizabeth F. Durbin at New York University investigated whether welfare programs affected the decision to work and concluded they did. Unemployment rates had been going down in New York; per capita incomes had been improving. And yet more and more persons were on welfare. Durbin concluded that the rolls had been rising because of an increase in acceptance rates, an increase in payment levels (which meant more persons would be eligible), but also because "the value of welfare (measured both in terms of basic allowance and of real value of goods and services) has risen much more rapidly than the equivalent income to be earned in a low wage job in New York."[12]

The president now was getting more and better information about the problem of welfare than any of his predecessors, certainly, and probably better than any of the governors or mayors who were dealing more directly with the issue. It is necessary, however, to be clear how limited the use of all this was. The routine myths, pro- and anti-, that surround the subject of welfare had been disposed of early on and played no part in the White House deliberations. This was no small thing, but it was nonetheless a negative achievement. It remained the case that no one could fully explain why the welfare rolls were soaring. Nor did anyone suppose there was an easy way to reverse this trend.

The one inescapable fact was that welfare was a problem that had created itself. The rolls rise because they are there. The French had no welfare problem: they had no welfare program. Which is not to say that there are no poor in France, no dependent persons. There is a sufficiency of both. But there is no program which caters to the special needs of the dependent poor, and which maintains a vast bureaucratic machinery that depends on this class of persons for its own existence. Harsh, essential facts. The French have family allowances, social insurance, medical care; if anything an overfull panoply of social services, but with it all the assumption remains that people have to look after themselves. The custodial quality of American welfare is not to be encountered elsewhere. In ways mass relief programs are an Anglo-American phenomenon. Tocqueville's prophetic insight that "Life would have no relish for [Americans] if they were delivered from the anxieties which harass them, and they show more attachment to their cares than aristocratic nations to their pleasures," corresponds to a not less sustained determination to think ill of ourselves where social-welfare matters are concerned. The tradition that charity has been heartless, moralizing, punitive, has been maintained perhaps not least in order to ensure that it be, if anything, just the opposite. (This rhetorical style was much in evidence in the 1960s. As the national government steadily escalated its levels of commitment to social change, there was an equivalent rise in accusations that it was behaving just the opposite. Often as not such charges were made by persons themselves on Federal payrolls, as if a system had been designed to ensure constant dissatisfaction and hence ever greater effort.)

The problem of the American tradition in welfare is that it may be more protective of weakness than of strength. Certainly few American social reformers would feel comfortable opposing welfare legislation on the ground that it would accommodate to the undercompetitive qualities of the poor, rather than otherwise. By contrast, the Webbs were openly disdainful of Lloyd George's reforms of the 1908–1911 period. Beatrice Webb later recalled:

To us, the compulsory insurance with automatically distributed money, allowances during illness or worklessness, with free choice of doctor under the panel system, would not and could not prevent the occurrence of sickness or unemployment. Indeed, the fact that sick and unemployed persons were entitled to money incomes without any corresponding obligation to get well and keep well, or to seek and keep employment, seemed to us likely to encourage malingering and a disinclination to work for their livelihood.[13]

The notion of an "obligation to get well and keep well," to "seek and keep employment," was not much in evidence among American social reformers in the 1960s. This was in part a consequence of ideology, if such a term may be used to describe the puzzled and uncertain impulses of the time, "The Age of Rubbish," as Richard Hofstadter was to describe it. The memory of the Depression and a penumbra of Marxism lingered on: individuals were not to be held accountable for their fate. A social-class problem was also involved. With the steady deprecation and isolation of the labor movement, upper- and middle-class progressives of the Northeastern or West Coast variety increasingly found themselves espousing the causes of persons and groups they did not know and were not known by. The social discipline which the Webbs expected of socialists (and required of the lower classes!) had simply no place in such a relationship. If deference of any kind was involved, it flowed from "top" to "bottom."

For all this, there was a more profound reality of poverty and blocked opportunity. Among the industrial democracies of the world (saving only Canada, which had had little choice in the matter) the United States alone had not instituted a postwar economic policy that gave the first priority to continued full employment. Accordingly, it became impossible to base other social policies on the presumption that all able-bodied persons in need of income would obtain it first of all by working. By contrast, for example, the French with perfect conscience could be severe on the subject, as suggested by a passage from a French government survey of social programs.

Having laid down the principle that all persons with dependent children are entitled to family benefits, the law then proceeds to make a restriction . . . by making the *exercise of a paid occupation,* or proof that the exercise of such an occupation is impossible, an essential condition, with a view to excluding the willfully unemployed who would be tempted to live on their children's allowances.[14]

Such an attitude was defensible on the most elemental grounds: there was full employment in France, no one need be without work.

Save for three wartime intervals, there had not been full employment in the United States in upwards of forty years. Unemployment persisted, and at times reached depression levels, among precisely those groups most likely to be told to "seek and keep employment." There were no jobs, or at all events those involved did not have jobs, and formal efforts to train and to place them had only begun and were not spectacularly successful. The fact of unemployment, having become almost a fixed condition of American society in "normal" times, imposed subtle, unspoken, but severe constraints upon social policy. Some measures simply were not to be considered.

Thus it was out of the question that anyone in the Administration should consider the one move with respect to welfare dependency that otherwise might reasonably enough have been inferred from the available evidence, namely, to abolish the welfare system. No other industrial nation in the world had a welfare system such as existed in the United States and no other had such a welfare problem. Female-headed families were not unknown in France, where the illegitimacy ratio had settled at about 6 percent, down from 9 percent in the early twentieth century, but about that of the early nineteenth. But there was no dependent class, simply—it must be assumed—because no provision was made for dependency. There were family allowances, maternity allowances, housing allowances, the Workingclass Family Help Association, and Family Holiday Hostels, with *aide sociale* funds available for emergencies. But these were universal provisions which made no distinctions whatever in favor of the female-headed household, in consequence of which, in the view in any event of French officialdom, there was no problem of dependent female-headed households. More than a century earlier, Tocqueville in his essay on pauperism submitted to the Royal Academic Society of Cherbourg commented with his unblinking brilliance on the great incidence of paupers (read "welfare recipients") in the England of that day—then the richest nation on earth—and their near absence in countries such as Spain and Portugal, for all the English pauper, on poor relief, was better off than the average of the self-sufficient citizens of the peninsula. He judged the phenomenon to be the combined effect of urbanization *and the existence of the poor-relief laws*.[15]

In such circumstances a case could be made for getting rid of such laws. In the United States a large and growing proportion of the dependent poor had got that way as a result of behavior not much sanctioned by the traditional moral standards of the society. A case could be made for raising the price of such behavior. But no such case was made. In the absence of a policy of full employment no such case could be made. The instinct of the president's advisers was to search for ways to provide more welfare rather than less.

If there was an exception it was Arthur Burns, in whom concern to control inflation in part at least by controlling government spending combined with an active skepticism about the intellectual substructure of the social programs of the Kennedy-Johnson period and the not notably different variations on many of the same themes now being produced for Nixon. Burns had not accepted outright the recommendations of the Nathan task force. Rather, he sent them to HEW with a request for further consideration. By February, however, it was clear that Finch and his associates were already leaning toward, if not committed to, the establishment of minimum national welfare standards, which the task force had recommended. It seemed both rational and humanitarian. It was directed primarily at the South, a familiar Federal concern. If white-dominated Mississippi was forcing black children to subsist on $8.50 per month, should not something be done about this in Washington? Moreover, within weeks of taking office the Administration was being urged by Northern Republicans to do something dramatic in this area.

On February 12, 1969, the Urban Affairs Council met for the third time. Governor Nelson A. Rockefeller presented a detailed analysis of the fiscal crisis overtaking state and local governments. His proposals were familiar enough, yet in sum constituted a significantly new style in Federalism. (One by one the Nixon Administration was to adopt all but one of his principal recommendations.) Addressing the president and the Council, Rockefeller called for the consolidation of Federal aid into block grants; for Federal standards and increased financial aid in welfare; for a national contributory health-insurance scheme; for substantially increased aid to elementary and secondary education (again through block grants); and for general per capita aid to state and local governments. Much of the discussion that followed centered on welfare. The governor noted that that winter, for the first time, New York City had applied a state law to a family of eleven which it was judged had come from Mississippi for the purpose of collecting welfare. The city bought them a ticket home. The governor took it as self-evident that the great disparities in payment levels between Northern and Southern states created an artificial and undesirable inducement to migration, or in any event a grievance of sorts which Northern states might well expect to see redressed.

That afternoon the president told Finch and members of the White House staff, "We have got to indicate we are going to do new things in welfare." If he had not already decided, before long it was clear that he, too, was in favor of national standards.

The events of February 12 anticipated much that was to come. A liberal Northern governor came to plead the cause of his state, and ended by moving the president further in the direction of massive aid for the South. It was a sequence no one intended, no one anticipated: it simply kept coming out that way. The proposal could be and was repeatedly made that the Federal government should assume more, most, or all the costs of welfare in the Northern states. But no one argued that the levels of welfare in those states were inadequate. (It appeared too probable that the levels of benefits were themselves part of the problem. This is not to say they were, but only that persons seeking to change the system did not generally direct their attention to increasing benefit levels in the high-benefit states.)

To the presidential government the proposal for "full Federal funding" had limited attractions. Billions of Federal money would be spent, without a single citizen getting an extra nickel. Poor politics. Further, to the president it seemed poor social policy. The proponents of full Federal funding, eminently respectable, perfectly decent men, nonetheless presented themselves as morally neutral on the subject of welfare. Some of the more fashionable mayors had gone through a step-right-up-and-claim-your-rightful-entitlement-long-denied-you-by-an-oppres-sive-bureaucracy-and-heartless-society phase, but such empathy had rarely lasted. It was replaced for the most part by silence. The old political taboos became if anything more compelling as the racial composition of the inner-city welfare rolls became more pronounced. For elected officials caught up with the problem, the "optimal" approach to welfare was to have no views on the subject as such while making every effort to get the Federal government to assume the cost. Thereafter, the rolls could climb as fast and as high as they would. If it did not cost the city any money, it would not cost the mayor any sleep. Any other approach involved too many political risks. The president, nonetheless, had another view. He was not neutral about welfare; he was against it. It was, to him, evidence of social failure and personal tragedy. Avoidance of dependency had preoccupied his family in his youth. He had never been a Boy Scout, he would recall. His parents could only afford to support one, and his older brother was chosen. When that one came down with tuberculosis, the family went as deep into debt as was necessary to pay the bills and avoid the county hospital. Nixon *knew* that welfare is stigmatizing. Liberals knew something different: that it ought *not* to be. Some found it possible to go from there to the view that it isn't; indeed, that welfare is good and what is bad is persons who don't see this. Such views enhanced the self-esteem of many persons, but changed reality not at all. Welfare *is* stigmatizing. To deny this fact is to be indifferent to pain. To contrive not to know it is—well, less than admirable. It was impossible for Nixon not to know it, and difficult for him to ignore it. His youth was still close to him. It had been shaped in considerable measure by this reality. The family had lived on tomato gravy. Meat once a week. He had gone on to become president of the United States.

This latter fact, more than any experience of poverty or tradition of self-reliance, distinguished him from the governors and especially the mayors who came through the White House in considerable numbers at this time, one more agitated than the other; some alarmist, some genuinely alarmed; pleading their bankruptcy, their impotence, their fears, and always soon or late getting to the subject of welfare. Whatever would be done, the mayors would not be remembered for doing it. The president would, especially if what he did somehow corresponded to the enormousness of the social problem that welfare surely reflected.

This then was an opportunity, as well as a problem. Indeed, it was not necessarily a problem at all. There was nothing the president *had* to do about welfare, as for example on taking office he *had* to deal with budgets and taxes and armaments, and so through the range of presidential subjects. Welfare was not such: never had been. Had he wished he could have left the subject for HEW to tinker with, while allowing it to be understood that any state or local official who made too much of the issue might find himself more accused than accusing. Two concerns argued a different course. First, he was not going to have many opportunities for domestic initiatives. It was soon clear that the budgetary situation was such that he would have very little free money in his first term, and, of course, he might not get a second. The Democrats in Congress would instinctively move to use up what little extra money came to hand by making small increments to the array of categorical programs that had started in the mid-sixties. A case could be made, and was, for proposing one or two major initiatives that would be unmistakably his and forcing the Congress to accept or reject them.

There was, further, the matter of his relations with Negro Americans. Nixon had had a good civil-rights record as vice-President, and could reasonably claim to be the inheritor of a fine Republican tradition in such matters. Yet the sixties had changed so much. Civil rights had triumphed; yet racial problems were widely perceived to have grown worse. More accurately, the problems of persons defined by race were seen to have grown worse. This was itself part of the difficulty. In the aftermath of the civil-rights movement of the sixties, no one could easily define the problem that remained. It was in most respects the problem of an urban lower class made up of persons fleeing a bankrupt agricultural system. But racial prejudice and hostility continued high among whites and began to be more openly espoused among blacks. Whatever the social-class components of the problem, the tradition of the civil-rights movement insisted that the issues be defined primarily by reference to race, and this view had been validated both by white liberals, in documents such as the Kerner Commission report, with its charge of "white racism," and also by white racialists, who were suddenly resurgent in the South, and, in the presidential candidacy of George Wallace, to be encountered across the Nation.

Nixon had won the Republican nomination as the result of the support of some such persons, symbolized by Senator Strom

Thurmond of South Carolina. His campaign had not been anti-black, but was notably reserved on the subject, at least by contrast to the Democratic position. Here, as in a number of areas, a considerable gap had developed between substance and symbol under his predecessors. The Nation was not "moving forward" on civil rights at the end of the Johnson years. The grand surge of events that had seemed so powerful at mid-decade had faltered and then subsided: overwhelmed by violence at home and abroad. Yet the Democratic Administration continued to make large pronouncements and to convey a sense of commitment. A number of civil-rights leaders and black professionals were on close terms with the White House, establishing both themselves and the advocacy of black interests as a normal aspect of government. This was an exchange relationship. The head of the National Urban League would travel to Vietnam and return with reassuring sounds. But the relationship was all the stronger for this: there was something to exchange—black political support. As time passed, however, the returns to blacks as a group were increasingly symbolic.

The quintessential sequence was that of the National Advisory Commission on Civil Disorders, appointed in an atmosphere of near panic in the summer of 1967. The Commission labored through the fall and winter devising new categorical aid programs to deal with what one Washington commentator of the period was fond of calling "the terminal cancer of the slums." Yet when the Commission's report was finished, the White House would not receive it. (Such matters are recorded in indirect ways. The report of the Kerner Commission begins with a Foreword. There is no letter of transmittal to the president.) The report called for more, far more, than the Administration could conceive the public wishing, or the Congress willing to provide. It was assumed that the civil rights ardor of the earlier period had waned, and it was—finally—understood and accepted that the war had preempted resources. And yet the promises persisted, not least because those who made them genuinely hoped that they might someday come true.*

* On the morning of the day the Kerner Commission was established by the president I appeared before a Senate committee which was moving to create a commission by statute. Before testifying I spoke on the telephone with a senior White House assistant, asking if the Administration had any plans I

In his study *The Lost Priority*, John Herbers writes, "One would have found it hard to devise in the spring of 1965 a course of action on the part of the government that would have been more devastating to racial amity."[16] Reality had to catch up with pretense, and there would inevitably follow a sense of letdown. Nixon *understood* that inasmuch as this would occur during his Administration, it would be ascribed to him. Whatever else the case, this would be the normal public perception, but in this instance it would be magnified by the fact that he had received virtually no Negro support in the 1968 campaign, and a bare minimum of Negro votes in the election. He was perceived almost as an enemy, and he came to office at a time of seemingly escalating black violence, of ever more horrendous rhetoric, the tradition of Martin Luther King, Jr., seemingly shattered, and the dementia of the Black Panthers seemingly ascendant. He was asked about this at his second press conference on February 6.

QUESTION: Mr. President, do you agree with those who say that you and your Administration have a serious problem with distrust among the blacks, and whether you agree that it is one of your more serious problems or not could you tell us specifically what you are doing to deal with what some consider to be this distrust among the blacks?

THE PRESIDENT: I am concerned about this problem; and incidentally, let me make it very clear that those who have raised this question are not simply those who are political opponents. My Task Force on Education pointed up that I was not considered—I think the words they used—as a friend by many of our black citizens in America.

I can only say that, by my actions as president, I hope to rectify that. I hope that by what we do in terms of dealing with the problems of all Americans, it will be made clear that the President of the United States, as an elected official, has no state constituency. He has no Congressional constituency. He does not represent any special group. He represents all the people. He is the friend of all the people. Putting it another way, as a lawyer, the president is the counsel for all the people of this country, and I hope that I can gain the respect and I hope eventually the friendship of black citizens and other Americans.

---

should know about. The answer was "No." There were no plans. My informant, who would spend the day drafting the president's television speech announcing the commission, was emphatic. "There is," he said, "no money."

This hope was not to be fulfilled in his first years in office. The Administration genuinely desired to win the blacks, but it also hoped to win the votes of whites, especially Southern whites. It had no more settled in office when the term "Southern strategy" began appearing in the press, more or less obviously the result of background conversations in the Department of Justice, where the long-range political calculations of the Administration were presumed to be made. A "Southern strategy" was quickly depicted as a bid for conservative-to-racist white votes in the South, and "backlash" working-class votes elsewhere. It was taken as given that this would mean the Administration would have to act in ways contrary to the interests of blacks. Certainly the immediate consequence was detrimental to a major symbolic interest of the group, namely, to have their concerns remain high on the national agenda, and detrimental to the personal interests of the black leaders who had enjoyed access and prestige under Johnson. There was a measure of feigning on both sides during this period. Civil-rights leaders would denounce the Administration one day, and the following day come to breakfast to discuss manpower training contracts. But the impression conveyed was one of growing hostility, and this was ineradicably confirmed in the winter of 1969–1970 by the nomination by the president of first one and then another Southerner for a Supreme Court seat and their rejection by the Senate ostensibly on grounds of racial bias.

Still, in the early months of the Administration these events had not yet occurred. Nixon hoped for something different. More importantly, he shared the anxiety of any sentient person in the capital that the spiral of increasing urban racial violence, now occasionally mixed up with other issues, had not ceased. In 1965 there had been four major riots and civil disturbances in the country. In 1966 there were twenty-one major riots and civil disorders. In 1967 there were eighty-three major riots and civil disturbances. In the first seven months of 1968 there were fifty-seven major riots and disturbances. From the time of the Detroit riots of 1967 a Civil Disturbance Task Force was operating in the Pentagon. Returning from Detroit, Cyrus Vance had reported "it would be desirable if the several Continental Armies were tasked with reconnoitering the major cities of the United States in which it appears possible that riots may occur." Following the riots associated with the assassination of Martin Luther King, Jr., the Department of the Army issued a Civil Disturbance Information Collection Plan providing for United States Army Intelligence Command personnel to engage, where authorized by Headquarters, Department of the Army, in covert operations directed against American citizens. In August 1968, Federal troops were "prepositioned" in Chicago in connection with the Democratic National Convention.[17]

In restrospect the domestic turbulence of the United States in the late 1960s may come to appear something less than cataclysmic. But this was not the view of men then in office. Mayors, governors—presidents—took it as given that things were in a hell of a shape and that something had to be done. Nixon's first sortie from the White House after becoming president was to visit a burned-out area of Washington, only blocks from the White House. The residents were surprised and pleased to find a president in their midst, but no one could take any pleasure from the scene he visited. The rubble, the ruin, left in the aftermath of the rioting associated with the death of Martin Luther King, Jr., was still there, virtually untouched, as if the events had occurred the previous week rather than the previous April. Photographers were sent round the country, and returned with pictures of the very same scene, North, East, West, everywhere seemingly but the South—and what would stay the course of insurrection there? Things weren't working. Some of the riot areas were two, three, three-and-a-half years old. Oceans of ink had proclaimed the citizens' coalitions and government programs that were to do something about them. Yet little, almost nothing, appeared to have been done.

This came as no great surprise to the Republican president. He was not disposed to think that much comes of such announcements. (Early in the Administration, there was considerable talk about "voluntarism," but little real belief.) Drucker's formula that modern governments were successful only at waging war and inflating the currency was not, in the end, especially amusing. For what *could* he do?

It had been easier for his predecessors. Even the smallest gestures were seen to have great significance at the outset of what became a vast transformation of racial attitudes and relations. But what could be done by "a stroke of a pen" had already been done. What commissions could do had been done. What could be done by enacting the unfinished agenda of the New Deal had all but been done, and if anything there seemed less a sense of achievement than ever. To compound the difficulty of devising a viable response there was then beginning to be voiced a generalized but powerful sentiment among the white working-class that *it* was being discriminated against, even exploited, in the interest of lower-class minorities. Simultaneously its sense of propriety and patriotism was being challenged, even taunted, by upper-class antiwar demonstrators. These were men and women in the middle. Inevitably politicians of the center would be concerned with them.* The Democratic strategists, Richard M. Scammon and Ben J. Wattenberg, at this time formulated their concept of "the social issue," a congeries of real enough grievances and alarms on the part of traditional working-class Democratic voters which, they reasoned, Democratic politicians had better pay attention to. (In 1967, when Harry McPherson, counsel to President Johnson, told Scammon he was thinking of writing a speech "decrying police brutality," Scammon replied: "Do you really want to help the President? Then get him photographed with a man in blue.")[18] By temperament and by the logic of his political situation, this was a group about which Nixon was equally concerned. Its disaffection both from traditional political liberalism and from the Democratic party was then being much exaggerated, but politics is shaped by such impressions and these were strongly voiced at the time, not least in the liberal media which was busily rediscovering the "white ethnics."

In the spring of 1969, Nixon read and was impressed by an article in *New York* Magazine entitled "The Revolt of the White Lower Middle Classes." In it Pete Hamill, a writer on the left,

---

* Political sociologists, most notably Andrew M. Greeley, have more recently demonstrated that the racial and social attitudes of "white ethnic groups" during this period continued to be considerably more liberal than those of "older" American groups. The upper class stereotype of the "hardhat" is probably best understood as simply the most recent manifestation of an enduring class and ethnic prejudice. It was, in reality, quite possible for workingmen to hold quite accepting attitudes on issues such as racial equality and social welfare, while taking offense at what they perceived as favored treatment of others. See, for example, Andrew M. Greeley, *Why Can't They Be Like Us? America's White Ethnic Groups*, New York, E. P. Dutton, 1971.

described the frustration and increasingly articulated anger of the Catholic working class of New York. Everywhere Hamill encountered fury, a sense of exclusion, of privileges lavished on others and denied to them. These were men who earned their living with their hands or their backs, as Hamill put it. "They do not live in abject, swinish poverty, nor in safe, remote suburban comfort. They earn between $5,000 and $10,000 a year. And they can no longer make it in New York." Nixon shared not a little of their resentment. (He came to refer to them as the "Five and Ten's.") During the campaign he had repeatedly spoken of the "forgotten Americans," those who "have not taken to the streets before, who have not indulged in violence, who have not broken the law." "These forgotten Americans," he had declared, "finally have become angry ———."

Hamill agreed, and his report confirmed, without any special intent, the degree to which welfare was an object of that anger.

"I'm going out of my mind," an ironworker friend named Eddie Cush told me a few weeks ago. "I average about $8,500 a year, pretty good money. I work my ass off. But I can't make it. I come home at the end of the week. I start paying the bills, I give my wife some money for food. And there's nothing left. Maybe, if I work overtime, I get $15 or $20 to spend on myself. But most of the time, there's nothin'. They take $65 a week out of my pay. I have to come up with $90 a month rent. But every time I turn around, one of the kids need shoes or a dress or something for school. And then I pick up a paper and read about a million people on welfare in New York or spades rioting in some college or some fat welfare bitch demanding—you know, not askin', demanding—a credit card at Korvette's. . . . I work for a living and I can't get a credit card at Korvette's. . . . You know, you see that, and you want to go out and strangle someone."

Cush was not drunk, and he was not talking loudly, or viciously; or with any bombast; but the tone was similar to the tone you can hear in conversations in bars like Farrell's all over this town; the tone was quiet bitterness.

They were angered too by the substance and style of antiwar protest, coming as so much of it did from a higher social class able itself to avoid the war. It was, in their view, "an American war, with Americans dying in action. . . ."

Hamill was worried. George Wallace had received ten million votes, "not all of them from red-necked racists."

That should have been a warning, strong and clear. If the stereotyped black man is becoming the working-class white man's enemy, the eventual enemy might be the democratic process itself. Any politician who leaves that white man out of the political equation, does so at a very large risk. The next round of race riots might not be between people and property, but between people and people. And that could be the end of us.*[19]

* Hamill's article is quoted because it was read by and probably influenced the opinion of the president and other persons concerned with this issue at this time. Two points may be stressed. Hamill was writing in a distinctly liberal journal, *New York*. Neither he nor his publishers could be assumed to take any pleasure in what he was reporting. Similar accounts were available from any number of cities. The following month John Askins in a series in the Detroit *Free Press* described the plight of poor whites in that city.

> It appears that social welfare programs in Detroit are failing to reach a great many poor people, and that most of the unreached are white.
> Why?
> To ask that question is not to imply that impoverished blacks shouldn't be getting the help, too. But it needs to be asked. There is the fact that the nation's welfare programs have become identified as black programs in the minds of many people. It is one reason why many poor whites, burdened by prejudice, have been reluctant to apply for help.
> It has helped advance the career of George Wallace. It has contributed in an unfortunate way to the resurgence of the Republican party. And it has threatened the existence of the War on Poverty itself: Congress would stand for a lot of waste and inefficiency if the OEO program were reaching a lot of whites.
> In Detroit, there seems to be a combination of reasons why it doesn't:
> · Poor whites are not organized, have no effective voice, have been unable to tell of their problems.
> · Poverty programs have been viewed by many as a means of preventing riots; the white poor have not rioted in recent years.
> · Poor whites are not heavily concentrated. They are therefore hard to reach, and, in an underfinanced program, expensive to reach.
> · Many poor whites are Southern migrants who, characteristically, refuse to admit they are poor, reject the concept of charity, and stay clear of what they regard as programs for black people.
> · Poor whites are, on the average, less poor than poor blacks; more of them are slightly above the official poverty income guideline and hence are ineligible for help—but are still poor.
> · A majority of workers in neighborhood centers are black, and their new clients tend to be black also.
> · Most neighborhood centers in Detroit are in primarily black areas.

Andrew Greeley of the National Opinion Research Center, while contending that the survey data of this period suggested that the overwhelming ma-

The president agreed with Hamill. "I find this to be a very disturbing article," he wrote, "What is our answer?"

As it happened, there was one. A body of social science had grown up in the late 1960s which viewed the Federal social programs of that decade as conflict-inducing. In the words of one sociologist writing the White House, "None of the objectives of social policy in recent years in the United States have been other than divisive. They have righted some moral wrong, benefited one group at the expense of another, but none could capture the involvement and imagination of all." From this point of view, new issues in social policy were needed. (The environment was an obvious candidate.) Yet the old issues remained to be resolved, the most pressing of which were the combined, interacting problems of race and poverty.

During the period that the problems of race had been attacked by a legal strategy, the courts had been the focus of the civil-rights movement, and remained so until at least the mid-1960s. The problems of poverty, of disadvantage, had largely been construed in terms of inadequate performance, in the individual or the group, and were approached through a services strategy, which, again, is the provision through external intervention of abilities and modes of behavior which were presumed to be the root of such disadvantage, or at very least a route out of it.

---

jority of all racial and ethnic groups in American cities still took a primarily moderate position, nonetheless saw welfare as a special problem. In October 1969, in a paper on "The Alienation of White Ethnic Groups," he told a Conference on National Unity:

> Given the fact that much of the tax increase, at least at the state and local level, is going into one form of welfare program or the other, and that large (though perhaps not large enough) amounts of federal moneys are also going into such welfare programs, it is understandable that ethnics feel that they are being taxed more heavily to subsidize other social groups. They will argue that no such subsidies were ever offered to them.

In May 1970, Gus Tyler, vice-President of the International Ladies Garment Workers Union, a forthright liberal sprung from the tradition of Jewish socialism, described attitudes among needle-trade workers possibly more sophisticated but hardly less angry than those of Hamill's Irishmen.

> [T]he mood today . . . is compounded of economic frustration, personal fear, and political fury. It has been produced by erosion of living standards that have been marginal at best in the 1960s, by the incompetence of government in dealing with social problems, and by the disorders and violence disrupting American life.

The legal strategy had had an heroic age of vast achievement, but this had begun to fade. There was a limit to the efficacy of rights without resources. The latter constituted the problem of poverty. Here the services strategy had less to report by way of achievement, perhaps especially in the field of social welfare, but if anything more dramatically in connection with efforts such as compensatory education. Vast promises had been made and not at all fulfilled. The cost-benefit ratios of service programs were, at very least, depressing, and became all the more unsettling as it became more clear that the costs were so heavily made up of transfer payments to middle- and upper-middle-class professionals. It would not be an exaggeration to argue that Hamill's ironworker was being taxed to pay for (and bid up) the salaries of college graduates in the services professions, or neoprofessions, whose accomplishments, on examination, proved evanescent at best. It was an arrangement easily enough caricatured as a system of feeding the sparrows by feeding the horses.

The alternative was an income strategy. The one seemingly fixed correlation in social statistics is that well-being rises with income. In David Riesman's term, "the more, the more." If what the poor lacked was money, giving it to them directly was, on the face of it, a reasonable response: direct, efficient, and immediate. The last consideration was not the least; anyone benefiting from such a program would *know* it. Just as importantly, although not a large consideration in White House discussions of the time, an income strategy would tend to provide some criteria for valuing the goods and services consumed by low-income families; *their* priorities would more often come to the fore rather than the priorities of others who "knew what was best." It would also restore—this *was* considered at the time—some sense of individual responsibility for outcomes. Where a services strategy tended to locate in government blame for services that do not succeed, an income strategy would tend to implicate the individuals, who would make their own choices in the market, in the results of them.

Finally, a large attraction of an income strategy was that, like the Constitution, it would be colorblind. The dispensers of services, as Hamill's workers knew well enough, were not. It was the style of the time to be rather contemptuous of the "hardhats," as they would soon be known. (This so few years after elites had declared the sturdy trade unionist the very model of Jeffersonian self-realization. The transformation of the symbolic New York taxi driver from the embattled proletarian of *Waiting for Lefty* to the loud-mouthed bigot of the Lindsay era took, after all, scarcely a generation.) It was correspondingly the style for professional groups and upper-middle-class elites to be avowedly partisan on behalf of the interests of the black minority, and, here and there, other such groups. This concern was regional in the extreme. It was hardly much in evidence in the South, where half the Negro population lived, and it is not at all clear how much it counterbalanced the ancestral prejudices against blacks elsewhere. But it seemed plain enough from the vantage point of a Brooklyn bar, and this had consequences for national social policy. Effective or ineffective, the *political* viability of a services strategy depended upon its appearing even-handed, or reasonably so. By the end of the 1960s this appearance was becoming difficult to keep up.

A tangential but exceptionally important development of the 1960s added further to these difficulties. America of the 1950s had been a settled society; in the decade that followed, it became an unsettled one. A confrontationist style borrowed from the civil-rights movement was transmuted and, after a point in some instances, perverted to often mindless assault on the civic and social order. (Nihilist terrorism made its appearance as children of the upper middle class began to blow up themselves, and on occasion, others, as they expressed their disapproval of this or that government policy.) For some time political scientists, notably James Q. Wilson and Edward C. Banfield, had been reporting a surprising shift in public-opinion surveys away from conventional concerns that had been the substance of politics for so long—employment, housing, transportation, and such— toward expressive issues that reflected alarm over the seeming erosion of standards of public conduct. The repeated plaint was the "people don't behave right any more."[20] In the case of a certain proportion of persons, this was certainly the case; but deliberately so. It was not just that the authority of many institutions was being challenged, it was also a matter of individuals and groups seizing for themselves authority that was presumably held and exercised by others.

This manner of behavior reached endemic proportions toward the close of the decade. Few institutions, few social classes, few regions, escaped it. But it tended to be most conspicuous among upper-middle-class youth and the urban poor, with some apparent interaction between the behavior of the two. Universities became the target of widespread assault, as did other institutions such as churches, courts, elementary and secondary schools, various government bureaucracies, business corporations, charitable foundations, and so across the spectrum of organized American society.

It was easy to become enraged by such antics; difficult to understand them. In the spring of 1969, Erik Erikson visited the White House in the company of a small group of academics invited to discuss the subject and provide the Administration with such understanding and guidance as they might have to offer. Erikson's analysis had considerable impact. What was being witnessed, suggested the noted psychoanalyst, was a widespread pattern of "role reversal." In one after another situation, the hierarchical roles played in the society were not so much being dissolved as being reversed. In most instances the effort was symbolic, but not in all, and potentially, not in any. The universities provided the most conspicuous and most prototypical examples. Seemingly everywhere students were exchanging roles with faculty and administration, all but mocking themselves as children playing grown-ups, but doing so with a certain cutting edge, adopting for example a moralistic harshness that was a caricature of the adult world.

Seemingly also, everywhere academics and administrators were joining in the play, submitting to each new, ever-harsher demand, fearful of the loss of love, terrified at what might prove even more devastating punishment. No one could know, but it was reasonable to suppose that this would increasingly be the lot of service-dispensing institutions in the society, not least those of government. An income strategy, to the degree it avoided concentrations of symbolic power, would tend to minimize the extent and the nature of such confrontation. This was no small consideration to the American national government in the winter and spring of 1969. It presented itself to the president as a specific option. He chose it.

Citations—Chapter II

1. E. W. Kenworthy, "McCarthy Upholds Wage Guarantee," *The New York Times,* April 12, 1968; R. W. Apple, Jr., "Kennedy Urges Research Funds Be Diverted into Job Aid Program," *ibid.;* Harold Gal, "Kennedy Opposes a Pay Guarantee," *The New York Times,* May 19, 1968.

2. Edmund K. Faltermayer, "A Way Out of the Welfare Mess," *Fortune,* July 1968; T. George Harris, "Do We Owe People a Living?" *Look,* April 30, 1968.

3. "The Negative Income Tax," A Ripon Research Paper, *The Ripon Forum,* April 1967, p. 1.

4. The Helstein quotation is from Harris, *op. cit.* The Friedman article is contained in Melvin R. Laird, ed., *Republican Papers,* New York, Frederick A. Praeger, 1968.

5. See Seymour Martin Lipset and Everett Carll Ladd, Jr., ". . . And What Professors Think," *Psychology Today,* November 1970. The findings of the Gallup Poll are reported in "Public Sees Itself as 'Middle-of-the-Road' or 'Fairly Conservative'," Princeton, New Jersey, May 12, 1971.

6. James Q. Wilson, "Crime and the Liberal Audience," *Commentary,* January 1971, p. 75.

7. The original chart, showing the years 1948 to 1964 comprised, in effect, the central argument of my paper *The Negro Family: The Case for National Action* prepared in the Department of Labor in the early months of 1965. My thesis at the time was that employment no longer controlled dependency, and that therefore large new measures of income maintenance would be necessary. Four years later the development had become unmistakable, at least so far as the statistical series were involved. See pp. 328.

8. Lawrence Podell, *Families on Welfare in New York City,* New York, The Center for the Study of Urban Problems, Bernard M. Baruch College, 1969, pp. 19, 27–32.

9. Perry Levinson, "The Next Generation: A Study of Children in AFDC Families," *Welfare in Review,* March–April 1969, pp. 5, 9; Thomas S. Langner and others, "Psychiatric Impairment in Welfare and Nonwelfare Children," *ibid.,* pp. 12–13, 21.

10. Department of Health, Education, and Welfare, Office of Child Development, "Achievement-Motivation in Welfare Youth: Preliminary Findings," unpublished memorandum, July 6, 1970.

11. Irene Lurie, *An Economic Evaluation of Aid to Families with Dependent Children,* Washington, D.C., The Brookings Institution, September 1968, p. 123.

12. Elizabeth F. Durbin, *The Effect of Welfare Programs on the Decision to Work,* New York, New York University, August 1968, mimeographed, pp. 138–39.

13. Beatrice Webb, *Our Partnership,* London, Longmans, 1948, p. 479. Gaston V. Rimlinger has shown that, where different notions of the obligations of beneficiaries of social insurance prevailed, different social security programs resulted. In his instructive paper, "Social Security and Society:

An East-West Comparison," *Social Science Quarterly,* December 1969, pp. 494–506, Rimlinger points out that different social conceptions of the meaning of "right to work" initially helped produce different social security programs in the industrialized countries. One understanding, supported by the left wing in the French revolutions of 1789 and 1848 and incorporated in the Constitution of the Soviet Union as one of the basic rights of Soviet citizens, emphasizes the duty of the individual to work; the other, deriving from eighteenth-century French liberalism, stresses the idea of access or opportunity to work, as embodied, for example, in Section 14(b) of the Taft-Hartley Act. This latter conception had a formative influence on social security programs in the United States and Great Britain, while the former affected Germany and the Soviet Union. Rimlinger suggests a number of reasons for the differences between social-welfare programs in these countries, as well as recent tendencies toward convergence.

14. *Social Welfare in France,* p. 449.
15. A. de Tocqueville, "Memoir on Pauperism," in Seymour Drescher, ed., *Tocqueville and Beaumont on Social Reform,* New York, Harper Torchbook, 1968.
16. John Herbers, *The Lost Priority,* New York, Funk and Wagnalls, 1970, p. 194.
17. See statement of Robert F. Froehlke, Assistant Secretary of Defense, to the Subcommittee on Constitutional Rights of the Senate Judiciary Committee, March 2, 1971.
18. Harry McPherson, *A Political Education,* Boston, Little Brown, 1972, p. 377.
19. Pete Hamill, "The Revolt of the White Lower Middle Class," *New York,* April 14, 1969, pp. 24–9.
20. See, e.g., James Q. Wilson, "The Urban Unease," *The Public Interest,* Summer 1968, pp. 25–39.

III

The Family Assistance Plan

Strategic abstractions—containment, massive retaliation, graduated deterrence—are common enough in foreign affairs, but relatively rare in social policy, where political leaders have preferred to assert goals rather than modes of achieving them. There is a sufficiency of reasons for this. Domestic policy is best described in general and reassuring terms, as the New Deal, the New Frontier, or even the War on Poverty. In part this reflects the instinct of the centrist politicians who have typically governed the United States, and who have wished social policy to be as little divisive as possible. In part it reflects the relative absence of thinking (not of necessity a fault) *about* strategies for social change within the centrist tradition. This pursuit has typically been the preserve of the left. Thus "socialism" is in essence a strategic statement. It is also divisive. The major American parties have been "capitalist" in this sense, but have hardly sought to popularize the term.

The concept of an "income strategy" entailed many risks—it could only, in the end, mean *income redistribution*—but it was still too novel to have acquired such an association, and too useful to an administration short on ideas to let pass. The new government adopted the concept. Increasingly it became a conscious, deliberate Administration policy, formally proclaimed in budget documents and publicized by Administration spokesman.

This had consequences, as abstractions do. One of the first

was the abolition of income taxation of the poor. One of the anomalies of the War on Poverty was that after proclaiming it the Federal government continued to collect income tax from a considerable number of persons it defined as living below the poverty line. A fair proportion of the budget of the Office of Economic Opportunity could be thought of as paid by income taxes collected from the poor. This is a loose idea—the taxes, doubtless, would have been collected anyway, since the poor receive more in America than they pay in taxes—but it illustrates the analytic power of the income strategy concept. From this point of view—given the further tendency of OEO to employ middle- and upper-class persons in its executive positions and, indeed, far down the line—the War on Poverty would have to be asked to explain in what way it was *not* an arrangement for transferring income *from* the poor *to* the nonpoor. It is entirely possible that had such a question been put, a satisfactory answer would have been given; it is nonetheless the tendency for such questions not to be asked *except* in the context of such general analytic conceptions. Certainly, for example, it is not a question that occurred to those of us who sat about the Peace Corps offices in the early months of 1964 drawing up the Economic Opportunity Act.

The actual proposal to abolish income tax on the poor came from the Department of the Treasury in April 1969. In 1967, the latest year for which data were then available, some twenty million tax returns had been filed by persons with adjusted gross incomes under $3,000. The Treasury estimated that in the five years, 1965 through 1969 roughly $1.5 billion of tax was paid by persons whose income was below the poverty level. To put an end to this anomaly the Treasury proposed adoption of a "low income allowance"' geared to the poverty level for different-sized households. *The allowance would be gradually phased out by a reduction of 50 cents for every dollar of income above the poverty level.* The estimated revenue cost was $625 million; it would remove 2,000,000 low-income families from the Federal tax rolls. The proposal was adopted almost without discussion in the White House, such was the import of an income approach, once resolved on. In a message of April 21, 1969, the president proposed the measure, which Congress promptly adopted, to go into effect in 1970. The income strategy was in place.*

In a series of messages to Congress in the spring and summer of 1969 the president elaborated his new strategy. On July 8,

* As readers will need to master the deceptively simple schedules of the negative income tax, it may be useful to reproduce the table prepared by the Treasury to illustrate the Low Income Allowance. In effect, the standard fixed deduction familiar to those who struggle through Form 1040 was replaced by a flexible allowance which declined as income rose, working against a base that had been raised to the poverty level.

Low Income Allowance

Family Size	(1) Present Level of Nontaxability	(2) New Level of Nontaxability[1]	(3) Maximum Allowance	(4) Level at Which Allowance Is Reduced to Zero[2]
1	900	1700	800	3300
2	1600	2300	700	3700
3	2300	2900	600	4100
4	3000	3500	500	4500
5	3700	4100	400	4900
6	4400	4700	300	5300
7	5100	5300	200	5700
8	5800	5900	100	6100

NOTE:
1. Column (2) is the HEW 1966 poverty levels increased by six percent (rounded).
2. Allowance is reduced 50 cents for each dollar of adjusted gross income over column (2) levels.

For 1972 and thereafter congressional action converted the Low Income Allowance into a new minimum standard deduction of $1,000 without any phase-out. The Treasury estimated that the cost of this new provision (at 1969 income levels) would be $2 billion by 1972. This was, in ways, the most important development to that date of the War on Poverty. It went all but unnoticed. A central theme of the discussion of FAP, as will be seen, is that taxation, negative or positive, is both a fundamental instrument of social policy and formidably difficult to explain. At higher income levels those affected have acquired the ability and will take the time to master the details. The unavoidable complexity of tax structures almost certainly works to the advantage of the well-to-do. One consequence of the complexity of the Family Assistance Plan was that the poor never showed any sign of comprehending the opportunity being offered them, nor of resenting those who in their name rejected the offer.

1969, he asked that an additional 4.8 million workers, including farm workers employed by large enterprises, be covered by unemployment insurance, and made the important proposal that henceforth the duration of unemployment benefits be *automatically* extended for further periods up to thirteen weeks whenever the national jobless rate of these covered by insurance rose to 4.5 percent or above for three consecutive months. On August 12, 1969, in a message on manpower training he proposed a "counter-cyclical automatic 'trigger' " which would increase manpower funds by 10 percent when the national unemployment rate exceeded 4.5 percent for three consecutive months. On September 25, 1969, in a message on Social Security, he proposed that "Benefits . . . be automatically adjusted to account for increases in the cost of living." No one of these proposals was altogether a new idea. Yet until then each had pleaded its case on its own merits. Now it was seen that each was related to the other, and part of a general scheme. The idea of an income strategy gave coherence to a wide assortment of proposals that provided *money* to persons in some form of distress. The president let it be known that he had adopted this view. At a Cabinet meeting on July 10, 1969, in the course of a long discussion of the perplexing problem of how simultaneously to combat a continuing inflation and an oncoming recession, he took pains to state that any new tax measure coming down from "the Hill" *must* provide for removing the poor from the income-tax rolls. He estimated about five million persons were involved—a quarter of the poverty population.

These proposals were reasonably straightforward. The inconsistency of collecting income tax from the poor while waging "all-out" war on poverty was evident enough once the subject was raised. The desirability of building a feedback mechanism into the unemployment-insurance and manpower-training systems was similarly evident, as was the case for automatic cost-of-living adjustments in Social Security benefits. All these proposals were fairly quickly adopted by Congress. The first major *test* of the Administration's commitment to an income strategy arose with reference to the far more emotional and politicized issue of hunger.

Food programs began during the New Deal, first as the distribution of commodities, and later through the provision of food stamps: a form of scrip purchased at less than face value. From the outset, the programs involved a curious assemblage of motives and attitudes. The desire to feed the hungry was much in evidence, but not less than the desire to maintain demand for farm products, or to use up the accumulations of government price-support programs. The desire to add dignity to the lives of the poor was similarly much in evidence, but so also was the concern that they might spend resources unwisely. Hence *food* stamps; no beer stamps. Kennedy had made an issue of the narrowness and inadequacy of the surplus-commodity program during the West Virginia primary campaign of 1960, and on the day of his inauguration directed, as his first executive order, an expansion of the program. Soon thereafter, the food-stamp program, which had lapsed during World War II, was revived. (A not inconsiderable part of both Kennedy's and Johnson's legislative programs involved the revival of New Deal programs allowed to lapse during wartime.) Toward the end of the 1960s, the combined stamp and commodity programs—a county could opt for one or the other—had grown to considerable proportions, and, although not widely perceived as such, had become one of the more significant of the Federal government's income-maintenance programs. As is not infrequently the case, the more government did to meet the nutrition needs of the poor, the more impassioned grew the insistence that it was not doing enough. When Nixon came to office, "hunger" was among the most emotional domestic issues awaiting him.

The food programs pursued an income strategy through a services technique, and combined the disadvantages of both. The tendency of services programs is to reach only a limited number of the persons nominally eligible for them. This was the preeminent fact about the food programs. The subsidy for those who got it was real enough, averaging at this time about $6.90 per person per month. But fewer than half the 3,049 counties in the Nation had adopted food-stamp programs and in those that had only about a fifth of the poor actually participated. Food stamps had to be purchased, the cost varying with family income and size. Typically, the poor, living from day to day, were asked to have a month's food money ready all at once. Few suburban housewives could do that; and even fewer of the poor did. Only 2.8 million persons were receiving food stamps in some 1,200 counties. Another 3.7 million received commodities in some 1,400 other counties and jurisdictions. Altogether only about one third of those with incomes below the poverty line were receiving food assistance when the new Administration took office, among them 40 percent of public assistance recipients. There were 480 counties or independent cities, where 10 percent of the poor lived, that had no food programs of any kind.[1]

There was at this time a good deal of malnutrition in the United States and probably also a good deal of hunger. The facts were not clear, indeed were more than normally suspect given the political uses to which they were being put, but the existence of a problem was not to be denied. In the spring of 1967 members of the Subcommittee on Employment, Manpower, and Poverty of the Senate Committee on Labor and Public Welfare visited the Delta area of Mississippi and discovered what they judged to be widespread hunger and malnutrition among the black poor. A surge of national publicity followed, and a political movement of sorts got under way. Much as the consumer movement was then being redirected from questions of value-for-money to matters of personal health and safety, an effort began to redefine the issue of poverty in terms of the *physical injury* done to the poor. By this time, the "liberal audience," in James Q. Wilson's phrase, had largely turned against the Johnson Administration over the war in Vietnam. Consistency required that it turn against his War on Poverty as well. Death in the Mekong Delta, death in the Mississippi Delta.

Senator Robert F. Kennedy, of New York, a member of the Subcommittee, was a central figure in both efforts. Soon after the visit to Mississippi, nine members of the committee wrote to President Johnson asking, among other things, that he make free food stamps available to persons in the Delta area without income and that he lower the food-stamp cash-purchase requirements for families in the area with low cash incomes. In some circumstances the proposal might have been cordially received, but not in those of April 1967. The move (as best one can judge) was half intended, and fully interpreted, as an attack by Kennedy on Johnson. The White House did not respond to the letter, but rather turned it over to OEO. The reply, in the words of Gilbert Y. Steiner, was "aggressive . . . irrelevant . . . defensive . . . argumentative. . . ."[2] One year later a "Citizens' Board of Inquiry" in Washington issued a report *Hunger, U.S.A.*, which described "unimagined" malnutrition and called on the president to declare a national emergency. A month after that, CBS television presented a documentary, *Hunger in America*, depicting the problem in the strongest terms. In the opening scenes a very small baby was shown receiving treatment in a hospital while the narrator stated: "Hunger is easy to recognize when it looks like this. This baby is dying of starvation. He was an American. Now he is dead." Later the Federal Communications Commission reported that the baby in question had been born prematurely as a result of an injury to the mother the previous day. It weighed two pounds, twelve ounces at birth and died, in a sense, of normal causes. The FCC found "no evidence to suggest that either the mother or the father was suffering from malnutrition."[3]

No one would wish to say whether deceit was intended, but the episode was representative of the period. Secretary of Agriculture Orville Freeman, a liberal Democrat, denounced the film as "biased, one-sided, dishonest."[4] It may have been. As the Johnson years came to an end, a combination of influences difficult to identify—having something to do with the necessity to outbid the already sufficiently extravagant rhetoric of the incumbent government, and perhaps also the continued general prosperity—tempted advocates of more rapid or extreme social change to espouse their causes in ever more extreme forms. If truth is one of the first victims of military war, it can suffer in a war on poverty as well. Freeman's retort was dismissed as routine and defensive, and he had been out of office nine months by the time the FCC came somewhat indirectly to his support. In the meantime a new Administration had arrived and the issue of hunger was awaiting it.

At the first meeting of the Urban Affairs Council, the president established a Committee on Surplus Food and Nutrition, similar to that on Welfare. Secretary of Agriculture Clifford M. Hardin was to be Chairman, with Maurice H. Stans, Secretary of Commerce, and Robert H. Finch of HEW as colleagues. In contrast to welfare, elements in Congress were pressing for action on "hunger" and the Administration was correspondingly pressed to assume a position of its own. The Committee report was presented to the Council on March 17. It was the first clear demonstration that the new "conservative" Administration could take positions at least as advanced as those of its "liberal" predecessor and possibly more so. (Before long, the episode also provided the first demonstration that such efforts would be greeted with great skepticism and even hostility by the groups that would most benefit by them, or which had most demanded them. A few of the persons most prominently associated with the hunger problem, notably Senator George S. McGovern, Democrat from South Dakota, were generous in acknowledging the Administration's actions, but the style of the hunger movement was attack, and it attacked whoever was in office, almost regardless of what the officeholder did.)

Hardin's committee had directed its concern to "poverty-related malnutrition," setting aside the more general question of unbalanced diets in the population at large. Once again, government knew something about the subject, more, certainly, than it would have known a decade earlier. The 1965 National Household Food Consumption Survey of the Department of Agriculture had reported that two thirds of households with annual incomes under $3,000 had diets that did not meet the Recommended Dietary Allowances for 1963 of the Food and Nutrition Board of the National Academy of Sciences–National Research Council. The National Nutrition Survey being conducted by the Public Health Service had by then examined some 12,000 persons, four fifths of whom had family incomes under $5,000. It had found "an alarming prevalence of characteristics associated with undernourished groups." Fifteen percent of the group was anemic. Five percent had traits associated with protein and calorie malnutrition. Seven cases of marasmus and kwashiorkor had been encountered. Hardin's committee concluded:

The exact extent of critical, poverty-related malnutrition in the United States is not fully known at the present time. Such knowledge as we do have indicates that malnutrition among the poor is in fact a serious problem.

The Food Stamp Program was judged to be far preferable to commodity distribution in principle, but deficient in practice, especially for "those whose income is too meager and too erratic to make periodic bloc payments." Food stamps were unavailable in most jurisdictions, and where available the program was afflicted by the familiar disparity in state standards, which at the lowest level cut off eligibility for a family of four at $1,920 in annual income, and at the highest at $4,140. The Committee report recommended that stamps be provided at no cost to those with incomes less than $50 per month for a family of four— there were some two million persons with incomes at this level; that the cost schedules be expanded so that no family need pay more than 30 percent of its income to obtain nutritionally complete diets (costing about $100 per month); and that the program be expanded to bring in 11.5 million people, about 5 million more than were then receiving food assistance of one or the other kind. Food stamps were budgeted at $340 million for the 1970 fiscal year. The Committee, in effect, proposed to increase the current cost of the program (FY 1970) to $1 billion, and to raise it to an estimated $2.5 billion by FY 1973.

This was the first large initiative to come before the Urban Affairs Council and the discussion went on at some length. To most of the Council members present, the attractive aspect of food stamps was that they were a form of currency, conferring on those using them the same status as purchasers in an open market. Further, while no one could say with certainty just how serious the hunger problem actually was, most saw that symbolically the issue was pressing. Hardin declared: "There is great urgency about this. This is the hottest item on the domestic front, and we must take the leadership ourselves."

The president agreed. "You can say," he told his Secretary of Agriculture, "that this Administration will have the first comprehensive, far-reaching attack on the problem of hunger in history."*

* The Administration remained faithful to this commitment. In the face of tight budgetary constraints, expenditures on all food and nutrition programs rose from $1,590,000,000 in FY 1970 to an estimated $2,783,000,000 in FY 1971, and were budgeted for $3,171,000,000 in FY 1972. That is to say, expenditure was scheduled to double over two budgets. (See Special Analyses, Budget of the United States, Fiscal Year 1972, p. 175.) In the spring of 1971 Sam M. Gibbons, a Democratic member of the Committee on Ways and Means from Florida, reported to the House: "Last March, only 5 million persons throughout the country were able to secure food stamps. As of this March,

The first message of the president to the Congress on a domestic issue of substance had dealt with the subject of poverty. This had been sent on February 19. The message declared, in effect, that the War on Poverty would go on, although with some new emphasis, especially on the "first five years of life."

In recent years enormous advances have been made in the understanding of human development. We have learned that intelligence is not fixed at birth, but is largely formed by the environmental influences of the early formative years. It develops rapidly at first, and then more slowly, as much of that development takes place in the first four years as in the next thirteen. We have learned further that environment has its greatest impact on the development of intelligence when that development is proceeding most rapidly—that is, in those earliest years.

This means that many of the problems of poverty are traceable directly to early childhood experience—and that if we are to make genuine, long-range progress, we must focus our efforts much more

some 10.6 million people were participating in the food stamp program." Nick Kotz in his book *Let Them Eat Promises: The Politics of Hunger in America* (Englewood Cliffs, New Jersey, Prentice-Hall, 1969), having obtained a copy of the minutes of the March 17 Urban Affairs Council meeting, suggests that the president's statement was openly cynical (p. 210). The minutes record that the president, after making his statement, added, "Use all the rhetoric, so long as it doesn't cost any money." This was intended and understood as a joke— mock consolation for Budget Director Robert P. Mayo. The president had just "broken" the FY 1970 budget. Hardin responded with the seriousness of a Cabinet officer who had just won a considerable victory. "This is specific, direct and basic," he said; "we can make this our showpiece in the whole poverty area." The president kept trying. "Make a speech tomorrow night," he said, and the minutes record, "and say you favor flexible price supports to pay for this." Humor is dangerous in politics, as is literalism in transcribing minutes. Even so, the "hunger lobby" repeatedly displayed a vindictiveness that was unwarranted and unecessary.

By the end of 1971, the Agriculture Department reported that government food aid to low-income families and needy schoolchildren had reached a record high. 10.9 million people used food stamps, an increase of 1.4 million since the end of 1970, while 7.8 million schoolchildren were served free or reduced-price lunches, some two million more than a year earlier. Even in the face of this record, criticism persisted. Early in 1972 Jean Mayer of Harvard, who had been brought to Washington by Nixon to chair the White House Conference on Food and Nutrition in 1969, wrote to *The New York Times* protesting a budgetary "freeze" on further growth in the program. In passing he noted that food stamp expenditures had risen from $250 million in 1969 to $2.2 billion in 1971. A nine-fold increase in three years had gone almost unnoticed, certainly unpraised.

than heretofore on those few years which may determine how far, throughout his later life, the child can reach.*

The message had called for experiment, and, more importantly, for an experimental mode.

. . . If we are to make the most of experimental programs, we must frankly recognize their experimental nature and frankly acknowledge whatever shortcomings they develop. To do so is not to belittle the experiment, but to advance its essential purpose: that of finding new ways, better ways, of making progress in areas still inadequately understood.

We often can learn more from a program that fails to achieve its purpose than from one that succeeds. If we apply those lessons, then even the "failure" will have made a significant contribution to our larger purposes.

I urge all those involved in these experimental programs to bear this in mind—and to remember that one of the primary goals of this Administration is to expand our knowledge of how best to make real progress against those social ills that have so stubbornly defied solution. We do not pretend to have all the answers. We are determined to find as many as we can.

The men and women who will be valued most in this Administration will be those who understand that not every experiment succeeds, who do not cover up failures but rather lay open problems, frankly and constructively, so that next time we will know how to do better.

In this spirit, I am confident that we can place our antipoverty efforts on a secure footing—and that as we continue to gain in understanding of how to master the difficulties, we can move forward at an accelerating pace.

The president's next major statement on poverty was contained in his Message on Food and Health, based on Hardin's report. It was sent to Congress on May 6, and followed the theme of the

---

* As will be evident, this statement reflected the summary of research, and the conclusions, of Benjamin S. Bloom's *Stability and Change in Human Characteristics*, New York, John Wiley, 1964. These ideas had not taken long to reach the presidency, but even as they were doing so many were being challenged. Psychologists were in less agreement as to the early "fix" of environmental influences, while geneticists and others began to contend that environmental influences, at whatever age, were being grossly exaggerated in both educational theory and public policy.

first message. The commitments of the 1960s were to persist, and if anything be expanded.

More is at stake here than the health and well-being of 16 million American citizens who will be aided by these programs and the current Child Food Assistance programs. Something very like the honor of American democracy is at issue. It was half a century ago that the "fruitful plains" of this bounteous land were first called on to do a great work of humanity, that of feeding a Europe exhausted and bleeding from the First World War. Since then, on one occasion after another, in a succession of acts of true generosity, America has come to the aid of one starving people after another. But the moment is at hand to put an end to hunger in America itself for all time. I ask this of a Congress that has already splendidly demonstrated its own disposition to act. It is a moment to act with vigor; it is a moment to be recalled with pride.

Little noticed in the message was the statement that one of the purposes of the legislation he would be submitting to Congress was to "ensure that the Food Stamp Program is complementary to a revised welfare program, which I shall propose to the Congress this year."

A week after the report of the UAC Committee on Food and Nutrition was presented to the full Council, the Committee on Welfare met to consider a draft proposal prepared in HEW for Finch and now submitted by him to the full Committee. The proposal was to replace welfare with a negative income tax (NIT).

To say it was "prepared" for Secretary Finch does not say enough. It had been prepared first for Secretary John W. Gardner, then for Secretary Wilbur J. Cohen, and *now* for Finch. Had he rejected it, it would have been prepared for his successor, Secretary Elliot L. Richardson. Bureaucracy was at work.

This statement, too, needs qualification. In the years 1966–1967, the echelon of social planners that had found a place for itself just above the career administrators of the government, and just below the political operatives of the Cabinet and sub-Cabinet, had been converted almost wholesale to the NIT, as it came to be known among them. In largest measure these men were professional economists. They were also professional reformers, in the sense that they earned their living and rather much defined themselves as men and women with special competence to devise solutions to problems which the society wanted solved, or which needed solving whether anyone wanted to do so or not.

The rise of the issue of poverty and the great difficulties which the poverty program thereupon encountered presented to this small group of government employees a challenge and an opportunity of the first order. Beyond that, it offered the opportunity to justify a newly established and somewhat precarious existence. In 1965 President Johnson had directed that the Planning-Programming-Budgeting System (or PPBS) that had been developed in the Pentagon be adopted by the domestic agencies of the government as well. The object of PPBS was that departments and agencies should "define clearly the major objectives . . . which they choose to pursue . . . [and] apply systematic analyses to the alternative ways in which those objectives are being—or may be—sought. . . ."[5] PPBS analysis, by focusing on the effectiveness of service programs, led directly to an income strategy.

In 1964 Congress had formally declared a national policy of eliminating the paradox of poverty in the midst of wealth. OEO had been established to focus this effort, but the policy objective was equally shared by HEW, Labor, the Council of Economic Advisers, the Bureau of the Budget, and so across the spectrum of domestic departments and agencies. From the first it was manifest that the OEO programs by themselves could not achieve the national policy. The community action programs, which received the most publicity, tended to be conflict-oriented, or came to be perceived as such, and soon were having political trouble with the White House and the Congress. The Job Corps and the Neighborhood Youth Corps, while useful, were from the outset limited by appropriations, and never reached more than a fraction of those for whom they were intended—a familiar sequence. Ventures such as Head Start were attractive but expensive, and of uncertain effectiveness. In short, the OEO programs had all the difficulties of a services strategy.

If an income strategy were to appear logical in any context, it would be so with respect to the task of eliminating poverty, and well before the advent of the Nixon Administration planners at OEO, HEW, and the Council of Economic Advisers were at work devising one. (If planning organizations are not given work, they will make it. Within months of the establishment in 1963 of the Policy Planning Staff of the Department of Labor, as noted earlier, a study of family allowances was begun.) The PPBS orientation gave a particular style to this approach. In the spring of 1968 five economists, John Kenneth Galbraith, Paul Samuelson, Robert Lampman, Harold Watts, and James Tobin, signed a statement, in which they were eventually joined by some 1,200 colleagues, calling on Congress "to adopt this year a national system of income guarantees and supplements." Lampman and Watts were then associated with the Institute for Research on Poverty at the University of Wisconsin, an enterprise founded by OEO. They were both much attracted to the NIT. Tobin was a declared advocate. Yet the statement avoided asserting a choice between that and a family allowance, inasmuch as opinions did differ and there was a case to be made that the latter, being universal, would be more acceptable politically. The academic economists were, after all, asking for political action. Curiously, the government economists took the more narrow professional view. With little public debate and almost no public notice the economist planners in government opted for negative income tax as the basic instrument of an income strategy. In a significant way this narrowed the president's options. By the time Nixon took office planning for a negative income tax was well advanced, and there were no plans for any alternative approach.

In effect, this meant the rejection of family allowances as an approach to the problem of poverty. The basic difficulty of family allowances was that of "efficiency." All families with children would receive benefits although only a portion of such families would be poor. If payments were made high enough to significantly change the circumstances of the poor, the total cost of the program would be enormous, with most of the payments going to families that could not be described as needy. This consideration touched also on the growing interest in a guaranteed income. In the course of the 1960s this idea had become steadily more familiar and reasonable-sounding, doubtless in part because it remained thoroughly general, even vague. In a strict sense the United States already had a guaranteed income in that some form of public assistance was available to almost anyone who was destitute. No one, save a few middle-class youths, slept under bridges and begged bread in the streets. But the idea of a guaranteed income went beyond subsistence. It envisioned a level of payment sufficient to maintain a reasonable, if low, standard of living. A negative income tax would provide just such a guaranteed income. In this sense they were identical proposals.

In another sense, however, they were profoundly different. The guaranteed income was an idea of the left; the negative income tax, an idea of the right. The original proponents of a guaranteed income tended to be apocalyptic about capitalism and more or less disdainful of bourgeois virtue. The original advocates of a negative income tax, by contrast, tended to be little impressed by social workers and still less by social visionaries. As the two ideas merged some of these distinctions in social purpose and political style were obscured, but they were never eliminated. The guaranteed income had begun to come under conservative attack as a proposal to put an end to work, while it has to be assumed that on the liberal side some anxiety was aroused by the possibility that a negative tax would be the pretext for dismantling the welfare state, as indeed was the avowed object of its intellectual mentor. Thus a political scientist might have foreseen the day when a "conservative" president would propose a negative income tax, while insisting that his proposal was not a guaranteed income and accordingly could be safely adopted. An observer of greater insight than is common among political scientists might also have foreseen that leading advocates of radical social change would take the president at his word and denounce his negative income tax on grounds that indeed it was *not* a guaranteed income. For the moment, however, the planners were absorbed with the technicalities of the subject, and pushing ahead on their own to learn more about it.

By 1968 the Institute for Research on Poverty was carrying out, with OEO financing, a sizable negative-tax experiment in New Jersey. Gilbert Y. Steiner describes it as "the most ambitious socioeconomic experiment ever undertaken in America without a base in legislation or executive order."[6] Shortly thereafter, the Social and Rehabilitation Service of HEW earmarked $1 million for initial funding of similar income-maintenance experiments in connection with the Model Cities programs of Gary, Indiana, and Seattle, Washington. Simultaneously, economic analysis of various guaranteed-income plans proceeded with some intensity. By the late 1960s sophisticated proposals were available to policy-makers. An inquisitive assistant secretary could, for example, learn from a paper on "The Effect of Nonemployment Income on the Work Incentives of the Poor" that

Leuthold's model includes minimum income and minimum leisure constraints which are asymptotes for the "rectangular hyperbola" indifference curves that follow from the Cobb-Douglas utility function that she maximizes.

OEO being rather out of favor in the latter Johnson years, HEW became the locus of this planning. By 1968, the PPBS operation was in the charge of Alice M. Rivlin as Assistant Secretary for Planning and Evaluation. Worth Bateman, as Deputy Assistant Secretary for Program Analysis (Income Maintenance and Social Services Programs) was directly responsible. In fairly short order he had established

as a long-term goal of the Department the development of a comprehensive income maintenance program which keeps those who can't work out of poverty and supplements the earnings of those who do work without destroying incentives. This goal implies substantially broader coverage than is provided by our present programs.

A November 1968 "Program Memorandum on Income Maintenance and Social and Rehabilitation Services Programs" for the period 1970–1974 spelled out the principles and the specifics of such a comprehensive income-maintenance scheme. A system was proposed which:

—keeps those who can't work out of poverty
—supplements the earnings of those who do work without destroying incentives
—does not stigmatize persons receiving aid or meddle in their lives
—strictly separates income assistance from the provision of social and rehabilitation services

The essence of the proposal was the provision of income supplementation for poor households headed by a male who works.

This clearly was the prime objective of the HEW planners, although in their detailed presentation they offered four "Alternative Income Maintenance Programs." The first entailed a Federal takeover of the existing welfare system; the second combined this with aid to the working poor; the third was a children's allowance of $25 per month per child; while the fourth was a straight-out NIT. For the first three plans the minimum payment standard for a family of four was to be $2,568; for the fourth, $2,136. The estimated additional annual cost in 1974 of the first, second, and fourth proposal was roughly equal, that of the NIT being $6.3 billion. By contrast, the estimated additional cost of the family allowance in 1974 would be $27.9 billion.

The HEW Program Memorandum gave cost estimates for fiscal year 1974. This reflected the assumption that there simply were not to be any such programs for FY 1970, the last budget to be submitted by the Johnson Administration, or the years immediately following. The memorandum stated that FY 1970 "is expected to be another year of fiscal restraint." All that could be hoped for in the immediate future would be a certain amount of tinkering, mostly with the AFDC program.

In preceding years, the *program* restraint of the Democratic Administration made a certain sense. There *had been* a shortage of funds, as a result of the Vietnam war, and a need to restrain expenditure as a result of the war-induced inflation. Certainly, there had been also the built-in hesitance of a party in power to propose measures which would redound enormously to the advantage of its normal supporters and not at all to the advantage of those who normally voted for the party in opposition. Unlike the family allowance, which would be universal in its coverage, the income-maintenance proposals envisioned by HEW, and the specific model then being tested in New Jersey, would benefit the twenty-five to thirty million persons in the nation living at or below the poverty line. (Much as the number of persons unemployed in the course of a year is larger than the average number of unemployed at any given moment, the poverty population is larger than the proportion of the population which at a given moment is poor.) Of these persons, a heavy proportion of the adults could be expected to vote Democratic in state and local elections, and, the Wallace phenomenon apart, could be expected to provide almost the same pluralities in national elections. To advance such a proposal in October 1968 might have brought charges of vote buying, and program planners might accordingly have felt restrained.

But no such inhibitions obtained in November 1968. The election was over. The temptation to propose a vast income-maintenance program that would fulfill the Administration's commitment to put an end to poverty was surely at its maximum probable point. What better promise of future performance to leave with the voters? What more painful choice to leave to the new Administration? There had been talk in the White House of leaving just such a legacy of brilliant, brave, forward looking legislative proposals. Certainly a guaranteed income would rank high on such a list. An interdepartmental task force on income maintenance had been set up early in the year. There were plenty of draft proposals available, plenty of staff work to back them up. *Yet nothing was proposed.*

The explanation, if there is one, derives from a combination of personalities and ideology. HEW Secretary Cohen had devoted his life to perfecting the Social Security System, conceived as an insurance program to care for the aged, the destitute, and the disabled. Just as the AFDC program detracted from the public image of social welfare, so concern with welfare legislation detracted from legislative efforts to extend and improve Social Security. The difference between a guaranteed income and old-age insurance was a difference of at least two generations in social thought. Cohen was prepared to believe that someday some such a proposal would be put forward, but he did not see this happening soon. Public opinion would need a deal of educating. The experience of Medicare—which had consumed decades of advocacy, and lobbying, and negotiating—appeared to confirm this view. It was, moreover, clear to all that President Johnson shared it. Those in direct contact with him on the issue would remark that for LBJ it was the Department of Health and Education period.

Johnson genuinely reflected the Southern and Southwestern aversion or professed aversion to any form of dependency—a *machismo* style. He felt the Democratic party was exceedingly vulnerable to the charge of piling people onto the dole. At the height of the rhetoric of the War on Poverty, he would talk of making "tax payers" out of "tax eaters," much as in 1934 President Roosevelt wrote Colonel House, "What I am seeking is the abolition of relief altogether. I cannot say so out loud yet, but I hope to be able to substitute work for relief."[7]

The central political fact about the negative income tax is that Democrats did not dare be first to propose it and Republicans did. This is a pattern not unknown to the two-party politics of Great Britain and the United States over the past century-and-a-half, but rarely has the irony of the process reached such heights. Rarely have the actors been so little capable of perceiving the irony. The men of this time were earnest and often, even, honest, but they were not much taken by nuance.

It is perhaps the ultimate irony that the Nixon proposal for a negative income tax was drafted by Democratic advocates who not months earlier had had the same proposal rejected by the Johnson Administration. (This in turn forced many liberal Democrats to reject the proposal, which, had it been put forth by one of their own would surely have been hailed as the largest social achievement of the second half of the century. But this exceeds the bounds of irony, and enters the region of political disorientation.) Rejection of the negative income tax was characteristic of the closing years of the Johnson Administration. It happened not just once, but repeatedly. Moreover, it went on almost to the moment the Administration left office, that is to say long past the point when those making the decision might have been deterred by considerations of immediate political consequences. More than any single circumstance—more than its blundering into the Vietnam war, more than its inability to get out, more than its inability to define the issue of social order in terms that would help restore it, more than its traumatized disinclination to mediate between the ethnic and racial groups which made up its electoral base—this suggests that by the end of the 1960s the Democratic party was near to having exhausted its potential as an agent of social change. The internal contradictions and conflicts of the party had come near to immobilizing it. The prolonged absence of serious political and intellectual opposition was in the end deeply debilitating. The Johnson Administration opposed a negative income tax not because it was politically risky, but primarily because the men in charge did not believe in such boldness. The Democrats had become the party of timidity.

The Democrats never thought of themselves as such and they had at their disposal the intellects to prove otherwise. By contrast, the Republicans had few intellects, and even less taste for being known as the party of audacity, but the facts are hardly in doubt. Had Nixon desired to do so, it was probably within his power in the first two years of his Administration to displace the Democrats as the party of the center. He did not do this: he did not even try. Rather, his political advisers, and he himself, set about narrowing rather than broadening the political and ideological base of the Republican party. This was their right, and they chose to exercise it. Inevitably the Democratic party benefited, and by the midterm elections of 1970 once again could think of itself as the majority party, the center party, and the party of social change. But this would have been hard to prove in 1968.

The details of the Democratic rejection of the negative income tax are not of special interest, but should be sketched. As time passed, the Johnson Administration had become more aware of the mounting problem of welfare dependency. In his Economic Message of 1967 President Johnson announced that he would establish a Commission on Income Maintenance Programs. But then he did not do so. A year passed and nothing happened. Then, of a sudden, he did do so. This was a pattern. The need for change would be perceived, if dimly, but the impulse to move toward change always somehow faltered almost the moment it appeared, only to recur once the perception recurred.

In such circumstances Congress has the opportunity to take the initiative, and sometimes does. In the course of 1967 both the House Ways and Means Committee and the Senate Finance Committee began looking more closely into welfare questions. The attitude in Congress was not necessarily, or uniformly, hostile to welfare; but it was no longer passive. For the first time welfare activists appeared on the scene, and the level of epithet rose among all parties. The result was the Social Security Amendments of 1967, which were both punitive and supportive, in an almost inextricable pattern. To begin with, Congress imposed a "freeze" on the number of AFDC recipients: no longer was this to be an open-ended program, immune to legislative review. Simultaneously, it established a Work Incentive Program (WIN) designed to help welfare mothers become self-supporting through job training and the establishment of specific incentives for getting and holding jobs. The incentive was reinforced by a *work requirement* which gave welfare authorities the power to withhold part of the AFDC payment from any family regardless of the age of the children, whose head was judged to have refused work or work training. The Amendments were seen in the welfare community as savagely punitive. Mayor Lindsay predicted social catastrophe. When the legislation came to his desk, early in 1968, President Johnson said nothing, signed the bill, and appointed the Commission on Income Maintenance Programs he had announced a year earlier.

In the meantime, his Administration was teeming with economist-planners drawing up various negative income tax schemes and trying to sell them to their superiors. In OEO James Lyday drafted a bill establishing an NIT which was introduced by Congressman William Fitts Ryan, Democrat of New York. While the Administration always in the end rejected such proposals, increasingly they would get as far as the Secretary's office in HEW, or the White House itself. The last of these many efforts began on July 26, 1968, when Joseph A. Califano, Jr., the President's chief staff aide for domestic affairs, established a task force on income maintenance headed by Merton Peck of the Council of Economic Advisers. The word was about that the president was thinking of one last bold set of proposals to bequeath to his successor. The political constraints were off. The sky was the limit. Negative income tax advocates were on the task force: those who had been blocked at HEW by Cohen, or at OEO by partisans of community action and other antipoverty program strategies, at last had direct access to the president, or at least to his staff.

But nothing came of it. The task force did *not* recommend a negative income tax. Its report of November 4 stated ". . . the Task Force sees no reason to make a commitment to any long-run income maintenance system at this point." It looked to the possibility, but that is about all. In doing so it looked also to the necessity for a work requirement.

While not all Task Force members favor the idea, all would be willing to accept the requirement that working-age males be willing to seek and hold training slots and jobs in order to receive assistance.

They judged this was an issue to be determined primarily in terms of the effect it might have on any new welfare legislation to be proposed, albeit they were not proposing much. Even the few measures they did propose—more Federal standards and the familiar tinkering—were rejected in a meeting in Califano's office on November 29 which Cohen attended.

If the report did not propose much that was new, it was critical of the established process of across-the-board Social Security increases every two years or so. As economists (in the main) the task-force members were seeking to "target" social expenditure. This was not Cohen's view, and the remaining recommendations in the report were turned down almost whole-sale.* On November 30 Peck wrote Califano, "we might be better off with nothing. . . ."[8]

Three months and a few days later, in the White House office immediately below Califano's the precise same negative income tax proposal that was *not* submitted to a Democratic president was being prepared for submission to a Republican one. Where previously the proposal had been blocked at HEW by the Secretary, or turned down in the White House if it managed to get by that barrier, the new Secretary, Robert Finch, had no such disposition and at the White House I, for one, was altogether in favor. It is necessary to say this if only because

* Historians of the Johnson Administration may find that this unwillingness to propose a second cohort of Great Society programs was repeated in other areas of policy. In 1971 the Johnson Library made public the administration's papers on higher education. A report in *The Chronicle of Higher Education* began: "The Johnson Administration, which in 1964 accepted pioneering proposals for the expansion of federal aid to higher education and got them passed by Congress a year later, by 1967 was rejecting ideas for further trail-blazing—including many that are still being debated today" (February 7, 1972). Specifically, the report of a 1964 task force headed by John W. Gardner was fully adopted, but that of a 1967 group headed by William C. Friday turns out to have been "almost completely ignored." *The Chronicle* noted that a number of the Friday task-force proposals are similar to those envisaged by the Nixon Administration in *its* higher education proposals. Perhaps most significantly, the Johnson papers contain the reports of three subsequent task forces in higher education. Each was made after the president announced he would not seek reelection and none, *The Chronicle* reported, was acted upon.

presidents rarely make decisions about issues that are not presented to them. The presentation process was crucial, albeit that the presidential decision was what finally mattered.

An account of the process is likely to seem incomplete because it was so simple. Finch and his associates were new to their jobs, flushed with the exhilaration and hopes of a new Administration. Their days were crowded, and not a little confused, as they rushed about accepting the fealty of one new fiefdom after another. There is nothing quite like the *ease* with which officials of a newly elected Administration take over the departments and agencies of government. Only later do the difficulties emerge. In the beginning a sense of immense power is conveyed. There are the great bureaucracies, the embodiment of plodding, incremental progress to the top, and of a sudden a handful of men, for the most part new to the experience, find themselves on *top* of them. The contrast is dizzying. For a short while anything seems possible. In Finch's case the exhilaration was compounded by his closeness to the president and his knowledge—shared by few— that of the time the president was giving to domestic issues, much was being devoted to welfare, that, he was getting long, complex memoranda on the subject from me, and asking for more. The scene had set itself for a large, complex proposal.

Each of the Urban Affairs Council committees was expected to propose a program. Most did. (In a succession of meetings in the late spring and early summer most of the committees presented reports usually containing "One Big Idea." In this sense a relatively temporary arrangement of work assignments led to the structure of policy.) As a basis on which to begin, Finch had before him the proposals of the Nathan task force. Burns, who had charge of these documents, had sent this one to HEW for review, with a clear enough indication that he thought the proposed measures too expensive, possibly too adventurous. But these were hardly concerns of Finch. He was not disposed to fear the adventurous, and even if he had been, he scarcely had time to look very closely at details. The *planners'* moment had come.

Finch turned the matter over to Veneman and Patricelli, who in turn assigned it to the professional staff who had been working on negative income tax proposals. Bateman was the principal HEW figure. He drew on the assistance of James Lyday of OEO and Greg Barlous of the Bureau of the Budget. They were asked to prepare a critique of the task-force report. They had, of course, already concluded that it was not possible to "fix up" the AFDC system, even at the large cost the task-force report envisioned. They wished to see the system scrapped, and replaced by a guaranteed income. They had a plan they had proposed to the preceding Secretaries, and they now proposed it to the new one.

The planners were fortunate in the political officers Finch had brought with him to the Department. Veneman had been the Republican spokesman on welfare matters in the California Assembly. He was a convinced and serious liberal. Patricelli had followed the issue in the United States Senate. Lewis Butler, who succeeded Rivlin as Assistant Secretary for Planning and Evaluation, was a lawyer of large intellect. Each had come to HEW to make a mark. A guaranteed income was their first opportunity and they seized it. Finch shared their excitement. By late February the first draft of a report proposing a negative income tax had been prepared, and by March it was ready for the Committee on Welfare. At a Committee meeting on March 24 it was presented as a more or less routine, commonsensical response to a difficult but not insoluble situation. The Administration was ten weeks in office.

The Finch proposal, christened the Family Security System,* was a straightforward NIT, limited to families with children. This limitation reflected both the welfare context in which the proposal was presented, and concern about cost. It could and would be argued that one advantage of the FAP proposal was that it would take several years at least to come into operation, by which time the budgetary constraints of FY 1970 would have long passed, but those constraints were very much part of the atmosphere in which the decision whether to propose a guaranteed income would be made. Fiscal dividend or no, the Nixon Cabinet contained more than its share of men who were simply conservative about spending public money. Finch proposed a basic income guarantee for a family of four of $1,500 per year. This would increase with family size on the basis of payments of $450 per adult and $300 per child up to a family of seven, which

---

* The name of the program was later changed to Family Assistance Plan (FAP). During the planning period it was known as the Family Security System and designated by the initials FSS. See p. 217.

would receive $2,400. For a family with income, the payment would be reduced at the rate of 50 cents for each $1 in earnings. Thus, a family of four would phase out of the system once its earnings passed $3,000; but a family of seven with earnings of $4,000 would still be getting a grant of $400. The schedule of payments was illustrated by a table in a detailed draft of the Committee report.

Amount of Federal Payment by Size of Family
and Amount of Outside Income

	AMOUNT OF OUTSIDE INCOME						
Family Size	0	500	1,000	1,500	2,000	3,000	4,000
2	750	500	250	—	—	—	—
3 (parent & 2 children)	1,050	800	550	300	50	—	—
3 (2 parents & 1 child)	1,200	950	700	450	200	—	—
4	1,500	1,250	1,000	750	500	—	—
5	1,800	1,550	1,300	1,050	800	300	—
6	2,100	1,850	1,600	1,350	1,100	600	100
7 or more	2,400	2,150	1,900	1,650	1,400	900	400

The Finch proposal was complicated from the outset by the need to accommodate the emerging food-stamp proposals. In the minds of most of the advocates of an income guarantee, food stamps were an anachronism that ought to, as soon as possible, be "cashed out" and incorporated into the primary income-maintenance system. However, within the Administration a major food-stamp proposal had already been presented to the president, who had indicated his general approval. Outside the Administration there was an intense, if limited, political demand for more food stamps, and no discernible demand whatever for a guaranteed income. Accordingly, a dual system was proposed. Income support would come partly in cash, partly in scrip, with both payment schedules declining as income rose. The report of the UAC Committee on Welfare illustrated the "preferred" option for a family of four.

Earnings	Cash Benefits	Total Cash Income	Food-Stamp Benefits	Total Income
0	$1,500	$1,500	$500	$2,000
500	1,250	1,750	425	2,225
1,000	1,000	2,000	375	2,375
1,500	750	2,250	325	2,575
2,000	500	2,500	250	2,750
2,500	250	2,750	200	2,950
3,000	0	3,000	125	3,125
3,500	0	3,500	0	3,500
4,000	0	4,000	0	4,000

It will be useful to pause at this moment to consider the nature of this proposal, and certain characteristics which would attend its subsequent reception.

First, *this was a guaranteed income.* Cavala and Wildavsky have usefully defined the proposition they predicted would not be proposed or enacted.

. . . we understand the series of proposals categorized under the concept of guaranteed income to embody at least the following four characteristics: (1) assistance is to be made available on the basis of need alone, (2) need and entitlement to public assistance would be objectively and uniformly measured throughout the nation in terms of the size and composition of the family unit, its income, and its other economic resources; (3) assistance should be paid in cash, not kind, and should be given for free disposition by the recipient, not earmarked for particular uses; (4) any tax placed on income earned in addition to that provided by the supplement should be less than 100 percent.[9]

Except that it would apply only to families, FAP satisfied these criteria.

Second, *FAP was a relatively sophisticated and complex form of guaranteed income.* In principle a guaranteed income need be nothing more complicated than an arrangement whereby an individual or household is regularly provided with a lump sum payment by the government in order that no matter what else occurs he will never have an income below that level. A negative income tax is at the opposite pole of sophistication. The principle is simple: every family above a certain income level pays a positive income tax, while every family below that level is *paid* a negative tax. That is to say, above the level the family gives money to the government: below the level the government gives money to the family.

The application is complex. Just as the positive tax is calculated by complex interactions of total income, total deductions, and family size, so the amount of negative tax is the result of interactions which seem simple enough to the initiated, but can be impenetrable to others. In order to grasp the process the mind must be capable of grasping the simultaneous process whereby income rises and the negative tax falls *or* whereby income falls and the negative tax rises. These are opposed movements, and are confusing, especially because in the area of positive taxation as income rises, taxes rise; as income falls, taxes fall. Up, up; down, down. A clear process. With the negative income tax it is the reverse. Up, down; down, up. An unclear process. Starting with a stated negative tax for families with zero income, the amount would gradually decline as income rose. A negative tax at zero income of $1,500 for a family of four would mean negative tax payments would continue until total income reached $3,000. The first dollar earned would reduce the negative tax payment from $1,500 to $1,499.50, while total income would rise to $1,500.50. That is to say $1,500 plus $1 minus 50 cents.

A third point follows from the second. Because the dynamic process of the negative tax is so difficult to follow, it appears that the normal reaction is to perceive it in static terms. The amount of negative tax is seen as the total amount of income, rather than a supplement to income which varies with different levels of earnings. *In consequence, the Family Assistance Plan always appeared much less generous than it was.* Mature editorial writers and legislators could be taken through the process slowly, carefully, step by step, agreeing all the way, only to end up saying, "Yes, yes, I understand. But how can a family of four live on $1,500 a year?" (Or $1,600, which was the amount of negative tax payment at zero income finally proposed.) Whereupon the recitation would begin again. It would be shown that this situation would never exist for the working poor, inasmuch as they by definition already were earning something and the FAP would add *further* to their income. It would be shown that for the welfare poor, primarily AFDC families, states would be required to supplement the amount of the negative tax at zero income, except in those states where total payments then in effect were less than that amount (e.g., Mississippi). Once again agreement. Once again the question, "Yes, but how can a family of four live on $1,600 a year?" This was peculiarly a problem for political liberals who saw themselves as knowledgeable about social policy. Less ambitious minds tended to assume that the president or the Chairman of the Committee on Ways and Means knew what he was talking about. But graduates of the best universities invariably wanted to know how a family of four could live on $1,600.

This misapprehension was compounded by the food-stamp provision, and by the statistical convention of calculating Federal programs in terms of a four-person family. Food stamps were income, albeit income that could only be used for limited purposes. In the Family Assistance Plan that finally emerged, the combined cash and stamp payment to a family of four came to approximately $2,460. However, because the stamp program already existed (even though the formulae were being made much more generous) the general perception was that this was nothing added to the income of the poor. No one ever asked how a family of four could live on $2,460 a year. FAP was always defined in terms of the cash payment at zero income.

Nor was it ever asked how a family of seven could live on $2,800 a year (or, with food stamps included, something like $4,000 a year). The Washington practice was to calculate family budgets, poverty levels, and such indices in terms of a family of father, mother, son, and daughter. However, among the working poor a primary source of poverty was large family size. The principal beneficiaries of a negative income tax would inevitably be families with low but not hopelessly low incomes who simply had more children than their income would support.[10] The lumberjack with five, the dirt farmer with six: for these men even the most modest income supplement would be important. But this was not easy to make clear. This circumstance was to assume greater relevance at a later period when it became the interest of many groups *not* to have it made clear.

However modest the payments might appear, they were higher than the level of monthly per person welfare payments then in effect in sixteen states, most of them Southern.* In these states, FAP would have completely replaced AFDC. Thus, a basic problem of the existing system would be attacked by establishing national standards. The remaining states would be required to maintain their existing levels of AFDC payments, which would mean supplementing FAP. Even so, in all but two states (New York and North Dakota), there would be a higher Federal contribution under the proposed arrangement than under the existing one. As it was also proposed to raise the Federal contribution to the "adult categories," that is to say Old-Age Assistance, Aid to the Blind, and Aid to the Permanently and Totally Disabled, even New York and North Dakota would end up with more Federal revenues than they were then receiving. Thus, a measure of "fiscal relief" was present in the proposal from the beginning.

The FAP proposal contained several further elements of great professional but, at that time, limited public interest. The most important concerned the "compulsory" aspect of the Work Incentive Program (WIN). This had been a congressional initiative. In no very subtle way it was intended and perceived as a rebuke to welfare administrators who, for all the promises they gave and support they received, manifestly were not cutting down the welfare rolls. Congress, as noted, had taken the matter into its own hands, and in the 1967 Social Security amendments established a program under which welfare mothers were to be offered work and work training, and in various ways encouraged to become self-supporting. The penalty for refusing to participate in such programs was a reduced AFDC payment. (The statute provided that "such individual's needs shall not be taken into account in making the determination" of the family budget.)[11] *The law made no exception for the mothers of small children.* The program was compulsory and was so intended. In actual operation it does not appear that any compulsion occurred. As with all service programs, the amount of money made available for WIN was much less than the "universe" of likely candidates would have required. The number of WIN "slots" always was exceeded by the number of persons voluntarily seeking training.

---

* As these states changed their own benefit levels, the number in which FAP would completely replace the AFDC program declined.

If anyone was being forced into training, no one at the executive level of HEW knew about it, but the *principle* of compulsion was nonetheless anathema to the career professionals, and their view was shared by the quasi-political officeholders to whom they reported.

Those who prepared the report for the UAC Committee strongly proposed that expanded job training be made available for AFDC recipients, and for the working poor, but with equal strength recommended that "market incentives and not compulsion determine participation in the new manpower program." Trainee motivation, the report continued, is essential to success. "Forced training, or training which is taken as a condition for assistance, would be detrimental in this regard." Moreover, "To offer a plan participant a choice of Labor Department job-training programs seems also to put a premium on the successful performance of the Department of their role under the various programs." (The Urban Affairs Council staff was then circulating a draft "Urban Affairs Policy" which put much stress on building incentives into government programs, both for individuals and for bureaucracies.) Later, FAP was widely seen as imposing a strict work requirement on recipients. In part this was the result of Administration rhetoric and was an intended result. (Although no one had wished to hear it described as "repealing the Fourteenth Amendment," which was one popular formulation on the left.) Terminology is tricky on this issue. It could reasonably be maintained that a "work requirement" in order to be such would require work as the condition of receiving *any* benefits. In these terms, neither the 1967 Amendments or FAP imposed a work requirement. Rather, they imposed a penalty for refusal to work. Under the 1967 Amendments, this penalty was on the large side, and could be imposed on most adult recipients. As will be discussed, FAP proposed that the penalty be reduced, and that mothers with infant children be exempt. However, all sides to the controversy concurred in referring to any such penalty as a "work requirement," and always for purposes of making it appear more severe than was the case.

The FAP proposal also provided for a general adoption of the practice, much favored by welfare administrators, of permitting recipients merely to declare their income (or lack of it) rather than having it determined by investigation. Under FAP, determination of income was to be made on a quarterly basis simply by the filing of a declaration. Payments would be made on the basis of an averaged income for the preceding twelve months. It was generally understood these declarations would be checked in the same manner and at about the rate that income-tax returns are audited. Finally, it was proposed that the income-supplement program be administered directly by the Social Security Administration, with no state involvement whatever. The administration of the adult categories and of the residual AFDC program would continue with the states.

The draft report was vague about cost. The "preferred option," as it was called, was estimated to require an additional $2 billion per year, exclusive of food and training programs. (A "secondary option," that of national standards for the existing welfare categories, was also spelled out in the paper, but with no great enthusiasm.) Of the $2 billion, it was estimated some $710 million would result in dollar-for-dollar savings by the states. Thus it was put forth that a guaranteed income could be had for $1.3 billion. This was no more than the cost of the proposed changes in the food-stamp program. If somewhat underestimated, even somewhat disingenuous—a considerable variety of related costs were not calculated—the figure faithfully reflected a powerful fact, namely that this guaranteed income was a relatively inexpensive proposal, albeit a radical one. Service programs were just as expensive, however partial their coverage, and in many instances were considerably *more* expensive.

The Family Assistance Plan which Nixon proposed in a television address of August 8, twenty weeks later, was not different in any essential from the Family Security System presented to the UAC Committee on Welfare on March 24. In the course of that period a great struggle, or so it seemed to those involved, was waged within the Administration, and within the White House itself, but this had little effect on the final product. The proposal might have been rejected in the course of this internal debate, but there was no way it could have been significantly modified. Cost precluded a family allowance. The political culture precluded abolishing aid to dependent persons altogether, or even cutting it back. The alternatives open to the president were to advocate some incremental changes in the existing system, or take the giant step to a guaranteed income. He chose the latter.

The battle was over by late spring, well before most of the combatants realized it.

Finch fell ill immediately after the March 24 meeting of his committee, and could not brief the president on his proposal. Nor could a report be readied for presentation to a meeting of the full Urban Affairs Council scheduled for March 31. It would never be ready. If liberals outside the Administration could never quite come to see the dimensions and the implications of the Family Assistance Plan, conservatives within did so instantly. The March 24 meeting had scarcely begun when Martin Anderson, representing Arthur Burns, declared that the committee was being presented with a negative income tax. "Let us call a spade a spade," he said. "Let us remember Oscar Wilde's conclusion," said I, that "anyone who would call a spade a spade should be compelled to use one." The general impression in the room was that of two academics fussing, but both of us knew well enough what we were fussing about. FAP, as was instantly obvious to anyone familiar with the dynamics of the negative income tax equation, would provide cash income supplements for an enormous population. It could not but have profound consequences.

If there is any meaning left to the terms "liberal" and "conservative" it emerges at such moments of decision-making on serious public issues. *No one could anticipate what would be the consequences of FAP*. Political liberals were willing nonetheless to take the chance, indeed were anxious to if only for the excitement of it all. Political conservatives were not. Michael Oakeshott, who succeeded to the chair of Harold Laski at the London School of Economics, has defined the conservative temperament in terms which showed with great distinctness, and not a little advantage, in the debate that followed.

Changes, then, have to be suffered; and a man of conservative temperament (that is, one strongly disposed to preserve his identity) cannot be indifferent to them. In the main, he judges them by the disturbance they entail and, like everyone else, deploys his resources to meet them. The idea of innovation, on the other hand, is improvement. . . . [A] man of this temperament will not himself be an ardent innovator. In the first place, he is not inclined to think that nothing is happening unless great changes are afoot and therefore he is not worried by the absence of innovation: the use and enjoyment of things as they are occupies most of his attention. Further, he is aware that not all innovation is, in fact, improvement; and he will think that to innovate without improving is either designed or inadvertent folly. Moreover, even when an innovation commends itself as a convincing improvement, he will look twice at its claims before accepting them. From his point of view, because every improvement involves change, the disruption entailed has always to be set against the benefit anticipated. But when he has satisfied himself about this, there will be other considerations to be taken into the account. Innovating is always an equivocal enterprise, in which gain and loss (even excluding the loss of familiarity) are so closely interwoven that it is exceedingly difficult to forecast the final upshot: there is no such thing as an unqualified improvement. For, innovating is an activity which generates not only the "improvement" sought, but a new and complex situation of which this is only one of the components. The total change is always more extensive than the change designed; and the whole of what is entailed can neither be foreseen nor circumscribed. Thus, whenever there is innovation there is the certainty that the change will be greater than was intended, that there will be loss as well as gain and that the loss and the gain will not be equally distributed among the people affected; there is the chance that the benefits derived will be greater than those which were designed; and there is the risk that they will be off-set by changes for the worse.

From all this the man of conservative temperament draws some appropriate conclusions. First, innovation entails certain loss and possible gain, therefore, the onus of proof, to show that the proposed change may be expected to be on the whole beneficial, rests with the would-be innovator. Secondly, he believes that the more closely an innovation resembles growth (that is, the more clearly it is intimated in and not merely imposed upon the situation) the less likely it is to result in a preponderance of loss. Thirdly, he thinks that an innovation which is a response to some specific defect, one designed to redress some specific disequilibrium, is more desirable than one which springs from a notion of a generally improved condition of human circumstances, and is far more desirable than one generated by a vision of perfection. Consequently, he prefers small and limited innovations to large and indefinite. Fourthly, he favours a slow rather than a rapid pace, and pauses to observe current consequences and make appropriate adjustments. And lastly, he believes the occasion to be important; and, other things being equal, he considers the most favourable occasion for innovation to be when the projected change is most likely to be limited to what is intended and least likely to be corrupted by undesired and unmanageable consequences.[12]

The FAP proposal could meet few of these conditions in the eyes of Burns and Anderson, and they said so. Few of the FAP proponents, for example, could foresee that one of the "unanticipated consequences" of the proposal would be that on the liberal left a demand would immediately arise for a level of negative tax payment so high as to constitute, if ever adopted, a political and social disaster. Those who wished, for whatever purposes, to disparage the program could readily depict the $1,600 "base" as shockingly inadequate, and just as readily depict a $5,500 or $6,500 level as a reasonable, even modest proposal. Some did this cynically, others out of genuine conviction that it was the case. (The audience, as it were, was similarly divided.) Almost no opponent on the left acknowledged, and probably few fully understood, that a $6,500 negative income tax would cost upwards of $100 billion, would provide an income supplement for three-quarters of the population, and would either wipe out the currency or bring on a truly draconic work requirement as a condition of keeping the economy alive. But if liberals thought of such things hardly at all, conservatives would think of little else. *They did not precisely foresee what was to come, but they were closer than were the Administration liberals.* In particular they saw that the proposal would in the end be used to damage the president's standing with precisely the groups whose interests he was most seeking to advance by the legislation. (But even Burns could not foresee that opposition liberals would bring the first black legislator elected in Mississippi since Reconstruction to Washington to testify *against* FAP.)

On the other hand, the Administration liberals did see that the existing system was going nowhere, did think of the children in Mississippi half-starved from the level of payments provided by state option, did see that the country and the president needed a big bold gesture to signify that things were going to be all right. Only a few years after the event the proposal of FAP is quite overshadowed by great initiatives in foreign policy and quite unexpected innovations in domestic economic policy. But it was important at the time, and may have done its healing work simply in being proposed. Here the liberals can claim their share of foresight.

In the meantime there was the battle to be fought. The dispute soon overwhelmed the committee-council structure which the president had set up only weeks earlier. The White House regressed to the primary mode of presidential government, namely, that aides advocate and the president decides. The struggle was in essence a competition to discover and set forth considerations that would appear decisive to him.

Political drama was such a consideration, possibly the most important.

Robert A. Nisbet has contended that one of the least appreciated forces in human events is boredom. It is an influence difficult to measure, but easy enough to detect, and it played its role here. A new president, a new Secretary of Health, Education, and Welfare. Were they merely to propose the same old things? Uniform national standards? Were they to wager their historical reputations on efficiencies to be achieved in job training? Was the measure of their magnanimity to be opposition to the man-in-the-house rule?

These were men capable of a larger sense of what they would do, and these were their first weeks in office. The presidency, for Nixon and for Finch, had been won at great cost. They had almost won it once. They tended to think in fact they had done so. The years that immediately followed had been humiliating, the years after that hard and chancy. But now at last their time had come. It was not to be frittered away. Not at that moment. Eventually the office came more and more to dominate the man. The war went on. Politics resumed. Everyone diminished somewhat; some a great deal. But this was March 24, the president's tenth week in office.

Finch's meeting took place at HEW in the late morning. Before the day was out Nixon was talking of the Family Security System. A memorandum from me two days later presented the case.

The essential fact about the Family Security System is that it will abolish poverty for dependent children and the working poor. The cost is not very great. *Because it is a direct payment system.* The tremendous costs of the poverty program come from *services.* . . .

The Family Security System would enable you to begin cutting back sharply on these costly and questionable services, and yet to assert with full validity that it was under your Presidency that poverty was abolished in America.

As executive secretary of the Urban Affairs Council it was nominally my task to guide the work of the Council and its committees so that the president would be presented with competently argued policy options. I chose now to become an advocate of a particular option. This was to have its costs, but much turned on the president's decision. No one could be neutral about it: to seek to appear so would have been an exercise more of duplicity than of discipline. In various ways the president indicated that he understood and accepted this changed role.

Motivation in such circumstances is personal and rarely disinterested. I had been an advocate of the income strategy: for the president to adopt it would be a triumph of sorts. *That* level of calculation. Poverty and deprivation and prejudice were real. They were forms of suffering. They seemed to be one source of social turmoil. (A turmoil that will most likely seem much less threatening in the perspective of history than it did at the time, but this was the time.) A guaranteed income would respond to this reality.

Moreover, evidence mounted that many services programs did not respond. A profound event, to my mind, had been the publication by HEW of the report *Equality of Educational Opportunity* in July 1966. James S. Coleman and his associates had carried out a massive inquiry into educational facilities and achievement levels across the Nation, fully expecting to find vast disparities in facilities, and to be able to demonstrate that these accounted for differences in achievement. They found nothing of the sort. Facilities for rich and poor, black and white, were, within geographical regions, surprisingly alike. If there was some tendency for the poor and the black to be less well provided for, this was by no means always the case, and the differences were almost always slight (save between regions). This finding was depressing in an almost ominous way. The polity *had,* it turned out, in a rough but essentially responsible manner, provided equal educational services for most groups in a vastly disparate land. Yet there was almost no social awareness of this reality.

The mindless celebration of American arrangements that prevailed in the 1950s now had its counterpart in an equally uncritical presumption of wrongdoing.

This attitude was accompanied by a yet more naive assumption that it was within the power of government to bring about great social change at manageable cost and at a steady, perceptible pace. Here the Coleman findings had been even more depressing. A significant relationship between educational inputs, of the kind associated with the Elementary and Secondary Education Act of 1965, and educational achievement scarcely existed. Great variations were found in achievement as between racial, ethnic, and class groups; but little was found in schools as such that could account for them. The instinct of the *political* leadership in HEW had been simply to conceal the findings, and this was done with some success, but the findings were well enough known within a circle of social scientists, and so also were the implications. By its very advances, social science was becoming a less confident guide to social policy. It had entered a period when it could with fair success predict failure, but had little else to add. Disraeli's dictum that "Few ideas are correct ones, and what are correct no one can ascertain," increasingly characterized the condition of learned men. His deduction that "with words we govern men" seemed more than ever the case. No large assertion is intended here, merely the description of a certain mood, and a minority one at that. But I was among the minority, and we had cause to think ourselves more right than otherwise. We no longer trusted the past, we were fearful for the future. Programs we had fought for had failed: so many. Now, most alarming of all, the bureaucracies behind such programs and their advocates in public life were failing utterly to see or accept what this might imply. A new style in social policy was needed.

Reflecting on not dissimilar events in foreign policy in the 1960s, Richard Neustadt in 1970 came to a conclusion very different from that he might earlier have reached.

Our contemporary "big" bureaucracy in national security affairs, so-called, is a blunt instrument. On the record of the past it is effectively responsive to blunt challenges when gripped by a blunt policy. Its character was shaped in World War and in Cold War. Yet the era of such challenges now seems to be behind us. Blunt policy no longer serves. Subtlety, however, is a thing for which this instrument was not designed, with which I have my doubts that it can learn to cope. What remains? Simplicity.[13]

Simplicity. Insistence that government stay close to what it knew how to do, and be rigorous in judging just what that was. (Neustadt notes that the American government in the 1960s knew next to nothing about Vietnam. The presumption otherwise made the disaster inevitable.) Laird had included in *Republican Papers* an article written by me in the summer of 1967 addressed to liberal Democrats, asking where had we gone wrong. Largely, I had argued, in assuming we knew things we did not know.

Somehow liberals have been unable to acquire from life what conservatives seem to be endowed with at birth, namely, a healthy skepticism of the powers of government agencies to do good.

The American national government is a superb instrument for redistributing power and wealth in our society. One person in ten in the United States, for example, now gets a Social Security check every month. But as an instrument for providing services, especially to urban lower-class Negroes, it is a highly unreliable device.

Within weeks of my returning to Washington this point was confirmed with some force. The president's February 19 message was about to be sent to the Congress, complete with a strong endorsement of Head Start, when word arrived for OEO that a massive evaluation study, carried out by the Westinghouse Learning Corporation and Ohio University, had come forth with the finding that had in effect been predicted by Coleman: Head Start wasn't working. The children were getting their teeth fixed, but little else that could be quantified. The president's message was modified, in an attempt, as much as anything, to telegraph the blow. Head Start was described as still "experimental," it had demonstrated not only how difficult but how important it was to get at the mysteries of early learning, it fixed teeth. The message ended with the nice passage: "We do not pretend to have all the answers. We are determined to find as many as we can . . . not every experiment succeeds. . . ." But this to small effect.

In *Republican Papers* I had written that a prime source of

liberal failure was the unwillingness to face the finding of failure where it appeared, as recurrently it did.

> In our desire to maintain public confidence in such programs, we have tended to avoid evidence of poor results, and in particular we have paid too little heed to the limited capacities of government to bring about social change.[14]

Response to the Head Start evaluation followed precisely this pattern. When it appeared, it was promptly dismissed as methodologically inadequate and, *sotto voce,* ideologically wicked. *The New York Times* discerned a White House scheme to discredit a fine and noble enterprise. If progressives had declined to acknowledge findings such as Coleman's, now, with Nixon in office, they were in a position not merely to ignore, but to accuse. *Why* did Nixon find that Head Start was "not working?" It availed nothing to respond that the president had had nothing to do with the study, had not even heard of it until its results were reported to him amid the din of his first weeks in office. The findings were negative, and accordingly the president would have to be blamed: not for the failure, but for the *finding* of failure.

The 1960s were a period during which "social science" prescriptions for social policy had much currency, and the style grew steadily more debased. In time the most trivial assertions of upper-class petulance or lower-class anger were likely to be received with respect, even awe. George Sternlieb has described the process.

> In this kind of "social science," anecdotal accounts began to pass as consequential theories and models for the design of new institutions. A typical specimen of the genus is the account of how I, a young draft dodger, full of beans and aware of the fact that I wasn't going to spend my career there, came into a class of young sullens; in six months they loved me. This sort of recital became dignified both as an indictment of the flywheels of our institutions and also possibly as a model for new educational institutions of the future. The former may well have validity, but the latter defies rationality. The wonder is not the existence of a number of these anecdotal descriptions, but rather the childlike acceptance of them as a vision of a future that

can be reproduced on a scale commensurate with the number of children and situations involved. The sordid fact that they enjoy such acceptance is but another indication of the extent to which we have begun to escape into fantasy.[15]

The unfailing thrust of this literature was to describe the institutions of society as victimizing one or another group, especially the urban poor. Any suggestion that such a group might be victimizing itself, or even that the institutions were essentially neutral, doing neither harm nor good, was subject to ferocious attack. Any evidence to this effect, especially evidence emerging from an evaluation of the more fashionable new experiments, was typically greeted with rage on the part of their sponsors or clients. Louis Wirth described this condition many years earlier.

The distinctive character of social science discourse is to be sought in the fact that every assertion, no matter how objective it may be, has ramifications extending beyond the limits of science itself. Since every assertion of a "fact" about the social world touches the interests of some individual or group, one cannot even call attention to the existence of certain "facts" without courting the objections of those whose very *raison d'être* in society rests upon a divergent interpretation of the "factual" situation.[16]

The president would no doubt have to persist with those programs that existed but it would be a poor risk to depend overmuch on them, and yet more "bad news" had to be expected. In the annual Report of the Social Science Research Council for 1968–1969, Henry Riecken set forth the president's problem with the authority of a disinterested and informed observer.

The difficulty we as a nation face in solving our problems is not will but knowledge. We want to eliminate poverty, crime, drug addiction and abuse; we want to improve education and strengthen family life, but we do not know how.[17]

Writing more than two years after these events, Sternlieb criticizes the Nixon Administration for its failure to recognize the "salutary placebo-effects of social programs" which might otherwise seem worthless on the basis of a strict accounting of results.

[T]hese programs have become forms of symbolic action. In their ritualistic aspects they are of particular value. They give psychic satisfaction to the patrons of the poor, convince outsiders—especially the media—that "something is being done," and indicate to the urban poor that someone up there really cares. In a word, these programs are placebos and they often produce all the authentic, positive results which placebos can have in medical practice.

Sternlieb's charge against the Administration is specific and cogent. It could only have come in the aftermath of the 1960s.

The failure has been not so much in what it has done, as in what it has called what it has done—not so much in the substance of its programs, as in its rejection of the gamesmanship which does not merely accompany programs but is central to them.

A reply of sorts may help explain the extraordinary set of decisions on domestic policy which did take place in the early Nixon period. One of the major components in Nixon's final decision to propose a guaranteed income was his distaste for some (not all) of the goals of the symbolic actions of the 1960s, and his simultaneous desire to make symbolic gestures in other directions. The president was not interested in providing "psychic satisfaction to the patrons of the poor." With exceptions, it was precisely this group in American public life which was most patronizing and contemptuous of *him*. The view was reciprocated, with little give on either side. Nixon was not opposed to trying to convince outsiders—especially the media—that "something was being done," but for all the public relations apparatus of his White House he expected few favors from the press. In any event, the record of the programs begun in the 1960s would make it nigh impossible to have yet another cluster of incremental gestures depicted as bold new departures.

Apart from any considerations such as these, Nixon was set on a course of making *his* symbolic gestures to a very different constituency from that which benefited from the programs of the Kennedy-Johnson era. The "psychic satisfaction" of the Nixon era was already, as it were, spoken for. There had been, as Woodrow Wilson declared when he took office, a change in government. Almost always this entails a redistribution of symbolic rewards, in almost precisely the manner, and with far greater consequence, as that in which jobs change hands. Symbolic gestures are the patronage awarded the electoral coalition that brings a president to office, or the one he hopes to shape for the next election. In Nixon's case this was a coalition of conservative "middle Americans," white Southerners, suburbanites, party regulars, and an undefined range of upper-working-class voters who found their Democratic loyalty strained by the symbolic gestures of the preceding two Democratic Administrations. Beyond this coalition there seemed to lie a fairly large electoral territory made up of blue-collar Wallace voters—it appeared that upwards of a quarter of trade union voters had been leaning to Wallace as the 1968 election approached—and ethnic groups in various ways estranged from their normal Democratic allegiance. These groups had benefited from some of the substantive programs of the 1960s—most, probably, from the Medicare legislation—but very little from the symbolic programs and politics of the period. They had all but deliberately been excluded, all but driven into a politics of resentment and anxiety, of the kind Wallace represented. No president in Nixon's position would see much advantage in this practice of his predecessors. His instinct was to cut it out altogether. As head of his party he could sense the effect the programs were having on a constituency he would be seeking approval from. As chief executive he was receiving competent reports that the programs were not accomplishing much anyway.

There was just perhaps an element of *Schadenfreude* in the new president's discovery that so few of the confidently proclaimed programs of his predecessors had much to show in the way of results. But, correspondingly, there had been a growing level of cynicism, or at least self-delusion, in the espousal of social programs by the Johnson Administration in its later years. In a long passage in his memoirs, *The Vantage Point,*[18] Lyndon B. Johnson evokes this period in his discussion of the Rat Extermination and Control Act of 1967. Republican conservatives in Congress had made the—typical—blunder of deriding a small categorical aid program for rat control proposed by the Administration. ("Mr. Speaker, I think the 'rat smart thing' for us to do is to vote down this rat bill 'rat now.'") Wherewith, Johnson writes, "The floodgates opened." More precisely, *he* opened them, taking the issue to the public, speaking about rats "in every public forum I could find. . . ." Thousands of persons, he recalls, especially those in slums, were bitten by rats every year. "The overwhelming majority of victims are babies lying in their cribs. Some of them die of their wounds."

That President Johnson was sincere, none should doubt. He had a singular capacity to care deeply about social legislation, to fight for it, and to win. If the Republicans wished to open themselves to the charge of not caring about children being bitten by rats, Johnson was fully within his rights to make the most of it. And yet there is a question of proportion. There *are* rats, they *do* bite persons, *including* children. But there was apparently no evidence on hand of children dying of such wounds. (Pet rats bite a large number of children, but typically on the fingers.) That wild rats should be controlled, no one would question, but it was not unreasonable to ask whether yet another Federal categorical aid program—a few million dollars to be spread over a continent—was the most sensible approach. And yet it could be made an issue, and President Johnson had done so.*

Nixon could not take up such issues. Once it might have been in him to do so, but no longer. Emotionally he was blocked: he could not bring himself to emulate, much less try to outdo, Lyndon Johnson in making the most of political opportunities of this kind. He could not bring himself intellectually to take such positions. He had spent too much time deriding such programs, and his derision, it began to appear, had not been unwarranted. Too many Potemkin villages were already on tour to add more. Nor could he wish to do so on political grounds.†

The result was one of high irony. With symbolic politics

* In 1971, with a program under way, there was still no knowledge in HEW of children dying of rat bites, although it appeared that earlier estimates of the number of such bites had been low. In 1967 the Public Health Service had been concerned about the prospect of bubonic plague spreading from Vietnam via returning ships and very much wanted the legislation. This, however, was not among the arguments the Administration could make for its bill.

† Presidents, observers had often noted, inevitably face conflicts in the demands of being simultaneously a "party leader" and "a chief executive." But for Nixon, in this instance, there was a degree of convergence. Embracing the issues and political styles of the 1960s would not enhance his standing among his supporters. At the same time—and perhaps most importantly in view of the programs he did endorse—the president was especially aware of the responsibility of his Administration to propose solutions to public problems arguably more effective than those of his predecessors.

barred, Nixon was led—it could be said he was forced—to put forth substantive legislative proposals of unprecedented magnitude for the abolition of poverty and inequality. In a steady succession of legislative messages he proposed to spend more money for the direct provision of the needs of low-income groups than any president in history. Early on an almost schizophrenic style took hold of his Administration. Symbolic rewards were devised for "middle America," while legislative proposals were drafted for the "other America." The latter ranged from high points such as the proposal of a guaranteed income and the provision of health insurance for the poor, to less-noticed proposals such as reformulation of scholarship aid so as to concentrate on youths from low-income families. In one form or another, the concern to make honest, substantive improvements in the life circumstances of the poor permeated the program and policy echelons of his Administration. National goals of great consequence were put forward. Thus, in a message to Congress on Elementary and Secondary Education sent in March 1970, he responded to the seeming ineffectiveness of compensatory education programs by asserting that the adequacy of education could no longer be measured by educational inputs, but would have to be assessed by the outputs, that is to say, not by what was spent on a child's education, but by what the child actually learned. Accompanying legislation, to establish a National Institute of Education to pursue the mysteries of the subject, proclaimed a national goal of "equality of educational opportunity" in realistic and powerful terms: an assertion of potentially enormous consequence.*

Congress did respond to some proposals. For example, the National Institute of Education was passed by both the House and Senate once a key group of Congressmen led by John Brademas, Democrat of Indiana, came to see that the president

* This followed directly from the Coleman report, *Equality of Educational Opportunity*. For all its other contributions to educational policy-making and the evaluation of social programs generally, the lasting significance of this study may be due more to its adoption of an output standard of equal opportunity. Other criteria, such as per pupil expenditures, qualifications of the teacher, or age and condition of the school plant, must be seen as inadequate in view of the report's findings that these measures had little association with scholastic achievement. See Frederick Mosteller and Daniel P. Moynihan, eds., *On Equality of Educational Opportunity*, New York, Random House, 1972.

was speaking a painful but necessary truth when he said that the processes of education among "disadvantaged groups" (or any other) were simply not understood to the point that anything like equal outcome could be achieved as between these and better-off groups. On balance, however, it did not. The Congressional reaction to reports that compensatory education was not producing was to increase appropriations, and defy the president to veto them. When he did so, it was established that he was an anti-education president.

If there was any doubt about this, the symbolic actions of the Administration settled the issue. It was deemed impossible that an Administration that assiduously and at times frantically cultivated the dingiest prejudices and anxieties of small-town, old-time white America could be anything but indifferent to the problems of urban and rural poverty of which President Johnson had been wont to speak with such passion. In particular, black leaders, who had been among the leading beneficiaries of the symbolic politics of the preceding Administrations, came to see that they could gain almost no rewards of this kind from Nixon, and were soon in open opposition. Some such leaders learned that they could get a great deal from the new Administration and that benefits would *not* be withheld because of public opposition. *Its* symbolic politics almost required that it be denounced by black "militants" and white liberals. A curious pattern resulted. Black leaders would obtain a major concession from the Administration one day, denounce it the next, and be back the day after for more. After a point a few seemed to find the arrangement almost agreeable.

It is unusual for dichotomies of this kind to be raised to the level of conscious, calculated behavior. Yet the Nixon Administration came close. In July 1969 Attorney General John Mitchell told a group of black representatives, "You would be better advised to watch what we do, rather than what we say." How more explicit can one be? He was saying that the rhetoric of the national government would now change, would now begin to reward other groups, but that the actual conduct of the Administration would not change. This is about what happened.

If, however, Mitchell expected blacks to see this as an improved, or even as an acceptable, situation he was, of course, asking for disappointment. Words are at least as important as deeds in politics and government, probably more so. Symbolic rewards are at least as valuable as real rewards, in ways more so. There do arise situations in which a constituency is sufficiently well organized and self-disciplined that it can trade substantive for symbolic rewards. Elements of business and the trade-union movement do this with fair regularity in national affairs. But for the American Negro to do this in 1969 would have required a godlike degree of insight and steadiness. Blacks chose, with every reason, to "watch" what the Administration said, *not* what it did. To expect black "leaders," of whom few save the officials of the NAACP had any solid organizational base in black communities, to trade benefits that redounded largely to persons such as themselves, that is to say, the symbolic benefits of being consulted, being invited, being included, for substantive benefits such as money in the pockets or food in the stomachs of Alabama dirt farmers was to expect what is rarely if ever encountered in public affairs. Symbolic rewards are immediate: program rewards in the best of circumstances are long delayed and often never do come to pass. In any event black leaders had legitimate organizational interests that had to be protected and advanced.

Nor was it possible—and here the otherwise reasonable-sounding position expressed by Mitchell must be seriously faulted—to expect even the informed public to follow the process. There is an element in public opinion, which is to say there are a number of citizens, capable of following dichotomous policies, even of approving them, given a certain rationale. But this is a tiny group. It is, moreover, at an unavoidable disadvantage in reaching a judgment. It is easy enough to "watch" what an Administration is saying. It is terribly difficult to see what it is "doing." Even those who can follow the legislative proposals, the legislation, the appropriation, the administrative follow-through, even such persons have no near-term way of knowing much about what actually happens. (Those who find this difficult to accept may wish to consider that in the mid-1960s the nation was led into a near full-scale war in Asia, and took almost two years to realize it.)

Few grasped that Nixon was putting forth a set of administrative and legislative proposals designed fundamentally—and deliberately—to fulfill the promises of the 1960s. An occasional journalist such as James Reston would see this and on occasion would say so. The right wing of the Republican party sensed it quickly enough, but their excoriations had no credence elsewhere. The liberal wing of the party said nothing. The more sensitive, conservative editorial pages, such as that of the *Wall Street Journal* and *Fortune* Magazine saw what was taking place, and commented with mixed but not hostile feelings. But on balance *this* reality was hidden from the public at large, which grew steadily more genuinely concerned that a major social retreat was under way at a time when, in fact, unprecedented social advances were being proposed. It is not likely that the Nixon Administration will ever be credited for what it tried to do, and there is a sense in which it deserves no credit. Sternlieb is almost certainly right: symbolic rewards can be as "real" as substantive ones. To deny them is to deserve resentment. There is little to add save that when the resentment arose and all but engulfed his presidency, Nixon did not change. It had come to seem his destiny.

That was ahead of him. In February and March and April as he worked to fashion a distinctive legislative program of his own, almost the only course open to the president, if he was to be responsive to the state of knowledge, and yet be responsive also to the problems that had so aroused the nation in the 1960s, was to move boldly toward an income strategy. (There would be other "new" programs, of course, primarily in the area of crime. It was to be assumed most would be worthless.*) So at least it seemed to me. There was no guarantee that FAP would succeed where other efforts had failed. Two centuries earlier Richard Burn had recorded in London, "Almost every proposal which

---

* At the end of 1971, it was becoming clear that the efforts of the Nixon Administration to reduce the incidence of violent crime were predictably ineffective. A Washington *Evening Star* report began: "Violent crime has not decreased in Washington since the Nixon administration made the city its law-enforcement model for the nation. Over-all, the number of crimes of violence—murder, rape, robbery and aggravated assault—has continued to inch steadily upward despite massive federal and local efforts to curtail the rise. . . . Washington seems assured of retaining its position among the most violent cities in the United States when the FBI releases its annual 'rankings' next spring." (December 20, 1971) Shortly afterwards, a study of the use of "preventive detention" in the nation's capital revealed that law enforcement officials had displayed little enthusiasm for trying their new powers, preferring instead to rely on other methods of pre-trial control of suspected offenders.

hath been made for the reformation of the poor laws hath been tried in former ages, and found ineffectual."[19] In particular, it was not clear how FAP would have any but the most indirect effects on the problem of welfare dependency as it had developed in cities such as New York. But it would put money in the hands of persons who all could agree needed money, whether or not they deserved it. It would blur racial distinctions that had become too sharp: 70 percent of the working poor were white. It would involve the Federal government's doing what it did best, namely, the collection of taxes and redistribution of income. Seek simplicity, Whitehead, too, had ordained. Thereafter distrust it, but first seek it.

There was also to be considered at this time an elementary question of balance in Federal expenditures. For all the talk of welfare, and Head Start, and such-like, the legislative record of the 1960s had if anything accentuated the imbalance between attention to the aging as against attention to the young. In the course of the decade, expenditures on the aged increased nearly $22 billion; those for the young, only $11.5. As the president was informed at the time, "Federal benefits and services of all kinds in 1970, including the social insurance programs, will average about $1,750 per aged person, and only $190 per young person. . . ." At an Urban Affairs Council meeting March 6, Veneman, substituting for Finch, had insisted that the rise in AFDC rolls was not a result of official leniency, but of home and family conditions. He urged that the Administration concentrate its energies and resources on children under ten. The president did not disagree; he had said as much in his message on poverty. The meeting was devoted to the problem. It ended with the president saying:

We must not let the public impression be that simply, here we are, and we'll make it work a little better. We can tackle it, and we can throw out these programs if we have better ones to replace them with. . . . The nation is aroused, but a large part of the people are frustrated, thinking that it has not worked [i.e., the poverty program]. We must show them we can make it work. . . . What we have to do is coordinate so that with the new Administration, we have *new* approaches.

Congress recessed for Easter. The president flew to Key Biscayne with a collection of notebooks filled with legislative proposals. Time was passing now. If he was to put forward a distinctive legislative program, he would have to make decisions.

The Urban Affairs Council staff proposed eight measures: the Family Assistance Plan, a First Five Years of Life program, reorganization of OEO into an Agency for Citizen Action, a Commission on Goals for 1976, reorganization of Model Cities into an Urban Systems Aid program, transformation of the Highway Trust Fund into a set of general Transportation Trust Funds, a set of proposals to aid Vietnam veterans, and, finally, a proposal for Home Rule, congressional representation, and other reforms in the District of Columbia. The FAP proposal came first:

FAMILY SECURITY SYSTEM

The Family Security System marks the first fundamental change in public welfare since the 1930s. In truth, it is in ways the most significant departure yet made from the Poor Laws of Elizabethan England from which our present practices have descended with all too little change.

It has been said, with justice, that the United States has tended to lag behind the other industrial democracies of the world in its public welfare provisions. With the enactment of the Family Security System we shall leap far ahead, for no nation has ever considered, much less adopted such a system.

Yet it is *simple*. It is relatively *inexpensive*—costing far less than the vast complex of service-dispensing programs which we have piled up, one on top of the other, in recent years. Above all, it is *sane*.

If there is one thing most thoughtful Americans would agree upon it is that the present welfare system established in the 1930s has failed. Moreover, all or almost all will agree wherein the failure lies. First in the fact that the Aid to Families with Dependent Children Program provides a positive incentive for fathers to abandon their wives and children to the welfare rolls. Second, that even when they do, in most states the AFDC payments are shamefully small. Less than $9 per person per month in one state. The products of this system are maimed by it, as surely as hunger, and deprivation, and stigmatization can maim.

The plan is simple.

Every American family with children is guaranteed a minimum income, according to the number of persons in the family. For those families with no income, this minimum guarantee is paid. But those families with income, especially the families of the working poor where an employed father struggles to maintain his wife and children on an income that is simply too little, there would also be a payment, so that total income would rise to more acceptable levels. The higher the family income, of course, the lower the Federal supplement. Thus a family of four earning $3,000 would receive no supplement.

In 16 to 18 states this program would eliminate the AFDC program altogether. The Federal minimum payments are higher than the existing AFDC payments. These are the poorest states in the Nation, whose people need it most. Not only will the poor get more in these states, but the state and local treasuries will be relieved of their present contribution to AFDC payments. In all but two other states the Federal minimum payment will be greater than the current Federal AFDC contribution so that those states may either raise total payments, or benefit from reduced payments which they would have to make, or both. In the two remaining states, New York and North Dakota, there will be savings from Federal participation in the home relief program.

The plan is inexpensive. The total cost of this program to the Federal treasury is likely to be only $2 billion per year. Of this about $700 million will be saved by state governments, so that the net cost to the public sector is about $1.3 billion. *This represents less than two weeks' growth in our Gross National Product. In return for which we will have abolished family poverty in America.*

The plan is sane. No longer will fathers have to leave their families in order to support them. No more will poor persons be driven out of one section of the Nation by inadequate or even punitive welfare legislation, and forced into crowded and hostile cities. It is not an accident that of the 16 to 18 states in which AFDC will be eliminated by the Family Security System, only *one* has taken advantage of the AFDC-U program, first enacted in 1961, under which a family with an unemployed father is eligible for benefits.

The proposal contains provisions to make job-training programs of all sorts available to current welfare recipients. This is meant to mesh with Labor Department reforms in the Manpower Administration. As part of the incentive for states to move as many of their welfare clients as can work onto training programs, the proposal is to have the Federal government pick up the state portion of AFDC payments in those states which have payment levels high enough that the Family Security System payments do not replace them.

A list of states in which AFDC is eliminated [follows]:

State AFDC Eliminated by Family Security Proposal

The elimination of AFDC is predicated on an average payment under the proposed plan of $31.25 per person per month. Under current state payment figures, this would swallow AFDC in 16 to 18 states (there being some monthly variation which makes exact prediction difficult).

States currently paying less than $20 per month
　　Alabama
　　Arkansas
　　Florida
　　Mississippi
　　South Carolina

States currently paying less than $26 per month
　　Georgia
　　Louisiana
　　Missouri
　　Texas
　　West Virginia (Has an AFDC-U program)
　　North Carolina

States currently paying around $31 per month
　　Arizona
　　Kentucky
　　Maine
　　Tennessee
　　New Mexico
　　Nevada
　　Virginia

Burns had by this time set up a staff in the Executive Office Building which competed at almost all points with the staff of the Council. Despite Burns' greater prestige, the tactical advantages were to the UAC. I operated from the White House itself—an intangible but unmistakable advantage—and through the UAC meeting schedule controlled a fair amount of the president's time and that of his Cabinet. It was probably also the case that as a Democrat and a complete newcomer to the president's circle I represented less of a threat to other members of the president's circle, who by contrast had to see Burns as a rival. Whatever the case, by late spring it was evident that the Urban Affairs Council agenda was having much more success with the president than were the various proposals emerging from Burns' operation: enough to cause trouble if the pattern became too evident.

It became necessary, in a word, for Burns to get something. His group was then developing a legislative version of a revenue sharing proposal, and while this properly belonged on the UAC agenda it was left to the rival group. It was understood fairly early on, however, that revenue sharing was to be a companion proposal to FAP, along with an enlarged and restructured manpower training program and a reorganization of the Office of Economic Opportunity. The shared feature of each proposal was the concept of an income strategy. Behind the idea of revenue sharing was the belief that the ills of urban government arose at least in part from the imbalance that had gradually developed between the revenue-generating capacity of the property tax, on which municipal government heavily depended, and the graduated income tax which provided revenue for the Federal government. The remedy for this imbalance was to begin sharing the proceeds of the latter tax with state and local government, leaving them to do with the funds exactly what they would, and requiring compliance only with general policies of the national government. At the Department of Labor, George P. Shultz was moving ahead rapidly on a general reorganization of manpower activities, and a proposal to turn much of the operation over to state and urban governments: again, an income strategy. In essence, the Federal government was to provide more resources and fewer prescriptions. The Labor Department would set forth fairly strict performance standards for manpower training, but leave it to local authorities to devise ways to meet them. The Federal government would impose strict civil-rights standards on the use of shared revenue, but would leave it to state and local governments to decide what to use the revenue on. There was the potential here for a fairly considerable redirection of government style.

On Good Friday, April 4, the president met at Key Biscayne with Finch, Burns, his legislative assistant Bryce N. Harlow, myself, and his counsel, John D. Ehrlichman, who was already assuming a pre-eminent role in domestic affairs. Whether by design or otherwise, the president has built a fairly considerable measure of conflict and advocacy into his White House staff. He needed a man who, up to a point, would be neutral, while being supportive of the contenders as their fortunes fluctuated, and he had found such a man in his counsel.

Ehrlichman greeted the party arriving from Washington with news that the president liked the feel of the FAP proposal. At the meeting Burns argued against it with force and with foresight. The Gallup poll showed the public was opposed to the idea of a guaranteed income. He foresaw, and stressed, that the $1,500-for-a-family-of-four figure would be turned against the president, who would be depicted as believing a family of four could live on $1,500 a year. Finally, he noted the proposal would add seven million persons to the welfare rolls. (The proposal, as it finally emerged, would have brought some thirteen million into the new system.) Harlow shared Burns's apprehensions about a guaranteed income.

Men who counsel caution in a president do him no disservice, but they do not add much to his day. At the very top of government there ought to be some occasional moment of high spirits, of brave abandon: "to seek a newer world." The constraints are everywhere. No one can get to be president without knowing almost too much about them. There are uses for a measure of incaution. Burns was no doubt right, but where was the glory in always being right if it meant never being bold? Why become president always to be careful? At the end of the day it was evident that the president was leaning toward FAP not least *because* of the risks involved. He would not be able to make many such decisions: he had as well make one. He liked FAP. It was not "tinkering." There it was left, but on April 7 in a note to Ehrlichman recording my understanding of the decisions reached at Key Biscayne, I wrote: "An Urban Affairs Council subcommittee report [on FAP] should be finished up this week. I will begin working on a presidential message."

Even so, the argument dragged on, and before long became public. On April 20, Vincent J. Burke of the *Los Angeles Times* broke the story. "The Nixon Administration," he reported from Washington, "is considering a dramatic proposal to provide Federal cash for the first time to fathers who work full time but don't earn enough to support their families." The proposal had "stirred intense debate." "This could be the most exciting feature of the whole Nixon domestic program," one source informed him, "but on the other hand it may never see the light of day." This was a fair assessment. No one knew the president's mind. Even so, the income strategy approach began to surface. On the same day, April 20, Don Oberdorfer of the *Washington Post* reported: "In an unexpected move to aid the poor, the Nixon Administration plans to ask Congress this week to eliminate well over a million low-income people from the income tax rolls—at the remarkably modest cost to the treasury of about $700 million." The next day the tax proposal was sent to Congress, followed on May 6 by the message on Food and Health. The possibility Burke had broached became more feasible: stories about FAP multiplied.

A measure of support began to come from outside sources. In the third week of May, Reverend Ralph David Abernathy, who had succeeded Martin Luther King, Jr., as president of the Southern Christian Leadership Conference, brought "Chapter II" of the Poor People's Campaign to Washington, this time accompanied only by a small group of symbolic representatives of the poor. He met with the president and the Urban Affairs Council on May 13. In a prepared statement, he presented a list of demands to the president, of which the first, and far the most detailed, concerned hunger. He acknowledged the president's message on hunger—"better than anything the previous Administration did"—but insisted it would not wipe out the problem. He went on for another two pages outlining specific formulas and needs. Only much later did he get to welfare, and spoke in general terms.

Fourth, I would emphasize the necessity for immediate action on welfare reform. A federal standard of welfare which will guarantee an annual income above the poverty line for all is essential now. Now is the time to repeal the repressive "freeze" on AFDC payments which Congress enacted in 1967. Now is the time to adopt a mandatory program of assistance for unemployed fathers. The tendency of the welfare system to cause family disintegration must be ended now.

It is not clear whether Abernathy was seeking higher payments under the existing welfare system or was proposing that it be replaced by an income guarantee. Apart from the reference in his statement, no mention was made of the matter in meeting.

In the aftermath, however, some of the problems the president would have with the proposal were rehearsed. Abernathy had been the quintessence of diffidence and civility in the Cabinet room. He expressed his "profound thanks and appreciation" to the president for the meeting. He then walked out to inform the press that it had been "most disappointing and fruitless." The position of black leaders of voluntary associations was by now badly eroded. They had needed, as Martin Luther King, Jr., had put it, "victories," meaning open concessions from the Federal government, to strengthen their leadership and legitimate their nonviolent methods. But they had had few. A rhetoric of generalized abuse evolved. In the course of the meeting in the Cabinet room, Mrs. Ellaweed Evans, a black mother from Birmingham, Alabama, described the misery of raising ten children in three rooms on beans and corn bread. "Mr. Abernathy," she said, "cannot solve our problem because he does not live with us." She spoke with passion of the folly of paying "thousands" of dollars to go to the moon. "God," she said, "is going to destroy us for doing it." Then, to the president of the United States: "If God don't destroy you, we will destroy you."

In such a climate, a leader such as Abernathy follows, and this generally was true of others like him. It was an interlude. The great charismatic leaders of The Movement were no more. The emergent elected, political leadership of the black central cities had not yet discovered itself as a "national" voice. The civil-rights image was blurred: Was it rights, or poverty, or race, or what, that they were making demands about? In such circumstances serious programmatic work is not done. The Family Assistance Plan, like the War on Poverty itself, was planned by whites for blacks.

If there was an exception to this it was Carl Stokes, mayor of Cleveland. Prior to the inauguration he had met with Nixon to discuss urban problems, and now on April 24 he brought a delegation of his fellow city mayors to meet with the president. In the meeting he was blunt, powerful, persuasive. Just as importantly, after the meeting he tried to help the president rather than harm him. There were things he wanted for Cleveland which only the president of the United States could grant. Further, he could see himself coming back for more such things. In the press conference that followed, he had little but praise for what was, after all, the only president then in office. In the meeting, Stokes pleaded, in effect, for a sense of alarm. The cities—his included—were turning into battlefields. Blacks were arming; whites were arming. Police cars were routinely shot at. Racial clashes were increasing. A pattern of calculated, planned attack was emerging. "Is there any city," the president asked, "better now than a year ago?" None.

"We are the victims," said Ivan Allen of Atlanta, "of the migration of twenty million people—all poor and most Negro." (In February the Illinois Department of Public Aid reported that the number of families in the unemployed segment (AFDC-U) of the welfare program had declined over the year, but that those in the father-absent category had increased by 19.6 percent. In Cook County, 62 percent of grantees came from Southern states; 83 percent were nonwhites.)[20] The states had done nothing to help, said the mayors. Many had encouraged the migration by welfare restrictions. The cities were the victims. Only the Federal government could help. One after another the mayors agreed. A number added that if tensions were high, the OEO programs had probably made them more so. Mayor Lindsay did not disagree. There had been some disasters in community action, he allowed, and yet he had also seen "power and responsibility work." *His* preoccupation was welfare; "The entrapment of welfare." He pleaded for uniform national standards. All present concurred.

If the states had not helped much in the past, the legislative atmosphere of early 1969 scarcely suggested they would do more in the future. The New York State legislature, after what *The Times* described as "more than six hours of acrimonious debate," adopted a budget which, as its headline put it, "slashed" welfare costs. Amid impassioned protests, few supporters spoke to defend the cuts; those who did argued only that they saw no viable alternative "in the light of the state's tight fiscal situation." The legislature changed the state-aid formulas for welfare and Medicaid, so that the state could contribute $123 million less than would have otherwise been forthcoming. That is to say, the state would not pick up its previous share of the rising costs. As legislation goes, it was harsh enough and it passed.[21]

On May 7, Lindsay sent a memorandum to the president on the subject of "welfare reform." "Welfare," he wrote, "is unpopular with all segments of society and, in its neglect of the working poor, increases polarization between the minority-group poor and the working class." New York had a system of general relief which included the working poor but the Federal government contributed nothing to it. The mayor urged that the Federal government enact such a program "perhaps at first as an option for the states, but eventually as mandatory."

A month later, Lindsay was back in the Cabinet room, addressing the twelfth meeting of the Urban Affairs Council on the specific subject of welfare. He was accompanied by Mitchell Ginsburg, Human Resources Administrator of New York, and Jack Goldberg, the city's Welfare Administrator. By now both the principle and the specifics of the proposed Family Assistance Plan had become generally known. Lindsay came to support the principle, and to propose changes in the specifics. He was successful in both efforts.

The mayor described the rise in welfare costs in New York City, reporting that the next year, for the first time, expenditures for education would be below those for relief. The charts were impressive. "That's happened since 1964? God!" said the president. The mayor replied:

Imagine the middle-class resentment of this—also that of the poor because of the welfare apparatus. The reason it is a hot political issue is that it has such terrific impact, not in the South but in the North. The message about the inequities of the burden is beginning to get through to the Northern middle-class taxpayer. They have less government services, and they pay more per income earned.

He noted further that New York City's major suburban areas, Nassau and Westchester, were experiencing even greater percentage increases in welfare than the city.

Lindsay's message was that the "North" had to be given greater consideration than would result from a straight-out negative income tax at a fairly low level with no shared costs above the national schedule. In a follow-up letter to the president of June 6, he noted:

. . . California and New York taken together have 18.7 percent of the country's population and 22.3 percent of its personal income. But they pay out 46.0 percent of all local and state expenditures on public assistance.

He acknowledged that a complete Federal takeover of welfare costs was still some way off, but made a strong case for some

Federal sharing of state supplements in the high-payment states. "The Federal reimbursement formulas," his letter insisted, "must reflect a state's fiscal effort and need as well as its wealth." With this he laid continued stress on work incentives. "What is required is an incentive above welfare levels so there is a *clear-cut advantage to working over not working.*"

By late spring the president had decided in favor of the Family Assistance Plan. No entirely satisfactory list of considerations and their respective weights is ever adduced to account for such decisions. In time, it is to be hoped, historians will have Nixon's own account. (And will, of course, speculate as to whether he knew his own mind at the time, and whether later he could reconstruct it!) A number of factors impressed me as a participant, of which the first may be the most important, namely, the necessity to make a decision. It is a matter of morale, as much as anything else, perhaps especially in the early months of an Administration when it is establishing its style. (Kennedy's dictum "To govern is to choose," was often turned against him. He had seemed not to make choices about some important things.) The Cabinet is buoyed by a man who will say yes or no. So probably is the Nation. And so, most importantly, is the president. Nothing simple comes to him. The decisions are difficult, and often close. He must prove to himself he can make them. Later, perhaps, a president learns to avoid making some decisions, but that, if it comes, is the wisdom of office and the most elusive of presidential arts.

In this particular instance, the White House was known to be split, and so also the Cabinet. A new president ought not allow such situations to go on too long.

To say there was a split and leave it at that would be to miss a fundamental dynamic that operated within the Administration, and was later to be seen affecting the Congress. In the atmosphere of that time, the more the issue of welfare dependency was disputed, the more all the parties to the dispute seemed willing to do in response to it. The dispute moved through a series of stages. At each one the participants appeared willing to do more than they had thought necessary or sufficient in the preceding stage. Burns, having at first been most skeptical about—probably opposed to—the establishment of national minimum welfare standards, ended by being much in favor of just that. (He

POLITICS OF A GUARANTEED INCOME | 171

would have made adherence to national standards a condition for the receipt of revenue-sharing payments.) Those, such as myself, who began as proponents of national standards for welfare, soon would settle for nothing short of a guaranteed income. The outcome of a dispute such as waged over welfare dependency during these ten weeks of the Nixon Administration "should" have been a compromise of some sort. A bit more than one side wished, a bit less than the other hoped for. But this precisely is what did *not* happen. The proposal finally adopted by the president was more ambitious and considerably more expensive than that which first appeared in the conference room of the Department of Health, Education, and Welfare on March 24. The larger the program became, the more the president was attracted to it.

An important element in the final outcome was that the initial reaction of the Cabinet and the White House staff had in fact been one of interest and of general approval. On April 26, a meeting took place in the Cabinet room attended by the principal contenders and half the Cabinet. Veneman briefed the group on the rising costs of the existing welfare system, pointing out that even so it covered only one third of the poor, and finally explaining the FAP proposal, noting in particular that 70 percent of poor families were white, so that the program would involve a gesture of reconciliation in that direction as well as for blacks.*

The general response was positive, even encouraging. Secretary of Labor George P. Shultz supported Veneman's case against the existing AFDC system, and spoke of the need to add greater work incentives and training opportunities to the FAP package. Secretary of Agriculture Hardin allowed he was more for FAP than anything else he'd heard of, asking only that the new food-stamp recommendations be part of the FAP proposal. Otherwise, he asserted, increased incomes would quickly be absorbed in increased rents and similar charges, with no improvement in nutrition. The Budget Director, Robert P. Mayo, wondered, as doubtless his predecessors had done, whether the new food-stamp program might not be paid for by reducing

---

* Families of the black poor being larger, some 43 percent of FAP *recipients* would be black, but the point was nonetheless valid.

payments to corporate farms under various price-support programs. Secretary of Housing and Urban Development George W. Romney thought some of the objectives of the proposal essential. Moreover, he liked the name "Family Security System." Secretary of the Treasury David M. Kennedy asked if the costs could be spelled out a bit more.

Paul W. McCracken spoke at some length, putting the question whether FAP was consistent with the basic Administration approach to social and economic policy, and concluding that it was. "We are trying to get to the individual," he judged. "We are a liberal Administration." This would give the individual purchasing power, it would bring forth market responses rather than bureaucratic ones. The critique of bureaucracy and of the services strategy was much in the minds of men such as McCracken. He felt there was a better way to do things: for him a guaranteed income was not only a logical idea, it was a familiar one.

Bryce N. Harlow, the president's lobbyist, brought mixed reports from Capitol Hill, which now knew something about what was going on. John W. Byrnes of Wisconsin, the ranking Republican member of the House Committee on Ways and Means, had indicated that the proposal for national minimum standards "might make some sense." Yet Harlow discerned grave problems with FAP. In the absence of a strong "work requirement" the opening Republican reaction, he felt, would be "absolute horror." (There were as yet no work provisions of any kind in the draft proposal.) For the president it would be a "political calamity." But—again the dynamic of the issue—Harlow did not leave it at that. He asked whether a work requirement could not somehow be factored in; whether a tougher system for checking up on incomes could be devised; whether the states might not be given a more prominent role. The "most critical weakness" would be the absence of a work requirement. With or without, however, no case could be made that the president would gain anything with Congress by proposing FAP. Whereupon Harlow, a deeply conservative Southerner, suggested that it might nonetheless have to be done. "It may be," he summed up, "this is a crisis decision."

By "crisis decision" Harlow meant, and was understood to mean, a situation of such gravity as to force a president to act, regardless of what he might deem to be his near- or long-term political interests. In this instance the question was whether the president should propose a politically explosive guaranteed income as an alternative to a socially destructive welfare system. If he did so he would have to expect formidable opposition from within his own congressional party. The Republican counterpart of the "small holders" of European parliaments could not possibly be attracted by such a proposal. (The most determined opponent of the bill when it reached Congress was to be Senator John J. Williams, Republican of Delaware, a chicken farmer.) On the other hand, it was probable that if he did make such a proposal he could expect some support from *big* business and *great* wealth—in approximate terms, the Rockefeller wing of the party, with which his relations had always been tentative, strained, or worse. (At this early point in his presidency, Nixon was rather disposed to expand his party base.) Earlier, Nixon had asked that FAP be checked out with businessmen around the country who had shown some interest in the subject of welfare. A fairly exclusive poll was taken: a partner of Lehman Brothers, the chairman of the Executive Committee of Inland Steel, the former treasurer of Eastman Kodak, the chairman of the Board of Governors of the New York Stock Exchange, the chairman of the Board of Marine Midland Bank, a vice-chairman of the Ford Motor Company, the chairman of the Board of Xerox. I reported back that "without exception they were enthusiastic, and stated they would unhesitantly support such a program were the Administration to propose it." In late June, Finch and I briefed the Arden House Steering Committee on Public Welfare on the tentative outlines of the Family Assistance Plan. Responding for the group, Joseph C. Wilson on July 2 expressed its "enthusiastic support" and promised the president it would press the measure in Congress.

In May further support came from a somewhat surprising source. In a special supplement on the United States, the deputy editor of the British magazine *The Economist*, Norman Macrae, set forth an assessment of affairs strikingly convergent with the general line of argument that was being made in the White House on behalf of FAP. He judged that Nixon had inherited from the Kennedy years "a continuing economic miracle" and from "the wreck of Lyndon Johnson's Great Society . . . a sociological mess." He called—as was pointed out to the president, who was in any event impressed by the article—for what amounted to an income strategy. He would place first emphasis on economic expansion and full employment. The next priority, as he saw it, was breaking up the great urban concentrations of low-income blacks which had become a symbol of a society divided along racial lines. To do this required reform of welfare.

The second great economic and social need . . . is the dispersion of population from the ghettos. A major requirement here is to get deserted welfare mothers and their large families out of the city centers instead of ridiculously saying that they can draw higher benefits only if they stay there. The need is to nationalize the welfare system, replacing it by a negative income tax.[22]

If American bankers and British editors could follow the argument, it could be assumed that congressional Democrats might do so as well. The congressional leaders, Michael J. Mansfield of Montana, Majority Leader of the Senate, and John W. McCormack of Massachusetts, Speaker of the House, represented an Irish, working-class, Democratic tradition which had been consistently "liberal" in social-welfare matters. The considerations that made it difficult for a Democratic president to propose a guaranteed income were not likely to weigh too heavily on Democratic legislators, especially if doing so were part of a general strategy of outbidding a Republican one. *This* became a consideration for Nixon.

It focused in the aftermath of a memorandum of May 24 from McCracken suggesting a possible compromise between "the Burns approach and the Family Security System." He began by observing that there was nothing like so sharp a difference within the Administration as everyone seemed to think. The new Administration food-stamp plan potentially provided income maintenance for *all* the poor. Finch had by then testified that the Administration hoped eventually to move toward cash payments rather than stamps. This, McCracken noted correctly, *"provides a substantial start towards a general income support program."* Burns had proposed that the Federal government impose national minimum standards, and also that it make the AFDC-UF program, that is to say, the unemployed parent segment, mandatory. The three measures, in concert, would be the beginning of a general income-support program. He suggested that the Burns proposals be put forth immediately, and that an Interagency Task Force be established to produce by early autumn "a more comprehensive support program as envisaged by the Urban Affairs Council."

McCracken's memorandum was an exemplar of the incremental style of policy change. All the parties to the dispute within the Administration, and presumably most of those observing it from outside, regarded the establishment of a guaranteed income as a profound departure from existing practice. Some were for it, some against: all agreed it would constitute a quantum change. And yet this was not quite the "reality." The food-stamp program was, in essence, a universal system of income support for the working poor. The changes in the existing welfare system which were being advocated within the Administration by the most conservative elements would cost billions and quite transform the impact of the previous arrangements. In a certain sense, the decision about a guaranteed income had already been made by the time the issue was put to the president in that form. McCracken proposed that the issue be viewed accordingly.

On the other hand, there is a sense in which no one knew this. The incremental reality had to be accompanied by a symbolic break if it were to have any of the political and psychological impact the advocates of a guaranteed income hoped for.* This was true in a large sense, and true also of the specific political and psychological gains which the president himself might reasonably hope for if he took initiative. In a response to the McCracken argument, on June 6 I contended that *"Timing is the issue."* Welfare reform was in the air. Dozens of proposals were being readied. One way or another the 91st Congress was going to take up the issue. The question for the president was whether the discussion would center upon *his* proposal or someone else's. President Johnson's Commission on Income Mainte-

* The distinction between an "incremental" change and a "quantum leap forward" is much in the eye of the beholder: this makes for the greatest difficulty in actually testing the Lindblom hypothesis. The general observation may be made that in retrospect programs such as food stamps will often be seen to have involved major changes in policy which were obscured at the time because the start-up costs of the program were small and because it was not presented as anything of extraordinary import.

nance Programs would by autumn be ready with its report which "will propose a system very much like Family Security, but somewhat broader." Finally, there was the matter of the budget. I wrote:

I am really pretty discouraged about the budget situation in the coming three to five years. I fear you will have nothing like the options I am sure you hoped for. Even more, I fear that the pressure from Congress will be nigh irresistible to use up what extra resources you have on a sort of ten percent across-the-board increase in all the Great Society programs each year. This is the natural instinct of the Congress, and it is hard for the president to resist.

If your extra money goes down the drain I fear in four years' time you really won't have a single distinctive Nixon program to show for it all.

Therefore, I am doubly interested in seeing you go up now with a genuinely new, unmistakably needed program, which would attract the attention of the world, far less the United States. We can afford the Family Security System. Once you have asked for it, you can resist the pressures endlessly to add marginal funds to already doubtful programs.

(In the course of the 1960s a major transformation occurred in the understanding of the budget process, and of the ability of the Federal government to forecast income and expenditure. In mid-decade the Bureau of the Budget began drawing attention to the concept of the "fiscal dividend," which Charles L. Schultze, one of the Budget Directors of the period, defines as "The difference between projected revenues and expenditures . . . the money available in future years for discretionary use by the president and the Congress to expand existing programs, to create new ones, to reduce taxes, or to hold as a surplus for economic stabilization purposes."[23] Because an expanding economy produces expanding revenue, it appeared that the difference between income and outgo at full employment would normally be positive, leaving the president and Congress something like $5 billion to $7 billion a year in "new" money, i.e., for which no prior claims or commitments existed. The magical property of the dividend was that, unless spent, it could not be depended upon to reappear. The phenomenon of "fiscal drag" would intervene.

POLITICS OF A GUARANTEED INCOME | 177

(This analysis—perfectly accurate so far as anyone could tell—served to ease concern in Congress about the prospective extravagances of the Great Society, and just as importantly for the first time established benchmarks which enabled national social policy to be pursued as something like an art of the possible. The Eisenhower years had demonstrated the great difficulty of abolishing existing programs; new initiatives would have to come from new money and now for the first time there appeared a general understanding as to just how much new money might be available. The onset of the Vietnam war, which began to have serious budgetary impact almost the very month that the Bureau launched the notion of the dividend, eclipsed the subject for a period, but it was waiting for Nixon on his return to Washington in the form of a twenty-five-page section of the 1969 *Economic Report of the President* consisting of the report of the Cabinet Coordinating Committee on Economic Planning for the End of Vietnam Hostilities. The report was a sober document representing itself somewhat otherwise. Assuming the end of hostilities in Vietnam and a 20 percent decline in real defense outlays, it estimated a "peace-and-growth" dividend for fiscal year 1972 of $22 billion, to be followed by an "annual peace-and-growth dividend" of some $7 or $8 billion a year. It was manifest that the "peace" portion of the dividend could only occur once, and the report was explicit that a simple "selection" of "highly eligible claimants" in the form of expanded existing programs and proposed new ones added up to $40 billion a year.

It is clear that the Nation cannot carry out all these activities—funding existing programs, undertaking new program initiatives, and reducing taxes—in the next few years from the peace-and-growth dividend; difficult choices based on a careful determination of priorities will be necessary.[24]

(Even so, the impression was probably intended and certainly received—it being generally in the air—that the end of the war in Vietnam would make great sums available for domestic programs. This was not the case, as those in the Nixon Administration who wished to avail themselves of these sums learned early on. The prospective growth of existing programs was greater than generally appreciated. The Vietnam war had given rise to a pattern of program initiatives which involved small-to-modest "start-up" costs, which thereafter grew to considerable dimensions. Vietnam had to a degree been financed by a run down of military stores, accompanied by the obsolescence of facilities and equipment elsewhere. Etc. With one thing and another it was clear that the president, whatever his wishes, would find budget room for only a very few major initiatives in his first term, and he was not guaranteed a second.) *

---

* In a 1970 publication, Schultze confirmed this after making his own fiscal and budget estimates. "In all these calculations," he wrote, "the amount available . . . is exceedingly small compared to the aspirations of various parts of the Nation for expanded Federal programs. . . ." In 1971 he extended this view into the following presidential term: "Between fiscal 1972 and 1974, there will be no fiscal dividend." Charles L. Schultze, et al., *Setting National Priorities: The 1971 Budget,* Washington, The Brookings Institution, 1970, p. 188; *Setting National Priorities: The 1972 Budget,* Washington, The Brookings Institution, 1971, p. 319. In the third volume in this series, *Setting National Priorities: The 1973 Budget,* Washington, The Brookings Institution, 1972, Schultze and his colleagues took an even stronger stand, arguing that new taxes would be necessary to meet projected expenditure. In this formulation the message got through somewhat, and there was considerable public comment.

The capacity of economists to agree on such issues across party lines marks the onset of a potentially important advance for reality-testing in government. On the other hand, there is likely to be a considerable lag of public acceptance of agreed on "facts," especially where they are disagreeable. There is a legitimate sense in which FAP was made possible by the "peace-and-growth" dividend. In effect it put the new administration on notice that it could not plead budgetary constraints if, as expected, it pursued a cautious social policy. I took the estimates at face value on first encountering them and argued that, for all the tight budget years immediately ahead, the prospect of the dividend meant the administration would have to have a *large* program ready to take effect two to three years hence when peace would surely have come. By early spring I was familiar enough with the forward budget estimates to know that there was not going to be any dividend, especially as Congress was moving toward further tax cuts, which in combination meant the Federal government was heading for a period of considerable financial imbalance. However, the political culture continued to insist that the public sector of the economy was "starved," for all that the political economy had become one of galloping public expenditure. This required an interim strategy which *also* argued for FAP, i.e. for the president to put together one package of "bold" spending proposals—FAP and revenue sharing—as a holding action until Congress and the public caught up with reality. Later I sought to hasten this process somewhat. At a press conference at San Clemente on August 25, 1969, two weeks after the measures were proposed, I stated in response to a question that there was not going to be any "peace-and-growth" dividend. I half supposed this was by then general knowledge in the press corps, and thought to enhance the stature of the new proposals by making clear that they had been made in the face of budgetary constraints that would have precluded any

Mine seemed a sensible argument to Nixon, who sent a copy of the memorandum to Mayo, who in turn distributed it within the Bureau of the Budget. From there it made its way into the press, which was now reporting the Great Debate with that curious mixture of precise information, gossip, speculation, and fantasy which makes up much of Washington journalism. This itself had become a factor for the president to consider. It was no longer possible for him to make a private decision, nor, if the matter went on too long, to avoid the appearance of inde-cisiveness.

In terms of the indications presidents give their staffs, Nixon's attitude toward FAP was positive from the outset, and if anything grew more so. He reached a decision well before he let on, although his intention was disclosed to a small circle. For a period beginning in late April, however, the proposal came under heavy attack from Arthur Burns. In the repeated pattern, this led to modifications in the final proposal which *increased* its scope and expense.

Burns was opposed to FAP at several levels. There was first a strong ideological distaste, which was probably held more strongly by his associates than by himself. In mid-April Martin Anderson, of Burns's staff, prepared "A Short History of a 'Family Security System'" in the form of excerpts on the history of the Speenhamland system, the late eighteenth-century British scheme of poor relief taken from Karl Polanyi's *The Great Transformation*. The account was vivid enough, and disturbingly familiar. In this view the Speenhamland system had been set up with the best of intent, but "in the long run the result was ghastly." It had been designed to prevent the proletarianization of the common people, and instead led to "the pauperization of the masses." Their productive capacity was drained, their inde-pendence destroyed, their self-respect shattered. Was it not the

---

but the most urgently important measures. Alas, the facts were not general knowledge, even to "insiders," and one learned anew the cost of bearing ill tidings.

It may be noted, however, that a seemingly haphazard political system can produce surprisingly stable results. Edwin S. Cohen, Assistant Secretary of the Treasury for Tax Policy, reported in 1972, that the reduction in individual income tax rates of 1964, 1969, and 1971 had the overall effect of keeping the effective Federal Income Tax level at about 10.6%, roughly the level it had averaged for the preceding fifteen years.

case, Anderson inferred, that FAP was merely Speenhamland writ large? Would it not have the same effect? A fair question. The president asked for a response.

The Urban Affairs staff rushed to the historians. Gertrude Himmelfarb was consulted at Brooklyn College, J. H. Plumb at Christ's College, Cambridge. As it turned out, Polanyi's view, widely held in England, had been rejected by American economic historians. Speenhamland had been no great success, but no great failure either. Unemployment, pauperism, agricultural productivity, in the eighteen Speenhamland counties had been no greater than in those without the system. One article concluded: "Far from having an inhibitory effect, it probably contributed to economic expansion."[25] The essential problem with Speenhamland was that it imposed a 100 percent tax on earnings up to the poverty line. The parish made up the difference between a man's income and his family's requirements, measured by a physiological standard of need. Below the "poverty level" each extra shilling of income meant a shilling less in his allowance from the poor rates.* FAP, as could be made unmistakably clear, did not do this.

On April 21 Burns submitted to the president a report entitled "Investing in Human Dignity: A Study of the Welfare Problem." It was an alternative to FAP. Reviewing the scant evidence relating to the rise of welfare rolls, he judged it to be an

* Two years after Anderson compared FAP with Speenhamland, the radical social-welfare theorists Frances Fox Piven and Richard A. Cloward did so as well. They observed:

> The most recent example of a scheme for subsidizing paupers in private employ is the reorganization of American Public welfare proposed in the summer of 1969 by President Richard Nixon; the general parallel with the events surrounding Speenhamland is striking. The United States relief rolls expanded in the 1960s to absorb a laboring population made superfluous by agricultural modernization in the South, a population that became turbulent in the wake of forced migration to the cities. As the relief rolls grew to deal with these disturbances, pressure for "reforms" also mounted. Key features of the reform proposals included a national minimum allowance of $1,600 per year for a family of four, coupled with an elaborate system of penalties and incentives to force families to work. In effect, the proposal was intended to support and strengthen a disturbed low-wage labor market by providing what was called in nineteenth-century England a "rate in aid of wages."

Frances Fox Piven and Richard A. Cloward, "The Relief of Welfare," *transaction*, May 1971, p. 39.

effect largely of higher benefits and more liberal or lax administration. He agreed with the view that there had also been a considerable rise in the proportion of eligible families actually receiving benefits. This led him to think the worst might be over: "It is possible that the crisis atmosphere surrounding the welfare problem will start to recede." He was alarmed that in an atmosphere of false crisis the Nation should make a fundamental shift in social policy.

The so-called Family Security System is a plan for guaranteeing incomes of people. In its technical form, it is simply a specific application of the negative income tax, as formulated by Milton Friedman.

It was this issue of principle that most troubled Burns.

The most basic concern is, or at least should be, that government seems to be shifting from a welfare policy aimed at those who cannot help themselves toward a policy of income maintenance. Put differently, we have been moving away from the concept of welfare based on disability-related deprivation and need to the concept of welfare as a matter of right.

He very much doubted that FAP "would have the beneficial effects on family structure that its proponents claim," and, as at Key Biscayne, he astutely foresaw that critics would make the worst of the plan, howsoever generous its intentions might be.

It would not be long before social critics point out that our very poorest families pay a marginal tax rate of 50 percent, whereas moderately well-to-do families pay only 20 percent or 25 percent.*

---

* Were this a personal memoir I should discourse at length on this remarkable man. It is enough, however, for me to say that our debate was never nasty and that, in my view, Burns was far more often correct in his forecasts than I was. An economist of formidable power, he is even more an intellectual in that singularly brilliant Middle-European Jewish tradition. Far better than I, he foresaw what would be the response to FAP among an element of academics and social welfare professionals. In Britain, for example, the Family Income Supplement introduced by the Conservative government has been assailed by poverty-oriented lobbies for imposing a "surtax" on the poor. Just the charge Burns anticipated. (See *Social Service Review,* March, 1972, p. 106.) If the point was not made in the United States it was surely because the anti-FAP polemicists preferred more global concepts such as the "abolition of the 14th

He reminded the president that during the campaign, in an address to the Association of American Editorial Cartoonists, he had spoken against such proposals, declaring

I take a dim view of these schemes that right off the bat would say: "Everybody whether he works or not, whether he's willing to work or not, is going to get something from the government." This, I think, would be the wrong approach. . . . One of the reasons that I do not accept and have not recommended, and at the present time do not see a reasonable prospect that I will recommend, a guaranteed annual income or a negative income tax is because of my conviction that doing so, first, would not end poverty, but second, that while it might be a substitute for welfare, it would have a very detrimental effect on the productive capacity of the American people.

Finally he noted the Gallup poll: 62 percent of the population opposed a guaranteed income: "Those opposing the guarantee exceeded those favoring it in every income category, including those at the very bottom of the income scale."*

Amendment." Welfare dependency grew enormously in the period immediately following Nixon's proposal, but is likely, owing to demographic forces, to reach a plateau by the mid-1970s.

* The Nixon quotation is from a question-and-answer exchange held May 17, 1968. Read in its entirety, Nixon's statement was considerably more positive than Burns recalled. He specifically stated, "I'm not prepared at this time to rule out the possibility of guaranteed annual income. . . ." He referred to the Canadian family allowance, and generally showed himself familiar with the subject. Nixon had spent the 1960s out of office, reading. Almost certainly he had read more of the literature on competing antipoverty strategies than did any of the various Democratic candidates of 1968. The transcript of the occasion includes the following passage.

> CARTOONIST: Mr. Nixon, do you feel that the guaranteed annual wage is the answer to poverty? And number two, do you think it is really possible to eliminate all poverty? Do you think, believe that all poverty in the country can be eliminated?

> NIXON: The objective of any great society is of course to eliminate poverty to the extent that it can be. Any realist knows that all poverty cannot be eliminated, because this finally comes down to individuals. And no matter how much you do for some individuals, unless they develop some responsibility, they're going to be poor. And that is a fact that I think those people who are in the Poverty March would recognize to be the case.

> Now as far as the guaranteed annual income is concerned, I'm not prepared at this time to rule out the possibility of a guaranteed annual income, or of a negative income tax—which as you know is one proposal of the more conservative group of people who are trying to find a substitute for welfare. That's why all this argument is taking place. Or what

Burns's memorandum then repeated the proposal he was known to favor: that each state be required to meet national standards of welfare payments, and to establish an unemployed-parent category of AFDC payments as a condition of participating in revenue sharing. These two measures, he argued, would respond to the problem of the "mercilessly low" benefits in the South, and would do as much as anyone could for the problem of family desertion. He went on, however, to propose large new programs to enable welfare recipients to obtain work. "Half of all AFDC mothers," he reported, "are not now employed either because they are deficient in labor-market skills or because their presence in the home is required for child care." He proposed special job training and job placement centers to work with those on welfare rolls and "those who are welfare-prone." Most importantly, he focused on the issue of day-care facilities, calling for a "substantial improvement and expansion." It appeared that, as of 1967, only 19,000 children, less than half of one percent of the children in AFDC families, were being cared for in such centers.

---

the Canadians have adopted, as we know, the family allowance plan, which is their answer as a substitute for welfare.

In my view, however, one of the reasons that I do not accept, and have not recommended, and at the present time I do not see a reasonable prospect that I will recommend, a guaranteed annual income or a negative income tax, is because of my conviction that doing so, first, would not end poverty, but second, that while it might be a substitute for welfare, it would have a very detrimental effect on the productive capacity of the American people. I do not agree with those who say that each individual has within him an urge to create as much as he can. I wish that were the case; I happen to believe that individuals need the carrot and the stick in order to create as much as they can.

And so under these circumstances, I want—whether we're talking about a guaranteed income or a negative income tax or a family allowance—I want enough leverage in any kind of a plan so that the individual receiving that kind of assistance feels that he has some kind of incentive to do more, to do better, to do something for himself. Let's face it—government could provide health, housing, income, clothing, for all Americans. That would not make us a great country. What we have to remember is that this country is going to be great in the future to the extent that individuals have self-respect, pride, and a determination to do better. And I am against any system which would destroy or reduce that incentive, that determination, that self-respect, and that pride. That's why I take a dim view of these schemes that right off the bat would say, everybody, whether he works or not, whether he's willing to work or not, is going to get something from the government. This I think would be the wrong approach.

Specifically, this Administration should commit itself to the inclusion of a comprehensive day care center program in its broad effort to improve human resources. The goal should be a nationwide network of conveniently located day-care centers, utilizing buildings currently in existence (schools, churches, factories, etc.) to the extent feasible. The successful experience we had during World War II with the Lanham Act demonstrates that such an effort can be effective.

It was probably at this point too late for Burns to reverse the course of events that was leading to the adoption of FAP, but it is near certain that his April proposal led to the modification and further enlargement of the program. The president had been satisfied with the rebuttal to the criticism of the Speenhamland experiment, *but these and other documents increasingly focused his attention on the question of work incentives.* FAP would impose a minimum marginal rate of taxation of 50 percent on the earnings of the working poor.* For them, and especially for AFDC families most of which would receive state supplements over and above the FAP grant, even higher marginal rates of taxation would take effect as earnings impinged on eligibility for a wide range of services, such as public housing, Medicaid, day care, and such. Burns, an economist of international reputation and a life-long friend of Milton Friedman, was not likely to overlook so crucial an issue as marginal rate of taxation on earnings. George Shultz, also an economist, and a colleague of Friedman's at the University of Chicago, was no less concerned. The president's interest in work incentives had a certain political edge to it; with Shultz it was altogether a professional matter. He was Secretary of Labor and concerned to increase employment. The interests of the president and the Cabinet officer were thoroughly compatible. At this point the president probably felt that Shultz, of all his aides, could give him an objective and professional appraisal of the FAP proposal. He asked him to appraise it from the point of view of work incentives.

On June 10, Shultz submitted a report to the president which proposed nearly to double the cost of the Family Assistance Plan. The proposal was promptly accepted.

* A marginal tax rate is the percentage of additional income which is paid in increased taxes. Thus, if a person's income increases by $500 and, as a result, he pays an additional $250 in taxes, the marginal tax rate is 50 percent.

Such was the repeated pattern. The more the problem of dependency was examined, the greater the difficulty seemed. From this it followed that even larger efforts would be required if any significant changes were to be effected. In part, this reflected the type of advisers he consulted, and in part the lessons those consultants had learned from the experience of their predecessors. The presidential advisers of the Kennedy and Johnson era had underestimated the difficulties of social change. This was, perhaps, a general characteristic of American governmental analysis in the postwar period: a naiveté born of noble purpose. The limits of policy were less and less emphasized while the potential for matters to get worse rather than better was increasingly ignored. By 1969, however, some of this had become clear. There was, further, a not unimportant convergence of political and analytical interests. Social issues needed more rigorous analysis; Nixon needed something to distinguish his Administration from that of his predecessors. I proposed a theme which quickly caught on in the president's circle, and which later became official: his was a *reform* Administration. It sought to change not the goals of American society, but rather the institutional arrangements by which the society sought to achieve those goals. This was the central assertion of the Nixon State of the Union Message in 1970, and again in 1971. (It does not appear to have been much of a political success. The president did not come across as a reformer. The Democratic party had no interest in helping him to do so. The press remained skeptical. But this *was* what Nixon himself felt to be the case.)

Burns, in his opposition to FAP, brought to the effort formidable analytic powers. Over and over again he would ask in what way FAP would contribute to family stability, an avowed objective. His question could not be answered because there was no answer. There was a hope that the provision of income support for "intact" families would in some way lessen the strains of life at the margin, and diminish the incentive for families to increase overall income by having the women and children go on welfare. But it was no more than that: a hope. There were no data. The opponents of FAP knew this. So did the advocates. It may well be that the quality of social-science analysis that went into the formulation of the Family Assistance Plan had not before been equaled in government. Unfortunately for the advocates, the state of social science at this time was such as to require repeated acknowledgment, if not assertion, that with respect to perfectly good questions there were simply no good answers.

(This most certainly had an effect on Nixon's later advocacy of FAP. The program was formulated in an atmosphere of sustained uncertainty. Two years after the event, Max Ways commented: "Supersalesmanship and 'bold' promises are often needed to overcome . . . inertia. President Nixon's 1970 support of FAP was hedged with such commendable caution that some observers called him lukewarm toward it."[26] Part at least of the difficulty FAP encountered arose from a conflict in styles of advocacy. Liberal Democrats, disposed to large solutions to social problems, had become accustomed, if not addicted, to having such proposals described in large, even loose, terms, as for example, the "all-out war on poverty." Nixon had grounds for wishing to distinguish the quality of his proposal from those of his predecessors, but this imposed a quality of restraint in his own pronouncements that made it genuinely difficult for persons who might otherwise have supported him to believe, or perhaps more accurately, to *feel,* that he was truly behind the measure he proposed. Social science does not much serve the symbolic needs of politics.)

Shultz, from the very beginning, had been a supporter and advocate of FAP, a fact the president knew well enough in asking him for comment. His report—it was more than a memorandum—was ready June 10. It began by asserting the complexity of the subject, and by deriving from that the conclusion that the only thing the government could be moderately confident about was that the most powerful motivation it could bring to bear on the poor would be money.

The AFDC program has brought the welfare system to the point where it is less a solution than a contributor to dependency. The most instructive lesson in this, as in the history of some other efforts to modify arrangements at the core of human existence, is that the changes in human behavior which are the key to the success of FAP* are extremely hard to predict.

* "FSS" in the original text.

The FAP* seeks to restore to the welfare system the purpose of reducing dependency by including the male *in* rather than forcing him out, by supplementing earnings from low-wage employment, and by building a Federal floor.

The prospects for success in this attempt hinge on the effects of human behavior in such basic matters as working, marriage, rearing of children, and family dissolution. Many of the most powerful forces involved are virtually invisible; but one, the ability to understand and the desire to follow economic self-interest is clear and clearly related to movement from welfare to work.

The Department of Labor knew something of this transition process. In fiscal year 1969, 17,500 public-assistance recipients received classroom training as part of the Federal manpower program. A year later, only 58 percent of those who completed their training were employed and, because of a high dropout rate, only 37 percent of all those who entered training were employed the following year. The jobs were nothing special. Of 1967 public-assistance women graduates, a quarter were earning less than $1.50 an hour, and half less than $1.75. The 50-percent marginal tax rate of FAP would reduce such earnings to a rate of 75¢ to 87½ ¢ per hour. Not much incentive.

Shultz went on to show what the tax rate would be in actual practice. It costs money to work. Estimates varied, but $15 per week was in the lower range of probability. It appeared likely, moreover, that a considerable number of welfare recipients had small incomes from casual employment that went unreported. A "rock-bottom" estimate of this unreported and untaxed income over the whole of the FAP population was $10 per week for men and $5 for women. In addition to the cost of going to work, this income would normally have to be given up by persons assuming a full-time job. In these circumstances a woman working thirty hours a week at $1.50 an hour would be hardly better off under FAP than if she stayed home. She would earn $45. Half of that—50¢ on the dollar—would be deducted from her FAP payment. It would cost her $15 to go to work and she would give up $5 in unreported earnings. The hypothetical woman worker would gain $2.50 by thirty hours work. Given Shultz's estimates, the hypothetical male worker would be *worse* off by $2.50. In

* "FSS" in the original text.

1967 there had been some 6 million full-time jobs paying less than $60 a week, which is to say $1.50 per hour. Under the original FAP proposal, the net additional income of anyone holding such a job would be $5 or $10 a week: too little to sustain the incentive for work. Thus appeared the all-important concept of *the cost of working*.

The Shultz paper was appropriately complex. The Federal government was about to try to improve the lives and change the behavior of millions of persons whose misfortunes were thought in some degree to have arisen in response to an earlier effort of the Federal government to improve their lives and change their behavior. No one could say for certain how the earlier effort went wrong. No one could say for certain what would go right. Nor why: "the most powerful forces involved are virtually invisible." At the very least, Shultz argued, the government ought not repeat the elementary mistake of the original ADC legislation, with its 100 percent tax on earnings. He had been able to demonstrate that in actual operation FAP would have almost the same effect. He therefore proposed an "earnings disregard" of $20 per week, that is to say, a zero tax rate on that much earned income, to be followed by a 50 percent rate. This would offset the cost of working. He estimated that the "earnings disregard" would increase the cost of FAP by $1 billion. He further estimated that a "significant though indeterminable" number of working poor would move "from work to FAP* and, perhaps then, to training and back to work." It would be foolish, he contended, to suppose that no one would leave ill-paid disagreeable work if a guaranteed income was available. Such persons, it was hoped, would then cycle through a training period and finally back to work. The costs of such cycling, in terms of increased FAP payments for persons who left the labor force, would be in the order of $600 million. The cost of FAP, with the earnings disregard and additional training and reduction in work would be $1.6 billion greater than the original estimate. Shultz presented a new cost table.

An item in the Shultz paper reported that the Bureau of the Budget was projecting the cost of the AFDC program by 1975 to be $8 billion. In this light, a $6.6 billion estimate for FAP did

* "FSS" in the original text.

Annual Costs and FSS (billions)

	Original Proposal	Amended Cost
Benefit payments	$4.4	$4.4
State costs	(2.7)	(2.7)
Federal costs	(1.7)	(1.7)
Earnings exclusion of $20 per week	—	1.0
Training and child care	.6	.6
TOTAL	$5.0	$6.0
Possible cost due to reduction in work	—	$ .6

not seem quite so formidable. No program with an annual cost anywhere near this was being considered in the White House, but here was an existing situation which it appeared was only going to get worse on its own, and might get better if the Administration invested a few extra billion at this early date.

These calculations from the field of political economy had large consequences, not least because they were reasonably well done—better surely than at any previous occasion. On balance, the statistical quality of the FAP planning was notable. The Federal government had acquired the habit of developing five-year forecasts of expenditures of major programs. Meant to inform policy, inevitably this practice influenced it as well. In the past, as welfare costs rose from year to year, it was possible to sustain the hope that perhaps the period of increase was over, that "next year" would see a leveling off. Generally, if not invariably, it was in the interests of welfare administrators to encourage this view, or at least not to resist it. This was now no longer possible. The Budget Bureau forecasts were not especially sophisticated, but neither were they simpleminded. They assumed trends would continue, barring some fairly powerful exogenous influence of a kind no one was able to define, much less detect. In a direct way these forecasts supported the case for a bold initiative in welfare. If the existing situation seemed bad enough, the prospective one was worse.

The advocates of FAP held out the hope—it was not more than that and was never stated in stronger terms—of a gradual decline in the total population receiving income supplementation as the combined effects of economic growth and income maintenance moved families out of poverty and dependence. It was contended that somewhere about mid-decade the costs of FAP would be lower than the costs of existing welfare, if the latter continued on its projected course. This was an argument of some force. The influence of such data was increased by the establishment of a "technical committee" headed by Paul O'Neill of Nathan's office, to make estimates of the costs of the various versions of the two basic proposals—Burns's and that of the Urban Affairs Council—which rather filled the air from early to late spring. All the contending parties were represented on the committee. Once it "costed out" a proposal, its estimates were never seriously challenged.

Even greater influence may be ascribed to the availability at this time of detailed information about the "poverty population." The FAP initiative was a second stage in the War on Poverty. It depended heavily on data gathering that had begun in the first stage, especially the 1967 Survey of Economic Opportunity carried out for OEO by the Bureau of the Census, in which a representative sample of 18,000 households was combined with an additional 12,000 poor, largely nonwhite units. By early 1969 a simulation model had been developed which permitted various versions of FAP to be "tested" and costs to be estimated. Most of this work was done by The Urban Institute, which made its information available to all who requested it. Thus, in time the Congress was to have before it the same data as the executive branch had worked from. So did persons outside government, persons for the program and persons against it. This was a situation probably without precedent in the development of major social legislation; it disciplined and informed the debate for those in any degree disposed to restraint in the discussion of public issues. Once the president had made the proposal, and congressional hearings were beginning, the Administration could in good conscience make statements about the effects it would have which never previously could have been made with any pretense to accuracy. Thus an October 2, 1969, statement sent by Finch to Congress:

The Family Assistance Plan is a revolutionary effort to reform a welfare system in crisis. With this program and the Administration's proposed Food Stamp Plan, the Federal government launches a new strategy—*an income strategy*—to deal with our most critical domestic problems. For those among the poor who can become self-supporting, this strategy offers an avenue to greater income through expanded work incentives, training, and employment opportunities. For those who cannot work, there is a more adequate level of Federal support.

If the Family Assistance and Food Stamp proposals are enacted, we will have reduced the poverty gap in this country by some 59 percent. In other words, these two programs taken together will cut by almost 60 percent the difference between the total income of all poor Americans and the total amount they would have to earn in order to rise out of poverty. In one particular category of the poor, that of couples over 65 years of age, the Family Assistance Plan will in fact raise recipients' income above the poverty line altogether.[27]

During this period the government was also sponsoring carefully designed negative income tax experiments in New Jersey, Iowa, and North Carolina (that is to say, one urban and two rural programs), and planning additional ones in locations such as Seattle. The New Jersey Graduated Work Incentive Experiment, conducted by the University of Wisconsin Institute for Research on Poverty in conjunction with Mathematica, Inc., a Princeton research firm, had begun in August 1968. It was to be completed in 1972. Events, in a sense, overran it. Well before it was completed, a president had embraced its principles and its hoped-for conclusions, to the extent at least of deciding that a "Graduated Work Incentive" system could hardly be worse than "welfare." Inevitably there arose a conflict between the methodological demands of social science and the political needs of Congress and the Administration, and, perhaps just as inevitably, the latter won out. In the course of the FAP debate, the persons conducting the New Jersey experiment "broke into" their data at the request of OEO. It was necessary that such findings as emerged be labeled "preliminary" and unavoidable that the experimental program would not exactly match the FAP proposal. (Four grant levels—50, 75, 100, and 125 percent of the "poverty" line were being used in New Jersey, and three negative tax rates—30, 50, and 70 percent.) Even so, the preliminary findings provide some information about an arrangement without precedent in social experience at a time when positive information was badly needed: 509 of the 1,359 participating families were "examined" and the results reported to a Cabinet meeting on February 18, 1970, by Donald Rumsfeld (who had become Director of OEO the previous May) and John O. Wilson, a Yale economist who had become Assistant Director for Planning, Research, and Evaluation. The findings, promptly given to the press, were emphatic enough, but also were stated in a way that did no injury to academic standards. Government was beginning to handle such matters in a professional manner.

CONCLUSIONS

This experiment was specifically designed to provide evidence about the effects such a program would have for the person it is designed to assist, give realistic cost estimates, and offer suggestions for implementation.

We believe that these preliminary data suggest that fears that a Family Assistance Program could result in extreme, unusual, or unanticipated responses are unfounded.

Furthermore, we believe these preliminary data from the New Jersey project indicate that a Family Assistance Program is practical. The data suggest that:

1. There is no evidence that work effort declined among those receiving income support payments. On the contrary, there is an indication that the work effort of participants receiving payments increased relative to the work effort of those not receiving payments.

2. Low-income families receiving supplementary benefits tend to reduce borrowing, buy fewer items on credit, and purchase more of such consumer goods as furniture and appliances.

3. The Family Assistance Program, excluding the Day Care Program and Work Training provisions, can be administered at an annual cost per family of between $72 and $96. Similar costs for the current welfare system run between $200 and $300 annually per family.

What would have happened had the findings been negative is impossible to say, yet it is the case that quite inconclusive findings on the question of family stability were reported in a straightforward manner.

Another important question is whether an increase in income would decrease the divorce, separation, and desertion rate among families.

While the experiment was not designed to specifically address this question, data . . . suggest that an increase of income of the levels examined in the experiment has little impact on family stability.[28]

The report noted that this finding conflicted with Census data "which reports that family stability increases significantly as income rises." A table showed the results.*

By mid-June the Administration was in something of an anomalous position. From almost the day that it had taken office five months earlier, an intensive, informed, and on balance competent policy debate had been going on. The president now knew more about the subject of welfare and negative taxes than any predecessor. He had, moreover, reached a general decision to propose a course of action without precedent in the history of social policy, one which also marked a singular departure from the posture of the Republican party through most of the twentieth century. That he was bent on this course was increasingly known outside the Administration, albeit the matter was not taken as settled, and its implications were scarcely appreciated. Yet he had as yet nothing *specific* to propose. There was no message to Congress, no bill. This was not a matter of oversight or sloth. To the contrary, it reflected a generalized condition that partly determined the fate of the proposal once it had been made.

The essential fact is that there never before had *been* "a welfare bill" of this complexity. The task of drawing one was as much an effort at codification as of simple drafting. There was no cadre of experienced technicians to fit the new part into the existing machinery. It was more a matter of designing a new

FAMILY STABILITY

	Control	Experimental
Husband present at start of program	92%	94%
Husband not present at start of program	8%	6%
Husband present at end of program	86%	85%
Husband not present at end of program	14%	15%

* The professional integrity of this report was later challenged in the Senate Finance Committee. See p. 511.

machine. Few persons in the executive branch had much relevant experience for this task, and there were fewer still in the legislature. The main consequence of this was to be an extraordinary preoccupation in Congress with those provisions that seemed familiar, which is to say the provisions surrounding the old AFDC program, in contrast to the provisions for the profoundly new proposal for a negative income tax. In general, this meant that the greatest amount of effort was expended on the least important matter. In turn, such efforts made marginal issues central: partly because of this, the bill finally was lost in the 91st Congress.

The president faced up to his situation in the aftermath of the Burns and Shultz memoranda, which provided him with the elements of a balanced, internally consistent, and imposing program. He needed to get a series of documents prepared, and to do so with as little further disruption within staff as could be managed. He assigned the task to Ehrlichman, who forthwith set up a working group headed by Edward L. Morgan, Deputy Counsel to the President. Nathan, Price, Anderson, and Patricelli joined the group, as did Jerome M. Rosow, Assistant Secretary of Labor for Policy Development and Research. (Rosow had drafted the Shultz memorandum.) The establishment of the Morgan group was an event of surprising significance. Until that moment the development of FAP had been very much in the hands of Democrats, either those held over from the previous Administration or, in my case, returned to Washington after having worked under Kennedy and Johnson. Now Republicans took over. Of all the Morgan group, only Rosow was a Democrat.*

The remaining members were young political executives, highly educated, and not less highly motivated. Morgan was the best young lawyer on the White House staff, probably the best in the Administration. Price had a superb sense for policy issues; Anderson possessed a devastating, if sometimes rigid, analytical

* For what institutional interest it may have, Rosow was the third incumbent of an Assistant Secretaryship that had been established in the Kennedy Administration, and which I first held. Concern with matters such as income and family structure persisted in the Department of Labor policy planning staff, where career officials such as Paul Barton became especially knowledgeable on the subject. This lent surprising continuity to the analysis of the problem of dependency from the beginning to the end of the 1960s.

mind; Patricelli, an unmatched sense of the Congressional process; Nathan, a driving but disciplined commitment to social
change. Rosow, an older man with business experience, brought
his own qualities of tempered idealism to the group, but its basic
ethos was that of Republican liberalism. Nathan, in particular,
espoused a "Republican style" of social planning, free, as he felt,
of the blowsiness that had characterized many Democratic initiatives in the preceding years. He and Price and some of the others
were more than a little aware that it had been given them to
mount a fundamental social initiative which had been available
to the Democrats, but which had been rejected in favor of highly
questionable alternatives.

This was a view I held, and did not conceal, but more
importantly it was affirmed in repeated exchanges with the economists of the Johnson Administration who had provided the
rudiments of FAP. They had been understandably put out by the
rejection of their proposals when their own party was in power.
They were now near to overwhelmed that the *Republicans* would
dare what the Democrats would not. They said as much. Within
OEO, for example, there had been from the outset a group of
economists who had felt that the community-action–Head Start
orientation of early years was a futile and wrongheaded strategy
with respect to problems of poverty. They knew well enough that
the confrontation politics of the community-action programs had
instantly aroused the suspicion and finally the fury of President
Johnson, who was trying to lead a great coalition only to find the
largest single agency in the executive office of the president
seemingly intent on tearing it apart. (What actually occurred in
the community-action programs around the nation is not the
point here: this is what Johnson perceived as happening.) Some,
at least, knew that even before Head Start was launched there
had been serious professional doubts that it would succeed, but
that these doubts had been swept aside on essentially political
grounds.

All this in turn was known or sensed by the Morgan group.
It lent an *esprit* to their work which was surely something new
for Republicans. Harlow was fond of recalling that when his
party had returned to office under Eisenhower there was no
Republican either in the White House or the Congress who knew
how to introduce a bill. Things were not very different sixteen

years later, but for the first time in a very long while there were young Republicans in positions of power and influence who were determined to learn.

Three documents were now required: a presidential address announcing the new proposal, a message to Congress proposing it, and a draft bill incorporating the measure. This work proceeded more in parallel than in sequence, with different persons doing different tasks. The address was given August 8, the message sent August 11, the bill finally arrived in Congress October 2.

These were splendid hours for the Nixon Administration: a time of immense promise. It was not to last. His "popularity" in the Gallup poll peaked at 68 percent in November 1969, and thereafter began a steady decline.[29] As with President Johnson before him, he became entangled with the war and with issues of race in ways that made him ever more vulnerable to attack. By the turn of the year the moment had passed. Still, the Nixon Administration too had its period of high spirits and great expectations as had those of Kennedy and Johnson. Things had not gone badly in the first half of 1969, but neither had there been much glory. Circumstances, advice, and his own predilections had initially led him into a dreary and divisive tussle with Congress in an effort to extend the surtax which had finally been imposed as an anti-inflation measure in response to war expenditures, and to authorize the continuance of the Anti-Ballistic Missile program. In this respect the beginnings of the Administration accurately anticipated the main course of later events. Symbolically, and in large measure substantively, Nixon adopted the foreign policy of the Johnson Administration and there commenced an extended, painful process whereby the Democrats dissociated themselves from that record and the Republicans embraced it. It mattered little that Nixon began to "wind down" the war, at least at the level of troop involvement, and that from the outset hoped to do so at an even faster rate than developed; nor did it make any difference that he never really publicly declared his support for the war. The only fact that mattered in terms of the national press and the liberal audience was that he did not denounce it and dissociate himself from it. Just as importantly, he enabled large cohorts of those who had begun that vastly misconceived calamity to rewrite their own history, and more or less to be believed. Very possibly this was inevitable, but it did not appear so in the summer of 1969, and never became irreversible until the "incursion" into Cambodia almost a year later.

In July of 1969 the events immediately in prospect were of a very different order. The flight of Apollo 11 was scheduled for the end of the month. With a near casualness that cannot have a counterpart in all of human history, the Americans were making arrangements to send a man to the moon and return him safely to earth; more precisely, they were to send three, two of whom were to walk about. As part of the entertainment, it was arranged that their president should be standing on the deck of a warship halfway around the world from the seat of government, waiting to greet them on their return. It all came off perfectly: the triumph of so many things, not least, as was noted at the time, the triumph of "straight" America, the greatest engineering feat in history. (How much America had changed could be judged from how quickly the miracle came to be seen as a commonplace. This was partly, no doubt, the effect of satiation with technological wonder, but also of cultural change. Increasingly, the culture would not approve what the polity could achieve, even an achievement that fulfilled a truly Appolonian challenge set by John F. Kennedy himself.) From the South Pacific the president continued westward, and arrived at length to a tumultuous welcome in Bucharest. He was thus the first American president to journey behind the Iron Curtain. (He began there, or at least stepped up, the process of rapprochement with Communist China.) The potential of a conservative Republican president to do things in foreign affairs unthinkable, or at least unmanageable, for a liberal Democrat, was unmistakably on view.

From Bucharest he returned to Washington, where he performed the same feat in domestic affairs. What a time! In a period of less than four weeks he sent three Americans to plant the Stars and Stripes on the moon, and was on hand to welcome them back. He then visited eight countries in nine days, talking of peace and giving rise to considerable expectation that he might bring about an end not only to the war in Southeast Asia, but, more importantly, that he might be arranging a dramatic restructuring of the whole of international relations, leaving behind the obsolete rigidities of the Cold War, moving into a new era of polycentric communism with the East interacting with a not less flexible *entente* of Western democracies. He returned home to a major restructuring of government, including the guarantee of an income for all Americans: a social program of unprecedented extent and presumed consequence.

These events, occurring in concert, reinforced one another. The improbable became commonplace. The anxieties and fears and suspicion which showed up early enough in the Administration, and which came later to pervade it, momentarily evanesced. The difficult was done promptly; the impossible took only a little longer.

A certain amount of confusion occurred. The president for a period planned to send the FAP message to Congress on July 14, before the flight of Apollo 11. Too much was going on to make this possible. On July 19, however, Press Secretary Ron Ziegler announced that on August 8, five days after the president would return from Asia and Rumania, "He will request national television time to outline to the Nation the Administration's new domestic program." This would include "a dramatic new proposal on welfare." At last things were coming together, and doing so in an atmosphere of exuberant success, seemingly in all things.

Still, somehow, the struggle over FAP continued. Early in July the Morgan group had been given the president's instructions. It was to take the basic FAP plan and add to it the work-incentive features proposed by Shultz, and the "work requirement" proposed by Burns. The question of cost had now to be faced. From the earliest discussions it had always been assumed that any welfare reform proposal would increase benefit levels and establish national minimum standards in the "adult" categories, which is to say, Old-Age Assistance, Aid to the Blind, and Aid to the Permanently and Totally Disabled. This was not only a matter of equity but of politics. The recipients of aid in these categories represented an important constituency of the Social Security Program. These were "deserving poor," and they were voters. Congress would very much want to associate any transformation of the AFDC program with improvements in these categories also. As with AFDC, benefit levels in adult categories ranged widely, "from $40 per month for an aged person in one state," as the presidential message was to declare, "to $145 for the blind in another." (Mississippi in the former case, California in the latter.) In 1968 the average of payments in Old-Age Assistance was $68 per person; for Aid to the Blind, $91; and for Aid to the Permanently and Totally Disabled, $81. These levels contrasted with an average payment per person under AFDC of $42. It was agreed to propose a minimum payment of $65 per month for all three adult categories, with the Federal government contributing the first $50 and sharing in payments above that level. It was estimated this would cost some $400 million per year.

The Schultz and Burns proposals now added further costs. It was decided to create an additional 150,000 training "slots" for welfare recipients who wished to take advantage of the work/ training incentives to be built into the benefit schedule, and to this was added provision for day care for the estimated 450,000 children of the 150,000 recipients. Once again the logic of the dependency problem was expanding the government response. Day-care proposals had been circulating in Washington for years, and the usual scattering of small programs had begun. This by contrast was a massive proposal, comparable to Head Start itself. Within the Administration it came to be seen as an essential element in the president's proposal. Schultz in particular felt that the availability of high-quality day care for children would be a more powerful incentive for mothers to take training than any income inducements *per se*. The program would be expensive. The combined training and day-care component was estimated at $600 million, but this almost certainly was low. All the same, in contrast perhaps to Head Start, it was a program that fitted into a larger proposal for social change and one which could reasonably be defended as necessary to the success of the whole.

The Bureau of the Budget had hoped to impose a $2-billion ceiling on the cost of welfare reform. (That is to say, $2 billion over and above the costs of the existing welfare system.) This never proved possible. The Nathan group produced a serious estimate of $4 billion for all the many new things involved, but even this was probably low, although not egregiously so. There would be a tendency for the costs of such items as day care to rise above the budgeted estimates, but the program was not open-ended. The benefits to families were estimated at $2.5 billion, which was a "hard" figure derived from the Survey of Economic Opportunity. There were state savings of some $700 million to be had from the new program, so that the overall "public" cost could be depicted as less than $4 billion, but this never weighed much with any of the principals. By mid-July it was clear that the president was heading for what was then an enormously expensive proposal.

As this emerged, grumbling in the Cabinet mounted; an uprising of sorts almost took place among the older, more traditional Republicans. Yet as had been the consistent pattern throughout the debate, even the most conservative members of the Administration found themselves advocating positions which a year earlier would have seemed at the very least advanced. On July 24, as an example, Secretary of Commerce Maurice H. Stans stated his strong opposition to FAP, but his not less firm support for Burns's alternative proposal of establishing minimum national standards and mandatory AFDC-U. He estimated this would cost $1 billion, and endorsed Burns's proposal to pay for it out of the first $1 billion of revenue sharing, which had for long been an agreed upon part of the "Administration's new domestic program" soon to be announced.

On August 4 the vice-president addressed a long memorandum to the president stating profound misgivings about FAP and displaying considerable insight into the dynamics of liberal politics. He favored the Burns proposals, as Stans did, and he was much interested in "foster care and liberalized adoption laws." But he did not care for anything else he was hearing.

For example, the liberal community has for years been drumming into every ear the idea that it is mean and wrong to keep a close eye on people who receive assistance. We have fallen into the trap of nodding our heads when this is said. I for one do not believe it.

It was a fair point. FAP would make some 24 million persons eligible for income maintenance on no greater certification process than their own say-so on an affidavit. A conservative, Agnew distrusted it. He felt thousands of recipients in New York City were already cheating under this system. (Two years later this would turn out to be the case, but it would have been thought quite reactionary to say so in August 1969.)[30] The vice-president wished to care for the dependent, but he was not disposed to do anything much beyond that. In any event, and most important, he felt FAP would be a political disaster.

Finally, Mr. President, as your principal political representative, I cannot overemphasize the danger in the Family Assistance Plan* as proposed. It will not be a political winner and will not attract low-income groups to the Republican philosophy. The $6 billion estimated for the program will be greeted on the Hill with shouts of derision, and the liberal Democrats will propose that three or four times that amount should be spent. After months of heated oratory, suitably whipped to a froth by the liberal press, the issue will be Nixon's niggardly ideas against the progressive proposals of the . . . Democrats.

It is important to realize how accurately professional politicians, like professional soldiers, can anticipate the tactics, if not always the strategy, of their opponents. *The vice-president's forecast of what would happen was more or less exactly what did happen,* with the important exception that by and large the "liberal press" did not give overmuch support to the Democratic effort to make the Nixon proposal seem "niggardly." It gave enough. The *Washington Post* was almost alone among national newspapers in trying to explain FAP and to explain what would be the cost of the Democratic alternatives Agnew had predicted would be proposed. (Some were to range as high as $100 billion.) The typical reaction elsewhere was that FAP was "inadequate, but . . ." Almost certainly Nixon would have been better off politically to have taken Agnew's advice, to propose no new program, to let the states and cities turn against welfare recipients, and to use his own money to give Great Society lobbies enough new funds to keep them satisfied. The country might not have been better off, but he would have been. But to the president's mind the matter had come to a choice between a patchwork effort on the existing system and the establishment of an altogether new system that had at least a chance.

This decision was past him, and his mind now focused on details of the program that were likely to make it more effective,

* "Family Security System" in the original text.

or to win more support. In Bucharest he decided that the $1,500 basic benefit for a family of four was too low. On August 1, Ehrlichman, who had traveled east to meet him there with the latest developments in the program planning, called Morgan from Rumania to ask what alternate formula could be contrived that would stay within the overall cost estimates.* In the days that followed a new formula was worked out. The basic benefit was raised to $1,600, and the "Shultz disregard" reduced from $1,000 per year to $720, thereafter described as $60 per month. A simple fact to record, but a complex achievement nonetheless. The new benefit schedule was *not* worked out on the back of an envelope, in the manner of presidential task forces and Congressional committees of the past. It was run on a computer, and the cost data that came back was probably as accurate as anything of its kind ever done in American government. Such tinkering seemed endemic to the program. It did not cease with the presidential announcement, but rather continued to the last week of the 91st Congress. In the end this may have led to a degree of confusion and uncertainty as to just what the program was, and this probably did some harm. And yet, nothing more faithfully reflected the state of mind of the planners, for whom the issue at stake was the replacement of a dependency-oriented welfare system with a guaranteed income. Within that framework, details were seen as largely optional. It was assumed there would be changes by Congress before enactment, and thereafter the program would be the subject of the ritual election-year adjustments that had become a feature of Social Security legislation.

The Albany meeting produced such a change even before the legislation had gone to Congress. Rockefeller was concerned that the "high payment" states such as his own would obtain little "fiscal relief" under the proposed legislation, inasmuch as the

---

* As it happened, Morgan received the call in the state Capitol in Albany, where he, Nathan, and I had just begun a meeting with Governor Nelson A. Rockefeller for the purpose of explaining the new program, and, we hoped, of winning his support. A sense of the extent to which the whole initiative seemed problematic to the White House staff up to the very end may be had from my own response to Morgan's being called out of the room to take a call from Bucharest. It *could* have been to report the president had changed his mind. Discretion required that a puzzled governor be forced to sit through thirty minutes of reminiscences of the Harriman Administration until Morgan returned to signal that all was well.

Federal government under existing matching formulas was already contributing nearly as much to AFDC payments as it would under FAP and it was assumed that no existing benefit levels would actually be cut back. By contrast, the low-payment states of the South and elsewhere would be completely or largely relieved of any further contributions whatever. Once again it appeared that the Federal government was intervening to reward most those jurisdictions that had done least. Rockefeller proposed a solution which was employed in New York State legislation where comparable situations repeatedly arose. All states would be relieved of at least 10 percent of the aggregate AFDC costs they were then paying. The proposal already provided that no state would be relieved of more than 50 percent of its current contributions. Rockefeller's proposal, which was all but accepted on the spot, led to the "50–90" formula, according to which welfare reform would insure all states of at least a 10 percent saving on welfare costs, and that for some the proportion would be as high as 50 percent.

At this time the decision was made that the president's address should not be confined to the welfare issue, but rather that this particular proposal should be presented as part of a fundamental reordering of governmental structure and technique. The president had by then fully embraced the concept that his was a reform Administration. His address on August 8 would begin with an assertion of the post-liberal condition

an urban crisis, a social crisis . . . a crisis of confidence in the capacity of government to do its job.

He would go on to list the reforms he had already proposed:

. . . a wide ranging postal reform, a comprehensive reform of the draft, a reform of unemployment insurance, a reform of our hunger programs, and reform of the present confusing hodgepodge of Federal grants-in-aid.
. . . major tax reforms, including the closing of loop-holes and the removal of more than 2 million low-income families from the tax rolls altogether.

These, he suggested, were preliminaries. The address of August 8 had a yet larger purpose: his first major statement in office of his own vision of how the nation could emerge from the crisis that gripped it.

My purpose tonight . . . is not to review the past record, but to present a new set of reforms—a new set of proposals—a new and drastically different approach to the way in which government cares for those in need, and to the way the responsibilities are shared between the state and the Federal governments.

Three major and one lesser proposals were set forth: welfare reform, revenue sharing, a major reordering of the manpower programs that had sprung up with such profusion during the 1960s, and a reorganization of OEO. Time will be the better judge of just how "drastically different" the Nixon proposals were, but it can be fairly asserted they were more complex than most previous formulations, certainly more so than those that had been standard Republican fare since the 1930s. The proposed redirection of power and responsibility was neither up nor down the Federal scale. The proposal was neither to weaken nor to strengthen the national government, nor state, nor local government. Rather, the effort was to redress imbalances that had developed in the Federal system, identifying what would be the major responsibilities of different levels of government and providing some rough correspondence between responsibility and capacity.

Welfare reform moved responsibility—and power—upwards. The ancient prerogatives of the county commissioner and the state board to set standards according to local or regional preferences and resources were to be reduced sharply, even, up to a point, eliminated. Poverty was a national problem, to be approached in terms of national standards, and dealt with in the largest measure with national resources, and by national bureaucracies. In a more subtle, but more important, way it asserted the primacy of national initiatives in the sense that the most important events would normally take place in Washington. Michael Harrington, a socialist much concerned with problems of poverty, would describe Nixon's proposal as "the most radical idea since the New Deal." And yet it was more than that. The New Deal had been, and remains, the central symbol of the national government taking the initiative in the face of national domestic crises. But even Roosevelt's initiatives were in considerable measure modeled on innovations that first occurred at the state level, notably New York and Wisconsin. There was no state antecedent to FAP. It was an arrangement no state could institute on its own; it was an idea that could be seriously implemented only by the national government, and on a national scale.

Beyond the specifics of the proposal, the decision to make income-support levels for the poor a national issue carried a built-in bias toward liberality, at least from the perspective of American political science. Party competition is most intense at the national level, from which, it has been argued, competition for votes leads to a fairly sustained bidding process by which benefit levels in universalistic programs tend to rise at regular intervals. This had been the experience of Social Security. It was assumed within the Administration that it would be that of FAP payments as well.

Revenue sharing moved power—and possibly some responsibility—downwards. As with the negative income tax, it was a proposal of large potential, a significant innovation in the development of American federalism. It was, however, a *conservative* adjustment, seeking to restore arrangements and dynamics that had fallen into disrepair and even disrepute over time. Like the NIT, it had also a complex political etiology.

In *Republican Papers* Laird himself wrote the chapter on "The Case for Revenue Sharing."[31] In 1958, he had been the first congressman to introduce general revenue-sharing legislation and was personally identified with the issue. And yet here again the proposal had *almost* been put forth by the Johnson Administration. This had occurred in 1965 under the sponsorship of Walter Heller, President Kennedy's first chairman of the Council of Economic Advisers, who had worked out a proposal in association with Joseph Pechman of the Brookings Institution. At the last minute the decision was reversed by President Johnson. Within his Administration it was generally understood that this was due to opposition from the labor movement, in the person of George Meany. Labor preferred to believe that national decisions concerning income redistribution tend to be more egalitarian than local decisions and held to its view. Historically labor had done little enough to raise such issues to the national level, but it had soon enough learned the advantages of the arrangement, and come to be protective of it.

But circumstances had changed since the New Deal. By the 1960s the basic equations of the American political economy reflected the fact that for every one-percent increase in the Gross National Product the revenue of the Federal government, derived primarily from the graduated income tax, and from business taxes, increased by one and one half percent. By contrast, the revenues of state and local governments, overall, increased by considerably less, or so at least was the understanding within the Nixon Administration. Similarly, it was assumed that a one-percent increase in GNP either generates or is accompanied by an equivalent increase in the demand for government expenditure. It followed that the capacity for new initiatives would flow abnormally to the national level, while protracted fiscal crisis would be the lot of state and local government. Reality was never quite so grim, but the general condition did obtain, and as talk of the "urban crisis" grew steadily more apocalyptic in the course of the decade, the case for some kind of response was strengthened. The fiscal arrangements of federalism were in pressing need of reform.[32] In his article Laird cited Murray L. Weidenbaum, a Republican economist, who was already an accomplished and energetic advocate of the reform.

. . . a basic conclusion . . . is that the nation will begin to solve its long-term governmental budget problems if it links its actions on the potential federal surpluses with the anticipated deficits in state and local budgets.*

More was at issue than merely the transfer of resources between levels of government. The hypothesis was at least tenable that the innovative capacity of state and local government was being lost to fiscal exigency. It was not less reasonable to argue that, for all its rhetoric, the priorities of the Federal government could all too easily be diverted from domestic matters, as had been so painfully evident in the final Johnson years. On this point Laird was able to cite my own remarks to a

---

* Weidenbaum became Assistant Secretary of the Treasury, with special responsibility for the revenue-sharing proposal.

National Board Meeting of Americans for Democratic Action in the fall of 1967.

> . . . liberals must divest themselves of the notion that the nation, especially the cities of the nation, can be run from agencies in Washington.
>
> . . . the biggest problem of running the nation from Washington is that the real business of Washington in our age is pretty much to run the world.
>
> As far as I can see, an American national government in this age will always give priority to foreign affairs. A system has to be developed, therefore, under which domestic programs go forward regardless of what international crisis is preoccupying Washington at the moment. This in effect means decentralizing the initiative and the resources for such programs.
>
> It is indeed a fact that it is so much more pleasant to be able to stroll across Lafayette Park to endorse or to veto a public works program than it is to have to go through the misery of persuading fifty state legislatures. But that has to do with the personal comfort of middle-aged liberals, *not with the quality of the government action that results,* and in a time of some trouble, comfort cannot be the sole consideration.
>
> The . . . theory involved is that the national government and national politics is the primary source of liberal social innovation, especially with respect to problems of urbanization and industrialization. *I do not believe history will support this notion.* The fact of the matter is that it has been from the cities and to a lesser extent the State governments that something like a preponderance of social programs have come in the twentieth century, for the most part, of course, cities and states of the North. There are many reasons for this, of which probably the most important is that until recently these have been the areas where such problems first appeared, and where the wealth and intellect—and political will—existed to experiment with solutions. . . . *If this potential has not been much in evidence of late, it is mostly, I believe, because we have allowed State and local government to get into such fiscal straits that they have no resources for innovation left to them.* But the impulse and potential remains, and it is to be found there rather than in Washington. [My emphasis.][33]

The essentials of the Nixon revenue-sharing proposal, as sent to the Congress on August 13, were those Laird had espoused. A stated percentage of personal taxable income would be distributed each year among the fifty states and the District of Columbia on the basis of population, adjusted for each state's revenue effort. The latter provision entailed a small bonus for those states that taxed themselves most heavily, moderating a presumed, if not proven, bias of categorical aid grants. "Budget stringencies" dictated a small beginning—$500 million for the second half of fiscal year 1971—but the amount would rise to $5 billion by mid-1975. As a proposal "to test new engines of social progress," Nixon's scheme had one provision that singularly contrasted with that considered by his Democratic predecessor. The Heller-Pechman plan, as it came to be known, had provided simply that Federal revenues would be shared with the states. The latter could then do with the money as they would. Whether they would devote it to resolving their local "urban crises" was something the national government could neither guarantee nor influence, withal that liberal doctrine generally held they would not. By contrast, the Republican proposal provided for an automatic pass-through of Federal revenues to cities and counties and subdivisions. Each unit of local "general purpose" government would receive an amount "based on its share of total local government revenue raised in the state." Once again there would be a reward for extra effort.

(Here it may be in order to observe that while Nixon's decisions were considerably influenced by social science findings concerning the nature of the problems with which he dealt, his *behavior* does not at all accord with what is generally supposed to occur. Nixon had been elected by white, middle-class voters who lived outside the South and outside the central cities. A theory of political behavior would hold that while the president had no large incentive to direct the benefits of his legislative program to this group, he ought to have concentrated on a group "nearest" to them in political attitudes and interests, in this case (such was the understanding of the time) the "conservative" upper-working class, in order to gain additional supporters. He did not do this. In two massive initiatives he proposed to devote almost all of the free resources he assumed he would have during his first term to precisely those who had voted against him and who were least likely to do otherwise in the future. The FAP proposal would cover 19,990,000 persons. More than half—52 percent—would live in the South. Almost one half—43 percent—would be nonwhite. More than one third of the nonwhite families in the Nation would begin receiving income supplementation under the program. In overwhelming proportion the adults in these various families would be Democrats. Increasing their incomes would almost certainly—by the witness of political scientists—increase their propensity to vote. Against Republicans.* Now, to compound matters, the president was proposing to share Federal revenues with his most natural of political antagonists, the big-city mayors. It was understood in the White House at the time the revenue-sharing proposal was finally agreed upon that of the twenty largest cities only the first and the nineteenth had Republican mayors, and of those two only number nineteen could be considered even reasonably reliable from a political point of view.

(Moreover, the president had not advocated either of these proposals during his campaign. His opposition to a negative income tax has been noted. With respect to revenue sharing he simply had no record, or at least none that had impressed his aides. On July 28 Burns had sent to him the report of the task force on revenue sharing which had assembled the Administration's program. The best it could evoke by way of a Nixonian antecedent was a singularly vague statement attributed to him "in 1968": "I plan a streamlined Federal system with a return to the states, cities, and communities of decision-making powers rightfully theirs."

(The mystery is not to be resolved. It is simply that presidents do not always behave as political actors ought. A political scientist might well have predicted Nixon would get little "credit" for his proposals among those who would be most benefited, and that correspondingly he would lose some support from those who might have expected him to give first priority to their claims. This is about what happened.)

---

* In the mid-term election of 1970—an election which the Nixon Administration viewed as crucial for the success of its legislative program—among the groups voting most strongly against Republican candidates were those likely to be the major beneficiaries of FAP. According to an analysis by the University of Michigan Institute for Social Research, 97 percent of the Negro electorate voted for Democratic senatorial candidates; similarly, Republicans gained only 29 percent of the Senate ballots cast by low-income individuals and 35 percent of those by Southerners. For all three groups, however, turnout was well below the average. About 38 percent of each group voted.

The third of the major proposals in the August address concerned manpower training, "one of those phrases," the president noted in his message to Congress of August 12, "with a fine ring and an imprecise meaning." He proposed a Manpower Training Act that would rationalize and in significant ways improve the various programs begun in the 1960s, and gradually turn their operation over to the state governments. Here the direction was both up *and* down. In March the president had announced a reorganization of the Manpower Administration of the Department of Labor—again an effort the preceding Administration had *almost* embraced, *almost* carried off; now he proposed to reorganize the whole manpower system on which expenditure had risen in short order to some $3 billion per year. The original Manpower Development and Training Act, one of Kennedy's major achievements, was to be merged with Title 1-A, the Job Corps, and Title 1-B, the Community Work and Training Program, of the Economic Opportunity Act passed under Johnson. The latter two programs had always been "intended" for the Department of Labor, or at least coveted by it. Chance had located them in OEO, but even so from the outset Labor had carried on the programs, such as the Neighborhood Youth Corps. Now they would come together in a unified statute, to be administered by a considerably more rationalized Manpower administration. There would be a large manpower program, with national standards watched over by a national agency. A "counter-cyclical automatic 'trigger'" would increase expenditures "if rising unemployment were ever to suggest the possibility of a serious economic downturn."

Simultaneously, the actual operation of manpower programs, that is, the decisions as to what projects to fund, would gradually be turned over to the state governments as each first achieved a "comprehensive manpower planning capability," then established a "comprehensive Manpower Training Agency," and finally met "objective standards of exemplary performance in planning and carrying out its manpower service system." At this point in time a vast manpower program was being administered in tiny detail from Washington. Yet the pattern was not fixed. Most of the programs involved were seven years old at most. There was still time to decentralize the effort, and there was reason to think this might have advantages.* The proposal made sense, and was later largely adopted by Congress.

In the presidential campaign Nixon had hardly held out the prospect of the establishment of a negative income tax, and had not really said anything about revenue sharing either. On the other hand, he *had* suggested he would abolish the Job Corps. Now he proposed to make this and comparable activities an established feature of the national manpower program. The matter came to this: in office his instinct was to continuity. Evaluations of the Job Corps performance, while nothing so dismal as those of Head Start, were hardly exhilarating. The expense was considerable and the results modest. The Civilian Conservation Corps analogy was not working out well, which is to say that the city youth of the 1960s did not readily take to life in isolated encampments. But, as with Head Start, it represented a promise made by the national government and the argument for maintaining the effort was stronger than that for reneging.

This judgment was most in evidence in the last of the president's August proposals, the reorganization of the Office of Economic Opportunity. The most popular OEO activities had now been transferred to regular departments. Of those remaining, the largest involved the Community Action Programs. These were not popular with the Congress, and were already being duplicated by the Community Development Agencies of the Model Cities Program. It would be easy enough in the circumstances to let OEO lapse, but the opposite decision was made. A major reorganization was proposed that strengthened program

* These were not necessarily the advantages either some of the supporters or the opponents of this decentralization might have expected. Martha Derthick has drawn a useful distinction between a primarily administrative decentralization in which certain operational responsibilities are delegated from higher to lower units and a decentralization of authority, enlarging the influence of diverse sets of public values on the nature of the programs being conducted. Administrative decentralization presumably permits greater flexibility in adjusting national programs to local conditions and, hence, produces more effective programs; the decentralization of authority would ideally enable state or city governments to decide, e.g., whether or not even to undertake a manpower program. Because of its gradual devolution of responsibility, under standards of performance established by the Federal government, the manpower reforms proposed by the Nixon administration are more of the first than the second type identified by Derthick. See Martha Derthick, *The Influence of Federal Grants,* Cambridge, Massachusetts, Harvard University Press, 1970.

activities which seemed most successful, particularly the Office of Health Services and the Office of Legal Services, and retained activities such as VISTA which were of considerable symbolic importance to the War on Poverty.* Most importantly, the president chose to give the most emphatic endorsement to the concept of OEO as an instrument of innovation and social experimentation, that is to say, the type of activity associated

---

* Nixon was especially supportive of OEO Health Services, which were heavily involved in birth-control programs. On July 18 he had sent to Congress the first presidential message on population, in which *pari passu*, he asserted, *"It is clear that the domestic family-planning services supported by the Federal government should be expanded and better integrated."* An estimated 5 million low-income women of childbearing age were without family-planning services "even though their wishes concerning family size are usually the same as those of parents of higher-income groups." He proposed the establishment as a national goal of the "provision of adequate family-planning services within the next five years to all those who want them but cannot afford them." Large families being a fundamental source of poverty among the population "at risk," this proposal, soon to be endorsed by the Congress, should be seen as an integral element of the income strategy the Administration had adopted and was now seeking to implement.

Yet this and similar proposals were not always seen as part of such a general approach to social policy. Andrew Billingsley, a vice-president for academic affairs at Howard University, has claimed that Negro leadership views family planning programs as attempts to "legitimize vicious extermination" and "conjure up the spectre of genocide." Speaking to the annual national conference of Planned Parenthood–World Population, Billingsley maintained that the black population is already so small that blacks have little impact on society: "Instead of trying to stamp out the black population," he told his audience, "you should enhance it." Birth control programs might be acceptable if they were controlled by blacks and were designed to enhance freedom of choice rather than "stamping out black children before they get on welfare." The audience gave him a standing ovation at the conclusion of his speech. (Reported in the San Francisco *Chronicle*, October 27, 1971, p. 2.)

There is, of course, a certain amount of overlap between a services strategy and an income strategy that helps to produce disagreement even among men with the best intentions. Programs of social services have not infrequently masked class or ethnic aggression, no less so, perhaps, in the poverty war of the sixties than in the temperance movement of earlier decades. Yet there is a fundamental difference between a program which provides for the distribution of only certain foodstuffs and one which allows a beneficiary to exchange stamps for foods of his choice; or, in the case at issue, provides the means for family planning rather than the requirement (not without advocates, past or present) to do so. That the effective use of birth control directly affects family income few, certainly, among the members of Planned Parenthood–World Population would doubt. That the provision of family-planning services could be portrayed as an insidious plot is, perhaps as much as anything else, a testimony to rigidity in thinking about strategies of social change, especially among leaders of groups most apt to benefit.

with the conceptual development of the negative income tax scheme, and the experimental mode illustrated by the New Jersey project. An Office of Program Development was to be created, and the Office of Planning, Research, and Evaluation strengthened.

The presidential statement (the reorganization did not require congressional approval) issued August 11 is quite the most exuberant of the series of documents that issued forth at this time. The spirit of Apollo 11 was much in evidence, as the president called for "a new spirit of adventure," for "social pioneering," for *"Bold Experimentation."*

We live in an exciting and difficult time. We possess great strength and skill; yet we are often unable to harness our strength in the service of our ideals. We sense new possibilities for unlocking the full potential of every individual; yet our institutions too often are unresponsive to our needs. We dream of what we might be able to make of our society; but we have not yet learned to achieve that dream.

Our nation will attain its social objectives, I believe, only if we develop a new spirit of adventure in their pursuit. We must become pioneers in reshaping our society even as we have become pioneers in space. We must show a new willingness to take risks for progress, a new readiness to try the untried.

Such an innovative spirit should characterize all of our institutions and all agencies of government. But it is in the Office of Economic Opportunity that social pioneering should be a specialty. It is the OEO that should act as the "R and D" arm for government's social programs.

On August 6 the last of the many meetings on FAP took place. The president summoned the Cabinet to Camp David, where, in Laurel Cottage, his decision to propose a guaranteed income was set forth to the discomfort, even the dismay, of most of those present.

He was not without his own doubts, and the next day said as much. He felt there had been only three members of the Cabinet with him, and puzzled particularly at the disaffection of the vice-president, who had, he recalled, spoken to him of the need for national welfare standards a full six months before the Miami convention. Still, the men closest to him were in favor of

the move. Before Nixon had left for the moonshot, Laird had
spoken to him for an hour on the subject, supporting the idea.
When the president returned they went over the same ground in
another long talk, and still the Secretary of Defense was for the
program. Finch was for it, if a little shaky at the end. Shultz
never wavered.* Still, the president's own doubts remained. He
did not know how many of the persons whose income would be
raised really were seeking more dignified, stable, comfortable
lives. "But we will do it anyway," he said, more to himself than
to those with whom he was talking. We would do it "because it
has to be done."

Three days earlier, August 4, he had himself gone over the
subject one last time. He asked *why* did it have to be done?
There were no certain grounds in evidence, nor yet in conviction, that it *did* have to. There was only the momentum of a
decision-making process that had reached the point where it
would at all events be proposed. He had *already* decided. But
why?

It came down to three propositions—each now asserted at a
higher level of confidence than ever had been the case earlier.
Each he accepted. First, the poor, especially the black poor, were
being destroyed by the existing welfare system. This was becoming the most serious social problem of the time. Second, after so
very long it was time to bring the South back into the mainstream
of American life. A tired image, but a pressing reality. What fundamentally kept the South apart, and kept the Nation incomplete,
divided, was poverty. Here was the one *"Bold Experimentation"*
that might bring fundamental change. Finally, it was necessary
to prove that government could work. There was, indeed, a
"crisis of confidence in the capacity of government to do its job."
The moonshot had been one kind of success; a guaranteed income would be another, at least as important, surely more
difficult. America needed some successes.

On August 7 he of a sudden appeared at the early morning
meeting of the senior White House staff. He'd gone round the
world, he said, and never saw an anti-American sign save on a

---

* The president probably underestimated his support. Rumsfeld had been made
a member of the Cabinet, and accepted the program. Others were not so much
against FAP as in favor of their own activities, many of which were directed to
the same ostensible social goals.

bearded American in India. Later in the day he remarked that he had been reading a biography of Disraeli and of Lord Randolph Churchill. "Tory men and Liberal policies," he mused, "are what have changed the world." He had come to a turning in much of what he stood for and espoused; possibly to a deeper understanding of what he might do, how he might change the world. All about him was busyness: briefing, drafting, coaching, collating. But at the center of the storm it was very quiet.

The briefing at Camp David was carried out by Morgan and his group. It had scarcely begun before a fact of first importance became unmistakably clear. *The proposal was hard to understand*. Burns, from the beginning, had sensed that this would make it easy to misrepresent, and in this as in much else he proved altogether correct. But it was difficult to grasp even for those most disposed to support it. There were too many moving parts; the interrelationships were too rapid, too complex to follow. At one point, as Patricelli, responding to a question, moved easily through an account of the particular process involved, the president turned to Laird and asked: "How do you get that smart?"

This may have been the single most important oversight of an otherwise impressive process that led to the formulation of the Family Assistance Plan. Much attention has been, or will be, directed to the limits of government understanding of social and political processes that led, in the 1960s, to grossly misconceived ventures, of which the war in Vietnam was the most singular. A corresponding reality is the limit of public understanding, especially in such areas as family income where individuals assume they are competent, and where for their own purposes they mostly are. This problem had been identified in the debate over children's allowances as against the NIT. Steiner reports the point having been made with considerable clarity at a private meeting at the Brookings Institution in October 1968, attended by economists, welfare administrators, tax experts, and journalists.

One of the problems of the negative income tax which is perhaps surmountable but not easily so is that it is so complicated. If you say to somebody, "Why don't we have a negative income tax," the first thing he says is "What is that?" It is not a self-explanatory thing that is easy to explain after half an hour, as compared to, say, a children's allowance. That is pretty simple. You are going to pay something to people who have children because it helps them support the children.[34]

The discussion at Camp David got so far and no further. Rather like members of the Senate Committee on Finance which took up the subject the following year, there were those present who became more difficult as their puzzlement became more public. In the end Laird broke the tension and, in effect, brought the meeting to an end, with the pronouncement that he was worried about the *name* of the new program. From its first appearance in March it had been known as the Family Security System. This sounded too "New Dealish." In a rush the Cabinet seized pencil and paper and began to compose acronymic formulations of conservative cast. (The next day the speech writers came up with Family Assistance Plan, which the President adopted.)

An opportunity was lost at Camp David. Apart from those personally and directly involved, the Nixon Cabinet never really fought for the president's most important domestic proposal. It wasn't theirs. They didn't quite understand it. It was enough that a Republican Administration had proposed it. Surely it was up to the Democrats in Congress to enact it. But in the upshot the Democrats, most of them, had much the same reaction. It wasn't their proposal; they didn't quite understand it. Moreover, it didn't sound New Dealish.

If these constraints were not fully understood, they were at least sensed. The briefing of the Cabinet was preceded and followed by extensive briefings of senators and congressmen and various interest groups. (The Republican congressional leadership was briefed on Monday, August 4, two days before the Cabinet.) The essential thrust of these meetings was to make the program seem simple, sensible, and relatively inexpensive. In the circumstances it was a sound enough decision, but it distorted reality. The program was not at all simple; it was sensible given certain assumptions about conduct, but not others, and it was not inexpensive. It was the most startling proposal to help poor persons ever made by a modern democratic government. The hope of the program's advocates was that "conservatives" would take the program at face value and that "liberals" would see the reality behind it. As things worked out, the opposite happened.

As an instance of this dualism, the decision was made to describe "the basic Federal benefit" as that for a family of four, $1,600. This, as noted earlier, was accepted usage. But as can be seen from the table on page 219, the *average* family size of persons who would be covered by FAP was 5.2 persons. For nonwhites the average size was 5.8 persons. The "basic Federal benefit" could justifiably have been described as $1,900, and with reference to nonwhites as $2,200.

Food-stamp benefits, in the neighborhood of $860 for a family of four, were never computed as part of total family benefit, although they clearly were such. (At a later date the Administration proposed to include a "check-off" provision whereby the cost of food stamps would be automatically deducted from the FAP payment, and the stamps mailed routinely to the recipients.) The true "basic Federal benefit" was rather more than $2,400 for a family of four with no income. A seven-person family with no income would receive $2,500 per year in cash, with food stamps added. (The benefit schedule stopped at families of seven.)

The central difficulty, however, lay in communicating the principle of the negative tax. As will be seen in the *Welfare Reform Fact Sheet* prepared at this time by the Social Security Administration, some effort was made to show that families of four would receive benefits up to total earnings of $3,920. "Families of seven would be eligible up to $5,720." Somehow, the idea would not take. The best estimates were that the average cash income of an FAP family of four in the working-poor category would be somewhat more than $3,700. Nonetheless, the proposal was almost invariably depicted in terms of the theoretical consequences for the *dependent* poor, that is to say those with no income, as against the *working* poor, for which it constituted so great an innovation. Inasmuch as the negative tax was lower than the "poverty line"—*and had to be lower unless large payments were to be made to families above the poverty line*— FAP, or any equivalent, could automatically be made to appear wholly inadequate to its presumed purpose.* Careful efforts were

---

* This difficulty did not lessen. Almost two years after the Nixon proposal, the House Committee on Ways and Means prepared to approve H.R. 1, a second version of welfare reform. In terms of benefits it was almost identical with

made to point out the provision that required all states to maintain existing levels of benefits for AFDC families, even though they might be greater than FAP payments, as was the case in most states. This, too, proved difficult if not impossible to convey. From the moment the program was announced, it was seen and depicted by many as an effort to *reduce* welfare payments.

Some difficulty was more or less deliberately created by the Administration. In his address of August 8, the president went out of his way to distinguish between his own proposal and the fanciful schemes of others.

This national floor under incomes for working or dependent families is not a "guaranteed income." Under the guaranteed-income proposal, everyone would be assured a minimum income, regardless of how much he was capable of earning, regardless of what his need was, regardless of whether or not he was willing to work.

The president knew what he was doing, and by most standards would be judged to have been within his rights to guard against an irrational response based on the negative symbolism of ideas such as a "guaranteed income." If, as he judged, the American people were willing to support the dependent poor altogether, and to give a hand to the working poor, it was hardly his responsibility to endanger this likelihood by insisting that doing so would involve embracing the principle of a guaranteed income, which he had every reason to think the public would not be willing to do. On August 6, William Safire, in response to a mild demur about the guaranteed-income paragraph in the draft speech, explained: "You miss Richard Nixon's main point, which is to make a radical proposal seem conservative." On August 7 the president confirmed as much. "I don't care a damn about the

---

that which the president first proposed, although, by eliminating food stamps, the basic benefit could be described as $2,400 rather than $1,600. The *Boston Globe,* which had been following the subject carefully for two years, nonetheless still could not grasp the distinction between the FAP benefit and actual family income. On May 14, 1971, it commented:

The welfare portion of his [Mills's] package has some of the defects of President Nixon's Family Assistance Plan on which it is patterned. It, too, puts a $2,400 a year ceiling on welfare benefits for a family of four, even though the official poverty level for such a family is $3,720.

Summary of Cost and Coverage of the Family Assistance Plan*

Characteristic	FAMILIES COVERED		PERSONS COVERED		Average Payment Per Family	Average Family Size
	No. of Families (thousands)	Percent of Total	No. of Persons (thousands)	Percent of Total		
Grand Total	3,857	100.0%	19,990	100.0%	$ 981	5.2
Sex of Family Head:						
Male	2,295	59.5	13,151	65.8	888	5.7
Female	1,562	40.5	6,839	34.2	1,116	4.4
Race of Head:						
White	2,390	62.0	11,482	57.4	876	4.8
Nonwhite	1,466	38.0	8,508	42.6	1,151	5.8
Age of Family Head:						
65 and over	222	5.8	1,070	5.4	901	4.8
Under 65	3,635	94.2	18,920	94.6	985	5.2
Region of Residence:						
Northeast	558	14.5	2,774	13.9	1,005	5.0
Northcentral	820	21.3	4,276	21.4	1,005	5.2
South	1,943	50.4	10,396	52.0	981	5.4
West	535	13.9	2,543	12.7	920	4.8
Work Experience of Family Head:						
Worked Full-Time All Year	1,304	33.8	7,304	36.5	742	5.6
Some Work Experience During Year	1,541	40.0	7,939	39.7	960	5.2
No Work During Year	1,012	26.2	4,746	23.7	1,320	4.7

* Estimates of the cost and coverage of FAP were continually revised as changes were made in the bill or better data became available concerning potential recipients. This table was derived from "Selected Characteristics of Families Eligible for the Family Assistance Plan, 1971 Projections," February 2, 1970, Office of the Assistant Secretary for Planning and Evaluation, Department of Health, Education, and Welfare. Data are based on the 1967 Survey of Economic Opportunity. They exclude Puerto Rico, Guam, and the Virgin Islands, and also recipients under the "adult categories." Subsequent versions of this table differ only in minor respects.

work requirement," he said. "This is the price of getting the $1,600."

Thus, at the outset of the public debate, there arose a tension between symbol and substance that was never to be allayed. The proposal *was* a guaranteed income, and there was *no* work requirement. As the Social Security Administration Fact Sheet explained, "Employable recipients must accept training or employment *or lose their portion of the family's benefits."* (My emphasis.) That is to say, there was to be a penalty for refusing to work: $300 in the bill sent to the Congress, raised to $500 by the Committee on Ways and Means. Refusal to work lowered the amount of the income guarantee. Nothing more. It would have made little sense to try for more, even had any of the principals been much disposed to do so. The essence of the Shultz proposal was that incentives could be established that would draw recipients into the labor market as a result of their own calculation of benefit. Only a *naif* would think that such an outcome could be obtained in any other way. The president could exhort, the Congress could demand: welfare administrators were not going to cut off welfare payments. On balance, then, it seemed fair to describe the very considerable work incentive built into the program as a work requirement, and to hope it would be understood.

And so the matter concluded. On August 8, 1969, in a television address, Richard Nixon undertook to change the history of social welfare, of his own party, and possibly of the Nation. His address dealt with four matters. He asked that they "be studied together, debated together, and seen in perspective," but the heart of the matter was welfare.

Good evening, my fellow Americans.

As you know, I returned last Sunday night from a trip around the world—a trip that took me to eight countries in nine days.

The purpose of this trip was to help lay the basis for a lasting peace, once the war in Vietnam is ended. In the course of it, I also saw once again the vigorous efforts so many new nations are making to leap the centuries into the modern world.

Every time I return to the United States after such a trip, I realize how fortunate we are to live in this rich land. We have the world's most advanced industrial economy, the greatest wealth ever known to man, the fullest measure of freedom ever enjoyed by any people anywhere.

Yet we, too, have an urgent need to modernize our institutions—and our need is no less than theirs.

We face an urban crisis, a social crisis—and at the same time, a crisis of confidence in the capacity of government to do its job.

A third of a century of centralizing power and responsibility in Washington has produced a bureaucratic monstrosity, cumbersome, unresponsive, ineffective.

A third of a century of social experiment has left us a legacy of entrenched programs that have outlived their time or outgrown their purposes.

A third of a century of unprecedented growth and change has strained our institutions and raised serious questions about whether they are still adequate to the times.

It is no accident, therefore, that we find increasing skepticism—and not only among our young people, but among citizens everywhere—about the continuing capacity of government to master the challenges we face.

Nowhere has the failure of government been more tragically apparent than in its efforts to help the poor and especially in its system of public welfare.

Whether measured by the anguish of the poor themselves, or by the drastically mounting burden on the taxpayer, the present welfare system has to be judged a colossal failure.

Our states and cities find themselves sinking in Federal quagmire, as case loads increase, as costs escalate, and as the welfare system stagnates enterprise and perpetuates dependency.

What began on a small scale in the depression '30s has become a huge monster in the prosperous '60s. And the tragedy is not only that it is bringing states and cities to the brink of financial disaster, but also that it is failing to meet the elementary human, social, and financial needs of the poor.

It breaks up homes. It often penalizes work. It robs recipients of dignity. And it grows.

Benefit levels are grossly unequal—for a mother with three children they range from an average of $263 a month in one state, down to an average of $39 in another state. Now such an inequality as this is wrong; no child is "worth" more in one state than in another state. One result of this inequality is to lure thousands more into already overcrowded inner cities, as unprepared for city life as they are for city jobs.

The present system creates an incentive for desertion. In most states a family is denied welfare payments if a father is present—even though he is unable to support his family. Now, in practice, this is what often happens: A father is unable to find a job at all or one that will support his children. So, to make the children eligible for welfare, he leaves home—and the children are denied the authority, the discipline, and the love that come with having a father in the home. This is wrong.

The present system often makes it possible to receive more money on welfare than on a low-paying job. This creates an incentive not to work; and it also is unfair to the working poor. It is morally wrong for a family that is working to try to make ends meet to receive less than the family across the street on welfare. This has been bitterly resented by the man who works, and rightly so—the rewards are just the opposite of what they should be. Its effect is to draw people off payrolls and onto welfare rolls—just the opposite of what government should be doing. To put it bluntly and simply—any system which makes it more profitable for a man not to work than to work, or which encourages a man to desert his family rather than to stay with his family, is wrong and indefensible.

We cannot simply ignore the failures of welfare, or expect them to go away. In the past eight years 3 million more people have been added to the welfare rolls—and this in a period of low unemployment. If the present trend continues, another 4 million will join the welfare rolls by 1975. The financial cost will be crushing, and the human cost will be suffocating.

That is why tonight I therefore propose that we abolish the present welfare system and that we adopt in its place a new family assistance system. Initially, this new system will cost more than welfare. But unlike welfare, it is designed to correct the condition it deals with and thus to lessen the long-range burden and cost.

Under this plan, the so-called "adult categories" of aid—aid to the aged, the blind, and disabled—would be continued and a national minimum standard for benefits would be set, with the Federal government contributing to its cost and also sharing the cost of additional state payments above that amount.

But the program now called "Aid to Families with Dependent Children"—the program we all normally think of when we think of "welfare"—would be done away with completely. The new family assistance system I propose in its place rests essentially on these three principles: equality of treatment across the Nation, a work requirement, and a work incentive.

Its benefits would go to the working poor, as well as the non-working; to families with dependent children headed by a father, as well as to those headed by a mother; and a basic Federal minimum would be provided, the same in every state.

What I am proposing is that the Federal government build a foundation under the income of every American family with dependent children that cannot care for itself—wherever in America that family may live.

For a family of four now on welfare, with no outside income, the basic Federal payment would be $1,600 a year. States could add to that amount and most states would add to it. In no case would anyone's present level of benefits be lowered.

At the same time, this foundation would be one on which the family itself could build. Outside earnings would be encouraged, not discouraged. The new worker could keep the first $60 a month of outside earnings with no reduction in his benefits; then beyond that, his benefits would be reduced by only fifty cents for each dollar earned.

By the same token, a family head already employed at low wages could get a family assistance supplement; those who work would no longer be discriminated against. For example, a family of five in which the father earns $2,000 a year—which is the hard fact of life for many families in America today—would get family assistance payments of $1,260, so that they would have a total income of $3,260. A family of seven earning $3,000 a year would have its income raised to $4,360.

Thus, for the first time, the government would recognize that it has no less an obligation to the working poor than to the nonworking poor; and for the first time, benefits would be scaled in such a way that it would always pay to work.

With such incentives most recipients who can work will want to work. This is part of the American character.

But what of the others—those who can work but choose not to?

The answer is very simple.

Under this proposal, everyone who accepts benefits must also accept work or training, provided suitable jobs are available either locally or at some distance if transportation is provided. The only exceptions would be those unable to work and mothers of preschool children.

Even mothers of preschool children, however, would have the opportunity to work—because I am also proposing along with this a major expansion of day-care centers to make it possible for mothers to take jobs by which they can support themselves and their children.

This national floor under incomes for working or dependent families is not a "guaranteed income." Under the guaranteed income proposal, everyone would be assured a minimum income, regardless of how much he was capable of earning, regardless of what his need was, regardless of whether or not he was willing to work.

During the Presidential campaign last year, I opposed such a plan. I oppose it now and I will continue to oppose it, and this is the reason: A guaranteed income would undermine the incentive to work; the family assistance plan that I propose increases the incentive to work.

A guaranteed income establishes a right without any responsibilities; family assistance recognizes a need and establishes a responsibility. It provides help to those in need and, in turn, requires that those who receive help work to the extent of their capabilities. There is no reason why one person should be taxed so that another can choose to live idly.

In states that now have benefit levels above the Federal floor, family assistance would help ease the state's financial burdens. But in twenty states—those in which poverty is most widespread—the new Federal floor would be above present average benefits and would mean a leap upward for many thousands of families that cannot care for themselves.

These proposals are of course controversial, just as any new program is controversial. They also are expensive. Let us face that fact frankly and directly.

The first-year costs of the new family assistance program, including the child-care centers and job training, would be $4 billion. I deliberated long and hard over whether we could afford such an outlay. I decided in favor of it for two reasons: first, because the costs would not begin until fiscal 1971, when I expect the funds to be available within the budget; and second, because I concluded that this is a reform we cannot afford not to undertake. The cost of continuing the present system, in financial as well as human terms, is staggering if projected into the 1970s.

Revenue sharing would begin in the middle of fiscal 1971, at a half-year cost of a half billion dollars. This cuts into the Federal budget, but it represents relief for the equally hard-pressed states. It would help curb the rise in state and local taxes which are such a burden to millions of American families.

Overall, we would be spending more—in the short run—to help people who now are poor and who now are unready for work or unable to find work.

But I see it this way: Every businessman, every working man, knows what "start-up costs" are. They are heavy investments made in early years in the expectation that they will more than pay for themselves in future years.

The investment in these proposals is a human investment; it also is a "start-up cost" in turning around our dangerous decline into welfarism in America. We cannot produce productive people with the antiquated, wheezing, overloaded machine we now call the welfare system.

If we fail to make this investment in work incentives now, if we merely try to patch up the system here and there, we will only be pouring good money after bad in ever-increasing amounts.

If we do invest in this modernization, the heavy-burdened taxpayer at least will have the chance to see the end of the tunnel. And the man who only looks ahead to a lifetime of dependency will see hope—hope for a life of work and pride and dignity.

In the final analysis, we cannot talk our way out of poverty; we cannot legislate our way out of poverty; but this nation can work its way out of poverty. What America needs now is not more welfare, but more "workfare."

The task of this government, the great task of our people, is to provide the training for work, the incentive for work, the opportunity for work, and the reward for work. Together these measures are a first long step in this direction.

For those in the welfare system today who are struggling to fight their way out of poverty, these measures offer a way to independence through the dignity of work.

For those able to work these measures provide new opportunities to learn work, and to find work.

For the working poor—the forgotten poor—these measures offer a fair share in the assistance given to the poor.

This new system establishes a direct link between the government's willingness to help the needy and the willingness of the needy to help themselves.

It removes the present incentive not to work, and substitutes an incentive to work; it removes the present incentive for families to break apart and substitutes an incentive for families to stay together.

It removes the blatant inequities, injustices, and indignities of the welfare system.

It establishes a basic Federal floor so that children in any state can have at least the minimum essentials of life.

Together these measures cushion the impact of welfare costs

on states and localities, many of which have found themselves in fiscal crisis as costs have spiraled.

They bring reason, order, and purpose into a tangle of overlapping programs, and show that government can be made to work.

Poverty will not be defeated by a stroke of a pen signing a check; and it will not be reduced to nothing overnight with slogans or ringing exhortations.

Poverty is not only a state of income. It is also a state of mind and a state of health. Poverty must be conquered without sacrificing the will to work, for if we take the route of the permanent handout, the American character will itself be impoverished.

In my recent trip around the world, I visited countries in all stages of economic development; countries with different social systems, different economic systems, different political systems.

In all of them, however, I found that one event caught the imagination of the people and lifted their spirits almost beyond measure: the trip of Apollo to the moon and back. On that historic day, when the astronauts set foot on the moon, the spirit of Apollo truly swept through this world—it was a spirit of peace and brotherhood and adventure, a spirit that thrilled to the knowledge that man had dreamed the impossible, dared the impossible, and done the impossible.

Abolishing poverty, putting an end to dependency—like reaching the moon a generation ago—may seem to be impossible. But in the spirit of Apollo we can lift our sights and marshal our best efforts. We can resolve to make this the year, not that we reached the goal, but that we turned the corner; turned the corner from a dismal cycle of dependency toward a new birth of independence; from despair toward hope; from an ominously mounting impotence of government to a new effectiveness of government, and toward a full opportunity for every American to share the bounty of this rich land.[35]

He had not long to wait for a response. The day before he made the address the White House received a public letter from the National Welfare Rights Organization, signed by the National Chairman, Mrs. Johnnie Tillmon, and the Executive Director, Dr. George A. Wiley. "This plan," the letter declared, "is anti-poor, and anti-black. It is a flagrant example of institutional racism."

Citations—Chapter III

1. These data, compiled from Department of Agriculture publications, were presented in the Report of the Committee of the Urban Affairs Council on Food and Nutrition, March 17, 1969, Washington, D.C.
2. Steiner, *The State of Welfare*, p. 223.
3. Federal Communications Commission, "Memorandum Opinion in re: Complaints covering CBS Program *Hunger in America*," Washington, D.C., October 15, 1969.
4. Steiner, *op. cit.*, p. 231.
5. Virginia Held, "PPBS Comes to Washington," *The Public Interest*, Summer 1966, p. 102.
6. Steiner, *op. cit.*, p. 96.
7. Quoted in William E. Leuchtenburg, *Franklin D. Roosevelt and the New Deal*, New York, Harper and Row, 1963, p. 124.
8. Franklin D. Raines, "Presidential Policy Development: The Genesis of the Family Assistance Program," unpublished senior thesis, Harvard College, Cambridge, Massachusetts, April 1, 1971, pp. 46–51.
9. Cavala and Wildavsky, "The Political Feasibility . . . ," p. 352.
10. See Daniel P. Moynihan, Foreword, in James C. Vadakin, *Children, Poverty and Family Allowances*.
11. Public Law 90–248, 81 Stat 891, Sec. 402 (a)(19)(F).
12. Michael Oakeshott, *Rationalism in Politics*, New York, Basic Books, 1962, pp. 171–2.
13. Richard E. Neustadt, *Alliance Politics*, New York, Columbia University Press, 1970, pp. 148–9.
14. Daniel P. Moynihan, "Where Liberals Went Wrong," in Laird, *Republican Papers*, pp. 132, 138.
15. George Sternlieb, "The City as Sandbox," *The Public Interest*, Fall 1971, pp. 14–21.
16. Louis Wirth, Preface, in Karl Mannheim, *Ideology and Utopia*, New York, Harcourt, Brace and World, 1936, p. xvii.
17. Henry Riecken, *Annual Report, 1968–1969*, New York, Social Science Research Council, p. 15.
18. Lyndon Baines Johnson, *The Vantage Point*, New York, Holt, Rinehart and Winston, 1971, pp. 83–5.
19. Richard Burn, *The History of the Poor Laws*, London, 1764.
20. Illinois Department of Public Aid, "A Special Report: The Question of Support of ADC Children in Illinois by Fathers Not Living at Home," Springfield, February 11, 1969.
21. Sydney H. Schanberg, "Welfare Slashed by Republicans in Assembly Vote," *The New York Times*, March 30, 1969.
22. Norman Macrae, "The Neurotic Trillionaire," *The Economist*, May 10, 1969, p. 61.
23. Charles L. Schultze and associates, *Setting National Priorities: The 1972 Budget*, Washington, D.C., The Brookings Institution, 1971, p. 319.
24. Cabinet Coordinating Committee on Economic Planning for the End of Vietnam Hostilities, "Report to the President," *Economic Report of the President*, Washington, D.C., January 1969, p. 190.

25. Mark Blaug, "The Poor Law Report Reexamined," *Journal of Economic History*, June 1964, p. 229.

26. Max Ways, "Don't We Know Enough to Make Better Public Policies?" *Fortune*, April 1971, p. 118.

27. Unless otherwise noted, statements and testimony which were part of the congressional hearings on the Family Assistance Plan may be found in the following:
   United States House of Representatives, Committee on Ways and Means, *Social Security and Welfare Proposals*, 91st Congress, 1st Session, 1969.
   United States Senate, Committee on Finance, *Family Assistance Act of 1970*, Hearings on H.R. 16311, 91st Congress, 2nd Session, 1970.

28. Office of Economic Opportunity, "Preliminary Results of the New Jersey Graduated Work Incentive Experiment," Washington, D.C., February 18, 1970.

29. The Gallup Poll, "Public Confidence in Nixon at Low Point: 48 Percent Approve of Performance," Princeton, New Jersey, July 10, 1971.

30. By the end of 1971, George F. Berlinger, New York State Welfare Inspector General, was reporting that an analysis by the Department of Social Services showed that 6 percent of New York City's welfare recipients (to whom nearly $4 million per month in benefits were paid) were "ineligible for assistance." When similar findings were reported by state or Federal officials previously, city officials had contended that their figures were too high; this time there was "no immediate response." Peter Kihss, "Six Percent on Relief Here Called Ineligible," *The New York Times*, December 12, 1971.

31. Melvin R. Laird, "The Case for Revenue Sharing," in Laird, *Republican Papers*, pp. 60–84.

32. For a somewhat more optimistic view of "fiscal federalism"—which, nonetheless, concludes that some large reforms are needed—see Richard A. Musgrave and A. Mitchell Polinsky, "Revenue Sharing—A Critical View," in *Financing State and Local Governments*, Proceedings of the Monetary Conference, June 1970, Boston, The Federal Reserve Bank, September 1970, pp. 17–51.

33. Laird, *op. cit.*, pp. 63, 73.

34. Steiner, *op. cit.*, p. 98.

35. Richard M. Nixon, Nationwide Radio and Television Address, August 8, 1969.

APPENDIX TO CHAPTER III

(Prepared by the Social Security Administration in August, 1969 for general distribution.)

Welfare Reform Fact Sheet
Background Material

I. *The Present System*

A. FAILURES

The present welfare system has been a failure; all indications are that its future will be worse, not better. In the last decade, the costs of aid to families with dependent children (AFDC) have more than tripled. The caseload has more than doubled.

Even more disturbing is the fact that the proportion of persons on AFDC is growing. In the past fifteen years the proportion of children receiving assistance has doubled—from 30 children per 1,000 to about 60 per 1,000 at present.

B. INEQUITIES

Serious inequities exist under AFDC between regions of the country, between male- and female-headed families, and between poor people who work to help themselves on the one hand and the welfare poor on the other hand.

Average benefits for a female-headed family of four persons vary from $39 to $263 a month.

Only twenty-four states provide federally matched assistance to male-headed families, and this is only done where there is an "unemployed father" in the house—one who works no more than thirty hours a week. In no state is there now federally matched assistance for a male-headed family where the father works *full time*.

The present AFDC system encourages dependency. The preferential treatment of female-headed families has led to increased family breakup. In 1940, 30 percent of AFDC families had absent fathers; today it is over 70 percent.

II. *The New System*

A. COVERAGE

The Administration's proposed welfare reform will provide direct Federal payments to *all* families with children with incomes below stipulated amounts.

The principal new group made eligible for cash assistance under the proposal is "working poor" families headed by males, employed full time. The Administration's proposed system would cover *both* "dependent families," defined as those headed by a female or an unemployed father, and "working poor" families, defined as families headed by a full-time employed male.

B. BENEFIT LEVELS
1. *Families with No Earnings*

The basic Federal benefit for a family of four would be $1,600 per year, $500 per person for the first two family members and $300 for each family member thereafter. A seven-person family with no earnings would receive $2,500 per year.

2. *Families with Earnings*

Families of four with earnings up to $3,920 per year would be eligible for payments. Families of seven would be eligible up to $5,720. All families would be allowed to "disregard" $60 per month ($720 per year) as work-related expenses—transportation, meals, clothing. Benefits would be reduced by 50 percent as earnings increase above $720 per year.

C. AN EXAMPLE

A family of four with earnings of $2,000 would be entitled to disregard the first $720 in earnings.

Subtracting $720 from $2,000, the remainder is $1,280. Fifty percent of this amount ($640) is subtracted from the family's entitlement for benefits, which is $1,600. The remainder

($960) is added to the family's earnings of $2,000. Its total income, therefore, would be $2,960. (See Chart II.)

A family of seven, with $2,000 in income, using the same arithmetic, would be entitled to benefits of $1,860, for a total income of $3,860.

D. STATE SUPPLEMENTAL BENEFITS

In order that present benefit levels not be reduced for families aided under the existing AFDC program, the new system would require the continuation of state benefits equal to the difference between the proposed Federal minimum and a state's present benefit level. All states, however, would receive fiscal relief under the proposed welfare program.

States would not be required to supplement "working poor" families.

E. THE WORK REQUIREMENT

A basic element of the Administration's welfare reform program is its emphasis on work, both a strong work requirement and the provision of incentives throughout the system for training and employment. (See Chart VI.)

All applicants for benefits who are not working are required to register with the Employment Service.

Employable recipients must accept training or employment or lose their portion of the family's benefit.

F. TRAINING AND DAY CARE

To insure that employable recipients become self-sufficient, the Administration's program provides a substantial increase in training opportunities and child-care services. Training opportunities will be provided for an additional 150,000 welfare mothers. Child-care services will be provided for an additional 450,000 children in families headed by welfare mothers.

G. ADMINISTRATION

Another important feature of the Administration's welfare reform program is the national administration of the basic Federal benefit for families. It is proposed that the administration of the system be assigned to the Social Security Administration in the Department of Health, Education, and Welfare. The administration of the new system by the Social Security Administration would be handled entirely separate from its responsibility for the wage-related contributory OASDI programs.

III. *Cost of the Program*

The estimated cost in the first full year of operation of the proposed welfare reform program is $4 billion. This is additional to present Federal spending for public assistance, estimated at $4.20 billion in Fiscal Year 1970.

Major cost components of the program are:

Benefits to Families	$2.5 billion
Adult Minimum Standards	.4 billion
Training and Day Care to provide Additional Work Opportunities for Cash Assistance Recipients	.6 billion
Other: Administration, effects on other programs, fiscal relief to States, and adjustments for lagged income reporting	.5 billion
TOTAL	$4.0 billion

A. BENEFITS TO FAMILIES

The estimate above of $2.5 billion in additional spending for benefits to families is based on an interagency analysis of data from the OEO Survey of Economic Opportunity. The economic model for deriving this estimate uses data on 14,000 low-income families and current research findings.

B. ADULT MINIMUM STANDARD

The Administration's welfare reform program also establishes a Federal minimum payment level of $65 per month for the three adult public assistance categories (aid for the blind, the disabled, and the aged) and provides for the administrative combination of these programs.

Under this proposal, the Federal government pays 100 percent of the first $50; 50 percent of the next $15, and 25 percent thereafter. Fiscal relief for State and local governments as a result of this Federal minimum for the adult categories is $400 million.

C. TRAINING AND CHILD CARE

The total cost for training an additional 150,000 welfare mothers and providing child-care services for an additional 450,000 children is $623 million.

Summary of Added Training and Child-Care Costs and Enrollments

	Persons Served (thousands)	Unit Cost (dollars)	Total Cost (millions)
Training	150	$1,110	$165
Incentive payments	150	180	27
Child care	450	858	386
Upgrading	75	600	45
TOTAL			$623

IV. *Fiscal Relief to State and Local Governments*

A. UNDER THE NEW WELFARE PLAN

Under the Administration's proposed welfare reform program, all states receive fiscal relief. Each state is required to spend at least 50 percent of the amount spent in the base year for the present public-assistance programs. No state, however, is required to spend more than 90 percent of expenditures in the base year for the four categories.

B. REVENUE SHARING

State and local governments are also aided under the Administration's proposed revenue-sharing program. The first full year effect of revenue sharing is $1 billion. The amount of revenue sharing increases annually in five steps thereafter.

C. COMBINED IMPACT OF WELFARE REFORM PROPOSAL AND REVENUE SHARING

Combining the welfare-reform and revenue-sharing proposals, $5 billion in new first-year funds is distributed as follows:

Cash Assistance Benefits for the Poor	$2.2 billion
Fiscal Relief for State and Local Governments	1.7 billion
Additional Training and Day Care	.6 billion
Other	.5 billion
TOTAL	$5.0 billion

The table attached provides state-by-state data on fiscal relief under both the Administration's proposed welfare and revenue-sharing reforms in their first full year of effect.

Impact on State and Local Governments of Welfare Reform and Revenue Sharing (First Full-Year Effect)

State	Revenue Sharing	Fiscal Relief Under Welfare Reform	Total
Alabama	16.1	11.9	28.0
Alaska	1.2	1.0	2.2
Arizona	10.1	3.4	13.5
Arkansas	9.5	6.2	15.7
California	112.5	179.5	292.0
Colorado	11.6	13.0	24.6
Connecticut	12.8	8.8	21.6
Delaware	2.4	1.6	4.0
Dist. of Columbia	3.4	4.1	7.5
Florida	30.8	8.5	39.3
Georgia	20.8	12.5	33.3
Hawaii	4.8	3.3	8.1
Idaho	4.0	1.0	5.0
Illinois	44.5	49.6	94.1
Indiana	24.2	5.0	29.2
Iowa	14.6	7.0	21.6
Kansas	12.1	6.6	18.7
Kentucky	14.8	10.6	25.4
Louisiana	20.3	18.9	39.2
Maine	5.1	2.0	7.1
Maryland	18.1	14.4	32.5
Massachusetts	29.6	30.1	59.7
Michigan	40.8	35.5	76.3
Minnesota	21.5	9.3	37.8
Mississippi	12.6	.9	13.5
Missouri	20.4	18.3	38.7
Montana	3.9	1.4	5.3
Nebraska	6.6	3.4	10.0
Nevada	2.5	.9	3.4
New Hampshire	3.1	.9	4.0
New Jersey	31.1	25.2	56.3
New Mexico	5.7	3.2	8.9
New York	117.1	43.9	161.0

State	Revenue Sharing	Fiscal Relief Under Welfare Reform	Total
North Carolina	24.2	10.4	34.6
North Dakota	3.5	.4	3.9
Ohio	41.2	32.0	73.2
Oklahoma	12.6	19.3	31.9
Oregon	10.4	6.1	16.5
Pennsylvania	53.3	43.2	96.5
Rhode Island	4.3	5.2	9.5
South Carolina	12.1	2.2	14.3
South Dakota	3.9	1.2	5.1
Tennessee	18.1	8.6	26.7
Texas	47.7	25.1	72.8
Utah	5.7	2.9	8.6
Vermont	2.4	1.2	3.6
Virginia	20.4	4.7	25.1
Washington	16.2	13.6	29.8
West Virginia	9.0	4.5	13.5
Wisconsin	24.2	12.4	36.6
Wyoming	2.1	.9	3.0
TOTAL	1,000.0	735.8	1,735.8

Proposed Benefit Schedule
(Excluding All State Benefits)

Earned Income	New Benefit	Total Income
$ 0	$1600	$1600
500	1600	2100
1000	1460	2460
1500	1210	2710
2000	960	2960
2500	710	3210
3000	460	3460
3500	210	3710
4000	0	4000

(For a four-person family, with a basic payment standard of
$1,600 and an earned income disregard of $720.)

IV

The Publics Respond

1. The Limits of Professionalism

As the delegates to Governor Rockefeller's 1967 Conference on Public Welfare came down the mountain road from Arden House they found waiting for them at the gates a straggle of demonstrators, mostly women, many black, identifying themselves as welfare recipients and protesting that *they* had not been invited to join in the discussions, as indeed they had not. There had been blacks present, but in such capacities as Dean of the School of Social Services of Fordham University, or Vice-President for Community Affairs of Pepsico, Inc. No welfare recipients were at the conference, nor anyone purporting to speak for them. Two years and some months later this was the first of the charges against the Family Assistance proposal made by the National Welfare Rights Organization (NWRO), which had been organized five months after the Arden House meeting. On August 6, just prior to the president's television address, the national chairman and executive director of NWRO wrote the president:

> You have already made a serious mistake. Poor people have again been ignored in the months of "research" and inside debate which has shaped your plan. All of the usual experts have been consulted but welfare recipients and poor people whose lives are most directly affected have again been left out.

By 1969 this had become, if not a serious charge, at least one which had to be attended to. It had acquired legitimacy through the convergence of forces set in motion by the poverty program, with its stipulation that community-action activities be carried out with the "maximum feasible participation" of the poor, and of the black assertion of autonomy and self-direction which followed the civil-rights activism of the 1950s and early 1960s.

The NWRO charge against Nixon was, strictly speaking, false. The organization had been consulted; its officers had been to the White House; George A. Wiley was regularly in touch.[1] The consultation had not been extensive, but until it was clear which way the president would decide, and even then until he announced his decision, there were limits to what any outside group could be told. The internal debate was not an ugly one, and neither side sought to make it so. Neither sought to drum up outside support for its position: it would have been improper and it would have been imprudent. As for the details of FAP, they were never closely held, and as for the general position of NWRO, it was understood to be strongly in favor of a negative income tax.*

* *Science News,* in its issue of June 7, 1969, two months before the NWRO letter and the president's address, carried a report of various developments which illustrate both points.

SOCIAL WORK
Choosing a New Way

The nation's welfare programs have been a thorn in the side of city governments for a decade or more. Recently they have become a national issue, and one which the Nixon Administration is girding its loins to handle.

Last week, as Mr. Nixon was trying to pick one of several plans to revamp the nation's welfare system, the issue erupted in a raucous invasion of the 96th annual forum of the National Conference on Social Welfare by a group of insurgents trying to finance their own activist organization.

The Administration is wavering between the idea of a straight Federal minimum for welfare payments, leaving the structure of the system relatively intact, and the more radical approach of the negative income tax, called the Family Security Plan by the White House. The FSP would supplement the income of families with low incomes and support those which had no income. Under the plan, a family of four, with no income, would receive $1,500 to $1,800 annually.

The Family Security Plan, being pushed by Secretary of Health, Education and Welfare Robert H. Finch and Urban Affairs Council Director Daniel P. Moynihan, would stimulate and reward poor people to get work rather than rely entirely on welfare payments. Under the present system,

Nonetheless, there is a larger sense in which the NWRO charge was true. The evolution of FAP was a quintessential example of the professionalization of reform, a process that had been gathering momentum for years and had now become a distinctive style—one of several—in the conduct of national affairs. From the first it has been associated with problems of income maintenance, the characteristic difficulty of industrial capitalism. In the United States, well before the issue of social insurance had attracted much political attention or support, at a time when the political culture was committed to a concept of individualism in which, to cite Oscar Handlin, "any social action seemed a threat to personal liberty," the American Association for Labor Legislation, an organization of university economists, began (in 1906) a sustained effort to bring about the enactment of a wide range of social insurance legislation, and comparable reform measures.[2]

The distinctive feature of this movement, associated with the name of John R. Commons and the University of Wisconsin, was the confidence that issues such as labor legislation could be dealt with on a "scientific" basis. The ideal was "scientific social engineering," an impartial, if meliorative, process for the achievement of social justice under the leadership of the universities. It is a close question whether the more remarkable fact about AALL was its presumption or its success. From Work-

---

if a father is employed, his family gets little aid, no matter how marginal his income.

Under the negative tax plan, recipients would be guaranteed a basic annual income. The amount they received would be reduced by half of what they earned: A family that earned $2,000 would have its welfare payment reduced by $1,000. When the family income reached a cut-off point—$3,000 in the Moynihan plan—the payments would stop.

At the prestigious social welfare conference, headed by former HEW Secretary Arthur S. Flemming, the concern among the 7,000 delegates was with the basic details of social work. Week-long meetings, forums and exhibits dealt with employment opportunities in social work, relations with the black community, work with the mentally retarded, the aged and the drug addict.

But outside the meeting halls, and sometimes inside them, the insurgent members of the National Welfare Rights Organization demonstrated for a revamping of the entire public assistance system. The group's demands are along the lines of the Moynihan approach: a guaranteed minimum income and a national minimum for public assistance.

men's Compensation to Social Security, nearly the whole of its agenda was enacted in the first third of the twentieth century, with the Association playing an important role almost at all times, often in opposition simultaneously to "business" and "labor," or at least elements of each. In general, trade unions opposed social insurance, fearing it would weaken attachment to the union, and doubtless also, in the words of George W. Perkins, president of the Cigarmakers, fearing "having any of our economic activities chained to the police power of the state." Samuel Gompers thundered against the "so-called American Association for Labor Legislation" and "government by commission." Compulsory health insurance seemed to him the work of the devil, and unemployment compensation hardly better.[3] By contrast, academic intellectuals turned as if by some tropic disposition to government as the agency through which their ideas might be implemented: a disposition to be noted in Plato and never long in abeyance since.

In the mid-twentieth century, however, changes of some consequence took place in this relationship. Initiative in social issues accrued to the national government. One man, the president, became an actor of incomparable influence. Simultaneously there occurred, in Karl Deutsch's term, a "revolution in competence" in the social sciences, primarily associated with the advent of the high-speed computer. Social science began to produce hypotheses, and on occasion demonstrations that approached the quality of proofs, which were much at odds if not incompatible with the political progressivism of the time. Typically, such assertions were set forth in a form essentially unintelligible to the political world. Jay W. Forrester laid it down that, "With a high degree of confidence we can say that the intuitive solutions to the problems of complex social systems will be wrong most of the time."[4] The good common sense of the people, or even of their leaders, was no longer to be trusted. Truly? None of course could say. A considerable range of phenomena is "counterintuitive" until finally understood. The leaders of American business, presiding over the most powerful economy in the world, had encountered great difficulty in grasping the seemingly counterintuitive principles of Keynesian economics, but at length the perceptions broke through and what had first seemed absurd came to seem obvious. Now, seemingly, it was the turn of social progressives to come to terms with complexity. With this and similar developments, organized society, for all its latent and even growing distrust of experts, became ever more dependent on them and increasingly required to accept their competence on faith.

A dual need arose: to use social science and not to misuse it. For all its advances, the limits of social-science information and understanding were immensely constraining. At times the greatest danger was the presumption of knowledge where none existed. Even so, some adaptation to the new possibilities was necessary. Joseph A. Califano, an assistant to President Johnson in domestic matters, later wrote: "The disturbing truth is that the basis of recommendations by an American Cabinet officer on whether to begin, eliminate, or expand vast social programs . . . nearly resembles the intuitive judgment of a benevolent tribal chief in remote Africa. . . ."[5] A better way had to be found.

As Nixon took office it was widely held that the American republic was caught up in "the most serious domestic crisis since the Civil War." The crisis was seen as primarily domestic, bearing on the fundamentals of civil authority and public order. Writing of the 1972 elections, Richard Rovere would add parenthetically, "Assuming that democracy in America survives that long." At the heart of the perceived crisis was the condition of the lower-income groups and lower classes of the cities, primarily black, and increasingly depicted as insurrectionary. The national government had anticipated at least some of these developments and had responded. Significantly, it did so with programs largely devised by social scientists. The poverty program, enacted by the Economic Opportunity Act of 1964, was the central effort. Five years later a debate of sorts was under way as to whether it had not been vastly misconceived. Whatever the case, the conceptions were those of social science. "Maximum feasible participation" was a social-science idea, a product of intellectuals, however much it might manifest itself—as on occasion it did—in demagogic, even anti-intellectual behavior. Social science was proving no more a guarantor of social peace than any other mode of policy formulation.

It may be that the sponsors of the participation idea had not foreseen this development—certainly it took the then president of the United States by surprise—but it remains that the government had acted in response to theories of social behavior that were all but unknown to the public at large. There had been no popular demand of any kind for the poverty program. (There was some demand for employment programs, but none of these envisaged the establishment of an Office of Economic Opportunity with a large experimental component.) A number of the programs were capable of *inducing* demand, and did so, none more successfully than Head Start. But here too the initiative had been almost wholly with elites. Sheldon H. White writes of the founding of Head Start:

There was social action dictated not by grass-roots demands but by the social diagnostician: there was the urge to establish a solution outside The System which had "failed": there was scientific backing offered by the expert-turned-advocate.[6]

The difficulty here is that the expert-turned-advocate too rarely reverted to being an expert when the experiments failed to produce the hypothesized results, as seemed, in 1969, to be the case with Head Start. If evaluations were disappointing the sponsors would, too often, content themselves with denouncing the evaluator, or redefining the putative objectives of the program. Only rarely would they respond to the dilemma in which government then found itself of having promised what it could not deliver and confronting, in a crisis atmosphere, belligerent accusations that it did not because it would not.

The issue of compensatory education arose early in the Nixon Administration, and influenced the adoption of FAP. It was an issue as closely connected as any could be to the achievement of racial equality, the minimization of social-class differences, and a general relaxation of the wrenching social tensions of the time. It had been generally supposed the principles of compensatory education were understood. By 1969 the best available opinion held that they were not. This "opinion," however, was all but inaccessible to the general or even the interested public. It took the form of yet unpublished papers, of works in progress, of judgments being formed by individual researchers and confirmed in the talking circles of Cambridge, Washington, Berkeley, and other such places. Thus, the Nixon Administration, on the basis of work being done in the Harvard University Faculty Seminar on the Coleman Report, had the strongest reason to believe, with respect to compensatory education, that "the least promising approach to raising achievements is to raise expenditures, since the data give little evidence that any widely used school policy or resources has an appreciable effect on achievement scores."[7] There is a legitimate sense in which it may be said that the president of the United States knew this to be so. But the Congress did not; *The New York Times* did not; the National Education Association did not; the Urban League did not. Moreover, the president knew they did not know. Further he had to be aware that this "best evidence" now available to him might be quite reversed by the next generation of studies. Or some startling "discovery" might take place. But for the moment this was the information he had to come to terms with.

It should be emphasized that the new "findings," while raising difficulties with the programs that had been developed on social-science advice in the course of the 1960s, when not in fact rejecting them outright, did not at all suggest government had been wrong to have sought or accepted such advice, or that it would be wise to avoid such counsel in the future. To the contrary, the perceptions of the social scientists as to the *nature* of a whole range of social problems had been startlingly confirmed. After four summers of urban riots it was considerably more evident something was amiss in poor neighborhoods, and that it involved the question of community. As one big-city school system after another began to sink into a slough of failed reform, declining achievement, and mounting recrimination it was not much to be doubted that received methods of education would be inadequate to the task facing them. A set of first-order responses had followed these original perceptions. OEO was established, and with it community action, Head Start, and VISTA; the Elementary and Secondary Education Act commenced a large program of additional aid to school districts serving poor children; Model Cities began; Parent and Child Centers began; street academies began; Methadone clinics began; minority business-loan programs began; a profusion of efforts of one kind or another started. It was only in the aftermath of such efforts that it became possible to assess the effectiveness of particular meth-

ods. Few outright successes could be recorded, although it may
be that in the large a quite successful undertaking had transpired.
Urban disorders all but ceased in the summer of 1969, while by
1971 the topic itself had receded from public attention.*

But in the winter of 1968–1969, as administrations
changed, no government could foresee this decline in overt
violence, and even had that been possible a responsible Administration would have had to regard the period as breathing space
at most. Not that much had changed. To the contrary, as more
came to be known about certain problems associated with race,
the more intractable some of these problems appeared to be.
None seemed more difficult than that of educational achievement, nor less responsive to established policies. Racial equality
could only be achieved through the occupational structure—it
could only be in terms of approximately comparable employment
and income levels that the concept would have operational meaning. To achieve this it would be necessary to attain something
like equal educational achievement. It was understood at the
time that the translation of educational achievement into occupational status and income was anything but perfect, but it remained the most likely-seeming strategy. It was all the more

---

* To return? No one, of course, could know. But the point should be made
that these programs were *visible,* especially in education. A 1970 study by
Robert J. Havighurst and others reported that large city high schools serving
low-status children were likely to be considerably "better off" than nearby
schools serving middle-class children.

> One change which is favorable to the low-economic-status schools is a
> result of the use of federal funds in the War on Poverty through the
> Elementary and Secondary Education Act and the Office of Economic
> Opportunity. The student-teacher ratio is now substantially lower in low-
> status schools than in high-status schools—the percentage of high-status
> schools with student-teacher ratios of 25:1 or less is about 42, compared
> with 70 percent of working-class schools. Also, the lower-status schools
> are generally employing more paraprofessionals than the higher-status
> schools—approximately 50 percent of the working-class schools employed
> 11 or more adult paraprofessionals, against 33 percent of the middle-class
> schools. [Robert J. Havighurst, Frank L. Smith, and David E. Wilder,
> *A Profile of the Large-City High School,* Washington, D.C., National
> Association of Secondary School Principals, November 1970, p. 10:6.]

The evidence of attention being paid, care being expressed may constitute far
the more important short-run result.

serious, then, to learn that the educational system was not producing, even in optimal circumstances, anything like equal achievement.

Nor were matters improved in the early months of 1969 with the publication of Arthur R. Jensen's article, "How Much Can We Boost I.Q. and Scholastic Achievement?" "Compensatory education," the paper began, "has been tried, and it apparently has failed."[8] Jensen argued that the essential source of the failure lay in the genetic inferiority of blacks to whites in those characteristics that make for success in intelligence tests, and, by extension, in school tests generally. This was no Southern exegesis of the Old Testament. Jensen was a liberal Democrat, a respected scientist, a professor at the University of California, Berkeley, publishing in the *Harvard Educational Review*. What was government to do with this proposition? If true, and if established as such, it would pose a problem for democracy different, surely, from any of the past. *The only responsible course government could take was to proceed as if the hypothesis—it was no more than that, nor was it asserted to be—was not true, and to hope to disprove it by a reordering of the environmental influences which, in alternative views, were the essential sources of inequality. Given the extremely weak effects of available services in bringing about changes in social status, the overwhelming logic of the situation was to move directly to raise incomes at the lower levels: an income strategy.*

Thus, on another score, the presidency was led to the issue of family and family income. The essential finding with respect to schools seemed to be that by the time children entered them they were practically fully formed adults in terms of their achievement relative to others. Eight or twelve (or sixteen) years of schooling would, in gross statistical terms, affect this ranking little if at all. Schools did not seem to make matters worse, but neither did they make them better, if "better" is defined as narrowing the achievement gap between social-class groups, these being often defined by their racial proxies. The earliest years of life appeared to be formative. This at all events was the best information available to the men assuming their brief authority in the White House. In Jerome Kagan's terms, "The differences in language and number competence between lower- and middle-class children are significant by the time the child is four years old, and are awesome by the time he enters the first grade." Richard Nixon had had nothing to do with the founding of Head Start, had probably been ambivalent about Federal aid to education in the first place, and had never heard of Professor Jensen. But these were realities confronting him as his presidency began, and they argued most powerfully for a system of family income maintenance.

The difficulty, to repeat, is that these were not public realities. Some glimmer of the analysis had made its way into the press, and, not least among former government officials, there was a limited audience that would hear out such an argument. But on balance earlier views persisted, and challenges to such views were met with suspicion or hostility. This defines one difficulty with which FAP made its way into the public consciousness. The legislation was almost altogether the result of professional analysis of what was wrong and what had to be done. There was as near as can be to *no* public support for a guaranteed income. (In this respect the development of FAP is altogether different from that of Social Security. By the time the national government got round to establishing a system of old-age insurance, the majority of states had established old-age pensions.) To the degree there was any formed public sentiment it was reflected in a 1968 Gallup Poll. Fifty-eight percent of the poll opposed the guarantee of a $3,200 annual income to a family of four, the government making up the difference between the family's earnings and that amount. Thirty-six percent were in favor. The typical sentiment reported was that "nobody should get something for nothing." At the same time, majority opinion was clearly disposed to favor plans for dealing with problems of poverty and welfare dependency so long as the stigma of "something for nothing" could be avoided. In 1968 a strong majority —78 percent—*supported* a plan that would guarantee enough work each week for all employable wage earners to bring their family income to about $60 per week, or $3,200 per year. In 1971, 67 percent of those interviewed by Gallup supported the proposition, based on a postwar German scheme in which companies were required to hire a percentage of welfare recipients, with government subsidizing their wages for a period. Nonwhites favored the proposition more than whites, 77 percent as against 66 percent; unskilled workers more than professionals, 71 percent as against 55 percent; and low-income groups considerably more than high-income groups.

There was also a general presumption that widely disparate welfare payments were leading to induced migration of the poor to the large cities. In March 1969, the Gallup Poll reported that 77 percent of the public favored the equalization of welfare payments, based on the cost of living in each area. But this was about the limit of perceived public interest in or support for new income-maintenance programs.[9]

The absence of support for a guaranteed income, the general lack of interest in the subject, was necessarily accompanied by a general inability to follow the intricacies of a negative income tax which was the basic mechanism of the Nixon proposal. In the debate that followed it was manifest that a large proportion of those dealing with the matter in Congress, reporting or commenting on it in the press, supporting or opposing it in various public forums, did not at all understand the principle.

This circumstance plagued FAP from the outset. The proposal was the purest embodiment of income redistribution. With a minimum of frictional costs, the Administration proposed to transfer income from high- and middle-income families to low-income families, and from small families to large families. Those opposed to such transfer could readily enough reckon what was involved. The overall cost of the program was publicly stated from the outset. However small the sum might seem to many, it was large to its opponents. With the added consideration that it would involve a transfer of income from white families to black families, those whose interests or values would not be served by the program had little difficulty grasping its implications. In the Congress, among the lobbies, and in the media an opposition bloc effortlessly assembled. By contrast, those whose interests or values disposed them to favor this kind of redistribution easily misled themselves, or were misled by others, into regarding the proposal as inadequate and to proposing or supporting increases in benefit levels which, seemingly modest, were in fact stupendous. Few perceived this, and almost no one pointed it out.

For all the rough-and-tumble of the internal debate and the Congressional proceedings that followed, FAP was a finely calibrated proposal. A sense of this may be had from the near precise correspondence of average FAP payment levels under

H.R. 1 (which, given the absence of food stamps, provides a better indicator) and the median income deficit of poor families, which is to say the difference between the poverty level and the median income of those below it.*[10]

	All Families	White Families	Black Families
Income deficit of poor families, 1970	$1,110	$1,024	$1,316
FAP payments under H.R. 1	$1,134	$1,027	$1,304

By contrast, NWRO, in its letter to the president of August 6, 1969, asserted that "Government research indicates that a minimum *adequate income* for a family of four is $5,500 a year." This was not the case—a fact which the Commissioner of Labor Statistics would protest in vain—but the claim did rough justice to the data. In April 1969, the *Monthly Labor Review* reported the costs of three levels of living for urban families of four in the spring of 1967. The "moderate" and "higher" budgets were $9,100 and $13,000 respectively. The budget for a "lower living standard," reflecting the needs of "families who were positioned—either temporarily or persistently—at the low end of the income distribution," was calculated to be $5,915.[11] This was not a *minimum* budget, but simply a lower-level one. Even so, "Fifty-five hundred or Fight!" became the rallying cry of NWRO and the not inconsiderable congeries of individual and institutional allies which responded to it. What few seemed capable of understanding was that using the FAP model—the actual NWRO legislation, to be discussed later, was slightly different—*a $5,500 benefit level in 1971 would cost some $71 billion and cover some 150 million persons.*† Half the beneficiaries would

* This relationship is only one way of assessing the adequacy of the FAP payment level. Using other criteria which take into account the distribution of prospective FAP recipients across income levels, the proposal was also carefully designed. For example, approximately 90 cents of each dollar of FAP payments would go to families with incomes below the poverty level, a ratio considerably better than that of proposals with higher payment levels.

† The actual coverage of the NWRO plan was difficult to assess precisely. Charles Schultze and Andrew Brimmer estimated that over half of the nation's population would receive some benefits, while estimates within the government suggested that the number of recipients would be closer to 150 million.

have family incomes over $6,000, and a third over $8,000. The break-even point would not have been reached for a family of four until $11,720, and would move even higher for larger families. Charles L. Schultze and colleagues have estimated that to pay for such a program would require a surtax of 78 percent.

(In 1971, after the introduction of H.R. 1, a compromise proposal of $3,600 was put forward by a number of national organizations, which in doing so gave no indication that anyone involved comprehended that even this amount would cost $25 billion, transfer income to about 69 million people, and, again in the estimate of Schultze and his associates, require a surtax of 28 percent.[12] The American income structure may be compared to a foreshortened diamond. On the lower half even small increments bring in large numbers of persons. Few persons in Washington in this period seemed to have any feeling for these numbers.)

A proponent of the Family Assistance Plan would be hard pressed to demonstrate that its benefit levels represented a definitive and conclusive response to the problem of poverty. Had the program gone into effect when proposed, 40 percent of persons then living in poverty would have remained poor. In large measure, however, these would have been childless couples, or individuals, or members of very large families. Budget constraints confined the program to families with children, and concern about possible criticism for providing a "baby bonus" imposed a cut-off point of seven-person families. But given those exclusions, the payment levels of FAP did come quite close to eliminating poverty as it was then defined, and were set at that level for just that purpose. This was particularly true for the families of the working poor—the largest category of FAP recipients—whose total income would presumably far exceed the basic FAP benefit level. The Commission on Income Maintenance Programs appointed by President Johnson in 1968, which

---

By "FAP model" I mean a negative income tax proposal that reduces the base payment by 50 cents for every one dollar of earnings above an income disregard of sixty dollars per month. I have also adopted the convention of discussing the cost and coverage of FAP and proposed alternatives as if all potentially eligible recipients would enroll. This is probably not a realistic assumption, but it is not clear what proportion of those eligible would enroll or how this proportion might vary among alternative plans.

issued its report two months after the president's speech, included childless couples and individuals in its program, but proposed benefit levels almost *precisely* those of FAP. (That is, $2,400 for a family of four, but no food stamps, in the one case; $1,600 plus $860 in food stamps in the other.) This was not accidental. Both programs were constructed from the same data base, the Survey of Economic Opportunity, and both sought to have the maximum impact on poverty with the minimum amount of money. This is no failing in public policy.

By contrast, the economic consequences of a negative tax at the level demanded by NWRO—two years later the amount was raised to $6,500, a position adopted by the Black Caucus in Congress—could have been nothing short of calamitous. The basic dilemma of a negative income tax—of *any* system of income maintenance—is its relation to work incentives. A point is reached, and more quickly than otherwise, when money gained from work becomes marginal, given the alternative availability of transfer payments. This, at all events, was the view of the planners of FAP. They took seriously the wide public perception that welfare softened rather than hardened people, that it could undermine habits of self-reliance, and that so, too, could a negative income tax, and on an even broader scale. In a paper prepared in the spring of 1969, Hyman P. Minsky argued that any but a quite modest negative income tax "may tend to induce inflation, reduce measured gross national product, and lower the measured rate of growth of the economy. As the induced inflation works its way through the economy the real disposable income of families with quite modest incomes will decline and the net benefits to the intended beneficiaries will be eroded." In Minsky's view a sizable negative tax would lead to withdrawal of labor from the market and increased consumption by those not directly beneficiaries. He was, and is, almost surely right. Large increases in welfare expenditures in Britain after World War II and the United States after 1964, he noted, were followed by periods of inflationary pressures and slow growth, albeit there may have been other circumstances contributing to this.[13] The planners of FAP were sailing close to the wind. They knew this. It seemed no one else did.

Some months later, the NWRO demand was incorporated in legislation introduced by Senator Eugene J. McCarthy, and in time became almost a talisman of advanced liberalism. Even the most ardent supporters of FAP—there were never many—felt routinely called upon to acknowledge that it was "inadequate." Simultaneously there developed a fierce opposition made up of those who would settle for nothing less than the $5,500 level. They were demanding economic ruin. But they did not know this, or if they knew it they did not care. The defeat of FAP became for many on the liberal left a truly impassioned cause. The issue became more and more divorced from anything approaching "scientific" social planning. To the contrary, it evoked an increasingly hysterical and irrational response. Surely the complexity of the proposal, and the clinical atmosphere in which it was developed, had consequences for its reception by the assortment of publics who had awaited the president's address.

2. Editorial Opinion

With the general public, as against organized interest groups, the president's address was nonetheless an overwhelming success. FAP was an extraordinary departure in proclaimed public policy, for which there was virtually no public demand, and with which there was no familiarity. It was for most purposes a brand new idea. But in broaching it the president had one large advantage: he was proposing to supplant the existing welfare system, which was widely regarded as a failure and about which something needed to be done. This proposition *was* familiar, and did have support, giving the president some leverage. The public perceived welfare as something that had somehow to be changed, but it had no strong feeling about how to do it. On the helicopter ride back from the meeting at Camp David, Maurice Stans, no friend of FAP but an experienced official, tore from that morning's Baltimore *Sun* a Yardley cartoon depicting the president at his desk, shuffling papers marked "Proposed Reforms" and looking up at a giant, tattered, tin-cup-rattling ghost labeled "Failure of Present Welfare System." "We've had you with us for thirty-four years," states the president. The cartoon was passed from one Cabinet officer to another to the nodding of heads. It was necessary to do *something*. This was the general perception. In such circumstances a president willing to lead is likely to be followed, for a time at least.

Elation is not too strong a term for the tone of the telegrams that poured into the White House. The permanent White House staff, looking back over years of telegram counting, could not recall a public response, on a domestic issue, of comparable magnitude and unanimity. Between August 9 and September 10, 2,757 letters and telegrams on FAP were received: 81 percent expressed unqualified approval; 10 percent had doubts about details or suggestions for modification; but only 9 percent were flatly opposed.[14]

The nature of the response may be suggested by one telegram, a favorite among the president's aides: TWO UPPER MIDDLE CLASS REPUBLICANS WHO WILL PAY FOR THE PROGRAM SAY BRAVO. A central fact about American politics at this time was that the educated, affluent business and professional class of the nation was probably the most disposed of any identifiable group to reformist policies in government. Intellectuals, now for the most part academic, had been in part immobilized by their intense distrust and dislike of first Johnson and now Nixon. The labor movement had no great demands to make of the society, while increasingly it found itself in the unfamiliar and uncomfortable position of having demands made of it, principally on issues of racial equality. The Civil Rights movement had exhausted its earlier agenda, and had not developed a new one. (The Urban League would periodically call for a Marshall Plan for the cities, but could never produce one.) The Southern-Midwestern coalition that helped elect Nixon had presumably done so under the impression he would *not* be proposing "radical" new programs. The Nixon-Wallace support combined accounted for 56.9 percent of the votes cast in 1968. All the more then, was the impact of this first large event of the Nixon presidency on that considerable public-regarding class of middle-class persons whose stake in the country and concern for social equity combined to produce an urgent sense that large measures of social reform were required. Significantly, the telegrams were almost exclusively concerned with welfare reform. This was the issue the president was seen to have faced up to, and it was this, with its dense penumbra of meaning and reference, which brought the response.*

The address was an enormous news story and was treated as such. It became the central feature of the news magazines, which without exception reported it as an event of the first consequence, and were scarcely reticent in implying their approval.

Newsweek

For more than six months, Richard Nixon bided his time, husbanding his domestic program. . . . Then last week, in a brisk 35 minutes of national television time, he unlimbered a set of reforms so sweeping that even some of his own Republican Cabinet Officers were left gasping for conservative breath, and some of his sternest foes had to hark back to the heyday of Democratic activism for a comparable summons to innovation in social policy.

Time

"What America needs now," the President told the nation last week, "is not more welfare, but more 'workfare.'" On the wings of that Nixonian neologism, the President proposed the first fundamental overhaul of the U.S. welfare system since it was created 34 years ago. . . . Although Nixon pointedly denied it, the notion is very much like a guaranteed income—with one crucial difference. For the able-bodied, willingness to accept "suitable" employment or vocational training would be the quid for the quo of assistance. In essence, Nixon notified the nation that his Administration is prepared to help those of the nation's 9.7 million relief recipients who try to help themselves.

U.S. News & World Report

Mr. Nixon blueprinted a sweeping program of welfare reform, including a form of guaranteed annual income for the poor. He zeroed in on other domestic problems—manpower training to cut ranks of the unemployed, revenue sharing to help ease the plight of cities, revitalization of the war against poverty. . . . The most massive overhaul of U.S. social-welfare programs since relief was started 34 years ago in the midst of the Depression has just been charted by the Nixon Administration.

---

* Intellectuals were not unmoved, but remained cautious. A telegram declaring I ALWAYS WAS SUSPICIOUS ABOUT YOU BUT AFTER YOUR SPEECH TODAY I GAVE UP ALL MY SUSPICIONS was signed simply SOCIAL SCIENTIST.

Business Week

The plan . . . submitted to Congress this week is far more than just an ingenious compromise of opposing viewpoints. It is a new and promising approach to a problem that never could be solved within the framework of the old system. . . . The President can and should insist on acceptance of his general framework. The principles of his proposal are sound, and the approach he is taking is the only one that promises to end the cruelties, inequities and inefficiencies of the present system.

The Economist (London)

It is no exaggeration to say that President Nixon's television message on welfare reform and revenue sharing may rank in importance with President Roosevelt's first proposals for a social security system in the mid-1930s, which were the beginning of America's now faltering welfare state. Any one of the three main proposals in the message would rank as major legislation—indeed historic legislation—and here they are combined into one.

Editorial comment was prompt and positive. A survey carried out by HEW found 95 percent of editorials in the country "favorable" to the new program, and the major newspapers in nearly all the twenty-five largest metropolitan areas "enthusiastic." Again, it was welfare that commanded attention, almost to the exclusion of the other components of the New Federalism. The *Los Angeles Times* (*the* Times in the Nixon White House) stated, "President Nixon laid out a bold new blueprint in his televised address on welfare and other domestic matters." *The New York Times* was pleased with the "overall design" and called the plan "a bold attempt to transform an apparatus thrown together thirty-five years ago to provide temporary relief that has now degenerated into a destructive and dispiriting way of life for millions of needy Americans." The Detroit *Free Press* termed FAP "more radical than virtually anything done by the Johnson Administration," and in a follow-up comment touched on a near universal theme: "The *status quo* is no answer—so the President's attempt, complicated and controversial as it is, is a better way to go." In Boston the *Herald Traveler* declared, "the thrust and scope of welfare reform under the 'New Federalism' deserve to be cheered." The San Francisco *Chronicle* observed that "the Nixon measure has the great advantages of being not only 'noble in purpose' but also suited to the needs of the day and the will of the people." The Chicago *Sun-Times* called it a "giant leap forward," the Des Moines *Register* said the plan takes "a middle ground, which if approved by Congress, would represent the most important and thorough-going overhaul of the federal-state welfare apparatus since its erection in the 1930s." This theme was stated most emphatically in the *Christian Science Monitor:* "It is hardly possible to over-emphasize the importance of President Nixon's new program for dealing with poverty in the United States. It is a major watershed —socially, economically, and politically."

The New York *Daily News,* with the largest circulation in the country, read, most probably, by more welfare recipients than any ten other newspapers combined, was cautious but not hostile. Even so, it would brook no nonsense about the nature of the proposal.

GUARANTEED ANNUAL INCOME

The Nixon people . . . feel that they have devised safeguards which could keep FA from degenerating into a straight-out dole with the reliefers forming an evergrowing pressure group demanding ever higher guaranteed incomes.

For one thing, reliefers who held paying jobs of any kind would be permitted to keep varying percentages of their earnings, and the "assured income foundation" would go down as those earnings went up.

For another, able-bodied unemployed fathers on relief, and mothers of school-age children, on FA rolls would be required to take jobs or job training. If they refused, they would lose their shares of the FA benefits—though the payments on account of the children would continue.

Day-care centers would be set up, where mothers at work or in job training could leave their children to be cared for during working hours. . . . The basic idea, then, is: Work or learn to work if you can, or no FA for you.

The *News* set a pattern that was to continue. Conservatives who were cautious about the program or opposed to it were typically quite accurate about its provisions. Liberals who thought the program inadequate typically were not. The *News* editorial, which appeared August 24, after details of the program had become available, got quite clear that the penalty for refusal to work was restricted to the adult involved and not to his or her dependents. On the opposite reach of the political spectrum, the "work requirement" was commonly represented as an automatic withholding of all benefits.

The Republican-conservative auspices of the program and the manner in which the president presented it paid off in the Great Plains, the Southwest, and the Far West. Reservations were expressed, but the general tenor of comment was positive and supportive. From Emporia, Kansas, William L. White, writing in the *Gazette,* recalled a "noble old song of childhood."

> Mother takes in washing
> And so does Sister Ann:
> Everybody works at our house
> But My Old Man!

"But no more," he continued. "Under the Nixon plan, anyone who works will be rewarded rather than punished. . . ." He was clearly moved: "The principle behind all this—that work should be rewarded while poverty is alleviated—is little short of magnificent. . . . It is a proud and happy day for those of us who . . . voted for Richard Nixon. He has fulfilled his pledge."

The Phoenix *Gazette* was more restrained, but not less supportive. The president's goal, it asserted, "to get able-bodied people off relief and onto payrolls, would bring a restoration of the pride in personal economic independence that made America great." In Utah, where Mormon attitudes might have been expected to produce outright rejection, the response was just the opposite. The Ogden *Standard Examiner* stated, "There is a revolutionary atmosphere around the broad-scale changes in public welfare methods and financing," and thought that many aspects of the proposals "should be thoroughly welcomed by all Americans—those of affluence and those who depend upon welfare payments for their existence." The Salt Lake City *Tribune* saw the address as "a turn toward more sensible, more compassionate and more imaginative ways to meet the challenge of rising welfare and local government needs. . . ." The *Deseret*

News, owned by the Church of Latter-Day Saints, thought the president might be rushing ahead to establish a guaranteed income before enough facts were in from experiments such as that under way in New Jersey, but the tenor of its comment was anything but hostile. The Portland *Oregonian* was fair to pugnacious on the president's behalf: "Congress will butcher this program at its peril, unless it has something better to offer." The Ottumwa, Iowa, *Courier* forecast events more accurately:

> The debate is on over President Nixon's new welfare program. And it will be a lively and long one, we may be sure.
> The President in all probability will be caught smack in the middle.
> There will be conservatives who will see the program as a giant federal guaranteed income dole and who oppose it on principle. And there will be politicians and militants who will oppose it because it wasn't their idea, or because they want the government to guarantee the poor much more.
> We believe Mr. Nixon's position will be tenable. Most legislation . . . is compromise legislation, a half-way point between extremes. Here is where Mr. Nixon seems to be right now. American middle-of-the-roaders eventually will approve of the over-all proposal, we confidently predict.

Although Southern congressmen were later to vote 5 to 1 against FAP, much of the most sympathetic and sophisticated comment about the president's address appeared in the Southern press. There was, to be sure, more outright negative reaction in the South than elsewhere. The Richmond *News Leader,* for example, recalled Edward Gibbon's dictum that "no state, without being soon exhausted, can maintain above the hundredth part of its members in idleness." The president, it averred, now proposed to maintain not one hundredth, but one tenth or more: "His proposals have left the liberal supporters of Hubert Humphrey and Eugene McCarthy gasping at an audacity their leaders never dared. . . ."

Yet a clear preponderance of comment was favorable. There was wide acknowledgment of the stigma associated with dependency, a phenomenon probably most pronounced in the South. The Anniston, Alabama, *Star* welcomed the president's address.

Three decades and the affluence of late years have made most Americans very fat and happy indeed, but unchanged is the attitude toward "those people" on the relief rolls—just keep them from starving to death. . . . But at last welfare, heretofore only a half-loaf—and a begrudged one at that—is going to become a whole loaf.

Possibly reflecting the intense and painful relationship Southern society has had with the Federal government, Southern editorials were far the most sensitive to the nationalizing implications of FAP, presidential rhetoric to the contrary.

Vicksburg, Mississippi, *Post:*

The President has couched his proposals in conservative language. He rang the changes on the theme that people should work—and be given opportunity to work—for their economic salvation. He called for a start on giving the states more of the responsibility for administering antipoverty and welfare funds; he scorned the federal bureaucracy and spoke of "a gesture of faith in America's states and localities, and in the principles of democratic self-government."

When one goes beyond language to substance, however, it becomes apparent that the President is putting forward anything but a conservative plan. What he proposes is indeed a replacement of the present welfare system. . . . Mr. Nixon has given a progressive, imaginative start to this process.

Greensboro, North Carolina, *News:*

In his criticism of the present welfare system, in his outline of the reasons for reforming it, President Nixon . . . hewed to a shrewdly conservative line. The President did not explore, with more far-reaching critics of "welfarism," the haunting likelihood that modern industrialism in its very dynamism will burden American society with its casualties and wounded, for all we may do. . . .

Instead Mr. Nixon appeals—because he assumes, no doubt correctly, that the country's mood and ethical traditions demand it—that Americans are above all a working people with a vision of public welfare that promotes, not discourages, gainful employment. . . .

Yet clothed in this Horatio Alger rhetoric Mr. Nixon has actually set before Congress and the citizenry an enlightened antipoverty agenda whose thrust is far less old-fashioned than his rhetoric.

More attention was drawn in the South to the guaranteed-income aspect of FAP than in other regions. The Anderson, South Carolina, *Independent* recalled Bagehot's rule that "To illustrate a principle you must exaggerate much and omit much," and deemed Nixon to have followed this counsel. It had learned, somehow, of the change in the title of the program, noting "the word 'assistance' having been substituted at the last minute to mollify the objection of Cabinet conservatives to the word 'security.' "

The President protests too much. In effect, a "guaranteed income" is what it is, under another name but with the hardly objectionable proviso of work incentives and, where possible, work obligations.

Other Southern journals repeated this theme. Nashville *Tennessean:*

The President unveiled what is in reality a guaranteed annual income for the poor. But he said he didn't want to call it that because he was against a guaranteed annual income. . . .

The President spoke as if he were half ashamed of recommending a guaranteed federal income. He shouldn't be. The guaranteed annual income is a respectable principle of modern industrial society. It has been advocated by some Democrats for years.

Bristol, Tennessee, *Herald Courier:*

President Nixon may never do a more un-Republican thing than proposing what amounts to a guaranteed annual income for all American families. . . .

Inherent in the plan, however, is the frank admission that something is wrong with the welfare system in this country, and this, in the long run, may turn out to be Mr. Nixon's most significant contribution. . . .

Southern editors could count. There was a fair amount of explicit or implied comment as to what FAP would mean for the South, especially with reference to existing payment levels for AFDC and the adult category programs. The Gainesville, Georgia, *Times* declared, "We have a tremendous opportunity to strike at root problems of the poor and our society at large." It would be, wrote the Marietta, Georgia, *Journal,* "One of the landmark acts of this administration and this generation." "From a selfish viewpoint," wrote the Little Rock *Democrat,* "the President's program would be great for Arkansas. . . . What we have heard so far sounds bold, dignified and workable." The Sherman, Texas, *Democrat* was abundantly clear that "The key to the President's plan to lift many out of poverty is his proposed aid to the working poor."

This aspect of FAP would necessarily have the most significance for the South, although it would turn out there were limits to the amount and kind of Federal aid the South would want. This wrenching ambivalence was first reported in an August 19 editorial in the Chattanooga *News-Free Press* commenting on the response of Democratic Senator Albert Gore. He had stated, "There are some counties in Tennessee in which nearly 78 percent of the population would be eligible for payments." The *News-Free Press* thought the idea of four out of five persons in a county dependent on the government for a living to be "shocking." Gore is reported as saying the Nixon proposal was a "bigger, more liberal, almost radically revolutionary program" than any had expected. The editorial reported that Gore himself, "a liberal Democrat, one who is generally a proponent of welfare handout programs . . . said he had some doubts about it." (Fifteen months later Senator Gore voted with fellow liberals on the Senate Finance Committee to kill FAP. By then, he considered it "utterly inadequate." But the general reaction in the region was abundantly positive and welcoming.

A clue to the eventual change of heart was that with few exceptions there was no mention in Southern editorials of race, or of the particular difficulties of the Southern Negro. The Atlanta *Constitution* contended, "What the President seeks is in large measure surely worthy. . . . The nation, more affluent and calmer now than in other times, should be willing to agree that welfare needs new directions." The nation *was* calmer. It had gone through the first spring-to-summer since 1963 with no major racial disturbance. The crisis rhetoric of the mid-1960s was fading. But neither this easing of tension, nor the preceding exacerbation of it, had yet produced a change of political cli in the South toward racial accommodation. It would too late to help FAP in the 91st Congress.

The response of the national columnists, while predictable, indicated that *they* had not predicted the event. Liberals were stunned but for the most part generous. James Reston, Mary McGrory, Max Lerner, were full of praise. Harriet Van Horne of the *New York Post* declared she must eat the words she had written before the election that no matter who was elected the human condition would not change. As she saw it, $1,600 a year would only be the beginning. With the Nixon plan, she judged, the Nation had "turned an historic corner. . . . We're on our way." Some held out. James Doyle of the *Boston Globe* thought the program too little and very late, and destined for bitter debate in Congress. David Broder of the *Washington Post* objected to the "gradualism" inherent in the plan, which he nonetheless described as "sweeping." He recalled the Kerner Commission warning that America was moving toward two societies, separate and unequal, based on race. "The welfare plan," he feared, "does not offer any hope that this trend will be changed overnight." This did not concern the Drummonds, who termed FAP "the most far-reaching, ground-breaking, daring social welfare reform since the early days of the New Deal." Which it was. Financial writers had no difficulty acknowledging this. In the *Washington Post,* Hobart Rowen called the Nixon program "far-reaching . . . far more liberal (and practical) than any of his political opponents would have guessed." Edwin Dale, Jr., in *The New York Times,* said it all added up to a "genuine revolution." Conservative columnists such as David Lawrence and Richard Wilson were openly pleased by the public success of the president's address, and joined in approval. James J. Kilpatrick wrote in the Washington *Evening Star,* "If the Nixon plan gains acceptance, most of the evils of the present system would be rooted out. . . . In my own view, a preliminary look at the plan discloses much more good than ill." Holmes Alexander grew near to overexcited about "the most cogent end-poverty plan that we've ever had."

It is not a pinch-penny program, but it will expend minibillions for a few years to save megabillions in the future. It does not sentimentalize the poor, but calls upon their "self-interest" in moving from welfare rolls to payrolls. It is the opposite of permissiveness, for it contains . . . [a] "compulsion" in sending nonworkers to jobs or job-training. This means in plain language that the poor may have to work-or-starve, and that "dependent children" will no longer be the excuse by nonearning parents.

Neither liberal fears nor conservative hopes were even remotely realistic. A primary difficulty of liberal rhetoric at this time was that it repeatedly demanded, on pain of apocalypse, that things be done in a time span in which they could not be done. Such terms were no sooner stated than it became evident that they would not be met, whereupon there seemed nothing left to do. The effect was immobilizing, and probably contributed to the *Weltschmerz* that became rather a fashion with the onset of the 1970s. Nor was conservative rhetoric, with its rousing promise of "compulsion" and stirring prospects of ne'er-do-wells stripped of spurious excuse, any closer to reality. Nothing of *that* sort was going to happen either. Hence also an unreality which translated itself as irrelevance.

It was the particular difficulty of the black community at this time that it was highly sensitive to both these extremes of viewpoint but somehow suspicious of positions in between. It had known more sustained cruelty, betrayal, and oppression than any other racial or ethnic group in the society. "Compulsion" was not an unthinkable prospect for blacks. The Land of the Free for them had been a land of slavery and later of peonage. Nor was apocalypse an impossible prospect. The urban violence of the 1960s had at its peak a *Götterdämmerung* quality, and had led to a competitive rhetoric of threat and abuse directed at white society, much of it suggestive of a reversal of traditional Southern roles. By no means all Negro leaders or institutions participated in, much less encouraged, this style, but by and large white institutions did. It was rewarded, often not least by the Federal government. (Typically, the Black Panther party had been founded in an OEO office in Oakland by two OEO employees, Huey P. Newton and Bobby Seale. Government mimeograph machines produced the first copies of the Party Platform, of which, interestingly, Point 2 called upon government to "give every man employment or a guaranteed income.")[15] At this time various elements in the Negro community began to give voice to profound anxiety about the future. The prospect of geno~ termination by whites was seriously discussed. (The ta~

education which Nixon appointed after his election in November reported to him a widespread conviction among blacks that concentration camps were being readied for them.) It may be much of this was a way of coping with fantasies of aggression against whites, but there were those who were seriously convinced that disaster was nigh.*

In any event suspicion of Nixon was profound. One conse-

---

* During this period I contended—with greater force than my data warranted, but not without data—that the Nation as a whole, black and white, was concerned about political stability and that the depiction of the black population as seething with rage, sunk in despair, or both was false, was a too-familiar projection of intellectual *Angst* onto the nearest putatively revolutionary proletariat. Recent research has confirmed this view.

In 1971 Potomac Associates published a study by Albert H. Cantril and Charles W. Roll, Jr., drawing on previous work by the Institute for International Social Research. Using the "self-anchoring striving scale" developed by Hadley Cantril and Lloyd A. Free they found Americans reasonably optimistic about their personal future: blacks no less—slightly more—than whites. A very different view was held of the state of the Union. A quarter of the population listed national disunity or political instability as a fear for the Nation—a threefold increase since 1964. Asked to rate where the Nation had been, was, and would be, they answered that the average of expectations was that in five years the Nation might get back to where it had been five years earlier. The authors write, "The importance of the drop in the ladder rating from past to present can scarcely be overstated. In the many studies in which the Institute for International Social Research used the striving scale technique, only once [the Philippines, 1959] did a present national ladder rating fall below that for the past."

The one exception to this finding was the attitude of blacks. Where whites saw the nation as having declined from past to present, blacks saw it as having improved. They saw the future as improving still more. This was the polar opposite of much opinion of 1969 and 1970 when the White House was seen as criminally insensitive to imminent racial disaster. This situation, however, strengthened the case that a large achievement such as a guaranteed income was needed for national morale. It might, among other things, ease intellectual fantasies about proletarian insurrection. To accomplish this can be a legitimate object of social policy. (See Albert H. Cantril and Charles W. Roll, Jr., *Hopes and Fears of the American People,* New York, Universe Books, 1971.)

One object of the present volume is to document the uses of social science in the formulation of a specific social policy. This has required some emphasis on the limitations of social science. Here, however, is a striking instance of its value. In 1969–1970 "informed" Washington opinion would have been near unanimous in assuming that black Americans were in a state of near-insurrectionary rage. They were not, but this could hardly be ascertained except through the use of a carefully instrumented social science survey. The White House view, or at least mine, was close to that of Cantril and Roll, essentially similar findings having been obtained from the Institute for Social Research at the University of Michigan.

quence was that by far the coolest reception to the president's address was in the Negro press. It may be that a certain alarm spread through the politically sensitive elements of the Negro community when the *president* raised the question of welfare dependency. This was a matter, for blacks, of the utmost sensitivity. In the post-bellum South the more or less conscious encouragement of black dependency had been fundamental for the maintenance of white supremacy.[16] It had been the means by which a particular kind of peonage had developed in which racial stigma was combined with economic thralldom. The "simple peasant folk," to use E. Franklin Frazier's term, was encouraged to incur debt, and characterized as improvident. Work was made disagreeable and workers were characterized as lazy. This memory surely persisted in New York and Chicago, and with it probably also the memory that by and large the technique had "worked."

Welfare dependency in the North was an even more sensitive subject. Especially in the aftermath of the Kerner Commission, political and social analysis tended to ascribe great guilt to whites for such difficulties as blacks might have. But only by argument too complex and subtle to be of political value could "white racism" be made to account for the AFDC population.* This subject, at the time, was being discussed with increasing frequency in the North, and almost always in a hostile, not infrequently racialist, manner. There was seemingly no good defense. Now the president himself was raising it; a president from whom little good was expected; a president who certainly owed no political favors to blacks.

The president had hoped for a different reaction. Black members of the Administration were invited to one of the many briefings arranged prior to his address; this one was held in

---

* Lee Rainwater in his study *Behind Ghetto Walls: Black Family Life in a Federal Slum,* (Chicago, Aldine, 1970) traces the connection. White cupidity, he argues, created patterns of social interaction among lower-class blacks which had led to dependency. Where these patterns became established, the end of white cupidity did not end the pattern of social interaction. Hence dependency could continue and even grow. This analysis was familiar to the planners of FAP, and seemed reasonable. It argued, in effect, against beating the dying horse of "white racism," and dealing instead with those patterns of social interaction that had resulted from it. But Rainwater's analysis, that of a white social scientist, had not at that time made any impress on black opinion.

Edward Morgan's office in the Executive Office Building, a short distance from an office Nixon used for working on speeches and such matters. On August 11 a report in the Chicago *Defender,* coming as it must have done from persons present, described a singular scene.

Suddenly, the President . . . strolled in to take over the briefing personally. For thirty minutes he made an impassioned appeal for understanding, leading one participant to believe that he had borrowed a page from Lyndon B. Johnson in "selling his product." The gist of Mr. Nixon's remarks was that he knew his black appointees had been getting a lot of flack that the Republicans didn't care about the poor; that he as President was bowing to Southern pressure and taking the country back down the road on civil rights.

The President assured his listeners that this was not so. He said he was totally committed to ending poverty, and he believed that his proposal was the strongest, most revolutionary ever made by any chief executive.

Mr. Nixon acknowledged that there were many people within his administration who did not share his commitment, but he made the hard decision and there would be no retreat in principle. It was a realistic, but massive program, and he was going all the way with their help, he wanted to convince black Americans, white Americans, all of the disadvantaged of the sincerity of his administration. He got a standing ovation.

Even so, he got no standing ovation from the *Defender.* Its editorial was not so much hostile as ambivalent, as is suggested by the concluding sentence: "At long last a journey that we desperately need to take has begun with the President's first timid step."

A difficulty for the Negro press was that no Negro of prominence, nor any black organization, said anything favorable about the new welfare program that they might report. NWRO had denounced the program before it was proposed. Immediately afterwards Reverend Abernathy pronounced it "oppressive." A Washington correspondent of the *Defender* reported Wiley Branton, a former director of the capital's principal antipoverty agency, as "alarmed" by some of the wording of the address. "Still others," the correspondent continued, "described the President's proposals as 'Viet Cong booby traps.' " The response of the

National Urban League was encapsulated in a *Defender* headline: "Nixon Welfare Plan Not Enough: Young."

There was nonetheless some editorial support. The Washington, D.C., *Afro-American* stated, "President Nixon is correct in attempting to evolve a new approach to the problem, and he needs all the help he can get." William Raspberry in the *Washington Post* felt, "Some of the critics . . . aren't being quite fair. . . . Little credit is being given Mr. Nixon for his courage . . . in moving to scrap a system of welfare whose chief result has been to entrap poor people in their poverty." Frank W. Mitchell, Sr., publisher of the St. Louis *Argus,* asked for understanding.

Man feels like he is man when he can stand independently and say I have done and I can see the results of my labor.

In this type of welfare set up the people will be more inspired to get jobs.

They will not have to bear cutting off or down on their monthly checks because of outside employment.

In this new bill it is encouraged that they do work.

Let us not overlook one of the greatest things Nixon may be doing in his administrative years as President.

Before you judge the man, look at his proposal with an objective thought, don't be blinded by the subjective prejudices that cause so many of us to fail.

In the black populace, as in others, there is a strong element of fundamentalism about work and family and responsibility, and this was voiced here and there, notably in an editorial, " 'Workfare' Welfare Makes Sense," in the Twin Cities *Courier*.

Perhaps the most impressive part of the new program is the family-assistance concept, that builds a floor under the family unit and holds it together, rather than ripping it apart as is now the case with AFDC. Only those who have seen a penniless, jobless, hopeless man unwillingly abandon his family to give wife and children a chance to survive, can fully appreciate the scope of this proposal. When any welfare system is predicated on the tragedy of broken homes, it is the worst possible solution to one of the greatest problems facing this country. That type of system eventually destroys any prospect of

266 | DANIEL P. MOYNIHAN

family unity, and undermines the very concept that lends meaning and dignity to life.

As for families who struggle to stay together, in the face of financial crisis, the welfare "dole" is disgraceful. Usually heads of these households are persons out of work and fresh out of luck through no fault of their own. Most are doing everything possible to get back on any payroll, willing to work at any job until something better comes along. When they turn to straight welfare in desperation, the minimal subsistence doled out compounds the disgrace, to say nothing of those unpalatable "surplus commodities" a woman is expected to transform into edible meals.

Since we subscribe to the credo, "honest work for an honest dollar," we particularly appreciate the work-incentives built into the "New Federalism." Only the handful who enjoy the idleness syndrome encouraged by programs launched during depression years, take a dim view of this prospect. But despite the system that built in human failure, the vast majority prefer to earn their own way, and ask only a hand-up over the rough spots. Penalizing families with the urge to work is perhaps the most devastating failure chalked up against the present arrangement.

But the prize of the week goes to the section giving consideration to men and women who doggedly plug away, day after day, on take-home pay that is a travesty on the government checks handed to high school drop-outs engaged in community organization.

Most comment, however, was negative, some hostile. The San Francisco *Sun Reporter* editorial was titled "A New Welfare Shell Game." FAP was described as a "confusing and misleading program, but the basic fact remains that it will not guarantee poor people an adequate income." The New York *Amsterdam News* took the same position: the program was "inadequate" and "disappointing." Sondra Matthews, a columnist in the *Greater Milwaukee Star,* put "Questions for Mr. Nixon":

· What recourse would there be for Blacks who say they are too sick to work? Who will be the judge?
· Why is it necessary to deduct fifty cents from every dollar in benefit after a person begins to receive more than $60 a month from a job?
· Why not start to deduct after the income reaches above the poverty level for that year? According to the U.S. Bureau of Labor Statistics it is now $5,915.
· Is the new program designed to control births of welfare recipients

since it is based on a two child family which is the present rate (2.2) of births for whites?

· If Nixon really feels this program will keep the family together, why can't some mothers remain in the home to raise their own children? . . .

· What guarantee does the Black recipient have that he will not be forced to take all of the dirty and sloppy jobs available in the sweat-shops of industry?

· Is this "get a job" a beginning of the old cycle around for the second time because white folks have run out of gimmicks with which to pacify the Blacks?

These were Northerners commenting on a program that would particularly benefit the South, where whites dominated. An incident during the briefings, later reported in the *Defender,* suggests the difficulty this raised for blacks. Clarence Mitchell, Jr., the congressional lobbyist for the National Association for the Advancement of Colored People, listening to the exposition in the basement of the White House, learning that as much as a third of the population of Mississippi would receive FAP payments, asked what if states like Mississippi decided not to partici-pate? The thought had simply not occurred to anyone in the White House, but it occurred to Mitchell: would Southern whites tolerate such largess? An answer of sorts was provided: if a state did not participate in FAP it would not be able to participate in any Social Security program: Old Age Assistance, Aid to the Blind, all that would have to be forgone. In the words of a *Defender* account of the meeting, "Mitchell's retort was that Mississippi could care less."

A number of editorials in the black press contained varia-tions on this theme, many reflecting a disinclination to see the South seemingly rewarded for its past failure to maintain decent standards. The San Francisco *Sun Reporter* depicted FAP as "simply another case of Nixon paying off his debts to Southern politicians." The *Amsterdam News* had a more complex view. It was "wary of whether or not those who need the help in Missis-sippi will actually get it," but its principal scruple was that "while the Nixon plan sounds great for Mississippi, it is penalizing New York and other industrialized states." (This view was shared by at least some Northern whites, including Senator Abraham A. Ribicoff, Democrat of Connecticut, who stated that the proposal seemed "great for Mississippi, but what does it do for Hartford?" Governor Rockefeller commented in similar terms.) Regional interest affected black response. The politically active Negro community was overwhelmingly Northern: wherever the majority of blacks might be, the interests of this community were those of the North. Inevitably this led to a primary concern for the condition of AFDC families, and something near to indifference to the problems of the working poor.

On balance, editorial opinion responded favorably to a strong presidential initiative without fully understanding it. What occurred was more echo than analysis. When opposition views were voiced, the press would echo them also. The initial response of public opinion was equally favorable. By contrast, it largely remained so.

3. Public Opinion

Public opinion was, if anything, ahead of the press. A week after the address Gallup began polling and found strong bipartisan support for "President Nixon's welfare reforms." Three quarters of those interviewed had heard of the proposals. Of these who had done so, 65 percent were favorable, 20 percent unfavorable, while 15 percent had no opinion. Little difference in opinion was found based on age, region, income level, or political affiliation. Many of those interviewed were impressed by the work incentives. Significantly, Gallup reported that "Public opposition to the proposals stems mainly from the belief that the new system does not go far enough toward meeting the increased needs of the poor."

In October the Harris Survey reported that one in three persons was not familiar with the welfare proposals, but that they received a "heavily favorable reception," a margin of 47 to 17 percent, from those who were. Harris found "easily the most appealing of the Nixon welfare package" features to be the inclusion of the working poor, supported 66 to 13 percent, and the work incentives, supported 63 to 18 percent. Only half as many persons reported themselves "not sure" about these features as of the overall program. To the negative statement "The trouble is that too much money will still be spent on welfare in this country," 37 percent agreed, but 38 percent disagreed, with 25 percent not sure. This tends to confirm Gallup's report of significant pro-welfare sentiment. The statement, "As some Negro leaders said, the program cuts out the part which helped blacks and helps whites instead," in the Harris survey produced only 7 percent agreement, with 62 percent disagreeing.[17]

Public opinion remained strongly in favor of FAP. A year after the president's address, the White House commissioned Field Research Associates to survey the issue among Californians. The results analyzed by William E. Bicker of the University of California, Berkeley, showed, in his words, "extraordinarily strong support" for the main features of the program. Aid to the working poor was approved by 76 percent of those polled; day-care services for working mothers by 86 percent; the requirement that AFDC mothers register for training or employment if their children were of school age or older by 85 percent. A full 92 percent favored the requirement that heads of families receiving benefits register for work and accept suitable employment on pain of losing their benefits, but not those paid to support a wife or children.

A negative question was asked to test the strength of belief: "Even if you are just bringing them up to the welfare standard, giving people who are fully employed money from the government is a bad idea because it just adds to the number of people who become dependent on the government for money." Forty-five percent of those polled agreed to this, but an equal 45 percent disagreed. In response to yet another question, only 4 percent criticized welfare as a waste of taxpayers' money. Bicker concluded: "Many people believe about the present welfare system what experts widely agree about the penal system: that it is merely custodial and not therapeutic or remedial in its effects and even rewards a tendency toward recidivism."

Thus FAP was proposed in a situation in which the public at large had come in preponderant numbers to believe that the existing welfare system was destructive and self-defeating. The editorial writer and the man in the street alike held this view, and did so with conviction. The president's proposal had begun with that premise. He then proposed that instead of being less generous with low-income persons, the Nation should be more, that is to say that a general rather than particular system of income maintenance should be established. Here it might have been predicted public opinion would be more divided. It was not. The predominant impulse was to be more generous rather than less. This disposition was abetted by the president's emphasis on work and work training.

Paul Fideler, a New England professor, unimpressed, wrote that the speech was straight out of Benjamin Franklin, that Nixon had "offered the poor the Protestant Ethic warmed over. Whether or not the poor would appreciate that, he was quite certain the middle class would; and, he was right." Leaving the president aside, this was an injustice to Benjamin Franklin, the American middle class, and possibly also the Protestant Ethic, now so little in favor in the institutions it had founded. The Nation had entered a period of great unrest, in which, regardless of ultimate or even proximate causes, a good deal of violence had come from low-income populations. An interpretation much preferred on the left was that such manifestations of impending social revolution would in the first instance lead to "repressive" rightist reactions on the part of the threatened bourgeoisie. Nixon's election was widely interpreted as such an event. Yet when this same president proposed, in substance, a guaranteed income, the public response was overwhelmingly favorable. This public, if anxious, was hopeful and willing. Whatever its previous disposition, it was prepared to change in response to a presidential initiative that made the necessary concessions to tradition and symbol.

4. Labor

It was characteristic of the New England professor to write of the president's audience as consisting of two groups, the poor and the middle class. A great shift in sentiment had taken place in upper-status reformist-to-radical circles. The working class, and its institutional embodiment, the trade union movement, had largely evanesced as an object of concern, sympathy, or admiration, and having vanished from sight was soon out of mind. In approximate terms, as such must be, advanced opinion held that

POLITICS OF A GUARANTEED INCOME | 271

the workers had "become" middle class. For those to whom this was a term of opprobrium, labor became opprobrious. Michael Novak described the intellectual's view of American labor as "vile."

This development had varied sources. The black assertion of the 1960s exercised a preeminent claim on liberal emotions and priorities. The legislative and social struggles of the labor movement were by and large past. Domestic politics in the 1950s had been much preoccupied with trade-union corruption (the issue that had brought the Kennedys to prominence). The protracted struggle over racial imbalance in the building trades impaired the "image" of the labor movement at large, while the impression of the affluence of these and other workers grew quite out of proportion. The median income of white men age fourteen and over in 1968 was in fact $6,267. Only 21 percent of all white men earned over $10,000; only 6.5 percent earned over $15,000.

As is common, ethnic/cultural forces had a part in the estrangement of the labor movement from the forces of "advanced" social thinking. American intellectual and cultural life was now heavily influenced, if not dominated, by Jewish cadres that, beginning in the 1930s, had appeared with such force of intellect and creativity. The leading intellectuals were preponderantly Jewish, while the labor movement (apart from the emerging public employee unions) remained the most Catholic of broadly based American institutions, and notably so in its head, George Meany. A Jewish-Catholic entente had operated in the labor movement and in politics generally during the Roosevelt-Truman era, but while the senior staff of the AFL–CIO remained heavily Jewish the larger entente did not survive the Cold War. The labor movement remained all but solidly in support of the war in Vietnam, while the intellectuals and academics turned passionately against it. By then, however, a vast estrangement had already taken place, asserting itself down to the level of ward politics, where, in cities such as New York, upper-status liberals attacked and in a measure were able to destroy the working-class political organizations that had governed for so long.[18]

By 1969 the "lib-lab lobby" which Stephen K. Bailey describes in his account of the enactment of the Employment Act of 1946 was recessive to the point it might have been thought not to exist. This would have been wrong. As the successful campaign to defeat the Supreme Court nomination of Judge Clement F. Haynsworth was to demonstrate, the lobby could be revived for specific purposes. The important point, however, is that these had to be *labor* purposes. It was labor that wished to defeat the nomination of John J. Parker by President Hoover in 1928, the last occasion on which such an event had occurred. Labor would join in some coalition efforts—the civil-rights acts of the mid-decade had been such—but on balance it stood apart, looking to what it perceived to be its own interests. It had reverted, its always lingering suspicions seemingly confirmed, to an earlier position of relative aloofness from the successive enthusiasms about *issues* that seize the *New Republic* or the undergraduates of the University of California at Berkeley.

If labor had lost popularity, it had scarcely lost influence. Of the public lobbies active in Washington, groups purporting to represent large numbers of citizens and claiming to speak for a generalizable public interest, labor remained far the most powerful. Its power was more negative than otherwise, but that is a general condition of power in Washington. It would in any event have been accorded a primacy of interest with respect to the establishment of a guaranteed income. No interest group could claim anything approaching the concern that the labor movement would have to have with such a proposal, nor would any be expected to have labor's technical competence in assessing one.

In the Johnson era the assumption had been that labor would automatically be opposed. "Labor unions," Cavala and Wildavsky had hypothesized, "fear that a guaranteed income would render them superfluous." As organizations their primary role, and justification, was to maintain wage levels: if government was now to do this, what role or justification remained to them. Alice M. Rivlin has commented that Wilbur J. Cohen, "this normally astute political forecaster," had been convinced that Congress would never enact a guaranteed income and suggests why he never even tried to get one proposed.

It would have been politically impossible for a Democratic administration to have proposed extension of welfare to the working poor.

Labor union opposition might have killed the proposal at the White House level, if not below.[19]

Cohen, who if anything had been *ab*normally astute about such matters, was at least not right about this one. The labor movement did not try to thwart FAP "below" in the bureaucracy; it did not intervene when it reached the White House; nor did it try to kill the legislation in Congress. *It could have done.* That is to say, it could have tried to block the program at any of those points, might well have done so in the White House, and certainly could have done so in the Congress. It did not. It was never enthusiastic about FAP. After a period some of the general positions taken by the AFL–CIO could be seen as negative, and some particular unions were hostile, but it was never given to be understood that the AFL–CIO was against the bill. By small increments an initial silence gradually changed into quiet support. More specifically, no decision was made at the outset to oppose FAP. Gradually, as testimony had to be prepared and general positions stated, labor detected features of the legislation—small ones—which it wished changed. This translated itself into a generalized commitment, and as the 91st Congress came to a close FAP ended up high on labor's list of "unfinished business."

As with the executive branch of government, the position of the AFL–CIO was determined primarily by its head, George Meany, who in this matter shared many of the fundamentalist views that had moved Nixon. The condition of the dependent, fatherless family in the slum seemed terrible to him, and for better or worse he was inaccessible to the notion that it was all functional and communal, quite advanced really. Nor did the notion that men should have to work strike the head of the American labor movement as the entering wedge of oppression. This is not said for purposes of caricature. One of the elements working in favor of FAP was the impatience of "middle Americans" with the political and cultural radicalism of the time. In the face of vastly publicized assertions that the family was finished, work was finished, the labor movement was finished, America was finished, FAP became an affirmation that this was not necessarily so. For the labor movement it would have been easy enough to turn on the proposal with the language of the various "militants" who did attack it; to charge that it would lead to substandard wages, forced labor, and punitive regulation; that it was "antipoor" and "antiblack." The price of doing so, however, would have been to be associated with viewpoints for which the labor movement had no sympathy.

Historically, labor had shown little enthusiasm for the kinds of social intervention represented by FAP, or in any case this enthusiasm had lagged by a generation or so. Once social insurance was established, for example, labor became the most significant lobby pushing for its extension, especially into the area of health care. The minimum wage had originally been suspect: would it be the maximum wage? Once it was established, however, labor became the major force pushing for increases. When the issue of poverty was raised in the mid-1960s, labor might well have insisted that the way to go about it was to raise the minimum wage and create jobs. Certainly it had misgivings about the style of the Office of Economic Opportunity. Yet the issue of poverty had a claim on its support, and its support was given. A similar situation arose with respect to FAP, only here the matter was even more touching, involving government supplementation of wages paid by private employers. Even so the issue involved was one which also had a claim on labor support, and once again support was given, albeit with some reluctance. Of first importance, labor's contacts with the Federal government were thoroughly established from top to bottom. It *knew* that, whatever the wisdom of the administration proposal, its purposes were the avowed ones. There was no hidden design to hold down wages, to flood the labor market, or whatever. Labor was capable of suspicion, but was not disposed to fantasy. The processes by which FAP was developed, and the reasons for its adoption, were easily enough established to the satisfaction of the headquarters of the AFL–CIO. Nothing sinister was afoot. As militant, left opposition to FAP increased, a number of middle class organizations grew uneasy, and some withdrew their support. Labor did not. For the officers of the AFL–CIO—Meany, Lane Kirkland, Andrew J. Biemiller—the rhetoric in which FAP came to be attacked was all too familiar. It was the rhetoric with which they were attacked. It may even have strengthened their willingness to see the program enacted.

Meany's disposition was revealed in a Labor Day interview

given several weeks after the president's address. Typically, the questioning began on the theme of whether labor had become a victim of its success, whether the working man had become middle class, whether labor was out of tune with the new generation, with the young, the black, and the poor. Meany replied that, "Labor leaders are out of tune with people who feel that they know better than labor does what is best for labor. We have always had that type of people." Labor, he said, had the most effective lobby in Washington and used it for labor's purposes. Labor was not attracted to militancy for its own sake. It was concerned about programs. It was prepared to accept that some things take time. (Meany's references ranged over half a century of labor history. Samuel Gompers, "Bob" La Follette, "Jimmy" Walker, Herbert Lehman, were as often cited as any contemporary. It may be recalled Meany headed an organization that had had three presidents over a period during which the United States had fifteen.)[20] As for black militants, he was not sure anything could be done for some of them. As for blacks generally, he said, "There is no question that they still have a long way to go. But there is no question that they have come a long way."

Next Meany himself introduced the subject of the welfare proposals: "That we don't agree with." Yet he agreed the issue should have been raised.

Now, of course, as far as the general picture on welfare is concerned, I give Nixon credit for bringing this welfare situation to the public from the White House. I think it is a wonderful thing that the President of the United States said: "There is something wrong with this. There are a lot of things wrong with this. It has got to be changed." I don't think anyone will disagree with him.

However, when he starts to specify the changes and what he wants to do, then, of course, we become very specific on the things that affect us. We are going to object to some of the changes. I think we will play a major part in shaping whatever bill comes out.

Predictably, he contended that the real problem was wage levels and that FAP ignored it: "The greatest contribution you could make to an attack on poverty, the greatest practical thing you could do would be to have a $2-an-hour minimum wage." He returned to the welfare theme later, mentioning the Administration tax proposals, stating that, "Merely by opening up this welfare thing," the president had done everyone a service, adding that it was hard to size Nixon up: "He has certainly done things to warm the cockles of Strom Thurmond's heart and, at the same time, he has been doing things that the civil-rights people think are all right too. . . ."

To the White House, this seemed a positive note on which to open the bargaining, and this impression was sustained. Labor was not stirred by the idea of a guaranteed minimum income. The AFL–CIO Convention in October 1969 endorsed the general position of liberal Democrats: full Federal financing of the existing system, mandatory AFDC payments for families with an unemployed head, and a higher minimum wage. Still it did not oppose FAP, either in public or in the committee rooms of the Congress, where its power was unmatched. In November 1970 the AFL–CIO Executive Council issued a statement on "The Unfinished Business of the Congress." Third on its list, following Occupational Safety and Health, and Social Security, was Family Assistance. The implied formulation of Meany's 1969 Labor Day interview was unchanged: labor favored welfare reform but required certain safeguards in the legislation.

The AFL–CIO reaffirms its support of the principles embodied in the Family Assistance Bill proposed by the Administration.

While proposed benefits fall short of need, the program of Federal benefits to all families with children whose income is below poverty levels is a step in the right direction.

But the bill . . . needs a number of improvements if it is to receive our support.

The demands were modest, although not necessarily obtainable. Labor wanted a statement of congressional intent that no one should live below the poverty level; with respect to training and work assignments for FAP recipients it wanted the same standards of "suitability" that had been adopted for unemployment insurance, and also desired that such work be paid the Federal minimum wage or the prevailing wage if higher. It wanted it established that when the Federal government took over welfare functions from state and local government existing collective bargaining rights would be protected.

This was the American labor movement as the 1970s began: particularistic, somewhat prickly, with a tendency to find fault and to withhold approval, but powerful, self-sufficient, and basically true to its professed ideals. There were, of course, widely ranging tendencies in the labor movement, including some far more "advanced" than the craft-union tradition which Meany embodied. And yet, in a pattern that was persistent in the debate over FAP, the most advanced elements, when not actually opposed to the proposal, showed little interest in it. At this time Walter P. Reuther had taken the United Automobile Workers out of the AFL–CIO and formed an unlikely Alliance for Labor Action with the International Brotherhood of Teamsters. When the House Committee on Ways and Means began hearings on FAP, Reuther appeared with a long statement on the need for reordering national priorities and raising social security payments, but completely ignoring FAP. When Representative James C. Corman, Democrat of California, tried to draw him out on the subject, he went on instead about the Employment Act of 1946. When the Amalgamated Clothing Workers of America and the International Ladies' Garment Workers presented a statement on welfare reform to the Senate Committee on Finance, its object was merely to insure that no Federal funds be used to train workers in the apparel industry, a condition they had successfully imposed on earlier manpower and poverty programs, out of concern for plant relocation in Southern and Southwestern areas. Ideological subtlety is no friend of principle. The president had proposed to give money to the poor. The plumbers were for this. The internationalist, socialist, militant unions were not sure.

5. The Urban Coalition

The first indication that labor would go along with FAP had come on August 14 when the program was "praised" and endorsed by the executive committee of the Urban Coalition Action Council, among those present being Andrew J. Biemiller, legislative director of the AFL–CIO. (The Action Council was the lobbying arm of the parent body, an arrangement necessary to maintain the tax-free status of the latter.) The Urban Coalition had been founded in 1967 in response to the urban rioting of the time, and the apparent inability of the Johnson Administration to respond effectively. It was now the closest counterpart of the "lib-lab lobby" of the Roosevelt-Truman era.

Organized labor had joined in founding the organization, as had a wide range of groups and individuals, not least big-city mayors, but from the first the distinctive feature was the participation and financial support of national business corporations. The meeting that endorsed FAP in August 1969 included the secretary of the Leadership Conference on Civil Rights, the mayor of Pittsburgh, the head of the National Council of Churches, and the president of Clark College, but it contained also the president of McGraw-Hill Publications, the chairman of the board of Aluminum Company of America, the chairman of the board of Time, Inc. As at Arden House, businessmen such as these came to the issues of "the urban crisis" comparatively open to new ideas. Their concerns were genuine. Business had been shaken by the rioting, its presumed interests threatened, but, just as importantly, a civic conscience had been aroused. (The "libs" of the earlier coalition had included a considerable number of businessmen and had been heavily financed by them. These tended, however, to be individual entrepreneurs rather than heads of large industrial or commercial hierarchies.) The theory of the Urban Coalition was that communication and cooperation had broken down among the various power centers and interest groups of the metropolis. It sought, by forming coalitions in individual cities, to make it possible to collect enough power and resources in one place to act in ways that would respond to the perceived needs of minority communities.

It was slow going. Indeed, by 1969 the Urban Coalition had few successes to claim for its local efforts. It was already, in this respect, a dying organization. But it had won a place for itself in Washington as an independent force of sorts, which had to be listened to if only because it had enlisted this extraordinary new element in reform, the national business corporation. When, for example, FAP was reported from the House Committee on Ways and Means in March 1970, the Coalition collected eighty-five "blue chip" industrial names to append to a statement urging the House to approve the legislation. This was new in progressive politics, and the Coalition lobbyists made the most of it. These purposes were uniquely served by the organization's chairman, John W. Gardner.

In March 1968 Gardner had resigned as Secretary of HEW to take this post. This gave it a leader and spokesman of national prominence. As a Republican, former Cabinet officer, former head of the Carnegie Corporation, Gardner could purport to speak, up to a point, for the traditionally conservative interests of business, commerce, and finance. (He was much helped in this by one of his co-chairmen Andrew Heiskell of Time, Inc.) His position was crucial in the debate over FAP. He could legitimate the idea, and attest, both in public and in private as he repeatedly did, to the soundness of the proposal, and the qualities of leadership that were manifest in the president's having proposed it. A Republican administration had done what Democratic administrations declined to do. None knew this better than Gardner. None knew more what had been involved, and few for that reason were more impressed. Over and again he so stated.

The general tone of Urban Coalition pronouncements at this time was bleak enough: bracing for the next round of riots and expecting government to do little to forestall them. In March 1969, on the anniversary of the publication of the Report of the National Advisory Commission on Civil Disorders, the Coalition, jointly with Urban America, Inc., issued a well-publicized study *One Year Later,* which concluded: "We are a year closer to being two societies, black and white, increasingly separate and scarcely less unequal."[21] The document shared what it described as the Kerner Commission's "relentless . . . emphasis on race." The white editors could scarce take their minds off the "headline phrase" of the Commission Report, "white racism."

Yet somehow the subject of welfare kept intruding. It was recorded that "the whirring economy" had slowed down "the cycle of poverty in the slums and ghettos," but also that dependency persisted.

Unemployment is down and income is up, even in the hardest-to-reach places and categories of people. But the cycle of dependence, measured by the number of welfare recipients, has accelerated more than the Commission anticipated.

How so? None could say. This "seeming paradox" was "partially due to special forces at work in the world of welfare." What forces?

Why are welfare loads rising in tandem with aggregate employment and income? A clue may be found in the fact that the number and proportion of Negro families in central cities headed by females continues to rise, and reached 30 percent in 1968. . . . For these broken families the vicious cycle of inadequate income and social disorganization continues unabated by general prosperity.

The Kerner Commission had laid it down that the welfare system "contributes materially to the tensions and social disorganization that have led to civil disorders." It did not say how, nor yet what to do about it. The Commission had proposed a war on poverty on four fronts. First, employment. Second, economic development of poverty areas and "encouragement of ghetto business ownership." Third, reform of the present welfare system. Fourth, in the words of *One Year Later* "(eventually, perhaps, the most costly) a national system of income supplementation."

The at-least-partial replacement of welfare with some form of direct income supplementation, the Commission's "longer-range strategy," remained in 1968 an idea whose time had not quite come.

The authors of *One Year Later* saw no prospect whatever of any action in pursuit of the Commission's "longer-range strategy" of income maintenance. The most that *One Year Later* looked for was that the discussion might continue, and that the debate over the relative merits of family allowances, the negative income tax, and other income-guarantee plans would be resolved by the report of President Johnson's Commission on Income Maintenance Programs later in the year.

That the Republican Administration might contribute anything to the debate, much less propose a guaranteed income, was a thought that simply could not have occurred to the authors of the report. The event, when it came about five months later, posed a test of character in which Gardner and the Urban Coalition did themselves credit. FAP was welcomed, endorsed, and consistently thereafter supported. Gardner knew well enough that much of the proposal was based on planning that had begun in HEW when he was Secretary. As a Republican he was not constrained by the doctrine that the duty of the opposition is to oppose, nor was he open to charges of letting down his party. The president's address presented an opportunity to form a coalition, with respect to the elimination of poverty, broader than any that had been imagined.

Gardner moved directly to join in the effort. He knew a guaranteed income when one was proposed, and he was sufficiently a student of Federal social policy to recognize the emergence of a family policy. In testimony prepared for the Committee on Ways and Means he began by acknowledging both.

First, we would offer a general word of praise for the emphasis on children that is at the heart of the proposals under discussion. It's about time.

Second, we would emphasize that, if the proposals are accepted, the Federal government will for the first time in history accept responsibility for providing a minimum level of payment throughout the Nation and for financing it. I would have been very proud had I been able to establish that principle during my tenure as Secretary of Health, Education, and Welfare. It is an historic step. All the details of the present proposals fade in significance compared with that major advance in Federal policy.*

On behalf of the Action Council he proposed some changes. He liked to assume the president intended, and hoped Congress would provide, for eventually increasing FAP payments to the poverty level. He hoped for "one-stop" administration of the program to eliminate local contrariness. With respect to the adult categories, he wondered if he might anticipate an eventual single income-maintenance system. As for the work requirement, he asked that the legislation specify job standards and wage rates for "suitable employment." He wanted careful definition of what constituted "refusal to work"—again for fear of local abuse. He asked that "The exemption from the work requirement granted to mothers with children under six" be extended to all mothers, while acknowledging it was often feasible for mothers with children over six to work, and that many did. He hoped for Federal

---

* The testimony, November 13, 1969, was presented by former Ambassador George McGhee.

standards for day-care centers, and that some provision be made
for job creation so that training would lead to work.

A fortuitous aspect of Gardner's leadership of the Urban
Coalition was that a prominent citizen's lobby now existed
headed by men who knew a great deal about the welfare system
but who were not themselves part of it. Many of Gardner's staff
at HEW had gone with him to the Urban Coalition, including
Lowell R. Beck, who became executive director. Most congressmen knew nothing of the intricacies of the subject and looked to
"the experts." Before long a fair number of experts were denouncing FAP in the strongest terms. The more important, then,
was the steady support of the Urban Coalition, led by men who
could speak with equal or greater authority.

In his study of the Employment Act of 1946 Stephen K.
Bailey concluded, "It would be difficult to prove that the direct
pressures of the Lib-Lab lobby changed a single Congressional
mind."[22] In the absence of a specific survey of those congressmen
who at one time or another voted on the issue, much the same
would have to be said of the efforts of the Urban Coalition on behalf of FAP. Yet this would underestimate its influence on the
atmosphere in which the debate took place. Left and right, hostility to FAP mounted. Fantasy flourished: these were *not* settled
times. Yet at the conclusion of the most eager exhumation of
malevolent intent, the most fevered extrapolation of prospective
evil, there awaited the question: How is it that the Urban Coalition
continues unwavering in its support? Why does it publish carefully edited booklets explaining the program, detailing its endorsement, and appending the names of board chairmen, college
presidents, mayors, bishops, civil-rights leaders, women voters?
(E.g., among mayors: Allen of Atlanta, Barr of Pittsburgh,
Cavanagh of Detroit, Daley of Chicago, Graham of Phoenix,
Hatcher of Gary, Lindsay of New York, Stokes of Cleveland,
Tate of Philadelphia. Among civil-rights leaders: Innis of
CORE, Wilkins of NAACP, Andrew J. Young, Jr., of the
Southern Christian Leadership Conference, Whitney M. Young,
Jr., of the National Urban League. Among businessmen, Henry
Ford II and David Rockefeller.) Even when individuals on the
list (in this case the Policy Council of the Action Council) later
took positions opposed to the FAP legislation an ambiguity

POLITICS OF A GUARANTEED INCOME | 283

remained. They had signed their names to repeated, emphatic endorsements of the principle. The support of the Urban Coalition established that men of experience, influence, and understanding were in favor of the principle and the program. As a result, any congressman disposed to favor it, or to follow leadership that did so, had available an impeccable endorsement of his position that was beyond party, regional, or even racial interest.

There were, to be sure, some issues seemingly beyond the power of the Urban Coalition or any other voice to clarify. Foremost of these was the FAP "work requirement" under which mothers of school-age children could be referred to work or training on pain of forfeiting $300—or, later in the evolution of the bill, $500—per year in payments. The preceding Congress had given to the states the power to refer *any* mother, regardless of the age of her offspring, to work or work training on penalty of forfeiting all that part of the AFDC payment that reflected "her" needs in estimating the family budget. This was provided in the "Welfare" Amendments of 1967. It was a severe regulation and intended as such. It was approved by an overwhelming vote of both houses. As noted earlier, FAP proposed to modify it. Henceforth no mother with a child under six could be required to accept work or training on pain of loss of benefits. Some 60% of the families headed by a potentially employable female had a child or children under six.

Gardner and his associates drew attention to this immediately. The August 14 resolution of the Executive Committee of the Action Council noted:

The plan proposed by the President exempts mothers of preschool children from the provision requiring recipients of assistance to register for work and training. This is a step forward over the present law and should be retained.

The Urban Coalition was not alone in this insight. Joel Handler, a member of the OEO-funded Institute for Research on Poverty at the University of Wisconsin, who opposed FAP as a "serious stepback" for the poor, nonetheless acknowledged the change from the "work incentive" features, known as WIN, *of existing law*. In an article early in 1970 he wrote:

The coercive feature in the WIN program is that if a person referred to the Department of Labor refuses without "good cause" to "accept employment in which he is able to engage which is offered through the public employment offices of the state" or rejects a *bona fide* offer of employment, then that person's needs will no longer be taken into account in determining the family AFDC grant. . . . The one potentially clear improvement of the FAP work test . . . is the flat exclusion of mothers of children under six from the coercive requirements.[23]

The Wall Street Journal, no friend of malingering, made the same point on March 30, 1970.

Even if a recipient's benefits are canceled for refusing "suitable" work, his dependents' benefits continue. For a family of four, the upshot is a cut of $300 in the basic $1,600 allowance, presumably with a similar reduction in state supplements—surely a meaningful sum to welfare families, but not so surely an infallible sanction.

But simple statements of a simple fact had not the least effect on the debate that followed. The issue of whether or not to impose a "work requirement" was argued with great passion with no acknowledgment on any side that a work requirement had already been imposed. Conservative congressmen declared it was time to crack down on chiselers, liberal congressmen were shocked by the inhumanity of the Administration's proposals. The debate billowed and swirled with no evident awareness on any side that most of the legislators involved had already voted for a far more restrictive position, which President Johnson had signed without a word of dissent. Gardner knew this. He was then Secretary of HEW; this had been HEW legislation. He was required to administer the new provisions. He knew that Finch and Nixon were now proposing to repeal them in part. But seemingly no one else could or would grasp this point, despite clear statements by Gardner and others. The limits of orderly and responsible assessment were quickly reached in the debate over FAP. Beyond those limits, the Urban Coalition could have little influence.

6. Business

It was the singular quality of the Family Assistance Plan that while it unified public opinion behind a large presidential initiative, it brought on crashing division and controversy *within* the various clusters of interest groups and organizations that make up the major lobbies in Washington. As against the general public, whose views are frequently passive, reflected, if at all, through reports of the several national polling organizations, there exist specialized publics which respond to such initiatives with much more energy and presumed influence. None of these is monolithic; internal divisions are recurrent; yet on important matters it usually proves possible to work out a bloc position, and to assert it with a fair show of unity. *Not* in the case of FAP. Organized labor achieved a measure of tolerant ambivalence that could pass for unity, although, as noted, even there a number of union leaders took independent positions. Elsewhere all was conflict. Civil-rights groups divided; social-welfare groups divided; liberals divided; conservatives divided—later both political parties divided; but nowhere did division attain the degree of clarity, precision, and completeness that occurred all but instantly among representatives of business.

At one level this was to be expected. A presumed conservative Republican president had taken a most radical position. Conservative Republicans were puzzled or aghast. (A similar reaction was to follow Nixon's announcement in July 1971 that he would visit the People's Republic of China.) TRB (Richard Strout) in a *New Republic* column wrote of "quivering conservatives gaping with dropped jaws at their peerless leader," adding, "if Truman had launched it, or FDR, or Kennedy or Johnson, the sonic boom of rage would have blown the petals off the cherry trees." Liberal journalists such as Strout (a convinced advocate of FAP) might take some pleasure from this spectacle, but the gaping, quivering conservatives could hardly have done so. They were presumably to abandon either their principles or their leader. Yet so many issues were involved, each with subtle or sometimes starkly differing values for individuals and organi-

zations that might otherwise seem similarly disposed. In per-
mutation they led to opposite outcomes. Sensitivities about race;
attachment to cultural orthodoxy; econometric sophistication;
class, ethnic, regional origin—all combined in unpredictable
ways. The advantage was not to any faction.

Business journals and organizations were reporting the
imminence of FAP well before labor and other such groups took
notice. The June 28 issue of *Business Week* featured an editorial
commenting on the debate going on within the Administration
and urging the president not to make the "mistake" of seeking a
"compromise." He should go all the way with a three-point program: "A negative income tax to guarantee a minimum of
income to all penniless families and subsidize the earnings of all
the working poor"; "strong work incentives"; and "more job-
training slots." Fifteen hundred dollars for a family of four—the
amount then being debated—seemed about right to the editors,
who wanted to make certain that "the negative tax is clearly tied
to a program to get its recipients working and earning."

Five days earlier *Washington Report,* a newsletter of the
Chamber of Commerce of the United States, carried an article by
Karl T. Schlotterbeck, director of manpower programs for the
Chamber, warning that "The idea that all Americans should be
guaranteed a regular income, whether or not they are able or
even willing to work, will soon be up for decisive action." The
Chamber's Committee on Welfare Programs after a six-month
study had proposed that elderly, disabled, and dependent persons
be provided for by the public, and that "Able-bodied adults in
need should be given opportunities and incentives to work," but
rejected the idea of a guaranteed income. The article was intended to alarm.

The businessman or anyone else who doesn't bother to learn what is
involved here, and make his opinion heard where it counts, may soon
come to realize that one of the proudest traits of the American people
has suddenly vanished while his back was turned; that self-reliance
has been reduced from an ideal to an option.

The article was not especially friendly to " 'hand-out' artists"
who argued there was "little work potential among welfare
recipients." This was an old enemy: the bureaucrat. But it was

not in any way hostile to or derogatory of welfare recipients themselves. An insert, "What You Can Do About Welfare," suggested how local chambers of commerce could help tackle the "manpower-welfare" problem of providing training and jobs, with associated programs of child and health care. This was a responsibility of business. "An appropriate slogan of the National Chamber referring to the welfare mother caring for dependent children is, *'If you won't hire her, don't complain about supporting her.'* "

Thus the range of business opinion was as wide as the subject permitted: from complete endorsement of a guaranteed income to complete rejection. Measured on a different axis, however, the extremes of opinion asserted themselves in a quite narrow spectrum of advocacy and of emotion. The "radicals" were not wild-eyed; the "reactionaries" were not apoplectic. (The hysterics of Chamber of Commerce opposition to the Full Employment Bill a generation earlier, which had so impressed and discouraged Bailey, were never displayed with respect to welfare.) It was all rather businesslike. Historians are likely to record that American business changed in that quarter century, becoming at once more civil and less vigorous.

The Arden House Conference had established among liberal businessmen a disposition toward a national system of income maintenance.* Advanced opinion had come to look with favor on the notion of a guaranteed income to deal with problems of poverty and dependency. On the other hand, there were not many men with fire in their belly on the subject. One was simply in favor of it. A hiatus followed the Arden House meeting. For the longest time there was no *next* event. The Committee for Economic Development took the matter under advisement, and established a Subcommittee on Poverty and The Welfare System chaired by Joseph C. Wilson, and including many members of his Arden House steering committee. Years went by as consensus was shaped. Steiner writes: "The same week the House of Representatives passed the family assistance bill, a CED crash program at last produced a welfare policy statement."

But it was not too late; the Senate had not voted. The

* Much earlier in the century, the National Civic Federation, largely supported by big business, was one of the leaders in the battle for the establishment of workmen's compensation laws.

statement, *Improving the Public Welfare System,* was a careful and valuable study, in the manner of CED documents. The press reported it as expressing "strong support" for FAP: a true statement but incomplete. The Administration's proposals were said to "represent a very important first step forward in revising the present welfare system." *First step.* The Research and Policy Committee of CED, chaired by the executive vice-president of the Standard Oil Company of New Jersey, with a subcommittee chaired by the head of Xerox, thought $2,400 a year in cash and food stamps a good beginning on a guaranteed income but asked that *"a priority claim against future available federal funds should be invoked to raise total assistance to more acceptable levels."* Wilson acknowledged to the press that the subcommittee was unsatisfied with that amount, but explained "we want to see this legislation passed." The statement specifically asserted, however, that *"neither training nor work should be made a condition for continuance of public assistance to women heads of households."* The group wished to see single persons and childless couples covered; wanted more day-care centers, extended to include two-year-olds; wanted more family planning; and called attention to the problem of high marginal rates of taxation on earnings when part of the negative tax was to be paid as food stamps. Advanced opinion was now considerably advanced!

That the Chamber of Commerce of the United States should take a position diametrically opposed to that of the Committee for Economic Development was part a matter of convention, part one of chance. The Chamber represented a tradition of business conservatism; the CED was formed partly in opposition to that tradition by men who had found they could make more money the other way. The two organizations were not social equals. Anyone can get into the local chamber of commerce: membership in the CED is restricted to two hundred "businessmen and educators." The style of the national chamber is not quite small-town, but it is some worlds away from the *haut monde* of the CED. An element of chance was also present. Both the Research and Policy Committee of the CED and the Committee on Welfare Programs and Income Maintenance of the Chamber were headed by oil executives: Emilio G. Collado of Standard Oil of New Jersey for the CED, and Myron A. Wright of Humble Oil and Refining for the Chamber. Collado was born in a suburban community of New York, attended Phillips Academy, Andover, took a B.S. at MIT, a Ph.D. in economics at Harvard, belonged to the American Academy of Arts and Sciences, the Council on Foreign Relations, and the Racquet and Tennis Club. He worked in Rockefeller Center. Wright was born in Blair, Oklahoma, attended Northwestern State Teachers College, and took *his* B.S. from Oklahoma A & M. He had been chairman of the board of the U.S. Chamber of Commerce, and was a member of the American Institute of Mining, Metallurgical, and Petroleum Engineers. He worked in Houston. FAP was of a class of social-economic issues in which the cultural divergences represented by these differing backgrounds routinely override similar economic interests.

The National Chamber of Commerce commenced a systematic campaign against the enactment of FAP. This began in a somewhat low key, and only grew urgent as it appeared the legislation might pass. When Ways and Means began to take testimony, Schlotterbeck appeared with a brief statement describing the Chamber's work in the field and stating simply that it opposed the provisions providing aid to the working poor.

The National Chamber is opposed to these provisions. They represent the beginning of a national guaranteed income arrangement. A Federal relief subsidy for these fully-employed fathers could tend to "lock" them in their present occupations. Such payments could prove to be a strong disincentive to improve their learning capacities.

The conditional voice should be noted: *could tend* to lock workers into their occupations, *could prove* a disincentive to improve earning capacities. The specific charge leveled against FAP was that the Government did not know enough to propose so massive an enterprise. A passage from Eveline Burns's paper prepared for the Arden House Conference was invoked.

When contemplating the policies that have been applied in the past and considering those which might be applied in the future, it is impossible not to be both impressed and depressed by the extent to which policy decisions are made and perpetuated on the basis of *beliefs* about facts rather than tested knowledge. . . .

At this time, for example, it was widely held that high AFDC payments had been a major incentive to migration, and that the program generally induced father desertion. Yet Schlotterbeck noted that a Cook County study had found nothing to support the migration thesis, while work by Podell in New York City had found that most desertions occurred *after* the receipt of assistance. (These specific points were valid. Whatever the probabilities appeared to be, no one could *prove* either the migration or the family-breakup thesis.) If the working poor were to be aided, the National Chamber proposed the matter be left to the states, some of which had programs that were already doing so.

In March 1970, as a decision in the House approached, the Board of Directors of the National Chamber formally declared its opposition to any Federal relief to fully employed family heads. An editorial in *Washington Report* began: "Congress is on the verge of taking the first step toward a guaranteed annual income from which there would be no retreat." Advertisements in the *Wall Street Journal,* the *Washington Post,* and the Washington *Evening Star* called attention to the issue. Lobbyists went to work. There was no congressional rush, however, to be recorded on behalf of the Chamber's position. Interviews with two Democrats on the Ways and Means Committee, Al Ullman of Oregon and Phil A. Landrum of Georgia, were reproduced, but even these congressmen were a bit puzzled, a bit ambivalent about FAP. Ullman was asked:

Isn't it rather unusual for the very conservative, prudent and knowledgeable Ways and Means Committee to offer a bill of this kind to the Congress? A bill which is going to cause us either more deficit spending, or which will lower the value of our dollars, or call for more taxes.

He replied:

In my judgment, it's almost unbelievable that, first, this Administration—which is supposed to be conservatively oriented—would propose this type of program, and it's equally unbelievable that the Ways and Means Committee would be reporting it out with such an overwhelming majority.

Yet Ullman went on to state he was not opposed to national standards for welfare and would be introducing legislation to establish "a basic Federal minimum of approximately the $1,600 base." It was only the guaranteed-income aspect of FAP that troubled him.

Once FAP had passed the House, in April 1970, opposition from the National Chamber became more sustained. The June issue of *Washington Report* carried an open letter from Arch N. Booth, executive vice-president, sounding genuine alarm, asking that members write or phone their senators and write the president. Booth wrote:

Never before has Congress considered a bill that more radically affects the relationship between government and the individual, or a bill that is *potentially as costly* to taxpayers.

The Chamber had by now discovered that there was technically no work requirement in FAP and made the most of this. Booth continued:

The Work "Requirement" Fallacy

The Administration will not admit to such rising costs—but says this program will lessen welfare costs because it is designed to get people off welfare and into jobs. They praise the bill's requirement that families must register for work or training, in order to qualify for the income payments. *However, they fail to emphasize that the bill does not literally require the father to work or train.* If he merely registers, but then refuses to work or train, his family's income supplement is reduced by only $300.

But if he were willing to work or train, one must question what sort of bureaucracy will be required to develop employability plans for the some three million adults who theoretically would register. The paperwork, the forms, the spot checking—and the frustrations—would be staggering.

One must also question the sincerity of any belief that this work-or-train feature will actually work. Welfare activists and other liberals insist that the income is a right, and that there must be no requirements to work or take training. The National Welfare Rights Organization has actually coached welfare recipients on how to avoid work or training. A newspaper article quotes one of the organization's

292 | DANIEL P. MOYNIHAN

attorneys as saying, "You can stay out . . . until Hell freezes over if you know how to do it."

Because the work "requirement" won't work as promised, the Administration bill will simply make *permanent* additions to the welfare rolls.

With 3,800 trade associations and local chambers of commerce, a direct membership of some 35,000 business firms, and, in its own formulation, "an underlying membership of approximately five million individuals and firms," it is fair to assume the Chamber's opposition had some consequence. It provided arguments for conservatives, never especially articulate, who had been taken by surprise when the proposal was first made, and thereafter half silenced by the strong national consensus that "something had to be done about welfare." At this time Governor Ronald Reagan of California discovered that FAP was a guaranteed income with no work requirement and came openly into opposition, a move the White House had feared. The Chamber did what it could to make the point that FAP was more complicated than a proposal for families of four to live on $1,600 a year, showing that large families would receive payments at income levels not at all associated with poverty. The geometric increase in costs that would accompany seemingly modest increases in benefit levels was also noted. It was asserted that a $3,600 payment level would cost $20 billion. But the Chamber made no noticeable effort to draw attention to the cost of a $5,500 level, which had become the standard of the liberal opposition. There was never any possibility of such legislation and it was ignored. The Chamber, though opposed, was not hysterical. It did not seek to frighten.

For how close a question it was! The National Association of Manufacturers, an organization not dissimilar in its membership from the Chamber of Commerce, and with, if anything, a more conservative past, looked at the very same aspect of FAP that preoccupied the Chamber and came to just the opposite conclusion. On August 26, 1969, a committee of the NAM produced a paper, later published, entitled *Incentives and the Welfare Programs*. It was a careful, competent statement, taking available research as far as it could be stretched, noting a study by Podell in which 60 percent of AFDC mothers with preschool

children stated a preference for work if there was a place for
their children to be cared for, and coming to the conclusion that
the president had *not* proposed a guaranteed income.

The guaranteed annual income concept, as the President noted, is
unrelated to work. It would provide cash for those with incomes below
some arbitrary level on a "no strings" basis.

The NAM did not testify on FAP before Ways and Means,
but when the legislation reached the Senate, and looked to be in
trouble, Archer L. Bolton, Jr., chairman of its Government
Operations Expenditures Committee, appeared as its representative before the Senate Committee on Finance and declared that
the NAM supported FAP. Senator John J. Williams, Republican
of Delaware, had to have this repeated.

SENATOR WILLIAMS: Do I understand that you are endorsing the
bill as recommended; its amendments by the administration?
MR. BOLTON: Yes, sir.

The NAM had suggestions for phasing out food stamps "which
raise income without commensurate work effort," and for perhaps putting off the effective date of the program, then July 1,
1971, by six months, but nothing more than that. It was persuaded that the work incentives would work. Bolton testified:

One charge against the bill has been that it inevitably will lead to a
flat benefit-guaranteed income for all. The critical factor, in our view,
is how the benefit incentive system is structured. If the basic allowance is a realistic minimum, and if the earnings disregard provides a
true incentive to work and advancement and if the work requirement
is strong, we feel such a program directs away from, rather than
closer to, a guaranteed annual income. We feel it strengthens rather
than weakens the connection between work and income and, most
important, strengthens the thesis that receiving public welfare is not
a blanket right but does entail responsibilities to society as well.

The NAM did not press its position, but it had taken it, and the
Administration made what use it could of this. (Williams, the
ranking Republican member of the Senate Finance Committee,
would not introduce the president's legislation. This was done by

294 | *DANIEL P. MOYNIHAN*

the second ranking member, Senator Wallace F. Bennett of
Utah, a past president of the NAM.)

The endorsement of FAP by the NAM, even more than
that of the Urban Coalition, strengthened the president on his
right. There was business-conservative opposition to FAP, but it
was never massive, and it was never unanimous. The NAM position suggests that the president had been sure in his instinct to
press the "workfare" aspect of the proposal, and within his
political rights, as it were, to differentiate between *his* program
and a guaranteed income. The president might say in an aside, as
in fact he did, that the "work requirement" was only a means of
getting the guaranteed income. He might, as he also did, increasingly use the term "guaranteed income" in semipublic remarks.
But by that term he did *not* mean freedom from a social responsibility of adults to support themselves by work. He had no
ambivalence about this issue, and the NAM was justified in
taking him at his word that FAP was not intended to produce a
nation of freeloaders.

The Chamber of Commerce was within *its* rights to note the
disposition of a certain type of middle-class professional to disparage "dead-end" jobs, and to encourage the view that the
correct attitude toward work programs was to evade them. This
was a position widely enough held in some circles, and anyone
might have been concerned as to what would be its eventual
impact on American society. *Any* system of income maintenance
poses a threat to work incentives, and FAP was the most extensive such system ever proposed. Nonetheless, the work ethic was
intact in America in 1969, and the NAM was not wrong to hold
that there was no evidence decent incentives would not lead
toward employment and away from dependency. FAP provided
an income floor, but it did not envisage a mass of persons settling
there as a permanent pauper class. Far from being a threat to old
standards, there is evidence that the FAP proposal was seen by
many as a reaffirmation of them. As the House readied itself to
vote in April 1970, the National Federation of Independent
Business, Inc., released a survey of 25,304 firms that showed 60
percent in favor of the Administration proposal to "give a minimum basic family income," and only 29 percent opposed.

7. Organized Religion

The struggle over the Full Employment Bill of 1946 was seen as one between the forces of business and of labor in a political culture increasingly defined in class terms. The failure to obtain a national commitment to full employment was a defeat for labor, just as the failure to maintain full employment over the next quarter century created the changed political culture in which FAP was debated. Although it became common to speak of FAP as the most important legislation since the New Deal, this was reference to legislation that was enacted. In terms of the issues involved, and the universal nature of the proposals, the Full Employment Bill was both a more recent and a more relevant predecessor. The debate over FAP, however, took place against a very different background. Race, rather than class, had become the fiery, presumptive issue of the time. Increasingly this brought organized religion into national politics to a degree that had had no equivalent since the prohibition movement.

In his study of the Full Employment Bill, Bailey refers twice to the National Association for the Advancement of Colored People, twice to the National Catholic Welfare Conference, and once to the National Council of Jewish Women, in the course of brief accounts of their marginal role in the "lib-lab lobby," itself an affair of no great moment. Those, plus a cross-reference in his index to the NAACP, are the sum of references to race and religion in *Congress Makes a Law,* a book, to repeat, about business and labor. In the period that followed there was a near reversal of roles. Organized labor and organized business remained enormously influential in national affairs. But, on balance, attention moved elsewhere. The primitive conflicts of industrialization had receded, to be replaced by the more advanced—or yet more primitive—issues of ethnicity, community, life styles, cultural values. Race and religion now acquired a saliency of their own.

A distinction can be made between social conflict which admits of contractual solution and that which does not. The clash of capital and labor did. This made possible a resolution of conflict and led to a strengthening of the contracting organizations, at least those of labor, and possibly those of capital also. The "urban crisis" of the 1960s admitted of no such outcome. To the extent that it manifested itself as "ghetto" riots, these were utterly unorganized. Attempts by the national government to create through community organization some potentially contracting entity achieved little. In the absence of particularistic organizations, it became logical to seek agreement at the generalized, universalist level of the social contract. Major legislation, constitutional amendments, even Supreme Court decisions when adhered to, frequently have the quality of agreements reached by contracting parties. FAP was an effort to fulfill an implicit commitment of the national society to the poor. The poor were not organized, nor perhaps organizable, and there were few representatives that could claim to speak for them save in a self-conferred capacity. Inevitably this concatenation of circumstances gave to those elements in organized religion seeking greater "relevance" an opportunity that had not previously existed, for who could better claim an institutional right to speak for the dispossessed?

This role had become prominent during the civil-rights struggles of the early 1960s. The issues of these conflicts did lend themselves to statutory contract, and had been successfully resolved. (E.g., the Voting Rights Act was in this sense an agreement by which the national government undertook to insure that specific rights of specific citizens would be protected and upheld.) Organized religion had played a role in this settlement. The Protestant, Catholic, Jewish triad that had become a fixture at inaugural ceremonies, and similar occasions of public piety, became a feature also of legislative lobbying.

In the aftermath of the civil-rights experience, the major religious organizations set much store by presenting a common front, and did so when possible. All of the more active groups welcomed the FAP proposal, and such a common front was readily established among the National Council of Churches, the U.S. Catholic Conference, and the Synagogue Council of America. However, as time passed, this unity fractured as Protestant support for FAP began to give way to doubts. Differences in religious political styles are only beginning to be explored, but they exist, and have consequences. A remark, only half-serious, of the period is suggestive. A pragmatic, highly educated Jewish aide to a liberal Catholic mayor of a Northeastern city was asked how things were going. "Not too well," he replied, adding, "it was a bad day for urban government when the Protestant clergy stopped believing in God." These different styles seemed almost assigned roles as the struggle for FAP progressed. Jewish support was throughout intelligent, practical, and offered more as advice than as pressure. Catholics behaved as idealists with responsibility for governing. Problems were real, resources limited, outcomes would be less than satisfactory, but things would have to go on. (John Cardinal Dearden, President of the U.S. Catholic Conference and Archbishop of Detroit, had asserted that the urban crisis was very close to a Catholic-Negro confrontation, which was certainly the case in his own and similar industrial cities. He was a member of the Policy Council of the Urban Coalition Action Council and a steady advocate of large social initiatives such as FAP.) Protestants, more than the others, behaved as men of the cloth. Their tendency was to apply to issues such as the work requirement in FAP a doctrinal more than a prudential standard. What was right? What was wrong? A Catholic official remarked on the reversal of roles. In the past Protestant representatives had upheld in interreligious councils the art of the possible, while Catholics had insisted on doctrine. Now it was the other way. Among liberal Protestants there had been a transfer to politics of a fair amount of religious conviction and impatience with the earthbound realities of budget constraints and legislative coalition building.

Concern for race was never far from the minds of their leaders at this time. Blacks were fellow Protestants; their ancestors had been Protestant slaves; the South was a Protestant region. As a result, perhaps, deference to the ways in which blacks defined black problems was strong. When black voices were raised against FAP the liberal white Protestants of the National Council of Churches grew uneasy, and at length uncertain. (When H.R. 1 came to a vote in the House of Representatives in June 1971 the Council opposed it as "racist.")

Still, a common front of the three major national religious bodies was maintained throughout the 91st Congress. Whatever the difference in individual styles, the more singular fact is that by the end of the 1960s the Protestants, Catholics, and Jews *in their national organizations* espoused almost identical views on social issues, views considerably more "advanced" than the politics of their coreligionists, Jews perhaps excepted. America had become a society in which the most vocal and uncompromising demands for social change came from the top.

The first formal response to the president's address came from the National Council of Churches, representing thirty-five Protestant, Anglican, and Orthodox communions. On September 12, its General Board adopted a resolution welcoming the proposal. The Board had recorded its support of a guaranteed income in 1968. However, it found the FAP payment level of $1,600 "less than adequate." Congress was urged to enact legislation with a higher level, to include individuals and childless couples, and to exempt all mothers with children from any requirement of employment or training. All in all, this response was a bit distant.

Catholic response was warmer. Family Assistance was, for them, almost a reward for a half-century of persistent exposition of social principles which on the whole had been misunderstood or ignored when not actually rejected. Organized Catholicism had been perhaps too successful in encouraging a virulent anti-Communism in American foreign policy, had been moderately successful in support of collective bargaining and the rights of labor, but had near to nothing to show for its assertion that family welfare must be a central concern of social policy. In a Labor Day address, just weeks after that of the president, Msgr. Lawrence J. Corcoran, executive secretary of the National Conference of Catholic Charities, hailed the event and called on Catholics to work hard for enactment of the legislation, although he noted risks. He, too, thought $1,600 too low, and was concerned about possible forced labor, depressed wages, and the absence of provision for job creation. A pastoral letter of the Catholic bishops in 1968 had called for a family allowance, and had related this to a general family policy.

Informed social critics are asserting that family instability in the urban areas of America is the result, in part at least, of our national failure to adopt comprehensive and realistic family-centered policies during the course of this century. The breakdown of the family has intrinsic causes, some of them moral, but these have been aggravated by the indifference or neglect of society and by the consequences of poverty and racist attitudes. The object of wise social policy is not only the physical well-being of persons but their emotional stability and moral growth, not as individuals but, whenever possible, within family units.

A resolution of the U.S. Catholic Conference in April 1970 urged the passage of the bill asking, nonetheless, that the $1,600 "be substantially raised." In the meantime the Family Life Bureau of the U.S. Catholic Conference, headed by Reverend James T. McHugh, began a sustained campaign on behalf of the legislation. Msgr. George G. Higgins, perhaps the one man to be involved in both the effort to enact the Full Employment Act of 1946 and now the Family Assistance Act of 1970, lent the full support of the Division for Urban Life, and of his influential column "The Yardstick—Catholic Tests of a Social Order."

Both Protestants and Catholics expressed essentially the same objections to FAP, but drew increasingly divergent conclusions from them. Without ever quite breaking with the others, the Protestants became less and less convinced that a bill need be passed in the 91st Congress. The Catholics became, if anything, more convinced. Jewish organizations tended to share this latter view, and no one expressed it with greater force than Hyman Bookbinder, the Washington representative of the American Jewish Committee. Bookbinder had been an official of the Kennedy and Johnson administrations, one of the group that put together the poverty program, later an assistant director of OEO, and still later an aide to Vice-President Hubert Humphrey. Under his influence, in order to support Family Assistance, the American Jewish Committee abandoned its practice of not normally becoming involved with legislation affecting specific social and economic programs.

Bookbinder's was the voice of battered idealism. In testimony before Ways and Means and the Senate Finance Committee he referred repeatedly to a life spent in the pursuit of social justice and asserted that FAP was "the most exciting and promising program in the domestic field for many, many years." He told the senators, "Frankly, I had not dared dream that *any* Administration elected in 1968 would offer such a daring proposal." In November 1969 he had said to the representatives, "It would be a great tragedy if the combination of those who think the program goes too far and those who think it does not go far enough should succeed in keeping this program from being launched." In August 1970, as that combination began to take shape, he told the Senate Committee, "It would be a tragedy of incalculable proportions if understandable concerns about some aspects of the plan should obscure [its] . . . basic ingenuity and purposes. . . ." He pleaded with fellow liberals not to let "the best . . . be the enemy of the good." As detailed objections piled up he kept insisting that the Administration was trying to be flexible, that "it is clear that no combination of suggestions would completely satisfy any member of the Congress, let alone *every* member."

On balance, Jewish organizations followed Bookbinder's lead, but the impulse to improve on FAP was strong. His own American Jewish Committee, in a statement adopted by the executive board, called for an increase in the $1,600 level, the inclusion of childless couples and individuals, and "flexibility" about work incentive proposals for mothers with children over six. This was a symbolic position. To ask that the minimum be raised, without specifying the level it should be raised to, was not to be seen as a serious objection. Nonetheless, most organizations felt called on to propose some improvement. A statement issued by the National Jewish Welfare Board asked, for example, that the public sector become the employer of last resort, in order, presumably, to make work incentives meaningful.

Shortly before the House vote, the Synagogue Council of America, the coordinating agency of Orthodox, Conservative, and Reform Judaism, adopted a resolution similar to those of the Protestant and Catholic bodies. With this action a formal tripartite position became possible, and in the name of the "Judeo-Christian heritage" members of the House were so advised. Thereafter the general secretaries of the three national organizations proclaimed June 1–7 "Welfare Reform Week" asking "religious leaders throughout the nation to join us in expressing their concern for welfare reform," and trusting that these expressions might reach a high point during the religious services of June 5–7. The Catholic instruction, sent to all dioceses, religious orders, institutions, and organizations was entitled "An Appeal on Behalf of the Family Assistance Program." It asked for activities to "inspire the United States senators to enact a strong bill."

In August 1970 the general secretaries of the three organizations appeared jointly before the Senate Finance Committee to present a somewhat stiff statement declaring that FAP merited their "endorsement and support," followed by a statement of general principles and a list of everyone's objections. A generalized defensiveness about the poor was much in evidence in this and in similar statements. The trio, for example, contended both that welfare eroded family stability, and that requirements that "mothers of young children must work or take job training as a *condition* for receiving welfare assistance" did so as well.

Again the wearisome comment is in order that it would be difficult to assess the results of the efforts of the religious organizations. The impression is that they became less effective as time passed. In the beginning the religious groups helped to lend legitimacy, even normalcy, to a proposal that conventional political wisdom assumed would be rejected as "too much." As time passed they inevitably lent support to the proposition that it was "too little." Bookbinder's bind. Some saw this clearly enough. In a letter to the Catholic hierarchy asking help with the Senate and informing them of the forthcoming tripartite testimony, John E. Cosgrove, Director of the Department of Social Development of the Catholic body, wrote:

While we will testify that there are weaknesses that need strengthening . . . the important thing is to establish a nationwide minimum family assistance benefit and to aid the working poor. This bill does these things.

Somehow this sense of urgency did not come through. The three general secretaries were followed at the witness table by representatives of the Federation of Jewish Philanthropies of New York, the Federation of Protestant Welfare Agencies, and Catholic Charities of the Archdiocese of New York and Brooklyn. Never to their knowledge, they testified, had the three local groups appeared before that or any other committee of Congress "To testify with one voice on behalf of any legislative proposal to aid the poor and needy." But only paragraphs later they were asking that the minimum be raised, that single persons and childless couples be included, and were describing the work requirement for mothers as "arbitrary and unnatural."

Increasingly this kind of testimony damaged the reputation of FAP among persons of doctrinaire bent. In what name of what higher good was Congress to impose an "arbitrary and unnatural" requirement on the mothers of children? Never mind that there was no such requirement in the legislation.

Assessing the impact of statements such as those offered by religious organizations on FAP is an exercise in nuance in which no one person's judgment is likely to satisfy another's. Statements differed more in tone than in content: near identical formulations were perceived as positive in the one instance, negative in the other. The essential fact is that Protestant support steadily eroded until it was understood in Washington that the National Council did not really favor FAP. The price of achieving agreement on a joint statement had been for the Catholics and Jews to play down their genuine support. In the end the churches and synagogues sounded a most uncertain trumpet.

8. The Social Welfare Profession

If the struggle over the Full Employment Act of 1946 was closest in time to the debate over Family Assistance, the National Insurance Act of 1911, enacted by Herbert Asquith's prewar Liberal government in Britain, was the nearest and in ways the only counterpart in substance and origin. It marked a quantum change in social policy, the beginning, in Bentley B. Gilbert's assessment, "of what might be termed the pioneering phase of social reform."[24] Until that moment reform in Britain and elsewhere had been a singularly incremental process.

Of a sudden, Winston Churchill, President of the Board of Trade, had drafted, introduced, and carried legislation establishing compulsory unemployment insurance. No nation, not even the Germans, had ever before dared insure its citizens against the risks of this prime disorder of industrialism. "To a more experienced social reformer," Gilbert writes, "unemployment insurance would have appeared impossibly dangerous." In part the danger derived from the absence of informed opinion that could be counted on to support such a measure. Social insurance given as a right was not a demand on the capitalist society that would have been put forward by socialists such as the Webbs, whose attachment was rather to the idea that, even after collectivism had taken over from capitalism, self-improvement, preachment and discipline in the working classes would be a precondition to an eventual classless society. Much as Nixon was to do long after, Churchill, in 1909, turned inward to government resources to draft his program, and then appealed primarily to the national political interests of party politicians to enact it.

It is the seeming nature of the chiliast to resist social changes which, however profound, are not perceived as somehow ultimate. Taken to its extreme, as certainly the Webbs did not, this disposition can create a *politique du pire,* not merely resistance to social betterment, but actual fear of it. By contrast, an aspect of liberal reform, as a political style, is a capacity to do large things without overmuch concern for large consequences. Both styles, the chiliastic and the reformist, tend, when they clash, to take seemingly incongruous positions. Thus the left in Edwardian Britain displayed much concern with the consequences social insurance might have for the character of the recipient, although their true concern was to transform the society. Churchill professed indifference to the character of the workman, asserting it was the duty of society to change the conditions in which he worked. Should a workman lose his job through drunkenness, the state would nonetheless pay him his insurance. "I do not like," he wrote at the time, "mixing up moralities and mathematics."

But, of course, his real concern was what *did* happen to the workman. Unemployment, as he saw it, was a risk in which "there is no proportion between personal failings and the penalties exacted. . . ." There was, he judged, "no reason to suppose that a mitigation of the extreme severities will tend in any way to a diminution of personal responsibility, but . . . on the contrary more will be gained by an increase of ability to fight than will be lost through an abatement of the extreme consequences of defeat."[25] Sixty years later, in not very different terms,

Richard Nixon, who was not the least disposed to utopianism, proposed a guaranteed income because he thought it must be dreadful to send one's daughter to the store with food stamps.

Churchill paid for his audacity. He had broken free, as Gilbert sums it up, of the influence of the Webbs and "their allies in the higher ranks of the civil service, in the Left Wing of the Labor movement, and among the Liberal intellectuals in the constituencies," and they in turn withdrew their approval. For the rest of his career he was known rather as an opponent of social reform. He was, in any event, hardly known as the author of what continues to be the boldest item of social legislation in the history of industrial democracy.

Nixon's reputation remains to be settled, but the reception of FAP within circles professionally concerned with social welfare was strikingly convergent. If there was a difference, it was mostly that by 1969 the size and influence of this group in the United States had significantly changed. Its influence derived from an ever larger audience of educated, well-to-do citizens who normally associate themselves with liberal social measures and follow the opinion of professionals, both in a strict and loose sense of the term. In turn, the number of professionals grew with successful efforts to obtain public funds to purchase their services, a process in which they, as other elements of the grants economy, both responded to and induced demand. This created a not always inchoate class interest.

Social work is one such profession. It is not large, but neither is it insignificant. A quarter of all master's degrees awarded in the social sciences are in the category of "social work, administration, and welfare." The National Association of Social Workers reports a membership of 50,000, to which must be added many practitioners not fully accredited. In a Senate speech in 1971, Abraham Ribicoff, Democrat of Connecticut, reported that the number of social workers grew from 41,000 in 1960 to 144,000 in 1968. As the services economy has grown, and as government employment has grown, this generalized group of educated persons in meliorative callings has burgeoned accordingly.

In a 1916 editorial in *American Federationist,* Gompers was singularly hostile to this still nascent development.

Some of these understudies to Providence, are actuated by generous and sympathetic emotions. They want to do good in the world—the majority, in truth, that they may feel that glow of gratification that comes from doing *for* others. They have a vision of a new world with themselves as the creators. The work of these creators and renovators has become commercialized and dignified by the title of profession— they are experts—experts in social welfare, experts on home life, domestic relations, child life, and the thousand and one problems that arise out of the lives of the poor. They are willing and feverishly anxious to be appointed upon commissions or as government agents to help the wage-earners to save their money; to secure minimum wages by law; to secure legislative provisions protecting their physical well-being. All these solutions are formulated along lines that necessitate governmental machinery and the employment of experts—the "intellectuals." The conclusion is inevitable that there is a very close connection between *employment* as experts and the enthusiasm for human welfare.[26]

The comment was not unfounded. Gompers acknowledged idealism of motive, while insisting that success would create institutional interests that would be—what?—as selfish and self-centered as any. It is difficult to reconstruct the clarity with which men such as Gompers perceived that the mind-set represented by the Webbs was essentially statist, and accordingly a threat to trade unions and all such voluntary activity. His task was the simpler because trade unionism existed as an alternative strategy for the worker.

A half century later, however, this did not appear as a viable option for the working and dependent poor, the former too scattered and marginal to organize, the latter having no effective sanction—equivalent to the strike—with which to bargain. The poor could be disruptive, but this did not transform them into a bargaining unit. In these circumstances the role of representing the dependent poor was assumed by individuals and organizations, increasingly tending toward professionalism, perceived vaguely but not inaccurately as the world of social welfare. They were with but not of the poor; they did not so much speak for them as they negotiated for them (as well as tried to serve them), which in most circumstances meant trying to get more money out of one or another level of government. A conflict of interest was unavoidable. Not only their clients, but they themselves were dependent on government (with exceptions, to be sure). They had their own interests, and it would have been singular indeed if they had not sought to advance them, increasingly through trade unions, and through professional accreditation systems that serve a similar function at a more exalted level. This trade unionism might have surprised Gompers, but little else. Weeks after the 1968 election Kenneth Boulding charged that what Gompers had feared had come to pass.

The New Deal and its successors were at least in part a fraud. Social democracy in practice has meant much more in redistributions toward the deserving middle class and the people who know how to get on the gravy train than it has for the poor.

The war on poverty, he speculated, "may well have distributed more to those who work as administrators than it has to the poor."[27] No final generalization is possible, nor is any necessary. There was as much or more good with the bad. It is only required that the question be raised: *Who* gets *what?*

Whatever is precisely the case, the general point is that the growth of welfare dependency and the initiation of federally financed welfare and antipoverty activities under successive Democratic presidents had by the end of the 1960s created a large and strategically placed interest group. This interest group had to be affected by the Family Assistance proposal, and this in turn would be affected by the group's response. How *would* the heirs of the Webbs, "their allies in the higher ranks of the civil service, in the Left Wing of the labor movement, and among the Liberal intellectuals in the constituencies," respond? In a word, they did all in their power to insure that a guaranteed income was not enacted.

From the first announcement of FAP, through its triumphant passage in the House, death by inanition in the Senate Finance Committee, and resurrection as H.R. 1 in the following Congress, the *de facto* strategy of social-welfare groups was to seek to kill the program, first by insisting on benefit levels that no Congress would pass and no president would approve, and, second, by raising issues about details of the legislation which allowed the entire initiative to be labeled oppressive, repressive, regressive, and worse. Those involved would probably deny any intention actually to kill the legislation. Nor should it be assumed that this was in fact a deliberate, conscious objective. But it *was* the consistent thrust of everything done.

The actual demands of the welfare professionals were not so different from those of organized religion or labor. Fairly early a consensus view was reached among most such groups, and was generally thereafter adhered to. But the style of the professionals, unyielding, often *enragé,* was quite different, while their assertions, delivered with the authority of persons who *know,* frequently approached and on occasion *must* have involved conscious dishonesty. (This may be harsh, but the alternative explanation—incompetence—is hardly less so. Social work training is both "soft" in a disciplinary sense, and—so it is contended—curiously distant from the realities of public welfare. In 1967 Steiner wrote that "professional social work, NASW* style, seems to have neither an immediate nor a direct tie to either public assistance workers or public assistance clients."[28] It may just be that the spokesmen for the social welfare profession—who were repeatedly *wrong* in what they said— were innocent of anything but pretending to a competence they do not possess in themselves nor inculcate in others.) It could not be demanded of a rabbi or a business-equipment manufacturer that he be thoroughly versed in the history of work requirements in the AFDC program, but this could be expected of a welfare administrator pronouncing on the subject *ex cathedra.* A labor leader, or an Episcopal bishop, might not have followed the subtleties of the negative income tax, but welfare professionals, who for decades on behalf of clients had been begging crumbs at the tables of the mighty, had a responsibility to acknowledge that now that the initiative had been taken by the government itself they were demanding the spoils of empire as a condition of beginning talks.

This does not exaggerate. In June 1970 the 98th annual meeting of the National Conference on Social Welfare called for an adequate, federally financed "income maintenance program" for the Nation's poor. In telegrams to all members of the Senate,

* National Association of Social Workers.

the Conference urged the adoption of a guaranteed annual income based on the BLS low-income budget, which their resolution stated to be $5,500 for a family of four. This was now almost a fixed demand. Had it been acknowledged that this meant providing income supplements to perhaps some 150 million persons at an annual cost of some $70 billion, it would have been at least an honest proposal. But nothing of this kind was done. Instead, the reasonable-sounding "BLS" $5,500 figure kept being invoked. In the course of a panel discussion, State Senator Barbara Jordan, of Texas, a black member of the President's Commission on Income Maintenance Programs, which by then had proposed an income guarantee at almost precisely the FAP level, explained, "We knew this was below the poverty level. But we chose it because it was a level that could be implemented promptly." The response of Whitney Young, Jr., then serving as president of the National Association of Social Workers, was simple moralism: "If Congress believes this is unrealistic," he was reported as stating, "then the values of our society are really twisted. We should be asking for what the Government itself says is the minimum for living."

The contrast with conservative criticism and commentary is surely to the disadvantage of the liberal social-welfare professionals, if advantage goes to clarity, thoroughness, and openness. At this time, for example, the American Enterprise Institute for Public Policy Research issued an analysis of FAP which point by point stated the case, pro and con, raising legitimate issues, as in this comment on day care.

The proposal would finance comprehensive care worth up to $1,600 to $2,000 per child for families whose incomes are low enough to qualify for FAP, say $3,500 a year, but not for those whose incomes are just a little higher, say $4,000.

Entitled *The Bill to Revamp the Welfare System,* the Institute pamphlet was lengthy and detailed. Its facts were accurate, and it raised what were, to conservatives, legitimate questions, often of some subtlety. By contrast, the charges of welfare professionals were frequently inaccurate, often grossly so. FAP would reduce benefits, deny benefits, hold up benefits. It would punish fathers, punish mothers, punish children. It was a "significant setback" for the poor in the editorial judgment of *New Generation,* journal of the National Committee on Employment of Youth.

Thus when FAP was first proposed it was at least generally agreed that the legislation exempted mothers with preschool children from the "work requirement." By the end of the 91st Congress, even this history had been rewritten. In December 1970 Reverend Theodore M. Hesburgh, Chairman of the U.S. Commission on Civil Rights, on behalf of the Commission, sent a letter to each senator urging approval of FAP.

I firmly believe this legislation rests on deep moral principles and its enactment will advance this Nation toward the just and decent society for which we all strive.

He noted, however, there were "problems," including *"the requirement that mothers of preschool children register for work"* (my emphasis). It was by this time almost routine for persons such as Hesburgh to make such mistakes, or, more probably, for the staff of the Civil Rights Commission to do so.* The reputation of FAP had been undermined. It might have been seen as a useful move, but never as a generous-minded one. As time passed amendments to the legislation demanded by Congress did give rise to legitimate qualms and objections from the point of view of welfare professionals. But the disposition to oppose was present from the outset. It merely gained force when it acquired substance.

The hostility and opposition of the welfare professionals flowed from a cascade of identifiable concerns, of which the first and most elemental was that the president had seized the initiative in an area that had theretofore been their preserve. It was utterly unexpected, and instantly compromised their claim to special knowledge and concern in the field. Some welfare groups had been tinkering with family-allowance proposals, most had got to the idea of uniform minimum standards in welfare, and there was a small shelf of reports proposing that the various categories of aid be collapsed into one general program of assistance based on need. (The most prominent of such documents was the 1966 Report of the Advisory Council on Public Welfare,

* Hesburgh's letter was dated December 11, 1970. A follow-up letter was sent as soon as the mistake was pointed out.

established by Congress to review the Social Security system, entitled *Having the Power, We Have the Duty*. In essence, this was a request for more money. The Advisory Council also proposed strengthened social services; legal representation and an appeal system for recipients or applicants; a positive program of informing recipients and applicants of their rights; the expansion of recruitment, education, and training of welfare personnel, including preprofessional, professional, and advanced social-work education. The list acquires a liturgical consonance.) Of a sudden a president assumed to be backward in such matters had submitted to the Nation a proposal that, regardless of what particulars might be cited in defense of the profession, was far in advance of it. In putting forth his proposal the president perforce declared the AFDC system over which the profession had presided to be a destructive failure, while one and all—outside the profession—agreed. (In truth the ADC program had been a large achievement in its time, and had meant life itself to millions of families in the years that followed.) All this was a shock only slightly foretold by the 1967 Amendments. Welfare had never before been such an issue. The only previous occasion on which a president had made any significant proposals had been in 1962 when, on the advice of the profession, John F. Kennedy had proposed more funds for training and employing professional workers. The only defense was attack, and attack they did.

Appropriately, the first hostile reaction to FAP came from the poverty program. If the legatees of the New Deal were somewhat disingenuously self-interested, those of the Great Society were avowedly aggrandizing: a matter of style. The 1960s quip that "There's money in poverty," was the least of it. There was power to be had as well, primarily through control of the community action agencies of the great cities. There was never as much money *or* power as was in some vague way promised or expected, but this hardly lessened appetites. The poverty program had begun in considerable confusion, but had evolved in the tradition of the Webbs. The poor were to be helped through strategies that would lead to individual improvement and collective self-realization, with a considerable degree of elite direction. An income strategy, as was the case with unemployment benefits paid impartially to the drunk and sober workman, was a threat to this strategy, and perceived as such. This may be too subtle: a proposal to put an end to poverty, or the largest share thereof, through direct cash payments was by any definition a threat to an agency proceeding at the same task by indirect means. Within a month of the president's address, the California CAP Directors Association adopted a "Position Paper on National Policies and Priorities" which denounced the welfare proposal and the Administration generally with an extravagance of paranoid and often incoherent insinuation. (Thus, it was asserted that the Administration, by reducing opportunities for the poor and disadvantaged, "may produce the volunteer military establishment desired by the Nixon Administration but it will also undermine the economics of family formation and stability needed by the total society." Some meaning was intended: just what no one will know.) It was a tract for the time.

The Nixon Administration is revealing itself to be the enemy of the poor and the disadvantaged and . . . is attempting to convert the local community action agency and organizations across the State into the visible and immediate instrument of new forms of neocolonialism.

The proposed Nixon welfare proposal to deal with family income maintenance is little more than a public relations gimmick to subsidize cheap labor and involuntary servitude. . . . All at the expense of the poor.

The rhetoric of moderation in which the Nixon Administration speaks to the people creates the illusion of new opportunities and benefits. Community Action organizations which have gradually assumed the role of advocates of the poor and deliverers of the needed services to the poor at the same time realize the illusionary quality of the political pronouncement and faced with budget reductions and program constraints cannot deliver. The people whose expectations have been aroused by the moderate rhetoric have no recourse other than to perceive the Community Action organization as no friend of the poor because of their inability to deliver.

Nixon's New Federalism, the rhetoric notwithstanding, represents the regeneration of domestic neocolonialism in dealing with the poor. . . . A regression into paternalism. . . .

The California CAP Directors Association recommends and urges the organization of an army of dissenters in every local community. . . . Our slogan shall be power to the people.

With this, the "deliverers of the needed services to the poor" raised the real issue.

We demand that the Nixon Administration commit itself to a program of block grants to community action agencies and organizations so that local determination has some meaning.

Without much straining the point, this can be seen as an effort to have the community action agencies legitimated as a unit of local government, so as to receive a share of the money Washington seemed intent on making available to localities. Their language was not perhaps that of most claimants on Federal resources, but in other respects the CAP directors were acting in a rational, traditional manner. The Federal government had set them up in business and they were being businesslike.

In September the board of the National Association for Community Development, a Ford Foundation project, approved the California resolution, and in October it was adopted by the annual meeting of the association in Washington, attended by a thousand delegates, for the most part OEO employees. The rhetoric of abuse had become so common as to have lost some of its impact, but more likely than not the event had consequences. A network of federally paid antipoverty workers committed itself near the beginning of the public debate to the assertion that FAP was "little more than a public relations gimmick to subsidize cheap labor and involuntary servitude." The last reference was, of course, to the charge that the program was antiblack.

The community action agency directors had at least some claim to speak for the poor. The next OEO-financed attack on FAP came from a cohort of upper-middle-class professionals who were almost a caricature of Gompers' vision of "intellectuals" doing well by doing good. OEO had established a network of centers, often university based, devoted to the study of poverty. Severe opposition to FAP now came from this area. In July 1970 *The New Republic* published a long letter from a staff attorney (a Smith graduate) at the Center on Social Welfare Policy and Law of Columbia University protesting a column by

John Osborne in which he proposed that, for all its imperfections, the Senate should enact FAP without delay. The letter declared that FAP was "pitilessly inadequate," and replete with "evils." None was more dangerous than the work requirement. "In the past New York has required physically ill men to cut brush in knee-deep snow as part of its General Assistance program. . . ." The states would be able to use the requirement "to channel cheap labor to local employers." "Judicial review of FAP administration is virtually emasculated. . . ." And so it went. The author asked consideration for the proposal put forward by the National Welfare Rights Organization.

It would guarantee $5,500 a year to a family of four, plus a work incentive; increase this floor according to regional living costs and unusual personal needs; provide assistance to all needy persons on an equal basis; and eliminate the work requirement.

In its request, then current, for further OEO funding, the Center on Social Welfare Policy and Law recorded that it had prepared during the preceding year a critique of H.R. 16311 (FAP) which, it said, despite some virtues, "perpetuates much that is wrong in technical and administrative aspects of current Aid programs."

Thus the times and mores. In the 1960s a combination of government and philanthropic activity had set up a fair number of persons in what Martin Mayer has called "the resentment business." What mostly they resented and decried was the actions of government. There is no counterpart to this modern social history: neither to the rewards in money and prestige that attended the role of government denouncer, nor to the absence of an equivalent subsidy for the supporters of government action. (By 1970 the total cost of OEO legal services was just under half that of the Federal judiciary.) It is witness to a certain flexibility in American politics that no one within the Administration grew especially exercised about the matter, although in the aftermath of the letter from the staff attorney a contributing editor of *The New Republic,* wrote the White House, "These are times that try men's tempers."*

* *The New Republic* asked me to respond to the critique of FAP by the Center on Social Welfare Policy and Law. I replied at length to the specific charges of

In this, as in a number of areas, the Republican Administration faced a profession whose political debts were largely to
the Democratic party. The social-welfare programs of the Nation
were preponderantly the creation of Democratic presidents, governors, and mayors. The government bureaucracies owed everything to the Democrats: not least their pride and sense of
purpose. Republicans had been more than aloof; from time to
time they had been hostile and destructive. The exceptions to this
general experience were rare and counted for little. The reluctance to cooperate with a Republican Administration was palpa-
ble, not least within the Federal government itself. For some

---

"pitilessly inadequate" base, "onerous" work requirement, *et al.,* but also dealt
with some of the unspoken implications of Miss Katz's letter:

> I was among those who drafted the Economic Opportunity Act in 1964.
> This may seem a long time ago to her; certainly it does to me. It was a
> moment of high, almost exalted aspiration. The bill proclaimed that we
> would "eliminate the paradox of poverty in the midst of plenty" in the
> United States. Its terms were absolute. Alas, its provisions were some-
> thing less. Money was scarce. A large-scale employment program for
> adult men was considered but rejected as far too costly. (The cost was
> about one-quarter that of the Family Assistance Plan.) In the end we
> settled for a youth employment program, and a variety of services.

> I doubt that any of us in those days could have imagined that in six
> years' time a President would be proposing a comprehensive system of
> graduated income maintenance that in one stroke would eliminate 60
> percent of the poverty in the nation. Still less would we have imagined
> that much of the sustained, detailed opposition to the new program would
> come from representatives of organizations such as the Center on Social
> Welfare Policy and Law, which is funded by the Office of Economic
> Opportunity. I say this because I am dismayed by the rhetoric of Miss
> Katz's letter. . . . Government needs criticism, and should not be loathe
> to pay for it. But do we really need the kind of relentless ascription of
> wrong-doing that pervades Miss Katz's letter?

> I believe I understand the motives of persons such as Miss Katz. She
> would hope for a genuinely marvelous program, with none of the
> strictures, or to use her term "oppressive features," of the present bill, nor
> the compromises with political reality which any legislation requires if it is
> to succeed. But as one who has been involved with this subject a long
> time, may I not plead that what we have before us is infinitely better than
> what we have now, and that everyone's help is needed if the bill is to pass.
> Increasingly it is being opposed by forces of the extreme right, and also
> by plain conservatives who simply don't believe in this kind of thing.
> It would be tragic if compassionate liberals added just that extra push
> that toppled the bill.

time a problem of discipline had been developing in the Washington bureaucracies. It was the foreign-policy and military establishments that had first begun resisting presidential leadership, primarily by going to the press, and by putting to new uses the old tradition of special connections with Congress. By the time Nixon took office the practice was more widespread. The lower echelons at OEO were by then confirmed in the practice of exposing—anonymously—the cruel conspiracies of those above them. This now began to occur in parts of HEW and similar agencies, sanctioned somewhat by the absence of a civil service tradition of apolitical support for the elected government and its policies. This older indiscipline now merged with a new assertion of the obligation of the civil servant, especially professionals, to retain professional autonomy. Here, as in much else, the Republican party suffered from its lack of intellectuals and publicists who could speak with authority to the concerns of this constituency. But the larger fact is that neither party met the standards which many social-welfare professionals looked for in society.

Political party distinctions in the United States tend to correspond to differences on broad areas of social policy, but never with enough clarity to satisfy the truly ideological. Democrats had enacted more welfare legislation by far than Republicans. But neither party, save in rare moments of stress, or in the pronouncements of insurgent candidates, ever adopted the approving, accepting, *loving* concern for the care of the poor which

---

I would return to my earlier theme, and cite Martin Mayer's excellent small book on the New York City teachers strike of 1968. It was a calamity, he reports, brought about by persons of great good will. Too many such persons, he suggests, have been set up in the "resentment business." Their job is to find things that are wrong; then to right them. If their efforts only make matters worse, well, they find something else wrong. There is a saying around the criminal courts, Mayer reports, that "the lawyer always goes home." I respect and admire the things the young poverty program lawyers are doing in this country. But I also have the strongest conviction that if the Family Assistance Plan is not enacted by this Congress it will not be enacted in this decade. I would remind those lawyers that if there is no bill for them to critique next year, they can always join a Wall Street firm. But the children of that Mississippi farmer will go on living the spare, bare life into which they were born, and from which they can be spared only by a large, bold national effort.

("Nixon's Family Assistance Bill: An Attack by Lucy V. Katz, A Defense by Daniel P. Moynihan," *The New Republic*, July 18, 1970, pp. 30–33)

was shared, in varying degrees of intensity to be sure, but withal shared by the welfare profession, and seemingly by so few others. A comparison of the welfare profession with the medieval church is not misleading: a vast institution serving varied interests—fat friars, wicked popes, and all—but institutionally committed to a humane and unselfish view of man's shared fate, and including at all levels men of pure spiritual commitment, whispering into the ears of monarchs, preaching to the masses, praying that men should come at last to see the truth of St. Paul's Epistle to the Corinthians: "And now abideth faith, hope, charity, these three; but the greatest of these is charity."

For such men and women—social welfare having the most equalitarian patterns of membership by race and sex of any profession—the American polity of the second half of the twentieth century presented a dilemma unique, surely, in the history of the relationship of humanitarian movements to the societies in which they arise. The experience of the past had been of sustained tension between ideal and reality, when, that is, the humanitarian ideal was accepted at all. In the West there has been a Judeo-Christian disposition to humanitarian ideals, but at most an intermittent impulse to put such ideals to practice. Social justice evolved from conflict rather than from condescension, much less a confessional renunciation of privilege. The constraints of scarcity mostly accounted for this contradiction, but something beyond that was also involved. The attachment to the ideal was imperfect. The preoccupation of nineteenth-century radicalism with "bourgeois hypocrisy" is suggestive, the term properly applying to discordance between belief and expression of belief, rather than between profession and practice. Belief in salvation by faith is abiding. Purity in conviction rather than faithfulness in practice is ever the first demand of ideologists, even the gentle ideologists of American social-welfare policy. Hence a profound problem arose for them when the American public reversed the old relationship between public ideology and public practice.

Ideologically the American public is conservative; in practice it is liberal. This is one of the most notable, if least noted, findings of American social science. No wholly successful explanation has been put forward to account for it. Probably in largest measure it arises from the intersection of a production-oriented past with the consumption-oriented present made possible by that past. Whatever the case, when presented with propositions scaled along a "conservative-liberal" spectrum, the American public emerges as strongly "conservative" in domestic matters; but when presented with questions that test approval or disapproval of large government social programs, the public preference is just as emphatically "liberal." Albert H. Cantril and Charles W. Roll describe the public response to program proposals in domestic matters as "overwhelmingly 'liberal.'" Describing the findings of a 1964 study, Lloyd A. Free and Hadley Cantril point to the dilemma for social policy arising from this peculiarly American antinomy.

While the old argument about the "welfare state" has long since been resolved in the operational level of government programs, it most definitely *has not* been resolved at the ideological level.[29]

As between national politicians of this period who understood and accepted this condition, and those who did not understand, or, understanding did not accept, there could be little agreement. A simple taxonomy emerges: those who understood and accepted, those who understood and did not accept, those who accepted and did not understand—this last group divided into subspecies of those who took ideological profession to be the dominant reality, and those who took their cues from practice. The three presidents of the 1960s each in his way understood and accepted. This is to say that, apart from personal preferences, they understood that the American public was willing to accept liberal programs *when cast in nonliberal terms*. By extension, this suggested that some programs were so "liberal" as to require not just conservative rhetoric but conservative sponsorship. Hence Johnson might talk of converting "tax eaters" into "tax payers," and his speech writers were certainly equal to the challenge of coining "workfare" or its equivalent, but only Nixon could hope to propose a guaranteed income without arousing genuine public alarm. It does not much abuse the term maturity to assert that the mark of the mature political mind in this period was the ability to understand and even to value this curious combination of liberalism and conservatism in American public mores. In effect the public asked little more than that change be

accompanied by continuity and deference to traditional pro-
prieties: no great condition to impose in a period of continuous
and rapid transformation, especially in technological matters.

More, probably, is obscured than clarified by speaking of
the genius of a people, but a certain prudence, even caginess is to
be seen in this American antinomy. In their ideological conservatism the American people had developed a kind of sea anchor
that had its uses. Some, innocent of subtlety, saw only the
conservative assertion and either approved or despaired. Still
others, innocent of ideology, saw only the practice and wondered
what the fuss was about. (This latter group would include many
of the "regular" Democrats of the industrial cities of the Northeast and Middle West. They had enacted or had helped enact
most of the liberal legislation of the twentieth century. They
seem never to have noticed this, anymore than did the ideological liberals who generally detested them, and at this time, were
steadily displacing them.) None of this was very satisfactory to
persons who understood the situation well enough, but who
could not accept it out of a penchant for tidiness or a taste for
the intensive politics that arise when profession and practice
reinforce rather than restrain one another. Still less was it satisfactory to those who simply did not understand, who, taking
words for deeds, could only see the American public as hostile to
them and indifferent to their purposes. Both these dispositions
were overrepresented in the social-welfare profession, with the
result that it could only respond with its own hostility or indifference to an extraordinarily advanced social-welfare proposal
which the "conservative" public had immediately embraced.

It is beyond the scope of this work to assess the state of the
social-welfare profession in this period, but some general obser-
vations are needed to place the opposition to Family Assistance
in a wider perspective. *Social Work,* the journal of the National
Association of Social Workers, was during these years a strange
melange of traditional articles on case-work and community
organization interspersed with black manifestos and rather unconvincing attempts by upper-middle-class white professionals to
demonstrate how radical and insurrectionary *they* were. Nixon
was an obvious target. Family Assistance was simply dismissed.
"Guaranteed Protestant Ethic," one comment was headed; "Mr.
Nixon's Speenhamland" another. This last article revealed that it

was all a diabolic scheme—"payment for services rendered" in the 1968 presidential campaign, precisely parallel to the older arrangement under which British capitalists battened on pauperized labor.

Small Southern business people, as well as business people elsewhere in the country (the sober, quiet middle class that works and does not demand)—the people who elected Mr. Nixon—could use some primary capital accumulation in this inflationary period. What better way exists to tie small business in the South and elsewhere to the Nixon Administration and build thereby a strong, viable Republican Party throughout the South. Statistics lend support to this view. . . .

The statistics were that 50.4 percent of FAP payments would go to families in the South. That the adults in these families most emphatically did *not* vote for Mr. Nixon posed no difficulty for the author. It was, generally, a "soft" discipline.

Yet a measure of compassion is owed the social worker. What was he or she if not a "sober, quiet middle class [person] that works and does not demand"? And yet the rhetoric of the period had devalued this role in their two primary communities, the campus and the slum. They were, after all, only trying to keep their jobs, keep up payments on the rather complex insurance arrangements the Association sponsored, and perhaps get promoted after accumulating a few more credits at night school. Nor was the profession lost to intellect. Articles such as "Mr. Nixon's Speenhamland" would often be followed by careful letters pointing out mistakes of fact. (At least one reader knew something about Speenhamland.) There were those who tried to maintain standards of analysis and debate, but it was difficult.*

---

* I should make clear with reference to the social work profession, and by extension to all those *employed* in various forms of social meliorism, that I speak only of the leadership cadres. For all I know—and it would not surprise me—there was no group more committed to getting some form of income guarantee —FAP if necessary—than the rank and file members of this profession. Issues of substance would be very close to them simply because their work is close to them. By contrast, the leadership of such groups maintains its own position, and to a degree that of the profession also, by trading in symbolic interests. For good or ill, this leadership at this time interpreted the symbolic interest of itself and the profession as being incompatible with the acceptance of a measure proposed by a Republican administration. It may be speculated that these middle class cohorts now see their interest as integrally associated with the expanding activity of the state, and associate this with the Democratic as

Nor should opposition to FAP be seen as primarily a reflection of upper-middle-class loathing for Nixon. If a Democratic president had proposed such a program he would almost certainly have encountered much the same scorn. The October 1969 issue of *Social Work* featured an article by Robert Harris, executive director of the Heineman Commission on Income Maintenance Programs (that is to say, a body appointed by a Democratic president), entitled "Selecting a System of Income Maintenance for the Nation." He analyzed the basic alternatives: a family allowance or a negative income tax. To eliminate poverty in families with children through a family allowance, he wrote, would cost "well over $100 billion." Obviously a negative tax could be more "efficient." However, he continued, such a tax would have to pay close attention to the question of work.

The issue of work incentives, relatively unimportant when considering the population that currently receives public assistance, looms large in considering programs that move beyond the existing welfare population. We do not want our income transfer system to eliminate financial incentives to work for those who are employable.

Harris' article appears to have been written before Nixon's August 8 address. In his conclusion he stated that there was no public support for *any* such program, and that until proponents of them persuaded the public that such "programs are really deeded to eliminate poverty and that they can be adopted without disastrous side effects," there was no possibility of any being enacted. Even so he came under sharp criticism for his presumed advocacy of work. One commentator wrote:

Work incentives are a questionable criterion, since the bulk of the poor should not be or are not able to be part of the labor force. Further, cost as a criterion can be questioned on the basis of both value and feasibility.

By following a policy based on work incentive we allow the poor again to carry the major human and dollar costs while protecting the taxpayers from bearing a greater tax cost.

---

against the Republican party. This could in part explain the curious post-war process whereby working class trade unionists—depending on the private sector for employment—grew more "conservative" while middle class trade unions and professional associations grew more "liberal."

As a profession that claims to honor the values of individual worth, humanitarianism, and social justice, it is time that social work gave up the nineteenth-century belief that only hunger will spur men to work. It is time to give up the means test. If we truly hold these values we do not have to accept . . . Harris or his value hierarchy that puts work incentive and cost above the values of social justice and human dignity.

Another commentator accused Harris of "scare tactics in citing a $100 billion bill for a children's allowance. . . ." Clearly, the rhetoric and doctrine of the social work profession had developed in a direction that was bound to make "workfare" anathema. By contrast, children's allowances had much greater appeal. (The editor of *Social Work* at this period, Alvin L. Schorr, was an early advocate of this form of income maintenance.) But the enthusiasm for children's allowances was scarcely visible until a president came along with an alternative proposal.

Thus only a *measure* of compassion should be accorded this group. They are not to be judged more greedy than the average interest group, but neither did they show themselves to be other than an interest group, one representing middle-class professional interests at that.[30]

There were individual exceptions. Among the welfare professionals who joined the debate over FAP, there were some few who could follow the presidential purpose. Of these Wilbur J. Cohen, who succeeded Gardner as Secretary of HEW in the last months of the Johnson Administration, was the most prominent. On television following the president's speech, he pronounced that FAP was, of course, a Democratic program, adding, in the manner of men and parties out of office, that it would cost considerably more than had been suggested. His position fluctuated, seeking advantage for the Democrats—he was by now as much a man of party as of profession—but with time his commitment to FAP became solid. It *was*, or he would have hoped it might have been, a Democratic program. He became increasingly active lobbying on its behalf and devising strategies for Democratic congressmen similarly disposed. In the course of the House debate on H.R. 1 he provided Representative Wilbur Mills of Arkansas, chairman of the Committee on Ways and Means, with a letter endorsing the legislation signed by himself and six previous Secretaries of HEW.

Mitchell I. Ginsberg, who had joined the Lindsay Administration in New York as Commissioner of Welfare, and was to become dean of the Columbia University School of Social Work, was more uncertain in his view, but in the end more intense in his commitment. His early reaction to FAP was that it was "a good idea as far as it goes." Its effect in reducing the rate of increase of welfare recipients, he felt, would be limited. He had presided over the transformation of welfare from a residual to a primary social problem of New York City. He had instituted reforms of now uncertain consequence, arguing for the concept of welfare as a right, and treating it as such through the substitution of the voucher system for the means test, and a generally accepting attitude to the growth in the welfare population. The Chamber of Commerce was fond of reproducing a statement of George A. Wiley that "Welfare is a right. We look upon the growth of the welfare rolls as a healthy thing." Ginsberg had been at least partly of this view. He had accommodated if not encouraged the increase in welfare dependency in New York City. But it had gone too far; the need for a nondependent system of income maintenance became evident. He had first favored some form of children's allowance. FAP was a more intensive response to the specific problem of low income and poverty, and he became an adherent. With Lindsay's approval, he gradually spent more time in Washington, ending the 91st Congress as the nearest thing to a full-time lobbyist the legislation had.

Cohen and Ginsberg were welfare professionals whose careers had taken them into or near to electoral politics at the level where men consider seeking the presidency, and some attain it. This is a moderating experience. In particular it is an experience of accommodating to public attitudes rather than seeking to change them. Others in the welfare profession were not required to submit to this discipline, nor yet to live with the narrow time perspectives of men holding or seeking public office. An abiding passion of many of these others was that the public should come to share their own accepting, approving view of welfare. That self-interest and not a little ambiguity might be found in this desire did not lessen it. For many it was a matter beyond interest, partaking of the quality of deep moral conviction. The public response to the president's address had shown with clarity that, properly understood, the American antinomy opened the possibility of extraordinary practical change: a system of income maintenance protecting every family with children in the land. In the short run this might appear an urgent goal for a nation shaken with violence and division, much of which was focused on issues of poverty and inequality. But for the long run it was possible to see it as a defeat: possibly a definitive defeat. The rhetoric of workfare fundamentally challenged the ideology of welfare. So at least, some welfare ideologists believed. The enactment of Family Assistance would enshrine precisely those attitudes which seemed most the enemy of a compassionate and generous attitude toward the poor.

Alvin L. Schorr, long an official of the Social Security Administration, latterly deputy chief of research and planning at OEO, and soon to be dean of the New York University School of Social Work, exemplified this view. Few contemporaries have written so well on the subject of children in poverty (as in his study *Poor Kids*), yet Schorr ended by seeking the defeat of Family Assistance. In an editorial in *Social Work,* in January 1969, he telegraphed his position. "Why, then, do programs for the poor as poor fail? The Protestant ethic of work as salvation is certainly at the heart of the problem." If this be doubtful theological history, it was a deep belief of these work-driven men and women. In a series of "Personal Statements" Elizabeth Wickenden, a widely respected authority in the field, explained "Why I Am Opposed to the Nixon Welfare Plan." "Statement Number 3" of April 23, 1970, went on at some length, but point one sufficed.

It [FAP] is based on the false premise that the causes of poverty lie within the poor themselves and, by derivation, within the welfare "system" designed to alleviate that condition.

Such statements, depicted in this instance as "a serious act of conscience," hardly made for dialogue. No person of consequence in the planning of FAP thought "the causes of poverty lie within the poor themselves," in the sense of ascribing blame. The belief that the welfare system wasn't helping seemed not unreasonable, although again no blame was ascribed. The planners of

FAP knew about all there was to be known on this subject, and they knew how little this was. The planners also knew that if the program was to be enacted the Administration would have to live with the tendency of American public opinion to operate at two levels: the one generous and easy, the other a bit censorious, a bit hard. Somehow the Wickendens and Schorrs could not credit such understanding or motive.

Their individual statements set the tone for organizational responses. Thus in August 1970, the Coalition for Health and Welfare Legislation, a group of thirty-five agencies and activities in New York City, including the "Welfare Division, Urban Crisis Task Force, National Association of Social Workers, New York City chapter" testified in opposition to FAP in just these terms.

The bill tends to look upon the recipient of family assistance as a person to be corrected by punitive measures rather than one who should be assisted by a whole series of incentives.

An effort of sorts developed within the Administration to speak to these concerns. I would make speeches declaring: "Simply put, [FAP] is a proposal to place a floor under the income of every American family. Whether the family is working or not. United or not. Deserving or not." The publications of the Chamber of Commerce gave ample space to such sentiments, but they never found their way into *Social Work*. As time passed, and the shock wore off, the professionals developed a more systematic rationale for opposition to FAP. The New York Chapter of the National Association of Social Workers informed the Senate Finance Committee that the plan as proposed by the president "was at first considered by many social workers as 'a foot in the door'—moving towards real reform. . . ." Now, however, it was seen to be a "regressive step." This was getting close to Newspeak. A paltering quality developed, as the designs of the Administration came to be fantasized. If anything was clear it was the intent of Family Assistance to set national standards in welfare, and as much as possible to begin direct Federal administration. Yet the point escaped Wickenden, the fourth of whose objections to FAP was

It puts into the hands of a local bureaucracy (new Federalism) instruments of control over the lives and livelihood of over twenty million persons. Since this cannot be exercised universally, it will in effect be exercised selectively (i.e. discriminatorily).

Just so the Columbia Center on Social Welfare Policy and Law found that "certain provisions of the bill may encourage administrative arbitrariness, racism, and family break-up."

Spokesman for the professionally less prestigious employees in the field were much more open about their interests. Jerry Wurf, head of the American Federation of State, County, and Municipal Employees, the largest public employee union in the United States, including, by his report, 30,000 welfare workers, wanted nothing to do with FAP. "This legislation," he told the Senate Finance Committee, "threatens to eliminate the jobs of our people." Federal jobs would replace state jobs. (Somebody *else's* union would pick up the new members.) The new contracts would not be as good. "We work a 35-hour week in New York City while Federal employees work a 40-hour week." Wurf may have spoken truer than he knew in a summary sentence: "Essentially, we have the same criticism of the legislation as the . . . National Association of Social Workers. . . ."

Concern over the ideology of welfare reform merged with concern for the specific provisions that would affect AFDC families. Great things might be afoot in the wide world of income guarantees and negative taxes: AFDC was the parish pump of the welfare worker. Unavoidably FAP threatened to disrupt this small world. All the rules would change, all agreements would be off. To those whose life had been lived with those rules, and whose skill was the knowledge of them, to those who had negotiated the agreements and watched over them, this could only be threatening. As the legislation evolved, efforts to satisfy senatorial objections led to amendments that would have meant reductions in AFDC entitlement and benefit levels for some groups. This came to preoccupy the social-work profession. Their indictments of FAP grew more detailed and more disagreeable, it being a feature of the denouement that those opposed to the legislation for the least charitable of reasons remained in the best of humor, while the bill was salvaged by those whose profession was charity.*

---

* These amendments will be discussed in Chapter V.

There was, perhaps, a failing of imagination here, but it was a near universal failing. The central innovation of FAP was to provide an income guarantee for the working poor. This was no small group. Some thirteen million persons would be newly covered, double the population of the dependent poor. (1.5 million persons already covered would receive higher benefits.) Vast social changes would be in prospect: a third of the population of Mississippi would receive income support: a third of the population of Puerto Rico: a fifth of the population of Georgia, Alabama, South Carolina. In Alaska, Guam, New Mexico, Aroostook County in Maine, the act would reverberate, would reach the lives of millions of persons, up every hollow, through every small town, into every great city of the Nation. But this population was utterly silent. In a year and a half of clamor and clash, not a sound was heard from the working poor. Very occasionally a legislator might mention their existence, but congressional opposition to FAP was strongest in precisely those regions where the number and proportion of working poor were largest. The politics of these regions, primarily the South, did not reward concern for the poor at the level of direct income redistribution to white, black, Mexican, and Indian alike.

The preoccupation of professionals with the AFDC program reflected more than absence of pressures from the working poor. Far more important was the rise of a militant organization of welfare recipients, the National Welfare Rights Organization. In May 1969, two years from its founding, NWRO took over the annual meeting of the National Conference on Social Welfare, barricaded the doors, and purportedly demanded $35,000 from the "welfare establishment" as a down payment on $250,000. Just as it was without precedent for the Federal government to have taken the initiative in expanding and transforming the concept of income maintenance, so was it unprecedented for the welfare recipients themselves to organize and turn their wrath on—the social-welfare profession. If the profession did not like, or did not trust, the president of the United States it was free to say so with whatever degree of directness it chose. But as a white (and black) middle-class profession it was utterly incapable of responding in any terms save agreement and concession (whatever private reservation and secret resolve might accompany them) to angry black women reviling the genteel world of the professional with disdain and disgust and dislike intended (at some level of perception and purpose) to reverse the terms with which the genteel dealt with the common, the powerful with the powerless, the secure with the insecure.

It was not fair. The social-welfare profession so wished to be understood as *not thinking any of those things*. It had grown accustomed to accusing *others* of having too much power and too little compassion. Now *it* was being accused of just that, and by just the kind of person it most liked to think it spoke for. Cavala and Wildavsky, in assessing "the political feasibility of income by right" offered the judgment that "It would not be too much to say that the social-work profession has been traumatized by the growth of black militancy." The militants were, even then, described as claiming "that the social workers are hostile to poor people and that their experience does not fit them to interpret these people's needs."[31] This may be the larger truth of the profession's response to FAP. All the reasons for opposition paled alongside the transcendent fact that the black militants were opposed.

9. The Welfare Militants

It was the fate of Family Assistance to be proposed at just the moment when there arose a mass organization devoted to the maintenance and manipulation of the existing welfare system. This was the National Welfare Rights Organization. It was not a mass organization in the sense of the International Brotherhood of Teamsters, the Methodist Church, or the National Association for the Advancement of Colored People. It had no such numbers, nor any comparable capacity to sustain itself over time. The half-life of such organizations tends to be brief; for NWRO it was probably all but over by the end of the 91st Congress. For the moment, however, it had some membership, and great saliency. (In the spring of 1969 *The New York Times* estimated the membership at 20,000, which appears close.[32] Soon NWRO was claiming 75,000, while *Newsweek* upped this to 125,000.) Whatever the numbers, the essential fact is that it *was,* as it claimed to be, an organization of welfare recipients. A convergence of circumstance had in this instance created what was in ways a *new social class,* heavily dependent on government, but seemingly atomized and incapable of organizing itself to bring influence to bear. Organization came about after the concentration of the population involved in a geographic area— New York City primarily—and the advent of charismatic leadership.

The leader, in the case of the welfare recipients, was George A. Wiley, a man of brilliance and energy, who perceived and defined the new social class, and focused its interests in ways that made organization possible. Wiley, a Syracuse University professor, had left academic life to join the national staff of the Congress of Racial Equality in the early 1960s. Later, after losing in the competition to succeed James Farmer, he turned to questions of poverty and discovered, in a sense, the problem of dependency.

A brief history is in order. In the winter of 1964–1965 I had made calculations at the Department of Labor which indicated there had been and would likely continue to be a rapid growth in the number of female-headed dependent families in Northern urban areas. I prepared for the White House a report, never intended to be published, entitled *The Negro Family: The Case for National Action.* It began: "The United States is approaching a new crisis in race relations." Its central statistical argument was that welfare dependency, in this instance the number of new AFDC cases, had for some fifteen years following World War II shown a strong correlation with the black male unemployment rate. The two curves rose and fell together with startling consistency (a coefficient of .91) until the early 1960s, when the relation suddenly weakened and then seemingly reversed. Unemployment then started to go down and new AFDC cases to go up.* If this continued, the report reasoned—if macroeconomic forces had lost their apparent influence on social structure—there would form an urban underclass which, because of its racial identification, would lead to a new and wholly unexpected range of social conflict. The day of civil rights was passing, that of welfare rights was coming. With this would

* This relationship is shown on page 83. As the chart indicates, the new trend noted in early 1965 persisted through the end of the decade.

come a complex of problems from reading retardation to prison riots that American society was relatively unprepared for.

So at least was the argument, and in this last formulation it was not long in being proved. The analysis was the basis of Lyndon B. Johnson's address at Howard University on June 4, 1965, perhaps the high-water mark of civil rights rhetoric in America, wherein he raised the question of family stability in an unthreatening way to a supportive audience. Within ten weeks, however, all had changed. With the outbreak of the riot in the Watts district of Los Angeles the black urban population became, in effect, an aggressor. This was a wholly new position for a racial group whose principal claim on the society had been that of a victim. The disorganizing impact of this on the established black leadership was at least as great as that on whites.

In this context the *Negro Family* report was released by the White House, specifically to assert that something was known about the otherwise inexplicable events in California. The document was not the least hostile. Chapter III traced the roots of the "startling increase in welfare dependency" to five influences: Slavery, the Reconstruction, Urbanization, Unemployment and Poverty, and the Wage System.[33] It was intended to support the Labor Department's adamant insistence that the problem of unemployment continued to be intolerable, and the growing conviction of the Policy Planning Staff that something like a family allowance would be necessary to offset the effects of "the wage system." It was the initial brief for an income strategy. Its publication, however, was seen as intensely threatening both by black spokesmen and white allies. For all the rhetoric that now developed about the Watts rebellion, revolution, or whatever, the basic fact was that for the first time in the 1960s it was the misbehavior of *blacks* that had to be accounted for. This was done in predictable ways, the basic argument being that riots resulted from intolerable racial provocation. But this in turn required the rejection of any information that suggested that what was involved was essentially a lower-class phenomenon. The *Negro Family* report was essentially of this order. In any event, the title and the subject itself stirred bitter racial memories. It was attacked with equal bitterness. The Johnson Administration promptly dissociated itself from the whole issue. In the way of the world, however, avoidance did not alter events. The report

330 | DANIEL P. MOYNIHAN

correctly forecast developments, which if anything came with greater speed than expected.

In this way a vacuum was created. No black would go near the subject, and until one did no white could do so without incurring the wrath of a community grown rather too accustomed to epithet. This was Wiley's opportunity. He understood the analysis of the *Negro Family,* and was not unsympathetic to it. More importantly, he understood that a real and increasingly near-to-desperate problem existed that commanded his concern. By rapid steps he moved to the center of the issue. In doing so he became the first black leader to define the problem of his people as in significant measure that of the female-headed family in the Northern urban slum.

Wiley's genius was to see that this segment of the black population had interests which could never be served by a strategy of avoidance designed more to maintain the self-esteem of those who did not need help than to help those who did. At a moment of much separatist activity he saw that dependency was an experience that united rather than divided: *half* of all AFDC mothers were white. He and his associates, and of course the women who followed him, made an imaginative leap that seemed to have large regenerative qualities. Instead of denying dependency, they asserted it. In asserting dependency they ceased in ways to be dependent. Large words: difficult of validation, and no doubt problematic for most of the individuals involved, but with a valid political meaning. The precursor of NWRO began as a "poverty rights" group in Washington in the summer of 1966. NWRO was founded a year later. Two years after that it was the unchallenged spokesman for blacks with respect to an issue which four years earlier the civil-rights movement had denied existed, but which was now near the center of national politics.*

The activities of NWRO reflected many influences, notably Saul Alinsky's organizing tactic of demanding concessions from someone with the power to grant them; of holding authorities to the standards of their own regulations—the reverse, in a way, of the trade-union tactic of working to rule; and of organizing

* I should like to acknowledge that during the events of 1965 Reverend Martin Luther King, Jr., was singularly supportive both in public and in private. He was alone in this, as in much else.

confrontations that gave the membership something to do. Some demonstrations seemed designed mostly to attract attention by a certain outrageousness, but others taught the lesson of how easily the poor could become so stigmatized that everyday things could seem "outrageous" when they did them. In 1938 in England under the auspices of the National Unemployed Workers' Movement a hundred unemployed men appeared at the grill room of the Ritz and asked for tea. In much the same way thirty years later NWRO mothers began to ask for charge accounts at department stores and special grants to buy Christmas presents. From his life as an academic and his experience in CORE Wiley acquired an organizing style of his own, and these were much in evidence in NWRO. He brought blacks and whites into the organization, both as members and as staff, and by and large was able to keep them together.[34]

The trade-union organizing tactics of Alinsky, and the Quakerish style of CORE were familiar dynamics on the national scene at this time. What was new was the role of the Federal government in organizing social protest. NWRO was in large measure made possible by the antipoverty program. The social-welfare theorists Frances Fox Piven and Richard A. Cloward of the Columbia University School of Social Work report that "most" of the early welfare-rights groups that preceded the national organization "originated in antipoverty agencies." Writing in 1971 they estimated that roughly half the sums raised to support NWRO had come from the Federal government and stated that at that moment "more than two hundred VISTA volunteers are engaged in welfare rights organizing," these having been "by any measure, NWRO's chief organizing resource."[35]

To Piven and Cloward, "The fact that the national government openly financed an organization of America's poor which was harassing local welfare departments," was a response by the institutions of society to the threat of lower-class violence, in this case black violence, that appeared in the 1960s. This is a complex argument beyond the concerns of the present volume. It rests on neo-Marxist premises which will puzzle persons who have been much involved in actual policy-making, but this does not invalidate the argument, which is fundamentally about systemic behavior. There are few motives that cannot be ascribed to public policies if it is first accepted that those involved need not be conscious of what they are doing.

Piven and Cloward, through their formulation of the "crisis theory" of welfare, on their own contributed a great deal to the early theoretical stance which NWRO assumed. In their view, many more persons were eligible for welfare than were then receiving it. They reasoned that

campaigns to double and triple the relief rolls would produce significant pressure for national reforms in the relief system. . . . Rapidly rising rolls would mean procedural turmoil in the cumbersome welfare bureaucracies, fiscal turmoil in the localities where existing sources of tax revenue were already overburdened, and political turmoil as an alerted electorate divided on the question of how to overcome this disruption in local government. To deal with these problems . . . mayors and governors would call upon the federal government with increasing insistency to establish a federally financed minimum income.[36]

For reasons that have been discussed, and almost certainly for others not yet perceived, relief rolls did double and triple, bureaucracies faltered, communities divided, and demand for national reform arose. However, the primary thrust of this demand as expressed by mayors and governors, and increasingly resonated in national Democratic circles, was merely that the Federal government assume the full cost of the existing welfare system: a budgetary rather than a structural reform. For his own reasons a Republican president instead proposed a "minimum income." Predictably, Piven and Cloward were not impressed; to them the proposal was a modern version of the Speenhamland system.* In this reaction, they exemplified the view Nathan Glazer has termed the radical perspective in social policy. He writes:

If the liberal, and increasingly the conservative, believes that for every problem there must be a specific solution, the radical believes that there can be no particular solutions to particular problems but only a general solution, which is a transformation in the nature of society itself.

* See page 180.

[E]ven if his policy is implemented, the radical remains firm in his faith that nothing has changed: the new policy is after all only a palliative; it does not get to the heart of the matter; or if it does get to the heart of the matter, it gets there only to prevent the people from getting to the heart of the largest matters of all. Indeed, one of the important tenets of radicalism is that nothing ever changes short of the final apocalyptic revolutionary moment when everything changes.[37]

If it was thus destined that the welfare-rights theorists should object to a guaranteed income when it was finally proposed, it was at least probable that the welfare-rights activists would do so also, although for quite different reasons. Piven and Cloward, more in sorrow than anger, have recorded their disillusion at the most recent of the long series of episodes in which the people have let the professors down.

. . . NWRO's contribution to the welfare explosion would have been greater had it devoted fewer resources to organizing existing recipients and placed more emphasis on mobilizing the non-welfare poor to get on the rolls. NWRO, however, has generally considered it more important to build up its membership rolls than to build up the welfare rolls (on the dubious premise that poor people can develop political power through permanent membership organizations).[38]

By 1971 Wiley was, indeed, speaking of the prospect of electing welfare mothers to Congress, presumably as representatives of a permanent constituency. But the indications are that his increasingly rigid desire to maintain his membership rolls *and* the welfare rolls was the consequence of the dynamics of his own organization rather than a predetermined objective. When the president announced his FAP decision Wiley indicated that while he would at first be opposed, his opposition would be tactical, and that he would end up supporting the program. His August 6 letter to the president did not demand an immediate income guarantee at the $5,500 level but rather that "The Federal government must take leadership in establishing *adequate income* for everyone as a national goal." He *could* have accepted the $2,400 level as a beginning. But this did not happen. NWRO opposition to FAP grew ever more determined until in the end it became obsessional.

There was a reason for this. The nominal objective of NWRO was a "guaranteed adequate income for everyone." It claimed to speak, as Mrs. Beulah Sanders told the Committee on Ways and Means, for "more than fifty million poor people— black and white, Puerto Rican and Mexican-American, and American Indians who do not have adequate incomes. . . ." Be that as it might, the actual membership of NWRO was (by all reports) made up overwhelmingly of black AFDC mothers. In a familiar organizational pattern, it is *their* interests that NWRO ultimately spoke for. These interests were not those of the working poor. Nor were they those of the dependent poor in poor states. Like the early trade unionists, the NWRO represented the aristocracy of welfare recipients. However bad their circumstances, those elsewhere were worse. Nearly a quarter of its membership was from New York, with two thirds from nine industrial states. These families had a guaranteed income, and not an intolerably low one. Schultze and his colleagues have estimated that the net income, in cash and kind, of a welfare family of four in New York City in 1971 living in public housing was $5,665. For those not in public housing the total benefit was $5,245. Either figure is roughly that of the NWRO demand of a guaranteed income of $5,500.[39]

The organizational interest of the NWRO was to improve the circumstances of this constituency, preferably in steady increments associated with crisis bargaining. Any large allocation of limited disposable resources to a new system and new recipients could not serve the interests of NWRO, especially when this was not to be accompanied by any guarantee of a rise in benefits for its membership. As trade unionists will strike in the name of the working class to maintain a differential in wages between themselves and another group of workers, so also the welfare mothers of NWRO who were ahead proposed to stay ahead. At the time of the President's address, AFDC covered only 35 percent of the poor children in the Nation: FAP would cover them all. NWRO represented children already covered, and could spare little concern for those not.

At its national conference in July 1970, NWRO issued a detailed statement "How the Nixon Plan Hurts Poor People." Seventeen detailed charges were listed, followed by a statement, "The Nixon Plan would do a few positive things." Some recipients in the adult categories, it was said, would be better off, some welfare families in Southern states. "The working poor will receive some additional aid." (Additional to what?) So much for the additional thirteen million poor who would be covered by the income guarantee of FAP. Disproportionate numbers of these working poor were Mexican-Americans, Indians, Puerto Ricans. These were not members of NWRO.

Whatever Wiley may have hoped for, his organization reflected the feelings of its officers, and these were not universalist. For all the wild inaccuracy of many NWRO statements—verbal demonstrations in their way—the organization was surely right in perceiving that the short-term effect of Family Assistance would be to improve the conditions of the nondependent poor relative to the dependent. The Administration knew this, but judged that the interests of welfare recipients in the poor states, and of the working poor, again especially in the South, had priority. In the long run—a decade or so—all would benefit. Theodore Marmor wrote at the time:

What is certain is that if the Nixon program is passed the large industrial states will immediately become the most visible advocates of more generous guarantee levels.[40]

But organizations such as NWRO live in the short run, and in that perspective there was little in FAP to attract NWRO.

If these circumstances did not insure NWRO opposition to FAP, another would have. *The organization could only appear strong when harassing persons and institutions sympathetic with its aims, or fearful of thwarting them.* Steiner writes:

To state it bluntly, at a time when other disaffections have made riots a terrible actuality or a fearful possibility in every large city, the cause of welfare change has been advanced by the organization of relief clients and the fear—which is not diminished by the absence of evidence to sustain it—that those organized clients will spark violent disorder.[41]

Officials of the Lindsay Administration could be called whatever names necessary to get into the newspapers, without fear of evoking more than another seizure of self-doubt on the part of the official. One could "liberate" the office of the Secretary of

HEW, as was done to Finch, in the assurance that his response would be conciliatory and that he would end by seeming weak. But there are United States senators who are not moved by such tactics, who, to the contrary, can make them serve their own purposes. In the course of consideration of the Social Security Amendments of 1967. NWRO attempted a sit-in in the Senate Finance Committee. This was as much as to guarantee that the Congress would do exactly what NWRO did not wish done. The term "Black Brood Mares, Inc.," was coined, and ascribed to Russell B. Long, Democrat of Louisiana, Majority Whip and Chairman of the Senate Finance Committee. It enjoyed a wide currency. Thereafter Long's office tended to be left alone. Of necessity NWRO's tactics came close to a policy of punishing friends and rewarding enemies: a portent of a short organizational life. Thus in 1969, appearing before Ways and Means, Mrs. Sanders, first vice-chairman of NWRO, threatened: "I am going to tell you right now, we are going to disrupt this Senate, this country, this capital, and everything that goes on. . . ." The one of *three* members of the House to have voted on the floor against the "Welfare" Amendments of 1967, James A. Burke, Democrat of Massachusetts, pleaded, "Don't make the task difficult for those who are fighting for you." He got little sympathy. Nor did the Administration that had proposed FAP.

It may also be the case that the middle-class organizers and supporters of NWRO had a separate agenda of their own. A quality of ambiguity accompanied much NWRO activity. Following the disruption of the National Conference on Social Welfare, meeting in New York City, a *Times* editorial, entitled "Welfare Wreckers," touched on a sensitive point.

The young terrorists who invaded a social work convention here last weekend and held 1,500 delegates prisoner for nearly an hour are obviously uninterested in aiding the needy Americans for whom they professed to speak.

Their imperious demands for cash with which to build a revolutionary organization of welfare recipients fits in with the current philosophy of disruption that is calculated to antagonize the rest of the body politic and promote right-wing action. It is no secret to its practitioners that the effect of such propaganda is to strengthen the repressive forces in the nation. Their undisguised hope is that the extinction of reform elements in a polarized society will check orderly movement toward correction of social ills and thus hasten a show-down in which society will go up in the flames of race, or class, warfare.

This evocation of the power of the right was the conventional liberal understanding, derived in part from the Weimar experience, in part from a need not to recognize how dominant liberal institutions and opinions were. But there was also a possibility of the direct assumption of power by the left. As the disruptions proceeded at the welfare conference, a featured speaker, the deputy mayor of the City of New York, explained, "Our experience is that some good can come of confrontation politics," adding that he thought that disruption was "time well spent." These were easily frightened men. On the other hand, liberal innocence seems to have been shared by the radicals. For reasons of their own, many felt that a right-wing repression would precede the revolution. There is no reason to suppose there were none who sought to hasten this process. The establishment of a guaranteed income by a conservative Administration acting from analysis rather than pressure in no way fitted this agenda. Some, clearly, determined that it should not pass.

In December 1969 the White House Conference on Food, Nutrition, and Health met in Washington, pursuant to the president's message to Congress of the previous May. The mood of the conference was radical and hostile to the Administration. Here NWRO raised the standard of "$5,500 or Fight," and found in Senator Eugene J. McCarthy a sympathizer and sponsor. McCarthy, along with Wiley, was one of the few persons seemingly to understand his bill, introduced April 30 as S. 3780, the "Adequate Income Act of 1970." The senator did not at first treat it as other than symbolic gesture. With no "work requirement," no "earnings disregard," and a 67 percent marginal rate of taxation on earnings, the bill would have created a massive work disincentive for almost the entire population. A family of four would have needed to do absolutely nothing to obtain an income of $2.75 for the average working year of 2,000 hours. A family of seven, earning nothing, would have an income equivalent of $4.25 an hour. Extra earnings would add little to income. The legislative analysts in the Department of Labor were hard put for words. One wrote:

These new minimum rates, available for no work at all, could not help but revolutionize the entire labor market. . . . Just to give some order of magnitude, in 1968 there were some 22 million male workers whose annual earnings were less than $5,500. . . . The inflationary impact of these developments, not to mention the social and political disruption they might cause, would be severe. In short, the direct and indirect cost implications of this proposal are simply too large for it to be taken seriously as a viable legislative program.

No one in Congress did take it seriously, but others did, and this had consequences. The most important was to deny FAP the support that ought to have been generated by its provision of income to the Southern poor. This was the one feature that could properly have been seen, especially after passage of the Voting Rights Act of 1965, as having the potential for major social change. For other parts of the country FAP was a stabilizing measure: its purposes conservative in that sense. Placing a floor under the income of every American family with children was elsewhere a preventive measure, with the disorganizing, destabilizing effects of the existing system at least attenuated. In the Old Confederacy the effect was expected to be very different. FAP had the potential of fulfilling the failed promise of the Reconstruction, and to do so while simultaneously benefiting poor whites. The civil-rights movement, or what was left of it by the end of the 1960s, had begun to perceive the need for a sustained antipoverty effort in the South. The Poor People's Campaign of 1968 was an effort to use demonstration tactics to force such a Federal response. It ended in muddy failure.

But the proposal of FAP might have broken that impasse *had* the older organizations been willing to rally to it, or even take the trouble to understand it. They were not. The strong impression of the time was that they did not dare to incur the wrath of the welfare mothers. Even relatively strong, new organizations such as the Urban Coalition, and later Common Cause, had to proceed with care. The charismatic qualities of Wiley and the threatening tactics of his followers were a clear and present danger. For a white liberal to support FAP was to invite retaliation: speeches interrupted, meetings broken up, offices occupied, the epithet "racist" hurled with indifference. In 1971 James Welsh in the Washington *Sunday Star* ascribed liberal ambiguity toward FAP primarily to deference to Wiley, "the most commanding figure among the plan's opponents." Even groups supporting it, he wrote, such as Common Cause, "tip-toe publicly on the subject so as not to appear too far removed from Wiley and his allies." For black groups this pressure grew over time. In 1969 all but one black member of the House of Representatives voted for FAP; two years later all but one voted against it.

The NAACP never actively opposed the legislation. A resolution adopted by its 1970 convention urged passage of the act, noting it would "entitle about twelve million additional people, who live mostly in the South and rural areas, to have their incomes supplemented. . . ." It asked the Senate to raise benefits to "the so-called poverty level." At this same convention, however, Bishop Stephen G. Spottswood, Chairman of the NAACP national board of directors, described the Nixon Administration as the first since Woodrow Wilson to deserve the label "anti-Negro." Clarence Mitchell, director of the Washington office of the NAACP, testified before both House and Senate committees, "in support of the broad objectives" of FAP, but his brief statements were desultory, devoid equally of information and enthusiasm. In no sense was this a priority concern of the largest of the civil-rights organizations.

In his appearance before the Senate Finance Committee, Mitchell also represented the Leadership Conference on Civil Rights. The Conference had almost decided to oppose FAP, but in the end had settled for a four-paragraph statement that declared the proposal "contains some basic innovative features," and noted that many of its 125 affiliated national organizations would seek "strengthening and enlarging amendments of varying types." For its part the Leadership Conference had two demands: that the law provide for Federal administration, with protection of the rights of employees moving from state to Federal administration, and that clear and adequate job standards be set for beneficiaries "required to accept training and/or employment as a condition for receiving aid."

The National Urban League in its response combined the traumatization of the social-work profession, the anxiety of white liberals, and the deference to NWRO of the civil-rights movement. The League, as Whitney Young, Jr., testified before the Committee on Ways and Means, was an "interracial social-work agency" with a thousand professional employees, many working on government contract. It was not a membership organization, and did not pretend to be. In his House and Senate appearances Young testified both as director of the National Urban League and as president of the National Association of Social Workers. He would express "strong support for the concepts" of the bill and then say he was opposed to it. At its 1970 convention, Mrs. Betti S. Whaley, director of program development, disclosed the League was opposed to FAP. "She said," reported *The New York Times,* "the League wanted a plan that had no punitive features and that was not 'predicated on the assumption that people don't want to go to work.' " The same issue of *The Times* carried a profile of Young noting his "scorn" for Nixon's "silent majority."

One result of this pattern of angry opposition or tepid support from civil-rights groups was that no congressman whose constituents included sizable numbers of persons who would benefit from FAP needed to fear opposing the bill. These constituents were silent and unaware, as best anyone in Washington knew. The organizations in Washington that might have represented them did not do so. The congressmen, for the most part conservative Democrats, found themselves in happy circumstances. A vote against FAP was completely justifiable: the congressman could agree with conservative opponents that it was a wild leftist scheme, and with leftist opponents that it was a sinister move toward oppression. Indeed, the main consequence of this pattern of opposition was that attention was directed away from Congress, where the decision would be made, back to the Administration, which came under near continuous demands to make first this change, then that, in legislation that had already gone forward, and which after a point had passed one body of the Congress. Mistakenly or no, the Administration tried to be accommodating, and in the process only confused matters, so that the distinction between supporters and opponents became ever more blurred. This worked solely to the advantage of opponents, especially ultraconservatives in the Senate, whose work was being done for them by others. In the House, supporters of FAP were in control of the committee structure, and so could bring the matter to a vote. Even there, NWRO pursued the matter to the end. Warren Weaver, Jr., of *The New York Times,*

reported that Wiley looked first to black congressmen to defeat
the measure and then "openly invited an alliance with conservatives who believe the program does far too much for the poor."[42]

On balance the welfare militants and the civil-rights organizations behaved in a "rational" manner. (Although it would
have to be asked how wise the Federal government was to help
finance an organization of one group of the poor that would help
defeat an effort to help another group.) But there may be some
attendant losses to these organizations as such. The presumption
of good will and of competence of many was compromised. In a
thousand private conversations in the capital men who would
never dream of saying so in public said in private that the individuals and organizations were acting out of selfishness, foolishness, or both. Twenty years earlier a similar judgment had been
passed on the trade unions, which never thereafter occupied
quite the same *future role* that until that time had been accorded
them by liberal opinion. This was a period of much progress for
some blacks. Daniel Bell wrote: "The black middle class has
been making faster advances than any ethnic group in our history in a comparable period of time." Where, then, was the
concern for those left behind?

There was an exception to this in the person of Andrew F.
Brimmer, a member of the Board of Governors of the Federal
Reserve System by appointment of President Johnson. He was in
this role perhaps the second ranking black official, after Justice
Thurgood Marshall, in the Federal government. As an economist
he was at home in the theory of income maintenance, and as a
governor of the Federal Reserve had access to the data. (This
meant no more than having research assistance: the relevant data
was available to anyone.) In an address at the Tuskegee Institute
in March 1970, he turned his attention to FAP and "the deepening schism" in the Negro community, presenting the most detailed
and competent discussion of the issue yet to appear at that time.
He took the audience through several illustrations of the principles
of FAP, and then discussed its global consequences.

About 3.3 million families would be covered; of these 2 million
(three-fifths) would be white, and 1.3 million (two-fifths) would be
nonwhites. These families would include close to 18 million persons—
of whom 44 percent would be nonwhites. Gross payments would

approximate $3.5 billion, and nonwhites would receive about $1.5 billion—or 43 percent. These annual payments would average around $1,060 for all families, about $1,000 for white families, and about $1,154 for nonwhites. However, since nonwhite families are expected to be somewhat larger (averaging 6.0 members vs. 5.1 members for whites and 5.4 members for all families), payments per capita would be about the same: $196 for whites, and $192 for nonwhites.

On balance, it appears that the new family assistance program would represent a considerable improvement—compared with the existing AFDC program—in about twenty states. Of these, fourteen are Southern states (with a heavy concentration of Negroes), and most of the remainder are Western states (with a sizable proportion of Indians and Mexican-Americans among their populations). In 1968 the average annual payment under AFDC in the fourteen Southern states was approximately $1,116. . . . [I]n some it is much below $1,000. Thus, given an annual payment of $1,600 for a family of four, there would be an increase of roughly $480 (or well over 40 percent). . . . [T]here appears to be no doubt whatsoever that the new proposal would result in real improvement.

In the remaining thirty states, assuming the 90 percent maintenance factor provided in the FAP legislation, he estimated an increase in overall AFDC payments of 15 percent. In addition there would be payments to the working poor, a larger population for the most part, receiving no income assistance whatever. Brimmer concluded:

So, while these estimates of the probable improvement which might accrue . . . are obviously crude, they are suggestive. They imply that Negroes—and particularly the poverty-stricken families headed by females—would benefit substantially. And above all, it would create a promising basis for checking the increased dependence on public welfare of a growing segment of the population. . . . [A] definite economic schism has arisen within the Negro community. Individuals in male-headed households appear to share fairly well in economic advances, while those in female-headed households are sinking backwards into poverty. . . . For this reason, the proposed family assistance program is pointing in the right direction, and— despite reservations many might have about some of its components— it should be viewed with greater receptivity within the Negro community.[43]

Not since E. Franklin Frazier had a Negro scholar been able to speak of such matters with authority and with unconcern as to who might take offense. A year later he returned to the subject in an address on "Race and Welfare." He spoke openly to an issue seemingly no other public person dared discuss.

[L]et me identify an economic issue whose resolution should have the highest national priority. This is the problem of public welfare. The simple fact is that the accelerated growth of dependency on public welfare is creating a permanent "underclass" in America. If allowed to continue unchecked, I am afraid that it may undermine further the already weakening support of efforts to bring about a greater measure of economic equality in the United States.

Moreover, the problem of welfare is increasingly acquiring racial overtones. The representation of blacks and other minorites in the welfare system is expanding at an accelerating rate—with a disproportionate share of the growth being accounted for by families headed by black females. While a number of factors help to explain this development (including the legacy of racial discrimination and segregation in this country), the central presence of the black female on the welfare state is inescapable.

Furthermore, the increased association of the welfare program with blacks has implications that are far-reaching. It has strengthened the distorted image (held by so many whites) of the black community as a subculture of American society plagued by poverty with little capacity to support itself. While the facts belie such a view, the actual dependence of a sizable fraction of black families on welfare casts a patina of incapacity on the community as a whole. This helps to obscure (for blacks as well as for whites) the real economic progress that blacks are making in the United States. Moreover, the apparent linkage between welfare and black people contributes hostility toward blacks—especially on the part of working (but lower income) white persons. Thus, an unfortunate by-product of the present welfare system is the aggravation of racial tension.

But the most tragic feature of the welfare system is the large number of the nation's children in families dependent on welfare. Black children make up a disproportionately large percentage of that total. Aside from the stigma of dependence that sets them apart— from affluent black children as well as from white children—there is a greater danger that the welfare system may sap the will and determination of these young people to make the necessary efforts (through the acquisition of marketable skills) to become self-supporting.

He allowed that he shared some of the reservations of others about FAP, but held "there are far more reasons to praise the plan than to damn it." Estimates of payments for 1972 now showed white families averaging $1,027 and nonwhites, $1,304. The proportion of male-headed families receiving aid would go from less than one fifth to one half; female-headed families would drop from four fifths to one half. He spoke forthrightly of the work and training proposals.

If this requirement is held to those actually capable in this regard, it would be not only an acceptable feature of FAP, but also a necessary part of a viable program for income maintenance. . . .

[The] effect of the work or training requirements under FAP un-doubtedly would be to encourage more welfare recipients to seek employment. However, this conclusion is not as strange (nor is the requirement as harsh) as it may appear to some observers. There is well-founded evidence (e.g., the results of the New Jersey Graduated Work Incentive Experiment) showing that poor people prefer to work —even when they receive an income supplement.

Finally, he turned to alternative proposals.

Even a figure of $3,600, compared with $2,400, would extend cover-age of FAP from 18 million to 69 million persons, and increase the net cost from $4.1 billion to $25 billion. Extending the minimum benefit to $5,500 would cost an extra $71 billion and cover more than half the population of the United States. The cost and coverage con-sequences of the $6,500 figure would be so large that it would be virtually impossible to carry on a meaningful discussion of the matter.[44]

He concluded with a plea for the enactment of legislation "with the broad features of the Family Assistance Plan."

This paper was given almost two years after the president had first proposed the Family Assistance Plan. In those two years various publics and various public men had commented on the proposal: extolling it, denouncing it, damning with faint praise, or supporting with mild demur. Yet on the record, Brimmer is virtually alone in having mastered both the subject matter and the legislation. There were some who did the one and some who did the other: only Brimmer, in a long list, can claim to have done both. The limits of social policy are determined not only by the creativity and boldness of those in office, but also, and earlier, by the capacity of the publics to comprehend and to respond. This limit came quickly where Family Assistance was concerned, as the Congress was to show.

Citations—Chapter IV

1. Gilbert Steiner points out, however, that intercession at the level of White House policy planning was not a major objective of NWRO. In part because the leadership of the organization felt that it lacked power and influence in Washington but also—and perhaps most importantly—because Wiley and his associates chose to concentrate their efforts on meeting the needs of welfare recipients at the local level, NWRO adopted a strategy of "directing [its] guns on the local welfare agencies." This was apparently an effective course of action in terms of building up the membership of the organization, but it also had the effect of making it inevitable that NWRO's national demands would reflect the particular needs of welfare recipients in areas where the group was strong. See Steiner, *The State of Welfare,* pp. 280–3, 310–13.
2. Oscar Handlin, Foreword to Roy Lubove, *The Struggle for Social Security 1900–1935,* Cambridge, Harvard University Press, 1968, p. vii. Lubove's is an excellent account. See also Daniel P. Moynihan, "The United States and the International Labor Organization, 1889–1934," unpublished Ph.D. dissertation, Fletcher School of International Law and Diplomacy, 1961, for a discussion of AALL.
3. Samuel Gompers, "Labor vs. Its Barnacles," *American Federationist,* April 1916, pp. 268–74.
4. Jay W. Forrester, *Urban Dynamics,* Cambridge, MIT Press, 1969, p. 110.
5. Quoted by Tom Wicker, "In the Nation: The Missing Ingredients," *The New York Times,* December 25, 1969.
6. Sheldon H. White, "The National Impact Study of Head Start," in Jerome Hellmuth (ed.), *Disadvantaged Child-Compensatory Education: A National Debate,* New York, Brunner/Mazel, 1970, p. 164.
7. Frederick Mosteller and Daniel P. Moynihan (eds.), *On Equality of Educational Opportunity,* New York, Random House, 1972, p. 42. The passage cited summarized the findings of Christopher S. Jencks. The seminar was chaired by Thomas F. Pettigrew and Daniel P. Moynihan.
8. Arthur R. Jensen, "How Much Can We Boost I.Q. and Scholastic Achievement?" *Harvard Educational Review,* Winter 1969, p. 2.
9. The Gallup Poll, "Public Opposes Guaranteed Minimum Income, Supports Guaranteed Work Plan," Princeton, New Jersey, June 15, 1968; "Public Favors Basing Welfare Payments on Cost of Living," Princeton, New Jersey, March 19, 1969; "New Welfare Plan Wins Wide Acceptance," Princeton, New Jersey, June 23, 1971.

10. These data, although not this specific comparison, will be found in Andrew F. Brimmer, "Race and Welfare: An Economic Assessment," Commencement Address, San Francisco State College, San Francisco, California, June 3, 1971, mimeographed.

11. "Three Family Budgets," *Monthly Labor Review*, April 1969, p. 5. The Federal family of four consists of a husband employed full time, a wife who does not work outside the home, and two children—a girl, eight, and a boy, thirteen.

12. Charles L. Schultze, *et al.*, *Setting National Priorities: The 1972 Budget*, pp. 187–8. This cost estimate was prepared by the Urban Institute, using the transfer income program evaluation model originally developed for FAP.

13. Hyman P. Minsky, "The Macroeconomics of a Negative Income Tax," unpublished paper prepared for the American Academy of Arts and Sciences, Conference on Income and Poverty. This meeting was one of a series which followed the Academy Seminar on Race and Poverty, 1966–68, in the course of which the concept of an income strategy was elaborated. See Daniel P. Moynihan (ed.), *On Understanding Poverty, Perspectives from the Social Science*.

14. There were 2,098 letters and 659 telegrams. President Johnson's announcement in March 1968 that he would not run for reelection had produced a larger response, but his statement was made in the context of foreign-policy issues, which routinely evoke a larger public response.

15. Bobby Seale, *Seize the Time: The Story of the Black Panther Party*, New York, Random House, 1970, p. 62.

16. See John Dollard, *Caste and Class in a Southern Town*, 3rd edn., Garden City, New York, Doubleday Anchor, 1957, pp. 428–31 and *passim*.

17. The Gallup Poll, "Nixon Wins Bipartisan Public Support for New Proposals on Welfare System," Princeton, New Jersey, August 30, 1969; Louis Harris and Associates, "The Harris Survey," New York, October 16, 1969. With respect to the proportion of persons who had not heard of FAP, it may be noted that in mid-1971 Gallup found that 45 percent of those interviewed had not heard or read of "the Pentagon Papers."

18. See Nathan Glazer and Daniel P. Moynihan, *Beyond the Melting Pot*, 2nd edn., Cambridge, MIT Press, 1970.

19. Alice M. Rivlin, *Systematic Thinking for Social Action*, Washington, D.C., The Brookings Institution, 1971, p. 27.

20. Gompers was out of office for one year in the 1890s, so that technically there have been four AFL presidents.

21. Urban America, Inc., and the Urban Coalition, *One Year Later*, New York, Praeger, 1969, pp. 4–28.

22. Stephen Kemp Bailey, *Congress Makes a Law*, New York, Columbia University Press, 1950, p. 97.

23. Joel F. Handler, "Lessons from the Past," *New Generation*, Winter 1970, pp. 10–16.

24. Bentley B. Gilbert, "Winston Churchill versus the Webbs: The Origins of British Unemployment Insurance," *American Historical Review*, April 1966, pp. 846–62.

25. Churchill to Llewellyn Smith, "Notes on Malingering," June 6, 1909, quoted in Gilbert, p. 856.

26. Samuel Gompers, " 'Intellectuals,' Please Note," *American Federationist*, March 1916, p. 198.

27. Kenneth Boulding, "The Many Failures of Success," *Saturday Review*, November 23, 1968, pp. 29–31.

28. Steiner, *Social Insecurity*, p. 204.

29. Cantril and Roll, *Hopes and Fears of the American People*, p. 41. Lloyd A. Free and Hadley Cantril, *The Political Beliefs of Americans*, New Brunswick, New Jersey, Rutgers University Press, 1967, p. 40.

30. See Edith G. Levi, "Mr. Nixon's 'Speenhamland,'" *Social Work*, January 1970, pp. 7–11; David N. Saunders, "Letter—Speenhamland: Superficial Comparisons," *Social Work*, April 1970; Robert Harris, "Selecting a System of Income Maintenance for the Nation," *Social Work*, October 1969, pp. 5–13; Miriam Dinerman, "Mr. Harris and the Elephant Game," *Social Work*, January 1970, pp. 114–18; Alfred J. Kahn, "Guaranteed Protestant Ethic," *Social Work*, January 1970, pp. 3–4. I should note that during this period there were a considerable number of unfriendly references to me in *Social Work*, referring to earlier writings. My association with FAP was made explicit: "the Nixon–Moynihan plan." However, I was not aware of any of this until the very end of the research done for the present volume. My views on the role of the National Association of Social Workers in the FAP debate were fully formed before reading any of these references, or the articles now cited.

31. Cavala and Wildavsky, "The Political Feasibility . . . ," p. 341.

32. For this and other data about NWRO I am indebted to an excellent doctoral dissertation prepared by Mr. Lawrence Bailis of the Department of Government, Harvard University, "Bread or Justice: Grass-Roots Organizing in the Welfare Rights Movement" (1972).

33. The "slavery thesis" is apparently to be undermined by the work of Herbert Gutman, who finds the origins of the female-headed family, the peculiar institution of the North, as it has been called, just there: in the North, a product of employment patterns developed in the late nineteenth century, as E. Franklin Frazier and other students of the Negro migration to the cities, have implied.

34. Steiner, *The State of Welfare*, pp. 283 ff.

35. Frances Fox Piven and Richard A. Cloward, *Regulating the Poor: The Functions of Public Welfare*, New York, Pantheon, 1971, pp. 320–30.

36. *Ibid.*, p. 321.

37. Nathan Glazer, "The Limits of Social Policy," *Commentary*, September 1971, p. 52.

38. Piven and Cloward, *Regulating the Poor*, p. 327.

39. Schultze, *et al.*, *Setting National Priorities: The 1972 Budget*, p. 187.

40. Theodore Marmor, "The Politics of Reform," *New Generation*, Winter 1970, p. 36.

41. Steiner, *The State of Welfare*, p. 282.

42. Warren Weaver, Jr., "Welfare Project Backed by Negro," *The New York Times*, June 6, 1971. The story refers to the support of Andrew F. Brimmer.

43. Andrew F. Brimmer, "Economic Progress of Negroes in the United States: The Deepening Schism," Address, Tuskegee Institute, Tuskegee, Alabama, March 22, 1970, mimeographed.

44. Andrew F. Brimmer, "Race and Welfare: An Economic Assessment," Commencement Address, San Francisco State College, San Francisco, California, June 3, 1971, mimeographed.

V

The Prospect
in Congress

1. The Prospect

The Family Assistance Plan was a product of the modern presidency, an institution now well advanced in its capacity to gather and process information and organized first of all to enable a single chief executive to reach decisions. That decision past, the proposal made its way to the Congress, a very different institution shaped by the technology and habits of a preindustrial age. *It* is first of all collegial. It is *able* to reach decisions, and does so regularly in adherence to formal rules of conduct, infrequently breached and rarely changed. But decision-making is not at the core of its being: representation is. Formally, and to no small degree in reality, the first loyalty of each congressman is to his constituents; where the view from the White House is directed to a more or less generalized national electorate, on Capitol Hill the specific problems of the 33rd Ward are as likely to command attention. Just as the president is not always a "chief executive," the member of Congress is not always a faithful representative. Yet it was the tension between these dominant inclinations of Congress and the presidency that most determined the fate of Family Assistance.

An imbalance in competence as between the presidency and the Congress has come about in modern times and has much affected the nature of American government. More and more Congress has come to wait upon the president, responding to *his* initiatives, working down *his* agenda. Inevitably the onesidedness of this relationship has affected the nature of the congressional response: more and more it assumes a symbolic nature, expressive rather than instrumental, designed to signal difference rather than to impose change, intended less to shape action than to dissociate the actors from the consequences of action. None of this has diminished the power of Congress: it has merely inverted it. If the president can dominate legislation, then surely the legislature can influence its administration. By no means does the development of congressional oversight of administration redress the imbalance—Congress's capacities for information gathering and processing are extremely limited, depending almost wholly on the erratic process of public hearings and the random inquiries of small and fragmented staffs—but it does provide congressmen so inclined with new, and often quite sophisticated, techniques to modify, if not to redirect completely, presidential proposals. Moreover, how better could a representative serve his constituents than by keeping a close eye on the workings of the bureaucracies?

The essential fact is that Congress as an institution has been on the defensive, and has reacted accordingly. It scrutinizes programs already enacted, and just as importantly, it declines to enact. As the modern presidency has become more active, processing more information, reaching more decisions, the opportunities for Congress to influence the executive simply by refusing to acquiesce in its judgment have correspondingly enlarged. Deadlock has become a recurrent condition of American national government. In mid-March 1968, following the New Hampshire primary election, President Johnson had confided to his aides Joseph Califano and Harry McPherson that he might not run for reelection. They protested. He asked three good reasons for doing so. The first, to McPherson, was that "nobody else could get a program through the Congress. Nobody else knows how." The president demurred. That might once have been the case, but it would not be with the 91st Congress. "Any one of 'em—Nixon, McCarthy, Kennedy—" he said, "could get a program through next year better than I could."[1] Getting a program through Congress has become almost the first measure of a successful presidency, and by that measure few modern presidents have succeeded, and never for long.

It is a question of *such* precedence that the planners of FAP hardly considered it. To dwell on how such a program might be got through Congress would have been to take the heart out of the enterprise: the chances were just too slim. The better part of wisdom was *not* to think about it. It would be enough that the president proposed the measure: in this instance a symbolic act by the presidency signaling to various publics that all was well and that the commitments of the 1960s would not be abandoned. The question of Congress would come in good time: the odds by definition were long.

Cavala and Wildavsky suggest what these odds would have been.

There is a high awareness of the failures of the present [welfare] system among members of the 91st Congress. Almost every member has a personal atrocity story dealing with the failure of the poverty program and the welfare system in his state or district. All are aware of the disincentives now built into our public assistance programs; almost unanimously they agree that the present approaches to the problems of poverty are not working and will probably not work in the future—fertile soil, it would appear, for the guaranteed income arguments. But rejection of present welfare policies has not yet been transferred into acceptance of income by right.

To the contrary, given the disincentives of the existing arrangements, "their answer . . . was to suggest that the welfare system be made more unpleasant." A guaranteed income was viewed, first of all, as immoral, in that it would destroy the work ethic, and second, impolitic, as it would require a large increase in income taxes. Those interviewed "did not believe that their middle-class and working-class constituents and their union leaders would support guaranteed income." One congressman judged it would be "political suicide" in his state; another, "extremely pessimistic." A few "safe-seat liberals" were in favor of such a measure, but that was about all. The political scientists had hypothesized that they would find a "middle group" that "could be reached by a combination of better information and a proposal modified to take their most serious objections into account." They found none. "The moderates were either opposed on moral grounds or frightened by the political consequences of the issue." Instead they favored job opportunities and food stamps. Southern members "talked in sentimental terms about the value and discipline of the old WPA and CCC camps. . . ."[2]

The planners of FAP did not have such concerns much in mind, but the president did. If no thought was given to the Congress in preparing the proposal, once the president had settled on it the *presentation* was shaped almost wholly with a view to reaction in Congress. This was not an avowed purpose: it was an automatic response. The president in office was a man of the center, and without so much as thinking about it, his speech, his message to Congress, and significant components of FAP itself, were crafted so as to exploit the one possibility the bill had, namely that the moderates would *follow* a president "who took their most serious objections into account." Cavala and Wildavsky had been told as much:

"Those boys," a Congressman said, referring to liberals from safe districts, "they don't have to worry about a thing back home in talking to voters, but for people like me—and there are quite a few of us here in the Congress—it's just too big an issue to stand up on alone. If the president was for it, then we could stand up with him."

On balance, this is what the moderates did. It was the conservatives and liberals who were to behave in strange ways as FAP began its way through the prescribed legislative course, which is to say first to the Committee on Ways and Means of the House; if successful there, to the full House; next to the Finance Committee of the Senate; then the Senate; next a House-Senate conference committee; back to House and Senate for final approval; and only then, should it somehow have survived, back to the president. This was not a hopeless prospect. Both houses had a substantial bloc of moderate Democrats, while presumably many Republican congressmen and senators would support their president's program. The chairmen of the respective committees were politicians of the center, and while each was a Southerner, the South had the most to gain from the measure they would consider.

On the other hand, these were very different committees from those which had welcomed the Great Society programs with intense, if brief, enthusiasm. The workings of Congress are affected by the separation of the authorization process from that of appropriation. Committees such as Education and Labor in the House, and Labor and Public Welfare in the Senate, the committees which would "logically" deal with a measure such as Family Assistance, are free to authorize all manner of similar programs without in the least obligating the appropriations committees to provide funds to pay for them.

FAP would face a different test. Technically it was a tax bill, part of the social-security system. It would thus be dealt with by the tax committees, whose only contributions to the Great Society—with the exception of Medicare, a holdover from Truman's era—were the "repressive" Social Security Amendments of 1967. If approved it would be a permanent statute, financed by automatic claims on the Treasury. This would constitute a far more serious commitment than, say, the Economic Opportunity Act, with its annual appropriations and—only after a considerable struggle—two-year authorizations. FAP would be the most serious test of congressional intent with respect to the issue of poverty and social equality since the New Deal.

2. The Liberal Democrats

In Paul Ricoeur's words: "The religious conscience says, 'If thou art not perfect in every respect, thou art not perfect at all.' Politicians are never subject to this 'law,' their achievements can never be more than relatively good. That is why the politician is faced by a terrible problem; it is not the problem of maintaining his innocence, but that of limiting his culpability."[3] To a marked degree the publics that responded to the president's address of August 8 did so free of any sense of their own responsibility—or culpability—for the state of welfare which he proposed to change. Most availed themselves of the opportunity thus presented to judge the proposal in terms of what *ought* to be. When, however, on August 11, the president sent a formal message to the Congress, he addressed a body that could not avoid responsibility for what *was*. There may have been a time when the welfare system had been the doing of a particular president, but that was a generation past. It was now also the work of the Congress, and in particular the Democratic majority in the Congress.

This was the majority party of the Nation; it controlled House and Senate, and had done so almost continuously for so long that with few exceptions all the major programs enacted in the middle third of the twentieth century were Democratic programs, welfare included. Any assertion that a major program had failed, any proposal to eliminate one and substitute another, was perforce a criticism of the Democratic record. When the proposed substitute was very near a quantum leap in the direction of progressive social policy, so long a Democratic monopoly, a singularly ironic political situation was instantly created. But more than politics was at stake. To a degree that could be obsessive, liberal Democrats had defined their belief and measured their worth in terms specifically opposed to that of Nixon. Now he had performed the ultimate perfidy. In triumph—as *president*—*Nixon* had proposed a measure of which even the most liberal Democrats had scarcely dared to dream. Accustomed to introducing vast visionary legislation by way of staking out a claim on the future, twenty or forty or sixty years beyond, when the Nation would finally catch up, of a sudden they found themselves behind. Behind *Richard Nixon!* In their syndicated column, Frank Mankiewicz, who had been Robert F. Kennedy's press secretary, and Tom Braden wrote, "The liberals and the welfare community, by and large, cannot take the Nixon reforms emotionally and cannot afford them politically." They cited Wordsworth: "There were none to praise, and very few to love."

Part of the difficulty the Democrats faced arose from the ambiguity of the Family Assistance proposal itself. The president had felt it necessary to do something about welfare: to limit culpability. The information available to him argued that the existing payment system rewarded self-defeating behavior in welfare recipients. But no information, no hypothesis even, offered the prospect of bringing about any great change in such behavior. Dependency had become a social condition beyond the apparent power of social policy to affect, save possibly at the margin. *This was the heart of the Administration's understanding of the matter.* It is not a judgment that will be found in the archives. It was not even a judgment. It was simply an awareness of the limits of knowledge that gradually emerged and thereafter did not need to be dwelt upon or even acknowledged.

This is not to say that the changes which FAP would bring

to welfare were thought unimportant or marginal. To the contrary, throughout the system there were wrongs that cried for remedy. Some were huge and unmistakable, as the difference between payments in Mississippi and payments in New Jersey, and responses to these, in this case minimum national payment standards, became prominent features of the FAP proposal. Other wrongs were obscure and even minor; the interstices of the legislation were filled with provisions setting them right, as right was then perceived by the career administrators in HEW. By and large the administrators were given a free hand to "fix up" in this manner. As time passed some such features of the legislation assumed far greater importance than was at first perceived. This was particularly so with respect to the establishment of national standards of administration and eventually, in H.R. 1, the equivalent of national administration itself. This was first seen as a way of protecting recipients, particularly blacks in the South, from punitive treatment by local administrators. How much of this there was none could say, but it was widely charged and widely believed that it existed. As more was learned about the actual workings of the welfare system, however, its random injustices emerged as near to scandalous.* Better administration came to be seen as an issue of substance bearing on a wide range of concerns.

When this is said, however, it remains true that within the White House it was judged that whatever was "wrong" with "welfare," a system of income conditioned on dependency, would stay wrong for a long while; that the situation would probably grow worse before it grew better; and that when it commenced to improve this would be the result of a concatenation of forces no analyst could prescribe, and certainly no government could contrive. *As a consequence of this belief, the thrust of the president's proposal was much more directed to the problem of poverty than to that of dependency*. It was assumed that there was a relationship between poverty and dependency; although how direct none could say. It was hoped that serious efforts at job training and job placement might move the welfare rolls downward. While it was readily enough agreed in the White

---

* A national survey by HEW in 1971 found that in a quarter of the cases, payments to welfare families were inaccurate: about half got too much, half too little.

House that if FAP was to have any chance in Congress it would have to be geared to "work," behind this tactical analysis was a strategic one that saw employment with income supplementation as the most likely long-run solution to the problem of dependency.

Most of the president's advisers gradually came to see the true nature of their proposal, but then only dimly, almost subliminally. It might have seemed obvious enough: under FAP thirteen million people were to begin receiving income payments who had not previously been receiving any. This surely was the largest feature of the proposal: a guaranteed income. Save for families in a few states which already provided income supplementation to low-income, intact families, none of the new recipients was "on" welfare and few were in circumstances in which they might readily expect to be. There is reason to believe the president saw this from the first: certainly he had little confidence in the regenerative qualities of a reorganization of the AFDC program. But his advisers, on balance, were generally content to think of FAP as the president's "welfare" program, even when they recognized that it was basically a proposal for *income redistribution.*

It was only when the proposal reached Congress that what had been little more than a convenience in terminology became a source of genuine confusion. If anything, the Administration now became more preoccupied than ever with the welfare details of FAP, and in this it was encouraged by the Congress. But the Congress itself—the key actors in the Congress—saw well enough what was at issue, that is to say, not welfare reform but income redistribution. While both matters might be of equal interest to a president, they have polar priorities in the scale of reckoning of the Congress. Except as it has symbolic uses, welfare is a matter of small import and less interest. By contrast, income redistribution goes to the heart of politics: who gets what and how, which in turn affects who votes and how. *To redistribute income is to redistribute political power. Family Assistance provided for the redistribution of income toward blacks, Mexicans, Indians, toward poor Southern whites, toward families with children.* (Twenty percent of Southern families were poor in 1966, as against 9 percent elsewhere. Half of all poor families lived in the South: two thirds of all poor nonwhite and nearly half, 42 percent, of poor whites.) Moreover, FAP provided a permanent mechanism for further redistribution at periodic intervals, as the Social Security system had done. *This* was not marginal to the political process. For each individual congressman or senator a particular income redistribution measure will have a particular effect. What can be quite general to the president must be most specific to the legislator. In this respect income redistribution is rather like reapportionment and evokes similar anxieties. *This* is what happened to Family Assistance in the 91st Congress.

Had FAP been only welfare reform, or only income redistribution, it would have posed fewer problems for the Democrats. In combination it made for genuine difficulties. There was a counterpart in Congress of the liberals and the welfare community Mankiewicz and Braden described as unable to take the Nixon reforms emotionally or to afford them politically. There was *also* the large and powerful bloc of Southern Democrats, of whom only a few had been able to rise above the fears of what a prosperous and libertarian South would be like. Income redistribution "threatened" Northern liberals and Southern conservatives, and accordingly both chose to concentrate on those aspects of FAP dealing with welfare. A casual observer of the committee hearings and the floor debate on the legislation might thus have gained the impression that it was the merits of FAP as welfare reform that determined its fate. This was not the case. It was FAP as income redistribution that decided the outcome.

Over a considerable range of programs the 91st Congress divided into a coalition of "left" and "right" against the supporters of the Administration. This was neither simply a partisan split, nor even an ideological one, as many of Nixon's proposals were nominally *of* the "left," or, more accurately, traditionally associated with the liberal left. The opposition of the right was readily enough explicable, but how to account for this other, seemingly unprecedented and noncompetent behavior? Mankiewicz and Braden were closest: on the liberal left FAP was threatening emotionally and politically, but the political threat involved more than that to its reputation for progressiveness. An income strategy threatened interests associated with a services strategy, and this was a direct threat to Democratic liberals. Nominally the party of the people, the Democrats through their patronage of and dependence on civil servants, intellectuals, the liberal as against conservative rich, had come also, and at times preponderantly, to represent the interests of these groups, manipulating the symbols of egalitarianism for essentially middle- and upper-class purposes. Much as earlier Republicans had promised the masses prosperity through business enterprise, Democrats now offered security through government enterprise. Either set of promises can lead to self-deception, and each is prone to rude awakening when what is said and what is done suddenly appear in hopelessly incompatible opposition. Much as the Depression shattered the Republican illusion, so the Northern riots of the 1960s shook liberal Democrats. Inevitably they looked to their shortcomings and found welfare among them. Here the record of liberal Democrats turned out to be singularly bad (which is not an obstacle to good legislation), but this in turn produced something like a bad conscience (which is).

The welfare record is of a long period of indifference followed by a decade of uninformed and uninspired tinkering. The latter resulted in the welfare amendments of 1962, in which Kennedy, Steiner writes, "passed over benefit inadequacy and bought the great rehabilitation thrust, that attractive gloss that the welfare professionals were selling as a cheap way of covering up an ugly and starving system."[4] In a sequence singular for its concision, this particular services strategy was proposed, was adopted, was put into effect, failed, and was judged to have failed. A degree of harshness is implicit in that judgment—who would wish to say that rehabilitation was adequately tried?—but none in authority demurred. Five years later, in 1967, the welfare rolls had increased so markedly that Congress, in the person of Wilbur D. Mills, chairman of the House Committee on Ways and Means, took matters into its own hands. Two ways to put an end to the increasing number of AFDC families were open: providing employment for the heads of such families so that they would not require welfare; or placing a fixed limit to the number of persons who might be supported, so that families otherwise eligible for welfare would not receive it. Congress did both. A work-incentive program (WIN) was established, administered by the Department of Labor, to train welfare recipients for jobs. It was provided that there would be no reduction of welfare payments for any earnings up to $30 a month, and deductions thereafter would exempt one third of the remaining earnings. (This came to be known as the "30 & 1/3" provision.) A day-care program was included. Simultaneously Federal matching funds for AFDC payments were frozen for cases attributable to desertion or illegitimacy. (Only about 6 percent of cases were then attributable to death of the father.) Except as population grew, Congress provided that the AFDC case load for which the Federal government would provide matching funds would be frozen on a state-by-state basis. Mothers would work and children would go hungry: was that to be it? Some saw the 1967 amendments in this light. One critic described the legislation as a reversion "to an Anglo-American tradition of total repression of the welfare poor that began in feudal England with the breakup of the manor lands."[5]

Nothing so harsh or punitive was intended by Mills or his Committee. The actions were essentially symbolic; the purpose, to declare that the Congress would no longer be passive about welfare, nor would it henceforth take for granted the good faith or competence of welfare administrators. By forcing the president to request a postponement of the AFDC "freeze"—something he surely would do—Congress was forcing *him* to acknowledge and become involved with the welfare crisis. By forcing local officials to try to train and find work for welfare recipients—something that would not happen on anything like a significant scale—Congress was forcing *them* to acknowledge that they were basically disposed to operating the system as it existed. What else, in the absence of a fully developed presidential proposal, *could* Congress do?

The Congress was then fascinated with manpower-training programs, a common feature of 1960s legislation. And again, no one had a better idea. An HEW task force had come to almost precisely the conclusion Mills reached. Welfare could be curtailed by work and training for mothers, combined with day care for children. (At this time a "diligent disciple of work" was made head of a new Social and Rehabilitation Service in HEW, which absorbed all welfare responsibilities.) The welfare community was appalled by the "slave labor" amendments, and the NWRO made its first appearance in Washington in an attempt to block them, but to no effect. In signing the legislation on January 2, 1968, President Johnson did not dissociate himself from anything the Congress had done. Rather he claimed credit for the work provisions, depicted other features as "severe," but expressed the desire that the Federal and state governments be "compassionate" in dealing with *"deserving* mothers and needy children."* (My italics.) Was there to be no consideration accorded undeserving mothers? He did not say. The AFDC "freeze" was, of course, directed to the problem of illegitimacy. The majority of illegitimate births were nonwhite. This was legislation unlike any that had passed the American Congress in its history. Yet it was approved by a president who probably cared more about civil rights than any of the men who preceded him in the office. This is not anomalous. Persons and organizations devoted to civil rights frequently found welfare a disturbing, contradicting, threatening subject. The president's brief signing statement conveys this torment.

Franklin Roosevelt's vision of social insurance has stood the test of the changing times. I wish I could say the same for our Nation's welfare system.

The welfare system today pleases no one. It is criticized by liberals and conservatives, by the poor and the wealthy, by social workers and politicians, by whites and by Negroes in every area of the Nation.

My recommendations to the Congress this year sought to make basic changes in the system.

Some of these recommendations were adopted. They include a work incentive program, incentives for earning, day care for children, child and maternal health services, and family planning services. I believe these changes will have a good effect.

Others of my recommendations were not adopted by the Congress. In their place, the Congress substituted certain severe restrictions.

I am directing Secretary Gardner to work with State governments so that compassionate safeguards are established to protect deserving mothers and needy children.

The welfare system in America is outmoded and in need of a major change.

A year earlier, in his Economic Message, Johnson had announced he would establish a commission on income-maintenance programs. A year passed and none was appointed. In the interval, as the president did not act, Congress did, and so that president found himself signing into law legislation which persons whose support he needed and deserved found hateful. It seemed time to appoint the commission, which he did when he signed the welfare amendments. The group of twelve members was headed by Ben W. Heineman, chairman of the board of the Chicago and Northwestern Railroads. The membership was distinctive in that no one was in any way associated with the existing welfare system. The number of members gradually increased to twenty-one, but this remained the case.[6] A staff was assembled, headed by Robert Harris, and the commission began what was to be a two-year study with a presidential directive to "examine any and every plan, however unconventional. . . ." Thereupon the liberal Democratic commission followed a course precisely similar to that of the conservative Republican Administration. *Faced with a welfare crisis it turned to the issue of income redistribution.* (Within the Johnson Administration itself, however, the avoidance of the issue of welfare was never overcome. No one on his White House staff knew much about the subject, and most of what they knew was wrong, apart from the innate conviction that the subject spelled trouble. The commission was a way of putting off the subject until after the election. There are no grounds, however, for thinking a newly elected Democratic Administration would have felt either the necessity or the opportunity to move with any daring. In any event, it fell to Republicans to make the choice.*)

The election of a Republican in 1968 freed the Heineman Commission of any concern it might have felt that its recom-

---

* Steiner writes of the 1967 amendments:

> Before the 1968 election, HEW prevailed on President Johnson—who did not make up his mind quickly—to support a one year delay of the imposition of the bill's freeze on federal payments for additional AFDC cases where the father is absent from the home. After the 1968 election, given the color composition of the AFDC rolls and the color composition of the Nixon vote, the way was paved for the new Republican administration to take a hard line on welfare, blaming the Democrats for gross blunders in policy and administration and blaming the recipients for existing. Instead, the Nixon administration approved outright repeal of the freeze and moved to overcome intolerably low benefits by making its first order of domestic business a federally financed cash floor under income of the working as well as the nonworking poor. (Steiner, *The State of Welfare*, p. 80.)

mendations might be so grandiose as to embarrass the president that had appointed it. It was thus a matter of some consequence that its report, issued November 12, 1969, three months after President Nixon's address, proposed in effect the Family Assistance Plan. There were important differences of detail, and with respect to the issue of work there was a difference of principle, or the makings of a difference of principle, but the commission proposal was a negative income tax that would eliminate the distinction between the working and dependent poor, and provide payments at almost precisely the level of FAP. In a letter of November 12, transmitting the report of the commission to President Nixon, Heineman wrote:

We feel that the Family Assistance Program that you proposed to Congress earlier this year represents a major step forward towards meeting the needs that we have documented. We are pleased to note that the basic structure of the Family Assistance Program is similar to that of the program we have proposed, although there are many differences as well. Both programs represent a marked departure from past principles and assumptions that have proven to be incorrect. And reliance on false premises for many years had led us to rely on inadequate and conceptually unsound programs.[7]

The commission proposed to "cash out" food stamps and to set the negative tax for a family of four at $2,400, the FAP combination coming to about $2,460. There was no "earnings disregard" in the commission plan; a 50-percent tax began immediately. This would have meant that persons with quite low incomes could be better off with the FAP combination. On the other hand the $1,600 base meant that cash payments "cut out" at $3,920 for a family of four, where under the commission's proposal they would continue to $4,800, so that persons with moderately low incomes would be better off under its plan. A major difference of detail was the commission proposal to cover childless couples and individuals. Altogether 36.8 million persons would be covered, half again as many as under FAP. This was more an issue of cost than principle, although the emphasis on children under FAP is a distinction that could be made. Under the commission plan, as under FAP, AFDC families in high-payment states would have needed a state supplement to maintain their previous level of benefits. (FAP required that such states continue supplementation so that no AFDC family would be worse off. This did not apply to the working poor.)

The Commission did indulge its right to look to a future when more funds might be available. It stated that the $2,400 level "has not been chosen because we believe it to be adequate, but because it is a level which can be implemented promptly. The commission recommends that once the program is launched the level of benefits be raised as conditions and experience allow."[8] Two black members of the commission, Clifford L. Alexander, Jr., and A. Philip Randolph, joined by a trade unionist, David Sullivan, asked for a $3,600 level. A third black member, Asa T. Spaulding, asked for $3,000. The report included a table showing that $3,600 would cost $20 billion and cover 75 million persons, assuming a 50-percent rate of tax on earnings.

The commission did not recommend any work requirement, or any penalty for refusal to work. This was the closest it came to a difference in principle with FAP. It *was* a difference in principle.* What is not clear is whether a difference in practice would have been the consequence of the adoption of one or the other plan. Family Assistance required that suitable work or training be accepted on pain of a small penalty. It was never the expectation of Administration officials that there would be any great use made of this power. The working poor were working; the AFDC mothers were either ineligible by virtue of having preschool children, or unemployable, or anxious for such work and training as might be available, the assumption being that there would always be more demand than supply. This had been the experience with programs under the 1967 amendments. In any event, the Administration wished to see the bill enacted, and there was no possibility without a "work requirement." Congress had made its view abundantly clear just two years earlier. A commission established by a previous president could, and the Heineman did, ignore it, explicitly rejecting a work requirement. The Democratic dilemma about welfare was nowhere more in evidence than on this point: The Democrats identified with low-income populations, but the basic party strength came from those just above. It was the party of the *working* man. To dis-

* Even so, both the Heineman Commission and its director were criticized in *Social Work* for their allegedly excessive concern with employment and work incentives.

sociate itself from the idea of the need for and dignity of work was something no Democratic leader in power would do. The one member of the Johnson Cabinet specifically on record as opposed to a guaranteed income was W. Willard Wirtz, Secretary of Labor. And yet the idea that welfare recipients needed to be required to work had racial, or at least class, implications, and this class, too, was made up of Democrats. Hence silence, avoidance, acquiescence in congressional restrictions, accompanied by the stated desire that administration be "compassionate."

In another perspective, the Democrats were the party of the intellectuals. For many in this group work requirements smacked of vulgarian slanders of "the young, the black, and the poor." Unavoidably the Heineman Commission reflected this view, as well as the general benevolent and libertarian views of its membership. Free of any constraint to please the White House, it expressed its own view that a work requirement in practice would be coercive.

Inevitably, any simple test designed to withhold aid from the voluntarily unemployed will deal harshly with some of those who cannot find work. Any degree of complexity involved in the test would introduce elements of subjective evaluation to be exercised at the lowest administrative level. We do not think it desirable to put the power of determining whether an individual should work in the hands of a Government agency when it can be left to individual choice and market incentives. Since we do not now have employment for all those who want to work, employment tests lose much of their meaning in the aggregate. But they allow abuses in individual cases.[9]

That this was a most decent view is not to be questioned, but it needs to be noted that it reflects a judgment, frequently to be encountered among well-to-do and successful liberals, that while the poor were almost always deserving, not much in the way of human kindness or qualities of any admirable kind will be found among persons at "the lowest administrative level." This is an attitude of large or little consequence according to one's preference. *The New York Times* report of the commission recommendations, written by a man who had been on the staff of the Kerner Commission, and could well have been on Heineman's, said:

Some commission conclusions paralleled Mr. Nixon's own welfare reform proposals. . . . But there were substantial differences, notably in fundamental outlook. Where Mr. Nixon stressed work as the antidote to poverty, the commission said that income from work was out of the reach of most poor people.[10]

Yet it should be recalled that FAP sought to *eliminate* the undifferentiated work requirement of the 1967 amendments signed by the president who had appointed this commission.

The Heineman report was a help to FAP. It put the national Democratic party more or less on record as favoring a proposal very like that of the president. (It was no secret in Washington that Heineman's staff had helped in the development of the FAP cost estimates, while both proposals drew on work done at OEO and HEW.) The Democratic National Committee had been at pains to find "flaws" in the Nixon proposal, and liberal congressmen had obliged with statements. Even so, it came to be seen that FAP was a measure *national* Democrats *had* to support. Initial comment by the Democratic National Committee had been ambivalent, almost defensive:

President Nixon's much-vaunted proposals to replace the present welfare program with a system of guaranteed income drew an initial response ranging from warm to wary. . . . In fact, Nixon—in making proposals along those lines—was to a limited extent simply carrying out provisions of the Democratic Party platform. . . . Where Nixon was criticized, it was not on the basis of general principles but on the basis of the ways to achieve the aims set forth in those principles.[11]

Now, however, the Democrats had a proposal of their own which they could claim was more generous than that of the Republicans, but which was fundamentally similar, if not identical, in principle. This made it easier for Democrats so disposed to vote for the president's proposal. It also made it easier for the Administration to defend the proposal against charges by some Democrats that FAP was so ungenerous as to be unacceptable. Had not a Democratic commission specifically rejected—by vote —the proposal to go beyond $2,400? FAP thus began to acquire a certain authority. It was where people who knew their business seemed to come out.

Yet even this development, seemingly so favorable, raised difficulties. In the aftermath of the Heineman Commission report it became possible for some Democrats to go beyond the charge that the president didn't really support his own proposal (a charge in which conservatives joined with an even greater will to believe) and actually to suggest that the president had made no proposal at all. No self-respecting commercial news network would air such a proposition, but it was well within the capacity of public television. In December 1970 *The Advocates,* sponsored by the Ford Foundation and the Corporation for Public Broadcasting, presented two teams debating the question, "Should the Federal government guarantee a minimum income to every American?" This proposition was defended by State Senator Barbara Jordan from Texas who had been a member of the Heineman Commission, and Theodore R. Marmor, a political scientist who had been a "special consultant" to it. Opposed were Governor Ronald Reagan and Roger Freeman of the Hoover Institute at Stanford University, who had been a member of Arthur Burns' staff in the White House when Family Assistance was developed. The two Democrats favored a guaranteed income, the two Republicans opposed. All references were to the Heineman Commission report. FAP for the evening had become a non-program.

It was perhaps to be expected that persons associated with public broadcasting would assume that a guaranteed income was a proposal that belonged to Democrats, whatever the facts might be, and surely not to the Republican who was then president. Perhaps unexpectedly, the audience of *The Advocates* voted, by mail ballot, three to one against the guaranteed income. Balloting was two to three times heavier than normal. The Democratic dilemma was thus compounded.

It was more than that. The liberal Democratic response to Family Assistance was conditioned by defensiveness about the party's past performance on welfare, by a loathing for Nixon which only intensified when he did what no Democrat had dared, and by the realization that any Democratic alternative would only further compound the Democratic difficulties. If it pleased the liberal enthusiasts it would almost certainly displease the Congress and the public. If it pleased the latter, it could scarcely be more than Nixon had proposed. This was commonplace enough; there had been hardly a moment in the preceding two decades in which such considerations would not have obtained. There was now, however, a further concern, a growing, pressing awareness that the Democratic prescriptions for social progress developed in the middle third of the century were somehow inadequate. The 1960s had begun with a confident faith; it ended in doubts. It appeared that an old agenda had been disposed of, but it hadn't really mattered that much. Not long after these events George Sternlieb gave voice to this premonition in terms stronger than most liberal Democrats would have used, but reflecting the same loss of confidence. Speaking of urban problems he said, "We're dead. We've used up the state of the art. We've come to the end of the line, and the end of the line is failure." But had not Senator Edmund S. Muskie, at the outset of his campaign for the Democratic presidential nomination, declared that "The blunt truth is that liberals have achieved virtually no fundamental change in our society since the end of the New Deal"? This was no bright confident morning of the Democratic spirit. Of happy warriors there were few; of determined reformers, none.

3. The Conservative Republicans

If the proposal of FAP was utterly unexpected by liberal Democrats, conservative Republicans were not less surprised and possibly even more disturbed. The Democrats, on balance, despised the president and could, as they chose, view his action as only the latest in a quarter-century history of deceptions. For congressional Republicans, especially the conservatives, who were far the largest group, this first encounter with their old friend as a new president was if anything more difficult. Wishing him well, they were nonetheless incomprehending: as much or more than Democrats. The difficulty of comprehension was compounded. Democrats had a record on welfare, howsoever unimpressive. Republicans had no record, knew nothing, and could not easily understand how it had come about that, with no notice and no noticeable desire, they were suddenly put in the position of having to manage in Congress the most important and complex social-welfare legislation of their political generation.

"The Kennedy-Johnson public assistance legacy to the new Republican President," writes Steiner, "was a services approach that had failed, a work and training approach that could not get off the ground, an asserted interest in day care but no viable day care program, a reorganization of the welfare apparatus in HEW, some procedural changes mandated in the lame duck period, and a steadily increasing number of AFDC recipients."[12] There was *no* Republican legacy. Even so, there was some reaction to FAP. Mayor Lindsay, then still a member of the party, called it "the most important step forward by the Federal Government in this field in a generation. . . ." So did some conservatives. Senator Peter Dominick of Colorado viewed it as leading to a "revival of the spirit and the dignity of life; a promise that more people can realize the 'American Dream.'" Loyalty to the new president was still reasonably strong, while a range of conservative forces vouched for the soundness of the idea. *Fortune* supported FAP throughout. More surprisingly, so did *Reader's Digest*. An April 1969 article, "Negative Income Tax—Better Than Welfare?," explained, "Here is a scheme which could provide help for our poor, offer incentives to work, and ultimately cost less than our present welfare system." The only negative Republican response to the president's address that received any notice was that of Governor Rockefeller, who welcomed the "needed new concepts," but complained that "states which have done the most to help those in need will receive the least benefits. . . . The proposals will not give significant relief to New York or other industrialized states, which bear the heaviest fiscal burden for public assistance." There was also some Republican opposition but, as with Democrats, it was divided between those who thought the program too much and those who saw it as too little. Thus, in March 1970 New York Republican Senator Charles E. Goodell denounced Family Assistance as "inadequate," "offensive," and "demeaning." He was defeated in the fall election by James L. Buckley, who declared that he, too, was opposed to FAP, preferring "a negative income tax that would give people a real incentive to work." Buckley was elected as a Conservative, but was accepted in the

Republican caucus of the Senate. Through all this period New York Republican Senator Jacob K. Javits was for the president's bill, but wanted an escalation of benefits built into it. Javits's was the more typical initial response of Republican liberals: support for the proposal with changes here or there.

This could not last and did not. Nixon in office acted in ways that somehow offended both liberals and conservatives. He was, to begin with, feared and hated by the former. As careful an observer as Richard Rovere could write in 1971 of the election in 1968 of a "stridently right wing Administration." This was not so. The new president was not strident, and was not right wing. In office he was doggedly centrist, with a respect for liberal traditions, if no great regard for liberals. One problem was that liberal doctrines had become fuzzy, even corrupted. If anything, Nixon in office was too attached to a traditional liberal view of the proper limits of government which had curiously weakened in liberal circles. It was typical of the time that the *New Republic,* ever vigilant for signs of repression from the Administration, could demand of the Congress legislation prohibiting Federal aid to colleges or universities that failed to provide for student participation in decision-making. It was left to Alexander Bickel to point out how illiberal it would be for Congress to set *any* conditions for the internal governance of institutions of higher learning, adding that "even" Nixon was opposed to such interference. Nixon assuredly was opposed, and his Administration exerted a good deal of energy in its first year in office to heading off congressional legislation designed to curb student demonstrators. Congress very much wanted to pass such a bill, but the president would not have it. Liberals took no notice of this. Conservatives did. A July 1969 article in *National Observer* noted, "The 'conservative' campus-unrest bill that was blocked in the House Education and Labor Committee last month was so mild as to be meaningless, but as mild as it was the legislation was opposed by the president." When, as was inevitable, the record began to sink in it became clear to ideological conservatives that Nixon was not going to be anything like the president they had hoped for. The president's troubles on the right now began.

National Review, the most thoughtful and prestigious of conservative journals, did not at first take an editorial position on FAP, but two articles in September issues argued against it. Henry Hazlitt saw "a giant step deeper into the quagmire of the welfare state." He contended that benefit levels would immediately begin to rise, while government-administered training programs would be feckless and would fail.

Most certain of all, the whole program of trying to force people to work for their benefit payments will soon be denounced as a sort of slavery. The work requirement will soon be quietly shelved.

James E. Estes allowed that the "concept of a guaranteed minimum decent level of income for all people in the United States is basically so simple and humane that it is difficult for anyone to challenge it." He nonetheless did so on grounds that it would demoralize the work force and inflate the currency. A long insert on "Julius Caesar's Poverty Program" recounted the rise of bread and circuses and the decline of empire in ancient Rome. Estes favored more vocational training and a direct employment strategy. By contrast, in January 1970 Ernest Van Den Haag undertook to refute both Hazlitt and Estes, with an aside for some of the objections George Meany had raised. He felt FAP to be "a step in the right direction" that would raise costs in the short run but probably eventually reduce them. "Whereas Mr. Hazlitt fears that the work requirements in the Nixon proposals will be neglected," he wrote, "liberal and labor critics fear that they may be applied." He raised the possibility of shunting aside the welfare professionals.

Attention should be paid to the social workers likely to administer Mr. Nixon's proposals. Those now coming from social work schools seem to contribute as much to the creation of social problems as they do to their solution. To the last woman, they are filled with utopian notions and psycho-moral clichés which distort their perception of society far more than simple ignorance could. In the past utopianism was wholly moral and religious. Now it is economic and political. Certainly no improvement.

He pointed out that certain of the advantages attending female-headed households would persist under FAP. He proposed a $100 bounty for any woman accepting a semipermanent or permanent contraceptive device, along with a somewhat bizarre notion to make it a Federal crime for a man to risk conception of a child he was not willing or able to support.

William F. Buckley, Jr., the editor of *National Review,* and the most authoritative of conservative publicists, at first declared himself open to argument about "this daring and attractive plan." He felt the president would have many questions to answer, but urged that they be asked, that the debate begin.

The appeal of Mr. Nixon's plan is its directness. It accosts, for the first time, the sprawling mess which has grown up around a few humanitarian postulates, grown utterly out of hand as witnessed . . . in New York City. . . .

The following April, however, Buckley pronounced "A Reluctant 'Nay' on Welfare Plan." He made the (accurate) point that FAP was not replacing other forms of public assistance, but merely adding to them. (This was a departure from the pure theory of the negative tax which called for sweeping away all such encrustations, replacing them with a single income-maintenance scheme from which there would presumably be no appeal.) He concluded that despite the sincere intentions of some, many persons behind the bill "talk about the 'workfare' aspects of the bill merely as boob-bait for conservatives." He feared the cost would rise greatly, and thought it especially unwise to commence such a program in an inflationary period. Insofar as in "this vale of tears we cannot have everything exactly when we want it," he concluded he would have to vote, "however reluctantly," against FAP.

Milton Friedman similarly cast a "reluctant 'nay.' " In May 1970 he described "the bill in its present form" as "a striking example of how to spoil a good idea." He made Buckley's point, which was of course his own, that to establish a negative tax without disestablishing the devices that preceded it was to compound calamity.

If food stamps, state supplements to existing Federal welfare, medical and housing assistance, and the entrenched welfare bureaucracy are all to remain largely undisturbed, there is no way to construct a sensible family-assistance program.

POLITICS OF A GUARANTEED INCOME | 371

His argument dealt mainly with the marginal rates of taxation on earned income under FAP as it would actually operate. He estimated this would be 40 percent on the first $720 of earnings, and 80 percent thereafter, owing to local regulations which sharply reduced eligibility for various benefits as income rose, and frequently did so on a "sudden death" basis whereby, for example, an extra dollar of income might disqualify a family for a $1,000 public-housing subsidy.*

Friedman was not wrong in this, although taxation rates would vary widely over jurisdictions, and were generally presumed to be worse under the existing welfare system. (His proposal to eliminate food stamps and raise the benefit level— "The farm block, not the poor, are the real political force behind food stamps"—was adopted in H.R. 1. He was correct in saying the Administration ought to have done this at the outset, and the Administration officials did testify in favor of "cashing out" stamps, but it was also the case that in this instance the farm block had working with it a notably abusive, accusatory lobby. As Buckley had noted, following the proposal of FAP "the executive director of the National Council on Hunger and Malnutrition . . . all but suggested that Nixon's program is designed to stimulate hunger and mulnutrition.") Friedman was surely within his rights to ask for a pure negative tax as he had conceived it, but no Administration could contemplate dismantling the whole system of social services that had developed over a century. Inadequate as some might be, others were indispensable and all were part of the legitimated expectations of the society.

Conservative opposition to FAP did not reassure liberals— workfare "boob-bait" remained "slave labor" for those so disposed—but it did cause doubts in the White House. Family Assistance had been the work of men for the most part strangers to Nixon's political cadres. Many of the latter were deeply attached to conservative ideology, and suspected FAP from the outset. When Buckley spoke, they listened, albeit they did not always follow. What they did understand quite well was the hard political calculations of columnists such as James J. Kilpatrick and Kevin P. Phillips, and the fire-and-sword fundamentalism of

---

* These "notch" effects are discussed in Chapter 7.

Human Events, "America's only large-circulation conservative news weekly." These became dead serious opponents of FAP. Kilpatrick, although at first responsive, began writing columns with titles such as "Nixon's Welfare Plan Now a Little Monster." He learned early enough that the work-training programs authorized in 1967 were not working especially well. FAP was modeled on them, he wrote, "and the model has flopped." More influential still was Kevin P. Phillips, author of *The Emerging Republican Majority* and, while serving as an assistant to the Attorney General, the presumed source of the press "backgrounders" from which emerged "the Southern strategy." After a period Phillips departed to write a syndicated column in which he regularly inveighed against FAP: "the 'mega-dole' as conservatives are beginning to term it. . . ." Phillips saw clearly that the essence of FAP was not welfare reform but income redistribution. He had sensed the nature of welfare bureaucracies and felt he knew what this would mean for any "work requirement." Mayor Lindsay, he reported in one column, "recently labeled as 'a return to the Dark Ages' the suggestion that able-bodied welfare recipients be put to work cleaning up city streets." It seemed clear to Phillips that whatever the legislation might mandate, the bureaucracies would take their cue from the Lindsays, and there would be precious few welfare recipients out cleaning streets. In the meantime the voters that Phillips felt the Republican party ought to be attracting would, as a result of an initiative by a Republican president, be forced to pay for the "mega-dole," through either taxes or inflation, and would get nothing in return. The beneficiaries of FAP could be counted on to vote against the Administration, and with money in their pockets were all the more likely to vote. It made no sense to him.

A fairly sustained effort was made to account for the president's move in terms of advice which he had accepted from me, neither a Conservative nor a Republican. Buckley, without malice, would refer to the "Nixon-Moynihan plan." Phillips, of a different temperament, took this further, writing in September 1970:

Because revulsion against this sort of welfarism helped put Richard Nixon in the White House, his support of a vastly inflated welfare program is puzzling. According to conservative Nixonites, the

President, preoccupied with his productive efforts to achieve peace in the Middle East and wind down the Vietnamese war, has been intermittently misled on the welfare scheme (especially the work incentive features that formed the basis of his initial approval) by elements of the White House staff. The same advisers who blueprinted the program have wrongly convinced the President that his prestige is at stake so as to oblige Mr. Nixon to pull their chestnuts out of the fire at his own political expense.

Thus many conservatives who believe that the welfare program is a sociological, economic, and political threat to the nation and the administration are hoping that the Senate Finance Committee will see that the prestige at stake is not the President's but that of the left wing of his White House staff, who will pay the piper if Congress rejects their handiwork.

Phillips was writing from knowledge. Within the White House, and the Administration, there developed a group that wished to see FAP defeated. The opponents of FAP never included any of the president's principal advisers, and the president himself was unwavering in his support. Albeit his attention was usually elsewhere, whenever the matter was raised he would assert without reservation that FAP was his "flagship," the pride of his legislative program, the warship from which his colors flew. There was nonetheless a fair number of persons, some of whom could at least suggest they were speaking for the president, who wished to see it scuttled. These, for the most part, were new recruits to the White House staff, which after a point greatly expanded. The new men were, on balance, lower-level political cadres given to a fundamentalist campaign conservatism. None had been in any way involved with the shaping of the president's proposal, and few knew much about it save that it was not what conservatives had bargained for. This reaction did not make its appearance until FAP, wholly unexpectedly, passed the House. But thereafter this somewhat nebulous White House group did have an impact among senators who wished to believe what such persons would intimate, namely that the president's support for the legislation was waning, or even that he had never really supported it to begin with. This released many conservative Republicans from obligations of loyalty, but curiously the influence was most noticeable among liberals of both parties. The latter in any event tended to believe that the White House was in the control of conservatives, and found in the theme that the president wasn't really for his own program sufficient excuse for them not to be. It was no accident, so this reasoning went, that the headline of *Human Events* on April 25, 1970, read:

HOUSE PASSES RADICAL WELFARE PLAN
Filibuster by Senate Conservatives May Be Only Way to Stop Scheme

Conservative attacks on the White House staff increased during 1970. *Human Events* wrote of the "Moynihan-Garment Duo Fueling Welfare Push," linking me with Leonard Garment, a former law partner of the president, and a former Democrat. Soon *National Review* was pointing to an "Ehrlichman-orchestrated policy of a move to the left." Attacks *from* the left rarely caused concern in the Nixon White House: certainly not on the subject of FAP. For the longest while liberals in the White House assumed that liberals in Congress would support the program. The problem always was assumed to be that of keeping conservative support. As finally assembled the proposal contained major components designed to respond to conservative concerns and to merit their backing. There was, doubtless, an element of "boob-bait" in the talk of "workfare," but there was also unprecedented provision to make employment possible and attractive to low-income persons, an issue of central importance, for example, to George Shultz. What this strategy could not take into account was that the president, forced toward the center by the dynamics of his office, or moving there of his own volition, would almost certainly provide an opening for an opponent on the right who would challenge him for leadership of that constituency and, in turn, for control of the Republican party. In the situation of 1969–1970 this opponent had to be Governor Ronald Reagan of California, and the most obvious issue on which to open his challenge was FAP. It was the optimal issue on which to begin— the president's major domestic proposal—to be followed by attacks on the Nixon record on school desegregation in the South, massive "full employment" deficits, arms-control talks with the Soviets, and the failure to dismantle the Great Society.

This might have seemed fantasy to the president's Democratic critics, but the prospect was extraordinarily vivid to the men who met in the Roosevelt Room at 7:30 each morning to plan the Administration's day. *From the right Nixon's record looked consistently left.* The right, in the person of Reagan, had come within breathing distance of the Republican nomination in 1968. The question had to be asked whether the president, who had barely held his conservative support in 1968, would not lose it in 1972. In any event, an attack on FAP led by Reagan raised the prospect of large defections by congressional Republicans more vulnerable than Nixon to charges of ideological deviation and with no commitment to welfare reform. Reagan would do poorly in the election of November 1970, and would recede as a threat on the president's right, but none knew this in August 1970 when *The Republican Battle Line,* newsletter of the American Conservative Union, wrote:

For the first time political observers have noticed a private, though not yet public, willingness on the part of Southern GOP leaders to admit they may have been mistaken in backing Nixon over Gov. Ronald Reagan in 1968.

A man of the center, Nixon was now under fire from both sides.

4. Southerners

The congressional response to a proposal such as Family Assistance may be analyzed formally in terms of the two parties, or of the two political tendencies, generally labeled liberal and conservative, but in reality the major question was how the South would respond. American domestic politics in the 1960s had been dominated by issues arising from the economic, social, and intellectual backwardness of this region. Much of American history had been taken up with the same issues. Always it seemed the South lagged behind, with little to offer the rest of the Nation save its problems. These were large problems, for the region was a larger part of the Nation than generally perceived.* A third of

* In Federal usage, the South comprises sixteen states: Alabama, Arkansas, Delaware, Florida, Georgia, Kentucky, Louisiana, Maryland, Mississippi, North Carolina, Oklahoma, South Carolina, Tennessee, Texas, Virginia, and West Virginia, and the District of Columbia. As will be clear, a number of these states were relatively prosperous, and most contained some prosperous areas.

the country's population lived there. In fiscal 1969 it paid 19.6 percent of Federal individual, corporate, and business income taxes.

It was to be the complex fate of Family Assistance, a program that would have its single largest impact in raising the income of the South, to receive less support there than from any other region. It got almost no active support from those with power in the South, nor any from those without power; little from the rich, less from the poor; not much from whites, nor much from blacks. This lack of support derived from a variety of reasons, not least—again a complex fate—the political and economic progress of the South in the 1960s.

Until 1964 national elections had been dominated by the political geography of the Civil War. North and South, counties that had settled their politics a century earlier in terms of that conflict of a sudden changed. Republican territory became Democratic, and vice versa. It was not clear how permanent this shift would be, but it raised for the Republicans, the minority party, the prospect of breaking into the theretofore "Solid" South which had long been a symbolic and in part a real advantage automatically accorded the Democratic candidate for the presidency. In 1968 Nixon had carried a number of states on the Southern perimeter: Virginia, Kentucky, Tennessee, and Florida. Although George C. Wallace's American Independent party swept the core South, winning as much as 66 percent of the vote in Alabama and 64 percent in Mississippi, Nixon carried both South and North Carolina. In the meantime Republican representatives and senators from the South began to appear in Congress. In the aftermath of the 1968 election, it was logical for the newly elected Republicans to look to ways to consolidate or expand their constituencies.

This led to the "Southern strategy" associated with Kevin P. Phillips. It was not a notably incisive analysis. It looked to a South that, having changed as much as it had, would now cease to change, coming to rest at just that point in the political spectrum where fear of further racial progress would turn a majority of whites against political liberalism, leading them out of the Democratic party and into the Republican. That *had been* a trend of the 1960s. Whole cohorts of liberal Southern congressmen had been defeated or had left the Congress. And yet this period too was transitional. Even at his worst as a segregationist, Governor George C. Wallace of Alabama projected himself as an economic populist. The South ·was too poor not to respond to economic issues once it had passed through the travail of desegregation. It was not to be doubted that a two-party system was emerging, but already the younger politicians had perceived that dividing the population along social and economic lines would leave a majority for the Democrats as the party of economic liberalism. The 1970 elections were to demonstrate how far this transition had progressed.

The "Southern strategists" of 1969 did not see this. Young men, or men new to politics, they took for granted that the South would remain very much the region they had first encountered one, or two, or three years earlier, when the reaction to the social liberalism of the national Democratic party was so powerful as to override any other consideration and seemingly to offer a genuine opportunity to forge a Republican majority there and in the Nation as a whole. A much more formidable analysis would have begun with the *need* of the South for economic liberalism and the residue of dislike for imposed social change. In that setting the obvious course for the Republican party was to embrace the first position and profit from the second. But this required more subtlety than is typically found among political strategists.

Dependent on the unchanging values of Dixie, Phillips was necessarily appalled by Family Assistance. It would ruin everything. "Poor people would be better off," he wrote in a column of July 25, 1970, ". . . but the middle class, as well as persons on fixed incomes, could be badly hurt." FAP was a threat to "Southern cheap-labor industry" because the work incentive had no "financial teeth." He concluded, "Bluntly put, the program would strike at the rual socioeconomic powerbase of Dixie's conservative Democrats."

True, but not so true as it had been. During the 1960s the long isolation of the South *was* ending. It was less and less a separate and different part of the country. In that decade, for the first time in modern history, the South gained population through in-migration as well as natural growth. A net gain of 1.8 million whites offset a net loss of 1.4 million blacks. (In 1970 53 percent of the total Negro population lived in the South, as against three quarters in 1940. These 12,064,258 persons accounted for 19 percent of the population of the region. In the Nation as a whole, black population grew 20 percent during the 1960s, as against a white increase of 12 percent, raising the black proportion of the total population to 11.2 percent, but the Negro population of South Carolina, Alabama, Mississippi, and Arkansas declined.) Overall, the population of the South grew 14.2 percent during the decade, an increase half again as great as that of the Northeast or North Central region, and second only to the West. The income gap was closing: for the period 1960–1969 median family income grew more in the South than in any other region, and grew faster for blacks than for whites. Black median family income doubled.[13] Economically, the South was enjoying more than its share of the fruits of the sixties.

Yet at the end of 1970 the *Wall Street Journal* reported on a survey of Southern opinion of FAP which, in a sense, confirmed Phillips's view.

Interviews throughout Dixie suggest that a few Southerners favor the bill, but that the vast majority of politicians and constituents alike agree with Senator Herman Talmadge, the Georgia Democrat, that the bill "would undermine the best qualities of this nation."

* * *

Senator Talmadge estimates that the new bill would channel at least some government money to 35 percent of the population of Mississippi, 25 percent of Louisiana, and 22 percent of Georgia. Phil Cawthon, director of Georgia's Department of Family and Children Services, estimates that eighty of Georgia's counties would discover that 50 percent of their families would be eligible for some welfare payments. . . . Southerners believe this could bring significant changes in the Southern way of life.

A considerable portion of the Southern opposition to the measure is couched in philosophical and pragmatic terms that omit any mention of race. For example Senator Talmadge, a leading critic, says "The Administration has sold this bill to the American people as a work incentive. It isn't. It's a work dis-incentive. We should pay people to work instead of paying them not to work."

* * *

Another big worry voiced by Southern opponents of the measure is what all that money would do to the low-cost domestic labor supply. "You're not going to be able to find anyone willing to work as maids or janitors or housekeepers if this bill gets through, that I promise you," says Lester G. Maddox, the peppery Georgia governor.

An official of the Citizens Councils of the region was quoted as acknowledging that FAP "would enormously increase the voting power of the poor people, and in the South an awful lot of poor people are Negroes." Whether or not the prosperous businessmen of Atlanta, Birmingham, or New Orleans were concerned with this forecast, the Southern delegation in Congress would have to be.

The view of a blocked and unchanging South implicit in the conservative "Southern strategy" had its counterpart among liberal Democrats, both North and South, who had become almost equally attached to a stereotype that indeed nothing *had* changed, and that any significant economic benefits flowing to the region would be little more than a reward for defiance. That there were psychological gains to be had from such a view will be evident enough. Less obvious is the degree to which it explained away the failure, or at least the inability, of previous liberal administrations to carry out measures to which they were nominally wholly committed, and possibly also the degree to which continued concentration on the sins of the South diverted attention from the shortcomings of other regions. All this animus came together in the issue of the dual school system.

In the fall of 1968 the Southern Regional Council issued a Special Report entitled: "LAWLESSNESS AND DISORDER: Fourteen Years of Failure in Southern School Desegregation." It reported the total failure of court orders to have any effect in the decade after the Brown decision, and the not far from total failure of administrative measures taken under Title VI of the Civil Rights Act of 1964. *As schools opened in 1967, 86 percent of Southern Negro students were still in segregated schools.* In Mississippi, the proportion was 96.1.[14] In December 1969 another Special Report was issued entitled: "THE FEDERAL RETREAT IN SCHOOL DESEGREGATION." It noted that the 1968 report "drew sharp criticism from some federal officials who felt that we were overly harsh in our indictment of their efforts." Be that as it may, the mistakes and failures of previous administrators "were never made in an atmosphere of outright intransigence." This had changed.

In 1969, it is no longer possible to be so charitable. This year there has seemed to be a deliberate effort at work in the federal administrative machinery to reverse such progress in school desegregation as has already been so dearly won. That effort, if not demonstrably successful in diminished percentages of students in desegregated schools, had cynically held out the hope to southern segregationists that the law of the land would not really have to be obeyed.[15]

Not two years later, as the 1970–1971 school year ended, the Associated Press led its dispatch with a statement few would have predicted:

Mississippi schools, the nation's most segregated two years ago, are now more integrated than those of California, Illinois, Michigan, Pennsylvania and Wisconsin.

The startling turnabout in Mississippi . . . dramatizes the South's emergence as the national leader in school desegregation. The shift concurred with worsening racial isolation in most big-city Northern districts.

The dual school system of the South had all but disappeared. Just as significantly, it had not been succeeded, or had not yet, by the Northern pattern of unitary school systems with *de facto* separation of the races in schools of predominantly white or black pupils. An AP dispatch reported the result of HEW's second national survey of racial and ethnic enrollment in public schools. It was found that in an eleven-state South the percentage of Negro students in majority white schools rose from 18 percent in the fall of 1968 to 39 percent in the fall of 1970.* The thirty-two Northern and Western states remained unchanged at 28 percent. Given considerable areas of the South where there is a majority black population, such that majority white schools are not technically possible in an integrated situation, the achievement was notable. The HEW release stated:

Tennessee and Virginia increased the number of Negro students in majority white schools one and a half times and Texas almost as much; percentages doubled in Arkansas, Florida, and North Carolina;

* The states were Alabama, Arkansas, Florida, Georgia, Louisiana, Mississippi, North Carolina, South Carolina, Tennessee, Texas, Virginia.

tripled in Georgia and South Carolina; quadrupled in Louisiana and Alabama; and increased fivefold in Mississippi.[16]

In the recent history of planned social change there can have been few efforts as successful as the dismantling of the dual school system of the South which occurred in the course of six weeks in August and September 1970. The Nixon administration did this. It may not have wanted to; it may have wished the courts had not forced it to; but nonetheless it did do it. The individuals involved were not different from those who had struggled with the task in preceding administrations. They were convinced of the moral and legal necessity of complying with the *Brown* decision. But they were different in the way they went about it. As a deliberate strategy the Administration set out to reward the South for obeying the law, rather than punish it for breaking it. In this, too, there was the tacit recognition that the South had changed and that, consequently, a new approach would be required to eliminate finally the dual school system.

Early in 1970 a Cabinet task force on education was established with this objective. The nearest thing to political considerations that entered its deliberations was the calculation that if this was to be done, "then 'twere well/It were done quickly." The vice-president was made chairman, with most of the duties falling to the vice-chairman, George P. Schultz, and the executive director, Robert C. Mardian, General Counsel of HEW. Biracial "Education Advisory Committees" were established by each of the seven states of the Deep South. Most of these were brought to the White House for a day's meeting with the committee: the Attorney General, the Secretary of HEW, the counselors to the president, and, not least important, Postmaster General Winton M. Blount, who would greet each new arrival in a deep Alabama voice. After a period the group would trek into the Oval Room, where the president would greet them, pass out trinkets and mementos, and then speak at some length, saying over and again one thing: In the fall of 1970 the people of the South of their own free will were going to disestablish their dual school systems because they had decided to do so. On August 14, 1970, the president, with seven members of the Cabinet, flew to New Orleans, where he met first with the Louisiana Advisory

Committee, just being formed, and then with the chairmen and cochairmen of the committees from six other Southern states. He declared, now for the public record, "The unitary school system must replace the dual school system throughout the United States. . . . And I shall meet that responsibility."

He chose to be unusually sensitive to the sensibilities of Southern whites. This was no doubt a political calculation, but it was more than this. The responsibility of government surely extended to some concern for outcomes. A decade of Northern lawyers poking Federal injunctions into the hands of Southern politicians and hastening back to Georgetown with tales of redneck vulgarity had produced—what? According to the Southern Regional Council, "Fourteen Years of Failure. . . ."

On September 1, two and one half weeks after Nixon's journey to New Orleans, United Press International reported: "The South calmly and peacefully—but not without difficulty— integrated more of its schools yesterday than on any previous day in history." The next day the president expressed his gratification. "The Nation has seen hundreds of communities achieve the transition from a dual to a unitary system smoothly, peacefully, and successfully." He thanked the news media for the "constructive" way they had covered the story. Writing shortly thereafter in the *Washington Post,* Henry Owen of the Brookings Institution approved the president's saying the end of legal segregation was "a tribute to the people of the South." This was not, of course, exactly so. There was not the least possibility that it would have occurred without the force of law and the prospect of bayonets. The Nixon Administration had done nothing whatever to bring the relevant law into being, but given the fact of it the Administration had worked with energy to obtain compliance. There was no great splendor in this; but there was much decent governance. Owen wrote that future progress would much depend on

whether the media and the intellectual community in the North make a serious effort to understand what is happening in the South, instead of simply repeating clichés of the 1930s. There is curious ambivalence in the attitudes of some Northern liberals on this point: Reaching out to students and other alienated elements is viewed as an act of statesmanship; but trying to understand the problems which a century of neglect have created in the South is considered political opportunism.*[17]

Owen argued, in effect, for subtlety; even for a measure of indirection. Nixon managed this with respect to school desegregation. It was assumed—not by all elements in the Administration, but by those that prevailed—that an end to the dual school system was indispensable to social progress in the South. The hierarchical relations of the races there were associated at least symbolically with the maintenance of a dual school system; this, at least in part, perpetuated the formidable gap between the educational achievement of Southern black and white children. With respect to this issue, as with respect to welfare dependency, the president had available to him fairly compelling social-science findings. Reanalyses of the data gathered by the Equal Educational Opportunity Survey of 1965, a counterpart in its way to the Survey of Economic Opportunity, established with some firmness that desegregation was the only readily available device that would narrow the achievement gap in a direct manner. The effect, it appeared, would not be so large as had been thought at first, and would depend crucially on the extent of accompanying social class integration, but there was some effect and no other known strategy could produce a comparable one.[18]

This issue settled—as much as such issues ever are—the question became that of how to bring about desegregation. Previous efforts had not much succeeded. In the meantime the edicts issuing from Federal courts were becoming overwhelming in their force and immediacy. Efforts to bring about compliance by withholding Federal education aid had not been more than marginally effective. The reverse idea occurred: to reward success rather than to punish failure. It had been the manner in the North to think and to speak of the issue in terms of justice. Now the discipline of government required that it be seen that the majority group involved, the Southern whites, saw it as an issue of *injustice*. If desegregation was to take place with anything like the necessary speed and at anything like an acceptable social

---

* Of the things the White House staff looked upon with pride from Nixon's first two years, probably the most vivid was that the schools of the South had been desegregated, as one of the president's aides put it, "without a single gun pointed at a single child."

cost, *that* perception had to be changed, or rather the intensity of the feeling associated with it had to be moderated. That this would be a less than straightforward process was a matter silently understood by all involved. Two tactics were employed. The president, by his general posture, and on occasions such as his address to the various State Advisory Committees, dissociated the idea of desegregation from that of surrender to Federal edict. Simultaneously, Federal funds were made available as a reward for those school districts that did in fact comply with what was, inescapably, the Federal command. It was a subtle strategy indeed.

On May 21, 1970, the president proposed the Emergency School Aid Act to provide $1.5 billion in aid to schools "undergoing desegregation either voluntarily or in compliance with court decisions." No great fuss was to be made about how the funds were used. A supplemental appropriation of $150 million was asked for the then current fiscal year, so that the program might begin immediately. The discussions in the White House with the State Advisory Committees made much of the prospective availability of these funds. But little help came from Congress, where a coalition of Southern conservatives and Northern liberals effectively blocked the legislation, although a supplemental appropriation of $75 million was passed for fiscal 1970. On September 26, 1970, the president wrote to Senator Ralph Yarborough of Texas, chairman of the Senate Labor and Public Welfare Committee, and Representative Carl D. Perkins of Kentucky, chairman of the House Education and Labor Committee, pleading for the bill as "one of the highest legislative priorities of the Administration." Eventually the House did pass the bill, but Senate liberals would not have it. Under the leadership of Senator Walter F. Mondale, Democrat of Minnesota, an alternative bill was drafted replete with precisely the kind of provision certain to arouse fears in the South (e.g., 3 percent of the $1.5 billion was to be reserved to pay plaintiff's attorney fees in desegregation and other civil rights suits affecting schools) and chock-a-block with compensatory-education schemes for which there was now scarcely a shred of respectable research support. The liberals did not trust the Administration's intentions, and they did not trust Southern school administrators. Yet while they still had grounds for distrust, their attitude and the actions it engendered belonged largely to an earlier era. By the fall of 1970 the evidence was unmistakable that the South was desegregating—had desegregated. The strategy of careful inducement could work. Still the liberals would not relent, and the Southern opponents of all such social change did not need to mobilize their formidable congressional resources to see the president's proposal blocked.* Even so, the dual system was ended.

Social policy, to succeed, must often proceed in the manner of diplomacy, seeking to influence position and judgment as a precursor of achieving desired actions. This proved possible with respect to school desegregation. The South was persuaded that further evasion was impossible—the work, in the main, of the courts—and that there might be some advantage to compliance, or in any event that it would not be disaster, an idea implanted by the president. At the same time, the relative status of those most committed to a peaceful transition was enhanced. A similar attempt at subtlety and indirection was made with respect to Family Assistance also, but here it failed. As a consequence, in a pattern too familiar, Southern opposition in Congress became unavoidable, for at issue was not a court order to be evaded, but a bill to be passed.

The potential effects of a guaranteed income in the South were impossible to conceal. The region would benefit hugely from such an arrangement, but it was also probable that the principal political actors involved, white congressmen and those who most influence them, would be injured by it. In the North, liberals might seek to misread the nature of the program or be persuaded to minimize its importance, but Southerners instantly grasped the reality. Family Assistance was income redistribution, and by any previous standards it was massive. It was a necessary and massive threat to an established political order that already knew itself to be half-disestablished. For Southern politicians there was nothing at all subtle about FAP.

Estimates by John F. Kain and Robert Schafer indicated, given the income and population distributions at the time FAP was being considered, that some 3,997,000 households would receive payments. Of these, 622,000 would be in the Northeast,

* The measure, raised to $2 billion, and more broadly defined, was finally incorporated in the Education Amendments of 1972, and signed by the president June 23, 1972.

898,000 North Central, 472,000 West, and 2,005,000 South.
FAP involved income redistribution between regions as well as
among individuals. Direct payments of $2,138 million would go
to low-income families in the South. Kain and Schafer estimated
that taxes collected in the South would provide $768 million of
this amount, while $1,370 million would come from taxes col-
lected outside the region. Funds flowing from outside the region
would have a multiplier effect, such that Kain and Schafer estimated a total rise in Southern income attributable to FAP of
$3,420 million. Poverty would be considerably diminished, espe-
cially among blacks, and low-income families generally. The
South would come into line with other regions with respect to the
proportion of families with incomes under $2,000. The typical
nonwhite family receiving FAP payments would increase its
income from $2,645 to $3,891. White family income would rise
from $2,619 to $3,578, the lesser increase being accounted for
by smaller family size. While it has never been established that
differential welfare payments have been an inducement to migration from the South, it is readily forecast by economists Kain and
Schafer that since FAP "would increase expected incomes in the
South by more than in the North, without presumably affecting
other nonmonetary returns from living in the two regions," the
result would be to reduce net migration from South to North.[19]

This, too, was a Southern strategy, if not a distinctive one.
Since the Civil War itself there has been a body of opinion that
has held that so long as the South remained poor, the Nation
would remain in danger. This was not exactly knowledge, but it
was a not unreasonable inference from the apparent facts of the
preceding century. Southern economic parity with other regions
would not bring an end to racial tension; it might even increase
it. But there is a difference between social peace and social
stability, and it was the latter, perceived as a rough equality of
the races, that the planners of FAP were seeking, albeit with
little more to go on than a conviction as old as Thucydides that
justice between unequals is impossible.

But to bring the races closer to economic equality at anything more rapid than the pace of the 1960s involved Federal
intervention so massive that it could scarcely be subtle and
assuredly not indirect. A competent journalist could discover this
with ease. Of the varied misfortunes which befell the legislation,

none was more ironic than an article which appeared in *Fortune* in June 1970 entitled "The Looming Money Revolution Down South." The subtitles alone were enough to spell disaster. "After long delay, integration is sweeping across the South. Now comes the startling Nixon program of a guaranteed income for every family." "Who's going to tote that barge?" "The last days of white supremacy." The article, by Richard Armstrong, was a careful work of investigative reporting about

the shanty-towns and rural hovels of the Deep South, down where the present welfare grant for a family of four is as little as $60 a month, and where fully half of the eligible families are excluded—in some cases because of registering to vote.

He described a family in the Alabama black belt, once cotton country, now "rich pastureland" where black Angus cattle graze on white-owned land, where, he might have added, the poor had become another surplus commodity brought about by a restructuring of farming patterns, feed-grain price supports, and the network of Federal agricultural policies.

In one of the most dilapidated of the shacks . . . four rooms hammered together with old boards and patched in spots with cardboard, Mrs. Adie Powell lives with her nine children, her parents, her sister, and her sister's six children. All these nineteen people now manage somehow to survive on $50 a week that Mrs. Powell makes on the assembly line at a local wood-processing plant, the sister's welfare check of $104 a month, and the $192 old-age and social-security pension that Mrs. Powell's parents receive.

Under President Nixon's family-assistance program . . . things would get quite dramatically better for Mrs. Powell and all her kin. As a member of the "working poor" Mrs. Powell could draw $3,552 a year in cash and food stamps to augment her earnings of $2,500 at the mill. Her sister, as an unemployed welfare mother, could draw $3,316 in cash and stamps, and the parents would collect $2,640. Thus, on the effective date of the bill, July 1, 1971, annual household income would almost double overnight from $6,052 to $12,008, the sort of money now enjoyed only by the white merchant and landowner class in Alabama's black belt.

The article continued in this mode. The Southern Regional Council, Armstrong reported, had recently completed a survey

of black families living in squalor and deprivation in and around
the little town of Louise in the Mississippi Delta. Average family
income was $1,538 per year, average family size was 7.1 per-
sons. He calculated that FAP would *treble* this income to
$4,493, "which should set off the greatest shopping boom ever to
hit sleepy Louise's fifteen stores." Georgia's welfare director
estimated that one third of the families in his state would qualify
for FAP, and that in eighty rural counties more than half would
be eligible. Armstrong estimated 40 percent of the population of
Mississippi would qualify. (In 1969 the average annual wage of
a Southern farm worker was $1,034. The income of the average
farm worker would have about tripled under FAP. Migrants
would especially have gained.)

The point was stressed by Armstrong that Family Assistance would have implications far beyond family budgets. A
young black activist told him that if a guaranteed income came
into effect, "I know a lot of white people who will get told to go
to hell." Armstrong added an interesting, if speculative, point:

Indeed, one of the odd features of the past decade of protest has been
the large role played by youngsters and old people, who had no jobs to
lose. A guaranteed income, under a Federal program with national
standards, fairly administered, could go a long way to lift black fears
of voting and speaking out. The day of black government may be
speeded in the hundreds of small towns and dozens of counties where
blacks are in the majority.

It seemed obvious to some, at least, that Family Assistance
would slow down the steady departure of blacks from the Deep
South, and possibly reverse it. Alexander Waites, a Mississippi
official of the NAACP, reported that the civil-rights legislation of
the 1960s and the spread of school desegregation was attracting
migrants back to the South. FAP would hasten this, said Charles
Morgan, regional director of the ACLU; "remigration is what
the bill is all about."

Predictably, Armstrong encountered "grave misgivings"
about FAP among "conservative white Southerners." Governor
Lester Maddox of Georgia was described as "horrified." Representative Phil Landrum was quoted as stating, "There's not going
to be anybody left to roll these wheelbarrows and press these

shirts. They're all going to be on welfare," noting that under the bill even if a family head flatly refused to work the family allowance was cut by only $300 a year, and not discontinued. The facts certainly suggested changes ahead. Armstrong stated what was no more than obvious, that "A realistic expectation is that there will be some defection from the work force. . . ." In one small Mississippi town he found that all but two of eighteen full-time maids would be eligible for FAP payments without having to work.

If it was possible for a competent investigative reporter to discern in straightforward terms what the economic impact of FAP would be in the South, it was much more difficult for political actors to judge what would be the impact on them. For one thing, support for FAP in the South was weaker than in any other region, both among blacks and among whites. In the fourth quarter of 1969, following the president's speech, the Survey Research Center at the University of Michigan conducted an economic behavior survey in which one question asked opinion about replacing welfare with income supplements for the poor up to "some minimum poverty standard." Responses were coded so as to record subtler variation in attitudes than can be had from the "Yes," "No," and "Don't Know's" of commercial opinion surveys. Otto A. Davis and John E. Jackson later summarized the results and found that support for a proposal such as FAP was rather less than the standard polls suggested. Of the sample, 46 percent favored the plan, but 41 percent were opposed. *The highest levels of opposition were in the South.* Blacks everywhere were more disposed to favor such a plan than whites—100 percent of urban blacks polled in the North Central region did so—but Southerners less than Northerners. *The blacks least likely to favor such a proposal were those of the rural South.*[20]

This might appear to be a problem of political rationality. In the case of FAP, however, something further was involved. Southern politics were in turmoil at this time. Old coalitions were breaking up, new ones being formed, allegiances were shifting, parties breaking up, parties starting up. None knew just what was best politically; few knew where they stood, and fewer still could predict where they would stand in the future. At the height of a populist-racialist reaction associated with Governor Wallace of Alabama, there of a sudden appeared (in the elections of

1970) a liberal resurgence which asserted that the issue of race was dead and that new issues should assume primacy. But before two years were out, race, in the form of the busing issue, had returned to the fore. In such circumstances politicians are as likely to think of danger as of advantage. For FAP this meant few Southern politicians were inclined to take a strong position one way or another.

If white Southerners understood the implications of FAP all too well, blacks seemed to understand them not at all. Or, if understood, they were for some reason not welcomed. Just what was the case is not clear, for the record, with one or two exceptions, is one of silence. With no black congressmen it is reasonable to assume that Southern blacks had only uncertain channels of information concerning legislation outside fields traditionally associated with civil rights. Even so, there was enough information to have elicited some response had not other considerations blocked it. The assessment in the White House at the time was that a generalized distrust of the Nixon Administration among blacks played a role, and that Southern blacks, to the degree they were organized, chose to associate themselves with Washington-based organizations that were familiar allies in civil-rights matters. In general these groups had declared FAP to be inadequate, and so, by their silence, did the one group in the Nation that stood most to gain from it. Representative Landrum knew that even if a family head flatly refused work the family allowance would be cut by only $300, and he felt he knew what this would mean. "I've been around long enough," he was quoted, "to know that most people would work until they made the extra $720, and then they would quit and go home." Yet Armstrong reported:

The Reverend Rims Barber, a civil-rights worker with the Delta Ministry in Mississippi, rails at this work requirement as "slave labor. That's just subsidizing lazy white women who shouldn't be allowed to have maids at that price."

The legislation provided that those states that desired to could turn over all FAP administration, including registration of recipients, to a Federal agency. Clearly the Federal government wanted to get administration *out* of local hands. Yet blacks were suspicious. The U.S. Employment Service, with its state-by-state structure, was suspect. The manager of a black farming cooperative whose members' incomes would quintuple under FAP was nonetheless "deeply suspicious." "I'll have to see it to believe it," he said.

Several months later Leonard Lesser of the Committee for Community Affairs, a Washington-based "nonprofit corporation organized to represent and speak for community organizations of the poor and disadvantaged," appeared before the Senate Finance Committee with Robert Clark, the first black member of the Mississippi legislature in almost a hundred years, and the only one. They appeared in opposition to FAP. Lesser referred the committee to the *Fortune* article, "which documents the abuses under existing programs and the likelihood that the family assistance program will fail if its administration is turned over to the states, as H.R. 16311 would permit." Clark spoke with unmistakable feeling.

I have come to recognize the overwhelming need for a change in our welfare system. I am hopeful that Congress will at least take steps to relieve the crying needs of my people. However, as a black man from Mississippi who has deep concern for poor of all races, I cannot support the bill.

So long as the administration of the proposed family assistance program is placed in the hands of the state governments it is bound to fail. I hope that you senators can understand what administration by the state means for the poor in Mississippi. The state will do the very least it can get away with. It will use every excuse imaginable to delay the program's implementation and see that its great purpose fails, some of which are blatantly illegal.

Clark declared himself in support of the NWRO proposal of "an HEW national minimum income floor of $5,500 for a family of four." He acknowledged that HEW Secretary Finch had over-ridden the veto by Mississippi Governor John Bell Williams of sixteen Head Start projects which "successfully involved poor parents in the education of their own children." But he could not trust the intentions of Finch's department with respect to the administration of FAP.

This episode, of no great consequence in itself, was symp-

tomatic of the confusion of liberal response to FAP that ultimately did have consequences. There was no state in the Union
where the legislation would have had more effect than Mississippi, and no people in Mississippi whom it would affect more
than blacks. Yet the first black Mississippi legislator since Reconstruction traveled to Washington to testify in opposition. A
failure of trust merged with a failure of imagination. Clarence
Mitchell had not believed Mississippi would let FAP go into
effect, neither did Representative Clark. It was too much. And
yet his response was to demand even more, as if testing to see
what would be the limits of this wholly new disposition. Nixon
had departed too much from his previous image, had proposed a
program too far ahead of any existing arrangement, for audi-
ences that had to be persuaded of his good will to find it credible.
In a political leader this may have to be judged a mistake.
Dishing the Whigs is one thing: smashing crockery is another.

Yet there was in evidence also a certain lack of candor
about FAP on the part of some liberals. Lesser was an experienced Washington operative, and by any standards one of the
more admirable. But he did not faithfully represent the tone of
the *Fortune* article, which was altogether optimistic about FAP,
and did not document *any* "abuses" of the existing welfare
system. It might have done, but it did not. Moreover, it made
quite explicit the Federal desire for national administration of
FAP.

In carrying out its mandate, HEW may either register applicants itself, through an agency as yet unnamed and not yet staffed, or it may
contract with state agencies to do the job, in which case HEW will
pay only *half* the administrative costs instead of all. As the financial
incentive indicates, HEW would like to take over the program entirely,
leaving only a welfare-service role to the state departments. "And
most states want to get rid of it," says John Montgomery, HEW's
director of family assistance planning. Even if some southern states
should elect to administer the program themselves, paying millions
yearly for the privilege, it is difficult to see how they could refuse to
register eligible applicants amounting, in some cases, to a third of the
population of the state. HEW retains final authority and states would
have no say about eligibility standards, as they do at present. One
of the virtues of the new program, administratively, is that *every*
family is eligible if its income is below the cutoff level, which in the

bill is $3,920 for a family of four. The minutiae of family history are irrelevant.[21]

The intentions of the Administration could not have been more clear in this matter. Montgomery, an experienced official, was then heading a staff of some 225 persons planning the implementation of FAP, including the establishment of Federal machinery to operate the program, it being assumed that the great majority of states would opt for that. Had Lesser and Clark been testifying before a committee anxious to do more than the president proposed, their position might have involved a more rational calculation. But this was the Senate Finance Committee, dominated by white Southerners whose clear disposition was to do nothing.

It may be that the nonresponse of Southern blacks was part of a more general style, then emerging, of being very little impressed with *anything* forthcoming from the majority white government. This certainly was the case with the achievement of school desegregation. Once again, Southern whites knew well enough what was going on. In a Senate speech in mid-July Strom Thurmond, who had been Nixon's Southern manager at the 1968 Republican convention, denounced the Administration moves in school desegregation as "arbitrary and discriminatory actions by the Executive branch, calculated to appease the anti-South elements in the Nation." He blamed the president's advisers, rather than the president. Nonetheless, six weeks later the public schools of his hometown of Edgefield, South Carolina, including the high school named for him, integrated their black and white pupils, the latter outnumbered two to one. The editor of an Edgefield weekly newspaper, a Wallace man, declared, "Strom and the Republicans sold us down the river. He told the whites that he and Nixon would never let this happen and they believed him."

So also, in a sense, had blacks, and events did not much change that belief. Rather, a familiar enough process began of redefining issues. The demand for "quality integrated education" began to replace the earlier insistence on the end of segregation. But where the president might have lost credibility with whites, he gained none with blacks.

The black position was in any event complicated at this

394 | *DANIEL P. MOYNIHAN*

time by a sharp dichotomy between the situation in the North as against the South. In the South local control was seen, with reason, to be a threat to black interests. Even if FAP was misrepresented as perpetuating local control, given that belief there was logic in opposing it. But in the North white theorists of black militancy perceived just the opposite threat. Writing in 1971, Frances Fox Piven described as "most portentous . . . the Administration's proposal for 'welfare reform' [which] would give the Federal government a much larger role in welfare policy, lifting the struggle for who gets what outside the arena of city politics where blacks had developed some power, and got some welfare."[22] Yet different theorists had yet different explanations of Administration malfeasance. In October 1969 Bayard Rustin, a black activist, wrote a denunciation of FAP for the magazine of Americans for Democratic Action. *He* saw the scheme as a reward for white Southerners.

. . . This bonanza for the South is entirely consistent with Nixon's famed "Southern strategy," which earned him the warm friendship of Strom Thurmond and which is guiding his opposition to Negro voting rights and to school integration.[23]

Some of this rhetoric reflected a concern that civil-rights issues were losing their priority in national affairs. Bishop Spottswood in labeling the Nixon Administration anti-Negro also complained that other issues, such as the environment, were claiming the attention of activist citizens. A fair number of established public persons felt it necessary to emulate the apocalyptic rhetoric of the radical left of the period, while even the most sober ones seemed to feel that in the absence of shock treatment the public as well as the government would lose interest. The Civil Rights Commission, under the chairmanship of Theodore M. Hesburgh, took to attacking the president in the strongest terms. After a period, civil-rights activities within the Federal establishment were markedly increased by the Nixon Administration. In a press conference in the spring of 1971 Hesburgh acknowledged that the president had asked Congress for a "substantial across-the-board increase in budget for civil rights." He acknowledged a list of similar measures, yet declared himself dissatisfied.

I have been dissatisfied with the leadership of the last four Presidents in this field. I suspect we'll always be dissatisfied. . . . I think one thing you have to say about Presidential leadership is it needs a little Presidential followership. . . . I have a feeling throughout the Nation there is a great reluctance to move forward in this field. And unless we have bombings and burnings and violence and disorder, people tend to go back to sleep again. . . . You could put the good Lord in as President of the United States and He couldn't solve this problem if everybody wouldn't cooperate.*

Hesburgh spoke from a past in which the issue of race was primary and could be judged in terms of the simplest of moral imperatives and constitutional dictates. If such a condition had ever existed, it was long past in the North, where the issue of race might mask that of social class, but in which the primacy of the latter was unmistakable to the close analyst. Increasingly, this was the condition of the South also. This was the reward for progress.

And so the Southern travail persisted. Had this been the 1930s, and had Roosevelt included Family Assistance in the Social Security Act, almost certainly the preponderance of Southern congressmen would have supported it. It would have caused no political problems and would have solved endless economic ones. Senator Huey Long of Louisiana, had he differed with the president on the issue, would almost certainly have done so by outbidding him. But much had changed. By the end of the 1960s few could summon the courage to take the leap into the future that a guaranteed income would almost certainly precipitate. This is not perhaps to be wondered at. Change was all but overwhelming the South as it was; men were preoccupied with what was already in process. It may be a time had come when a program, to win political support, had to be undersold, rather

---

* Early in 1972 the White House issued a summary of "Civil Rights and Related Social Programs" of the Nixon Administration which stated: "In 1969 $75 million was budgeted for *civil rights enforcement activity* compared to 1973's recommendations for $602.1 million—an eightfold increase over a five-year period." An increase of this magnitude did occur, and as a matter of deliberate policy. Such changes do not, however, necessarily lead to greater satisfaction on the part of bodies such as the Civil Rights Commission. Eight times as many investigators leading to eight times as many complaints *could* create an atmosphere in which matters seemed eight times worse. This is a common dilemma of social policy.

than otherwise. Family Assistance, even as "workfare," was too obviously too great a leap into the future for Southern whites to accept, and possibly for Southern blacks also. There was simply no way to be subtle about a guaranteed income: it *did* raise the prospect of "fundamental social change."

This is not a proposition easily established, but there is evidence that is at least suggestive. Thus at this time Senator Ernest F. Hollings, Democrat of South Carolina, became deeply involved with the issue of hunger and malnutrition among poor blacks in his state. He became an impassioned congressional advocate of expanded food programs. In private conversation he would acknowledge that food stamps were a halfway house toward a guaranteed income, and that a full-fledged proposal such as the Family Assistance Plan would accomplish even more of what he hoped for. But, he felt, the South was not ready. In the 1980s perhaps, not in the 1970s. And so he took to denouncing President Nixon for the inadequacies of the Administration's food programs.

Citations—Chapter V

1. McPherson, *A Political Education*, pp. 427–8.
2. Cavala and Wildavsky, "The Political Feasibility . . . ," pp. 323–29.
3. Quoted by Kenneth Thompson, "The Forgotten Niebuhr," *World View*, July–August 1971, p. 3.
4. Steiner, *The State of Welfare*, p. 79.
5. James J. Graham, "Public Assistance: Congress and the Employable Mother," *University of Richmond Law Review*, Spring 1969, p. 259.
6. Wilbur Cohen was briefly a member, but did not sign the final report. Another member, Margaret Gordon, had been involved with social-security matters, but primarily in the field of unemployment research.
7. The President's Commission on Income Maintenance Programs, *Poverty Amid Plenty: The American Paradox*, Washington, D.C., November 1969, p. iii.
8. *Ibid.*, p. 58.
9. *Ibid.*, p. 59.
10. Jack Rosenthal, "Presidential Panel Favors Income Aid Based on Need," *The New York Times*, November 13, 1969.
11. Democratic National Committee, *Demo Memo*, Washington, D.C., August 25, 1969.
12. Steiner, *The State of Welfare*, p. 105.
13. Median family income computed by John F. Kain and Robert Schafer, Harvard University, published in "Regional Impacts of the Family Assistance Plan," Cambridge, Massachusetts, June 1971, mimeographed.

14. Southern Regional Council, "Special Report, LAWLESSNESS AND DISORDER: Fourteen Years of Failure in Southern School Desegregation," Atlanta, 1968, mimeographed, p. 5.
15. Southern Regional Council, "Special Report, THE FEDERAL RETREAT IN SCHOOL DESEGREGATION," Atlanta, December 1969, mimeographed, p. iii.
16. The news release from the Department of Health, Education, and Welfare was dated June 18, 1971. Shifting court definitions of acceptable standards of integration make it difficult to compare statistics in this field, but the "majority white school" definition is as good an indicator as any.
17. Henry Owen, "North-South Breach Is Slowly Healing," *Washington Post,* September 14, 1970.
18. See the papers contained in Mosteller and Moynihan (eds.), *On Equality of Educational Opportunity.*
19. Kain and Schafer, "Regional Impacts of the Family Assistance Plan," Tables 6, 7, 9 and *passim.*
20. Otto A. Davis and John E. Jackson, unpublished paper presented at a conference on "The Political Economy of Income Distribution," The Urban Institute, Washington, D.C., March 1972.
21. Richard Armstrong, "The Looming Money Revolution Down South," *Fortune,* June 1970, p. 152.
22. Frances Fox Piven, "The Urban Crisis: Who Got What and Why," mimeographed, 1971, p. 42. (Scheduled for publication in Robert Paul Wolff (ed.), *1984 Revisited,* Random House, January, 1973.)
23. Bayard Rustin, "Nixonism vs. Welfarism," *ADA World Magazine,* October 1969.

VI

Congress: The House of Representatives

1. The Committee on Ways and Means

Room H-208 on the second floor of the Capitol is small by the standards of Imperial Washington, but choice in terms of the Capitol itself, a corner suite just a few feet off the House Chamber. It is a privileged position, shared only by the Appropriations Committee on the southwest corner opposite. Ways and Means, established in 1802, the oldest standing committee of the House, is charged with drafting revenue legislation, which must originate in that chamber. Until 1865 it also handled appropriations. *That* committee, in the manner of its era, has got hold of three rooms, but Ways and Means, with a certain republican restraint, contents itself with one. It is a cluttered room with one large table, worn chairs, and a sign on the wall that reads, "Due to the lack of experienced trumpeters, the end of the world is postponed for three weeks."

An organization such as Ways and Means has an institutional role so pronounced as to shape political behavior by its structure as much as by the individual interests of its members. It might have been supposed that liberal Democrats would have supported FAP because it was a liberal program, conservative Republicans because it was Republican, Southerners because it aided the South. On closer scrutiny it developed that within each of these groups countervailing interests might overcome the expected tendency. Now, however, the institutional traditions of

Ways and Means provided another set of incentives which reversed that reversal. For a period, liberal Democrats, conservative Republicans, as well as some Southerners, behaved as they "ought" to have behaved. Structure imposed rationality.

The chairman of the committee, Wilbur D. Mills, was in this period generally held the second most powerful man in Washington, following only the president. His position, powerful in any circumstances, was enhanced during the 91st Congress by the salience of legislation—taxation, social insurance, tariffs, welfare, revenue sharing—which came under his jurisdiction. When the 91st Congress organized, more than half the standing committees of the House were chaired by Southerners. Of the twelve most important, Southerners chaired nine. Of these men, Mills and Carl D. Perkins of Kentucky were the only ones not somehow flawed by the Southern experience. From near reactionary to near radical—the range of manner and opinion in the others was wide—the shared quality of all was that of having come of age in an embittered, poor, racialist South or Southwest and having been formed by that experience. Somehow the experience did not get to these two as it had got to the others. Mills attended a good Methodist college, Hendrix in Conway, Arkansas, followed by Harvard Law School. He became first a judge and then a congressman, and thereafter gave his life singularly to this vocation. There were more than a few qualities he shared with the president; he was, of all things, lawyerlike.

He had helped assemble a committee markedly in his own image. It was by region and politics as near as could be to the center of the Democratic party. The only old-fashioned Southern member was Phil M. Landrum of Georgia. The second-ranking Democrat, Hale Boggs of Louisiana, was a Catholic, a liberal, a man of New Orleans. Big-city Democrats were automatically present: Dan Rostenkowski of Illinois, who spoke for the Cook County delegation; Jacob H. Gilbert of the Bronx Democratic organization; William J. Green, son of the former Democratic leader of Philadelphia. The ranking Republican, John W. Byrnes of Wisconsin, an experienced and humane man, a Catholic with six children and no fortune, was also very much of the center of his party and a legislator as gifted as Mills. A Republican member of the committee observed that "The mindless operation of the seniority system has somehow brought the two natural leaders to the top. Mills and Byrnes, under any rational system, would be the leaders." The Democratic members of Ways and Means serve as the Committee on Committees in the House, so that party balance is a prime concern in their appointment. As a separate committee serves this function for Republicans, with them a tradition has grown up that Ways and Means members must first of all be from safe seats (also the case with the Democrats), leaving them as little as possible exposed to constituent or other pressures. Of the ten Republicans, four—Herman T. Schneebeli of Pennsylvania, Barber B. Conable, Jr., of New York, George Bush of Texas, and Rogers C. B. Morton of Maryland—were liberal, well-to-do Protestants educated at Ivy League colleges. Any of them might have sent the telegram the president received following his August 8 address from the "two upper-middle-class Republicans." Each was also the sort of congressman most receptive to the efforts of Laird and others to formulate "constructive" Republican alternatives to the Great Society programs.

There is a sense in which the special quality of the committee was its normalcy. These congressmen knew their assignment was important. The workload was heavy and complex, but, for those members who wished it, there was the opportunity to participate directly in shaping major legislation. Where so many political institutions are skewed in one direction or another, and much taken up with the advancement of particular positions or causes, much concerned with the symbols of politics, Ways and Means was almost wholly taken up with its substance. Its members did not have to be known to the public: they were known to the Congress; known to almost all with serious interests at issue in politics. The sheer *consequence* of Ways and Means has seemingly shaped both the style of the members and the substance of the committee actions. In his study of the committee John F. Manley writes of a "vital integrative norm" that tempers the behavior of its members: *"the norm of restrained partisanship."*[1] It dictates that members pay close attention to the technical details of the legislation, and that, while they may disagree on what to do, they nonetheless will agree on how to decide. This ideal may be best thought of as a distillation of the norms of the House of Representatives itself. "Within such an organization," Manley writes, "the ideologue who cannot contain his fervor, or the man who is so fired with his vision of the truth that he brooks no dissent, are unlikely to do very well." The generalization may be made that behavior least recognized by the news media is most recognized by the House, and that recognition commonly takes the form of a seat on Ways and Means, whose members Manley describes as, "in general, pragmatic in their outlook on politics, patient in their pursuit of objectives, unbending on few things, and inclined to compromise on all but the most basic issues."*[2]

This was eminently the case with the Ways and Means committee of the 91st Congress. Its Democrats were liberal, but not fervid; its Republicans were conservative but not unyielding; its Southerners were moderate by standards of the racially aroused South. Advocates of "fundamental social change" would have tended to expect little from such a group, any more than from the Nixon White House. Yet these were the two institutions in which the idea of a guaranteed income took shape and prospered.

Mills led his committee but did not coerce, much less disdain it. The committee would do nothing he was opposed to, but he would not normally support anything the committee opposed. Where most other committees had fractionated into subcommittees presided over by the members with seniority competing with one another, Ways and Means remained one committee with one chairman. It always met as a whole and its decisions were almost always near to unanimous; major differences were compromised within the committee. In particular almost everything Mills did was done in concert with Byrnes; they were not to be separated save by the rarest of circumstance. The issues with which the committee dealt were too serious to

---

* The "norm of restrained partisanship" has not always characterized the behavior of the members of Ways and Means, although recent exceptions are rare. However, in the period 1933–1939, the first three Congresses during Franklin D. Roosevelt's tenure, the committee's activities, reflecting in part the large Democratic majorities in both the Senate and the House, were intensely partisan. At times, Republican members of Ways and Means were locked out of the committee's office during executive sessions. Manley reports, however, that the major exception during this period was the handling of the Social Security Act of 1935. Of all the bills in the thirties studied by Manley, he feels that the handling of the Social Security Act most resembles the current practice of Ways and Means with respect to its restrained partisanship. (*The Politics of Finance*, p. 170.)

permit of slender majorities: experience had taught this lesson. Equally, the issues were too complex and too easily susceptible to the influence of special interests to allow them to become the object of competitive bidding on the floor, or so the leadership felt. Bills reported from Ways and Means typically went to the floor under a rule that permitted no amendments or very few. The House was to vote Aye or Nay; it was not to redraft the legislation. All but invariably the vote was Aye. These arrangements were of the first consequence for Family Assistance. The proposal had emerged from a decision-making process in the White House in which sufficient power was concentrated in one man that a decision was possible. It now went to the House of Representatives where substantially the same condition obtained.

To appearances, Ways and Means knew little of welfare matters, and might have been expected to be unresponsive. Yet again, the White House parallel obtained. To come relatively new to the subject was to be more open about it, the more so as Ways and Means, again as with the White House, was relatively immune to pressures directed to the maintenance of the existing system (as, indeed, it was comparatively aloof from the publics interested in tax bills and other areas of its business). In any event, appearances were somewhat deceptive here. Ways and Means *was* involved with welfare, having responded to the presidential initiative that led to the welfare amendments of 1962, and having, on its own initiative, launched those of 1967. It understood the subject to be a troubled one, and by now tended to look upon the various welfare lobbies as being at least in part a source of the trouble. It was above all open to information.

This did not guarantee an immediate welcome for FAP. The committee had not been consulted in advance and more or less had to respond to it in the first instance as a proposal to spend a great deal of money. On September 18, Mills announced he would hold joint hearings on the president's messages on Social Security and on welfare.* These began October 15, with Robert Finch in the witness chair. Representative Al Ullman, the

---

* The Social Security message, sent September 25, proposed a 10 percent increase in benefits, effective April 1970, automatic future adjustment of benefits to reflect cost-of-living increases, similar adjustment of the taxable wage base to reflect wage increases, and provisions enabling pensioners to earn more income without loss of benefits.

fourth-ranking Democrat, opened the questioning by declaring himself "shocked . . . almost to the point of being speechless" by the Family Assistance proposal. "It looks to me," he said, "like you are opening up the Treasury of the United States in a way it has never been opened up." Others were shocked that the president had proposed only a 10 percent increase in Social Security benefits, when 15 percent was called for. The press headlines—not large—were not encouraging: "Democrats Assail Nixon Welfare Plan," "Democrats Score Nixon Relief Aim." The stories were in the same vein.

This atmosphere did not, however, persist. The Administration witnesses were by now in fair control of the intricacies of the subject and a rapport with the committee was established. The committee members and the Administration officials were united in the awareness that they both knew a great deal more about welfare than almost anyone else, and also that they did not know much. Finch sought to explain the process by which the Administration had come to the conclusion that "a radical reform of the structure of welfare is needed." He stressed four points: the gross inequities under the existing system between categories of persons equally in need; the gross inequities from state to state; the "increasingly complex and controversial management crisis in welfare"; and the economic incentives "which in the present system weigh more in favor of continued dependency and family breakup than the reverse." The fiscal relief of state governments was emphasized. Data was provided on prospective benefits in the eight states (Alabama, Arkansas, Georgia, Louisiana, Mississippi, Missouri, South Carolina, and Tennessee) which then provided less than $1,600 per year for an AFDC family of four. The proposed expanded child services were described. A new cost estimate of $4.4 billion was revealed, the increase of $400 million resulting from a decision, made after the president's address, to treat only half of unearned income* as earned for purposes of the "disregard." The chief actuary of the Social

---

* "Unearned income" is just that: money obtained other than through employment. There is a great variety of such income, ranging from annuities and interest on savings, i.e., income derived from property, to gifts from relatives. An income strategy must determine whether to treat money obtained in this manner differently from that received from employment. The presumption, carried over from tax policy, is that such income is somehow different. Again, an added complexity in social policy.

Security Administration had been asked to make an independent estimate of FAP costs, and had come up with a figure close to that of the interagency group. So it went.

On the afternoon of October 15 HEW Undersecretary John Veneman made the crucial point that FAP was building on the WIN program which the committee had put together two years earlier. The hearing began to become a dialogue. He explained that the work incentives under FAP were stronger than under WIN, that there would be virtually no discretion as to who would be required to register for work or training, and that the first $60 rather than $30 of monthly income exempt from taxation. Robert Patricelli, now a deputy assistant secretary of HEW, outlined the planning that had gone into the work-incentive provisions. "We hope," he said, "there will be a much more efficient procedure of linking [those registered] . . . with a training opportunity or a job opportunity." Byrnes responded by stating a central belief of the Committee on Ways and Means:

Frankly, in my judgment, this bill is going to rise and fall not on a hope. It is going to rise and fall on the question of whether there can be a conviction that you are really going to go through with it, and it is going to be effective.

The Labor Department's Jerome Rosow, who was present, quickly joined in.

May I, with your permission, Mr. Byrnes, respond to your strong statements, which we endorse wholeheartedly, and on which we have been working very carefully over the past months, to design the proper language in the proposed legislation . . . as . . . will be represented by Secretary Shultz tomorrow. . . .

Shultz appeared the second day, a superb witness. His first words were "this is not a proposal for a guaranteed minimum income. Work is a major feature of this program." Family Assistance, he said, was a composite of "work incentives, training and employment opportunities, child care, and income allowances." Work was his central theme.

My responsibility lies not with the whole of the family assistance plan, although I am interested in the whole plan, but particularly with its relationships to the labor market. It is my concern that the program be structured in such a way as to protect work incentives and that the program in its total design be one that creates the strongest possible conditions for moving people from welfare into employment.

He reported on WIN, the responsibility of the Department of Labor, repeating that the 1967 amendments "established a foundation on which to build a larger training program in support of the Family Assistance Act." There was not a great deal to report. The program had begun in October 1968, had enrolled 92,000 persons by September 1969, of whom 13,000 had by then gone on to get jobs. Altogether in the Nation fewer than two hundred persons had been denied benefits for refusing work or training, none of them mothers. Shultz sought a balance between a strong conviction that Family Assistance should lead to work training and to work, and an equally strong determination that it not adversely affect wage rates or working conditions. He was persuaded that the welfare community, especially in the "liberal" states, had gone off in a mistaken direction with respect to work and training. Under the WIN program state welfare agencies were required to refer "appropriate" recipients to the employment service. In New York only 7 percent of those screened by the welfare agencies were deemed "appropriate" for such referral. In Utah the proportion had been 97 percent. (Within the Administration it was taken as given that the welfare bureaucracy in New York City, for example, has become politicized and would resist any work program. It was also assumed that the Utahs would tend toward their extremes. All the more was there a case for fixed national standards.) FAP almost entirely eliminated local discretion. The legislation described six categories of persons who did not have to register with the local public employment office: those ill, incapacitated, or of an advanced age; a mother or other relative caring for a child under six; the mother if the father or another adult male relative is in the home; children up to age 21 if attending school; a person needed in the home to care for an ill member of the household; and those working full time. All others were to register. Shultz estimated the total would come to 1.1 million family heads.

The Secretary of Labor explained the work test. An FAP recipient would be denied benefits if he refused "without good cause to accept suitable employment in which he is able to engage." He stated the known facts about this criterion.

> The key word is "suitable." It is a test that has long been used in unemployment insurance, and over the years, through agency and court interpretation, a large body of case law has established its meaning in different situations.
>
> We expect that a similar process will occur in the case of family assistance. It will be applied on an individual by individual basis, under guidelines that the Secretary of Labor will be responsible for providing to the state agencies. There will be appeals, and there will be hearings on those appeals. Cases may be taken to court where matters will be finally settled.
>
> . . . We intend to follow the same policy with respect to wages as we now do in WIN, and in the proposed Manpower Training Act. We do not require a person to take a job that pays less than the applicable minimum wage, or the prevailing wage, whichever is higher.
>
> But a policy of this sort does not contain the whole story. Our objective is to move people out of poverty and off welfare. We are not going to be out looking for low-wage jobs. We want the highest wages possible. And to the maximum possible extent we are going to train people for jobs at decent wages, whenever we find that they cannot get good jobs with their present skills.
>
> There is no intention of doing anything that would undermine existing wage levels. We are not going to open up a new cheap labor supply to employers who are not paying the going rates.

Either there is a public trust or there is not. The intent of the work requirement could not have been more plainly stated by a person more qualified to do so. Veneman had already told the committee that the penalty for refusal was the loss of $300 a year in benefits. Shultz went on to point out that the current rate of disqualifications in the unemployment insurance program—using the "suitable" criterion—was "less than 0.1 percent of claimant contacts." He stated with perfect conviction that low-income persons desired to work. (A month later he wrote Mills with the information that half of all women with children of school age, including 47 percent of those with a husband and two thirds of those without, were in the labor force.) He pointed to the continued inability of the economy to produce day-care facilities: only 2 percent of the children of working mothers were being cared for under group-care arrangements. He added a personal conviction that had been with him from the earliest discussions of FAP.

If somebody asked me what is the most important thing in this whole plan, I would say it is the idea of quality child care. I recognize the plan has a lot of dimensions to it and a lot of important aspects. But I think that is what I would put my emphasis on.

He pleaded for the working poor: half lived in the South; one in three of the family heads had less than eight years of education; four in ten did not get a full year's work; one in three was black.

The following week Finch and his associates returned for a day of questioning which went over the same material, and then, for the Administration, the hearings were over. Another fifteen days of testimony followed, much of it devoted to Social Security matters. On November 13 the hearings concluded. It is difficult to assess their impact. Those members of the committee who wandered in and out of the large hearing room could pick up a fair amount of odd-lot information. (If they did not know that welfare in New York City was a mess they could have learned from Jack R. Goldberg, Commissioner of Social Services in the Lindsay administration, that the average case-worker had a case load of 71 cases and that the average turnover of case-workers was about 42 or 43 percent a year.) Gradually the basic dimensions of the Family Assistance proposal emerged. The Administration witnesses had explained that 13 million new beneficiaries would be included under the working-poor category. This would be in addition to 6.5 million AFDC recipients. (Of the latter, 1.2 million would automatically receive increased benefits under FAP.) It would not be a small operation. FAP would require 25,000 new Federal employees, and would cost $250 million a year to administer, perhaps more. Some details got straightened out. Children's earnings would not be counted in family income, nor would food stamps or home produce. The resources allowed a family of the working poor would be on the generous side: up to $1,500, a home, household goods, all personal effects, and such other property as determined by the Secretary of HEW to be "so essential to the family's means of self-support as to warrant its exclusion." This clearly could include a farm. The estimated cost of day care would be $1,600 per year per child. Although the singular feature of FAP was the inclusion of the working poor, it turned out that 22 percent of this population was already receiving income assistance of some kind, as against 81 percent of the nonworking poor.* The gross variations and contortions that had grown up in the fifty-plus separate systems were dramatized, although they could hardly have been news to the committee. The Administration had settled on five goals for the Family Assistance Plan, and these were the subject of a fair amount of drill.

GOALS OF THE FAMILY ASSISTANCE PLAN

1. *National standards*
     Payment floor
     Eligibility requirements
     Move toward national administration
2. *Equity for the working poor*
3. *Work incentives*
4. *Family stability incentives*
5. *Expanded job training and child care*

The fact that AFDC covered 35 percent of poor children and FAP would cover 100 percent was repeated and repeated.

The committee was not unimpressed, but neither did it appear to be taking FAP seriously. Social-security benefits had to be raised, and this was why hearings were being held. The Administration did make some points, but this was not evident at the time. Byrnes and a number of Republican colleagues, especially Conable and Schneebeli, asked supportive questions which, for example, enabled Finch to put into the record a lengthy analysis of the undoubtedly powerful and positive response of public and editorial opinion to the president's address. Byrnes brought up the New Jersey income maintenance experiment and the Administration produced a brief but positive report: the experiment was going well; there were no "spending

* This estimate was made in 1965. Some states were doing this by defining a male head of family working less than 35 hours a week as unemployed and accordingly eligible for AFDC-U payments.

sprees" in evidence, "no perceptible" reduction in work effort; much was being learned.*

The most persistent, and not wholly friendly, questioning came from Michigan Congresswoman Martha W. Griffiths, who, two years earlier, had been chairman of the Joint Economic Committee's study of income maintenance programs and was both knowledgeable and concerned about welfare. Although much a part of the liberal wing of the Democratic party, her attitude toward the AFDC program was not at all complaisant, and her questioning went directly to the issue before the committee. She wanted to know what FAP would do about *welfare:* about illegitimacy, about desertion, about dependency. There were no very good answers. The Administration witnesses had grilled one another to the same purpose and with no greater success. She went straight to the point with Finch on the first morning of the hearings. Representative Ullman had finished by contending that FAP would lead to disaster. "This was our problem two years ago in the welfare program, to try and close it in so that we could keep it under control." The Administration, in his view, was now proposing to treble that same welfare program. Griffiths was much the more perceptive questioner.

Far from Mr. Ullman's viewpoint, my viewpoint is that all you have added to this program is money and I believe that money is never going to do it. You are going to have to do something far different if you are ever going to cure the problem of welfare.

I think the place where you are applying the money . . . is not in the cities that need the remedy.

She would not let go of the subject.

A teacher told me that she had a very bright little girl in her class. She worked very hard with her. She was an illegitimate child. Her mother was drawing AFDC. The little girl became pregnant at about thirteen and the teacher was absolutely sick. So she called the kid in and talked to her and said "What are you going to do?"

* This was merely an administrative observation. In February 1970 the committee was presented with the controversial "preliminary" findings of the experiment, discussed below, which dealt with specific data rather than general impressions.

And the kid said, "Why, I am going to get my own case-worker. That is what I am going to do."

And that is what you are going to do.

She asked if the Administration would accept an amendment requiring a mother of an illegitimate child to remain in school or be deprived of AFDC payments. From her point of view it was absurd that a mother with children under six should be exempted from training. She viewed this as a form of denial.

I just feel that the moment has come when you have to direct the money and the action towards the source of the problem, and the real problem is these young women. And your bill in my judgment doesn't do a thing for them. Ten years from today you can come back and you will not have solved the problem.

All Finch could reply was that the bill was "betting on instincts."

This piece of legislation proceeds from the premise that most people want to be with their families, the husband wants to be with the wife and vice versa, and the children there, too. Also, given two courses of action, work or nonwork, a man does want to get up in the morning and go off and do some work that is fulfilling and gives him some dignity.

It was a reply not without conviction. The witnesses were trying to be honest, but eight months with the issue of welfare had shaken all certainty on the subject of dependency.

The most damaging admission concerning FAP was made by Shultz in his prepared testimony when he explained the consequences of a dual system of Federal and state payments for the marginal rate of taxation on the earned income of welfare families. Forty states would be required to supplement FAP payments in order that benefits would equal the levels of July 1969. The working poor were excluded from this provision, but families eligible for AFDC support were guaranteed payment levels at least as high as those then in effect.* However, it was

---

* Later, the Ways and Means committee required supplementation of FAP payments up to the benefit levels of January 1970, unless these happened to exceed the poverty level. For the first time an official "poverty level," ranging from $1,920 for a single person to $6,120 for a family of seven or more, was being incorporated in legislation.

felt that supplementing states ought to be able to reduce their payments as earned income increased, just as would the Federal government. *This meant increasing the negative tax rate.* States were required to "disregard" the first $720 of earnings, but thereafter could reduce payments by varying amounts per dollar. This could lead, Shultz stated, to a total marginal tax rate on income of 67 percent, or more.

A yet more damaging case could have been made, and three weeks later Milton Friedman made it in testimony stating that, while he strongly endorsed the basic principles of the president's proposal, he was concerned that the marginal tax rate be kept low enough to provide a real work incentive, which he estimated to be no more than 50 percent. He pointed out that Social Security taxes at 4.8 percent would also be collected on most income of welfare recipients, bringing the *de facto* marginal tax under FAP to 71.5 percent.* Food stamps had *their* rate of taxation, the president's proposal being that stamp payments (a form of scrip) start at $1,200 (for a family of four) and be reduced by 30 percent of income, including FAP benefits, until the allowance was exhausted; i.e., at $4,000 of income. Pending adoption of the income-tax–reform proposals, the Federal government would begin collecting taxes on earnings at about the $3,000 level. State and local income taxes might compound the tax rate further. No one case would be like another, each the consequence of decisions widely separated in time and jurisdiction, but nonetheless these factors had combined to influence the growth of welfare dependency, and were not addressed by the new legislation. Friedman was restrained and friendly in his testimony, but any who listened would have had difficulty denying his conclusion that the various tax rates, each suddenly entering or leaving the family budget calculation, especially in the range of earnings from $720 to $3,920, promised little change in the condition of welfare families, as contrasted with

---

* In most states and over a wide range of incomes below the FAP break-even point of $3,920 for a family of four. As will become apparent later, estimates of the tax rate, coverage, and other features of FAP are conditioned by a number of factors, such as other programs operating in the same jurisdiction, amount and source of other income, and size of family. The reader who is interested in these details is advised to consult the record of the hearings, which is replete with charts and calculations.

the working poor, for whom FAP would be a straightforward benefit.

But it was not clear who if anyone in the Congress was listening. Forty-five representatives and one senator testified at the Ways and Means hearings. The senator and thirty-four of the representatives concerned themselves exclusively with Social Security matters, all supporting some expansion or increase in benefits, while ignoring Family Assistance.* Among these was Carl D. Perkins, chairman of the House Committee on Education and Labor, which was responsible for the poverty program. The subject simply had not impressed itself. A few congressmen mentioned FAP, favorably or unfavorably, without going into great detail. Democratic Representative Shirley Chisholm, of the Bedford-Stuyvesant area of Brooklyn, appeared to add her voice, as she put it, to the "chorus of critics" of the president's proposal. The benefit levels were "patently inadequate"; the compulsory work aspect smacked of "involuntary servitude." She sensed that the Administration was in any event preparing to allow the proposals to die. "If they were allowed to die," she concluded, "it would not be a great disaster—except for the Southern and rural states that stand to benefit most by the proposal." Another Democrat, Clement J. Zablocki of Wisconsin, suggested that the president's welfare proposals be "scrutinized carefully" to see if they would make welfare more "efficient and effective." Two Republicans spoke up for the president. Frank Horton of New York stated he was "enthusiastically" cosponsoring the proposals. Thomas J. Meskill of Connecticut asserted his fundamental agreement with the principles of FAP. Of some significance, Phillip Burton, Democrat of California, chairman of the Task Force on Health and Welfare of the House Democratic Study Group, began a statement on Social Security with the observation that while he was not prepared to speak about FAP he thought "the Administration should be commended for

---

* Ways and Means was considering concurrently with FAP a Social Security measure which, among other things, would have provided the usual election-year increases in insurance benefits. Although it was not originally a matter of design, it soon became apparent to advocates of FAP both in the White House and in Congress that this coincidental union might have its advantages; support for the Social Security provisions might also assist in passing the welfare titles of the bill. This apparently favorable arrangement proved to be much less of an asset in the Senate.

having what I think is essentially as sound a format as any other that I have observed to get us out of this impossible and contradictory family welfare morass." Two New York Democrats, Allard K. Lowenstein and James H. Scheuer, also spoke to the issue, the former asking that the FAP base be doubled to $3,200, the latter concerned that there be more job-training and family-planning services.

Three congressmen—a large or a small number according to one's expectations—had developed a detailed alternative to the president's plan. On August 12, John Conyers, Jr., Democrat of Michigan, Charles W. Whalen, Jr., Republican of Ohio, and Jonathan B. Bingham, Democrat of New York, had introduced legislation establishing a National Living Income Program, describing it as similar to the president's, "a radical departure from the present welfare system." The bill was based on the version of a negative tax developed by James Tobin at Yale. As far back as 1966, in a *Public Interest* article, Tobin had distinguished between "structural" and "distributive" strategies in combating poverty. The former sought to build up the capacities of the poor to earn decent incomes; the latter assured a decent income regardless of capacity. As of then, Tobin stated correctly, the "war on poverty" as embodied in OEO had given rise only to structural strategies. Moreover, the established system of public assistance, he argued, was replete with "perverse incentives to those dependent upon it," of which the most serious was the AFDC incentive to the breakup or nonformation of families. With the "buildup" in Vietnam he conceded the time was not at hand for an income guarantee but declared there would be no victory in the war on poverty without one and pleaded that when the moment next arrived that "fiscal drag" became a problem to be solved, "let us not repeat the great tax rate reduction of 1964–1965, but instead concentrate the benefits on those whose need is greatest."[3] Congressman Whalen, a professor of economics, testified that the basic principles of FAP and of the National Living Income Program Act were "virtually identical," although the latter set a $3,200 base for a family of four, and was universal in coverage. The NLIP, as he termed it, would cost an estimated $20 billion, an amount he allowed might not be available under the existing budgetary circumstances. It was his hope, and that of his two colleagues, that the two bills together "might serve as the basis—the beginning point—of exhaustive congressional discussions . . ." of the blight of poverty. His cosponsor Bingham, a reform Democrat of New York, was one of a small group of congressmen who, the preceding July, at the invitation of the New York Citywide Coordinating Committee of Welfare Groups, had lived for a week on the sixty-six cents per day per person allowed for food in New York City welfare budgeting. He presented to the committee a list of the items purchased with the $9.24 allowed him and his wife for the seven days, together with menus his wife had worked out. He reported having been hungry much of the time, and feeling a loss of energy and initiative. Conyers, a Democrat representing a black constituency in Detroit, emphasized in his testimony the stigmatizing aspect of a "policy of coercion to work."

William F. Ryan, Democrat of New York, was also cosponsor of the NLIP, but testified on behalf of his own measure, the Income Maintenance Act. This was a modified version of the one he had introduced in May 1968, drafted for him in the Office of Economic Opportunity by James Lyday, which Steiner terms the "first guaranteed income bill ever offered in Congress."[4] Ryan congratulated the president, stating "he made respectable the concept of a guaranteed annual income, although he refused to characterize his proposal as such." His own measure was particularly close to FAP: a family of four with no income could expect $2,004 per year. He provided for a staged increase in benefits, and, as in NLIP, for regional cost-of-living differentials.

This then was the sum of it. Of 435 congressmen and 100 senators, six had something of substance to say about a guaranteed income; four had bills. Of the six, four were New York reform Democrats; all were relative newcomers to the Congress, only Ryan having served as long as nine years. The president, as Ryan said, had made the issue respectable, but he had not made it popular. But neither was it unpopular. The "chorus of critics" of which Mrs. Chisholm spoke consisted of the NWRO and its minuscule constituency. Few congressmen indicated their opposition to FAP, and little outside conservative opposition made its appearance during the hearings. By contrast, two spokesmen of stature did speak on its behalf. Henry W. Maier, mayor of Milwaukee, on behalf of the U.S. Conference of Mayors, asked that some such program be adopted but that coverage be universal, and that the benefit levels of FAP be "improved." Nelson A. Rockefeller, on behalf of the National Governors' Conference, asked that FAP be adopted as a "workable first step" toward a 100 percent federally financed welfare system with adequate standards of assistance for all in need. "The president's proposal," he told the committee, "may well be the most significant Federal domestic legislation put forward in a generation."

This was testimony from a real world: from men who themselves *levied* taxes. Mills was then resolutely opposed to revenue sharing on the grounds that only the Congress should spend money raised by the Congress. He would not even hold hearings on that aspect of the president's address of August 8. Yet he knew as well or better than most congressional leaders that the Federal revenue structure had become so much more powerful than that of state or local governments that *some* kind of fiscal relief had to be considered. Family Assistance did provide some such relief. The governors and mayors had testified in support of it. This was a point.

Mills was struggling with himself and the subject. He was by temperament, perhaps by role, a fiscal conservative. This had given him an aura of conservatism on social issues which was not altogether deserved. If in the 1960s he held up the administration-sponsored Medicare legislation until the pressure for it became overwhelming, in the 1950s he had himself sponsored universal unemployment compensation, and had taken the measure from a divided committee to the floor of the House where he suffered one of his rare defeats. He was pragmatic: above all, open to information. As he learned more about welfare he more and more came to feel, as had the president, that something had to be done. Like the president, he did not have to involve himself with the subject, but chose to do so. As early as 1962 he had voiced his concern about the direction in which the program was heading. Now Mills and his committee decided to take the president's proposed reform seriously and to proceed from there. With that decision the case for an income guarantee was largely won, however little he, or the president before him, might have realized it.

On the last day of hearings Mills entered into a long exchange with Mitchell Ginsberg, appearing on behalf of New York City and the National League of Cities. Ginsberg supported FAP but wanted, at very least, more fiscal relief for cities such as New York. He and Mayor Lindsay, he said, and "all of us in the city" were "deeply gratified" by the Administration's initiative. The proposed redefinition of eligible families—the inclusion of the working poor—was "a historic and far-reaching reform." However, as the bill stood, "it would do nothing for the poor of New York or any other large city." He proposed that the legislation provide for an eventual full assumption by the Federal government of all costs of income maintenance, and that at the outset there be 50 percent matching of the state supplement, a principle included in the Administration proposal for the adult categories. Mills pressed. Did Ginsberg really want the Federal government to take over? "I have never known of any program that the Federal government ever took over that I thought was better than the state-administered program," the chairman mused. If the Federal government took over, would there be any local incentive left "to work on the real causes of poverty?" It had been the pleasure of critics to describe Mills's 1967 welfare amendments as punitive and even vengeful.[5] Yet this surely was not the legislator who confronted Ginsberg with one set of facts after another contradicting the standard wisdom of the welfare profession. Mills fair to pleaded for knowledge, at the same moment despairing of it.

I am perfectly willing to spend almost any amount of money within reason to help individuals to help themselves when they are in this circumstance, and perhaps we haven't done enough in the past—certainly we haven't—in trying to prevent the need for assistance.

It just seems to me, though, that we go in the opposite direction when we don't do first those things that should be done to correct a circumstance. Instead we recognize a circumstance exists, but put more and more money into the continuation of that exact circumstance.

There is nothing in welfare that I see, just welfare alone, that does anything except barely keep an individual alive. It doesn't motivate a person to change his circumstance. There is nothing within welfare itself that gives him any opportunity or motivation for improvement or self-reliance.

Why can't we develop some kind of a program that would tend to motivate these people? It is not a sin to be poor. I think it is a sin on the part of all of us to do nothing about it, nothing more than just trying to maintain that status in life. And I am convinced from the people that I talk to, who are able-bodied people, that they would much prefer an opportunity to be self-reliant and they seek it. But in many instances they are without any success whatsoever.

But I don't see anything in the program before us any more than in existing law that will motivate these people or give them the opportunity to be motivated.

Wilbur Cohen, he continued, had told him that before the 1970s were past as many as 10 percent of the children in the Nation would be on AFDC. Did Ginsberg agree? Ginsberg did: *at least* 10 percent. What then? Who was to say? The chairman concluded his part in the hearings on a note of perplexity.

I am trying to get at the basic facts. I can only make a decision and I can only propose something, so far as I am individually concerned, to the Members of the House when I have facts, and I can substantiate it, but I cannot do these things on the basis of some of the specious arguments that have been made in the past to justify some of these steps.

Four days later, November 17, Ways and Means began executive sessions on the proposals before it, returning from the vast hearing chamber to its small corner room in the Capitol. HEW and Labor officials were regularly called in.* This was practically a change of venue. The hearings on FAP had taken place in a general atmosphere of dissatisfaction with, or indifference to, the president's proposal. If Representative Ullman was not being "shocked" at the extravagance of the legislation, some well-paid representative of the poor was being shocked by its

---

* It is never really the case that, once an Administration's officials have completed testimony during public hearings, their participation in the legislative process is over. This is especially true of Ways and Means. Over the years, especially with regard to tax legislation, the committee has made a practice of working closely on technical issues with Administration representatives, who are almost always invited to executive sessions, at times outnumbering the members present. Dependence on the assistance of HEW and Labor officials was particularly necessary in the case of FAP because the committee's own staff specialized primarily in tax and trade matters, not welfare bills. Although this situation was, by and large, advantageous to the Administration, it should not be thought that members of Ways and Means more readily acquiesced in presidential proposals than other congressmen. Indeed, the record would suggest that they were, if anything, more resistant.

inadequacy. Back in H-208 the committee sat together around a table and began to think what to do. Veneman began to impress the point that the Administration had been as puzzled as the committee, had gone through the same travail of doubts, but had come at last to the conviction that Family Assistance offered some chance, while nothing else offered any chance. *Was* there anything else? There was not. No member of the committee had a bill. There were no experts to whom the committee would any longer turn who had any different idea. The Heineman Commission proposal was only a variation on FAP that cost more. Soon or late the committee would have to decide yes or no on the president's proposal. Although no one paid much heed, on November 18 Byrnes told the Women's National Press Club that he thought the committee would be "responsive" to welfare reform and would report legislation as early as March.

The decision, ultimately, was for Democrats to make. Both in Ways and Means and in the House, they were the majority, and for the first time in recent political history their credentials as the party of progress and innovation were being seriously challenged. Not surprisingly, their response was uncertain. The situation was described by Alice M. Rivlin in a *Washington Post* article in December 1969, entitled "What's Happened to the 'Good Guys'?"[6] These were the congressmen who really cared about poverty and social injustice, the shifting coalition, mostly Democratic, who were responsible for Medicare, and Headstart, and Vista, "the guys in the white hats whom people were counting on for leadership in attacking the massive problems of poverty, racial inequality, and urban blight." What had happened, she wrote, was that the "good guys" appeared to have gone "berserk." As had been forecast, congressional liberals in the face of the Nixon presidency had moved directly to increase appropriations more or less across the board on the categorical aid programs of the 1960s. What had not been foreseen was a move for general tax reduction which steadily gained momentum during 1969, won approval in Ways and Means, and eventually became law. A good deal of the fiscal dividend of the 1970s was being given away. Charles L. Schultze had been appalled and had said so in print. Those, he said, who talked continually of national priorities were now revealing what their priorities really were: consumption goods. Rivlin was even less forgiving.

Where are the "good guys" when they are needed most? Incredibly, they are passing a tax bill that will cripple efforts to solve social problems for a decade to come. . . . These legislators are not only behaving irresponsibly on taxes. They are also adding scarce dollars to ineffective programs that meet no one's test of high social usefulness.

Nixon had proposed shifting money to educational experiments to find more effective teaching methods. "The Congress," Rivlin wrote, "(including most of the liberals) slashed the experiments and added a billion dollars to the Office of Education appropriations," primarily for categorical aids and "impacted" areas, two scandalously unproductive forms of expenditure. Rivlin accounted for the "dilemma of the 'good guys' " in terms of three factors. First, "real progress" on social problems was going to be truly expensive and everyone knew it. Second, "there are no obvious prescriptions for social ills." Disillusion with the underfinanced efforts of the Kennedy-Johnson years had set in. (She noted, with justice, "Oversold programs are now being over-attacked.") These in themselves need not have been disabling difficulties: it was the third that hurt.

. . . [M]ost devastating, the Nixon administration's domestic program has not been nearly as bad as some of the liberals feared—or hoped. Not that the administration has taken much action; it has certainly not provided leadership in changing national priorities. But its few actions on the domestic front are hard to fault.

The administration budget for fiscal 1970 did not slash Great Society programs, as some had expected it would. In fact, it moved most of them forward about as fast as they had been moving in the last two years of the Johnson administration. The Nixon administration's welfare reform, while far from perfect and much too small, is the first really progressive step in this difficult area in many years.

A President who is inching in the right direction is a poor target for the liberals, especially when moving faster would take more money than anyone thinks there is. So the "good guys," lacking a positive program of their own and reluctant to accept the administration's few good initiatives, are venting their frustration by lashing out at the administration in irrational ways such as reducing taxes and adding to ineffective programs.

In the October 1969 issue of *The Progressive* Rivlin had written of FAP that "The President was not playing the game according to the rules, and the liberals were not sure what their next move ought to be."[7] She now repeated the complaint, and asked that the "good guys" get behind a constructive and realistic program of some kind. This was easier to envisage than to achieve. For one thing, there was now underway a crisis of liberal belief about their traditional approach to problems. The Vietnam war—in no small way, liberalism's war—was seen to have been profoundly misconceived. In the penumbra of this intense moral revulsion, questions arose about the whole of liberal doctrine in its applied forms. Had they opted for a meliorative view of events that was not sufficiently demanding of either intellectual or political effort? Had they allowed a genuine passion for racial justice to degenerate into something ominously close to acquiescence in self-defeating behavior that perpetuated racial inequality? Had they held to a model of social processes that vastly exaggerated the potential of mild governmental interventions? And yet *Nixon* did not seem to be challenging these positions. To the contrary, he seemed to endorse them. He had not, as Rivlin noted, slashed Great Society programs.

On the surface this seemed to legitimate them, and so dulled the impulse to reappraisal. In truth the Administration's decision was shaped by wholly different considerations. Programs were continued not because they were thought effective, but because it was not thought worthwhile to try to discontinue them. The Model Cities program was such an instance. The president's first impulse was to close it down. He was dissuaded on grounds that while the program was almost certainly useless, if not indeed fraudulent, the press believed it to be an enterprise of great consequence and would judge the Administration's commitment to the "urban crisis" by its commitment to Model Cities. There was no possibility of getting the press to see otherwise. The Administration was going to be accused of abandoning the cities regardless of what it did (*any* administration would have been so accused) but it was worth $100 million or so to keep the accusations from becoming too concrete.* In any event, com-

* It may be hoped this comment does not appear either excessively critical or unnecessarily cynical. It is simply the fact that by 1969 the difficulties of achieving social goals through the general strategies of the 1960s were evident

mitments had been made to persons in Model Cities neighborhoods which the Federal government had to honor, regardless of how foolish it might have been to make them in the first instance, or of the fact that there had been a change of Administration.

In consequence of all this the Democrats found it difficult to position themselves *in opposition* to the president. For the first time in modern history Republicans had taken the initiative in social legislation away from them, but had done so by seemingly going *beyond* what they stood for. In doing this the Republicans could draw on the resources of the presidency and also enjoyed a certain margin of competence, which, while not flaunted, was nonetheless visible to the inquiring congressional eye. In these circumstances the only viable strategy of moderate opposition was to cooperate at least somewhat. This led to the passage of Family Assistance in the House.

The process was in part mechanical: that of a weaker force giving way to a stronger one. In January the president delivered his first State of the Union address to the Congress. It was, wrote

---

to many analysts who had watched from a distance, but were not yet recognized by many of those who had been involved and who placed great hopes on their success. An example would be the New Towns In-Town program launched by President Johnson in 1967 with great fanfare. The idea, seemingly flawless, was to use surplus federal land in urban areas to build housing for the (black) populations of the inner city, in the process avoiding the disruptions and delays of the urban renewal process. A study by Martha Derthick, summarized in the newsletter of the Urban Institute, found the program to be a nearly complete failure. For all the sound coming out of Washington, only seven cities were enlisted in the program.

> Three years later, the program was dead in three cities—San Antonio, New Bedford, Massachusetts, and San Francisco. In Louisville the program was in limbo. And remnants of the program are sputtering along in Washington, D.C., Clinton Township (adjacent to Detroit), and Atlanta. As of mid-1971, fewer than 300 housing units in these three cities were under construction (*Search,* January–February 1972.)

A great expenditure of presidential time and prestige, and of comparable executive resources elsewhere in government, produced, in the course of four years, some three hundred housing starts.

By 1969 this outcome, and similar outcomes for similar programs, seemed an ineluctable pattern to me at least. But I also believed—I may have been wrong—that this condition had barely made an impress on the public or the press, and that for the president to speak his mind would be calamitous. Perhaps because the president had always assumed that such programs fail, it was too much to hope that an assertion by him that they *had* failed would be accepted as reflecting a fair-minded reading of the evidence.

Reston, a "magnificent" speech. He had assumed the initiative in
international affairs with the doctrine announced in Guam of
limiting the extent of American commitments to internal conflicts abroad. He proposed to move from "an era of confrontation to an era of negotiation." Stragetic-arms limitation talks
with the Soviet Union were developing nicely, with both sides, it
was hoped, "motivated by mutual self-interest rather than naive
sentimentality." In that spirit, he noted, "we have resumed discussions with Communist China. . . ." The main thrust of his
domestic proposals was in the area of the environment. Was it
not time, he asked, to "make our peace with nature and begin to
make reparations for the damage we have done to our air, to our
land, and to our water?" But first he had spoken to three areas of
"urgent" priority that "demand that we move and move now."
Number one was welfare reform.

When a system penalizes work, breaks up homes, and robs recipients
of dignity, there is no alternative to abolishing that system and adopting in its place the program of income support, job training, and work
incentives which I recommended to the Congress last year.

He then asked for the reforms associated with revenue sharing
and finally civil-rights goals.

We can fulfill the American dream only when each person has a fair
chance to fulfill his own dreams. This means equal voting rights,
equal employment opportunity, and new opportunities for expanded
ownership.

These were conciliatory statements of a president asking a
Congress in the hands of the opposing party to join him in the
large enterprises of the day. A week earlier, on January 13,
1970, in a blunt, belligerent speech to the National Press Club,
Finch had indicated what might be the political consequences of
the Congress refusing. As Rivlin had indicated, the Democrats
were then in the process of adding $1 billion to HEW education
funds, almost all of the additional funds to go to the most questionable programs. In any event the money was part of an
appropriation bill for a fiscal year that had begun July 1, 1969.
How, asked Finch, was he supposed to spend the money with less

than six months left in the fiscal year? Why, he asked, would Congress not give him money for experimental programs which were needed—because knowledge was needed? Not to know that was to have missed the 1960s. Why, he asked, was he being directed instead to spend more money for old discredited programs such as aid to areas "impacted" with Federal employees. In his former hometown of Pasadena, he recalled, such money had been used to buy the "best football uniforms and the best band uniforms around," for the children of well-paid Federal scientists and engineers. All this was being done in the name of liberalism, but what, asked the Secretary, of welfare reform?

The most revolutionary social proposal since the '30s—and that is not my phrase but the characterization of the plan made by several newspapers and magazines—this revolutionary proposal is being threatened with death by invisibility at the hands of a Congress apparently too preoccupied with other matters even to offer alternative reform proposals of its own.

He pointed, as was his right, to the apathy of groups that would "be pressuring Congress like crazy for this if a Democrat had come up with it." He asked where labor stood on the issue, saying it had "not been hostile," but had tended to be "cautious and neutral." "The odds for reform," he concluded, "are running against us." Stating only that the basic principles of FAP were nonnegotiable, he asked Democrats to produce alternatives of their own.

    Political Washington had by this time almost managed to forget that Family Assistance had ever been proposed.* Finch's speech put it back on the front page and on editorial pages around the Nation, where "death by invisibility" was deplored. Finch had asked that a major proposal sent by the president to Congress be debated and voted on there, a point difficult to object to.

---

* "Restrained partisanship" required a certain amount of judiciousness on the part of the Administration and other supporters of FAP, as well as the members of Ways and Means, as long as the process of legislative scrutiny proceeded apace. In this respect Finch's remarks reflected the great importance of the bill to the Administration inasmuch as they suggested that Ways and Means was not acting with its customary nonpartisanship in considering Family Assistance—a serious charge.

It was now up to the Democratic leadership in Congress to move. No formal announcement was made, but in the opening weeks of the 2nd Session of the 91st Congress, it began to be understood that the House leadership was disposed to let the president have his Family Assistance bill if, as he had declared in his State of the Union message, this was his first domestic priority. Reaffirming the existing welfare system was out of the question, while those Democrats who had studied the issue proposed changes noticeably similar to those of the president. The leadership could not force the bill from Ways and Means, and would not dream of attempting to do so. But they were prepared to welcome and support it if the committee did so and the committee was, after all, composed of good party men whose normal disposition was to support the party leadership.*

Mills kept his counsel. A committee staff report contending that FAP did not have the work incentives claimed for it made its way to the press, but the staff was not going to make the decision. The American Conservative Union began raising an alarm, but it would not make the decision. The *Wall Street Journal* ran some skeptical articles, but the press would not make the decision. Mills would make the decision. He would do so with a range of considerations in mind, but from the position of a man of great power which had been acquired by the responsible exercise of the duties of the chairman of Ways and Means. It was

---

* As Nixon began his second year as president, there were other indications that he had had some success in broadening his base of support. As 1969 ended, his popularity among the public reached its highest point before or since. Writing in January 1970, John Osborne, who watched Nixon for *The New Republic*, said that the presidency had been a good experience for him:

> After the Johnson years, we know how much the country needs a credible President, and to the extent that Mr. Nixon has given us one he has served us well. With his declared and, I believe, genuine intent to disengage from the Vietnam war, and with proposals that constitute an enormous advance toward a humane and sensible welfare system, he has recognized and moved to meet at least some of the country's larger needs. I value and quite possibly overvalue these aspects of the first Nixon year because they indicated to me a capacity, limited though the demonstration has been . . ., to be a better President than I thought the candidate of 1968 capable of being. If so lame and grudging an apology for Richard Nixon makes me a candidate for membership in his silent majority, so be it. I suspect that his majority includes a great many Americans who expected little that was good from him and are therefore pleased with the little more that he gave us in his first year.

not open to him to act on the assumption that he would not be the cause of whatever was going to occur: he would be. He could prevent a bill's being reported. That point was absolutely clear. If he did so there would be no welfare reform. He would be responsible. This was not unthinkable. For years he had blocked Medicare in the face of the most urgent wishes of two presidents of his own party. That had been a matter of his not wishing to commence a practice of which he did not approve. In this respect, welfare was different. It already existed. There was no way to remain innocent. The existing system was not working. A reasoned proposal had been put forth that might work, that is to say might reverse the seemingly inexorable trend to ever higher levels of dependency. Government is frequently in the hands of foolish or inattentive men. Mills was not one of these. During the calendar year 1969 the number of persons receiving AFDC benefits increased, nationwide, by *one third* (32.1 percent). Anyone with a feel for the situation could sense this happening. Mills had felt it, and so had the committee. At some point in mid-February he decided that Family Assistance should be reported out of Ways and Means.

The nature of his decision is suggested by the fact that he made no significant changes in the proposal, and did not at first indicate that he would necessarily vote for it on the floor. On February 26 the committee decided to report a bill and directed the staff to prepare a formal draft. In a news conference Mills said he was "going into a retreat" to think through his own position, but added that even if he decided to vote against the measure on the floor, he would not lead a fight against it. On the other hand, he would not be floor manager. One week later, March 5, the Committee on Ways and Means voted 21 to 3 to report the Family Assistance Act of 1970. Three Democrats, Al Ullman of Oregon, Phil Landrum of Georgia, and Omar Burleson of Texas, voted against FAP, charging it was a guaranteed income.*

The committee report stated that, with certain exceptions, the bill was "essentially patterned after the proposals of the president," which was so. The original theme was unchanged.

---

* The one potential Republican opponent, James B. Utt of California, had recently died.

The bill is intended to convert the existing program from one which results in people remaining in dependency to one which will encourage people to become independent and self-supporting through incentives to take training and enter employment.

In this way continuity with the WIN program was established, and that is about as much social commentary as the committee report contained. A number of changes had been made in the legislation, of which the most important concerned the "savings" which would redound to state governments under the new arrangement. The Administration had proposed a "50–90" rule which would ensure that no state would be relieved of more than half its current expenditure, nor be required to continue spending more than 90 percent of it. The latter provision meant a small saving for the high-benefit states, but it could hardly be described as "fiscal relief." As he was not moving ahead with revenue sharing, Mills had an incentive to add something more by way of fiscal relief to the FAP legislation. In this case it was provided that the Federal government would pay 30 percent of state costs incurred in supplementing the payments to AFDC families (although not the working poor). This was a provision of considerably more substance to states such as New York.

In other changes the committee was sometimes more generous, sometimes less. All unearned income, rather than only half, as proposed by the Administration, would be offset against FAP payments. Child-care projects would be funded at 100 percent Federal cost rather than 90 percent. New authority was added to establish a Federal claim against a deserting parent or spouse for the amount of Federal welfare payments subsequently made to his or her family. States agreeing to Federal administration would be absolved of any cost, rather than having to pay half. Fathers of families in the working-poor category, even if employed full time, would be required to register with the employment office. The attractiveness of the bill was enhanced by increasing the income floor for the aged, blind, and disabled from $90 per month to $110. The Administration had hoped the FAP legislation might be included in a general social security "package." Mills had not permitted this, but the provisions for the "adult categories" now became sufficiently attractive to make it difficult for a congressman to vote against the bill, whatever might be his views on FAP.*

Upon the release of the committee report the president issued a statement welcoming the action. "Not every Congress has the opportunity to enact a fundamental reform of our basic institutions," he said. "The 91st Congress now has that historic opportunity." At a White House press conference, Veneman was asked how he thought it had come to pass. He couldn't precisely say: it was just a matter "that many of the members of Congress finally realized where we were going under the present system."

Veneman's statement is deceptively simple, but as near to precisely accurate as a summary judgment can be. The 21–3 margin by which Family Assistance was reported from the Committee on Ways and Means reflected, more than any other single factor, the judgment of the House that "something" had to be done about welfare; it was perfectly willing to trust to the competence and prudence of the committee to offer the course of action that seemed best. The traditions of Ways and Means, in turn, dictated a process of careful deliberation and judicious compromise aimed at furthering the business at hand. This was the integrative function of the committee. Interest groups had scarcely any influence with it, but it systematically responded to the opinion of the representatives in Congress and helped organize that opinion into an effective majority in support of a course of action. Further, the committee, under Mills's leadership, had established a record of thoroughness and prudence in the execution of its highly technical and consummately important work. As far as can be known, it decided in favor of FAP by much the same process and on much the same grounds that had determined the president's decision; that the president's decision had already been made was an added influence, not least because of the political implications which that held for the Democratic party. Mills was equally capable of assessing those implications and responding in a purposeful manner, joining and supporting the president rather than thwarting him. So too, at the end, was his committee. This had been a successful response during the Eisenhower presidency: it seemed, for the moment, even more necessary with Nixon. In any event, Mills was a positive man.

* The social security amendments were later reported in H.R. 17550.

Some weeks later, speaking at Hendrix College, Finch called Mills "easily one of the ten outstanding legislators in the history of the Republic." He spoke of the qualities of "high intellect, an open mind, patience, and the tenacity to stick to an orderly decision-making process that ultimately brought him to reverse his initial skepticism" about Family Assistance. He might have said it anyway, but he did mean it.

2. Passage in the House

The surprise of the committee action of March 5 was the revelation that Mills had decided to sponsor the bill, which now became H.R. 16311, the "Family Assistance Act of 1970" introduced by him "for himself and Mr. Byrnes of Wisconsin." A month later he went before the House Rules Committee to obtain clearance for the legislation to go to the floor, and recounted his "personal conversion" with a zeal—passion would not be too strong a term—that the Capitol had not before seen in the chairman of Ways and Means. He spoke of Family Assistance as the "only ray of hope" for ending the "welfare mess." In a passage that became the Quotation of the Day in *The New York Times* he explained, "When we were boys and a man's barn burned down, all the neighbors pitched in and helped him build another one. All we're doing here is pitching in and helping this man to help himself." The phrase "personal conversion" was cited by Marjorie Hunter in the *Times* news story: "Mills Tells Panel of His Conversion to President's Income Plan for the Poor." He was unyielding in defense of the inclusion of the working poor. The welfare poor and the working poor all want work, he insisted, but the existing system dragged people into dependency. "I've concluded," he said, "that if we don't lend a hand of assistance to those working full time but not earning enough to live on, it won't be long until they are all on welfare." *He declared that $1,600 was enough to "start" and pledged to the committee, in association with Byrnes, that if the "other body" were to raise this ceiling Ways and Means would not go to conference and there would be no bill.* James J. Delaney, Democrat of New York, observed that the existing welfare system was everywhere criticized, but that the president's proposal was also being criticized. "We're damned if we do," he mused, "and damned if we don't." "No, sir," Mills exclaimed, "we're saved if we do and damned if we don't!"

It is not truly within the powers of social science to account for such a conversion: it happened. Earlier a similar change of mind had happened to Mills with respect to Medicare. Not entirely similar, for Mills had opposed Medicare and *then* changed his mind. This was his first encounter with the Family Assistance proposal. His first reaction had been to say nothing, and then, after a period of silence, he said yes. This was almost precisely the route the president had followed. Each man was of an analytic frame of mind, and each saw his role as one of decision-making. Each decided: there is little to add, other than that Mills's decision was accompanied by a general decision of the House leadership to support FAP. The chairman of Rules, William M. Colmer, Democrat of Mississippi, a member of the House since before the passage of the Social Security Act, was bitterly opposed. (Eight of the fifteen members of his committee voted against the bill when it did reach the floor.) As he later told the House, he tried to impose a modified closed rule on the bill, which would have permitted a vote "as to whether this guaranteed income phase of the bill," the working poor, should be stricken. By Colmer's testimony, both the Democratic and Republican leadership opposed him, and the bill was given the closed rule forbidding amendments traditional for legislation introduced by Ways and Means.

This is turn ensured the passage of FAP in the House. The combined leadership had more than sufficient votes. Rarely since becoming chairman in 1958 had Mills failed to carry a measure he had brought to the floor. In the singular circumstances of FAP, a form of guaranteed income proposed by a Republican president and supported by the Republican leadership, he had little to fear. The committee had done the work of the House, *for* the House. All the major political tendencies of the members were represented on the committee. The past record, supported now by a 21–3 vote, suggested that a consensus had been reached which a majority could "live" with, if not, indeed, warmly support. The pressure of legislative business in the House rewards such a record, according, in effect, deference to the committees that achieve it. This was deference to reasonable, moderate men. Ironically, or perhaps typically, it resulted in legislation singularly vulnerable to attacks that were to come much later from unreasonable and immoderate men.

The debate took place April 15 and 16. It was not undistinguished. Mills and Byrnes made formidable opening statements, explaining the legislation and the process by which they had come to support it. They stood back to back on the issue, and drew regularly on statements from other members of the committee, which behaved very much as a collegial body explaining to the House why it ought to endorse legislation it did not, perhaps, fully understand. In this process some facts about the committee's own deliberations emerged. Mrs. Griffiths, rising "in support of the president's bill," explained that she had unsuccessfully offered an amendment to require pregnant teen-agers to continue in school after the birth of the child, or to receive training, and stated her opposition to the provision that women with children under six might stay at home. It was her view that such women wanted to work but were dissuaded by social workers. Three Republican committee members, Conable, Harold R. Collier of Illinois, and Charles E. Chamberlain of Michigan, spoke with understanding and emphasis on various points at issue. The central argument of all those supporting FAP was put by Collier.

I urge every Member of this House to give welfare reform a chance. To do anything less is to accept the present program, with all of its present shortcomings, and its inevitable social doom.

This was a respectable, if not conclusive, argument. The Congress was legislating in the same condition of uncertainty which had afflicted the Executive. The need to do something was evident, even though the alternative of doom was not. Howard W. Robison, Republican of New York, in effect commented on this in remarks on the Administration's adoption of an "income strategy." The "overwhelming fact" of the debate, as he saw it, was that no one was prepared to defend the existing welfare system. To him, the manner in which it was proposed to replace that system was as important as the replacement itself.

[W]e do not herald in this program with slogans which go far beyond this one bill's promise; we do not guarantee to the American people that this bill alone will still the turmoil in this Nation; we do not insure that poverty will hereafter disappear or that the program will meet everyone's need in every way. Rather, from the President on down, effective action has been quietly taken without the necessary bravado which, in the past, has so often come back to haunt us.

This *was* the tone of the debate. In the closing hour Gerald R. Ford of Michigan and Carl Albert of Oklahoma, minority and majority leaders, exchanged remarks commenting on the broad, bipartisan agreement that *something* had to be done. Mills may once have spoken of "salvation," but he now resumed his formal manner. Byrnes was careful, correct, sensible. Family Assistance was a sensible proposal.

This was not strategem: no more so in the House leadership than in the president. These were pragmatic, centrist politicians moved to the adoption of an extraordinary measure by the logic of a situation that seemed to admit of no better response. Mills, for one, argued, as had the president, that FAP was not a guaranteed income, inasmuch as men would have to work for their living. He went on to argue that the existing welfare system was *itself* a guaranteed income, and the worst kind. This pronouncement, in effect, marked the permanent separation between symbol and substance in the FAP legislation. As a *symbol* the adoption by the United States of a guaranteed income would have marked a major ideological shift: victory for one set of dispositions, defeat for another. But neither Mills, nor Nixon before him, was moved by any desire to win an ideological victory for the principle of a guaranteed income. They were merely trying to respond to a specific problem they felt to be serious enough to warrant large risks. It is not to be supposed that anyone involved thought the matter through in these simple, opposed, terms. Rather, those involved acted in a situation in which solving one set of problems only created another. They were working, in a sense, at the limit of the system's capacity.

There were two symbolic issues at stake. On the one hand, welfare reform: on the other, the guaranteed income. In substance the measure involved both: it *was* reform, it *was* an income guarantee, but much more assuredly the latter than the former. The state of knowledge, if anything, exaggerated the distinction. That FAP would establish a guaranteed income was demonstrable: a fact of definition. That it would reform welfare could at most be hoped for, and hopes were minimal.

Nonetheless, Mills and Byrnes preferred to reverse the order of asserted significance. This was easy for them to do, as they themselves would have been uneasy with legislation that not only provided a guaranteed income but also proclaimed, in a more or less explicit manner, that it was no longer necessary to work to gain some kind of living. The hard fact is that Family Assistance *did* establish this principle. It did not proclaim it. To the contrary, first the president and now the bill's managers in the House went out of their way to deny any such intention. To have done otherwise would have doomed the measure at the outset, and in any event it was not the intention of Nixon, or Mills, or Byrnes to abolish the wage system, to put an end to work, to transform the social values of late capitalism. They were, instead, trying to reassert those values and to support them in the face of an existing welfare system that did the opposite. To all three, doing so seemed to require a substantial change, yet one which need not appear unprecedented.

The major danger that might have arisen at this point was a coalition of Southerners and conservative Republicans, which had put an end to dozens of lesser measures in preceding Congresses. It did not form. In some measure this reflected the leadership of Mills and of Hale Boggs, both certified Southerners, whose efforts left the South free to vote against FAP without having to crusade against it. As *welfare reform* it could be seen as marginal to Southern interests: there was no welfare problem *there*. But the crucial role was that of Byrnes, who bent the GOP to the president's purpose. This is the presumed role of the congressional "leadership," but only rarely is it performed with the quiet competence Byrnes brought to the occasion. In effect, those opposed to change of large magnitude and in a "liberal" direction were assured that nothing much was being changed. The evidence suggests that conservative leaders in the House were not much taken in by this. Rather, they behaved as if there was a clear distinction between substance and symbol in legislation such as Family Assistance and that they could afford to concede the substance so long as the symbolic loss was kept to a minimum. In congressional politics as in much else, the things that do not happen are often the most revealing.

All sensible enough, save that it conceded nothing to those, opposite to the conservatives, who could afford to forgo the substance of legislation such as Family Assistance as long as the symbolic gain could be pressed to a maximum. John Conyers, Jr., Democrat of Detroit, expressed a general view of the emerging black caucus in the House, and of many liberals.

A major shortcoming of the president's categorical assistance plan is that it departs little from the social theories behind present welfare programs. We believe, on the other hand, that the Government of the richest nation on earth must insure a living income for every American as a basic right. Only such a restructuring of the basic premises of public assistance will yield a program that will meet the real needs of the poor. . . .

Louis Stokes, in his first term as a Democrat from Cleveland, asked no one to expect that he or his colleagues "will walk from the floor in any state of euphoria." And, he added, "we promise you that we will be back."

Not all conservatives were willing to settle for the fact that Conyers and Stokes were dissatisfied. William M. Colmer, in his 19th term as a Democrat from Pascagoula, had moved a long way from his youth when he had campaigned as a New Dealer. As a conservative of the Deep South, the substance of FAP was as important to him as its symbolism. The fourth-ranking member of the House, he pleaded against the enactment of "a guaranteed income."

Unquestionably it is the most controversial, it is the most important, it is the most complex and disturbing piece of legislation that I have had occasion to consider in my whole career here as a Member of this body.

I am very much disturbed about this bill. I am very much disturbed about the threat that it poses to our system of government, to our way of life.

He knew very well what the bill entailed.

He pleaded to a near empty chamber. When the motion to

recommit came to a vote, there were only 129 members on
hand: an opponent of FAP obtained a ruling that there was not a
quorum present. This reflected the certainty of the outcome, but
also the difficulty of answering either set of objections: Conyers's
or Colmer's. The traditions of the House imposed a restraint on
language—Colmer had thanked the "gracious" chairman of the
Ways and Means Committee for yielding him ten minutes in
which to plead that he not bring down the Republic—but the
intensity of opposition FAP had already aroused among its
various publics was present in the Chamber also. It was not dealt
with. From the point of view of the long-term success of the
measure it would probably have been best if the benefits to the
South had been made so explicit as to caution Southern conservatives who might thereafter wish to oppose it and, correspondingly, if the great cost of larger measures had been made so
graphic as to give pause to Northern liberals thinking to outbid
the Administration and the House leadership. Neither argument
was driven home. Mills made the point on the floor that half the
working poor were Southern, but the very language of the
debate—a debate over *welfare*—obscured this. The negative tax
was only dimly understood. Southern politicians remained free to
ignore it: word never reached their constituents. Northern liberals either had fewer constituents who would clearly benefit one
way or another or had welfare constituents whose interests were
not those of the working poor. Thus in the moment of victory in
the House the conditions were established for defeat in the
Senate.

But then how were Southern conservatives to be forced to
acknowledge what FAP had in store for the South in the face of
statements such as this from Stokes?

My primary objection to H.R. 16311 concerns the payment provisions. . . . It is disgraceful . . . that the eight Southern states
that have done the very worst job of providing for their needy citizens
are rewarded in this legislation by allowing them to terminate all state
payments.

How were Northern liberals to be persuaded that $1,600 was a
realistic beginning level of payments, which could only rise, in

the face of statements such as this from Joe D. Waggonner, Jr., Democrat of Louisiana:

As was to be expected, the minute this guaranteed annual income feature was unveiled last year, the bandwagon started to roll. The predictable gaggle of liberals, leftists, and radicals were, at first, astounded that a supposedly conservative Republican administration was proposing national welfarism in a greater magnitude than even the most liberal Democrat in the history of the Nation. They regained their composure quickly, if not their intelligence, and began an out-pouring of statements, position papers, and conferences calling for increases that stagger the imagination and would empty the pocket-books of the working public.

If the liberal representatives could balk at providing aid for the South, then conservatives, with far more experience in the tactic, could threaten to resist increased benefits for the North.

Yet, the actual likelihood was fairly clear. Patricelli had told a meeting of Catholic Charities of the Archdiocese of New York that, "When the budgetary situation improves, we might look toward increases in the Federal base payment." Much was made of this by conservatives, but it made no apparent impact on liberals. Bingham set forth the NWRO demand for a $5,500 base, saying it would be "tragically mistaken" if this were to be viewed as a "radical demand not to be taken seriously." He noted that a task force of the White House Conference on Food, Nutrition, and Health had called for $5,500 and a good deal more. Earlier I had told the National Jewish Welfare Board that the essence of FAP was a floor under the income of every family with children, "Whether the family is working or not. United or not. Deserving or not." Coming from the "spiritual mentor" of the program, this statement was obviously disturbing to con-servatives. It somehow revealed just what they feared, and they said so. But it did not reassure liberals such as Stokes, who said of FAP's provisions:

[M]ost pernicious of all, the whole scheme seems to still be premised on the attitude that the recipient is basically a lazy, booze-guzzling ne'er-do-well—an attitude proved totally fallacious long ago to all who cared to listen.

Edward Hutchinson, Republican of Michigan, had already told the House that the penalty for refusing to work was a loss of $300 in total family benefits. Would that dissuade a genuinely "lazy, booze-guzzling, ne'er-do-well?" But neither set of opponents conceded anything. Conable cited Pope, "All looks yellow to the jaundiced eye."

Earlier in April, Phillip Burton, Democrat of California, as chairman of the liberal Democratic Study Group's Task Force on Health and Welfare, had issued a task-force report recommending approval of FAP as "a sound step toward the elimination of poverty." This was accompanied by a fact sheet on the program, prepared by Richard Merrill of the DSG staff, which was detailed and fair-minded. Burton, a fourth-term congressman, would probably be judged the most informed liberal in the area of social insurance then in the House. He had been a "seatmate" of Veneman in the California legislature. His support of FAP was as consistent as his criticism. In combination he undoubtedly assured the votes of most of the hundred-odd members of the DSG. In the debate he rose to record his "support" for the legislation and "commendation" of the Administration. (He noted that the change from the Administration's proposal to permit all unearned income to be "disregarded" would cost poor families some $600 to $700 million.) He then, however, introduced into the Record a resolution signed by himself and thirty members which was more negative. "We criticize as inadequate the income level. . . . While . . . most of us intend to vote for H.R. 16311 . . . we nevertheless retain these serious reservations about the inadequacy of the Family Assistance Plan." Seven of the nine black members of the House had signed the resolution along with Bingham and Ryan and like-minded reform liberals.*

The problem was that the conservatives had the better case that *their* principles *and* their interests were assaulted by the legislation. Burleson was entirely correct in stating:

If this had been proposed during the Kennedy administration or the Johnson administration, there would have been holes in the top of this ceiling right over here on the Republican side of the aisle.

---

* Congressmen William Dawson of Illinois and Adam Clayton Powell of New York did not join their more junior black colleagues in signing the Burton resolution. Neither was especially active in the Congress at this time.

Mills and Byrnes had to think most of this group, which had far greater strength in the House than did members who thought it inadequate to commence a guaranteed income with a $1,600 negative tax. When it came to making a symbolic concession, it had to be to the conservatives. Partly as a gesture, and partly to preclude a straight vote on the merits, Collier introduced a motion to recommit which instructed Ways and Means to amend the provision that a recipient might be denied benefits for having "refused without good cause to accept suitable employment" by deleting the term "suitable." (Under House rules only one motion to recommit was possible.) The issue of the term "suitable" had been repeatedly raised by conservatives in the debate. (Would the Employment Service ever really judge a job to be "suitable"?) Simultaneously the committee was instructed to add a clause that no family might be denied benefits for refusal to work "if the individual has the demonstrated capacity, through other available training or employment opportunities, of securing work that would better enable him to achieve self-sufficiency." The one change negated the other. The Employment Service was left with statutory instruction to do the best it could by everyone. This motion passed 248 to 149. Twenty-five of Burton's thirty who were on hand voted against. Conversely many Southern conservatives voted in favor.

Immediately thereafter the House voted on the Family Assistance Act, which passed 243 to 155, with thirty-two not voting.* This time all of Burton's group who voted were for the bill, save Chisholm. (Diggs, the dean of the black delegation, did not vote.) By contrast, the Southern delegations voted overwhelmingly against. Of 102 votes cast from Alabama, Arkansas, Florida, Georgia, Louisiana, Mississippi, North Carolina, South Carolina, Tennessee, Texas, and Virginia, 17 were for, 79 against. Alabama, Georgia, Mississippi, and South Carolina cast

---

* On April 15, the House voted on the motion to give the bill a closed rule. By a tally of 205 to 183, the motion was passed and the bill was then debated with no amendments permitted. This vote was also, in part, a test of the support for Family Assistance in the House. In this instance, unlike the actual vote for passage, the margin in favor of FAP was only 22 votes and twelve more Republicans opposed than supported the measure. However, since many members of the House vote in principle against giving bills closed rules, and for other reasons as well, the April 15 roll call is not as direct a test of the support for FAP as the vote the next day.

zero votes for, and in sum 29 against. The two favorable votes from Florida were Miami congressmen. The one favorable vote from Louisiana came from Hale Boggs, who had spoken vigorously for the bill during the debate. Texas voted 16 to 4 against, with only two Mexican-American Democrats, Republican George Bush and Democrat Bob (sic) Eckhardt supporting the bill. (Bush was to be reminded of this months later when he ran for the Senate against a Democrat who accused him of having voted to put millions more on welfare.) By contrast, the strongest votes for FAP came from prosperous states which would benefit least. Wisconsin, 8 to 1; Minnesota, 8 to 0; Washington, 7 to 0; California, 29 to 3.

Both parties mustered a majority for the bill, Democrats voting 141 to 83 in favor; Republicans, 102 to 72. The proportions were almost identical, 63 percent of Democrats and 59 percent of Republicans. Immediately preceding the vote Ford told of a telephone call from the president urging all Republicans to support FAP. They did not do badly. The Democrats on their own could deliver one third of the House for such legislation. The remainder had to come from moderate or conservative Republicans, and probably only would have done so in these rare circumstances.

Citations—Chapter VI

1. John F. Manley, *The Politics of Finance: The House Committee on Ways and Means,* Boston, Little, Brown, 1970, p. 64.
2. *Ibid.,* p. 47.
3. James Tobin, "The Case for an Income Guarantee," *The Public Interest,* Summer 1966, pp. 31–41.
4. Steiner, *The State of Welfare,* p. 117.
5. Myself included. See Daniel P. Moynihan, "The Crises in Welfare," *The Public Interest,* Winter 1968, pp. 3–5.
6. Alice M. Rivlin, "What's Happened to the 'Good Guys'," *Washington Post,* December 21, 1969.
7. Alice M. Rivlin, "Nixon's Welfare Reform, 'Good, But Not Enough'," *The Progressive,* October 1969.

VII

Congress: The Senate

1. The Senate Finance Committee

If Congressman Stokes and his colleagues did not leave the floor in a state of euphoria, others did. For the House to pass such a bill by such a margin was an extraordinary and a cheering event. The Nation's troubles were hardly over, but here was a sign that the divided government in Washington could not only function, but for certain extraordinary measures might function *better* than governments of the past. The Administration was jubilant. The president issued a statement cast in this perspective.

Years from now, when historians look back on our times, I believe they will say that this welfare reform is the most important piece of social legislation in almost four decades.

*   *   *

The House has done its duty. Now the Senate has the opportunity to act with the same responsiveness and the same responsibility. The poor and the helpless—and the taxpayer—need welfare reform now.

In part the surge of optimism was due to the view, widely held, that the Senate was more "liberal" than the House. If FAP could pass by a large margin in the House, it would surely pass the Senate: eveybody—anybody—knew this, and for those who did not, journalists explained.

The assumption was wrong, first of all for applying the inapplicable spectrum "conservative-liberal" to the question.

"Unhappy is a society," writes Daniel Bell, "that has run out or words to describe what is going on," but this was the unhappy state of affairs. Family Assistance was neither a conservative nor a liberal measure in the meanings intended by those terms. It threatened "conservative" interests and "liberal" interests also, not least the liberal interest in appearing liberal. That there was a sizable liberal element in the Senate only meant that enemies towards the "right" would be joined by not less determined enemies towards the "left."

Optimism was misplaced, secondly, because the Senate had become less competent as a legislative body than the House, and this was more significant than its ideological makeup. Competence declined during the 1960s in inverse relationship to the rise of the Senate as the nursery of presidential ambition, and, ultimately, of presidential candidates and presidents. With revenue matters, which by definition included welfare legislation, these tendencies were if anything exaggerated. The fact that such legislation must originate in the House places the Senate in a conflicted role. It is a junior partner in the legislative process, technically denied initiative of its own, but at the same time influential as an appellate body to which appeals from House decisions can be taken. To a "Ways and Means Democrat" cited by Manley, the Senate and its Finance Committee act precisely as an appellate court, and "like most courts of appeal . . . [are] wrong most of the time." Wrongheaded may be a better term. The Senate and its committee can alternate between decisive and indecisive leadership, but where finance issues are concerned it tends to be almost deliberately unpredictable, as if still smarting from an intended slight received at Philadelphia in 1787. The House had maintained discipline and protected its prerogatives. The Senate had allowed both to deteriorate. All the while presidential politics dissipated its energies and cohesion. It had become a chamber erratically exposed to interest groups. FAP was soon to evoke intense pressures from a range of such groups having nearly opposite social purposes, but a common interest in preventing its passage. All that was required was inaction, the response the Senate was best equipped to provide.

These groups are most conveniently divided according to their perceptions of the symbolic import of FAP. While the substantive content of the bill was firmly enclosed as H.R. 16311, symbolically it could be located at almost any point on a spectrum ranging from a prudent and cautious reform of welfare payments to a climactic abolition of the wage system. The Administration had opted for welfare reform as the symbolic meaning of Family Assistance. The House had gone along. But organizations such as the National Chamber of Commerce and the American Conservative Union and journals such as *Human Events* were astonished and alarmed by the FAP victory in the House. Few had thought this likely, least of all liberals, and no very great effort had been made by conservatives to prevent it. A last-minute effort was put together, but *Human Events* reported, "The lobbying efforts by the Administration were enormous," and some of the staunchest conservatives could not resist the pressure to "go along with the president." Now, suddenly, the press was proclaiming the advent of a "guaranteed income," in that the Senate was bound to be at least as liberal as the House. No evidence is at hand to suggest that conservative opposition significantly enlarged in scope as a result of this suddenly changed situation, but it became more intense, and had a greater claim on the attention of its audience. Something large was indeed afoot —and it was something much more discontinuous than "reform."*

Among liberal Senate Democrats and their supporters a more complex process took place. Family Assistance came to the Senate both as a major proposal of a Republican president *and* as a measure enacted by a Democratic House of Representatives. This made straight-out opposition difficult, even though it might not have been in the interest of Democrats to allow a Republican president to outdo them in social policy. Yet neither could they risk being associated with the defeat of a bill already endorsed by a broad spectrum of their party in the House and congruent, in

---

* In June 1971 the House again voted on FAP, now incorporated in H.R. 1. The Family Assistance title passed 234 to 187, a somewhat reduced margin. Fewer Republicans voted for the measure the second time, and eleven of the now twelve Negro Democrats in the House were also opposed. *Battle Line*, the newsletter of the American Conservative Union, published an "Anti-FAP Honor Roll" consisting of "Congressmen who opposed FAP (excluding radical Democrats)." Disillusioned with Nixon at this point, the publication was no longer *The* Republican *Battle Line*. (My emphasis.)

substance, with the declared aims of their social policy. The Administration, however, had identified FAP as a reform measure. This left some liberal Democrats free to assert that nothing less than a guaranteed income would satisfy *them,* so that accordingly they could not be satisfied with FAP. A somewhat diaphanous position perhaps, but sufficient to conceal the disarray of a party temporarily as much at odds with itself as with its nominal opposition. This in turn made for a seeming movement to the left of the Democratic center. A situation began to emerge not unlike that in which Goldwater followers became the most dynamic element in the Republican party following the defeat of Nixon in 1960. As James Q. Wilson observed of the Democratic left in the early 1970s, it had never suffered the electoral defeat of the Republican right, and so was more difficult to argue against.

In his Press Club address Finch had said it would be helpful if there were Democratic alternatives on the table so that the cause of welfare reform need not be identified solely with a Republican president. The following week, on January 20, Senator George McGovern, of South Dakota, speaking to the Citizens' Committee for Children in New York, responded by proposing a children's allowance of $50 to $65 a month, accompanied by the abolition of income-tax exemption for children, which was then $600 per child per year and scheduled to rise to $750. (This was proposed as part of a Human Security Plan which would "guarantee a job at a decent wage" for able-bodied workers, improve Social Security for the elderly and disabled, and establish a Special Public Assistance program for the few who might still need such assistance.) McGovern presented the classic arguments for this form of social insurance. "The United States," he said, "stands alone among advanced nations in its failure to provide its people with a progressively taxed system of Children's Allowances." He added a critique of "separate services" for the poor which was gaining currency in social-welfare circles, and applied this to Family Assistance, which he termed "the poor people's program par excellence," an approach to the problems of the poor which "divides them from their fellows—strips them of the political support which they need—and furthers the explosive divisions which threaten to tear our nation apart." He spoke with some force.

Over the past ten years we have sought to end poverty with programs which have driven wedges of misunderstanding between our people. In our anxiety to put a quick end to the suffering of the poor, we have pursued the gods of "efficiency" and "poverty-effectiveness." In order to partake of our paternalistic programs, we have required that men humble themselves in proof that they are destitute and "worthy." Our programs have been efficient—deadly efficient. You recognize the programs to which I refer—medical care in public clinics, public assistance, and public housing. All were started by reformers with high hopes. All have turned out badly. . . . These programs have efficiently demeaned the poor. They have efficiently alienated the non-poor. They have reinforced the mythology of poverty, fostered racial prejudice and earned us the title "limousine liberal."

One would think that we might have learned from the experience. Yet, now we rush to embrace as new, radical, and a departure for the '70's, a Family Assistance Program which simply isolates the poor and their supporters more efficiently.

* * *

If the President wants to submit a plan whose greater virtue is that it gives money only to the poor and only because they are poor, that is his problem. But if we rush to support that program as the push button answer to poverty, we are wrapping our hopes for those 10% of our citizens who are poor up in a neat little package, addressing the package to Strom Thurmond and hoping that he will deliver it to the needy.

McGovern's plan was not worked out at the time of his speech, and he so stated. His cost estimates were confusing. The children's allowance, he said, would cost $10 billion "the first year," and, when fully implemented "could reach close to $35 billion dollars per year by 1976." This was close as such estimates go. As of July 1, 1969, there were in the Nation an estimated 70,759,000 children under eighteen. Of these 10.7 million were poor. A $50 per month allowance would cost $42.5 billion per year. Eliminating the income-tax exemption would reduce the cost to $32.5 billion, of which approximately $6 billion would go to poor children. A $65 per month allowance would have cost $55.3 billion per year, reduced to $45.3 billion by the elimination of the income-tax exemption. Of this some $8 billion would go to poor children.

A tract for the times. There had emerged in the sixties a rejection of scarcity as a political constraint. This development was perhaps encouraged by aspects of the ecological movement which depicted a world groaning under the burden of abundance, but in the main it was simply that politicians in an era of inflation and economic growth became accustomed to using ever larger numbers. The costs of the war were cited as a justification for programs costing three and four times as much as the war. The Apollo flights gave rise to a form of argument that began, "If this Nation can afford to go to the moon it can . . ." The argument was not illogical, but became unrestrained. In the House debate Colmer had recalled Macaulay's fear that American government would be all sail and no anchor, that the day would come (in Colmer's words) "when the demands of the people upon their elected Representatives would be so great that they could not be met and the whole American dream would collapse." Certainly the idea of limits was not much in fashion, nor was much thought directed to the contradictions, which Nathan Glazer pointed out, between increasing insistence on individual freedom and demands for ever more complex forms of social intervention. This was a time of expressive politics. Anyone who asked what would follow this or that grand gesture—unilateral withdrawal from Vietnam, a $3,600 or $5,500, or $6,500 guaranteed income—was likely to be charged with opposing the ends as well as the means.

The controversy over the "inadequacy" of FAP displayed this tendency in an advanced form. *A guaranteed income, like a minimum wage, must be an exercise in restraint. Too high a level defeats its purpose.* It may be argued, for example, that the intense employment difficulties of Negro youth in the 1960s reflected in part the effect of the minimum wage. (When teen-age unemployment was first measured, just after World War II, it was low for both black and white youth, and lower for blacks than for whites.) Too large a guaranteed income would bring on immediate inflationary pressures, unless matched by tax increases, which would be unlikely. A further inflationary effect would presumably follow if the income guarantee was so high as to lead to large withdrawals from the work force. The planners of FAP did not have any fixed judgment as to just how much would be too much, but it was assumed that the critical zone would be reached fairly soon after the $3,000 mark, and that a negative tax of $5,500 or $6,500 would bring economic disaster. Total adjusted family income in 1966, as estimated by Joseph A. Pechman, was $659 billion. To increase this amount by $50 to $100 billion simply by printing checks would be . . . well, disaster. The virtue of FAP was that it was small enough to be fitted into a routine budget, yet large enough to make a difference to those who would benefit. Pechman estimated that in 1966 the lowest fifth of American families, those with less than $3,070, received only 3.2 percent of total money income.[1] In round numbers this would have been less than $20 billion in 1966. Additional FAP transfers in the neighborhood of $5 billion obviously would have consequences for this group without at all "distorting" the economy. This was an economy already (in 1969–1970) far weaker than many seemed to realize.*

The FAP planners knew that when their program went into effect it would have consequences not just for recipients but for the economy as a whole, and these could be good or bad. There was a mood of genuine caution which few not altogether opposed to the program seemed to share. The newsletter of the Urban Coalition Action Council, reporting passage of H.R. 16311 in the House, referred to a statement issued by Gardner on the occasion on which he congratulated all concerned, but added:

The Action Council will work in the Senate for increased benefits rising over a specified time to the poverty level. Such a provision is essential to breaking the poverty cycle. The necessary funding must be given priority in the Federal budget.

Mills and Byrnes had given their word to the Committee on Rules, and to the House, that if the Senate were to go one cent beyond $1,600 there would be no bill. Most likely the Action Council saw this as a negotiable commitment and assumed the Senate could carry out its role as an appellate branch without endangering the legislation. It was a large presumption, but a general one. On balance liberal spokesmen and commentators

* Any even half-competent member of the Johnson or Nixon Administration knew that devaluation of the dollar, in one form or another, was coming.

proceeded as if the House action was a flawed beginning to an enterprise that could still be made splendid in the Senate, where such matters were understood.

In a general perspective, Nixon's proposal of a guaranteed income may be thought of as a disequilibrating act. Both liberals and conservatives suddenly found themselves in unfamiliar and uncomfortable positions arising in the main from a conflict between their ideological dispositions and their party responsibilities. Liberals faced the prospect of having to support a presumably conservative president at the cost of aiding his party and yielding their own position in the vanguard of social progress. Conservatives faced the prospect of having to support a radical social measure while yielding their party's role as the restraining influence in social policy. Four distinct responses to the president's initiative occurred, each of which can be seen as an effort to restore equilibrium, defined for this purpose as a state in which there is sufficient agreement as to whose interests are represented by whom. These could be designated as the strategies of denial, of cooperation, of realignment, and of outbidding.

The strategy of denial appeared first. The benefit levels of FAP were described by liberals as "piteously inadequate," the work requirement a form of "involuntary servitude," the distribution of benefits yet another manifestation of the "Southern strategy." The thrust of this critique was to deny that FAP was a guaranteed income. For their part conservatives denied that it was welfare reform. The Administration might have genuinely desired to find work for welfare recipients, but conservatives could point out that the legislation did not contain as much a work requirement as did existing law. The Administration might seriously have hoped that Family Assistance would, subtly but powerfully, so alter incentive structures that the incidence of female-headed dependent families would decline, but conservatives could point out that under FAP, no less than under AFDC, any low-income family with an employed head could substantially increase the "cash flow" through its various pockets and pocketbooks by the simple expedient of breaking up and putting the women and children on welfare. Reform indeed!

In order of divergence from the previous equilibrium, the next strategy was that of cooperation, as evidenced by Mills and the Ways and Means Committee, and as hinted at earlier by the

Democratic National Committee and by Wilbur Cohen. This was to accept the president's proposals, describe them as essentially Democratic in origin, modify them somewhat, and adopt them. H.R. 16311 was *not,* after all, the bill introduced, following the president's address, by Ford and Byrnes and other Republican legislators. It was a bill to reform welfare, written by the Committee on Ways and Means and introduced by Mills for himself and Byrnes. It passed the House as a Democratic bill with Republican support, albeit it was seen as the president's proposal. In this strategy equilibrium would be restored by depicting the president as having proposed something Democrats had been for all along and which they accordingly supported. In this new constellation the president would have to be depicted as less illiberal than in the past, but the national Democrats would remain the party of social progress and initiative.

A third strategy was that of realignment. The parties were caught up with a conflict of substance and symbol in their respective positions. Among both Democrats and Republicans there arose an impulse, sometimes errant, sometimes sustained, to make the most of it, to go all the way, to espouse the substance of their new symbolic position, or to embrace the symbolism of their new substantive position. Some Democrats began talking of the needs of the middle classes, as had McGovern in his proposal of a large family allowance, the greatest portion of which would benefit middle-income families. Some Republicans began talking of the rights of the working class and the poor. In his first two years in office Nixon adopted a legislative and administrative program that was not so much liberal as progressive, similar in ways to that of Woodrow Wilson, whom he admired most of twentieth-century presidents. It would be too much to assert, with George McGovern, that of the array of liberal programs of the 1960s, "All . . . turned out badly," but not very many had turned out very well, while accompanying social trends had ranged from the disappointing to the terrifying. Nixon did not so much proclaim new social goals as propose new means of attaining old ones. Thus the results of the 1962 welfare amendments with their concentration on social-work rehabilitation had turned out to be, in the estimate of George Hoshino, writing in *Social Work,* "dismal."[2] Hence Nixon moved from a services strategy to an income strategy but was *still seeking substantially the same results*. The strategy of denial on the part of liberals, accompanied by the tendency of the Administration to protect its rear by often flamboyant conservative rhetoric, tended to obscure this development, but in a curiously assertive way reality impressed itself on the political mind, and many Democratic politicians at least toyed with the idea that if Nixon had come over to their side, they would go over to his. Thus Democratic Representative Ullman had opened the hearings on FAP by declaring himself "shocked"—at the extravagance of the proposal.

McGovern now followed suit. His analysis of the state of affairs—the seeming failure of the poverty programs, the alienation of the nonpoor—was close to that of the FAP planners. Nixon, occupying the presidency, opted for an income strategy that would deliver resources directly to the poor, but in a manner that was automatic, was color blind, was unobtrusive. Or so it was hoped. McGovern, seeking the presidency, took up an opposite position. Nixon, he charged, had adopted a "poor people's program par excellence"; he would opt for a program designed to aid the middle and working classes as well. This was logical for him in any event. The poor would not be voting in the upcoming primary campaigns, and McGovern, the obverse of Nixon, would have trouble winning the confidence of the "5 & 10's." Support of the "limousine liberals," who would provide most of the campaign funds, could be had by rhetoric concerning the poor. But primary election votes would have to be won from persons whose class interests were those of neither the wealthy nor the poor. A large family allowance—worth in the range of $2,000 per year for the average factory worker—would, if persisted in, appeal to that particular class interest. It is precisely McGovern's integrity as a political person that suggests the validity of a mechanistic analysis of this kind. Thus in an earlier period of consolidating his Senate position he became the leading congressional advocate of greatly increased food programs, and chairman of the Select Committee on Nutrition and Human Needs. In this position he could appeal to the national liberal audience by his concern for the poor, while serving his farm constituents of South Dakota. There was nothing cynical about his earlier position, nor about this later one. It simply made political sense.

The response of realignment was not limited to welfare

matters. In the spring of 1970, the president sent messages to Congress on elementary and secondary, and on higher education. Both concentrated on problems of low-income students. It was proposed greatly to increase scholarship assistance to low-income—again disproportionately black—students and to cut back on aid to middle-class students. Congress was not amused. Eric Wentworth of the *Washington Post* caught the irony of the situation in reporting Finch's testimony before the Education and Labor committee.

NIXON EDUCATION PROPOSALS SCORED

Liberal Democrats attacked the Nixon administration's higher education proposals at a House hearing yesterday, claiming they shortchanged the middle-class "Silent Majority."

These Democrats usually concentrate on the needs of the nation's poor. But they found the administration has already provided for low-income students in its proposed overhaul of student aid.

Rep. Edith Green (D-Ore.) and other members of her subcommittee chided Health, Education and Welfare Secretary Robert H. Finch and Education Commissioner James E. Allen, Jr., because the Nixon proposal would make students above a certain income level eligible only for government-guaranteed but unsubsidized loans from colleges or private lenders. A "National Student Loan Association" would increase the volume of these loans by creating a secondary market.

Mrs. Green quoted Saul Alinsky, radical community organizer, on the alienation of the middle classes. If the administration proposals became law, added Rep. John Brademas (D-Ind.), "then the great 'Silent Majority' would become very vocal indeed." Rep. Hugh Carey (D-N.Y.) warned against driving middle-income families deeper into debt.

* * *

. . . Mrs. Green insisted the proposals would limit freedom of choice for middle-income students. Unable to pay the more costly tuition at private colleges without financial aid, she said, they would be forced to attend public institutions.

A year later the president resubmitted his proposals, the essence of which was "that no qualified student who wants to go to college should be barred by lack of money." Mrs. Green was still in opposition. The UPI reported her as saying:

There is no mention of help for students of middle-income families. . . . I think it's highly unfair to ask middle-income taxpayers to foot the bill for someone else's child to attend an expensive school while they can't afford to send their own children to such a college.

The report added:

Both Mrs. Green and [Representative Carl D.] Perkins cited lack of help for private colleges, other than Mr. Nixon's statement that black universities must get increased help.*

* A study should be written of liberal response to Nixon's education proposals, which, as with his welfare proposals, were generally *more* liberal in the established sense than anything proposed by his predecessors. The following account, taken from the Comment section of *The New Republic* for November 13, 1971, suggests the striking similarity of reaction.

THE GREENING OF EDUCATION

It was time again last week in the House to vote for a new higher education bill—a potpourri which each year gets more expensive, more complex. But this round, *the administration endorsed a unique proposal to give financial help to more poor college students than ever before; and liberal Democrats, including the black caucus, defeated it in a 257–117 vote.*

The debate centered on how the government should distribute educational opportunity grants, scholarships for the needy. Traditionally, the U.S. Office of Education has parceled money to the states, which divide it among the schools. Financial aid officers at each university decide which students are "needy" and how much they'll get. Congress has long believed that such a flexible system allows universities to respond sensitively to hardship cases—for example, to students whose families must put several offspring through college, or those who have high medical expenses. But the system has been abused: "needy" may describe a good left tackle and *not* a troublesome activist. Poor students shop around for the college which offers them the most aid—but once they are accepted, there's no guarantee they'll continue to get it.

The administration proposal, a bipartisan amendment offered by Republican Albert Quie and Democrat Donald Fraser of Minnesota, would have changed all that. The government would automatically guarantee up to $1,400 for needy students, depending on how much their families could afford to contribute. Students would receive the scholarships no matter where they live or what college they attend. The poorest would be helped first.

It was an antipoverty crusader's dream. But Edith Green (D-Ore.), who firmly chairs the subcommittee that wrote the education bill, preferred the current method with minor changes, and she had her way, with the help of the black caucus. Why? For one thing, the Quie-Fraser amendment carried an administration taint. "We don't trust the Nixon administration," a caucus aide said flatly. "I don't think the black caucus members under-

To the extent such positions are seen as realigned, it is primarily at the symbolic level that a shift has occurred. A politician may occasionally espouse the interest of a particular class, but the more general behavior is to represent the interests of as many groups as possible. In any event, the Democratic party contained a large and influential element of middle- and upper-class voters, while Republicans had reason to believe that they were beginning to appeal to blue-collar workers. Both parties, then, envisioned the possibility of increased support by *explicitly* serving these somewhat nascent, but nonetheless distinct, class interests.

The strategy of outbidding was an extension of the strategy of denial. If Family Assistance wasn't enough, it was logical to offer an alternative that was. The most important alternative, apart from Senator McCarthy's sponsorship of the NWRO $5,500 proposal, was offered on February 10 by Senator Fred R. Harris of Oklahoma, the retiring Democratic National Chairman, and a member of the Senate Finance Committee. Harris declared the $1,600 level of FAP "would mean for many a sad plunge into the lower depths of ever greater poverty." (The theme that the president's proposals would somehow lead to greater poverty had become common to both the denial and the outbidding strategies.) Harris offered instead the National Basic Income and Incentive Act, which was Family Assistance starting at the level of $2,520 and raised over three years to the poverty level. (The press generally interpreted this to be $3,600 for a family of four, but it was then already $3,740.) The Harris bill provided payments for individuals and childless couples, excluded any mother with a dependent child from a work-training program, and included somewhat vague provisions such as "Refusal to participate in work-training program if the program

---

stood what was going on," said another, "This is technical stuff." Yet all of the black representatives, except the three who sit on Mrs. Green's committee, signed a statement in June supporting the Quie-Fraser amendment. Ronald Dellums, the fiery California Democrat from Berkeley, even wrote a "Dear Colleague" letter warning that Mrs. Green's bill "would be tragic for thousands of low-income students." Yet all black members of the House ended up voting against the amendment, along with white liberals. John Brademas (D-Ind.), who worked closely with Quie on the amendment, gave in at the last minute, so as not to jeopardize some pet legislation included elsewhere in the education bill.

would not prepare the individual for a suitable job which will be available when training is complete will not disqualify one to benefits."[3] Harris did not demean Family Assistance. He told the Senate Finance Committee, as it began hearings on H.R. 16311, "This bill is important because, if adopted, it would establish the principle of a federally guaranteed minimum income for all Americans and replace the outdated and unworking system of welfare. . . ." His own proposal would ultimately cost $20 billion and cover 75 million persons. The president had put up close to $5 billion. By scrapping the revenue-sharing proposal, Harris proposed to get another $5 billion, the rest to be had somehow. This was in the range of political realism.

The distinction between outbidding the president and co-operating with him could become quite narrow. Within the Administration it was always assumed that the Democratic majority in Congress would insist on adding some attractive feature to the president's proposal before accepting it. Mills had done this by increasing payments in the adult categories. Harris hoped to incresease payment levels to the working and dependent poor. Harris, however, was not a member of Ways and Means, an institution which rewarded cooperative and restrained behavior. To the contrary, he was a member of the Senate Finance Committee, an institution which, like its parent body, made individualist behavior more rational than not and was governed less by formal norms than by an informal code. In the House Harris's bill might have been taken up by his colleagues as a serious alternative to that of the president *and thoroughly looked into*. In the Senate it was just another speech. Whatever his personal inclinations, Harris found himself in an institutional setting in which the incentives for outbidding the president were stronger than those for cooperating with him.

By contrast, however, Senator Ribicoff was from the first disposed to cooperate with the president, and remained so. Unlike Harris, whose political base in Oklahoma was now rapidly eroding, and who would soon be seeking the presidential nomination by a "populist" appeal directed to the liberal-left of his party, Ribicoff's political position was secure. As Secretary of Health, Education, and Welfare under Kennedy he had sponsored the welfare amendments of 1962, and knew well enough what had followed. He was, moreover, the only member of the

Senate Finance Committee who could assert any particular authority in the field. He expected the committee to look to him for initiative in the matter, and had an understanding to this effect with the committee chairman, Russell B. Long of Louisiana. From the first Ribicoff sought to produce a somewhat "better" bill than the president's, and to have it pass. Four days after Family Assistance was approved by the House he made public fourteen amendments which he would offer to H.R. 16311. The form of his proposals was itself a declaration of intent: he sought merely to amend a bill now passed by the House and soon to be before the Senate. The amendments began with the assertion of a national goal that would assure all citizens an adequate income by 1976. FAP payment levels would be raised to $1,800 in 1972 and $2,000 in 1973. Ribicoff proposed to include childless couples and individuals over the age of twenty-five, to increase the Federal share of state supplementation from 30 percent to 40 percent, and similar measures on which no issue of principle and only relatively narrow ones of cost separated him from the Administration. He proposed to exclude mothers of children under fourteen from the work requirement where no adequate child-care facilities were available. Told that this was a symbolic issue of great importance to conservatives, he allowed that he was himself not sure how much support he would have for such an amendment. On April 28 he indicated to the White House that he anticipated the Finance Commitee would report out a bill by mid-June. For all the centrifugal tendencies of the Finance Committee, Ribicoff assumed it would get right to business on this issue, and that he would be closely involved in bringing the matter to a successful conclusion.

Hearings began the next day. Two days later Family Assistance was dead.

American national government is like that. Through the twentieth century the powers of the presidency have steadily increased, but the powers of the standing committees of the Congress, which Woodrow Wilson had once described as the true locus of governmental power, had not correspondingly diminished. Rather, their activities have shifted. Their most significant role is that of oversight: accepting presidential initiatives, but thereafter scrutinizing executive performance. Such scrutiny can be devastating, especially as government has grown more ambitious, and embarks on more high-risk enterprises. Personal dispositions and politics apart, Family Assistance came to grief when the Senate Finance Committee chose not to deal with it as a new initiative presented by the president for which he would be ultimately held accountable, but rather to review it as an ongoing program that was not working well. There was a touch of destiny in this. Had the president, or Ways and Means, proclaimed FAP to be a guaranteed income, Senate Finance would almost certainly have sensed that this was something *new*. But as *welfare reform* it was by definition something old. The Finance Committee accordingly proceeded to inquire into the workings of the existing welfare system that purportedly needed reforming. At last, the committee discovered welfare. It was horrified: or chose to appear so. It never did get to considering the new elements of FAP until the very last moment. It was by then much too late, but in any event, the Senate Finance Committee had none of the institutionalized competence of Ways and Means to deal with an initiative as divisive on ideological grounds and complex in technical detail as Family Assistance.

The term "incompetence" is used partly in the medical sense of the "inability of an organ to perform its function adequately." (Webster's Third New International Dictionary) The difficulty was in part organizational, and in part political. The composite result has been summarized by the *National Journal:* "Few congressional committees have been as much vilified as Finance—partly because of its role as the visible point of access for pressure groups; partly because of the wheeler-dealer reputations of some of its most influential members, past and present; and partly because, as a committee, it has long been ideologically out of step with the Senate as a whole."[4]

As one of the most powerful of Senate Committees, Finance was inevitably the subject of pressures, but this can have the effect, as in Ways and Means, of producing strong leadership and a measure of cohesion, even *esprit,* in the group as a whole. Senator Harry Byrd, Sr., of Virginia, had given it a dominant chairman into the early sixties, with Robert Kerr, of Oklahoma, preserving the oil depletion allowance and other revenue measures of crucial concern to one or another group. But this was the kind of power exercised by an appellate body, in large part negative. The Finance Committee was rarely a positive influence, and now, under the leadership of Russell B. Long of Louisiana, was even less so. Long had once appeared destined for a large role in Senate affairs, but his position declined in the latter half of the 1960s. At the opening of the 91st Congress Senator Edward M. Kennedy of Massachusetts took from him his position as Majority Whip. While this left him with only the Finance Committee as a power base, it did little for the Committee itself, which, unlike Ways and Means, had never acquired the individual and group discipline and work habits necessary to mastering a new and difficult subject. In part this reflected differences between the House and the Senate. The size of the House imposes certain kinds of discipline if *any* work is to be done and makes it necessary for much to be done in committee. The smaller size of the Senate, combined with the greater prestige of its members, permits more business to be transacted on the floor, with all members participating, so that, consequently, the committee dominance of a given issue, though impressive, is less pronounced. In any event, the Finance Committee, like Ways and Means, had almost no experience with welfare issues, and could not expect any great deference to its judgments in the area on grounds of expertise. Nor could it command respect by virtue of the distinction of its membership. It was a powerful committee, but by and large its membership was no longer made up of the most powerful senators. Another misfortune for FAP, but American government can be like that, too.

The political problem was not that the Finance Committee was more "conservative" than the Senate as a whole. In one test after another FAP had survived the scrutiny of conservatives. What it could not survive was a committee dominated by Democrats representing Southern states where FAP would have its greatest impact on the social order, and Republicans representing Western states where welfare was a minimal problem, and reform a marginal concern.

This was the anomaly of the Finance Committee: one of the most powerful of the Senate committees, it was one of the least representative. The membership of Ways and Means was a faithful reflection of the American population, and especially that portion which votes Democratic. The big Northern Democratic cities strung from the Atlantic to the Great Lakes were represented with meticulous concern: Boston, New York, Philadelphia, Cleveland, Detroit, Chicago. Finance had Vance Hartke, Democrat of Indiana, and Ribicoff of Connecticut, but no Democratic senator from a state where welfare had become a serious problem. There were other Democratic liberals on the Committee: Clinton P. Anderson of New Mexico, Albert Gore of Tennessee, Eugene J. McCarthy of Minnesota, and Harris of Oklahoma, but none of these represented a constituency much involved with welfare issues. Counting Gore and Harris, six of the ten Democrats were Southerners. Three of the Democrats, Long, Herman E. Talmadge of Georgia, a senator of considerable influence, and Harry F. Byrd, Jr., of Virginia were themselves sons of Southern political leaders.

If the Democrats on the committee represented the South, the Republicans represented the Great American Desert and the mountain and plains country adjacent: Arizona, Utah, Nebraska, Iowa, Idaho, Wyoming. The seven Republican members came from states that sent fourteen senators but only nineteen representatives to Congress. In part this reflected the importance of the committee to oil, gas, and mineral interests, but also the workings of seniority. The only Eastern Republican on the committee was the ranking minority member, John J. Williams of Delaware (still a Southern state by Census classification), then the tenth-ranking member of the Senate, who had announced he would retire at the end of the 91st Congress. Williams's prime concern was that citizens derive as little financial gain as possible from government, whether by theft, welfare, bribery, or whatever. Though Delaware was one of the richest states in the Union, its welfare payments were among the meanest.

A further influence in the consideration of FAP involved the staff of the Committee, headed by Tom Vail, a tax attorney. Social security and welfare matters were assigned to Michael Stern, a former HEW employee. It was a new staff, recruited by Long when he succeeded to the chairmanship. (The senior Byrd did not believe in staff. He perceived that staff members inevitably exercise some of a senator's powers, but for their own purposes.) There was, in any event, no established staff tradition, and little competence in the field of either welfare or income redistribution.

None of these obstacles having to do with the makeup of the Finance Committee and the capacities of its staff need have been fatal. The problem was far more intractable. With the exception of Ribicoff there was not at the start one member of the committee who supported the president's bill. Even Ribicoff's support was conditional, so that in effect *no* member supported the bill. In particular, not a single Republican member supported it, while the senior Republican, Williams, was adamantly opposed. In any event the Finance Committee as an institution was erratic and centrifugal. Its decision would not be shaped by one man, as had been the case in the White House and in Ways and Means. It would not necessarily even seek to reach a decision. It was capable of aggressive hostility, but equally capable of fecklessness. The onset of Senate hearings should have been perceived by the White House and by HEW as a moment of great danger, requiring the closest attention. It was not.

This being the fact, the Administration has to be charged with inattention. No one was guilty of grievous dereliction of duty, much less was there deliberate disloyalty. Rather, a combination of small failings and failures produced an attitude of insufficient concentration on these seventeen senators. No one quite sensed their hostility. In part this was due to the experience in the House, where Ways and Means had been friendly enough to Administration witnesses at the outset and had finally persuaded *itself* that the legislation should go forward. In part there was a failure of legislative liaison. No Senate lobbyist came back with the bad news that the bill was in deep danger. (Lobbyists have that weakness.) Similarly, Long gave it to be understood that he wanted and expected a bill, and very probably he did. Nonetheless he could be driven by his own rhetoric into intransigence, and this might have been anticipated.

A more generalized and characteristic executive myopia was also involved. The White House and the Cabinet departments live surrounded by essentially liberal media—*The New York Times,* the *Washington Post, Time, Newsweek,* the television commentators—which in the most natural way concentrate on events that occur in what might be termed the liberal spectrum. Thus if a rump caucus of a White House Conference on Food, Nutrition, and Health resolves that sixty or so billion dollars should be spent on income maintenance, reporters are there, television cameras are there, the event makes an impression on the executive branch. It is a minuscule event: often as not staged, faked, contrived. Compared with the impressions of welfare which the sixth-ranking Republican member of the Senate Finance Committee might have got that same day from a visitor from back home seeing him on quite different business it is an event of no significance. Yet the one is reported, the other not. Over the winter far too much attention was paid within the Administration to individuals and groups involved in outbidding FAP. This was in part a personal reaction by men who felt they had done something large and expansive, and who too easily became defensive and hurt when it was charged that their work was mean and repressive. Additionally, the Administration fell victim to the then generalized Washington understanding that the Senate was a distinctly more liberal body, and also a more competent one than the House. The planners of FAP had by now acquired their own version of the "liberal audience." Their realignment had won a measure of approval, and the portent of more. The success of FAP would be the great triumph: a *liberal* triumph. By contrast, conservatives who regarded the legislation as profligate and near demented had no power to wound, and so it was possible to overlook their power to destroy.

Long gave warning enough of what was to come. In the tradition of "waiting on the House" the Finance Committee took no action on FAP until it had passed there. This was April 16. On April 17 he announced that the committee would receive a staff briefing in executive session on April 22, and that public hearings would begin with Finch on April 28, followed by Shultz, and thereafter public witnesses. On April 23, the day after the briefing was scheduled, Long delivered a near hostile speech on the floor of the Senate. More ominously, it was a profoundly confused one. Based on the committee's "first look" at the bill, he said, "it looks like a reenactment of the work incentive program Congress wrote into law in 1967 . . . and an expansion of welfare to make 15 million people eligible . . . in addition to the 10 million now on the rolls." He spoke of his sponsorship of the WIN program, and of sabotage of the program by the executive branch. The Labor Department had entered a contract with the NWRO "for about $430,000 [to] . . . show people how not to go to work." He cited a year-old account in the *Washington Post* of an NWRO conference held in the capital.

> At one conference session yesterday . . . participants got a two-hour course on how they could avoid job training or work under the city's new Work Incentive Program. . . .
>
> Steven Wexler, a lawyer on the National Welfare Rights Organization staff, told them how they could "exhaust appeal after appeal. . . ."
>
> "You can stay out of the program until Hell freezes over if you know how to do it," he said.

(His staff's briefing paper was notably harsh on the subject of the WIN program. For fiscal 1969 Congress had appropriated $117.5 million; the executive had expended $37.4 billion; 69,400 trainees had been projected; 15,200 had been taken in. These and similar data were followed by the laconic observation, "The Administration states that it will seek funds for 225,000 additional training slots for the first full year of the Family Assistance Plan.") Long charged that the previous Administration, and holdovers from it, had deliberately frustrated the desire of Congress to provide work training for mothers and day care for children. "Instead they frittered away government money hiring professional troublemakers and professional agitators. . . ." He charged that the NWRO had sought to intimidate the committee with a "sit-in strike" during the consideration of the 1967 welfare amendments. He was disturbed by the Labor Department contract, and would not be assuaged by assurances later given him by Rosow that there had been "some positive sides" to the uses to which Wiley and his associates had devoted the money. *The Finance Committee staff depicted FAP as a proposal that would encourage and facilitate just the kind of work avoidance and welfare maximization which Long associated with NWRO.* The chairman concurred.

> . . . Senators should be aware that the welfare bill before the Finance Committee today does not solve the problem—it just makes it cost $4 billion more. Under the bill, a fully employed father of a family of four with low earnings could increase his family's total income if he quit work, or if he reduced his income.

The tone of Long's speech, if seen as the commencement of a process of bargaining, was not especially portentous; but the content was. He had chosen to take the Administration at its word and to view FAP as *welfare reform*. How much reform, he asked, did the legislation in fact provide?

The question was fatal. Doubly so. First, the main thrust of the legislation was to establish a guaranteed income for the working poor. To concentrate on the welfare aspects of the proposal could only divert attention from its most significant feature. Second, the changes in the existing welfare system which were contained in FAP were preponderantly directed toward making the system more accessible and more liberal. (E.g., the AFDC-U program was to be made nationwide; minimum national benefit standards were to be established for AFDC families.) From the point of view of the liberal social reformer such measures were readily classifiable as reform. But this was a minority view. To men such as Long—and he was not at all unrepresentative in this—the term "reform" applied to the subject of welfare had but one meaning: the curbing of abuse. Welfare reform to such minds meant dealing with cheating, with absurd advantages made available to manipulative clients, with lax and even corrupt practices indulged in by indolent or insolent administrators. Nixon had made some concession to this view in his proclamation of "workfare," but his legislation contained scarcely a clause that could be depicted as "tightening up" the system. In this respect the president had sent forward a pure product of the welfare bureaucracy which for a decade and more had been openly at odds with legislative critics, denying or avoiding any evidence that their program did indeed need tightening. The various welfare publics were well enough aware of attitudes such as Long's so that the mere assertion by the president that he sought to "reform" the system caused great anxiety. Ultimately it would be charged that the proposals were indeed oppressive, while early on the income provisions were dismissed as trivial, and the process of outbidding the president began on his left.

Now a precisely comparable response began to his right. *Conservatives began to outbid the president with respect to welfare reform.* While the left got more press, this tactic on the right was far the more devastating. It was difficult to argue persuasively that FAP did not provide income for the poor: it did. But

it *was* difficult to demonstrate that FAP provided welfare reform
in terms of the general expectations of a man such as Long: it
did not. The measure was *not* directed to correcting abuses. In
part this reflected a concern for sensibilities such as those of the
NWRO. But also, in part, it reflected plain ignorance. The
planners of FAP had no idea how absurd the welfare system had
become. It *did* invite abuse, and needed changes directed to the
elimination of abuse. Once the Senate Finance Committee began
to press the point, the case for FAP as welfare reform was bound
to collapse. By proposing to leave the existing welfare system
essentially intact, the Administration was made to appear to
sanction it. FAP, having first benefited from the near unanimous
judgment that *something* had to be done about welfare, now
began to suffer as it was revealed that it appeared to do little.

The issue had appeared, tentatively, in the hearings before
Ways and Means, but *that* committee chose not to press the
matter. The country had got itself into a fix it could not get out
of. The House, finding the welfare situation seemingly intractable, acquiesced in the Administration's proposal to create a
general system of income maintenance, which would at least, it
was hoped, diminish the attractions of and the pressures toward
welfare dependency in its AFDC form. This subtlety—some
might call it subterfuge—was never successfully communicated
to the Senate.

In part it was obscured by the effort to avoid the label
"guaranteed annual income," which it was thought would destroy any chance the legislation might have had. In his prepared
testimony for the Finance Committee, Finch had to go round on
that subject yet again.

Certainly the most widely discussed question is whether Family
Assistance is really in fact a "guaranteed annual income," and to this
question I can emphatically answer "no."
. . . There are critical differences in concept and in program
operation between Family Assistance and such plans. Under guaranteed-income plans, the government would allow people to abdicate
their responsibilities for self-support by assuring a basic income regardless of whether they are willing to work or not.
Under Family Assistance, however, income is not provided
regardless of personal efforts or attitudes.

Technically this was inaccurate. FAP did guarantee an income to families with children regardless of "personal efforts or attitudes." But, for practical purposes, so did the AFDC program with respect to female-headed families. It would nonetheless profoundly distort the purpose of the Administration to see it as proposing an even wider guarantee and planning to leave it at that. Finch, Shultz, Veneman, Nathan, myself—all those principally involved, and first of all the president—looked on welfare dependency as a woeful condition which society must minimize. This was a company as capable of moral judgment as the next, and this subject was viewed in moral terms. FAP, it was hoped, would affect the situation, both directly and indirectly. It would make certain types of dependency less attractive, and—the deep conviction of all—would make more attractive and viable the transition to self-sufficiency. But it promised no cure. The "advantages" of dependency would persist.

No great subtlety was needed on the part of the senators to perceive that the system as it then existed, based on laws already enacted, did make for absurdity if not abuse, as in the evolution of the AFDC-U program, which authorized payments to families in which a male head was unemployed. Plain enough in intent, this program, enacted in 1961, became anything but simple in execution. *Who* was unemployed? HEW regulations left this to the determination of state administrators, but permitted the definition to include anyone working less than 35 hours a week, whereupon a common tendency came into play. In the absence of a general system of income maintenance, *some* welfare administrators did all they could to stretch existing law to create such a system, or at all events to be as generous as they could by defining underemployment to be unemployment. The result was a "notch." A man working for low wages in a high-welfare payment state would have his income supplemented as long as he remained underemployed, i.e., worked less than 35 or 30 hours per week. By working one hour beyond that limit, however, he would lose *all* his supplement. An extra dollar of earnings would cost hundreds of dollars of welfare. The Medicaid program provided that any family receiving AFDC or AFDC-U payments was automatically to be covered for medical expenses as well. Hence an even sharper "notch." An extra dollar of earnings

POLITICS OF A GUARANTEED INCOME | 463

would cost hundreds of dollars of welfare, *plus* hundreds of dollars of paid health care.

Then came the welfare amendments of 1967 fashioned to encourage work by its "30 & 1/3" formula. Welfare mothers who worked were permitted to keep $30, *plus work expenses,* out of each month's earnings, with no loss of welfare payments. (State limits for work expenses were set as high as $100 per month.) Thereafter payments were reduced by 66⅔ cents for every dollar earned until by this process total earnings exhausted the "standard of need" established by each state for families of various sizes. *This* meant that a mother in a high-payment state could have quite considerable earnings while still receiving welfare supplements, but also that a point would come when a small increase in earnings would bring on a sharp "notch" that would reduce true income by considerable sums. It was moreover possible—again the effort to stretch the system—for a mother to begin receiving AFDC payments at a point where her earnings were lower than the state "need standard" and to continue receiving them even after earnings rose *above* that standard until the amount was exhausted under the "30 & 1/3" formula.* Finch had illustrated both processes in tables prepared for Ways and Means in February.

Incentive for Men to Work Part-Time Under AFDC-U
(Assume a State with a $3,000 Need Standard and Payment Level)

	Earned Income	Welfare Grant	Net Income
Father works 20 hours a week at $1.70 an hour; earns $1,664 a year with $210 in work-related expenses, is eligible for welfare.	$1,768	$2,197	$3,775
Father works full time at $1.60 an hour with an estimated $420 in work-related expenses, is ineligible for welfare.	$3,536	—0—	$3,116

* A state could have a "need standard" which it did not in fact meet under its payment schedule, electing instead to pay only a portion of the standard.

Treatment of Working Women Under AFDC
(Assume a State with a $3,000 Need Standard and Payment Level)

	Earned Income	Welfare Grant	Net Income
Mother earning $2,500 with $420 in work-related expenses, is eligible for welfare.	$2,500	$1,781	$3,961
Mother earning $3,500 with an estimated $420 in work-related expenses, is not eligible for welfare.	$3,500	—0—	$3,080
Mother already receiving welfare increases her earned income to $3,500 with $420 in work-related expenses, and remains eligible.	$3,500	$1,161	$4,341

The FAP formula, which did not permit state-to-state variations in work expenses, all of which were subsumed under the $60 per month, or $720 per year, "disregard" and which anticipated that state supplements would be reduced at a rate of two thirds of earnings after the disregard, had the effect of *lowering* the eligibility ceilings in all states, many of which were in the $6,000 and $7,000 range. In New York the state payment level for a family of four was $3,756. Under the "30 & 1/3" plus work-related expenses formula, earnings could go as high as $7,074 to $7,344 before eligibility for AFDC payments was exhausted. Under FAP the new ceiling would be $5,947.50. *Thus it was true that FAP would have reduced benefits to some welfare families.* Patricelli later explained to the Finance Committee that this was one of the trade-offs necessary in setting up a reasonably uniform national system.

We did not feel that a small loss of welfare benefits to people who have relatively high earnings was in error. This is one of the choices that has to be made between having a very high ceiling on welfare benefits and adjusting work expenses, and the proper level of the basic payment, and all of the rest.

The reaction of the members of the Senate Finance Committee was astonishment that the Administration was proposing to continue a system in which a family of four earning almost $6,000 per year might still be receiving welfare. The point somehow never got through, which can only mean it was never adequately made, that the existing AFDC arrangements permitted payments to families with even higher incomes. Once again the Administration faced the dilemma of dual audiences with nearly opposite values where welfare was involved. But even so the level of umbrage and misunderstanding in the Finance Committee at times seemed gratuitous.

The staff of the committee seems to have had some responsibility for the committee's attitude. In his April 23 speech in the Senate, Long told of his concern about work disincentives, drawing on material prepared by the staff.

A typical aid to families with dependent children payment for a family of four today in many states is $250 a month, or $3,000 a year. A father in a family of four who earns $2,000 annually will be eligible under the bill for welfare payments of $960, bringing his total income up to $2,960. This is less than what he would get if he were totally unemployed. In other words, he can increase his family's income $40 a year by quitting work entirely. But that would not be his best move. For, by working part-time, he could increase his family's income substantially by reducing his earnings to $1,000 a year. Instead of $2,960 his family's income would jump to $3,813— $853 more than if he continued working full time.

That . . . is obviously a ridiculous situation. . . .

Long was relying on a table prepared by the committee staff said to illustrate these anomalies. (See table page 466.)

The situation was more complex. The unemployed father with no earnings would receive $3,000 under FAP *or under existing AFDC-U.* (The "U" was omitted in the committee print.) If *under existing law* he earned $2,000 per year by working 35 hours a week or more, he would not be eligible for any AFDC payment. However, *under existing law,* if he earned $2,000 by working less than 35 hours per week, he might be classified as unemployed, and therefore be eligible for an AFDC payment of $2,267. In the latter case the FAP formula would provide somewhat less. Further, it was a distortion of reality to concentrate on AFDC-U families. Of almost two million families receiv-

Impact of H.R. 16311-State A

Needs standard for family of 4—$3,000; full need met; families with unemployed fathers now aided

Family of 4 headed by—	Income under present law		Income under H.R. 16311	
Mother, earnings of $2,000, work expenses $30 per mo.	AFDC Earnings	$2,267 2,000 —— 4,267	FAP Suppl't Earnings	$ 960 1,187 2,000 —— 4,147
Unemployed father, no earnings	AFDC	$3,000 —— 3,000	FAP Suppl't	$1,600 1,400 —— 3,000
Unemployed father, part time earnings of $1,000, work expenses $15 per month	AFDC Earnings	$2,753 1,000 —— 3,753	FAP Suppl't Earnings	$1,460 1,353 1,000 —— 3,813
Employed father, earnings of $2,000, work expenses $30 per month	Earnings	$2,000 —— 2,000	FAP Earnings	$ 960 2,000 —— 2,960
Unemployed father, earnings of $2,000, work expenses $30 per month	AFDC Earnings	$2,267 2,000 —— 4,267	FAP Suppl't Earnings	$ 960 1,187 2,000 —— 4,147

ing AFDC payments, only some 90,000 were in this category. Still, legislators seize on such details.

What baffled Long and the committee was that a man earning the same amount of money—$2,000 per year—could end up with $2,000, or $2,960, or $4,147, according as one or another of these arrangements obtained. This was surely ridiculous. But it was not a situation FAP proposed to create. It was the *existing* situation FAP proposed to accommodate to by continuing the AFDC-U program. Long denounced these "fantastic, illogical incentives for people to quit work." He inserted into the record a story from the Washington *Star* two days earlier which described a Washington mother of five, whose husband had recently left home, being advised to quit her $1.80-per-hour job in order to be eligible for AFDC payments. The object of the story was to illustrate the attractions of the FAP principle of aid to the working poor. The reporter concluded:

All this might not have come about if the Nixon administration's welfare reform plan, passed last week by the House, were in effect. The program for the first time would benefit the working poor by giving cash grants without requiring the head of the household to be unemployed.

Long seems to have got just the opposite impression. He commented:

. . . In this article it is explained how welfare workers have advised this very fine Negro mother here in Washington how she must not work so she can increase her income. . . .

* * *

The bill before the Committee on Finance is not much better. It, too, would provide an incentive for many low-income working people to quit work, rather than try a little harder to improve their condition and that of their families.

This had been the message of the staff briefing, prepared as a 51-page pamphlet. Other Administration arguments were challenged, especially the estimates which showed that the number of families receiving FAP would decline over time, so that by 1976 families with income supplemented by FAP would be fewer than the number that would be receiving AFDC support if no change were made and existing trends continued. (HEW contended the number of FAP families would decline from 3.7 million in 1972 to 2.7 million in 1976, while AFDC families would otherwise rise from 2.2 million to 3.1 million.) The good-faith administration of the WIN program was not-too-subtly called into doubt. But the principal thrust of the staff paper was that FAP did *not* provide the work incentives claimed for it. To the contrary, it was asserted, it would create yet greater work disincentives.

There was an ironic truth to this. One of the least noticed features of Family Assistance was that it mandated the AFDC-U program in *all* states. This was in line with the principle of national standards, and concern for family stability (albeit no evidence linked the two). At the time FAP was proposed, twenty-three states had an AFDC-U program. Not one was of the Deep South. The staff briefing noted that, owing to the AFDC-U provision, "An estimated quarter million persons in families with an unemployed father would become eligible for assistance for the first time under H.R. 16311." This would make such families eligible also for state supplemental payments. (It would also make them eligible for Medicaid.) A table was prepared illustrating the hypothetical impact of AFDC-U on "State B," which had not had such a program.

Impact of H.R. 16311-State B

Needs standard for family of 4—$2,200; full need met; families with unemployed fathers now aided

Family of 4 headed by—	Income under present law		Income under H.R. 16311	
Mother, earnings of $2,000, work expenses $30 per month	AFDC Earnings	$1,467 2,000 ――― 3,467	FAP Suppl't Earnings	$ 960 387 2,000 ――― 3,347
Unemployed father, no earnings	None		FAP Suppl't	$1,600 600 ――― 2,200
Unemployed father, part time earnings of $1,000, work expenses $15 per month	Earnings	$1,000 ――― 1,000	FAP Suppl't Earnings	$1,460 553 1,000 ――― 3,013
Employed father, earnings of $2,000, work expenses $30 per month	Earnings	$2,000 ――― 2,000	FAP Earnings	$ 960 2,000 ――― 2,960
Unemployed father, earnings of $2,000, work expenses $30 per month	Earnings	$2,000 ――― 2,000	FAP Suppl't Earnings	$960 387 2,000 ――― 3,347

The man who earned $1,000 ended up with more than the man who earned $2,000. The man who earned $2,000 but managed

POLITICS OF A GUARANTEED INCOME | 469

to be classified "unemployed" would get yet more. This lesson was capped by a table contrasting the "Work Incentive Features" of the present law and H.R. 16311. It was revealed that under present law "Persons must be placed in employment, training, or work project," while under the latter the issue is "Left to discretion of Department of Labor." H.R. 16311 was made to appear deliberately and pervasively permissive. In the context of Administration rhetoric of work, it almost seemed as if the Congress was being lied to.

The hearings were a calamity. The senators had all but made up their minds that FAP would provide disincentives to work, *and that this could be shown*. The Administration was not sufficiently aware of the danger. In some measure this was a weakness born of gathering strength. Administration officials responsible for FAP, after a year and more with the subject, had come to understand it about as well as such complex measures are ever understood, which is to say they knew most of what was knowable, and had educated guesses concerning that which was not. Ways and Means had caught on to the subject quickly enough. People who were willing to listen seemed to end up satisfied. Twenty-one out of twenty-four members of Ways and Means had done so. The altogether different mood of the Senate Committee was not sensed.

Even so, Finch's opening statement was the most informative exposition of the subject yet made. He offered the first clear statement of the true nature of Family Assistance.

The family assistance payment is not intended to substitute for welfare payments now available to those who for one reason or another cannot work. State supplementary programs in all but five or six States will raise the payments to such families significantly. The family assistance payment is intended primarily as an income supplement to reinforce the work efforts and family stability of the millions of poor heads of families who can work and are working but who, because of limited education, or opportunity, are not able to provide adequately for their families.

He presented the crucial facts concerning the effect the proposal would have on the working poor. The average family would have 5.6 members. It would receive an FAP payment of $742 and a food-stamp payment of $564, raising its average total income from $3,400 to $4,706, slightly above the poverty line. (Many families of the working poor would already have been receiving some food-stamp benefits.) Where AFDC currently covered 17 percent of the poor and 35 percent of all poor children, FAP would cover 65 percent of the poor and virtually all poor families with children. Taken together, FAP and food-stamp transfers would close the poverty gap by about 60 percent, although (a point developed in the hearings) only about 18 percent of AFDC families would automatically receive higher payments.

Finch presented data that argued that welfare was indeed a "problem" that caused itself. The closer welfare payments approached earning levels actually experienced by welfare mothers, the heavier the case load.

Relationship Between Earnings of AFDC Mothers, AFDC Grant Levels, and Case Loads per 1,000 Poor Persons in the Population, for 11 Cities

	1	2	3	4
City	Median Best Wages[1]	Grant Level	Difference Between 1 and 2	Case Load per 1,000 Poor Persons
New York, N.Y.	$274.56	$278.00	$ −3.44	200.7
Philadelphia, Pa.	237.60	213.00	24.60	84.1
Providence, R.I.	264.00	266.00	−2.00	76.7
Chicago, Ill.	264.00	279.00	−15.00	72.5
San Jose, Calif.	315.04	221.00	94.04	71.8
Phoenix, Ariz.	230.56	134.00	96.56	41.7
Rochester, N.Y.	281.60	278.00	3.60	40.9
New Orleans, La.	220.00	116.00	104.00	39.7
Atlanta, Ga.	221.76	125.00	96.76	36.4
Memphis, Tenn.	220.00	120.00	100.00	32.0
Raleigh, N.C.	220.00	144.00	76.00	23.7

[1] Self-reported, highest wages of AFDC mothers as reported in survey interview. NOTE: Columns 3 and 4 have a statistically significant correlation of −.57.

Finch pleaded, in effect, the case against raising the FAP base, noting that it was only a base and acknowledging the proliferation of special aid and bizarre formulae which had come into existence.

A low income woman and her family can receive food stamps, State supplementation, Medicaid benefits, public housing, day care, legal services and a variety of other services benefits. For example, a non-working mother with three children in New York City who receives State supplementation, Medicaid, food stamps (using the current schedule), and public housing, has a total income—of both money and in-kind payments—of $7,405, exclusive of day care benefits. This same figure in Chicago would be $5,541.

He did his best to demonstrate the "disadvantage" of work under the existing AFDC system. One table showed what a 4-person nonwelfare family had to earn in various states to be as well off as a welfare counterpart.

What a Working Man Must Earn to Be As Well Off As a Welfare Family
(Based on data available January 1970)

State	Welfare payment to 4-person family with no income (Per month)	Required gross earnings for 4-person nonwelfare family to achieve same net disposable income as a welfare family[1]	
		(Per month)	(Hourly wage)
California	$221	$288	$1.67
Connecticut	294	358	2.08
Illinois	269	319	1.85
Indiana	150	185	1.07
Louisiana	104	154	.90
Massachusetts	307	372	2.16
Michigan	263	333	1.94
New York	313	383	2.23
Nebraska	200	250	1.45

[1] Assumes that work-related expenses are equal to the average allowance for work-related expenses including taxes currently made in States shown. These work-related expenses do not include day-care costs.

A third table showed the effect of state supplementation. In New York, two families earning the same amount of money, one receiving welfare supplementation, the other not, ended up with a $148 difference in net disposable monthly income, the advantage being to the welfare family. FAP, said Finch, would clear out this thicket of absurd rulings and regulations.

Comparison of the Net Disposable Incomes of 4-Person Welfare Families and Nonwelfare Families Earning the Same Amount of Wages—Monthly Estimates for Selected States (Based on data available January 1970)

State	Amount of Earnings (1)	Net disposable income of a welfare family earning the amount shown in Column 1[1] (2)	Net disposable income of a nonwelfare family earning the amount shown in Column 1[1] (3)
California	$288	$371	$221
Connecticut	358	433	294
Illinois	319	395	269
Indiana	185	300	150
Louisiana	154	208	104
Massachusetts	372	451	307
Michigan	333	394	263
New York	383	461	313
Nebraska	250	400	200

[1] Assumes that work-related expenses are equal to the average allowance for work-related expenses including taxes currently made in States shown. These work-related expenses do not include day-care costs.

The committee did not believe him. Hearings began Wednesday, April 29. Regardless of what witnesses said, the senators asked about the staff table which "showed" that under FAP it made sense not to work. A typical exchange:

THE CHAIRMAN: . . . You say that the present AFDC program "makes it possible for many welfare families to receive more money from welfare (or a combination of welfare and work) than other equally needy families who must rely solely on a low-paying job." Is it not true that this situation would still be largely true under the bill before us?

SECRETARY FINCH: It would not be true with regard to women. It would be less true than it is now with regard to men.

Not a satisfactory answer. Long in particular was preoccupied with the notion of work, and it availed nothing to argue that the existing system might be worse than the one being proposed.

Senator Talmadge now made his appearance in the debate. He asked Finch what would be the impact of FAP on Georgia, adding that he believed "in many areas we might have over half the people in individual counties on welfare." Finch did not know. The senator asked Veneman about the cash penalty for a man refusing to accept work. It was not much.

SENATOR TALMADGE: So he could do a little casual labor on somebody's yard from time-to-time and maybe sell a little heroin or do a little burglary and he would be in pretty good shape, wouldn't he?

MR. VENEMAN: He would be in about the same shape as under the present program.

Finch intervened to plead: "What we are trying to do is to take care of the children. The question is: If a man takes the attitude that he refuses to work, should we penalize his children?" The senator asked why the WIN program had been such a "dismal failure," especially in New York.

"Let me ask you," Senator Byrd then began, "why do you wish to add fourteen million people to the welfare rolls?" Finch did his best. Veneman was asked whether it was true that of the total "fiscal relief" provided by FAP 30 percent would go to California, and another 38 percent to New York, Massachusetts, Illinois, Pennsylvania, and Ohio. Veneman replied, "That is approximately correct, Senator." (California had a large case load in the aged category.)

No senator spoke a word in support of the president's bill. Some, notably Gore, McCarthy, Hartke, and Fulbright, either stayed away from the hearings or said nothing. Ribicoff was not hostile, but he too was thrown off by the staff briefing, to which the Administration did not seem to have sufficient answers.

SENATOR RIBICOFF: Mr. Secretary, if your objective is to supplement the income of the working poor, how do you explain the low category of the working poor and that he has been discriminated against under H.R. 16311?

SECRETARY FINCH: Senator Ribicoff, a "notch" effect is there, but we have cut it about in half with our proposal. We recognize that there is still some disincentive left.

Finch estimated it would cost another $2 billion to supplement the earnings of the working poor up to the potential level of AFDC and AFDC-U families. Patricelli added, "Senator, the Administration is proposing to spend $4.4 billion to try to eliminate, or at least drastically reduce, the penalty that exists under the present law." No reply was simple because nothing *was* simple.

Now Senator Harris came in from the left, asserting, "We have heard all of these pious statements about putting people to work and we have heard a lot of to-do about forcing people to go to work," but, he put it to Veneman, "Where are the jobs?" Unemployment was rising.

SENATOR HARRIS: What are we going to do about that under your bill?

MR. VENEMAN: I don't think our bill touches that problem.

He wanted to know whether the $1,600 floor could not be raised by abolishing the ABM or the SST programs. He felt the payment levels of FAP were not adequate, noting that most AFDC mothers would not receive increases, and that the day-care provisions would not meet the potential need. So it went. No one was satisfied.

As Frank C. Porter of the *Washington Post* wrote, the bill "was listing badly when Senator John J. Williams torpedoed it. . . ."[5] Williams, attacking from the right, hit upon a devastating polemic. Where the committee staff had merely calculated the "notch" effects in the operation of the various income formulas of welfare itself, Williams extended this to the full range of potential benefits and services available to poor families which Finch had mentioned in his testimony. With lethal attention to detail he had persuaded HEW to construct a set of tables illustrating the "Combined Benefits and Reduction Rates Under

Combined Benefits and Reduction Rates Under Selected Income-Tested Programs for a 4-Person, Female-Headed Family in Phoenix, Arizona[1]

Earnings	FAP Benefit	State Supplement[2]	Total Money Income	Federal Income Tax[3]	State Income Tax[4]	Social Security Tax[4]	Food Stamp Bonus or Surplus Commodity Value[5]	Average Medical Vendor Payment per AFDC Family[7]	Public Housing Bonus[8]	Total Income: Money and In-Kind From All Sources	Cumulative Marginal Reduction Rate (Percent)
0	$1,600	$404	2,004				$441	(6)	1,176	$3,621	
$720	1,600	404	2,724			$37	441		1,176	4,304	5
$1,000	1,460	357	2,817			52	441		1,176	4,382	72
$2,000	960	190	3,150			104	441		1,104	4,591	79
$3,000	460	23	3,483			156	441		1,032	4,800	79
$3,140 (State breakeven)	390		3,530			163	441		1,032	4,840	71
$3,920 (FAP breakeven)			3,920	$17		204			948	4,647	125
$4,000			4,000	28		208			936	4,700	34
$5,250			5,250	212	$18	273				4,747	96

[1] A woman with 3 minor children where State pays $2,004 to a family with no other income.

[2] Calculated according to the family assistance State supplementary formula, but assuming exercise of secretarial discretion to hold reduction rate to 67 percent, as authorized in sec. 452(b)(2).

[3] Federal income tax calculated on the basis of tax provisions in effect in 1972, assuming no surcharge.

[4] Current State tax schedule.

[5] Social security tax of 5.2 percent will be in effect Jan. 1, 1971.

[6] Arizona has no food stamp program, but has a surplus commodity program with an income eligibility ceiling of $3,072 for a family of 4 with earnings and $3,552 for a similar family with earnings. Not all eligible families participate in the commodities program. Such families' benefits and cumulative reduction rates would be lower.

[7] Arizona has no title XIX program.

[8] Public housing bonus is the public housing agency estimate of comparable private market rental ($1,680 yearly) minus amount of public housing rent paid. Calculated for 3-bedroom unit from data supplied by local housing authority, including any allowable deductions for employment costs and payroll deductions, but not including deductions for day-care costs, health-related expenses, earnings of minors, or any other deductions allowed. Maximum admission limit is $4,200 of countable income; for continued occupancy $5,250. These figures should be used with caution since the great share of AFDC recipients do not live in public housing, and hence would neither receive subsidized housing or face the high cumulative reduction rate. Precise figures unavailable for Phoenix, Ariz. of number of AFDC recipients living in public housing.

Combined Benefits and Reduction Rates Under Selected Income-Tested Programs for a 4-Person, Female-Headed Family in Wilmington, Delaware[1]

Earnings	FAP Benefit	State Supplement[2]	Total Money Income	Federal Income Tax[3]	State Income Tax[4]	Social Security Tax[5]	Food Stamp Bonus or Surplus Commodity Value[6]	Average Medical Vendor Payment per AFDC Family[7]	Public Housing Bonus[8]	Total Income: Money and In-Kind From All Sources	Cumulative Marginal Reduction Rate (Percent)
0	$1,600	$188	$1,788				$661	$437	$480	$3,366	[9]
$720	1,600	188	2,508			$37	661	437	540	4,109	72
$1,000	1,460	141	2,601			52	661	437	540	4,187	
(State breakeven) 1,850	1,035		2,885			96		437	540	3,766	150
$2,000	960		2,960			104		437	528	3,821	63
$3,000	460		3,460			156			432	3,736	108
$3,920 (FAP breakeven)			3,920	$17	$12	204			348	4,035	68
$4,000			4,000	28	13	208			342	4,093	18
$6,450			6,450	417	60	335				5,638	37

1 A woman with 3 minor children where State pays $1,788 for a family with no other income.

2 Same as table for Phoenix, Arizona, p. 475.

3 Same as table for Phoenix, Arizona, p. 475.

4 Same as table for Phoenix, Arizona, p. 475.

5 Same as table for Phoenix, Arizona, p. 475.

6 Delaware has no food stamp program but has a surplus commodity program with an income ceiling of $2,580 net income (earnings less mandatory payroll deductions). Not all eligible families participate in the commodities program. Such families' benefits and cumulative marginal rates would be lower.

7 Based on estimates of medical vendor payments, May 1969. In view of the seasonal variation in medical care costs, it was assumed that May 1969 represents 1/12 of the annual 1969 payments. Income eligibility is AFDC cutoff for AFDC recipients or $3,000 for medically indigent nonrecipient family of 4.

8 Public housing bonus is the public housing agency estimate of comparable private market rental ($1,560 yearly in city-leased housing) minus amount of public housing rent paid. Calculated for 3-bedroom unit from data supplied by local housing authority, including any allowable deductions for employment costs and payroll deductions, but not including deductions for day-care costs, health-related expenses, earnings of minors, or any other deductions allowed. Maximum admission limit is $4,800 of countable income; for continued occupancy $6,000. These figures should be used with caution since the great share of AFDC recipients do not live in public housing, and hence would neither receive subsidized housing or face the high cumulative reduction rate. For example, only 29 percent of AFDC recipients in Wilmington, Del. live in public housing.

9 The increase in the public housing benefit increases money income by 103 percent of earnings.

Combined Benefits and Reduction Rates Under Selected Income-Tested Programs for a 4-Person, Female-Headed Family in Chicago, Illinois[1]

Earnings	FAP Benefit[2]	State Supplement[3]	Total Money Income	Federal Income Tax[4]	State Income Tax[5]	Social Security Tax[5]	Food Stamp Bonus or Surplus Commodity Value[6]	Average Medical Vendor Payment per AFDC Family[7]	Public Housing Bonus[8]	Total Income: Money and In-Kind From All Sources	Cumulative Marginal Reduction Rate (Percent)
0	$1,600	$1,496	$3,096				$408	$789	$1,116	$5,409	
$720	1,600	1,496	3,816			$37	312	789	1,116	5,996	18
$1,000	1,460	1,449	3,909			52	312	789	1,116	6,074	72
$2,000	960	1,282	4,242			104	312	789	1,116	6,355	72
$3,000	460	1,115	4,575			156	228	789	1,116	6,612	74
$3,920 (FAP breakeven)		972	4,892	$17		204	288	789	1,116	6,864	73
$4,000		908	4,908	28		208	288	789	1,116	6,865	99
$5,000		241	5,241	172	$11	260	288	789	1,116	6,991	87
$5,362 (State breakeven)			5,362	230	14	279	288	789	1,116	5,955	387

1 A woman with 3 minor children where State pays $3,096 for a family of 4 with no other income.

2 Same as table for Phoenix, Arizona, p. 475.

3 Same as table for Phoenix, Arizona, p. 475.

4 Same as table for Phoenix, Arizona, p. 475.

5 Same as table for Phoenix, Arizona, p. 475.

6 Food stamp bonus is the difference between the value of the coupon allotment and the purchase price of the coupons. Based on current food stamp schedules, with mandatory payroll deductions subtracted from gross income in determining purchase price and eligibility. Income eligibility limit is AFDC breakeven for AFDC recipients or $3,600 net for nonrecipients. Not all eligible families participate in the stamp program. Such families would have lower benefits and cumulative reduction rates.

7 Based on estimates of medical vendor payments, May 1969. Income eligibility ceiling is AFDC breakeven for AFDC recipients or medically indigent nonrecipient family of 4.

8 Public housing bonus is the public housing agency estimate of comparable private market rental ($2,076 yearly) minus amount of public housing rent paid. Calculated for 3-bedroom unit from data supplied by local housing authority, including any allowable deductions for employment costs and payroll deductions, but not including deductions for day-care costs, health-related expenses, earnings of minors, or any other deductions allowed. Maximum admission limit is $6,000 of countable income; for continued occupancy above $8,400. Since continued occupancy at higher incomes for increased rent is permitted, no cutoff point for eligibility for public housing is shown in this table. These figures should be used with caution since the great share of AFDC recipients do not live in public housing, and hence would neither receive subsidized housing or face the high cumulative reduction rate. Approximately 18 percent of all AFDC recipients in Chicago, Ill. live in public housing.

Combined Benefits and Reduction Rates Under Selected Income-Tested
Programs for a 4-Person, Female-Headed Family in New York City[1]

Earnings	FAP Benefit	State Supplement[2]	Total Money Income	Federal Income Tax[3]	State Income Tax[4]	Social Security Tax[5]	Food Stamp Bonus or Surplus Commodity Value[6]	Average Medical Vendor Payment per AFDC Family[7]	Public Housing Bonus[8]	Total Income: Money and In-Kind From All Sources[9]	Cumulative Marginal Reduction Rate (Percent)
0	$1,600	$2,108	$3,708				$522	$1,153	$2,052	$7,435	
$720	1,600	2,108	4,428			$37	522	1,153	2,052	8,118	5
$1,000	1,460	2,061	4,521			52	522	1,153	2,052	8,196	72
$2,000	960	1,894	4,854			104	522	1,153	2,052	8,477	72
$3,000	460	1,727	5,187		$6	156	522	1,153	2,052	8,752	72
$3,920 (FAP breakeven)											
$4,000		1,574	5,494	$17	21	204	522	1,153	2,052	8,979	75
$5,000		1,520	5,520	28	26	208	522	1,153	2,052	8,985	92
$6,000		853	5,853	172	53	260	522	1,153	2,052	9,095	89
$6,279 (State breakeven)		186	6,186	336	80	312	522	1,153	2,052	9,185	91
			6,279	386	90	326	522	1,153	2,052	7,529	694

[1] A woman with 3 minor children where State pays $3,708 to a family with no other income. The standard in New York State was adjusted to include the rent as paid to a public housing authority ($101 a month) for a typical unit. Does not reflect increased standards as of May 1, 1970.

[2] Same as table for Phoenix, Arizona, p. 475.

[3] Same as table for Phoenix, Arizona, p. 475.

[4] Same as table for Phoenix, Arizona, p. 475.

[5] Same as table for Phoenix, Arizona, p. 475.

[6] New York City has a surplus commodity food program with an eligibility ceiling of AFDC break-even levels for AFDC recipients or $4,200 for other low-income families of 4.

[7] Based on estimates of medical vendor payments, May 1969. Income eligibility ceiling is AFDC breakeven for AFDC recipients or $5,300 for medically indigent nonrecipient family of 4.

[8] Public housing bonus is the public housing agency estimate of comparable private market rental ($3,264 yearly in city-aided apartments) minus amount of public housing rent paid. Calculated for 3-bedroom unit from data supplied by local housing authority, including any allowable deductions for employment costs and payroll deductions, but not including deductions for day-care costs, health-related expenses, earnings of minors, or any other deductions allowed. Maximum admission limit is $6,900 of countable income; for continued occupancy $8,800. These figures should be used with caution since the great share of AFDC recipients do not live in public housing, and hence would neither receive subsidized housing or face the high cumulative reduction rate. Approximately 8 percent of all AFDC recipients in New York City live in public housing.

Combined Benefits and Reduction Rates Under Selected Income-Tested Programs for a 7-Person, Female-Headed Family in New York City[1]

Earnings	FAP Benefit	State Supplement[2]	Total Money Income	Federal Income Tax[3]	State Income Tax[4]	Social Security Tax[5]	Food Stamp Bonus or Surplus Commodity Value[6]	Average Medical Vendor Payment per AFDC Family[7]	Public Housing Bonus[8]	Total Income: Money and In-Kind From All Sources	Cumulative Marginal Reduction Rate (Percent)
0	$2,500	$2,792	$5,292				$846	$2,017	$2,052	$10,207	
$720	2,500	2,792	6,012			$ 37	846	2,017	2,052	10,890	18
$1,000	2,360	2,745	6,105			52	846	2,017	2,052	10,968	77
$2,000	1,860	2,578	6,438			104	846	2,017	2,052	11,249	77
$3,000	1,360	2,411	6,771			156	846	2,017	2,052	11,530	77
$4,000	860	2,244	7,104			208	846	2,017	2,052	11,811	77
$5,000	360	2,077	7,437		$ 6	260	846	2,017	2,052	12,086	72
$5,720 (FAP breakeven)		1,957	7,677		19	297	846	2,017	2,052	12,276	74
$6,000		1,770	7,770	$ 14	26	312	846	2,017	2,052	12,336	80
$7,000		1,103	8,103	156	53	364	846	2,017	2,052	12,445	89
$8,000		436	8,436	297	80	406	846	2,017	2,052	12,568	88
$8,658 (State breakeven)			8,658	398	104	406			2,052	9,802	520

[1] A woman with 6 minor children where State pays $5,292 to a family with no other income.

[2-5] Same as table for Phoenix, Arizona, p. 475.

[6] Food stamp bonus is the difference between the value of the coupon allotment and the purchase price of the coupons. Based on current food stamp schedules, with mandatory payroll deductions subtracted from gross income in determining purchase price and eligibility. Income eligibility limit is AFDC breakeven for AFDC recipients or $6,060 net income for nonrecipients. Not all eligible families participate in the food stamp program. Such families would have lower benefits and cumulative reduction rates.

[6] New York City has a surplus commodity food program with an eligibility ceiling of AFDC breakeven levels for AFDC recipients or $6,060 for other low income families of 7.

[7] Based on estimates of medical vendor payments, May 1969. Income eligibility ceiling is AFDC breakeven for AFDC recipients or $7,200 for medically indigent nonrecipient families of 4.

[8] Public housing bonus is the public housing agency estimate of comparable private market rental ($3,264 yearly) minus amount of public housing rent paid. Calculated for 3-bedroom unit from data supplied by local housing authority, including any allowable deductions for employment costs and payroll deductions, but not including deductions for day-care costs, health-related expenses, earnings of minors or any other deduction allowed. Maximum admission limit is $8,084 of countable income; for continued occupancy $8,800 for federally aided projects. These figures should be used with caution since the great share of AFDC recipients do not live in public housing, and hence would neither receive subsidized housing or face the high cumulative reduction rate. Approximately 8 percent of all AFDC recipients in New York City live in public housing.

Selected Income-Tested Programs for a 4-Person, Female-Headed Family" in Phoenix, Arizona; Wilmington, Delaware; Chicago, Illinois; and New York, New York. The effects of Federal and state taxes, Social Security tax, food-stamp or commodity benefits, Medicaid payments, and the public housing "subsidy" were calculated on total family income under a system in which FAP payments and state supplementation were available. The tables "demonstrated" that after the $720 "disregard" was reached, earnings for female-headed families in the hypothesized circumstances were soon subjected to near confiscatory marginal rates of taxation, or worse.

In Phoenix $1,000 in earnings produced a total income "money and in-kind from all sources" of $4,382. Earnings of $3,140 netted $4,840; earnings of $5,250 netted $4,747. A rise in earnings of $2,110 resulted in a drop in income of $93.

In Wilmington earnings of $720 produced income of $4,109. Earnings of $4,000 netted $4,093. A rise in earnings of $3,280 resulted in a drop in income of $16.

In Chicago zero earnings produced income of $5,409. Earnings of $5,362 netted $5,955. A rise in earnings of $5,362 resulted in a rise in income of $546.

In New York City zero earnings produced income of $7,435. Earnings of $6,000 netted $9,185. Earnings of $6,279 netted $7,529. A rise in earnings of $279 resulted in a drop in income of $1,656.

Tables were also constructed for 7-person female-headed families. In New York such a family with zero earnings had an income of $10,207. Earnings of $8,658 netted an income of $9,802.

In the image of game theory the tables were a form of threat analysis in worst-possible-case condition. This was the "worst" the situation could get. It assumed a welfare family was in public housing; the great majority were not: only 18 percent in Chicago; only 8 percent in New York. It assumed the family members were ill, hence the Medicaid payments. It involved the bluntest of notches, as with Medicaid, which typically ceased the moment the last dollar of AFDC aid was used up in the "30 — 1/3" formula. It dealt with notches over which the Federal government had no control, as in much public housing.

The tables distorted reality. HEW probably ought not to

have prepared them. But to have refused would have been to deny the Senate its role of oversight. Whatever the case, the tables were prepared, and revised, and revised again to the Senator's obvious pleasure. Williams's questioning was relentless. Patricelli bore the brunt of it manfully. He knew more about the intricacies of the legislation than anyone on the HEW team. But there was no way out.

> SENATOR WILLIAMS: . . . If they increase their earnings from $720 to $5,560 under this bill, they have a spendable income of $6,109, or $19 less than if they sit in a rocking chair earning only $720. Is that not correct?
> MR. PATRICELLI: That is correct. . . .
> SENATOR WILLIAMS: They are penalized $19 because they go out and earn $5,500. Is that correct?
> MR. PATRICELLI: That is correct.
> THE CHAIRMAN: . . . What possible logic is there to it?
> MR. PATRICELLI: There is none, Senator.

Probably without fully intending to do so, the committee reached a point where it was established that *no* bill could really meet its conditions.

> THE CHAIRMAN: What is the point of requiring the man to go to work if he's going to end up with less money? That is the point. Why do that?
> MR. PATRICELLI: We agree wholeheartedly. All we have been able to do in the Family Assistance Act is remove some of the notches. We have not been able to rewrite the commodity program, the Social Security program, the food-stamp, the Medicare program.

In fact, the Administration food-stamp proposal provided for a tapering-off process rather than a blunt notch. A proposal had also been made to set rents in federally assisted public housing as a percentage of income to avoid that "notch," and also to retain tenants who managed to raise their income. But these issues could not be dealt with in the Senate Finance Committee. If one bill had to deal with them all, there would be no bill.

Questioning the next morning was desultory. At 11:35 Long recessed the hearings to meet with Finch in executive session. He emerged with the announcement:

The Secretary of Health, Education, and Welfare has agreed to coordinate an effort among the executive departments concerned with income maintenance programs to devise an overall plan for welfare reform which will take account of benefits such as public housing, food stamps, etc., which are made available to low-income families. When this plan is submitted to the committee, it will be published. We will then proceed. . . .

The worst had come to pass. The welfare system was "exposed" for what it was widely supposed to be: a vast swindle in which work was penalized and dependency rewarded. Family Assistance was "exposed" as a proposal to increase the dimensions of the problem from some ten million welfare recipients to twenty-four million. There *was* such a case to be made. It was doubtless unfair to the vast proportion of recipients, but not unfair to all. But fairness had nothing to do with the matter. A system had been created—not, surely, by the recipients—which in certain circumstances rewarded behavior that the generality of the public would find unacceptable. An "advanced" element of opinion tended to find this attitude of the *public* unacceptable, but that was of little consequence. What mattered was the attitude of seventeen senators, most of whom shared the general view. The very intensity of public feeling on the subject made it difficult to oppose welfare reform, but when first the committee staff, and then the ranking Republican senator, succeeded in casting doubt on the assertion that Family Assistance *was* reform, the matter was lost.

A different committee might have produced a different outcome. Certainly, once seized of the issue, Ways and Means would never have sent the legislation back to the Administration. If the bill was to be revised, Ways and Means would have felt fully capable of doing the revision. In any event the committee's leadership would not have permitted the fate of the bill to linger on while other business was pressing. But the Senate Finance Committee was not bent to any such norm of prosaic, workmanlike persistence. The senators were individualists, and more than a normal quota were exhibitionists as well. At the expressive, symbolic level of politics they are hardly to be faulted, but there was lacking an eventual seriousness which is the mark of mature government. The older battles against the "welfare state," not the newer concern with welfare reform, were the real objectives of the conservatives on Senate Finance. Even Harris, a self-proclaimed populist, friend of the dirt farmer, the Indian, the black, the dispossessed everywhere, showed no real interest in getting a bill. To the contrary, he seized upon the discomfiture of the Administration witnesses as an opportunity to suggest dark doings in high places. Charging that the Administration had made "the most ill-prepared presentation" he had seen since coming to Congress, he told Finch:

. . . I will just be very frank with you. Rumors are circulating very strongly in this room today and yesterday that the Administration intends to abandon this bill in this committee and that the presentation has been lukewarm and confused purposely to sabotage the bill.

What true populist would not prefer an unimagined conspiracy to a guaranteed income? But the trouble went beyond personality. The Senate Finance Committee, as then constituted, simply was not capable of carrying out its assigned functions.

2. FAP Revised

The Administration was trapped. In retrospect this is clear. It could deal with those seeking to outbid FAP as a guaranteed income. That issue was definable, a matter of expenditure. Most congressmen, and in particular the leadership of Ways and Means, could be expected to side with the president against increasing the proposed base, and a persuasive case could be made for not doing so. Those seeking to outbid FAP as *welfare reform* were, however, in a much more advantageous position. To begin with, their strategy was not perceived. It had been taken for granted that conservatives would attack the $1,600 base as too high, or else concentrate on opposing *any* payments to the working poor. The thought had never occurred that Williams would all but ignore the guaranteed-income aspect of FAP and concentrate almost solely on the "abuses" of the existing system. In this he could expect support from other congressmen. Moreover, he could expect support from the proponents of

FAP. What responsible parent, as I put it in an address at the time, would earn an extra $1 if it meant $500 less in medical care for his children? No one could defend such practices. Yet, there was no politically viable solution. The system was in place and would stay in place until another set of influences—possibly a guaranteed income—obviated its need.

Nonetheless, accepting the challenge to their own competence, the Administration planners went to work on the issues raised in the brief Finance Committee hearings. A great deal was done in a very short while. As in the past, as difficulties were encountered the program became larger rather than otherwise. It *seemed* as if yet further advances in social policy, comparable in their way to the guaranteed income itself, were emerging from the process. It was a brief, but heady experience, not unlike the spring weeks of 1969. No one perceived that the new proposals would make no impact whatever. The congressional debate over FAP, which began on the issue of adopting a major forward movement of the welfare state, had been transformed into an argument as to whether a welfare state should have been started in the first place. When the Administration had first confronted the state of welfare there seemed two options: to tinker, or to go forward to a guaranteed income. There was, of course, always the third option: to go backward and abolish welfare altogether as a social contagion that manifestly induced undesirable behavior. Not a moment's thought was given to this option, and scarcely more to the question of "abuses" which raised it.* But now, by agreeing to attempt to perfect reform, the Administration would find itself advocating a great act of confidence in the social dividends to be had from generosity in the context of a detailed inquiry into the foolishness of it.

Just as seriously, the Administration advocates were taking punishment and would never again join the encounter with quite the same *elan*.

Robert L. Bartley has written of the Washington press corps that it has "real talent at reducing the great issues to

* In the 92nd Congress the Senate Finance Committee produced a bill, as a substitute for H.R. 1, which in effect did abolish the AFDC system, providing instead that jobs be made available and everyone be required to work. *The New York Times* described the measure as an "abomination," to no noticeable discomfort of the Finance Committee. *The New York Times*, June 26, 1972.

POLITICS OF A GUARANTEED INCOME | 485

matters of personality. Given, say, a new legislative proposal, its attentions turn instinctively to a range of questions including, will it pass? what effect will it have on the personal standing of A, B, and C? and on the presidential campaigns of X, Y, Z?"[6] This is more than a style of journalists. It derives from the politics of a capital in which power is systematically fractionated by the Constitution, and randomly diffused by a party system that exerts a minimum of discipline, such that majority coalitions in Congress are typically across rather than within the parties. In such circumstances personalities become a surrogate for ideas, and the rise and fall of the latter are typically reported in terms of the former. The *Washington Post* account of the Senate committee action described it as "a major defeat for the so-called liberal wing of the Nixon Administration—particularly Finch, Moynihan, and Shultz," who were credited with having persuaded the president and Ehrlichman to support the measure, "which many conservatives regard as socialistic."

This, within limits, was true. "So-called" was perhaps the highest degree of liberalism a member of the Nixon Cabinet* might be accorded by the liberal press, but within the Administration, and by all indications the Republican party organization as well, a fairly pronounced majority of the more senior persons had felt that in proposing Family Assistance the president had acted on doubtful advice which he would one day regret. It appeared that day had come. FAP had not been defeated; it had been humiliated. *Human Events* summed up the event as a "massive setback" for the proposal, and a "serious loss of prestige" to its sponsors within the Administration and the House of Representatives.

How come, it is now being asked, that neither Mills nor such White House architects of the plan as Daniel Moynihan could see the grave defects in the program, flaws which both liberal and conservative members of the Finance Committee saw instantly?

How come, *Human Events* continued, the Labor Department was paying the NWRO half a million dollars "to show able-bodied people how they can avoid going to work"? Senator

---

* I had been appointed a Counselor to the President and a member of the Cabinet in October, 1969.

Long's question, it felt, had not been answered, nor had a long list of comparably damning revelations been explained.

It appeared the "liberals" had been made fools of. From Sacramento, Governor Reagan suddenly attacked FAP as an expensive expansion of what was already a "costly and unworkable welfare system." He told a news conference, "This would put one out of every seven of our citizens on welfare." It would cost, he said, not an extra $4.4 billion, but as much as $15 billion. Reagan was almost certainly then, as a Gallup Poll showed him to be a year later, the first choice for president of Republican voters should Nixon not run again. The Finance Committee hearings enabled any who wished to do so to identify the president's proposal of "welfare reform" as a near-mindless welfare expansion. The fortunes of those originally identified with the proposal accordingly declined and the whispering that the president wasn't really for the bill intensified. A subtle loss of momentum took place.

There was no preventing this. It was in the nature of the charge to be unanswerable without giving up the game. The planners of FAP knew well enough that the AFDC program could be abused by recipients as well as by administrators. They had nonetheless decided that the existing system, for all its absurdities, was best left largely undisturbed while the new influences gradually took hold. This was not an oversight: it was a calculation, not unlike that made with respect to continuing the Model Cities program. The existing arrangements were a form of rights-in-being. To disturb them—to withdraw them—without simultaneously providing a manifestly preferable arrangement was to arouse just the kind of turmoil and mistrust the Administration hoped to diminish. The transformation, when it came, would be a calculus of millions of individual choices. The art of government would be to bring it about without forcing it.

British politics are more amenable to such strategies. When the time comes, as repeatedly it does, that the failure of a given line of policy becomes unmistakable it is usually possible for a British government to reverse itself, or its predecessor, without too grisly an exhumation of guilt. The Administration and the Ways and Means Committee hoped, in effect, for the same silent reconciliation with the past. These hopes were lost in a sudden, vengeful onslaught of fundamentalist hostility to what the welfare state had become.

The *Washington Post* was almost certainly correct in the judgment that "perhaps more than any other man" Senator Williams was responsible for the defeat of Family Assistance, having led a campaign, "and brilliantly so," of like-minded Republicans and Democrats to keep it off the floor of the Senate. But advantages fell to him that could not have been anticipated.

Finch had spent himself in this and a dozen struggles, harried from left and right. The end was now at hand. Rather as the vice-president had been able to forecast liberal reaction to FAP, both Finch and the president had anticipated the likely fate of a liberal Republican in HEW. The president had urged him to become his Attorney General instead, foretelling a terrible time with the Democratic bureaucracy of HEW and its often punishing ideological attachments. Finch had nonetheless decided to go where he felt he was most needed: the country *did* look to be coming apart at the end of 1968, and HEW seemed to be a place where a "determined broker," in Finch's terms, might put some things back together. He had said at the time that the point would probably come when he would have been used up, and it came sooner than even he had anticipated. On May 18 just before he was scheduled to meet a group of angry HEW civil servants dissatisfied with the Administration's policies toward minorities, he collapsed. On June 6 it was announced he would come to the White House as a counselor to the president, and would be succeeded at HEW by Elliot L. Richardson of Massachusetts, then Under Secretary of State. Richardson was a liberal Republican with a background in state government and party politics not unlike Finch's. His interest in welfare problems was established well before he came to Washington, and he assumed the Family Assistance brief with energy, competence, and complete conviction. He was soon a master of the subject. But it was too late: the Administration had entered its time of troubles.

On April 30, the second of the three days of Finance Committee hearings, the president announced the United States' "incursion" into Cambodia. The war in Asia, which, in the face of the Nixon Doctrine and the steady withdrawal of American troops, had greatly receded as a political issue, suddenly rose up and bid fair to consume the Nixon presidency, as it had done that of Johnson. Meeting with the Cabinet and congressional leaders before his television address, the president announced his decision in a voice and manner that made clear he expected little support. That day a senior Republican senator had told him the decision would mean he would be a one-term president. He was prepared, he said, to accept that price. Across the land there was an unprecedented rising of critics determined to exact it. The first nationwide strike of colleges and universities began. Students were killed by National Guard troops at Kent State University in Ohio. Violent talk and violent acts once more dominated domestic politics.

The president's address, which ought to have communicated limited purposes, did just the opposite. It was as if the 1960s had not occurred. Whatever faith he had in the military and intelligence bureaucracies upon whose advice he acted, no such confidence remained among the educated classes of the Nation. Nor was there much of such confidence within his own Administration. If there were such a thing as a Cabinet vote, a vote on April 30 could well have gone against the decision.

A persistent theme of Vietnam criticism was that the war absorbed resources and energies in government that otherwise would have been available and—a leap in conjecture—would have been used to resolve social problems at home. The evidence for this contention is mixed. As already noted, to the extent the war created full employment it was an incomparable weapon for fighting poverty, and to the degree it made demands on all citizens it was a powerful inducement for a democratic government to be concerned about inequality. There are, however, two senses in which the resources-diverted argument has validity.

First, the war brought on an ever-mounting level of political militancy, and varying levels of internal political violence. Urban rioting had consumed the domestic energies of the Johnson Administration in its last phase. (When the Nixon staff took over in the White House it was presented with pads of forms to be used for calling out the National Guard. Blank spaces were provided for date, time, and place.) A year later urban explosions most often occurred in well-to-do neighborhoods where young nihilists were learning to make bombs, but this too could absorb the energies of government. In the summer of 1970, for example, the White House staff was near to preoccupied with the doings of the Commission on Campus Unrest, headed by former governor William W. Scranton of Pennsylvania, which had been appointed in the aftermath of Cambodia. This meant energy diverted from other subjects, including problems of poverty and proposals such as Family Assistance, which had quite absorbed the Administration when it first took office.

Second, groups outside the Administration that might have been looked to for support of initiatives such as Family Assistance were now once again preoccupied with the war, and were almost totally in opposition to the president. Further, with the Cambodian incursion the Democratic party came to life. Of a sudden it seemed possible that Nixon could be beaten in 1972. Six months later it would be widely held by journalists and politicians in Washington that it was impossible for him *not* to be beaten. Such opinions are subject to change, and in time this would change too, but it grew if anything stronger as 1970 and the 91st Congress progressed. Democratic candidacies began to take shape in the Senate. By mid-1971 one out of every six Democratic senators was an announced or potential candidate to run against Nixon for the presidency. The atmosphere of opposition took hold quickly. Moreover, the presidential Democrats ranged from liberal to left on domestic issues at this time. Family Assistance was an achievement any of these Democrats might have dreamed of for his own presidency: "the most important domestic legislation since the era of Franklin D. Roosevelt." For the political heirs of Roosevelt to preside over its enactment was altogether fitting. A reluctance inevitably arose to let history record that it had happened under Nixon's brief incumbency.

Dispositions varied. Senator Edward M. Kennedy, as Majority Whip, supported the legislation throughout. Senator Edmund S. Muskie fairly early endorsed the legislation in principle, but came to have unresolvable objections to the work requirement. This, too, was part of the changed atmosphere. Most of these men did not trust Nixon; few liked him. Had it been assumed he would be president through most of the 1970s, there would have been a case for accepting his bill, however imperfect. The prospect now arose that his time was all but half passed. In such circumstances a prospective Democratic presidential candidate might in good faith conclude it was best to wait and do the job decently. It was not in the nature of political men to dwell overmuch on the possibility that a liberal or left government in office might be utterly powerless to bring off any such achievement. There is little success in politics; most men are broken by it. But those are not the expectations with which the battles are joined.

On the same Friday that Long recessed the hearings on Family Assistance, the president appointed and announced a special committee to revise the measure in the aftermath of the Senate action. The group set to work in good spirits, with no feeling of restraint. At the close of the second day of Finance Committee hearings, Patricelli had prepared a memorandum describing the four "notches" that had to be dealt with: Medicaid, food stamps, public housing, and the AFDC-U program. Each was dealt with in turn, and as had been the case in the first round of planning, the more the issue was looked into, the broader the proposal became, and the more costly.

On June 10 the president announced the revised Family Assistance proposal. The revisions began, John Osborne wrote in the *New Republic,* with "the nation's first federally subsidized system of health insurance for the poor. . . ." FHIP—the Family Health Insurance Program—joined FAP in the acronymic jargon of the capital.

The history of Medicaid had been almost a saga of welfare mindlessness. As Title XIX it accompanied Medicare into the Social Security Act in the rush of legislation that followed the presidential and congressional elections of 1964. Medicare—health insurance for the aged—had been debated nearly two decades. It was a symmetrical addition to the general social-insurance system established thirty years earlier. So in its way was Medicaid. The one enhanced the security of the aged, and was the subject of great attention. The other added to the incentives of family dependency, and was hardly noticed at the time. The original Social Security program had done both these things: the introduction of medical-care payments a generation later did so as well.

Just as Old Age Assistance, and Aid to Dependent Children—categorical programs—accompanied the original Social Security provisions as more or less interim measures for persons not yet covered by Social Security insurance, Medicaid provided, at state option, noncontributory health-care payments—hospital and nursing-home services, physicians' services, dental care, prescribed drugs, and the like—to certain *categories* of the poor who were without insurance. The Federal government shared the cost, according to familiar complex formulae having to do with the fiscal capacity of the state and the need of the state's population. The Federal contribution in different states ranged from about 40 percent to 82 percent, with an average of 51 percent. As of the time of the FAP revision, all states but Arizona and Alaska had opted to participate in the principal option of Medicaid, coverage of all public-assistance recipients, that is to say all persons eligible for the four categorical public assistance programs: aid to the aged, the blind, the permanently and totally disabled, and families with dependent children. Twenty-eight states had also extended coverage to the "medically needy," defined as "categorically related" persons whose circumstances —as for example being blind—would make them eligible for one of the four categorical aid programs, save that their income exceeded the public-assistance levels. The Federal government would match benefits given to such persons whose income after medical costs did not exceed 133 1/3 percent of the state payment level. Seventeen states had exercised a third option to provide care for the *children* of the working poor, defined as families that did not qualify for cash assistance under the categorical programs, but whose income was less than 133 1/3 percent of the amount paid an AFDC family of comparable size, or whose income after medical expenses was below that level.

The Medicaid legislation was signed by President Johnson July 30, 1965. In Fiscal Year 1969 the total program cost was $4.1 billion. Nothing near that amount had been foreseen by Congress. The Federal share was $2.1 billion, as against $1.7 billion allocated to AFDC payments. Almost half (46.3 percent) of all Medicaid recipients were members of AFDC families.

A range of indictments may be directed against Medicaid. It poured demand into a market where little provision had been made to increase supply. By 1969 the informal judgment of Bureau of the Budget examiners was that half the cost of the program was being consumed in inflated prices.* It took a re-

* National expenditures for personal health care nearly tripled between 1960 and 1970. Price increases accounted for 43.9 percent of this rise.

gionally imbalanced system of medical care and, because of the extensive state options, did little to redress the imbalance, and may have contributed further to it. Of $4.1 billion spent in calendar 1968, New York alone spent more than a fourth. Relative to population, the ten states with the highest expenditure per population were all Northern or Western (California) save only for Oklahoma. By 1965 such tendencies were well enough established to warrant greater concern than either HEW or Congress showed. Was the South to become *yet* further behind?

But the prime charge to be made against Medicaid is that it considerably enhanced the advantages of dependency. The "rewards" to the female-headed poor or near-poor family were sharply increased, especially where that family was dependent on public assistance. The cost of moving out of dependency was accordingly also sharply increased. The low-income male-headed family received some benefits in seventeen states, but none whatever in the remainder. (New York State, in its role of confounding the argument of the income strategy, *did* provide Medicaid coverage for adults in low-income families. This was done without Federal contribution.) Once again the tendency of the South to slight its children in favor of its aged was abetted. In 1968 Louisiana led all the states in the rate of recipients of "medical vendor payments" among the aged. Simultaneously Louisiana had one of the lowest recorded proportions of child recipients.

FHIP was to Medicaid as FAP was to Aid to Families with Dependent Children. A background paper which accompanied the president's June 10 announcement described the advantages of the new proposal in now familiar terms. It would;

—cover all poor families with children, bringing equitable treatment for the working poor.
—require a modest contribution from participating families which will be scaled to increase with income so that there is no work disincentive "notch."
—provide a Federal floor of medical services nationwide which the states could supplement in a manner similar to their role under Family Assistance.

It was envisaged as providing a health-insurance policy that would cost about $500 in the open market to some five or six million families, a total of 25 to 30 million people. The premium schedule was to be graduated from zero for families with income between $0 and $1,600, to about $500 when family income reached the cutoff point of $5,620. Participation was compulsory up to the FAP cutoff point of $3,920, at which point the family contribution was estimated at $160. Medicaid would continue for the aged, blind, and disabled, but not for AFDC families.

The program was not worked out in finished detail. The president's statement described it as "the second legislative stage of the Administration's income strategy against poverty." It had been planned for introduction in 1971, and all that could be proposed in June of 1970 was that the FAP legislation include language requiring such a submission by February 15 of the following year. Still it was a clear commitment to a major principle. Osborne wrote:

How the enormous increase in the demand for medical services that would result is to be met is a problem the Administration leaves to future solution. That and many other questions are sure to be raised. But they are outweighed by the real significance of the proposal, which is that it puts the country on the way to the comprehensive national health care that should have been instituted long ago.

The food-stamp proposals also dealt with "notch" problems, while expanding the program. It was proposed to smooth out the stamp schedule "so that no work disincentive notch" remained. FAP recipients would be enabled to "check-off" on their application the amount of cash they wished applied to purchase stamps, and the cash and stamps (or a voucher for stamps) would be sent to them in one transaction. (It was assumed that a "check-off" system would considerably expand the use of stamps, and hence the cost of the program.) The administration of the food-stamp program was to be transferred to HEW. The commodity program was to be phased out, and wholly replaced by food stamps by the end of the first year of operation of FAP. Agriculture Secretary Hardin joined the press conference announcing the proposal, which would also require legislation by the next Congress. He noted that with twenty days to go the Administration pledge to have commodity or food-stamp programs in every county and independent city by July 1970 was near to being met. There had been 440 jurisdictions with no program a year earlier; the number was now reduced to 47.

In respect to public housing the June amendments simply called attention to the Administration's proposed Housing Act of 1970 under which a family in such quarters would pay as rent 20 percent of income under $3,500 and 25 percent thereafter. "As its income and rent increase, the housing subsidy declines to zero without any sudden termination of benefits or a work disincentive." The Administration had a theory—an income strategy— and was trying to apply it.

Finally, it was proposed to abolish the AFDC-U "notch" by abolishing that category of assistance, which accounted for 5 percent of AFDC cases. All male-headed families would be covered under the negative tax formula of FAP with no state supplementation. Henceforth "all male-headed families would be treated alike and always have an incentive to work more hours and earn more money." The alternative of extending state supplementary benefits to the working poor had been rejected as costing about an additional $1 billion.

The June 10 announcement also promised a proposal on "a reform of the social services program as a companion piece to the Family Assistance plan." This was sent to Congress June 18. It provided for the separation of federally supported social services from cash assistance, both in administration and eligibility determination. Any low-income family would be eligible, and participation wholly voluntary. Federal appropriations would be for a fixed amount, rather than being open-ended, and state governors would be given discretion in transferring funds from one category to another (the theme of decentralization). A sevenfold increase, from some $25 million to $175 million, was proposed for Federal foster-care and adoption programs. This was to correspond to the proposed increases in day care under FAP.

These were no small proposals. The themes of the president's original address were working their way through the government with a measure of analytic power. The social-services proposals were much influenced by Richard Nathan in the new Office of Management and Budget, but they were also the work of the bureaucracy. It had become possible, as it surely was necessary, to restore a measure of balance to the antiservices bias

of the Administration's early days. Services were necessary and
social workers were valuable. The art of administration was to
create conditions in which they could best function. The proposed reforms of "Individual and Family Services" called for a
truce of sorts, as suggested by a passage from the background
papers.

Present social services do not effectively fulfill the needs of their
clients:
  —social workers spend most of their efforts on the investigation
and paper work associated with eligibility for cash assistance, putting
services in direct competition with enforcement and serving neither
purpose well;
  —because they control the flow of welfare dollars to recipients,
social workers often seem to their clients to be snoopers or policemen
and cannot effectively perform a helping, service role;
  —the caseworker system has overemphasized counselling activities and underemphasized the provision of "hard" services such
as homemaker care when someone is sick, housing assistance, foster
care, and the like. . . .

If this is some distance from the simple faith of the 1962 amendments that casework could accomplish almost anything, it was
equally distant from the assumption that it could do nothing.
Social workers *could* "effectively perform a helping, service
role." The new legislation was designed to enable them to do
this. Right or wrong, it reflected a belief that there *was* such a
thing as effective social work, and that something had been
learned as to why this effectiveness had been thwarted in the
past.
  The requirement to eliminate "notches" also provided the
Administration with an opportunity to propose changes in the
FAP legislation itself along lines it was assumed would make it
more attractive to the Senate Finance Committee. A lengthy list
was proposed. The penalty for "Refusal to Register for or Accept
Employment or Training" was increased from $300 to $500. A
permanent "hold harmless" provision was included such that no
state would have to spend more on welfare than its estimated
projected costs under existing law. (This responded to generalized Southern fears about increasing the "welfare rolls.") The
discretion of the Secretary of HEW in administering the program

was more closely defined, again responding to Southern concerns. Small details were attended to. It was provided that benefits would be calculated using income *after* the payment of Federal income tax. "This change will result in a lower total reduction or marginal tax rate on earnings and increases work incentives."

A new cost estimate was submitted: $4.1 billion. The savings from elimination of AFDC-U were offset by an estimated increase of $400 million in food-stamp costs, for a net reduction of $300 million. Detailed data on eligibility by various categories, including a state-by-state breakdown, was provided. The South, sixteen states and the District of Columbia, would in 1971 contain just half the male-headed families receiving FAP payments, and just over one third the female-headed families, 49.5 percent and 35.8 percent respectively. The South would have 42.7 percent of all FAP families. A new estimate was presented of racial distribution: 61.4 percent of FAP families would be white, 38.6 percent nonwhite. The significance of family size in poverty became more explicit: 23 percent of FAP families would include seven or more members. Senator Williams's tables were reconstructed to reflect the new provisions, both including public housing, which was stated to be available to only 6 percent of FAP families nationwide, and excluding it. Either way, each of the four cities showed, as earnings increased, a smooth progression of total net money and in-kind income. No "notches."

The "committee print" of the material submitted in connection with the June 10 revisions came to 308 pages. In its way it is an indictment of the state of readiness with which the Administration had entered the hearings six weeks earlier. Questions were now answered which could have been answered earlier but were not. The Finance Committee had, after all, authorized both the Medicaid program and the WIN program. In both instances cost estimates and operating expectations had turned out to be very shaky. It was reasonable for the senators to want to know how the cost estimates for FAP had been made, to inquire as to the number of additional Medicaid recipients that would result from an increase in AFDC recipients in Southern states where higher payment levels would make more families eligible; to ask, at very least, just how many FAP recipients, state by state, were anticipated. These were normal issues for Senate Finance to raise in its appellate role. None was an issue of great substance—had there been such, Ways and Means would have become involved rather than being content with rough approximations—but the role of the senators was to be, or to appear to be, concerned.

When the hearings had begun on April 29 the Administration did not have "hard" answers to most of these questions. Administration witnesses, for example, knew well enough how the program costs had been estimated, and had reason to be proud of the procedure, but this was not something easily communicated to skeptical senators. By contrast, the June submissions began with a detailed account of "Costs and Caseloads under the Family Assistance Plan." A concise description was provided of the committee headed by the chairman of the Council of Economic Advisers, which had developed and agreed upon the final data, using and building on the estimating procedures developed by the President's Commission on Income Maintenance Programs, which in turn had used data contained in OEO's Survey of Economic Opportunity. It was reported that a one-percent change in unemployment rates would result in a $100-million change in FAP payments. The committee had pressed the Administration witnesses on this point. (FAP estimates were based on 3.5 percent unemployment, already a thing of the past.) An answer that 5.5 percent would only involve an extra $200 million in costs would have been considerably more reassuring than the we-will-get-that-information-for-you-Senator responses which had generally been given. (The hearings were recessed before Shultz, the upcoming witness, could appear. Unfortunately, most of the questions put to the Secretary of HEW were of a kind the Secretary of Labor was best equipped to answer.) The Administration had simply not anticipated the oversight style which the Senate Finance Committee would adopt in considering even an altogether new proposal.

Nonetheless, within forty days the Administration had provided answers, had revised its program to meet objections, and had outlined a major new program of a kind typically associated with the Democratic party, and now submitted to the Democratic Senate.* These actions could be expected to win FAP some

---

* This was not, however, a case of the president flatly reversing himself. During the 1968 campaign he had declared himself opposed to "a national compulsory health insurance program," although as with his statement that *"at*

friends, but also to lose some. The president's statement of June 10 concluded:

Nowhere has the failure of government been more tragically apparent in past years than in its efforts to help the poor. The 91st Congress has an historic but rapidly vanishing opportunity to reverse that record by enacting the Family Assistance Act of 1970. Let there be no mistake about this Administration's total commitment to passage of this legislative milestone this year.

That commitment ought not to have been doubted, but the Administration had lost the capacity to fulfill it.

3. Down to the Wire

Cambodia broke the Administration's stride. The June 10 announcements were made in the midst of a protracted civil crisis. Where earlier the spectacle of the Nixon Administration proposing a national compulsory health insurance scheme would have elicited interest, speculation, even awe, it now passed all but unnoticed. Once again the issue of the internal stability of the Republic had come forward in the most dramatic and unsettling manner. There was little time for anything else.

Even so, the outcome might have been different. The situation in the Senate was not hopeless, and the Administration was clearly willing to go to great lengths to be flexible. Had it been possible to organize the various publics that also supported the measure, it might have succeeded. This was the moment when the various publics tend to have their largest influence. The Senate was hesitant. A rush of public support could have forced a decision, and the decision, in those circumstances, would prob-

---

the present time I do not see a reasonable prospect that I will recommend —a guaranteed annual income or a negative income tax," his position on health insurance was hedged somewhat. It continued: "I want to see that every individual who needs medical care is able to get it. But I want it to be good medical care. That's why I want to keep the doctors free from government control as much as possible and oppose extension to a national compulsory health insurance program for everyone." FHIP could be reconciled with this position.

ably have been favorable. But no such surge of support took place, first because of the war, which greatly aroused the old distrust and hatred of the president, and because of the predicament Williams had created. After a point the war receded somewhat as an issue, but by this time the consequences of trying to respond to the conservative demand for welfare reform had become evident. Rights-in-being, as for example the AFDC-U program, were in fact scheduled to be abolished—not many, but enough to give substance to the claim that the measure was restrictive. (It had become restrictive with respect to *some* measures for *some* groups.) First the president lost friends for FAP, and then FAP on its own began to lose friends. Its enemies remained constant, its friends did not.

Donald A. Webster, Assistant to the Secretary of the Treasury, had been brought to the White House to keep track of the bill, and the White House now received regular reports of great intelligence and candor. The first certain sign of trouble was the failure of the Finance Committee to reschedule hearings. On June 29 Webster reported that the committee had met to discuss FAP, and in the words of the Chief Counsel, the senators "wouldn't even talk about it." Accordingly, resumption of hearings was "indefinite as to time." Congress was already talking of finishing its business and adjourning by Labor Day.

Senator Curtis had led the opposition to rescheduling hearings, insisting that nothing be done until HEW provided him with an alternative bill eliminating coverage of the working poor, and providing for a tax that would pay for the increased welfare costs that remained. Curtis, who had been floor manager for Barry M. Goldwater at the 1964 Republican National Convention, was appalled by the FAP initiative, and determined to see it fail. Webster's informants had told him that while some Democrats on the committee were very much for the legislation, "they would not mind seeing it fail, especially as a result of Republican opposition." The chairman was said to be in "mental turmoil," his mind "sowed with seeds of doubt" that FAP would correct the problems of the present system. Until there was Republican support for the bill on the committee, Webster continued, the Democrats would not move. It was urgent, he felt, that the president step in forcefully: "Anything short of this risks loss of the bill."

This asked something different of the president: his time, rather than simply his support. It was one thing to let his advisers work up a national health–insurance scheme and sent it to Congress with his approval. It was another for him personally to begin lobbying for a welfare bill in the midst of his first great military-diplomatic-political crisis, especially as he would be asking precisely those senators he could count on for support in Vietnam to change their minds about FAP. Later he did intervene personally, and even now he gave the subject some attention, but the timing of the dual crises was ruinous. So, equally, was the Republican membership of the committee. Williams and Curtis were firmly opposed. Only Bennett and Jack Miller of Iowa could be counted on to support FAP, and "with no great enthusiasm," reported Webster. Len B. Jordan of Idaho, Paul J. Fannin of Arizona, and Clifford P. Hansen of Wyoming were disturbed by the legislation, which they deemed fundamentally at odds with their "philosophical" principles. Once the legislation failed, any number of persons who had done nothing to help it had the grace to charge the president with having failed to do so. There is something to the charge: presidents are accountable: their legislation passes or it does not; their party supports them or it does not. But by July 1970 there simply was no prospect of any but the faintest support for Family Assistance from the Republican members of the Senate Finance Committee. (In matters of both lesser and greater importance to him, Nixon had asked senators for support and when refused hastened to say that he understood, that he, too, had been a senator.) In the meantime the few Republicans he *could* count on to support FAP were denouncing his Vietnam policy.

Hearings were at last scheduled to reconvene July 21. Once again the committee staff prepared an analysis of the Administration proposal. Even allowing an element of staff hostility, the 58-page booklet reflected the near total opposition of the committee members, and with fine impartiality provided ammunition for all opposition views. Chart 1 revealed that the number of "welfare recipients" in the first year of the revised law would be 24 million, unchanged from the original proposal. The number of aged, blind, and disabled would increase somewhat; the number of persons in families would go from some 7 million to 21 million. Chart 2 showed the impact of this increase on selected

In 16 States, more than 15% of the population will be on welfare under the Administration revision

12%	U.S. AVERAGE

35%	Mississippi
25%	Louisiana
24%	Kentucky
22%	Georgia
20%	New Mexico
19%	Alabama
19%	North Carolina
19%	Tennessee
19%	South Carolina
19%	Arkansas
18%	Colorado
17%	Indiana *
17%	South Dakota
16%	North Dakota
15%	West Virginia
15%	Maine

* NOTE: The Department of Health, Education and Welfare subsequently revised its estimate of the number of persons on welfare in Indiana under the Administration revision; under the new estimate, 6% of the Indiana population would be on welfare.

In 13 States, the welfare rolls will be more than tripled under the Administration revision

8.9 times as many persons on welfare	Indiana *
5.9 times	South Carolina
5.8 times	North Dakota
4.9 times	North Carolina
4.9 times	South Dakota
3.9 times	Virginia
3.8 times	Nebraska
3.8 times	Mississippi
3.6 times	Tennessee
3.2 times	Arkansas
3.2 times	Colorado
3.2 times	Texas
3.1 times	Georgia

2.3 times	U.S. AVERAGE

* NOTE: The Department of Health, Education and Welfare subsequently revised its estimate of the number of persons on welfare in Indiana under the Administration revision; under the new estimate, the welfare rolls would be increased 3.2 times.

states. Chart 3 showed these proportions as rates of increase. In Charts 2 and 3 a miscalculation by HEW concerning Indiana was let stand, but corrected in the small print. The suggestion that the Administration did not have its facts straight was a continuing theme in the hearings. Having demonstrated that welfare rolls would be swollen, the committee analysis *then* proceeded to show that *current* recipients would be denied benefits. In 23 states 450,000 persons in AFDC-U families would no longer be eligible for state supplementation. In 22 states welfare payments to certain AFDC families with income would be reduced or even cut off. Chart 7 showed this process in 11 states: 8 of these were also included in Chart 2, where the impending welfare inundation had been shown.

What was going on? Was there to be an explosion of welfare rights, or the abolition of welfare rights? A new and simple system of income maintenance, or a yet more irrational one? No straight answer seems possible. Had the planners of FAP been free of any restraint, a straight negative income-tax system could have been devised that would indeed have been simple. But they were forced to superimpose a new system on an old one and at points did not so much compound complexity as expose it. It was equally fatal.

Observe the "galloping supplement," a mystery of welfare practice which was to be "reformed" by the revised FAP, thereby bringing about the benefit reductions indicated in Chart 7. At this time there were 11 states that made cash assistance payments lower than their standard of need. In these states earnings were not subjected to the "30 & 1/3" formula until the combination of earnings and payments equaled the need standard. This was—again—a device for boosting recipient income within the confines of the AFDC system. The result was yet more complexity and variation. The FAP revision provided that the Secretary of HEW would set minimum state supplementation with reference to the single criterion of actual payment levels as of January 1970 for families with *no other income*. This would result in a lower state supplement for families *with* income. As a result, such families would be somewhat worse off under FAP than under AFDC. The revisions created a similar problem in 11 other states, which the staff paper also illustrated. Altogether 300,000 welfare families faced reductions in income.

Welfare Reduction or Cutoff in 22 States under Administration revision

11 States now pay a portion of unmet need

		Welfare payment to family of 4 with countable income of		
		$1,000	**$2,000**	**$2,400**
Alabama	H.R.16311	$ 616	$ 266	$ 126
	Admin. revision	600	0	0
Arizona	H.R.16311	1,512	822	547
	Admin. revision	1,208	208	0
Florida	H.R.16311	1,006	406	166
	Admin. revision	608	0	0
Kentucky	H.R.16311	1,097	232	
	Admin. revision	956	0	
Louisiana	H.R.16311	738	228	25
	Admin. revision	600	0	0
Mississippi	H.R.16311	600	235	115
	Admin. revision	600	0	0
Nevada	H.R.16311	1,521	1,321	1,241
	Admin. revision	716	0	0
New Mexico	H.R.16311	1,292	392	32
	Admin. revision	1,196	196	0
North Carolina	H.R.16311	1,120	320	
	Admin. revision	920	0	
South Carolina	H.R.16311	716	196	
	Admin. revision	600	0	
South Dakota	H.R.16311	2,367	1,417	1,037
	Admin. revision	2,312	1,312	912

The staff next revealed that the marginal rates on *low-income* earnings were higher under the revised FAP than either the original or the existing law. The trade-offs the Administration could not avoid in successive versions of Family Assistance are to be seen in these marginal rates of taxation. The original

Senate Finance Committee – Chart 9 (June 1970)

Diminished Incentive for Low-Income Work under the Administration revision

For family of 4 headed by a woman, the net value of each dollar if she moves from unemployment with no income to full-time work at the minimum wage

	Present Law	H.R.16311	Administration Revision
Phoenix, Ariz.	62¢	60¢	28¢
Wilmington, Del.	71¢	67¢	23¢
Chicago, Ill.	54¢	38¢	27¢
New York, N.Y.	60¢	44¢	30¢

(NOTE: value of public housing excluded)

proposal permitted sharp "notches" at "high" income levels. At a certain point for certain recipients the marginal rate of taxation exceeded 100%. An increase in earnings of one dollar resulted in a decrease in income of more than one dollar, as when a single increment of income made a recipient no longer eligible for Medicaid, or food stamps, or public housing. However, in this situation there were low marginal rates of taxation for recipients

with low incomes. *Their* extra dollar of income did not diminish
Medicaid or other benefits. As Patricelli told the resumed hearings, the necessary mathematical consequence of eliminating the
work disincentive of the "notches" at higher levels of income was
to flatten the curve and thereby raise marginal rates of taxation
at lower levels. HEW prepared graphs to illustrate this process in
Senator Williams's four cities. The principle can be illustrated in
simplified form.

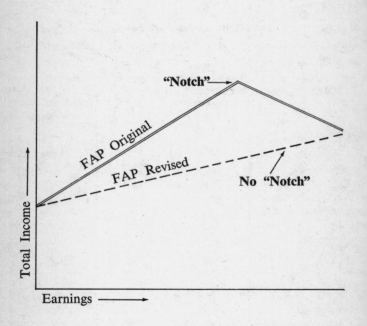

The staff paper set the tone of the resumed hearings: the
program was both too much and too little; too radical, too reactionary; too comprehensive, not comprehensive enough. In his
opening statement Long said, "In significant respects the new
plan is a worse bill—and a more costly bill than the measure
which passed the House." He cited three areas of "deterioration"—the elimination of AFDC-U, the reduction of state sup-

plements in 22 states (including Louisiana), and the expansion, as he judged it, of the area of Secretarial discretion in administration. He estimated the latter might add $1 billion to the cost. Harris declared himself "appalled" by the "regressive" changes. Both senators, however, agreed that the Senate should be given an opportunity to vote on welfare reform before Congress adjourned.

Richardson came to the hearings fresh, confident in his knowledge, and fixed in his purpose, which was to persuade the committee that the complexities, contradictions, and ambiguities they had been discovering were arguments *for* Family Assistance rather than against it. If the committee knew the half of it, he suggested, they would be even more astonished: that is what had moved the president to propose radical change.

I want to emphasize again that this Administration did not enter office determined to put into effect the specific kinds of welfare reforms which we have proposed. Neither the philosophy of the president nor our currently restricted budgetary situation would have permitted us to propose such revolutionary and expensive legislative initiatives unless we were convinced that they were inescapably necessary.

It was, he continued, "impossible to cure one defect in the system without in some cases, in most cases, raising some other problem." He came prepared to trade and to placate. Right off he proposed that families facing reduced benefits because of the elimination of the "gap filling disregard" be "grandfathered" for a period of two years from the effective date of the bill. During that period they would receive payments based on the old formula. New families coming into the system would receive payments based on the new formula. As for the marginal rates of taxation at low-income levels, he pointed to the specific statement in the material prepared for the committee by HEW which explained that this was the necessary result of the changes the committee had requested for high-income levels.

It is far more a tradition in the Senate than in the House that the whole body be given a chance to pass on important measures. Had there been sufficient good will—had there been any good will—in the committee toward the legislation, or unambivalent support from the publics, Richardson's testimony and that of James D. Hodgson, the former Under Secretary of Labor who succeeded Shultz when the latter became director of the new Office of Management and Budget, would have provided the basis for some committee action to report a bill to the floor. But the good will was missing. Williams had seen that he could worry the bill to death, and proceeded. Up went the charts; down went the charts; on went the questioning. Under the House bill, he would point out, a "man" in Phoenix doubling his income from $3,000 to $6,000 would gain $592 in income. Under the revised bill he would gain only $510. No matter that the chart referred to a female-headed family, no matter that Patricelli pleaded, "The critical thing is that we are making progress." The committee had asked that the notches be removed; it now objected to the consequences of that removal.

Harris was equally adamant. His suspicions of the Administration were not to be overcome. He told Richardson:

[I]n every instance that you have mentioned . . . when you have made an effort to rationalize what is a very irrational system, and avoid these notches that apply, disincentives to work which presently exist, you have done it to the detriment of the recipient. He winds up being the victim of rationality.

Harris began to sense an issue. For the first time, with the abolition of the AFDC-U program, it could be charged without refutation that Family Assistance would deprive deserving persons of existing benefits. He waxed oratorical.

Mr. Secretary, you have said . . . that this only involves 90,000. That reminds me that Senator Richard Russell told me once that when he came to the Senate, the then Senator from my hometown, Thomas P. Gore, a blind man, was chairman of the Armed Services Committee; he said they had a meeting about benefits for the widows and orphans of those who had been killed in the Spanish-American War. Senator Russell said, "I was a rather young man, and I said, 'well, I don't know how you can call it a war. There were only 385 people killed in the whole engagement.' " And he said that Senator Gore looked at him, almost as if he could see him with his sightless eyes and said, "Son, for those 385 it was a hell of a war." I think that might be said for those 90,000 you are talking about. I don't think it is good to say, "Well, there are not very many of them." For those people, that is a very, very serious matter, as well as for those who are going to be in that position in the future.

Richardson let it be known that the 90,000 AFDC-U families could be "grandfathered" also, but to no effect. Liberals on the committee showed no interest whatever in the Family Health Insurance Plan, nor did conservatives, save Miller, who quizzed Richardson for a bit on the fee structure, but soon left off to state that both he and his fellow Iowans were concerned at the prospect of one fourth of the population of Kentucky being on welfare.

What Richardson got from Harris, Hodgson got from Long, whose implicit position it was that the WIN program had failed because the Department of Labor had not wanted it to succeed, and that the work incentives under FAP would fail for the same reason.

The hearings went on and still nothing happened. Or rather, something less than honorable happened. It is not unknown for congressional committees seeking to scrutinize the activities of the executive to end up instead trying to discredit it. Williams now moved in this direction, raising the question of whether the Administration had falsified evidence presented to Congress. It had not, but, as is frequently the case, the suspicion lingered, and the charge served its purpose.

The last Administration witnesses were not heard until August 18, when John O. Wilson, Assistant Director of OEO, reported on the New Jersey income–maintenance experiment. The "preliminary results" of the experiment, released February 18, 1970, had made the important statement that, "On the basis of these data, we can say that work effort did not decline for the group analyzed. . . . There is, in fact, a slight indication that the participants' overall work effort actually increased during the initial test period." At Williams's behest, the General Accounting Office had audited the OEO findings, which were actually the findings of contractors conducting the experiment. In June the GAO presented to the committee its "Preliminary Comments," in which it characterized the OEO conclusion as "premature." Between these two events an article had appeared in *The New York Times Magazine* recounting the findings, and stating the inquiry derived from an exchange in which I had told Wilson that FAP was in trouble, and that we should take the risk of breaking into the New Jersey data in the hope that it might support our case. "He got me so mad," Wilson told Fred J. Cook, the author of the article, "that I said, 'Damn it, I'll get some answers.'" Cook went on to state that the release of the preliminary data had had "a profound impact upon Congress," that the grumbling that the "Nixon Administration's income-maintenance plan was visionary and impractical virtually ceased," and that Mills thereupon threw his prestige behind it.[7]

(The actual sequence of events was as follows. On January 20 the staff of the Ways and Means Committee issued a "confidential committee report" on "Issues Involved in Provisions of H.R. 14713 Relating to Family Assistance Payments for the Working Poor." It challenged the assertion that AFDC led to family breakup or that FAP would reverse this trend. The document promptly appeared in *The New York Times* and caused a stir. At OEO Wilson prepared a draft "reply," sending me a copy. On January 29 I wrote back that his was "a valiant but unavailing effort." There *was* no hard evidence for our case, and we both knew it. He came to the White House, where I asked about the New Jersey experiment. He replied that its results, if any at that early stage, would only bear on the question of work effort. The meeting ended with no agreement whatever as to what Wilson would do. However, the discussion made him "mad" enough or interested enough to think of "breaking into" the New Jersey data. This turned out to be feasible. I was not told this was being done. The findings were presented to the Cabinet meeting of February 18, 1970. I was in the Southwest, did not attend, and to the best of my recollection did not even know the New Jersey data were on the agenda. In any event, the study was carried out without any participation by me. In a letter of July 23, 1971, to Professor Walter Williams of the University of Washington, Wilson states that I "was not even aware of our decision to examine preliminary data.")

Williams now confronted Wilson with the *Times* article and with the GAO auditors, who repeated their conclusions. The senator asked, "Is this a political report to justify a conclusion or do you think it is based on fact?" The preliminary findings had undergone further scrutiny since February, and OEO was unmoved in its conclusions, given that they were tentative and so described. The GAO had not found any tampering with the data, it had simply concluded—a professional point—that the conclusions were "premature." OEO had said they were "preliminary." Wilson replied to Williams, "If we had found 10-percent decline in work effort, that is what we would have stated. If there had been a 20-percent decline, we would have stated that." But the case was shaken simply in that it was challenged.* The chairman

* Williams continued to press the issue after the hearings, and in so doing offered yet another instance of the difficulties in the use of social-science information in the formulation of social policy. In mid-December two journalists uncomfortably close to the White House, Clark Mollenhoff and Richard Wilson, published reports, ostensibly given them by Senator Williams, that I had ordered the results of the New Jersey Graduated Work Incentive Experiment "rigged" to "make them appear favorable," and with these results had persuaded the president to propose Family Assistance.

Mollenhoff wrote:

New Jersey tests that were the basis for Nixon administration confidence in the family assistance plan were "rigged," Senator John J. Williams (Rep.-Del.) said Saturday.

He told *The Register* that the record of the Senate Finance Committee will demonstrate that White House Counselor Daniel Patrick Moynihan had a key role in "the rigging" of reports to make them appear favorable.

* * *

The Senate Finance Committee record shows the following:

Moynihan was put on notice by Dr. John Wilson, OEO research director, that the test period was too short and the data inadequate.

Moynihan directed that Dr. Wilson prepare the report, and under this pressure the report was prepared last February.

The White House staff used the OEO report to prepare charts to sell the family assistance program to President Nixon and to sell it to the House Ways and Means Committee.

* * *

Senator Williams said he is certain President Nixon had no knowledge of the maner in which Moynihan and the Department of Health, Education, and Welfare used the OEO tests to sell the family assistance plan.

Senator Williams said that he questioned Dr. Wilson and obtained verification that he had objected to using the data, but had given in.

(*Congressional Record,* December 15, 1970, p. E 10416. Congressman H. R. Gross, Republican of Iowa, introduced into the record the article which appeared in the Des Moines *Register*.)

Wilson's column was in the same vein.

According to Sen. John J. Williams (R-Del.), Moynihan simply rigged up a favorable report, on the basis of a New Jersey test, which purported went on to ask for an explanation of a newspaper report of a pamphlet "Know Your Welfare Rights" prepared by the Tulare County (California) Legal Services Association which advised readers: "If you don't want to work: There is no good reason why welfare can force you to work, no matter what your [social welfare] worker says."

Delay now became an open tactic of those opposed to FAP and time the greatest enemy of those who supported it. Ways and Means had taken its time with the bill, but had used it. The longer it had considered the measure, and the more changes it made, the more it became committed to the final product and the more acceptable that product became to the members of the House. The Senate Finance Committee, by contrast, was doing nothing. The longer it delayed, the more it seemed probable that the legislation would become lost amid end-of-session business; alternately, the longer it held the bill, the *less* it seemed likely that the final product would be acceptable, for Senate Finance was decidedly not an integrative institution. The bill, accordingly, was dying of inanition.

When the July Fourth weekend passed and the Senate committee still had not resumed hearings, an effort began within the Administration to arouse a measure of alarm among liberals. In a widely reported speech I forecast that if Family Assistance were not enacted by the 91st Congress it would not be enacted for a decade. There was some response. Leonard Woodcock, the new head of the United Automobile Workers, called to say he did not wish to be among those who merely watched this happen.

---

to show that recipients of income support payments show no increasing disinclination toward work.

*   *   *

On the basis of this report . . . President Nixon bought the family assistance idea.

*   *   *

Moynihan is being severely criticized in his numbered days in the Nixon administration for the alleged rigging. This conceivably could be Moynihan's most costly mistake.

The president, of course, proposed FAP in August 1969, while the New Jersey data became available six months later, and thus could have had little influence on the earlier event. The more important charge is rigging. The charge was a lie, but probably was believed. Experimentation in social policy is vulnerable to such charges, perhaps because the methodologies are still in a formative state.

A senior official of the United Community Fund called to state his concern at the "complete lack of support from the health and welfare agencies for Family Assistance." He suggested it was distrust of Nixon on the one hand and fear of the Chamber of Commerce on the other: he would do what he could. Tom Wicker of *The New York Times* declared that "the political imperative is still for the Democrats to move the family assistance plan out of the committee and into debate on the Senate floor, with or without the support of the Republican minority. . . ." If it languished much longer in the committee, he judged, it would be dead for 1970, "and no one can say when anything like it might get another chance." *The Progressive* took much the same view. Worth Bateman and Alice M. Rivlin wrote in the *Washington Post* that "liberal Democrats have been reluctant to embrace FAP because they apparently do not want to see the President winning points for welfare reform." They urged Democrats in Congress nonetheless to support the bill with a provision for a maximum 50 percent tax rate on earnings, which they estimated would cost $200 million in additional Federal expenditure, and $400 million in forgone state savings.

This was about the extent of the stirring. The idea of even sharing "points" with Nixon had become intolerable to many liberals. The publics could not be aroused. Few abandoned FAP outright, but it was no longer an enterprise touched with glory. The publics that might have been indomitable in their determination to see the measure through now, in general, lapsed into passivity: willing to see it happen, not willing to do much of anything to make it happen. This disinclination was strengthened when the NWRO emerged in open and determined opposition.

On July 25 its annual conference adopted a detailed resolution in opposition to the bill, which divined malevolent motive in every title, every amendment. Even the proposed Social Service Amendments came under attack, being revealed as a device whereby "states would be encouraged to put children under foster care and into adoption programs rather than provide emergency needs and other benefits to enhance family relationships." This line of argument responded to an understandable desire of the NWRO membership: benefits now. Other aspects of the attack on FAP responded to a different clientele, seeking to establish the theme of incipient Fascism under Nixon. The resolution declared:

> While this legislation would offer increased benefits for a few people in the South, some low income working people, and the recipients of Old Age Assistance, Aid to the Disabled and Blind, we must conclude that it is, on the whole, an act of political repression.

Later, an article in *Social Policy* by Wiley concluded, "The Nixon plan must be defeated."[8] This was strong language, and had its effect. It came to be perceived as something of a risk for a Washington liberal concerned with credentials in civil-rights circles to persist in support of FAP. When in doubt there was always the liberal editorial assurance that the $1,600 floor was "grossly inadequate."

Help—some worse than no help at all—came from various organizations, of governors, county executives, and mayors, when the Finance Committee began hearing public witnesses in late August. Governor Warren E. Hearnes, a Democrat of Missouri, representing the National Governors' Conference, testified that H.R. 16311 was "a step toward the position supported by the Governors. However, it is not as positive as we would like to see. . . ." They would have liked to see "full Federal financing and full Federal direction." Hearnes offered the comment that the House might have moved a "little quickly," and urged the Senate to "give a great deal of time and study before [the legislation] . . . is finally enacted into law." Such an endorsement on September 10 (the last day of hearings) with election campaigns already under way was the equivalent of asking that the bill be put over to the next Congress. The National Association of Counties, represented by Bernard Hillenbrand and a group of officials, was more positive. They proposed an end to the two-tier system of welfare payments, and had other concerns, but basically supported FAP.

The most vigorous endorsement, however, came from Carl B. Stokes, Democratic mayor of Cleveland, representing the National League of Cities and the U.S. Conference of Mayors. Putting aside his prepared text he asked, in effect, what in the hell was going on.

Mr. Chairman, about two and a half years ago, in June of 1968, when I was privileged to attend my first conference of the U.S. Conference of Mayors, I introduced a resolution which was subsequently adopted that provided for a national minimum assistance program for families coupled with a public services jobs program in the amount of some $1 billion together with the necessary social services.

That resolution, which was adopted by the Conference of Mayors, was subsequently reaffirmed by them in 1969 and 1970, and the National League of Cities has itself endorsed the proposal and called upon this Nation, this Congress, if you would, to initiate this plan.

This idea, obviously, did not originate with me. In fact, it has been in the Democratic Party record for over 10 years. However, so far as I know, no Democratic President ever introduced this plan for the consideration of Congress, for the benefit of our Nation.

Interestingly enough, a Republican President, Mr. Nixon, did introduce it, and it is now pending before this Congress. I say interestingly, because I am a Democrat, and I never would have thought Mr. Nixon would introduce what is essentially a Democratic proposal. And yet, I find a Congress that is heavily composed of Democrats for whom this has been a policy position for many years, and of Republicans whose leader proposed the program, apparently having some problem in the enactment and the adoption of the program.

Now, we pay tribute here, of course, to the distinguished House of Representatives which, under the leadership of the chairman of the House Ways and Means Committee, did pass this bill and send it to the Senate, where it is now being considered, and I hope favorably, by this committee, and that in very short order it is going to be adopted for our Nation.

* * *

Now, I do not know how many more bombings we need, I do not know how many policemen we need to have shot, I do not know how many more police stations we need to have shot at, I do not know how many more babies need to die in the first year of their birth, I do not know how many more functional illiterates we need to cultivate within the borders of our cities, I do not know how long we are going to continue to subsidize the decline and deterioration of the great centers of our Nation that have spawned a civilization and a culture and an economy unmatched by any in the history of mankind, before we turn our attention to some of the basics, one of which is standing here before this committee.

Stokes had a story to tell: He was mayor of the eighth largest city in the Nation. He paid taxes on $40,000 a year in income and $100,000 in property. His brother was a member of Congress. His mother resided in Shaker Heights, "one of the most exclusive suburbs in the United States." His son attended "one of the most exclusive private schools in the United States . . . a feeder school for Yale University." But from the age of two, when his father died, until seventeen, he had been on welfare. He had dropped out of high school. "Fortunately, the Army came along, and following my service in the Army, because of a Federal subsidy program, the GI Bill of Rights, and some good discipline that I got both from my mother and from the Army, I returned to school and was able to go to college." He was not ashamed of subsidy and not afraid of work. "The League of Cities and Conference of Mayors," he told Long, "endorse unequivocally the mandatory work component recognizing mothers of young children as an exception." An exchange with Ribicoff suggests how a subtle political imagination could beat the work issue *by joining it.*

SENATOR RIBICOFF: . . . [D]o you think these people could be used to make Cleveland a little more beautiful and cleaner?

MAYOR STOKES: Just cleaning up, just basic housekeeping?

SENATOR RIBICOFF: Just basic housekeeping.

MAYOR STOKES: Unquestionably. . . .

SENATOR RIBICOFF: . . . There is nothing disgraceful for a person to be a white wing.

MAYOR STOKES: . . . After all, white wing jobs used to be jobs, some people, when times were much harder, worked awfully hard and used every kind of political device to get, because we do have to have people to clean up debris. There are people who just cannot be an engineer.

SENATOR RIBICOFF: That is right.

MAYOR STOKES: There are people who have to be barbers and there are people who have to be laborers.

SENATOR RIBICOFF: Even today people sweep up city hall, right? . . .

MAYOR STOKES: Most of the time.

The exchange harked back to one between Ribicoff and Mayor Lindsay, who on August 24 had been the first public witness before the committee. The senator had asked about the prospect of using welfare recipients to clean up New York, which had become, he said, "without question, one of the filthiest cities anywhere." Lindsay was understandably defensive. Ribicoff told of an early walk along Fifth Avenue. The mayor, coming from the world of the well to do, countered that the poor had neighborhoods of their own to clean, and spoke of Model Cities programs. Stokes, coming from the world of the poor, was not required to make this response. Ribicoff asked Lindsay the number of able-bodied men and women on welfare in the city. Commissioner Ginsberg said there were 14,000 men. The number of women, please, said the senator. "160,000 to 165,000 mothers," replied the commissioner. "14,000 men and 100,000 women . . . could make New York sparkle," said the senator. ". . . How much training do you have to have," he asked, "to have a stick, a broomstick, with a spike in it to pick up a piece of paper." The mayor invited him to New York, "[t]o see the sanitation effort being made by people in those three poor areas."*

Lindsay's testimony was subtly but devastatingly damaging. He made clear, as did other witnesses in much the same position, that the prospects for the passage of FAP were not good enough to warrant taking any risks with the good opinion of the liberal audience and the militant blacks to whom he looked for support in other matters. Stokes wanted a bill and to get one was willing to concede a little to senatorial virtuousness. But the ship was foundering, and to more sophisticated minds the order of the day was *sauve qui peut.*

The Ribicoff-Lindsay colloquy prompted a long lead editorial in the *Washington Post,* one in a series written by Meg Greenfield that was to keep track of the legislation for the rest of the year with dispassion, intellect, and a considerable capacity for identifying motive. Lindsay had found Ribicoff's work pro-

*One year and two days later a *New York Times* headline announced "Employable Welfare Recipients Put to Work Cleaning up Parks." Some 30,000 to 50,000 men would be going to work, reported Murray Schumach, "with rakes, shovels, brooms and pointed sticks—known as 'stabbers,'" clearing litter and doing other municipal chores. They were part of "a small army of welfare recipients who under state law are being assigned to public works." This was one of the series of "welfare reforms" imposed by the 1971 New York State Legislature.

posal reminiscent of the "dark ages." The *Post* was not much impressed, and went on to say of Ribicoff that "among the liberal Democrats on the Finance Committee which is holding the welfare bill prisoner he has uniquely involved himself in a serious effort to find some ideological middle ground that will permit the bill to be reported out." This now became the central issue of tactics on all of the many sides of the issue: would the Senate be permitted to vote? On September 2, one of the three journalists best informed on the subject gave the White House a private count of sixty votes for FAP. The varied opponents of the bill obviously had much the same count. They would lose a vote on the floor, and had also to fear that if a Social Security bill went to the floor FAP could be added as an amendment. The *Post* asked for a vote.

[T]he administration is trapped in its efforts to get the bill out of Senate committee between the hostility of numerous Republican members and the apathy of the Democrats. Each prospective concession to one side makes the bill less palatable to the other. If there is anything, therefore, that is not needed at this time . . . it is the growing exchange of animus between liberal Democrats and the administration over whose fault the hangup is. . . . [T]he principal delayers of this bill in committee have been Democratic Chairman Long and Republican Senator John J. Williams. And it is equally true that by and large the Democrats have responded from the beginning on this bill by rock-throwing criticisms or plain indifference or the introduction of alternative measures that are beyond the wildest budgetary possibilities of the moment—or of the near future for that matter. And meanwhile this utterly important, innovative domestic measure is stuck in committee.

The *Post* asked that more senators of Ribicoff's persuasion interest themselves in the issue. The "middle" of the Senate supported the bill, but was not involved with it. If it were to become involved, there was still hope.

The *Post* was not altogether alone. *Life* carried a long editorial analyzing the obstacles to the bill. There was first the "vast welfare bureaucracy," 170,000 employees with a "built-in resistance to change." There were those Americans "who think stigma and humiliation should be the proper lot of those 'on welfare.' . . ." There was Senator Long referring to welfare mothers as "brood mares." There were the "welfare militants . . . convinced that a comfortable income for which they don't have to work is a moral 'right.' " (What, asked the editors, could be less "meaningful," more "dead-end" than the "passive use of an income provided at taxpayers' expense . . . ?") Then there was the president, who had so far made "scant" effort to persuade the seven Republicans on the Finance Committee to support his bill. A *Fortune* editorial concurred.

These were by way of warnings to the president, but they were more than that. It was no longer to be questioned that the Senate Committee on its own would not move the bill, and that the various publics would not seriously strive to make it do so. The only hope lay in direct presidential intervention, and this now occurred. Much as he had assumed control of the original debate over FAP within the Administration, he now took over tactical direction of the final effort to get it enacted.

The Cambodian storm had passed. The president was spending more of his time on domestic issues, thinking, too, of the November elections. He could not let himself be charged with having abandoned Family Assistance, and he did not want to do so. The strategy of denial was working better than might have been expected. Even persons who supported FAP got into the practice of suggesting that the president didn't: if the bill passed it would be their achievement, not his. In September 1970 John Gardner left the Urban Coalition to found Common Cause, a general-purpose citizens' lobby. It promptly took up the cause of Family Assistance, hoping to organize Senate liberals for a floor fight. Jack Moskowitz of Gardner's staff explained to the Washington *Evening Star:* "We're going on the assumption there is now a vacuum of administration leadership, and we have to assume the administration may make a deal to get the bill out of committee, and that this will produce a weaker bill than now exists." A member of Harris's staff told a reporter there was a widespread conviction that "the Administration will sell its soul just to get something out of committee." Thus, some liberals took the position that the Administration was indifferent to the bill, while others asserted it was so eager for *something* as to be willing to take *anything*. Either way the effect was to make support for FAP more a matter of individual choice, and less one of party or doctrinal imperative. In parliamentary imagery, the liberal whips were removed. Similarly, for conservatives, the more attention was concentrated on the president—what did he *really* think? what were his *real* objectives?—the less pressure there would be on the Finance Committee to do anything.

The president countered by trying to create a center bloc in the committee which would move the program. It was rather a lonely business. Not that many persons of influence within his own Administration were for the bill. Even at the beginning the Cabinet was divided and in the year that had passed, new issues—or diminished energy—weakened the commitments of those who had supported it. Not unexpectedly, the Republican party organization showed no great enthusiasm, nor did the minority leadership in Congress. Again, like many Democrats opposite, Republicans in the Senate were willing to have a bill, but increasingly less willing to do anything much to get one. Not unlike liberal Democrats, the typically conservative Senate Republicans found FAP disequilibrating, too.

At such moments the power of the presidency, to those close to events, appears almost institutionally inadequate to its tasks. Presidents nonetheless persist. In August Nixon began to lobby for Republican votes. He met with minority members of the Finance Committee. Bennett began to emerge as a supporter of legislation of some kind. Next the president made a large gesture toward Ribicoff. Even before Senate hearings had resumed, Webster had picked up the impression that the committee would probably end voting simply for FAP pilot projects. On July 8 the committee staff had itself been briefed by OEO representatives on similar experimental programs. During the hearings Long raised this possibility with Hodgson. "Before embarking on such a vast program," he inquired, ". . . it might be desirable to try it on an experimental basis. . . ." He cited the experience of Medicare; he suggested that alternative schemes might be tested. With no instructions, the Secretary of Labor replied that he felt this would be "temporizing," but the idea persisted. With Administration assistance, Ribicoff now produced an amendment which provided for a twelve-month period of "field testing" to begin January 1, 1971. This was not, strictly speaking, to be an experiment. The program would go into effect January 1, 1972, regardless. But it was a concession to those who foresaw administrative difficulties, while putting off the effective date of the program six months was suggestive of fiscal prudence. On August 28 the president announced from San Clemente that if the Senate accepted Ribicoff's amendment it would be acceptable to him. He emphasized his own support for FAP, listed the speeches he had made, and revealed that he had been having private conversations with committee members. He pleaded for a floor vote, for what he now described as one of the dozen or half dozen most important pieces of domestic legislation in the Nation's history.

We have made numerous proposals for modification in the plan to meet the objections of Committee members. But ultimately the Senate as a whole must be given the chance to work its will on this issue and this bill. I urge this great and conscientious Committee of the Congress to get down to the hard business of marking up a bill as expeditiously as possible.

Finch, Veneman, and I presented the statement to a press conference, evoking all the sense of urgency we could. The statement was the featured news that day from the Western White House and was received as an important presidential initiative, but it made no converts. The *Washington Post*'s story quoted Wiley as saying Nixon was "backing down . . . because he doesn't even want to spend $4.1 billion more for the poor."

Next, six members of the Finance Committee were invited to a State Dinner being given the president of Mexico by President Nixon in San Diego on September 3. An Air Force plane flew five senators, Long, Ribicoff, Byrd, Bennett, and Miller, and their wives, save Mrs. Ribicoff who was ill, from Washington to San Diego, where Senator Fannin joined them. On the morning of September 3, Marine helicopters took the party to San Clemente, where the senators met with the president while Mrs. Nixon showed the ladies the Western White House. As presidential attentions go the arrangements were not inconsiderable.

Four months earlier the event might have been formative; even now, in the ambience of military deference and splendor, of high diplomacy mixed with small courtesies, John Wayne and Mexican folk dancing, the senators found themselves asserting that of course a bill of some sort *had* to be reported out. By accepting the Ribicoff proposal for a pretest, the president had established that the Democrats might share the glory, if any. Ribicoff, at least, sensed the reciprocal reinforcement which the division of political power in Washington made possible at that moment. The night before leaving Washington he had told Long that no Democratic president could ever have proposed Family Assistance. Long seemed disposed to agree that an opportunity of a rare sort still existed.

It was now a year since the president had made his proposal, and he did not, in truth, have much to show for it. It had produced deep misgivings within his Administration and his party; the most open-minded response from his opposition resembled that of Metternich at the Congress of Vienna, who on learning of the death of the Russian Ambassador is said to have asked, "What can have been his motive?" Still the tone with which he sought the support of the six senators was remarkably like that in which the previous summer he had talked to his own staff about his decision. Historians may come to regard this compartmentalization of issues as a mark of his presidency. This, together with a quality the British journalist Peregrine Worsthorne was to describe as immunity to hate. He had expected no credit, and he had got none. This was about his assessment of liberal response. Actually he had got a fair amount of praise from liberals but this had been balanced by about an equal amount of abuse. In any event, it didn't affect him much. Three days before the San Clemente meeting Hyman Bookbinder had testified that the president's speech of August 1969 had led to "excitement, even euphoria," but "now, many months later, there is uncertainty, even despair." The president had been touched by the euphoria, but had got hold of himself quickly enough. From the first he knew that the decision on Family Assistance would be made by men who had been not the least euphoric in the aftermath of his address. He was now talking to them around the Cabinet table at San Clemente.

What he sought to convey was that he had been through the same travail they were experiencing and had nonetheless come down on the side of a powerful new initiative. FAP, he said, was a "controversial move, an unpredictable program." Anyone looking at it might well throw up his hands and conclude there were "too many risks." He no less than any other. "What convinced me," he said, "to take the risks was what was going on."

New York City: "an unanswerable argument for doing something." His options had been to tinker with the existing system or to propose a completely new approach. A majority of the Cabinet had been against FAP; he had nonetheless decided in favor. The Senate Finance Committee, he continued, "must write this bill." He wanted a good bill. "If what comes out of the Committee is an uncertain trumpet . . . ," or if the Committee goes wild, "I might have to veto the result." (There was always the possibility that the congressional Democrats would solve their dilemma by giving him *more* than he would accept.) He ended with an appeal as likely as any to influence these six senators, not least because the president of the United States was telling them the absolute truth.

We might be at one of those historic points in history where a great step forward is going to happen because a few men have had the boldness and the stamina to do so. If we go on as we have been there will be a general national revulsion [to welfare]. I am for Family Assistance because while (a), It is a possible disaster, (b), AFDC is a certain disaster. . . . The future . . . lies with the men in this room.

He turned then to Long and asked, "Russell, is there a chance?"

Long had consistently taken the position in public, and in quasi-public situations such as this meeting with the president, that there was. As he recessed hearings on May 1 he had said, "We do want to pass a bill." He now told the president that cost was not the problem, that the "objection is to paying people not to work." A majority of the committee, he judged, was in favor of supplementing the income of the working poor, but there was a "rising objection to people who lay about all day making love and producing illegitimate babies." Bennett made the suggestion that the program separate the working poor from the welfare poor: that the emphasis be on leading the dependent toward jobs, creating jobs if necessary; that the program be seen as a transition system from dependence on welfare to independence in the private economy. (This distinction was adopted in H.R. 1, with responsibility for the working poor assigned to the Labor Department. The senators made clear that experience with the WIN program had finally persuaded them that a welfare bureaucracy would never cooperate in a work program.) Bennett, representing a Mormon constituency, explained, "I would have to go back to Salt Lake and say this is a job-producing program." He asked only that it be that, which is no more than the president had been asking, although the Administration had not yet faced the fact that even with these senators the argument that for "workfare" to work the government must create jobs as well as training slots was seen to have great force. Bennett, too, concluded, "we have an historic opportunity."

In the legislative manner, the committee chairman and the ranking minority member had spoken. They seemed in agreement with one another and with the president. Spirits rose. Miller, Byrd, and Fannin spoke as if well disposed. Ribicoff, the one senator most committed to the legislation, did what he could to get agreement that his amendment resolved many difficulties that had been mentioned. He, too, adopted the president's tone: "As I get older," he said, "I become less certain of anything." But surely, he allowed, FAP was worth testing. Long had persistently raised the possibility of a system that would subsidize private employers who engaged low-skill workers: this, too, Ribicoff suggested, might be tested. As a counterpart, the government should put up money to create jobs in the public sector. He wanted the system to be universal; he wanted more help for the more generous states; he wanted the floor raised by increments to $2,000; but most of all he wanted a bill. He was, he said, a liberal, Bennett a conservative, Long a populist. "There are enough of us," he said, "to write a good bill."

There were enough senators, but there was not enough time. In a plain perspective this may be all that happened to Family Assistance: time ran out. But behind this was the calculation of any number of the players that time *should* run out. With each successive day it became an even better tactic for defeating FAP. Nonetheless, a considerable effort was made to maintain the initiative seemingly won by the president's moves at the end of the summer. On August 29, the day after the president declared that "the Senate as a whole must be given the chance to work its will on this issue," the Senate Democratic Leader, Mike Mansfield, stated that he shared that view precisely. In an interview he said, "any bill of this nature, prepared by the president, should be given the courtesy of being proposed to the Senate." He acknowledged doubts in his own mind about the bill, but insisted: "The Administration's wishes should be taken into consideration. As far as I'm concerned it will be considered, debated, and disposed of for no other reason than as a courtesy to the President."

When a democratic system is working, the spoils of political conflict are melted down to the coinage of trust among politicians. Legislatures uniquely depend on personal integrity, especially in dealing across political lines. Mansfield's pledge was taken at full face value—probably no other man in Washington at this time was held in so much respect—and was understood to be a pledge, not "to deliver," but to do his best. His powers, too, were limited. But they were sufficient to quite restore hope within the Administration that the bill might yet pass. All that was needed was a vote on the floor. September filled with strategy meetings, interspersed with optimistic public forecasts. On *Face the Nation,* September 13, I allowed there was a solid 60-vote majority for FAP in the Senate. Ten days later at a meeting with Minority Leader Hugh Scott in his Senate office a rough tally showed 62 votes—41 Democrats, 21 Republicans—for FAP. (There were then 57 Democratic senators, 43 Republican.) Some liberal Republicans were soft: but some conservatives, notably Baker of Tennessee and Dole of Kansas, were thought quite solid. All that was needed was a floor vote that would get the bill to conference, it being assumed any final legislation would be drafted by a House-Senate conference committee meeting in private in room H-208. Mills would dominate the conference, and the Administration would get a good bill.

If only the committee would act. Bennett had become committed to the enterprise, and would vote for any version that would get the issue to the floor. He counted three Republican colleagues against any measure, and three who would go along with a "pretest" bill. Talmadge had told a White House legislative aide there was a solid Southern bloc in the committee against the bill. The committee staff indicated that only a pilot project could be reported out. For all the cordiality of the San Clemente meeting, the conversations on the flight back to Washington had dwelt almost exclusively on various combinations of pilot projects, with much emphasis on Long's wage subsidy. All that really emerged was the addition of job creation to an already overlong list of changes somebody wanted made.

Wilbur J. Cohen now began trying to find an acceptable formula for the Democratic side. He wrote, "The situation is very complicated and cannot simply be solved by dealing with general principles." A number of other supporters of FAP began to increase their efforts in an atmosphere of mounting interest and even excitement. Somewhat earlier "Welfare Reform Legislation Bulletin" No. 11 of the Board of Social Ministry of the Lutheran Church in America had responded to my "warning" that failure to adopt a bill in the 91st Congress would put off welfare reform for a decade by asserting that "little more than what the administration proposes can be expected to win approval in both houses at this time." It proposed a detailed and urgent lobbying effort.

If your Senator is Fred Harris or Eugene McCarthy ask them not to sacrifice welfare reform but to vote for the Administration's bill if legislation they plan to introduce fails to win approval in the committee.

If your Senator is Republican remind him of the President's oft expressed desire for this legislation and of the party support it received in the House.

If your Senator is a Democrat remind him that Democrats are a majority on the Finance Committee and that his party will likely get the blame if Welfare Reform is killed in Committee.

The National Association of Manufacturers stood firm, a factor of some hoped-for consequence. Common Cause began to organize a lobby made up of representatives of groups such as the Lutherans. On September 25 the White House was informed that this group would seek four amendments: the restoration of the AFDC-U program; Federal administration, or something approaching it; legislative work standards; and legislative commitment to an eventual payment level equal to the poverty standard. (Note that the concept of a *negative tax* never really got through. Even this sophisticated group could only think, or would only speak, in terms of benefits paid to dependent persons with no income.) More welcome, the following day the U.S. Catholic Conference, in the manner of the Lutherans, inquired as to what bishops might do to be of help, with no conditions attached. In the meantime Hale Boggs and Phillip Burton began to involve themselves in the subtle maneuvers by which committees in one body of the Congress influence committees in the other.

Time slid by. On September 1 the White House legislative liaison reported that Mansfield was talking of a postelection session. This would mean a rapid run-down in activity in the weeks immediately ahead. On September 10 he announced he hoped to achieve *sine die* adjournment by mid-October by putting the Senate on a two-shift basis, with the equivalent of two concurrent legislative calendars. Nine items were scheduled for the first shift, beginning with the pressing issue of a Constitutional amendment providing for direct election of the president and continuing with much mandatory legislation, not yet enacted, such as appropriation bills. (The debates on Administration foreign policy had affected the progress of Senate business, too.) FAP was at the bottom of the list, to be voted on "no later" than October 9; not much of a chance. In making his announcement, Mansfield agreed that the prospect of clearing even his limited agenda by mid-October was "questionable." At the same time Scott predicted that only a limited Family Assistance Plan could be approved by the Congress in the time remaining.

The final blow came with the November election. On the same day Mansfield announced his legislation schedule, Vice-President Agnew began an election tour appealing to "the workingmen of the country" to give the president a Republican Congress and denouncing the "radical liberals" who exercised such influence among the Democrats. The Administration did not know but that it was on the verge of a decisive electoral victory. In part, it would appear, through a misreading of Richard Scammon's and Ben Wattenberg's *The Real Majority*[9] its tacticians were persuaded that the "social issue" would be dominant in the campaign and set out not merely to pick up seats in Congress, but just possibly to change the social structure of the American party system. Out of office, Democratic activists seemed at times determined to dissociate themselves from the mass base of the party in favor of a political posture Tom Wolfe termed "radical chic." Simultaneously, the GOP, the presumed party of elites, found itself increasingly abandoned and repudiated by the newest generation of the old families that had meant much to it. The finest prep schools, colleges, and universities, the "best" newspapers and magazines, the most respected television commentary, *all* seemed now to be in the hands of Democrats, or residual Republicans more embarrassed than not by their past, and perhaps the more determined to live it down. The blue-collar vote beckoned, the desertion of the social elites rankled. The logic of an attack against the Democratic *coalition,* rather than policies or personalities that had emerged from it, was compelling.

Scammon and Wattenberg, and many journalists, seemed to confirm this analysis. What few persons on the Republican side seemed to grasp was that most of these writers, especially the authors of *The Real Majority,* were writing to warn the Democrats what would happen if they did not prepare for such a Republican attack and indeed make ready their own counterattack. (Scammon lectured Democratic congressional candidates in 1970 on how to turn the "social issue" to *their* advantage.) It turned out, of course, that liberals had war records too. In any event, the most elemental of political rules is that law-and-order is an issue for the party-out-of-power. The economy, moreover, made for Democratic weather. In the event, the elections were normal-seeming enough: a relatively mild mid-term trend away from the party of the president. But in truth a much larger battle had been fought and lost. The Democratic coalition survived, seemingly even strengthened. Democrats emerged as the party of peaceableness and reason: the Republicans as an extreme, if not extremist. The Democrats emerged also with a candidate to run against Nixon, Senator Muskie of Maine whose election-eve telecast had contrasted so favorably it was said with that of the president.

This could only mean the worst for Family Assistance, and for the same complex of reasons that had thwarted it all along. The invitation for me to appear on *Face the Nation* September 13 came in response to the sudden round of Administration activity on its behalf. George Herman, a television journalist of the first capacity, began the questioning by probing the Administration's most vulnerable point.

HERMAN: Dr. Moynihan, the Administration is exceedingly anxious to obtain Senate passage of the new welfare bill. You yourself have said that if it doesn't pass this year, it won't pass for a decade. Do you believe that Vice President Agnew's sharp new attacks on some six to eight radical liberals, as he calls them, in the Senate, will help or hurt the passage of the welfare bill in the Senate?

MOYNIHAN: Well, to the degree that they are radical liberals they will be for the bill. . . . [A]t this point the more serious problem is with conservatives.

But the next questioner asked, "Are you not in fact having some troubles from . . . the radical liberals of the Senate, who are against some parts of the welfare bill?" True enough, I countered, there is "no one group in [the] ideological spectrum that fully approves it. I expect no one group fully understands it. It's very complicated legislation. It's the first welfare bill in history . . . to be sent to the Congress." It was a bill of the center. Accordingly, the next questioner asked, if it were the case that our main problems were with conservatives, was I "making a case for electing more Democrats or more liberals to the Senate . . . ?" A fair response would have been that apart from Williams and Curtis the most determined opponents of FAP were Southern Democrats and the least dependable allies were to be found among liberals. But the dialogue was already too complicated.[10]

From mid-October to the November election, Nixon campaigned intensively for Republican senatorial candidates. A set stump speech developed which began with troop withdrawals from Vietnam, went on to deplore "Big Spenders" in the capital and the bomber Left on campus, and ended with an account of the Administration's "reform" programs, including Family Assistance. Typically, the speech would balance the floor under family income with the "work requirement" directed to men able to work. Later, Democrats would charge that these speeches gave an indelible cast of accusatory conservatism to welfare reform, such that the symbolic significance outweighed and more than negated whatever substance the bill might have. There is truth to this and truth also to the counterclaim that the voters, especially those he was addressing, would support workfare but not welfare. By no standard could the passages on FAP be interpreted as an effort to arouse any animus against welfare recipients under the existing system, which is to say "welfare mothers." The workfare references were to able-bodied men who were to receive income supplements under the new program. "If a man is able to

530 | DANIEL P. MOYNIHAN

work, if he is then offered a job, and if he refuses to work, he should not be paid to loaf by a taxpayer in the State of . . . or anywhere else." It was also the case that on more than one occasion the president was defending a Republican candidate against Democratic charges that he wished to put half the state on the dole. The rights and wrongs of the matter are not, however, to be settled by reference to the texts: the determining fact is that most of the Republican candidates lost.* As of November 4, any partisan Democrat who wished to deny that the president supported Family Assistance was in a politically viable position to do so. The advantage to party of doing so was considerable, and the risk

---

* Among these was George Bush, running in Texas against a Democratic opponent who made a specific issue of Bush's vote for FAP as a member of Ways and Means. Nixon spoke to the matter at a rally at Longview, Texas, October 28. His remarks then were about as strong and detailed as any he made.

> Rather than pouring billions of dollars into old programs, programs that have failed, we say the time has come to look at our education program, to look at our health program, to look at our welfare program, and to reform those programs. . . .
> Let me take one that I understand has become an issue here in this Texas campaign.
> I want to talk about the welfare program. I want to talk about it very directly and I want to talk about it with the concern that every good Texan has for anybody who needs help.
> First, we in this country, because it is a rich country, do want to provide assistance to any family that needs assistance. But when we look at the present welfare program, do you know what has happened?
> We have found that millions more have been added to the welfare rolls at a cost of billions of dollars with no end in sight. I will tell you why it is wrong.
> When a program makes it more profitable for a man not to work than to work, when it encourages a man to desert his family rather than stay with his family, it is time to get rid of that program and get another one in its place.
> So, this administration stands for a new program, one that will provide a floor of dignity without the degrading aspects of welfare for those families that need it.
> But, one that will also have a work requirement and a work incentive. I will put it very bluntly: If a man is able to work, if a man is trained for a job, and then he refuses to work, that man should not be paid to loaf by a hardworking taxpayer in the United States of America.
> That is the program we stand for. It is the program that George Bush and John Tower stand for. We need that kind of reform. It is something that all of us want.

Public Papers of the Presidents of the United States, Richard Nixon, 1970, p. 979.

to conscience small. The Republicans were on their way out; it would be but a short delay before the job could be done right by a Democrat. A year earlier Republicans had done splendidly in state elections, adding New Jersey and Virginia to their pronounced majority in the Governors' Conference, and who could say they were not headed for a sweep in Congress? As the president had entered the Cabinet meeting of November 5, 1969, the room rose in applause. One year to the day later there was no sound. The president sat down, explained it could have been worse, and went straight to business.

More than its immediate predecessors, the Nixon Administration separated its program staff from its political cadres. With the election over, the original Family Assistance team reassembled at the White House on November 11 to plan the campaign to put the legislation through the Senate in the remaining days of the Congress. A systematic and sustained effort followed. The *National Journal* wrote: "The Administration has devoted more manpower and manhours to the Family Assistance Plan . . . than to any other single piece of domestic legislation it has proposed."[11] Cabinet officers and their aides now roamed the corridors of the Senate Office Building during the first full "lame duck" session of Congress in twenty years. Veneman, Patricelli, and Rosow manned a continuous watch. Legislative liaison officers, notably Howard A. Cohen of HEW, came into their own. Intelligence reports came hourly to the White House. The president talked to congressional leaders, and was available for other chores. Once again morale rose. What no one realized, or wanted to acknowledge, was that all was different in the aftermath of the campaign. The president was viewed by the Democrats not as having tried to win a ball game, but as having tried to steal the ball. There was some bitterness, much vindictiveness, and a minimal disposition to enable him to recoup his position by an epic legislative achievement cast precisely in the mold Democrats claimed for their own.

The Finance Committee had already voted once on FAP, a motion to accept the House bill rather than draft a distinct Senate bill. This had failed 14 to 1, with only Harris approving. Now a second vote approached, based on the "October version" of the "June version" of the original. The Ribicoff pretest provisions had been incorporated, along with various "grandfather clauses" of the kind Richardson had offered in testimony. The date for the vote, it became clear, would be November 20. That morning the president showed up at the Washington headquarters of the Retail Clerks International Association, AFL–CIO, to thank the members for their support of FAP. (This rather puzzled the union officials. They had taken no position, and understood the AFL–CIO executive council to be opposed.) He needed all the support he could get, and needed to give every evidence of his own. The day before, Richardson had supplied him with a vote count of the committee. One vote shy.

Richardson counted for the bill two Republicans, Bennett and Miller, and six Democrats, Long, Anderson, Ribicoff, Harris, McCarthy, and Fulbright. A majority of nine was required. There were three "possibles," Jordan, a Republican, who had said he would vote to report the bill, but only if his vote was necessary, Gore who would not be present but would have a proxy, and Hartke who was being approached through other channels. (Both Gore and Hartke had been prime Republican targets in the election just past. Gore, after thirty-two years in Congress, had been defeated; Hartke had barely survived.) But the vote went very differently from the vote count.

On Tuesday, November 17, Common Cause scheduled a meeting of organizations supporting the legislation, to be joined by Richardson, to plan a unified, mass lobbying effort in the seventy-two hours to come. Each group was to send one, two, or three representatives, with perhaps 150 persons expected altogether. Wiley insisted on bringing 100–200 welfare mothers to expound the NWRO position. Gardner spoke with Ginsberg and others planning the campaign. They agreed that Wiley's only purpose for attending the meeting would be to wreck it, and that if they went ahead without him the NWRO would be outside the doors, in front of the television cameras. They decided to cancel.

NWRO had not yet, however, run its course. Rebuff could still be turned to account on the still credible theory that it reflected the rightness of the cause rather than the obstinacy of the tactic. Senator McCarthy was approached, as sponsor of the NWRO legislation, and agreed to conduct "people's hearings." These were held the following two days, November 18 and 19, in the Senate Office Building. In an atmosphere of intense emotion the Family Assistance Plan was denounced as all things evil.

Mary McGrory described the scene as one "where scores of militant welfare mothers bellowed their opposition to being driven out of the house to do underpaid work." One liberal columnist privately described the hearings as a "lynching bee." For the first time the full emotion of the welfare movement was displayed on congressional precincts in a supportive, even encouraging atmosphere. It made a powerful impression: enough —such is the evidence—to switch the vote of Harris, and with that the vote of the majority of liberal Democrats on the Finance Committee, against Family Assistance.

The Times had the story on the morning of the twentieth. A front-page report by Warren Weaver, Jr., was headed: "PRESIDENT LOSING WELFARE SUPPORT, Senator Harris Is Turning Against Proposal—Other Liberals May Join Him." In an interview Harris stated: "I had hoped we could improve on the Administration bill, but I'm despairing more and more that it can be done. Every Administration change has made the bill worse. If its bad features can't be eliminated, I think it ought to be killed, and we should start all over." Weaver added, "The only prospect for Senate approval of the plan has been based on solid support by liberals and moderates of both parties. Liberal Democratic defections of even modest proportions appear almost certain to doom any such majority."

Hours later the vote was taken; Family Assistance was defeated 10–6. Harris voted against, and cast proxies for McCarthy and Gore. Anderson voted against, owing, it was generally held, to Harris's influence. Byrd and Talmadge were against. Four Republicans joined them in opposition: Williams, Curtis, Fannin, and Hansen. Three Democrats and three Republicans voted for Family Assistance: Long, Fulbright, and Ribicoff; Bennett, Jordan, and Miller. Hartke was not present and did not vote. Wiley declared himself "very pleased," and credited the "people's hearings" with the outcome. "It's a big win," he told the Washington *Evening Star,* which described the NWRO response as "jubilation."

Next, by a 13–3 vote the committee authorized the Family Assistance Plan to be tested, along with other proposals including Long's wage-subsidy plan and a Bennett proposal to set up a public corporation to train and place welfare recipients. No plan would go into effect without further legislative authorization.

The three votes against this measure were those of Harris, McCarthy, and Gore.

The Administration liberals felt betrayed. Richardson was quoted: "I just couldn't believe he [Harris] had changed his vote." Harris and others hastened with their explanations. "It's not a reform bill," he told *Time,* "it's regressive." A relatively rare event, a number of journalists volunteered their personal impressions of these conversations as they called the White House for its side of the story. One senior correspondent reported that after an hour's explication of the punitive features of Family Assistance, "I felt I had to clean the phone." This was not surprising. There are standards of behavior in Washington by which men are judged, albeit privately. Kennedy's maxim, "To govern is to choose," is generally accepted, and is central to a certain code of conduct. Public men are expected to make choices in conditions of uncertainty, and to accept the consequences. Nixon had done this; Mills had; so, in his way, had Williams. Harris had not. He wished to be both for the bill and against it. His conduct was not unjustifiable, it was merely weak. But government is often more an affair of personal strength and weakness than of good and bad.

The November 20 vote established, in some circles, that the liberals killed FAP. Seven of the ten Democrats, in effect, voted against it. This misreads the event. Liberal votes defeated Family Assistance, but this in the main was the triumph of conservative strategy. Williams killed FAP, with the considerable assistance of Talmadge. It was remarked at the time that if a John W. Byrnes rather than a John J. Williams had been the ranking Republican on the committee, FAP would have passed, and within the limits of such assertions, this almost certainly is true. Once Williams had demonstrated that Family Assistance, when combined with a range of other programs, could produce sharp work disincentives, the Administration, because of its own characterization of the program, was forced to try to eliminate them. It could never do so completely, and so could never satisfy the conservatives. Simultaneously, with each adjustment to eliminate "notches" and "galloping supplements" *some* family *somewhere* was deprived of a right-in-being. This could only arouse the liberals, none of whom, save Ribicoff, had any great knowledge of the field, to a not unfamiliar self-certifying fury. More cunning probably ought not to be ascribed to the conservatives than they claim, but the liberal senators were reactive throughout, and it took no excessive skill on the part of Williams and his allies to obtain the desired response.

FAP was defeated on a Friday. The following Tuesday, November 24, the Finance Committee gave any who cared to learn a lesson in what repressive legislation could be like. As if to exorcise the fantasy of the president's incredible plan to put 24 million persons on welfare, the committee set to work cutting down welfare eligibility under the existing AFDC law. In the face of clear Supreme Court rulings as to the unconstitutionality of equivalent state regulations, the committee restored the "man-in-the-house" rule and the one-year residency requirement. This was done by voice votes, with Ribicoff reportedly the only opposition. Harris, who was not present, cited this committee action as yet another reason he had voted against Family Assistance four days earlier.

In a *Washington Post* story headed "Panel Move on Welfare Jolts Liberals," Eve Edstrom described many senators as quite surprised by this "double whammy to the Administration's welfare reform objectives." And yet was it not more likely that the Family Assistance debate had merely held off this kind of action through most of the 91st Congress? Now, with that debate over, Congress was reverting to its normal disposition. A week later, on Debember 2, by a vote of 10–4 the committee re-affirmed its "man-in-the-house" and one-year residency decisions, and went on to forbid the Office of Economic Opportunity legal-services program to finance lawsuits designed to "nullify" Federal statutes or policy on welfare matters. The committee voted also to require the mother of a welfare child to reveal the name of its father; to allow states to require the entry of case workers into a welfare home; and to exclude from the AFDC-U program families with unemployed fathers who worked ten hours a week or more. It was revealed that earlier the committee had tentatively decided to make it a Federal crime for a father to cross a state line to evade child support. The chairman was quoted as explaining that by its "man-in-the-house" ruling the committee did not mean to have families pushed off welfare simply because a mother "from time to time was 'friendly' with" a man not acting as head of the family.

How to state it indirectly, yet with sufficient clarity? It did not require special sensitivity to racial nuance to grasp that the function of these actions by one of the most powerful committees of the United States Senate was to confirm—after a period of distraction to reassert—the view of welfare as a problem of race. Yet there was near to no protest against these purposely punitive measures. For here there was no guilt, no fear, no good will, to exploit and ultimately to suborn.

Still the struggle for FAP went on, gaining new support here and there as reality encroached. On December 2, the day the Finance Committee voted its grim agenda, Senator Hartke addressed the Senate pledging his support for the Family Assistance Plan. It was the first speech of its kind given in the Senate chamber. There were no conditions to his support. He acknowledged criticism that the bill did not "go far enough" but asked that his colleagues go at least that far. He cited the increase in AFDC costs, state by state, from August 1969 to August 1970: Indiana, 53.2 percent; California, 34.9 percent; Texas 67.6 percent; a national average of 28.3 percent. "The longer we allow a system of national failure to create a culture of personal failure," he said, "the larger the costs of redeeming ourselves will become." More than a week earlier, on November 23, the president had made the same point in a meeting in the Cabinet room with representatives of the National Association of Counties. He was caught, he said, between left and right, between those who claimed FAP was a guaranteed income, and those who thought the work requirement repressive. The outlook was not good. *But,* he continued, the welfare crisis he had predicted a year earlier had come to pass. It would not go away without fundamental change or . . . fundamental indecency to the recipient class. Family Assistance, he pledged, would remain the major domestic goal of his Administration.

Yet another revision of FAP now took place. With Ribicoff and Bennett as allies and cosponsors, the Administration began plans to offer FAP as a floor amendment to the Social Security bill the Finance Committee was expected to report momentarily. On December 2, Ribicoff gave Richardson a list of ten changes he and Bennett would make in the then-current version of the bill, asking the Administration to support as many as it could, but not requiring support for all ten. On December 3 Common

Cause convened a meeting of supporting organizations to hear Richardson's response, which had been approved overnight by the White House. Richardson once again described the proposal, and made a point that might have been made by others.

[A]lmost 14.5 million people will be eligible for benefits that will make them better off than under current law. Anyone who contends that this bill is somehow worse than current law, or should be defeated if it is not further liberalized, must answer to these 14.5 million people.

Praising Ribicoff and Bennett as having been "magnificent in their commitment," he accepted, item by item, seven of their ten proposals, and offered counter-proposals on two others. AFDC-U was to be restored; current AFDC benefit levels were to be made mandatory; the Federal government would administer the FAP program, public-service jobs would be created. The Administration was firm only on the basic $1,600 payment level, and that by reason of "budgetary limitations." The statement was thoroughly conciliatory; in any event the most important of the new "concessions" represented provisions that had been in the original Administration bill.

It was no use. The NWRO still found the bill inadequate. Harris thought it improved, but called for yet further improvement. A member of Ribicoff's staff was quoted as saying, "Harris just seems to want more and more and more. Our negotiations just seem to have ended."

The Finance Committee now produced the Social Security Amendments of 1970. The *Washington Post* commented, "It is as if the Finance Committee had set about to create a memorial to Rube Goldberg. . . ." In addition to authorizing the FAP experiments, the bill contained the new welfare restrictions, a 10-percent across-the-board increase in Social Security payments, a new protectionist trade policy complete with import quotas, and a "catastrophic illness" insurance plan covering 170,000,000 people with a first-year estimated cost of $2.2 billion. Just where the latter had come from no one seemed to know. Or care. The whole thing, said the *Post,* was a "Godzilla-like monster." It was a "disgrace." And now, the editorial continued, Family Assistance was all but doomed.

Again, not quite. The Senate leadership was cooperative in trying to get the Ribicoff-Bennett amendments before the Senate. Long introduced the committee report on December 16: "the most significant social insurance legislation Congress has ever considered." The Ribicoff-Bennett move was expected the next day. The Vice-President was put on the alert in case of a tie. But a filibuster immediately broke out over a foreign aid supplemental authorization which was deemed by opponents of the Cambodian incursion to lend congressional sanction to it. Another filibuster was threatened by opponents of import quotas. Labor let it be known that inasmuch as Ribicoff and Bennett had adopted the Administration proposal on a wage minimum of $1.20 it would rather have no bill at all. In any event, the Senate could not pass a serious bill.* In a terse statement, as to an unruly class being called to order, and suddenly, awkwardly silent, Mansfield told his colleagues they had made a spectacle of themselves. There was nothing to do save wait until January and start again. In his address to the Democratic caucus on the opening of the 92nd Congress, he reminded the senators of the unfinished business carried over from the agenda of the 91st. First he mentioned the supersonic transport, next the Family Assistance Plan, a matter "of national importance and deep presidential interest."

It truly was. To grant this is neither to approve nor disapprove of the president; it is merely to acknowledge a fact. On December 13 the president was scheduled to address the decennial White House Conference on Children. Given the conference subject, and with the fate of the last legislative push for FAP to be decided in the coming week, some reference to the legislation was in order. I prepared notes; Raymond K. Price, Jr., produced a finished speech. But the president arose at 4:30 on that Sunday morning to write his own. At long last he deter-

---

* Actually, the Senate did pass something. After a prolonged series of parliamentary maneuvers, interrupted by a recess for Christmas, the Senate unanimously approved an omnibus Social Security bill on December 29. The legislation contained provisions amending the Social Security, Medicare, and Medicaid programs, as well as the restrictive welfare regulations; by a vote of 49 to 21, the Senate had earlier adopted a motion by Senator Long to delete the welfare pilot projects. The omnibus bill did not become law, however, as Mills and his colleagues on Ways and Means refused to join a conference committee in the closing hours of the session.

mined to say in public what he had been saying all along in private.

I would like to speak briefly tonight of one government program presently being considered by the Senate—which I believe particularly deserves your support.

The great issue concerning family and child welfare in the United States is the issue of family income. For generations social thinkers have argued that there is such a thing as a minimum necessary family income, and that no family should be required to subsist on less. It is a simple idea, but profound in its consequences.

On August 11, 1969, I proposed that for the first time in America's history we establish a floor under the income of every American family with children.

We called it the Family Assistance Plan. It has in turn been called the most important piece of social legislation in our nation's history.

You know the story of this legislation. In April it passed the House of Representatives by a margin of almost two to one. Then it became mired down in the Senate.

It is still stuck, but it is not lost. There is still an opportunity for the 91st Congress to change the world of American children by enacting Family Assistance.

In these closing days of that Congress, I want to emphasize once again, unequivocally, my support for welfare reform *this year*.

In the last ten years alone the number of children on welfare has nearly tripled, to more than 6 million. Six million children. Six million children caught up in an unfair and tragic system that rewards people for not working instead of providing the incentives for self-support and independence, that drives families apart instead of holding them together, that brings welfare snoopers into their homes, that robs them of pride and destroys dignity.

I want to change all that.

The welfare system has become a consuming, monstrous, inhuman outrage against the community, against the family, against the individual—and most of all against the very children whom it was meant to help.

We have taken long strides toward ending racial segregation, but welfare segregation can be almost as insidious.

Think what it can mean to a sensitive child. To take only one example—the free lunch program—my daughter Tricia does tutoring at an inner-city school, and she tells me of her deep concern each day to see the welfare children herded into an auditorium for their free lunch, while the others bring their lunches and eat in the classroom. We have got to find ways of ending this sort of separation. The point is not the quality of the lunch—in fact, the free lunch is probably nutritionally better than those the others bring. The point is the stigmatizing by separation of the welfare children, *as* welfare children.

I remember back in the Depression years of the nineteen thirties, how deeply I felt about the plight of those people my own age who used to come into my father's store when they couldn't pay the bill because their fathers were out of work, and how this seemed to separate them from the others in the school. None of us had any money in those days, but those in families where there were no jobs, where there was nothing but the little that relief then offered, suffered from more than simply going without. They suffered a hurt to their pride that many carried with them for the rest of their lives.

I also remember that my older brother had tuberculosis for five years. The hospital and doctor bills were more than we could afford. In the five years before he died, my mother never bought a new dress. We were poor by today's standards. I suppose we were poor even by Depression standards. But the wonder of it was that we did not know we were poor. Somehow my mother and father with their love, with their pride, their courage and their self-sacrifice were able to create a spirit of self-respect in our family so that we had no sense of being inferior to others who had more than we had.

Today's welfare child is not so fortunate.

His family may have enough to get by on. They may even have more, in a material sense, than many of us did in those Depression years. But no matter how much pride and courage his parents have, he knows they are poor—and he can feel that soul-stifling, patronizing attitude that follows the dole.

Perhaps he watches while a case-worker—himself trapped in a system that wastes, on policing, talents that could be used for helping—while this case-worker is forced by the system to poke around in the child's apartment, checking on how the money is spent or whether his mother might be hiding his father in the closet. This sort of indignity is hard enough on the mother—enough of a blow to her pride and self-respect—but think what it must mean to a sensitive child.

We have a chance now to give that child a chance—a chance to grow up without having his schoolmates throw in his face the fact that he is on welfare, and without making him feel that he is therefore something less than the other children.

Our task is not only to lift people out of poverty, but from the standpoint of the child to erase the stigma of welfare and illegitimacy and apartness—to restore pride and dignity and self-respect.

I do not contend that our Family Assistance Plan is perfect. In this confused and complex and intensely human area, no perfect program is possible—and certainly none is possible that will please everybody. But it is a good program, and a program immensely better than what we have now, and vastly important to the future of this country and especially to the neediest of our children. For the Senate to adjourn without enacting this measure would be a tragedy of missed opportunity for America and particularly for the children of America.

I have dwelt at some length on Family Assistance because of its vital and even historic importance, and because now is the time of Senate decision.

Mary McGrory, as old an antagonist as any the president had in the press, wrote that it was a "magnificent, emotional appeal." If only, she implied, it had come sooner: "[B]ureaucratic and parliamentary failures would have meant little if the President's true mind had been known. . . . The speech was splendid—and too late." Perhaps. Perhaps, to the contrary, it was only after the bill was defeated that his opponents could accept that he had been serious.

But it had been a good run. Many of the institutions and individuals involved showed themselves to advantage. Failure was relative. The presidency had shown itself equal to a complex task of analysis and of decision-making. Congress did not do badly. If the measure was defeated it was in the main because the Senate desired this. The center, temporarily perhaps, was overcome. This was at least in part a problem of understanding—the subject was new and complex—but the state of politics was also involved. As the end approached, the *Washington Post* commented: "There has been meanmindedness on the right and showboating on the left and mostly apathetic silence in between." But the silence in between reflected prudence more than indifference. Lined up, the left and right had, on this issue and at this time, a capacity to punish that made silence a rational response. It was the case, then, that income by right proved *almost* feasible. But to enact it required as much discipline and boldness as to propose it. These were lacking in the Congress not because those concerned were unequal to the challenge, but because they chose not to accept it.

Such prudence is normal to politics, and occasions no alarm. The more remarkable fact is that some persons did choose to run this gantlet, and few were seriously injured in the process. The president was not. He emerged rather strengthened by not having succumbed to the punishment from left and right. He had shown that something could be done that it had been thought could not be done. A month after he addressed the White House Conference on Children, a story in *The New York Times* noted, "Even Richard Nixon came out for income maintenance payments that would be paid to desperately poor families, with no questions asked." Not "even." Among presidents, "only." That is not the least reward of an otherwise difficult job. Nor a bad portent for the future of effective government.

Citations—Chapter VII

1. Joseph A. Pechman, "Distribution of Federal and State Income Taxes by Income Classes," Presidential Address, American Finance Association, New Orleans, December 28, 1971, mimeographed, Tables 1, 2.
2. George Hoshino, "Money and Morality: Income Security and Personal Social Services," *Social Work*, April 1971, p. 20.
3. This is from a summary of the bill presented by Harris to the Senate Finance Committee, April 29, 1970.
4. Frank V. Fowkles and Harry Lenhart, Jr., "Congressional Report/Two Money Committees Wield Power Differently," *National Journal*, April 10, 1971, p. 780.
5. Frank C. Porter, "Hill Unit Sends Welfare Bill Back to Finch for Overhaul," *Washington Post*, May 2, 1970.
6. Robert L. Bartley, "The Press: Adversary, Surrogate Sovereign, or Both?" Paper prepared for delivery at the 1971 annual meeting of the American Political Science Association, September 7–11, 1971, mimeographed, p. 3.
7. Fred J. Cook, "When You Just Give Money to the Poor," *The New York Times Magazine*, May 3, 1970.
8. George Wiley and Jonathan Kaufman, "Adequate Income vs. Nixon's 'Welfare Reform,' " *Social Policy*, November–December 1970.
9. Richard M. Scammon and Ben J. Wattenberg, *The Real Majority*, New York, Coward-McCann, 1970.
10. CBS News, *Face the Nation*, Produced by Sylvia Westerman and Prentiss Childs, with George Herman, David Broder, and Dan Rather, September 13, 1970, mimeographed transcript.
11. John K. Inglehart and Dom Bonafede, "Welfare Report/Nixon's Family Assistance Plan Faces Showdown on Senate Floor," *National Journal*, December 5, 1970, p. 2633.

VIII

The Future of Reform

For those concerned to see the national government assume an innovative and responsible role in the resolution of social conflict and inequity, the history of Family Assistance provides grounds for optimism. Not for congratulations. Few men of large capacity and sufficient courage are to be encountered in this narration, and few indeed within the ranks of those nominally committed to the kind of social change FAP represented. Even so, here was a fundamental innovation, a nonincremental change of policy addressed to issues of unquestioned relevance.

Two essential features of a mature policy-guidance system were to be seen. First, a capacity for correction. By the late 1960s Americans had somewhat mastered the technique of tracking various social situations and comparing actual movements with expected or desired ones. If this was far from the sophisticated navigation some envisage for the future, it was equally distant from the dead reckoning of the past. This was accompanied by a considerable willingness to acknowledge error. The proposal of FAP involved the recognition—in some ways the assertion—that two large social programs had not succeeded. The Social Security legislation of the 1930s had not led to the "withering away" of dependency. The antipoverty legislation of the 1960s had not brought an end to poverty. (In 1971 Wilbur J. Cohen told an audience at the National Bureau of Economic Research, "The OEO program . . . has probably taken three people out of poverty since 1964." Allowing for hyperbole, three less persons poor is not much of a result for the expenditure of ten or so billion dollars.) Neither program promised to do better. Whereupon the president proposed an altogether different approach that had been conceived by critics of the earlier ones, and the proposal received substantial support in the Congress.

A second feature of a mature policy-guidance system is a capacity to maintain a sufficient correspondence between the social assumptions on the basis of which specific programs are proposed and the social realities that are the context in which the programs will operate. By the 1960s the United States was approaching the condition of a postindustrial society. *Some* of the disciplines of earlier economic life were no longer necessary, while others were no longer even desirable. At the same time large new initiatives in social policy *had* become possible, notwithstanding superficially "conservative" public attitudes. A guaranteed income marked a sharp break even from the insured labor market economy of the past, but it *had* become possible, *and the possibility was perceived.* This perception greatly expanded the range of policy options which the president and Congress considered. It freed policy from constraints within which earlier decisions had been made. The inability, for example, of the Johnson Administration to propose a guaranteed income was in essence born of the presumption that the constraints which had shaped policy since the 1930s were still operative. As it happened, they were not. That the next Administration was able to perceive this was more the reflection of a steadily developing policy system than of any distinctive individual bent.

The events of the 91st Congress have, if only temporarily, placed income-by-right on the national agenda of pending legislation. Although Family Assistance may be no more certain of passage as a result of this, it is nonetheless now within the' domain of normal politics, and likely to remain so until either enacted, or discredited by information and events.

This last possibility ought not be dismissed. The attempt to establish a guaranteed income failed in the 91st Congress owing for the most part to the well-known institutional restraints built into American government. But an observer of the process may also note the potential for the system to become quite unrestrained. The proposal of a guaranteed income predictably aroused opposition from groups that had reason to oppose income redistribution. Predictably also—Cavala and Wildavsky anticipated this—it aroused opposition from groups whose status derived from the manipulation of the existing welfare system and the management of class grievances of the kind that had acquired status (with concomitant rewards) under the antipoverty program. But *unpredictably* the competitive outbidding process among liberals set off by the proposal of a modest income guarantee ended with positions verging on the fantasized. The demand arose not for guaranteed income but for guaranteed wealth. It began to appear that fundamental reform could become fundamental temptation, specifically that upper-middle-class liberals, having lost a sufficient awareness of the privilege—the singularity—of class position, now proposed privilege for all: an attractive thought, but as unattainable as it is illogical.

This impulse followed a pattern well established in American history and successful up to a point, but not guaranteed of success. What will come is hardly likely to be stayed by analysis, but these various "surprises" raise several points on which some general observation seems warranted.

As the study of government has become part of what Boulding has called the "movement of the social system into self-consciousness," fewer aspects of politics are attributed to chance, or so it would seem to those so inclined. Yet Manley has correctly pointed out that political science lacks a theory of non-incremental change. Although one case can hardly offer enough material for construction of a theory, the experience of Family Assistance provides ideas that will be useful in removing some of the mystery of how fundamental reform occurs.

Of major importance in the events that led to the president's address of August 8, 1969, was the network of policy advisers assisting him and operating largely through the formal mechanism of the Urban Affairs Council. It may be the general rule that as the presidency becomes more institutionalized, social policy tends to become more ambitious. The Family Assistance Plan was a product of the Urban Affairs Council, in ways a consequence of it; barely three months after his inauguration, Nixon had accepted the central thrust of the proposal, as drawn up and presented by one of the Council's committees. The UAC never achieved the professionalism of the Council of Economic Advisers, nor the power of the National Security Council, nor has the Domestic Council which succeeded it. Yet, these are essentially similar mechanisms, and reflect the trend of creating more and more policy-making machinery under the direction of a presidential assistant rather than a Cabinet officer. The Bureau of the Budget was such an organization, but its evolution led it to a different purpose, that of imposing restraint rather than conceiving initiatives. It was staffed by an elite corps of the permanent government and kept a certain distance from the presidency no less than from the Cabinet departments. By contrast, the newer organizations are personal instruments of the president-in-office and tend to measure their success by the number of things they get started.* That this trend continued and may even have accelerated under a nominally conservative Republican president suggests that general forces are at work.†

The council structure serves the president well if an activist social policy is desired. In this instance it organized Nixon's policy staff so as to maximize the likelihood of cooperative behavior and disposed both the White House and the Cabinet to seek out larger rather than lesser problems with which to deal.

---

* When the Office of Management and Budget was established in 1970, the first director moved into the White House itself. His office on the second floor of the West Wing was a tiny affair with a post in the middle, nothing approaching the General Grant splendor of the old Budget Director's suite in the Executive Office Building, but two hundred yards and four minutes closer to the person of the president. Proximity had become crucial.

† The Social Security Act was also the product of a Cabinet-level coordinating committee. In order to develop a comprehensive program for presentation to Congress in 1935, President Roosevelt appointed during the preceding summer a Committee on Economic Security composed of the secretaries of Labor, Treasury, and Agriculture, the Attorney General, and the director of the Federal Emergency Relief Administration. The committee was instructed ". . . [to] study problems related to the economic security of individuals and . . . report to the president not later than December 1, 1934, its recommendations concerning proposals which in its judgment will promote greater economic security." Assisted by a technical committee of government professionals, this advisory group recommended a program designed to be both "practical and effective" and to incorporate the best features of the many plans for social security available at the time, while avoiding the excesses of the Townsend Plan and similar designs. The result was a proposal of broad scope and intricate detail. For an account of the work of the committee on Economic Security, see the memoir by its executive director, Edwin E. Witte, *The Development of the Social Security Act,* Madison, University of Wisconsin, 1962.

The Urban Affairs Council provided an agenda and a timetable for decisions, determining when and how the president would come to terms with an issue. Through its Cabinet-level membership, the recurrent ideas of professional bureaucrats gained access to the president, while the diversity of political stances represented within the policy-making group (not necessarily an automatic tendency of the institutionalized presidency), as well as the variety of policy interests (which probably is inevitable), required some form of bargaining over these and other ideas. The need to develop a presidential program dictated some form of compromise; the desire to produce the president's *own* program biased the outcome toward the innovative. Functioning smoothly for however short a period, this particular advisory mechanism produced a proposal which bore the stamp neither of a crusading individual, nor of an ascendant clique in court politics, but was, rather, a relatively genuine, cooperative solution. For that reason, it was also an ambitious one.

The presidential council structure is not, obviously, without risks, some of which were evident in the case of Family Assistance. An "institutionalized" presidency may be disposed to larger decisions, but not necessarily better ones. Had the White House debate on FAP lumbered on, or at least not been resolved so readily, the Administration might have been better prepared for the hard questions posed by the Senate Finance Committee; had the process of policy formation not been so institutionalized, perhaps the president's commitment to the bill would not have been as easily challenged. Yet these are manageable hazards. A more intractable dilemma is that the advisory council's program is never *entirely* the president's. No collection of aides and high-ranking officials can ever be sufficiently sensitive to all the important political considerations the chief executive is swayed by. An intricate professional conception such as a guaranteed income, is inevitably modified in becoming a presidential program. To what effect is beside the point. The alternative would place an unsustainable burden upon the advisory mechanism, requiring essentially that all recommendations be seen from a purely presidential perspective. In such circumstances, it is unlikely that a program such as Family Assistance would have been proposed at all. Yet where the presidential perspective remains the province of the president, advisers are in fact free to advise, if only that.

The development of the "institutionalized" presidency under Nixon, however, is not sufficient to explain the proposal of Family Assistance. Lesser options of an alternative sort were available—national minimum benefit levels, Federal assumption of all welfare costs—which would have posed far fewer short-term political problems for the president. That a bolder course was taken was only partly the result of bargaining among advisers; it also reflected the understanding of those involved that the problem of welfare dependency required a fundamental reform of existing social policies. This is a simple enough explanation, but one not always emphasized by process-oriented students of government. It may be that what is distinctive about a nonincremental change in public policy is just this: the perception that marginal changes, "tireless tinkering," will no longer do. How such a perception occurs, and how it becomes sufficiently widespread to permit, if not encourage, boldness are questions concerning which the experience of Family Assistance can only be suggestive.

The development of the plan was influenced by social science, but not at all in the way generally supposed. There *was* good data available by the time Nixon became president and this made possible relatively decent estimates of the cost and coverage of various proposals for reform. In the aftermath of much undisciplined program innovation in the 1960s, this was crucial in winning confidence in the proposal both within the Administration and, later, in the Congress. Moreover, social-science evaluations suggested that the AFDC program wasn't doing its recipients very much good (nor were many other programs of more symbolic attraction such as Head Start). There was much data to document that things were not getting any better with respect to the problem of dependency and some support also for the proposition that "welfare" was becoming a divisive issue in the Nation; yet these judgments could readily have been made without the benefit of social science. On the other hand, evidence was at best mixed as to how the public might respond to a guaranteed income. Nor was there evidence of any kind as to *what* effects a guaranteed income would have. A negative income tax experiment was under way at the time the issue arose, but it had not the slightest influence on the president's decision. (Nor are the final results, when they come, likely to be nearly as supportive of the decision as has been hoped.) In particular there was no evidence to suggest that a guaranteed income would have any immediate impact on dependency. Far from providing unequivocal guidelines for fundamental reform, social science emphasized the limits of knowledge.

But the fact that "experts" could not (or did not) "prescribe" did not at all inhibit the decision-making process. That they could provide, with seeming objectivity, evaluations of current programs and estimates of the costs and coverage of potential alternatives was sufficient; such advice was a necessary precursor to any break with past assumptions. The more important contribution of social-science advice was to suggest to the president that, inasmuch as there was no way to know what the correct course of action would be, he had as well choose what he felt to be the wisest and most distinctive. The experience of Family Assistance suggests that while social-science advice might tend to restrain social-policy expectations, it does not restrain social-policy decisions. The essential fact is that a nonincremental change in public policy was proposed notwithstanding the obvious limits of comprehension.

This further suggests a gloss on the concept of the professionalization of reform. In its early stage this style of decision-making in government involved a heavy reliance on the professional judgment of persons trained to careers in various types of service functions. Such training typically emphasizes the autonomous judgment of the professional. In Everett C. Hughes's formulation, "Professionals profess. They profess to know better than others the nature of certain matters, and to know better than their clients what ails them or their affairs."[1] The welfare amendments of 1962 were the products of this kind of professional advice and, typically, they were oversold. Theodore J. Lowi notes they were proclaimed as evoking a "new spirit" and constituting a "completely new philosophy . . . in welfare."[2] Professionals of this order do—must—try to instill trust in their clients, including, when it comes to it, Cabinet officers and presidents. Trust is their placebo, and it can work. It can also fail.

At a more general level of social science, however, advice tends to stress how little is known, or at least will do so if the advisers are persons of competence and integrity. This does not preclude large, nonincremental changes of policy. The history of

FAP demonstrates that American government is capable of this, that it does indeed have "a limited tolerance for the intolerable." Nor did a grand design for the "reconstruction" of society prove necessary, only some reasonable-sounding ideas. Indeed, by emphasizing the limits of knowledge, by establishing the unlikelihood of much good coming from prevailing practice or minor variations, the president's advisers probably disposed him toward the larger of his options. The inability of policy-makers to comprehend the complex effects of large changes can be seen as an argument for making only small ones, but the FAP experience of little knowledge impelling a fundamental reform should be seen as an important modification of a general rule.

By the same token, the limits of information about the effects of public policies focus primary attention on the behavior of the political actors involved in deciding. By emphasizing that nobody really knew very much, social science required that the initiative in proposing Family Assistance be taken in the one place it could be taken: the presidency. Nixon's attitudes toward welfare, his conception of the presidency and of what might be his role in history, influenced in an as yet unknowable way his decision to propose FAP. More traditional categories of political explanation are seemingly less fruitful; the immediate gains to the president and his closest supporters were real enough, but there were losses also, and these had been predictable. But the men involved did gain a sense, not unimportant for being intangible, of having done what it was necessary to do, of having acted constructively, of having responded to the concerns of the Nation expressed however imperfectly during the presidential election. (Does not political leadership in a democracy consist of translating these inchoate sentiments of the governed into policies of the government?) These might not be the worst terms by which to understand the genesis of nonincremental change. "Politics," Michael Oakeshott has written, "is not the science of setting up a permanently impregnable society."[3] It is at most a matter of prevailing over dangers near enough to be perceived, which may, at times, dictate ambitious enterprise, such as Family Assistance. Qualities of energy and courage are at least as relevant for success as power of analysis. Of these qualities, political science has little to say, only to note their necessary primacy for responsible and effective government.

To leave the discussion of Family Assistance at this point would, however, be unsatisfactory. Courageous and energetic leaders may take costly and reckless actions; to decide on the basis of a little knowledge is not necessarily to choose wisely. The incrementalist hypothesis is not just descriptive, it is also normative: it asserts that change in a democratic society not only has to be incremental, but ought to be. Marginal reforms, it is held, by never altering too much, being always subject to relatively easy corrective measures, produce better decisions and pose less of a threat to democratic consensus. They are *understood*. They respond, in Lindblom's term, to "the intelligence of democracy."[4] Does the experience of Family Assistance offer any modifications of this aspect of the incrementalist hypothesis?

This is a more difficult question to answer. Whether a guaranteed income, such as FAP, constitutes a fundamental change will only be known (and then never for certain) if one is adopted and is accompanied by fundamental effects. Not all of these, perhaps not any, will be judged as desirable. It was a *large* correction, and it could turn out that in proposing Family Assistance the president set in motion forces tending toward income redistribution and currency inflation that future presidents will not be able to control. In a survey of the Boston metropolitan area conducted in the spring of 1971, Lee Rainwater found quite exceptional support for and awareness of the president's proposal, which was almost invariably seen for what it was, a guaranteed income. There was, however, almost no grasp of the workings of a negative tax. Asked what a minimum FAP income ought to be, the modal respondent stated $5,500, precisely the original NWRO demand. The expected modal tax rate on earnings was computed as 73 percent.[5] These findings, added to the evidence of three years of public debate over FAP, suggest that negative tax proposals (or programs) will experience strong upward pressures tending to set the "base" at the poverty level, or higher, accompanied by necessarily high marginal rates of taxation to limit coverage. Thus, a negative tax seems likely to degenerate toward a flat grant system, paying a large benefit to recipients.* This could have consequences as difficult as any ascribed to the existing welfare system.

* H.R. 1, the version of Family Assistance introduced in the 92nd Congress, set the basic benefit level at $2,400 for a family of four and the marginal rate

Such a future is not an inevitable one. However unprecedented as a social program, Family Assistance was nonetheless fairly described as an effort at reform. Through the 1960s evidence mounted that established modes of social meliorism were not succeeding and, indeed, may have begun to reinforce some of the problems they were intended to resolve. In the meantime, social discontent was rising. The presidency responded with a proposal explicitly directed toward the achievement of well-established goals—an end to poverty, the diminishment of inequality—but taking a different approach. Society was not asked to change values so much as methods, on the ground that the methods were not proving effective. But it was more than that: society was not only to change methods but also to take them more seriously. It is one thing to experiment with programs unlikely to have more than marginal effects; it is altogether different to try a strategy that could not but have a large and direct impact on the distribution of income, and perhaps of political power as well. It is one thing to proclaim an all-out "war on poverty"; it is another to enact one.

The designers of FAP knew this, or at least had some sense of the risks inherent in the course they were pursuing. For that reason, they undertook their task both seriously and cautiously. (Indeed so much so that the final product could be readily depicted as less than the innovative reform it truly was.) But if such initiatives are to attain their goals, and to avoid the excesses of which they are capable, much will depend on the development of a comparable competence—analytic as well as political—among the publics and Congress.

The events of the 91st Congress do not inspire great confidence that this will occur. Men such as Mills and Byrnes understood FAP well enough: institutions such as Ways and Means were capable of taking it seriously. But these were exceptions. After a year and a half of debate it was not likely that as many as a dozen United States senators understood the bill. When, early in 1972, Senate Finance Committee hearings revealed that the

---

of taxation at 67 percent. Both of these elements were higher than the corresponding features of the legislation considered in the 91st Congress. Some economists, such as Joseph Pechman and Alice Rivlin, were quite critical of the increased tax rate, while endorsing, however faintly, the new benefit level. Professional criticism notwithstanding, future negative tax proposals are likely to continue to evolve in this fashion.

then most recent set of Ribicoff amendments would produce a program covering some 70 million persons and costing $42 billion when fully in effect in 1976, the senator was genuinely appalled and temporarily withdrew his support for *any* version of FAP.[6] Ribicoff regained his composure and resumed his lonely effort in the Senate to enact some version of welfare reform. Yet he had been shocked. Elementary information as to the large cost and great coverage of plans with seemingly only slightly higher benefit levels could not make its way into the consciousness of even concerned legislators. Adding $1,000 or $1,500 to the benefit levels of the president's proposal seemed modest, reasonable, liberal. Whereupon it would be learned that this would add 25 or 50 million recipients, and the liberal would feel trapped, exposed to the devastating charge of recklessness. Some chose, in effect, to brazen it out. When modest proposals turned out to involve quite immodest costs, they would claim to have known it all along and to desire precisely that outcome. But the evidence is otherwise: for the most part those who got involved in outbidding the president appear to have had little notion of the numbers with which they were dealing.

Nor was there any cost to be paid for such lack of competence. One liberal journal, the *Washington Post,* sought in its editorial comment to impose some discipline on the debate in its later stages. A number of more conservative publications, such as the Washington *Evening Star,* kept some feet to the fire. But more typical was the editorial position of the *Boston Globe,* which viewed neither Nixon's nor Ribicoff's plan as "adequate in the amount of money provided."

Political systems operate well enough without analytic competence; the experience of Family Assistance is an adequate demonstration. Among the public, and in Congress, for example, FAP was accepted on its symbolic merits, and the confidence that the substance of the measure corresponded to its symbolic content was well enough justified. Yet to no small degree its ultimate defeat was brought about by persons and organizations most committed to its purposes. Seeking to get yet more than the president proposed, liberals misrepresented the substance of the measure, and ended by getting nothing. In the process they also affected the symbolism: a measure intended to be generous, and which was generous, came widely to be perceived as punitive.

Had there been more general analytic competence on hand, it is not likely that the measure could have been so utterly misrepresented—which was recurrently the case—with near total impunity. Social policy has entered a stage in which the ambitiousness of government must be matched by analytic competence if the nation is to avoid a condition—more common elsewhere in the world than perhaps realized—in which the grandiosity of official pronouncement is equalled only by the absence of result.

In the end, the effort to enact Family Assistance failed. It had been close, but nothing can be known of the future. A comparable effort may yet succeed, or it may be that a guaranteed income will elude the Nation, that its destiny is to be Sisyphean, rather than Promethean, almost but not quite capable of fundamental change. The incrementalist view that this is not the worst condition, and in any event is the only possible one, is not disproved; whether the Nation is capable of maintaining a balance between expansion and restraint in the evolution of a guaranteed income must await its enactment. There are grounds for optimism, and for pessimism also.

With time the ambiguities of the experience impressed themselves upon the president. In the fall of 1971 he read Nathan Glazer's essay, "The Limits of Social Policy," delivered the previous year as the Jacob C. Saposnekow Memorial Lecture at the City College of New York and subsequently published in *Commentary* Magazine. Glazer argued that "the line dividing liberals from conservatives grows steadily fainter" in American politics, as illustrated by the proposal of Family Assistance, "the great reform in welfare policy." Increasingly, he judged, both conservatives and liberals believe that for every problem there must be a specific solution, and search for such solutions. Glazer was not optimistic. He offered two propositions.

1. Social policy is an effort to deal with the breakdown of traditional ways of handling distress. These traditional mechanisms are located primarily in the family, but also in the ethnic group, the neighborhood, and in such organizations as the church and the *landsmanschaft*.

2. In its effort to deal with the breakdown of these traditional structures, however, social policy tends to encourage their further weakening. There is, then, no sea of misery against which we are

making steady headway. Our efforts to deal with distress themselves increase distress.[7]

Family Assistance? He admired it. But was wary. To Glazer the largest question concerned "how we might prevent further erosion of the traditional constraints that still play the largest role in maintaining a civil society." Of these, the first is that "most people still feel they should work. . . ." He was more than wary: he worried.

The Administration proposal is a heroic effort to improve the condition of the poor without further damage to those social motivations and structures which are the essential basis for individual security everywhere. But does not the history of our efforts to expand policies of income support suggest that inevitably improvement and damage go together.[8]

The president worried also. But he did not know, and there was no prospect of knowing.

Citations—Chapter VIII

1. For the general concept, see my article, "The Professionalization of Reform," *The Public Interest*, Fall 1965, pp. 6–16.
2. Theodore J. Lowi, *The End of Liberalism*, New York, Norton, 1969, p. 231.
3. Michael Oakeshott, *Rationalism in Politics*, p. 58.
4. Charles E. Lindblom, *The Intelligence of Democracy;* see also David Braybrooke and Charles E. Lindblom, *A Strategy of Decision*, New York, Free Press, 1963.
5. Lee Rainwater, *It's A Living: Explorations in the Social Meanings of Low Incomes*, forthcoming, chapter 8. The term "modal" is an approximate description of a somewhat complex averaging.
6. Marjorie Hunter, "Ribicoff Abandons Drive for Nixon Welfare Plan," *The New York Times*, January 29, 1972.
7. Nathan Glazer, "The Limits of Social Policy," p. 52.
8. *Ibid.*, p. 57.

Afterword

Events recur, Marx agreed. "The first time as tragedy, the second as farce." "Tragedy" is not so much a strong term as an exact one. It probably could not be shown that Family Assistance was *fated* to fail in the 91st Congress, albeit there was a certain inevitablity to it all. For the 92nd Congress, however, "farce" is surely the appropriate term. There were men and women who behaved as if the proposal were still a serious one, requiring disciplined understanding and adult judgment. But these were few. In the main the tendency was to exaggerate and to caricature, the more so as the presidential election approached. The general principles developed in the preceding account of the first round will serve the reader who might wish to make sense of the second. Withal, the nation and its system of government showed a continuing, if somewhat conflicted, disposition toward generous social policies. A continuing issue will be whether generosity can be matched by competence.

In politics a certain patience is demanded. The idea of a guaranteed income came precipitously to public affairs. Few were prepared. Time should remedy this. Economists will surely impose some discipline on the discussion. For those who would wish to see a guaranteed income established, the greatest danger is that before this happens the general idea will have been discredited by the extravagance of so many of the proposals put forth as alternatives to FAP. Whatever happens, the issue of income distribution is likely to absorb much energy in the years ahead. The nation's wealth grows, but the distribution of it remains almost frozen. This may be unacceptable in principle; in reality it may be a condition of growth. Or it may be that a wholly new set of understandings will emerge. Considerable competence will be needed to carry this debate forward to a rewarding conclusion.

Among conservatives the case against a guaranteed income continued to build, especially with regard to work incentives and disincentives. Liberals showed less interest in the subject as such, being preoccupied with positioning themselves on the issue so as to gain an advantage over some other liberal holding a different position—higher or lower or whatever. A vast inflation of proposals occurred. Serious conservatives were fairly confident as the election year took shape that the idea of *any* guaranteed income was being discredited.

New proposals came forth, now more openly redistributionist. Each exhibited that tendency of intellectuals Bertrand de Jouvenel found so "absorbingly interesting" in his Boutwood Lectures delivered at Cambridge University in 1949; to conceive too high an income floor *and* ceiling to be feasible in a stable political economy. A clearly persisting habit of mind was at work.

Index

Index

About the Author

DANIEL P. MOYNIHAN, recently named United States ambassador to India, has served in the subcabinet or cabinet of Presidents Kennedy, Johnson, and Nixon. He is the only person in public life to have maintained this continuity of involvement with domestic social issues through the 1960s and into the present decade.

In 1963, as Assistant Secretary of Labor for Policy Planning and Research, he began consideration of family allowances as a measure to offset the persistence of poverty in the midst of American affluence. In 1965 he was a member of the White House task force that drafted the Economic Opportunity Act of 1965. That year, for his service as "an architect of the nation's program to eradicate poverty," he received the Arthur S. Flemming Award as One of the Ten Outstanding Young Men in Government. After a period in academic life, he returned to Washington in 1969 as Assistant for Urban Affairs, later Counselor to the President. In this role he pressed an "income strategy" on social issues which was embodied in the Family Assistance Plan proposed by President Nixon in August 1969.

Professor Moynihan is a member of the Faculty of Arts and Sciences of Harvard University and of the John F. Kennedy School of Government. He is a member also of the board of directors of the American Association for the Advancement of Science, has received twenty honorary degrees, and is an Honorary Fellow of the London School of Economics and Political Science.

VINTAGE POLITICAL SCIENCE
AND SOCIAL CRITICISM

VINTAGE HISTORY—AMERICAN

VINTAGE WORKS OF SCIENCE
AND PSYCHOLOGY